Merry Christmas
Charlie, Cammy & Alethea

TENNESSEE ❧ A SHORT HISTORY

TENNESSEE

 A SHORT HISTORY

Stanley J. Folmsbee
Robert E. Corlew
Enoch L. Mitchell

THE UNIVERSITY
OF TENNESSEE PRESS
KNOXVILLE

Library of Congress Card Number 69–20114
Printed in the United States of America
Copyright © 1969 by The University of Tennessee Press
Knoxville, Tennessee
All Rights Reserved
Second printing, 1972

Illustrations

viii   TENNESSEE, A SHORT HISTORY

FOLLOWING PAGE 411: *Governor's Mansion / Albert Gore / Howard H. Baker, Jr. / William E. Brock III / Knoxville / Capitol and state buildings, Nashville / Industry / Dairying / Cotton / Tobacco / "World's most modern waterway" / Graphite Reactor / Gaseous Diffusion Plant / Great Smokies / Country Music Hall of Fame / Recreation*

FOLLOWING PAGE 475: *Seven state universities and Two institutions for medical education*

Abbreviations

AHM	*American Historical Magazine*
AHR	*American Historical Review*
ETHS *Publ.*	East Tennessee Historical Society's *Publications*
GHQ	*Georgia Historical Quarterly*
JAH	*Journal of American History*
JNH	*Journal of Negro History*
JOP	*Journal of Politics*
JSH	*Journal of Southern History*
MVHR	*Mississippi Valley Historical Review*
NCHR	*North Carolina Historical Review*
WTHS *Papers*	West Tennessee Historical Society *Papers*
THQ	*Tennessee Historical Quarterly*
THM	*Tennessee Historical Magazine*

Preface

Few states have had as fascinating a history as Tennessee. Across the pages of its past have moved Indians, frontiersmen, three future Presidents of the United States, and such colorful personalities as Daniel Boone, Davy Crockett, Sam Houston, "Parson" Brownlow, Alvin York, and "Boss" Crump. Interestingly, many other states owe a debt to Tennessee for providing pioneers and statesmen who built their states into greatness.

Physically, the state of Tennessee is long and narrow and with such a wide diversity of topographical features that the people in its three "grand divisions" have had difficulty in communicating with and even understanding each other. Within this diversity, however, is a plethora of natural resources that has made rapid economic development possible.

First occupied by prehistoric Indians, the Tennessee country was later claimed and used by the Cherokee, Chickasaw, Creek, and Shawnee tribes. During much of the colonial period, these Indians and their neighbors, and the white traders who lived among them, became pawns of European diplomacy; the ultimate success of the English in the intercolonial wars meant that Tennessee would be English in cultural and economic background rather than French. Thereafter, the periodic Indian wars, the step-by-step removal of the Indian title and of the Indian himself from the land, and the conflicting interests of land speculators and pioneering settlers in the development of a land system were signal milestones in Tennessee's early history.

During most of its pre-statehood period, Tennessee was North

Carolina's claim to Western land. That colony's lack of interest in the West was one reason why the first permanent Tennessee settlers found it necessary to govern themselves under the semi-independent Watauga Association. Following the Revolution, North Carolina assumed a belated, albeit mercenary, interest in Tennessee, but by that time Tennesseans were determined upon separating from their neglectful parent. After a rebellious interlude of the "Lost State of Franklin" and intrigues with the Spaniards at New Orleans, separation became a reality. The United States Congress then designated the Tennessee country as the "Territory of the United States South of the River Ohio"; thus, prior to its admission into the Union, Tennessee was the first state to pass through a period of territorial government.

At the time of its admission as the sixteenth state in 1796, Tennessee was still a frontier, with primitive agricultural practices and living conditions. Some beginnings had been made in organized religion and education, but these first attempts only partially alleviated the prevalent outlawry. Moreover, the new state suffered from disgrace and discord among its most illustrious leaders. One of the state's first two senators was expelled from the United States Senate, and politics became so personal that Tennessee's two outstanding leaders, John Sevier and Andrew Jackson, became embroiled in a bitter feud.

The independent spirit of Tennessee's people has become the state's hallmark. Not only at King's Mountain during the Revolution but also during the War of 1812, a tradition, symbolized by the nickname "Volunteer State," was created and later exemplified in the Mexican War and other conflicts. This individuality, however, went further than nationalistic ardor. For instance, the Creek War and the Battle of New Orleans brought Andrew Jackson to national attention, and Tennesseans basked proudly in reflected glory as his presidential aspirations achieved success. When, however, they believed that Jackson himself was becoming too domineering and that some of his policies were not in accord with the economic interest of Tennessee, it was independent-minded Tennesseans who spearheaded a revolt against his leadership.

The movement against Jackson resulted in the formation of the Whig party, which carried the state in every presidential election from 1836 to 1852—even including a victory over James K. Polk, who was elected President in 1844. In state elections, the strength of Whigs and Democrats was evenly matched, and, consequently, this era was one that included many exciting political battles. Eventually, in the 1850's, the Democrats emerged as the dominant party, mainly because the national Whig party split over the question of slavery. Most Tennessee Whigs, remaining firm to their political beliefs, then joined the new Know Nothing party. They supported John Bell and the Constitutional Union party in the election of 1860 and led the fight against secession until Lincoln's call for Tennessee troops ended hopes that the state would remain in the Union.

Tennessee divided along sectional lines during the Civil War, with East Tennessee remaining loyal to the Union and Middle and West Tennessee supporting the Confederacy. With its Tennessee and Cumberland river systems and its important rail centers at Nashville and Chattanooga providing ready access to the heart of the Confederacy, Tennessee's strategic location made it the major battleground of the West. More battles were fought on its soil than in any state except Virginia. Nashville, the state capital, fell early in the war, and Military Governor Andrew Johnson suppressed disloyalty with such vigor that he became Lincoln's running mate in 1864; thus, Johnson succeeded to the presidency after Lincoln's assassination.

With the close of the war, Tennessee escaped the evils of carpetbag government only to endure the even more rigorous rule of home-grown Unionists led by William G. (Parson) Brownlow. Brownlow's regime was created by disenfranchisement of Confederates, was maintained by force, and was infused with corruption. It collapsed in 1870, leaving the state with a heritage of bitterness and a mammoth state debt.

Like other Southern states, Tennessee, in the years after Reconstruction, was governed politically by the ex-Confederate leaders, or "Bourbons." Their rule was challenged by the industrialists and by a rising group of small farmers who flirted briefly with the imported radical doctrines of the Farmers' Alliance and Populism. In time, control was wrested from the hands of the Bourbons, and by 1896 most of the scars of war had been obliterated.

A new century brought new opportunities and new responsibilities to the people of Tennessee. Industrial growth increased at such a rate that it challenged agriculture as the major source of state wealth. Then the machine age, combined with greatly improved methods of agriculture and super highways, brought about the development of urban centers in the state.

Later changes within Tennessee's borders—the TVA, the great atomic power plant at Oak Ridge, and the various armed services projects at Memphis, Millington, Tullahoma, Nashville, Chattanooga, and Knoxville—have also resulted in drastic changes in the population distribution and have further revolutionized the character of economic life. Today, the people of Tennessee are still adapting to the new age of industry and science without seeming to have lost the independent characteristics of the frontier and agrarian periods.

Tennessee, A Short History is a condensation and revision of the two-volume *History of Tennessee* written by the two undersigned authors and the late Enoch L. Mitchell. The original volumes were published, along with two other books of "Family and Personal History," in 1960 by the Lewis Historical Publishing Company, Inc., New York.

The undersigned authors wish to express their sincere regret and great sense of loss at the inopportune passing of Professor Enoch L. Mitchell, one of the original contributors to the two-volume work. Although Professor Mitchell died while this condensed and revised version of the history of Tennessee was in its first planning stages, his work on the original edition has provided a foundation for the revised edition. His name, therefore, properly belongs to this first edition of *Tennessee, A Short History.*

To the many historians, librarians, archivists, and others who provided invaluable counsel and assistance in preparing the original edition of this work, we would again like to express our appreciation.

For their generosity in furnishing photographs that appear in *Tennessee, A Short History,* we wish to thank the following: the Tennessee Conservation Department for pictures of Governors William Blount, John Sevier, James K. Polk, DeWitt Clinton Senter, Gordon Browning, Prentice Cooper, and Buford Ellington and for photographs of David Crockett, Mrs. James Robertson, Andrew Jackson, Nathan Bedford Forrest, Kenneth D. McKellar, Cordell Hull, Edward Crump, Albert Gore, the Indian burial grounds, Rocky Mount, the block house at Benton, the Dean Cornwell murals, homes of James K. Polk and Sam Davis, Fort Donelson, governor's mansion, tobacco and cotton scenes, Country Music Hall of Fame, and state buildings at Nashville; S. N. McMinn of Lascassas for Governor Joseph McMinn; the Greene County Chamber of Commerce for Andrew Johnson's tailor shop; The University of Tennessee Library at Knoxville for the print of Governor John Buchanan; the Walden S. Fabry Studios of Nashville for the photograph of Governor Frank G. Clement; the Nashville Chamber of Commerce for pictures of Fort Nashborough and the Hermitage; the Knoxville Chamber of Commerce for Blount Mansion and the aerial view of Knoxville; the Memphis Chamber of Commerce for the photographs of the city and the W. R. Grace Company; the Chattanooga Chamber of Commerce for the aerial of Chattanooga; the Tennessee Valley Authority for pictures of Norris Dam, dairying, river transportation, and recreation; the Minnesota Historical Society and Stanley F. Horn's *The Decisive Battle of Nashville* (Knoxville, 1968) for the reproduction of the oil painting of the Battle of Nashville by Howard Pyle; the Wiles-Hood Studio of Nashville for the William Jennings Bryan group; Thompson's of Knoxville for the Great Smoky Mountains scene; the Public Relations departments of Tennessee's seven state universities and of Vanderbilt University for pictures of their institutions; and the United States Atomic Energy Commission for photographs of a graphite reactor and an Oak Ridge plant.

To Mary Scott Corlew we wish to express our appreciation for preparing the index.

In the present volume, Professor Folmsbee is the author of Chapters 1–10, 15, 25, 26, 29, and 30. Professor Corlew is the author of Chapters 11–14, 16–24, 27, 28, and 31.

Stanley J. Folmsbee
Robert E. Corlew

TENNESSEE ❧ A SHORT HISTORY

1. ⟨⟩ The Land: Boundaries and Physical Features

T ENNESSEE is characterized by an amazing diversity of physical features, its borders having been determined by the accidents of history rather than by logic. Had the natural contours been followed, Tennessee would be three states or parts of three states, instead of one. Divided into three "grand divisions" of East, Middle, and West Tennessee, the state has been plagued throughout history by sectional bitterness; from another point of view, regional diversity has been a blessing as well as a curse.

Boundaries ⟨⟩ Long, narrow, and rhomboidal in shape, Tennessee extends 432 miles from the Unaka range of the Appalachian Mountains on the east to the Mississippi River on the west. Its greatest width from north to south is 110 miles. With a total land and water area of 42,244 square miles, Tennessee ranks thirty-fourth in size among the fifty states. The eastern and western boundary lines are largely natural in character, one following for most of the distance a mountain crest and the other the course of a river. But the northern and southern lines, which were supposed to follow the parallels of latitude 36° 30′ and 35° because the charter bounds of the colony and state of North Carolina once included all of Tennessee, suffered from inaccurate surveying and interstate controversies.

As a result, the northern boundary has a particularly uneven or jagged appearance. Its most eastern section, to a place called Steep Rock Creek (now Laurel Creek) on the edge of Johnson County, was surveyed in 1749 by a joint commission headed by Peter Jefferson, father of the future President. Thirty years later the survey was continued by another joint commission created by the now independent states of Virginia and North Carolina. After reaching Carter's Valley, west of the Holston River, the representatives of the two states disagreed, separated, and proceeded to survey parallel lines about two miles apart as far west as Cumberland Gap. There the North Carolinians abandoned the survey, but the Virginians continued with what became known as the Walker line to the northward-flowing Tennessee River. Even this line, incorrectly marked by faulty instruments, continued to creep northward until it was about twelve miles above the true 36° 30′ parallel at the Tennessee River. Before that fact became known, however, Tennessee induced Virginia in 1802 to accept a compromise line east of Cumberland Gap equidistant from the Virginia and North Carolina surveys of 1779. Years later Virginia attempted to have the boundary moved to the true parallel, but the United States Supreme Court in 1893 decided that long usage, legislative acceptance by Virginia, and implied acceptance by Congress had made the line of 1802 final.

Kentucky was somewhat more successful than Virginia in its negotiations with Tennessee. In 1818, when the region west of the Tennessee River was about to be opened to settlement as a result of Jackson's Chickasaw Purchase, Kentucky authorized an accurate survey of the 36° 30′ line between the Tennessee and the Mississippi rivers. Two years later that state negotiated a settlement with Tennessee which accepted this new line as the boundary between those rivers, but the old, inaccurate Walker survey between the Tennessee River and Cumberland Gap was allowed to stand in order to avoid disturbing the citizenship status of the many Tennesseans residing north of the line.

The southern boundary of Tennessee is still in dispute, but the principle asserted by the Supreme Court in the case of *Virginia* v. *Tennessee* in 1893 would seem to indicate that the line as surveyed somewhat inaccurately in 1818 will never be disturbed. As late as 1971, however, Georgia officials resumed their efforts to have the line replaced by a more accurate survey of the 35th parallel, which would, incidentally, put a narrow slice of Chattanooga in the state of Georgia. Those officials also claimed that the colonial charter of 1732 entitled Georgia to a boundary considerably north of the

35th parallel. That claim is inadmissible, however, since the Georgians in 1787 accepted in negotiations with South Carolina the 35th parallel as the state's maximum northern boundary.

At the time of that agreement, many believed that South Carolina was entitled to a narrow strip of land south of North Carolina's claim to what is now Tennessee. The alternative to the 35th parallel in the agreement of 1787 was a line running west from the source of the Tugaloo-Chatooga branch of the Savannah River in case that source was south of the 35th parallel. Since this branch rises north of 35°, the South Carolina claim was geographically nonexistent. Even so, that mythical claim, formally ceded by South Carolina to the United States in 1787 and by the United States to Georgia in 1802, is shown on every map of the Western claims of the original states to be found in American history textbooks and atlases.

Physiographic Regions ⮞ Topographically, Tennessee is divided into six major and two minor physiographic regions (see the Physiographic Map of Tennessee on pages 534 and 535). The most eastern is the Unaka Mountains; next is the Great Valley of East Tennessee, followed by the Cumberland Plateau. The fourth region, the Highland Rim, surrounds the fifth, the Central Basin. At the western edge of the Highland Rim is one of the minor regions, the Western Valley of the Tennessee River. The sixth major region is the Gulf Coastal Plain of West Tennessee. The western part of this plain is the second minor region, the Flood Plain of the Mississippi River, sometimes called the Mississippi Bottoms.

These natural regions are reflected in the political subdivisions of the state known as the "grand divisions." The grand division of East Tennessee is made up of the first two physiographic regions and about half of the third, Middle Tennessee extends from the middle of the Cumberland Plateau to the northward-flowing Tennessee River, and West Tennessee from the Tennessee River to the Mississippi. Before 1818, when the area west of the Tennessee River was opened to settlement, what is now Middle Tennessee was called West Tennessee. The present West Tennessee was then called the "Western District." Beginning in 1835, the legislature has designated the counties to be included in the three grand divisions. At that time two counties, Hardin and Perry, were bisected by the northward-flowing Tennessee, and the legislature assigned Hardin to Middle and Perry to West Tennessee. Ten years later, when the portion of Perry County lying west of the river was made into a new county, Decatur, the legislature neglected to reassign Perry to Middle Tennessee. Later legislatures continued that neglect until 1965, when Perry County finally was shifted from West to Middle Tennessee.

The six major physiographic regions are merely sections of larger regions which extend far beyond the borders of the state. For example, the Unaka range of mountains (sometimes erroneously called the Alleghenies) is the western front of the "Blue Ridge province" of the major geographic division called the Appalachian Highlands, or more familiarly the Appalachian Mountains. The boundary line between North Carolina and Tennessee in general follows the Unaka range, and only the portions of these mountains lying west of that line are in Tennessee. Through them several branches of the Tennessee River have found their way, thus dividing the Unakas into sections with local names such as Stone, Bald, Great Smoky, and Unicoi.[1]

The northern part of the North Carolina-Tennessee boundary was surveyed in 1799 and the remainder in 1821. When the members of the joint commission of 1821 reached the Hiwassee River, they realized that they had come to the end of the Unicoi Mountains. For that reason, or possibly because of their haste to refresh themselves at a nearby tavern, they surveyed a line due south to the Georgia boundary. They could have argued with equal justification that the line should follow a mountain crest all the way to Georgia and therefore should run along the top of Frog Mountain, in effect a continuation of the Unicoi range, to the Georgia boundary. Had they surveyed such a line the rich copper deposits in the Ducktown-Copperhill region of Polk County would be in North Carolina instead of Tennessee.

The Unaka Mountains in Tennessee vary in width from two to twenty miles and cover a total area of about 2,600 square miles. The

[1] Some geographers have been inclined to use the name Unaka to apply only to the upper part of the western prong of the Blue Ridge province, from the Big Pigeon branch of the French Broad River northward, and to extend the use of the name Great Smoky Mountains to all of the southern part of the range.

range presents the highest and most rugged surface in the state and has several peaks with elevations of more than 6,000 feet. The highest, Clingman's Dome, rises to a height of 6,643 feet. The region is drained from the southeast to the northwest by the branches of the Tennessee River, which occupy steep-sided valleys and afford many excellent power sites. Despite the gaps cut by these rivers through the mountains, the Unaka range and the Blue Ridge to the east have constituted an almost impenetrable barrier between the Tennessee country and the Atlantic Coast. Because of their isolation, the mountaineers of the Unaka region have retained until recent times a relatively pure Anglo-Saxon character, still continuing to use many Elizabethan forms of the English language and passing down through generations variants of old English ballads.

The rocks in the Unaka area are composed of granite, gneiss, schist, shale, slate, sandstone, conglomerate, and quartzite. During the mountain-building period these rocks were folded and faulted by great crustal movements. Erosion of the more soluble rocks resulted in the creation of many beautiful valleys and coves. Some of the valleys have agricultural possibilities, but more important economically are the rich forests which have made lumbering an important occupation throughout the range. A considerable part of the forest land has been set aside as the Cherokee National Forest.

A notable feature of the mountain area is its scenic grandeur. It is also a "paradise" for the botanist because of its remarkable plethora of botanical specimens at various climatic levels. The creation of the Great Smoky Mountains National Park, together with improved access by modern highways, has made the tourist business an important source of revenue, rivaling the receipts of the "moonshiners" and the lumbermen. About one half of the area of the park, which is the most visited one in the nation, is in Tennessee.

The Great Valley of East Tennessee, the second natural region, referred to by some geographers as the *Ridge and Valley* region, extends from southwest Virginia into northern Georgia. It is a segment of the Ridge and Valley province of the Appalachian Highlands that runs from New York to central Alabama. In Tennessee the Great Valley varies in width from thirty-five to fifty-five miles and covers about 9,200 square miles. It slopes gradually from northeast to southwest, with elevations dropping from 1,600 to 700 feet, and is made up of long, narrow ridges with broad valleys lying in between them. Clinch Mountain, in the northwestern part of the region, rises about 1,000 feet above the floor of the main valley.

The underlying rocks are almost wholly sedimentary and in large measure of a limestone character, but also include some harder shales and sandstones. The wearing away of the soluble limestone gave rise to the long, fertile valleys, while the more resistant sandstone and chert beds remained as ridges. The area is drained to the southwest by the Tennessee River and its tributaries.

The Great Valley, lying between two mountainous regions, was seriously isolated from the rest of the country until the building of railroads overcame some of the transportation difficulties and revitalized the agricultural and industrial potentialities. Since the creation of the Tennessee Valley Authority in 1933, the area has been dotted with artificial lakes behind the several dams constructed to supply electric power and aid in flood control, as well as to improve navigation facilities. These lakes flooded much good bottom land, but even so the Great Valley contains nearly one-fifth of the farm land in the state. Although there is considerable specialization in tobacco in the northern half of the valley, most of the land is devoted to general farming. The valley contains significant mineral resources and is an increasingly important industrial area. Knoxville and Chattanooga, two of the four large cities of the state, and many smaller cities, such as Oak Ridge, are significant manufacturing centers.

The Cumberland Plateau, extending from central Alabama to southern Kentucky, constitutes the southern segment of the Appalachian Plateaus province of the Appalachian Highlands, which terminates in the Catskill Mountains in New York. It is an erosional remnant of what was once an extensive peneplain. In Tennessee the Cumberland Plateau has an area of about 5,400 square miles and varies from about fifty to seventy miles in width. The elevation ranges from 1,800 to 2,000 feet except in the northeast corner, where the Cumberland Mountains rise to an elevation of about 3,500 feet and somewhat resemble the Allegheny Mountains of Pennsylvania. The eastern segment of the Plateau in Tennessee is called Walden Ridge, the edge of which was described by one writer as a "formidable, gray, rocky, cliff-lined rampart." The western edge is much more irregular because of the entrenched streams that flow to the west. Numerous small parts of the Plateau have been separated from it by erosion. For example, Lookout Mountain, geographically a part of the Great Valley, is geologically a separated piece of the Plateau.

The Plateau includes a unique irregularity called the Sequatchie Valley, a great cove extending almost halfway across the state from the Tennessee River at the Alabama line to the Crab Orchard Mountains. The floor of the valley, which averages about five miles in width, lies about 1,000 feet below the surface of the adjoining Plateau.

The rocks on the Cumberland Plateau are sedimentary in origin and consist of conglomerates, sandstones, shales, and limestones deposited during the latter part of the Paleozoic era. Coal is especially important, as it underlies much of the Plateau. The colorful sandstones are used extensively as a building material. Tributaries of the Tennessee River drain the southern and eastern parts of the Plateau, but the central and northwestern parts are drained by the Cumberland. Many of the streams which flow to the west and northwest have cut deep and narrow gorges. Although called in the early days "The Wilderness" because of the severely limited agricultural possibilities, the Plateau in recent years has seen some success in the cultivation of Irish potatoes.

The Highland Rim, the fourth physiographic region, forms an encircling rim that almost completely surrounds the fifth region, called the Central, or Nashville, Basin. Both are segments of the Interior Low Plateaus province of the Interior Plains physiographic division extending from northern Alabama to beyond the Ohio River. The portion of the Highland Rim in Tennessee has an area of about 10,650 square miles, exclusive of the Elk River Valley, considered by some geographers to be a part of the Central Basin. The Rim ranges in width from about twenty-five miles in the eastern part to about seventy-five in the northwest. The eastern section is a gently rolling plain about 1,000 feet lower than the Cumberland Plateau and about 400 feet higher than the Central Basin. It is divided from the Plateau by a steep and uneven escarpment and from the Basin by a rough, hilly region. The western part is similar in formation but somewhat lower. At its western edge is the narrow

Western Valley of the Tennessee River, the first of the two minor physiographic regions in Tennessee.

The rocks in the Highland Rim are sedimentary in origin and are chiefly limestones and shales but include some sandstones. Especially in the eastern part there are many sinkholes caused by the solution of the limestone by water in underground channels. Some of the soils near the inner edge of the Rim contain small pieces of rock called chert. This area has been called the "Barrens," although it is not entirely lacking in fertility. Other parts of the Rim are more productive, particularly the narrow strips of bottom land in the valleys of the larger streams. Cotton is grown in the southern part of the Rim and tobacco in the northern, in the valley of the Cumberland River. The Rim also has timber and mineral resources.

The Central, or Nashville, Basin is almost entirely surrounded by the Highland Rim. Ranging from 50 to 60 miles in width and about 100 miles in length, it covers an area of about 5,500 square miles and has an average elevation of 600 feet. Although its borders are very irregular, the Basin has been compared by Joseph B. Killebrew to "the bottom of an oval dish, of which the Highlands form the broad, flat brim."

The Basin came into existence as a result of erosion on a great anticline that extends from northern Alabama into Kentucky and Ohio, which also created the similar Bluegrass region of Kentucky. The outcropping rocks are largely limestones and shales. The northern part of the Central Basin is drained by the Cumberland and its tributaries and the southern part by the Elk and the Duck, two branches of the Tennessee River. The soils are quite fertile for all crops suited to the latitude, and the region has been called the "Garden of Tennessee." Before the Civil War much cotton was grown in the region, but now its chief crops are grains, hay, vegetables, tobacco, and livestock. Its race horses were once almost as famous as those of the Bluegrass region of Kentucky, and the Tennessee walking horse still has considerable fame. Located in the region is Nashville, the capital and second largest city in the state and also an important transportation and manufacturing center.

The Gulf Coastal Plain of West Tennessee is a segment of the physiographic division called the Coastal Plain, which includes the plain along the Atlantic Coast as well as the one along the Gulf of

Mexico. In Tennessee it covers an area of about 9,000 square miles, and is divided into two parts, the Plateau, or Slope, of West Tennessee (but which extends across the river far enough to include most of the Middle Tennessee county of Wayne) and the Flood Plain of the Mississippi River, frequently called the Mississippi Bottoms. The latter is the second of the minor natural regions of the state. Even the former lacks the rugged features which characterize the remainder of Tennessee, the only hilly region being a belt of land lying just west of the Tennessee River. From an elevation of between 500 and 700 feet along that watershed the Plateau slopes gently westward to elevations of from 300 to 400 feet along the bluffs overlooking the Flood Plain. At several points toward the south this plateau extends all the way to the bank of the Mississippi and forms the Chickasaw Bluffs, familiar landmarks to the boatmen on the river.

In the extreme northwest corner of the Flood Plain is Reelfoot Lake, a hunting and fishing "paradise" and the only natural lake of significance in Tennessee. It was formed by the New Madrid earthquakes of 1811–12, which blocked off the natural outlet of Reelfoot River, thus creating the lake.

The strata outcropping in the Gulf Coastal Plain area consist of loosely consolidated beds of sand, clay, and shell marl. In the western part there is a deposit of loess, seen in almost vertical cliffs. The soils of the Plain are very productive, and this area is the chief cotton-growing region of the state. Although the dense forests of both hardwood and softwood trees once covering much of the area have to a great extent been cleared away, Memphis, the metropolis of the region, is still the leading hardwood manufacturing center in the world. But much of the wood is now imported from outside West Tennessee. Memphis, the largest city in the state, is an important distribution as well as manufacturing center.

River System ॐ With the exception of one small area in the southeast, the entire state is drained by the Mississippi River system, most of it by two branches of the Ohio—the Tennessee and the Cumberland—and their tributaries. In the western part, however, the rivers flow directly into the Mississippi.

According to modern nomenclature, the Tennessee is formed by the junction of the Holston and French Broad rivers a few miles above Knoxville. The Holston, earlier called the Hogohegee by the Indians but renamed for an early settler along its upper course, rises in southwest Virginia. Its two main forks converge near the famous "Long Island" at Kingsport, after the South Fork has received the historic Watauga, which rises in North Carolina. The French Broad and its tributary the Nolichucky, and the Little Tennessee and the Hiwassee, eastern branches of the Tennessee, also rise in North Carolina. From the west the upper Tennessee receives the Clinch (named for a hunter) and its branch the Powell, which rise in southwest Virginia, and the Emory, from the Cumberland Plateau.

Through the years the changes in the nomenclature of the upper Tennessee and its tributaries have caused much confusion among historians. After using various Indian names, the early French and English visitors gave the name Cheraquis, or Cherokee, to the Tennessee and Little Tennessee rivers because they found the Cherokee Indians living on the southern bank of the latter stream. Then, learning that one of the leading towns of those Indians was named Tenase or Tennessee, they gradually shifted the name from Cherokee to Tennessee. The visitors obviously considered the present Little Tennessee to be a part of the main stream, and the present Tennessee which joins with it at Lenoir City to be merely a branch. Consequently, the name Holston was used not only for the present river of that name, above the junction with the French Broad, but also for what is now called the Tennessee, between the mouths of the French Broad and the Little Tennessee rivers. This nomenclature was illogical, however, since the Little Tennessee was much smaller than its Holston "branch." Beginning about 1820, therefore, the name Little Tennessee was given to the present river of that name, and the Tennessee was considered to be formed by the junction of that stream with the "Holston" at the site of Lenoir City. It was not until about 1880 that the name Tennessee was given to the part of the river between Lenoir City and the mouth of the French Broad, above Knoxville. This was done presumably so that federal appropriations for the improvement of the "Tennessee River" could be applied all the way to Knoxville. Before that time Knoxville was situated on the banks of the Holston rather than the

Tennessee. Thus is explained why the "Treaty of the Holston," negotiated at the site of Knoxville in 1791, was so called.

Near Chattanooga the Tennessee River abruptly changes its course several times as it cuts through Walden Ridge into the valley of its unique tributary, the Sequatchie. Before the Tennessee was tamed by TVA, fearsome perils, such as the "Suck" and "Boiling Pot," confronted navigators along that tortuous course through the "Narrows." Emerging from Sequatchie Valley, the river resumes a southwest course as far as Guntersville, where it turns northwest across Alabama, creating an even more famous river hazard, the Muscle Shoals; near the head of Muscle Shoals the Tennessee receives the Elk River, which rises in Middle Tennessee. Below Florence, Alabama, the Tennessee turns northward and flows for nearly two hundred miles, crossing Tennessee a second time and Kentucky, before emptying into the Ohio at Paducah. On its northward course across Tennessee the most important tributaries received are the Duck, entering from the east, and the Big Sandy, flowing from the west. As a result of dam-building by TVA, much of the course of this river system is now made up of artificial reservoirs, such as the Kentucky, Chickamauga, and Fort Loudoun lakes in the main stream and the Norris, Melton Hill, Cherokee, Douglas, Holston, and Watauga lakes in various tributaries.

The Cumberland River, the other major stream besides the Tennessee which flows through the state, rises in southeastern Kentucky, runs across northern Middle Tennessee, and then parallels the Tennessee River on its way across Kentucky to a junction with the Ohio. Its southern tributaries, the Obey, the Caney Fork, the Stone, the Harpeth, and the Yellow, drain most of northern Middle Tennessee. One northern branch, the Red River, rises in Tennessee, flows for a few miles through Kentucky, and enters the main stream near Clarksville. The Cumberland system is also being converted into a series of artificial reservoirs.

The most important of the rivers which flow across West Tennessee into the Mississippi is the well-named Forked Deer. Its largest branch, the Obion, also has two major "forks" as well as a small branch coming from Reelfoot Lake. Farther south the Mississippi River receives the Hatchie (once called the Big Hatchie) and the Wolf, both rising in Mississippi, and between them the smaller Loosahatchie, which rises in Hardeman County. Near the mouths of these streams are the Chickasaw Bluffs, with Memphis, near the mouth of the Wolf, occupying the fourth and most southern of the series.

Natural Resources ૭᥍ The soils of Tennessee constitute the state's most important natural resource. Throughout history a majority of the people of the state have farmed or fabricated products of the soil. Although the soils in the Unaka Mountains region are rocky and shallow, those in the Great Valley and the Cumberland Plateau are of varying fertility. Much of the western Highland Rim is more productive, but the most fertile areas of the state are in the Central Basin and in the Gulf Coastal Plain.

Closely identified with agricultural potentialities are climate and weather. Tennessee has a mild climate with an average annual temperature of 60° F. The length of the growing season varies from about 150 days in the Unaka Mountains to about 220 days in West Tennessee. The prevailing winds are westerly or southwesterly. Those coming from the Gulf of Mexico are usually moisture-laden and provide the state with an adequate rainfall, averaging about fifty inches per year.

The principal cash crops are tobacco, cotton, and soybeans, but in acreage and farm value corn, hay, wheat, fruit, vegetables, and livestock are also important farm products. Tennessee is the leading dairy state in the South and second in the production of hogs. All the major cities are important meat-packing centers, and Memphis is one of the leading cottonseed processing centers in the world.

Forests have been among the state's most important natural resources; but in contrast to an earlier time when most of the land was covered with trees, less than half of the state's area is in forests today, including regions leased or owned by the state and federal governments. The most productive forest areas are in the Unaka Mountains, in the Highland Rim, and in the lowlands of West Tennessee. About two-thirds of the state's current lumber production is from hardwoods, making Tennessee the South's leading producer of hardwood lumber. Oak provides about 40 per cent of that production. Cedar, pine, and hemlock are the leading softwood trees in the state, with Tennessee having about 60 per cent of the commercial red cedar land in the nation. Because of wasteful exploitation and delay in instituting adequate reforestation programs, Tennessee's forest resources had been seriously depleted by 1930. Since that time rapid progress in the conservation movement has revitalized the lumbering industry.

Tennessee, one of the leading states in the South in the variety and value of its mineral production, has about thirty minerals of notable importance but a complete list would include more than fifty. In the order of their current values of production (1967) the most important are stone, zinc, Portland cement, coal, phosphate, and copper. The total value of production in 1967 of all minerals was $182,745,000, and Tennessee ranked first in the production of ball clay, pyrite, and zinc and third in phosphate rock and dimension marble. Iron ore, found in the Unaka Mountains region, in the eastern base of the Cumberland Plateau, and in the western Highland Rim, has been exploited spasmodically over the years, so its significance in the state's economy was relatively greater in the past. Until 1958 bituminous coal ranked first in tonnage and in value of production. Its availability, on the Cumberland Plateau, has been an important factor in the industrial development of Tennessee. The rise of stone to the first position has been due mainly to the great increase in the demand for crushed stone for highway construction, but involved also has been a decline in the production of coal and an increase in value of marble being mined. Marble is found primarily in the Great Valley, with Knoxville the chief center of the marble industry in the state. Tennessee marble has been widely accepted throughout the nation, particularly for constructing many notable public buildings. The copper deposits in the southeastern corner of the state were opened in 1847 and have been worked almost continuously since that time. Sulphur fumes resulting from the smelting process of copper destroyed practically all the vegetation in the surrounding area until it was discovered that the fumes could be utilized in the production of sulfuric acid, a by-product even more valuable than the copper.

SUGGESTED READINGS

General Accounts
    Donald Davidson, *The Tennessee, I: The Old River* (New York, 1946);
N. M. Fenneman, *Physiography of Eastern United States* (New York, 1938); Stanley J. Folmsbee, Robert E. Corlew, and Enoch L. Mitchell,

History of Tennessee (2 vols., New York, 1960), I, Ch. 1; John Haywood, *Civil and Political History of the State of Tennessee* (Knoxville, 1823; reprinted, 1969); Haywood, *Natural and Aboriginal History of Tennessee,* ed. Mary U. Rothrock (Jackson, Tenn., 1959); Joseph B. Killebrew, *Introduction to the Resources of Tennessee* (Nashville, 1874); Harry L. Law, *Tennessee Geography* (Norman, 1954; reprinted, 1963).

Specialized Accounts

E. Merton Coulter, "The Georgia-Tennessee Boundary," *GHQ,* XXXV (Dec., 1951), 269–306; William R. Garrett, "The Northern Boundary of Tennessee," *AHM,* VI (Jan., 1901), 18–39; Cecil C. Humphreys, "The Formation of Reelfoot Lake and Consequent Land and Social Problems," WTHS *Papers,* No. XIV (1960), 32–73; James R. Montgomery, "The Nomenclature of the Upper Tennessee River," ETHS *Publ.,* No. 28 (1956), 46–57; Joseph H. Parks, *Felix Grundy: Champion of Democracy* (Baton Rouge, 1949), 122–33; Laura Thornborough, *The Great Smoky Mountains* (Knoxville, 1956; revised, 1962).

2. &✌ *Indian Inhabitants*

HUMAN HABITATION of Tennessee began far back in the dim recesses of time. Thousands of years before this country was inhabited by the Cherokee and other historic tribes found here by the first white explorers, prehistoric Indians had found their way into this region. Knowledge of these "first Tennesseans" was rather scanty and somewhat inaccurate until after the Tennessee Valley Authority was created in 1933. At that time scholars pointed out that within the area to be covered by the waters of Norris Lake there were Indian mounds and village sites. To prevent the irretrievable loss of priceless archaeological data, the Authority and The University of Tennessee inaugurated a program of scientific excavation, which later was expanded to include many other parts of Tennessee. Reports of these excavations have been published, and the skeletons, pottery, arrowheads, and other artifacts uncovered have been deposited with The University of Tennessee's McClung Museum in Knoxville.

Prehistoric Indians &✌ According to most authorities, the American Indians came from Asia during the last Ice Age, when that continent was still connected with North America at what is now Bering Strait. These "first Americans" have been given the name Paleo-Indians because they lived in ancient times. They were nomadic hunters who wandered southward, probably reaching Tennessee about ten or fifteen thousand years ago. Recent excavations in the neighborhood of Kentucky Lake indicate that the lower Tennessee Valley was more densely populated by Paleo-Indians than most other parts of the United States.

About eight or nine thousand years ago[1] these people were succeeded by the Archaic Indians, who settled in villages, built houses, cooked their food over open fires, and began to shape and polish their stone spear points and other weapons and tools. In this period before the use of bows and arrows, one of the chief weapons was a spear-thrower, which could hurl spears through the air at animals or enemies. These Indians had domesticated dogs, engaged in fishing, used shells and bones as ornaments, and had the unique practice of burying their dead in trash heaps of clam shells and animal bones. An early site of these Archaic Indians was located near the town of Eva in Benton County; another was in Henry County on the Big Sandy River.

The next inhabitants of Tennessee have been named Woodland Indians because their culture occurs in the eastern woodlands, extending from Canada to the Gulf of Mexico. They probably came into Tennessee about 1000–500 B.C. and gradually developed a more settled way of life, based on agriculture. The Woodland Indians used bows and arrows as well as spears, made pottery, including large vessels for cooking, and introduced the cultivation of corn into Tennessee. Their houses were circular huts, or "wigwams," made by sticking small saplings into the ground and bending them over to form a dome-shaped framework.

Later generations of the Woodland Indians were responsible for many of the Indian mounds so widely scattered over Tennessee. Early writers were inclined to refer to all of the prehistoric inhabitants of the area as "Mound Builders," but most of the mounds built by the Woodland Indians were exclusively for one purpose, the burial of the dead. The growth of a belief in a life hereafter led to ceremonial burials and the placing of various articles alongside the bodies which might be helpful in the spirit world. The finding of tobacco pipes revealed that these Indians had developed the practice of using tobacco for ceremonial and other purposes. As other bodies were added, these burial mounds increased considerably in size,

---

[1] With the advent of the atomic age a new method of dating prehistoric remains, called the radiocarbon process, was invented. A geiger counter is used to determine how much the radioactivity of a type of carbon found in all living organisms had declined since the death of the organism, plant or animal, had occurred.

reaching heights of ten or fifteen feet. One of the largest was found in Stewart County. For many years it was thought that possibly Welshmen in the twelfth century had built the "Old Stone Fort" near Manchester, in Coffee County, but excavation and subsequent radiocarbon dating by University of Tennessee archaeologists in 1966 showed that the "fort" was actually constructed by Woodland Indians about 100–500 A.D. The Indians, however, probably used it for ceremonial purposes rather than as a fortification.[2]

Another group of mound builders constructed even larger mounds, which were named temple mounds because of their use as substructures for temples or community buildings. These builders were the Early Mississippian Indians, so called because they concentrated in the Mississippi Valley. East of the river they were mainly of the Muskhogean language group.[3] They came into the Tennessee area about 1000 or 1100 A.D.

A unique feature of the temple mounds, revealed by excavation of the mounds on Hiwassee Island in the Tennessee at the mouth of the Hiwassee River, is the composition by several layers of earth. Apparently, as a group of two or three temples built together wore out, the structures would be razed or otherwise destroyed, and several feet of soil would be added to the remains; then another group of temples would be constructed on the new summit. This process was repeated several times, with the top one or two layers seemingly being the work of later historic (or proto-historic) Indians who either succeeded the Early Mississippian tribe or amalgamated with it. Hence, the temple mounds grew to great size. One of the largest, the Pinson mound on the Forked Deer River in Madison County, is more than seventy feet high, the second highest in the United States. Since it is not typically Mississippian, however, it may have been built by Woodland Indians.

The Early Mississippians constructed rectangular dwelling houses by setting long saplings upright in trenches to form the walls and then bending over the tops and weaving them together to make a base for a thatched roof. Their pottery work was quite distinctive and they raised beans, potatoes, squash, and pumpkins, as well as corn. No graves of the Early Mississippians have been found; possibly they

---

[2] Faulkner, *The Old Stone Fort*, 23–26.

[3] The Indian languages of the United States have been classified into several groups, the Muskhogean, Caddoan, Iroquoian, Siouan, and the Algonquian.

cremated their dead or, according to archaeologists, stored the bodies in "bone houses" which were later destroyed.

Proto-historic Tennessee Indians ε➤ Prehistoric Indians lived before the time of written records, so for information concerning them we are dependent largely on the results of archaeological investigations. The historic Indians came into contact with white people, who left written descriptions of that Indian civilization. For Tennessee Indians, however, there is a gap of more than a hundred years between the visits by the Spanish De Soto and Pardo expeditions, 1539–67, and the first French and English contacts in 1673. It was not until near the end of the seventeenth century that Indian-white relationships became sufficiently frequent to constitute a real beginning of the historic period. It is to the preceding twilight zone back to the time of De Soto that the term proto-historic has been applied, a period for which archaeological data are supplemented by a small amount of historic information.

The Tennessee Indians of that period had a Late Mississippian culture and were called by names which continued in use in modern times. The Creeks and the Chickasaw, like their neighbors the Choctaw of south central Mississippi, were of the Muskhogean language group, but the Shawnee, Yuchi, and Cherokee were not. The Chickasaw, who seceded from the Choctaw, lived in northern Mississippi but they claimed all of West Tennessee and part of Middle Tennessee as their hunting grounds. They did not have any towns in what is now Tennessee until about the time that state was admitted into the Union and a trading post had been established at the site of Memphis.

Excavations in East Tennessee, however, unearthed much evidence which, when related to other data, indicates that much of this area was occupied by the Creek Indians from before 1300 to about 1700 or 1715. The name "Creek" came to be applied to this great confederacy of tribes because some of them resided along Ocheese Creek (the present Ocmulgee River) in Georgia and the name "Ocheese Creek" was shortened to Creek. The confederacy included tribes residing in Alabama and Florida as well as Georgia and, for the period mentioned above, Tennessee.

The Creeks had two types of towns: "red" ones devoted to making war and "white" towns to preserving peace. The towns agreed that war should never occur between them, so instead of war they substituted "brother of war" ball games, the ancestor of modern lacrosse. They also played another game called chunkge (or chunkey). Since the Indians acquired a passion for gambling, spectators often bet everything they owned, including their clothes, on the results of the games.

It was the custom of the Creeks for each family to bury its own dead, in graves dug near the house, and to inter food and weapons with the bodies, for use on the way to the happy hunting ground. Examination of skeletons has revealed that few adults lived more than forty or forty-five years and that infant mortality was excessive. The Creeks indulged in a purification practice of diving four times into water immediately upon arising in the morning. This was required of all, regardless of age or sex or even the coldest weather; however, if there was snow on the ground they would roll in the snow. Upon assembling in the morning the men further purified themselves with a "black drink" (as the traders called it), which induced vomiting; then the men smoked the ceremonial pipe.

These Indians called themselves "people of one fire"; their principal chief was known as "miko" and the vice-chief as "twin miko." Life in a Creek town concentrated in its public square, an outdoor council ground flanked on all four sides by buildings and centered by a sacred fire, symbol of the heavenly sun. Each building was open on the side facing the square and was supplied with two tiers of mat-covered benches. In the square were held the daily council meetings, and impressive assemblies of the whole confederacy occurred periodically. One such festival, held in midsummer, was the "Boskita," shortened by traders to "Busk."

Another tribe, of uncertain origin, which temporarily occupied East Tennessee during the proto-historic period was the Yuchi (or Euchee), who claimed to be "Children of the Sun." They were referred to by various other names. It is probable that they were the Indians of the "Chisca province" mentioned in accounts of the De Soto expedition. Juan Pardo, the Spaniard who invaded their land in 1566, described these people as living in houses built partly underground in a fortified village; later excavation of Yuchi sites in East Tennessee confirmed his description.

It was the powerful Cherokee Nation which forced both the

Creek and the Yuchi Indians to migrate from East Tennessee in the early 1700's. In 1714 the warriors of the Yuchi town of Chestowee on the Hiwassee River, fearing capture and enslavement by the Cherokee, massacred their fellow townsmen and then committed suicide. Soon thereafter the remaining Yuchi moved to the Chattahoochee Valley in Georgia and affiliated with the Creek Confederacy.

Another non-Muskhogean tribe, the Shawnee Indians, occupied the Cumberland Valley in Middle Tennessee during and shortly after the proto-historic period. The French had a trading post at the site of Nashville, 1710–14. On early French maps the Cumberland River is called the Chaouanon, the French name for Shawnee. About 1714 the Cherokee and Chickasaw combined forces to drive the Shawnee out of the Cumberland Valley. Most of them settled north of the Ohio River.

The Cherokee Indians After the Creek, Yuchi, and Shawnee Indians had been expelled during the early years of the eighteenth century, the Cherokee were the only Indians who actually occupied any land in Tennessee. Their towns were located in the Southern Appalachians—in East Tennessee and in the neighboring regions of North and South Carolina and Georgia. Cherokee claims to hunting grounds extended to the Ohio River on the north, to the Kanawha and its branch the New River on the east, and to the northward-flowing Tennessee (in conflict with the Chickasaw) on the west. In view of the absence of Indian towns after about 1715 in all of Tennessee except the southeastern corner and in most of Kentucky and western Virginia, this immense area was an Indian "no man's land" traversed by many tribes with war and hunting expeditions but where none had permanent homes.

The Cherokee Indians were the largest and one of the most important tribes in the Southeastern United States, justifying the name they gave themselves of *Ani-Yunwiya* or "principal people." They were kinsmen of the Iroquois and of that language stock. Their Muskhogean neighbors called them "Tciloki" or "people of a different speech," which was transcribed "Achelaque" by the Spaniards. The Cherokee themselves adopted it in the form "Tsalagi." From these words the name Cherokee is derived.

Authorities now believe that the Cherokee first came into the Southeast and into Tennessee more than a thousand years ago. At the beginning of the historic period their estimated population was about 22,000 and they were living in about eighty towns distributed among four large groups. The Lower settlements were along the Keowee and Tugaloo rivers in South Carolina and Georgia; the Middle settlements, the heart of the nation, were located near the headwaters of the Tuckaseegee and Little Tennessee rivers in North Carolina; and the Valley towns, also in North Carolina, were along the Valley, Notteley, and upper Hiwassee rivers. The fourth group, the only one in Tennessee, was the Upper or Overhill towns, located on the other side of the mountains from the Carolina settlements, chiefly along the Little Tennessee River but with a few towns on the Tellico and the Hiwassee. Early English traders, however, divided the towns into three groups instead of four, considering the Middle and Valley towns as one group—the Middle Cherokee.

Although the Cherokee Nation as a whole had a principal chief, the political, military, and religious life was centered in the towns, which varied in size from a dozen to around two hundred families. Each major town had a "King" and a "Great War Chief." On the west side of the public square in the center of each town was the council house or temple. Grouped around the temple and square were the dwelling houses, which like those of other Late Mississippian Indians were built of upright logs. In the center of the dirt floor was a scooped-out fireplace, flanked by a hearth stone for use in baking corn bread. At one end were the beds, made of saplings and woven splints. In cold weather the families slept in the adjacent "hot house," a small, dirt-covered, cone-shaped structure, also supplied with beds and a fireplace in which a fire was kept burning all day and banked at night. Similar hot houses were used by the medicine men for giving "sweat baths" as a means of treating certain diseases and also as a purification ritual.

The council house was used mainly as a temple for religious rites but also as a public hall for civil and military councils. Usually large enough to seat 500 persons, it was seven-sided to correspond to the seven clans of the Cherokee Nation, with each clan being given seats in a particular section. Seven large pillars outlined the outer walls, and within were two concentric series of seven posts each as well as a large central pillar. Three tiers of benches lined the walls, with one area, near the sacred seventh pillar of the outer wall, being reserved for the main officials, three of whom had special seats with high backs. Near the central pillar and in front of the officials' seats was the altar, at which a fire was kept perpetually burning except for periodic and ceremonial extinguishing and re-kindling. Lieutenant Henry Timberlake, who visited the Cherokee in 1761–62, described the town house at Chote as having "the appearance of a small mountain at a little distance." He commented on its gloomy interior, "extremely dark, having, besides the door, which is so narrow that but one at a time can pass, and that after much winding and turning, but one small aperture to let the smoak [sic] out, which is so ill-contrived, that most of it settles in the roof of the house."

Cherokee society was based on the family and the clan, with descent being on the maternal side. Nevertheless, each individual had a close relationship to his father's clan and was ordinarily permitted to marry into the clan of either of his grandparents. Intermarriage within the clan was strictly forbidden. In any particular town all seven of the Nation's clans[4] had members; thus, all the Cherokees were linked by bonds of kinship.

The national government paralleled the local. A principal, or paramount, chief for the Nation had the aid of seven counselors in conducting civil and religious affairs. There was a separate military organization headed by the Chief Warrior, or "Greatly Honored Man," whose insignia of office was a raven's skin hung around his neck. He had three assistants and seven counselors. The government also had numerous minor officials, including medicine men, or conjurers, whose duties were a combination of magic, fortune telling, practical surgery, and spiritual comforting. Women had an important role in time of war, particularly the "Honored Woman" who had a vote in deciding for or against war and the power of life or death over captives. The last and most noted of these "War Women," as they were called by the whites, was Nancy Ward, who has been credited with warning settlers of the danger of attacks and with saving at least one white captive from being burned at the stake.

The religious organization was closely related to the civil government. The expected holders of office, especially medicine men, were

---

4 The seven clans were named Wolf, Deer, Bird, Red Paint, Blue, Wild Potatoes, and Long Hairs.

dedicated in early childhood and received special training. The leading conjurer, or "High War Priest," performed the usual functions of a holy man, resorting to superstition, prestidigitation, and showmanship to achieve his aims. Dietary habits were influenced by superstition. Good health resulted from the practice of throwing fat into the fire prior to eating a meal, even though the Indians had never heard of cholesterol. Certain herbs, such as ginseng root, as well as the rites of the conjurers, held miraculous powers. Entirely apart from superstition, white people were eventually to learn of the benefits obtainable from Indian herbs and drugs.

As was the case with other Indians, the Cherokee had a vague conception of Creation as well as a belief in life after death. Personal possessions of the deceased were placed in the grave for use on the way to the happy hunting ground; presumably the sitting position of the corpse assured a good start on that journey. The Cherokee believed in a mysterious Being called "Yowa,"[5] conceived of as a unity of three "Elder Fires Above," who had created the sun, moon, and stars, and all living things. The moon was the deity which controlled Cherokee ceremonial life and determined the times for the holding of the seven sacred festivals which were held regularly, six of them every year and the seventh every seven years. These ceremonies were characterized by special dances, ritual bathing, crystal-gazing, extinguishing and rekindling the sacred fire, fasting followed by feasting, and prayers and sacrifices to the Supreme Being.

Before the beginning of historic times the Cherokee had become farmers, although they still depended on hunting and fishing for their meat supply. The chief crop was corn, which was so much their staff of life that two of the seven ceremonies were the New Green Corn and the Ripe Corn festivals. Other crops were beans, squash, gourds, pumpkins, and sunflowers. Farming was carried on mainly by the women and old men, since warfare and hunting absorbed the time of the able-bodied males. Between wars, however, men did more of the work. As a means of preventing starvation, each town had a communal granary, supplied in part from the "town plantation."

The specialties of the Cherokee in crafts were stamped pottery

---

[5] The similarity of that name to the Hebrew "Yahweh" (Jehovah) led the author-trader, James Adair, to believe that the Indians were a lost tribe of Israel.

and skillfully carved stone pipes in the shapes of birds, animals, or occasionally human beings. The Cherokee were also adept at wood carving and in weaving baskets and mats out of colored strips of cane. Clothing was made of turkey feathers as well as of animal skins, and feathers of more brilliantly colored birds were used as trimmings or headdresses.

The women wore skirts and shoulder mantles, and the men breech clouts and sleeveless shirts. Both wore moccasins. The men's garb was gaudier than that of the women, and included earrings, neck-pieces, and bracelets to supplement the painting or tattooing of the body. At the time of a visit to London in 1730 of several young Cherokee chiefs, a newspaper described their attire when presented to the royal family:

> The Indian King had on a scarlet jacket, but all the rest were naked except an apron about their middle and a horse's tail hung down behind. Their faces, shoulders, etc., were spotted with red, blue and green. They had bows in their hands and painted feathers in their heads.[6]

The Cherokee were somewhat taller and more robust than other Southern Indians; they had coarse, black hair, but rather light complexions. Timberlake described them as having an "olive colour" and noted that the men usually shaved their heads or had all their hair plucked out by the roots "except a patch on the hinder part of the head, about twice the bigness of a crown-piece, which is ornamented with beads, feathers, wampum, stained deers hair, and such like baubles." He also said they slit their ears and stretched them to an enormous size in order to adorn them with pendants and rings, but he explained that this custom was borrowed from the Shawnee Indians. The women wore their hair long, "sometimes to the ground, club'd, and ornamented with ribbons of various colours."

Marriage customs seem to have been influenced by the near equality of the sexes which resulted from the matrilineal system of the Cherokee. Elaborate negotiations were carried on by the kinfolk of the couple. The groom would send the bride a piece of venison as a pledge that he would provide an ample food supply; and the bride would send the groom an ear of corn as a token that the crops would be tended and the food prepared. But it seems that the life of

6 Williams, *Early Travels*, 129n.

Cherokee women was not one of drudgery and unrequited toil. They were a respected group whose family ties were important. Marriages were of short duration, however, and adultery so prevalent as to provoke comment from early European visitors. The trader James Adair attributed this adultery to these Indians' "petticoat government."

Effects of Indian-White Contacts ᘒ Before the coming of the white man the life of the Cherokee and other Indians was leisurely and pleasant. There was an abundance of game and the streams were well stocked with fish. Without much cultivation the fertile soil produced corn and other vegetables. There was plenty of time for fun and entertainment. The Cherokee as well as the Creeks indulged in the "ball play" ancestor of lacrosse and also played chunkey, and gambled on the results of the games.

Large-scale wars were not prevalent before the whites came along and incited one tribe to war against another. Neighboring tribes engaged in commerce, transporting goods along Indian trails and on the rivers in dugout canoes. But with the development of trade relations with the whites, wars became more prevalent, and hunting became a business instead of a sport. As their primitive weapons for war and hunting were replaced or supplemented by firearms, the Indians became dependent on the whites for a regular supply of ammunition. Other European goods gradually became necessities. From the whites the Indians obtained horses and other domesticated animals and learned better methods of agriculture; the Indians were taught the doctrines of Christianity, but while adopting the white man's religion and customs, they acquired many of his vices to add to their own.

In a similar way white civilization was influenced by contacts with the Indians, with both beneficial and injurious results. The white man's diet was greatly enriched by food products contributed by the American Indian, and the billion-dollar tobacco industry had its origin in a weed first cultivated by those aborigines. The natives also taught the white pioneers how to survive in a wilderness environment. On the other hand, in retaliation against the savages' methods of warfare, the whites came to adopt practices equally savage in character. The opportunity to occupy great stretches of Indian country stimulated the white man's greed, and the natives were frequently dispossessed by dishonorable means. Although the Indians were the inevitable casualties of the march of civilization, we cannot ignore the marks which the struggle left engraved on the characters of the people, both white and red.

SUGGESTED READINGS

General Accounts

Robert S. Cotterill, *The Southern Indians* (Norman, 1954), Chs. 1–2; Folmsbee, Corlew, and Mitchell, *Tennessee*, I, Ch. 2; Philip M. Hamer, *Tennessee: A History, 1763–1932* (4 vols., New York, 1933), I, Ch. 1; Haywood, *Natural and Aboriginal History*; Thomas M. N. Lewis and Madeline Kneberg, *Tribes That Slumber: Indians of the Tennessee Region* (Knoxville, 1958; reprinted, 1960); Lewis and Kneberg, *Hiwassee Island: An Archaeological Account of Four Tennessee Indian Peoples* (Knoxville, 1946); James H. Malone, *The Chickasaw Nation* (Louisville, 1922); Robert A. McGaw and Richard W. Weesner, "Tennessee Antiquities Re-Exhumed: The New Exhibit of the Thruston Collection at Vanderbilt," *THQ*, XXIV (Summer, 1965), 121–42; Charles H. Nash, "The Human Continuum of Shelby County, Tennessee," WTHS *Papers*, No. XIV (1960), 5–31; Theodore Roosevelt, *The Winning of the West* (4 vols., New York, 1904), I, Part 1, "The Spread of English-Speaking Peoples," Ch. 3 (one-vol. abridgment, New York, 1963, Ch. 2); John R. Swanton, *Early History of the Creek Indians and Their Neighbors*, U. S. Bureau of American Ethnology, *Bulletin* No. 73 (Washington, D. C., 1922).

Specialized Accounts

The Cherokee: John P. Brown, *Old Frontiers: The Story of the Cherokee Indians from Earliest Times to the Date of Their Removal to the West, 1838* (Kingsport, Tenn., 1938); William H. Gilbert, Jr., *The Eastern Cherokees*, U. S. Bureau of American Ethnology, *Bulletin* No. 133 (Washington, D. C., 1943); Lawrence H. Gipson, *The British Empire Before the American Revolution* (12 vols. to date, New York, 1936–), IV, 49–83; Henry T. Malone, *Cherokees of the Old South: A People in Transition* (Athens, Ga., 1956); James Mooney, "Myths of the Cherokee," U. S. Bureau of American Ethnology, *19th Annual Report*, Pt. I (Washington, D. C., 1900); Charles C. Royce, "The Cherokee Nation," U. S. Bureau of American Ethnology, *5th Annual Report* (Washington, D. C., 1887); Grace D. Woodward, *The Cherokees* (Norman, 1963).

Travels: James Adair, *History of the American Indians*, ed. Samuel C. Williams (Johnson City, Tenn., 1930); William Bartram, *Observations on the Creek and Cherokee Indians*, American Ethnological Society *Transactions*, III (New York, 1853); Edward G. Bourne (ed.), *Narratives of the Career of Hernando De Soto* (2 vols., New York, 1922); John R. Swanton (ed.), *Final Report of the U. S. De Soto Expedition Commission, House Executive Document*, No. 71, 75 Cong. 1 sess. (Washington, D. C., 1939); Charles H. Faulkner, *The Old Stone Fort: Exploring an Archaeological Mystery* (Knoxville, 1968); Frances Harper (ed.), *The Travels of William Bartram* (New Haven, 1958); Samuel C. Williams (ed.), *Lieutenant Henry Timberlake's Memoirs, 1756–1765* (Johnson City, Tenn., 1927; reprinted, Marietta, Ga., 1948); Williams (ed.), *Early Travels in the Tennessee Country* (Johnson City, Tenn., 1928).

3. ⁊⁖ *The Europeans Struggle for Control*

THERE IS A LEGEND that some Welshmen under the leadership of a prince named Madoc came to the Tennessee country by way of the port of Mobile in the twelfth century. Although there is a highway marker for the Old Stone Fort near Manchester which suggests that possibility, the visit remains a legend rather than a provable fact. As indicated in the preceding chapter, it is now known that the "Fort" was a ceremonial structure built by Woodland Indians about 100–500 A.D.

First Explorations ⁊⁖ The first Europeans in Tennessee probably were the members of the expedition of Hernando De Soto, whose exact route is still a subject of controversy. It is believed, however, that in 1540 these Spaniards from Florida came into Tennessee along the Hiwassee River, where they found the Cherokee Indians, and then followed an Indian trail to the Tennessee River. They camped for some time at the Creek town of Chiaha on an island a few miles below the site of Chattanooga. The Spaniards played and swam with the Indians until the natives abandoned the town because of De Soto's demand that they provide female companionship for his soldiers. De Soto sent out two scouts to locate a province called Chisca which the Indians said was rich in gold and copper, but their search was in vain.

After cutting across Alabama, De Soto's expedition passed through the Chickasaw country in northern Mississippi and reached the Mississippi River in May, 1541, at the Indian town of Quizquiz (pronounced Keeskees).[1] De Soto died in the Arkansas country, but in 1566 and in 1567 another Spaniard, Juan Pardo, led other expeditions into the Tennessee region seeking alliances with the natives as well as gold in the Chisca province. His soldiers became involved in hostilities with what probably were the Yuchi Indians, and built forts for defense. One of them was located at the Creek town of Chiaha, and probably was the first fort built by Europeans on Tennessee soil. The forts were soon abandoned, however, and the Spaniards did not establish any settlements in Tennessee.

Of greater significance was the almost simultaneous appearance of the English and the French at the eastern and western extremities of the future Tennessee about a century later—in 1673. The Englishmen, James Needham and Gabriel Arthur, were sent out from Fort Henry, at the site of Petersburg, Virginia, by a trader named Abraham Wood. After passing through the Occaneechi villages in the Piedmont, they encountered a party of Tomahittan Indians, who led them across the mountains to their towns, located somewhere in East Tennessee. Most writers have identified the Tomahittans as Overhill Cherokee,[2] but recent archaeological research indicates that they were the Yuchi Indians, living along the Hiwassee River. The Englishmen learned that these Indians had been trading with the Spaniards in Florida, but that some of the tribe had been captured and enslaved. Therefore, the Indians were interested in trading with the English. Leaving Arthur with the Tomahittans, Needham took several of the Indians to Fort Henry, where they were entertained by Wood. On the return journey Needham was killed by his Occaneechi guide, who told the Tomahittans to hasten home and kill the other Englishman. His aim was to preserve for his tribe the position of middleman between the English and the Western In-

[1] According to the 1939 *Final Report of the De Soto Expedition Commission*, the site was in Mississippi, but Memphians have long contended that it was in Tennessee. Recently, an Indian town located between Memphis and the Mississippi line has been excavated and restored, and arbitrarily given the name of Chucalissa. West Tennessee archaeologists believe that it may have been the Quizquiz town visited by De Soto, and that it was then occupied by the Tunica Indians, kinsmen of the Natchez tribe. Nash and Gates, "Chucalissa Indian Town," 103–21.

[2] Grace Woodward in *The Cherokees*, p. 28, even interpolates within a long quotation from Wood the name of a town, "Chote," and the words "the Cherokees" without the customary brackets to show they were not in the original, merely because the late Judge S. C. Williams said the Tomahittans were Cherokees and guessed that the town mentioned was Chote.

dians. Arthur was saved, however, by the intervention of a chief, and he was permitted to accompany the Indians on several war and hunting expeditions before returning to Fort Henry. Following these visits, the Virginians developed trade relations with the Tennessee Indians, but they were later outstripped by the more advantageously located traders from Charleston, South Carolina.

Meanwhile, the French, from their colony in the St. Lawrence Valley, began to explore the western country. In 1673 Father Jacques Marquette, a Jesuit missionary, and Louis Jolliet, a trader, floated down the Mississippi as far as the mouth of the Arkansas. On the way they probably stopped on Tennessee soil. In 1682 Robert Cavelier de la Salle led an expedition to the mouth of the Mississippi. Near the mouth of the Hatchie on the first or second Chickasaw Bluff, he built a fort and named it "Prud'homme" after a member of the expedition who had become lost. La Salle stopped again at Fort Prud'homme on the return journey to the Great Lakes.

The next Frenchman known to have visited Tennessee was Martin Chartier, who married a Shawnee woman and lived with her people on the Cumberland River near the site of Nashville. In 1692 he led a party of Shawnee eastward; later they settled on Chartier's Creek in Pennsylvania. By 1696 Jean Couture had become the first of several renegade French traders who found their way from the Mississippi River to Charleston. On a French map of 1701 the Tennessee River is called the "road to Carolina." The French renegades stimulated abortive efforts of Dr. Daniel Coxe and others to establish an English colony on the Mississippi, which in turn led to more successful efforts on the part of the French to assume a dominating position in the Mississippi Valley and along the Gulf of Mexico.

The French established trading posts throughout the area, at Biloxi, Mississippi, in 1699, and at Mobile, New Orleans, and in the Illinois country, north of the Ohio, early in the next century. There was a temporary trading post at the site of Nashville, which therefore became known as "French Lick," from about 1710 until the Shawnee were driven out of the Cumberland Valley in 1714.[3] More permanent was a French post, Fort Toulouse, at the site of Montgomery, Alabama, which had a great influence on Tennessee history.

In an attempt to bolster their claims, the French distorted geog-

[3] The name of the trader is unknown, but the name of his youthful assistant, Jean du Charleville, has been preserved.

raphy in drawing maps of North America. Since the Tennessee and the Cumberland rivers (after the expulsion of the Shawnee) were in Cherokee and Chickasaw country, nations that adhered to the English instead of the French, those rivers were drawn without their bends, or curves, southward. In contrast, the rivers flowing into the French-controlled Gulf of Mexico were shown as rising far to the north, within present-day Kentucky. Some of these maps were copied by the English. Also, according to tradition, the French Broad River was given that name because it flowed through the mountains into the French country, whereas another Broad River, rising near its source, flowed eastward to the Atlantic. Some Englishmen in the colonies, however, demanded that the French be driven out by force, so that the "sea to sea" clauses in several colonial charters could become valid.

Indian Trade and Anglo-French Rivalry In the imperial contest to determine whether the eastern part of the Mississippi Valley, including Tennessee, would be under the control of Great Britain or of France, the Indians and the white traders played a conspicuous part. The Indians were increasingly dependent on goods of European manufacture, especially gunpowder, and they tended to favor the European country that was the most generous and consistent in supplying their needs. Within most Indian nations there was one faction favoring the British and another favoring the French. In general, however, the French were able to control the Creeks and the Choctaw, while the British usually held sway over the Cherokee and the Chickasaw. But each country and its traders continued to try to break the other's monopoly. The result was lack of harmony within each tribe and frequent wars between tribes, with one contestant being supported and supplied by the British and the other by the French.

Very important in Tennessee history was the Europeans' trade with the Cherokee, especially the Overhill group, who after about 1715 were the only Indians whose towns were located on Tennessee soil. From the British angle, the traders from South Carolina were able to supplant those from Virginia, but the situation was complicated by spasmodic efforts of the Virginians to recover the trade. The first Carolina traders with the Overhill Cherokee were Eleazar

Wigan (or Wiggan), Alexander Long, and Cornelius Doherty, who became active during the first two decades of the eighteenth century; but it is probable that the trade began during the last years of the preceding century.

The Indian trade was based largely on credit, extended by British merchants to those in Charleston buying the trade goods, and then in turn selling on credit to the traders, who carried the goods into Indian country to exchange for skins and furs. In the early period the Indians sold to the traders members of other tribes captured in war. They were sold as slaves in Charleston and sent to the West Indies or New England, but the practice of enslaving Indians gradually died out in the British colonies. The leading commodity supplied by the Indians was deerskins; in 1748, for example, approximately 160,000 skins worth £250,000 were exported from Charleston. Much smaller quantities of beaverskins and other pelts were also involved in the trade.

In exchange for the skins, but sometimes on credit, the traders supplied a variety of goods, including clothing (especially blankets, the Indians' "dress suit" for ceremonial occasions), shirts, laced hats, petticoats, colored stockings, striped calico, ribbons, and buttons. For personal adornment there were beads, bracelets, ear bobs, vermilion, and looking glasses (largely for the men). Also supplied were kettles, hoes, axes, scissors, knives, hatchets, guns, gunflints, gunpowder, and bullets. Despite regulations to the contrary, liquor was sold, usually at so many mouthfuls of rum for a deerskin; the customary practice was for the buyer to select a man with a large mouth to do the measuring. The Indians, like children, always expected presents; sometimes this increased the traders' overhead expenses, but frequently the government supplied the presents.

The journey from Charleston to the Overhill country required three or four weeks. Usually two or three traders traveled together as a caravan, requiring as many as a hundred horses to carry their goods. During most of the year the traders lived at an Indian village with their Indian wives and halfbreed children. Some of these halfbreeds later became prominent chiefs of the Indian nation. After the Indians returned from the hunt, they swapped skins for trade goods, and then the trader took the skins to Charleston. Sometimes the trader would not have enough peltry to pay off his debt to the Charleston merchant. If that occurred too frequently, he was in danger of confinement in a debtor's prison unless he could first obtain a "protection" from the colonial government permitting him to make some arrangement with his creditors. In petitioning for such a "protection" the trader would not hesitate to enlarge upon his service to the colony in maintaining the good will of the Indians toward the English. Such was not always the case, however. There were some dishonest traders who regularly cheated the Indians and occasionally became involved in brawls with them, thereby doing the British cause serious harm. Despite meticulous regulations and even the supplying of iron yardsticks, which could not be broken—but which were easily misplaced—many instances of Indian dissatisfaction with British traders developed.

The Cherokee country was called the "key to Carolina" because of the ease with which the colony of South Carolina could be invaded through the Cherokee domain. In 1725, Colonel George Chicken returned from a Cherokee visit to report that some of the Overhill towns were inclined to favor the French. Four years later an English visitor to South Carolina, Sir Alexander Cuming, determined to correct that situation and to win the unalterable allegiance of the Cherokee to the British crown. He entered an assemblage of warriors at Keowee, one of the Lower Cherokee towns, fully armed—a serious violation of Cherokee custom—and required the Indians "to acknowledge his Majesty King George's Sovereignty over them on their Knee." This was a submission, he boasted, which they had "never before made either to God or man." Later he met with delegations from all the Cherokee towns and named one of the chiefs, Moytoy of Great Tellico, as emperor of the whole nation.

Of even greater importance was Cuming's decision to take six young Indians to London with him. Included in the group was Attakullakulla, the Little Carpenter, who was destined to become the chief diplomat of the Cherokee and a powerful force, during most of his later life, in maintaining their friendship with the English. He never forgot his experiences on the journey and hoped for another opportunity to visit the "great white chief" across the waters. After being presented to King George II, the six Cherokee, on behalf of the tribe, signed a treaty in 1730 that promised everlasting friendship with the British and willingness to fight against their enemies. An important provision, which later caused trouble, stated that if an Englishman killed a Cherokee Indian, he would be punished as if he had killed an Englishman; "in like Manner, if an Indian kills an Englishman, [he] shall be deliver'd up to the Governor, and be punish'd by the same English Law as if he were an Englishman."[4]

Although Cuming's work considerably strengthened British influence among the Cherokee, that influence has been exaggerated by some writers. Actually, the English had serious difficulties with the Cherokee within the next three or four years. The selection of Moytoy of Great Tellico as emperor had antagonized another Overhill town, Chote, the traditional capital of the Cherokee Nation, even though Moytoy was not commissioned by South Carolina until 1738. That action came as a result of the disturbing influence of Christian Priber, a German socialist, who had arrived at Great Tellico about a year earlier to establish his communistic "Kingdom of Paradise." The English trader-author, James Adair, said that Priber "ate, drank . . . dressed, and painted himself with the Indians," learned their language, and "by gradual advances impressed them with a very ill opinion of the English." He also "inflated the artless savages, with a prodigious high opinion of their own importance in the American scale of power." According to another trader, Priber said that in his "Kingdom," which he also called a republic, "all things should be in common" among the members, "even their wives." There would be no marriage contract, and women would be free to exchange husbands every day. Children were to be "looked upon as Children of the Public and be taken care of as such and not by their natural parents."

Priber told the Indians to consider both the English and French "as interlopers"; but since the English had a near monopoly of Cherokee trade, he advised those Indians to play off the French against the English. Considering Priber to be a French agent, the English tried to arrest him, but the Cherokee would not permit it. Later, in 1743, he was seized in the Creek country by English traders and taken to Georgia, where he was imprisoned for the remainder of his life.

Despite the anti-English influence of Priber and a French captive, Antoine Bonnyfoy, who was adopted into the tribe and resided at Great Tellico for several months, that town (along with its

4 Williams, *Early Travels*, 140–41.

neighbor Hiwassee) was the center of the pro-English sentiment. This was due largely to the recognition in Charleston of Moytoy (and after his death, his son) as the emperor of the Cherokee Nation. It was the offended Chote and the other towns along the Little Tennessee River which were for a considerable period of time most susceptible to the French influence.

French imperialism not only challenged the dominant position of the English among the Cherokee Indians but also among the Chickasaw, who lived in northern Mississippi but claimed all of the western part of Tennessee. English traders, such as Thomas Welch, had begun operations among the Chickasaw before the end of the seventeenth century and had encouraged their hostile attitude toward the French. The resistance of these Indians near the Mississippi River enabled them to disrupt French communications between the trading posts near the Gulf of Mexico and those in the Illinois country and in Canada. Many French boats on the Mississippi were ambushed.

Unable to lure the Chickasaw away from their adherence to the English, the French adopted the policy of destruction, first by inciting the Choctaw against the Chickasaw and then by force of French arms. So serious was the danger that the Cherokee offered the Chickasaw a haven in their country. Determined to hold on to their lands, however, the warlike Chickasaw succeeded, in 1736, in defeating two French expeditions before they could make a united assault. Three years later a much larger expedition of 3,600 Frenchmen and Indians rendezvoused at the site of Memphis, and the Chickasaw sued for peace. Under the harsh French terms, the power of that tribe was considerably weakened, and raids on the French convoys on the Mississippi River became less frequent; but the Chickasaw still remained a problem to the French.

The Building of Fort Loudoun ⧉ The contest between the English and the French for control of the eastern part of the Mississippi Valley, including Tennessee, erupted into a series of wars from 1689 to 1763 between those nations and their allies in Europe as well as between their colonial inhabitants. There were interludes of peace in Europe, but they were not always observed by the colonists and their Indian allies. The last of these wars, called the French and Indian War in America, actually began in the New World in 1754. In its American as well as its international aspects, the war ended in a complete British victory. One factor, of some slight influence in its outcome, was the building of the most western English fort in America, Fort Loudoun, on the bank of the Little Tennessee River.

The idea of a British fort in the Overhill Cherokee country had been suggested as early as 1746, when Chote and the other Little Tennessee River towns, under the leadership of Old Hop and the Little Carpenter, were still the center of the pro-French influence. When, about 1752, the English finally dropped Moytoy's son, the "Little Emperor," and recognized Old Hop of Chote as the emperor of the Cherokee Nation, the way was paved for the shifting of his faction to the English side. There was increased need for a fort to protect the Overhill towns from raids by French-controlled Indians, and to provide security for the women and children while the warriors were on the warpath. "They pray for it as a favour," wrote Governor James Glen of South Carolina to the British Government, "so it would probably fix their friendship for the English at present, but as the Indians are pretty fickle should they ever afterwards meditate mischief, it would enable us immediately to curb their insolencies and prevent things from coming to a head."[5]

When the English in 1753 built Fort Prince George near the Lower Cherokee town of Keowee, the Chote faction in the Overhill region renewed its contacts with the French, using French John, a slave of Old Hop's and the leading French agent in the Cherokee country, as messenger. The Little Carpenter, Old Hop's "Right Hand Man," also had been influenced by the French while spending several years as a captive and then as a visitor among Francophile Indians. He hoped that Cherokee relations with the French could be used as a lever to bring about improvement of the unsatisfactory trade conditions with Carolina.

Although the French and Indian War began in the distant region of the upper Ohio Valley, because of the efforts of the French to prevent the settlement of that area by the Ohio Company of Virginia, both the English and the French attempted to obtain the aid of the Cherokee. At first the Cherokee repulsed the French overtures and even promised a thousand warriors to Virginia to assist

[5] Hamer, *Fort Loudoun*, 4.

an expedition against the French Fort Duquesne at the site of Pittsburgh, hoping thereby to induce the Virginians to break the Carolina monopoly of the Cherokee trade. But angered by the failure of the British to build a fort in the Overhill country and frightened by French threats of invasion, the Cherokee promised the French to be neutral. Therefore, no warriors went to Virginia. While the Braddock expedition against Fort Duquesne was meeting disaster in the summer of 1755, five hundred Cherokee were meeting with Governor Glen at Saluda, where they ceded sovereignty over all their lands to the English in exchange for the promise that a strong fort would be built in the Overhill country.

The building of the fort was delayed, however, by lack of funds and lack of cooperation between the governors of South Carolina and Virginia. In July of 1754 the British government ordered Glen to build the fort, and instructed Lieutenant Governor Robert Dinwiddie of Virginia to send him some portion of the ten thousand pounds Dinwiddie was being given for the prosecution of the war against the French. Glen asked Dinwiddie for seven thousand pounds, but Glen received only one thousand, which was woefully inadequate. It was not until December, 1755, when a delegation of 150 Cherokee, including the Little Carpenter, went to Charleston demanding action and threatening to join the French, that the South Carolina legislature was moved to appropriate two thousand pounds as a loan to the British crown to start the fort. Since the assembly failed to levy a tax to raise the money, patriotic citizens of Charleston had to subscribe the amount.

Glen began assembling an expedition, appointed Captain Raymond Demere as commander, and sent an agent to the Cherokee country to select a site for the fort. Early in June, 1756, as the expedition was about to start, William Henry Lyttelton arrived from England to replace Glen as governor. Lyttelton also was instructed to build the fort, but with funds supplied by an outright grant from the assembly rather than by a loan. Captain Demere was sent on to Fort Prince George, where he waited for three months before the reassembled expedition finally arrived.

Meanwhile, Virginia hoped to get some Cherokee warriors for a second expedition against Fort Duquesne. At a conference with the Cherokee on the Broad River in North Carolina in March, 1756, the Virginians promised assistance in the building of a strong fort, and the Cherokee promised to send four hundred warriors to Virginia within forty days after the fort had been completed. Having learned that Glen was organizing an expedition, Dinwiddie sent Major Andrew Lewis and sixty men to the Overhill country to help the South Carolinians build the fort; Lewis was then to return with the promised warriors.

When Lewis arrived late in June, the South Carolinians were not there, but he was met with a demand from the Indians that two forts be built, one on the north bank of the Little Tennessee River and another on the south bank after the South Carolinians arrived. Lewis reluctantly acquiesced and built a small log fort across the river from and about a mile above the town of Chote. After learning that the Cherokee were in contact with the French at Fort Toulouse, Lewis surprised their leaders in secret council, whereupon he was told that they had agreed to send a letter to Captain Demere at Fort Prince George telling him to return to Charleston and that the Indians would make slaves of the few soldiers already in their country. Although the message was changed at the insistence of Lewis, he left for Virginia in August with only seven warriors and with the impression that the Cherokee were very undependable and in constant communication with the French.[6]

Eventually the South Carolina expedition, financed by four thousand pounds Lyttelton obtained from the South Carolina assembly, was ready to depart. The expedition of about two hundred men included one company of royal troops and two companies of South Carolina militia, commanded by Captains John Stuart and John Postell. The engineer to supervise the building of the fort was William De Brahm, a German who earlier supervised the fortification of Charleston. The Demere expedition left Fort Prince George on September 21 and followed the old trade route down the Hiwassee River to the site of Murphy, North Carolina, and thence across to the Tellico River. Above the town of Great Tellico, the English-

---

[6] Lewis returned to Virginia by way of the Carolinas and reported to Governors Lyttelton and Dobbs. Dr. James G. M. Ramsey in his *Annals of Tennessee*, published in 1853, repeated the errors made by earlier historians of South Carolina and Georgia (Alexander Hewat, 1779) and of North Carolina (F. X. Martin, 1829) who said that Lewis had been sent by the Earl of Loudoun (instead of Governor Dinwiddie) and had built Fort Loudoun (instead of a smaller fort which was never garrisoned). Unfortunately, many later writers followed Ramsey in perpetuating those errors. See Folmsbee, "Annotations," in 1967 edition of Ramsey's Annals, 751–52.

men were warmly received by the Little Carpenter and other chiefs and escorted to the towns on the Little Tennessee.

The construction of the fort was begun after a dispute between Demere and De Brahm as to its location had been settled in favor of De Brahm. The site selected was on the south bank of the Little Tennessee near the mouth of the Tellico, partly on a ridge above the river, which De Brahm considered an essential factor in the fort's defense. Roughly diamond-shaped, the fort had a bastion projecting from each corner, each of which was to mount three cannon. Around the fort a ditch or moat was dug and locust trees were planted in it; the trees' long, sharp thorns, De Brahm declared, would render the fort "impregnable at least against Indians who always engage naked." The embankment along the ditch was also provided with a palisade fifteen feet in height. Twelve small cannon were brought to the fort on the backs of horses by John Elliot, an unfortunate choice because he was the trader most disliked and distrusted by the Overhill Cherokee.

Despite protestations of friendship by those Indians to Captain Demere, a pro-French conspiracy centered in the town of Great Tellico was condoned by the emperor, Old Hop. It was carried further than he desired, however, when a treaty was negotiated with the French governor at New Orleans. The French also built a fort near the mouth of the Tennessee River, and they promised adequate trade and a fort in the Overhill country if the Cherokee would first drive the English from their towns. As rumors of an imminent French attack became current, the isolated English detachment faced the danger of mutiny. Demere had to read the articles of war to the soldiers when Postell's company threatened to go home after De Brahm discharged them from working on the fort. On December 22 De Brahm departed for Charleston, although the fort was far from complete. Old Hop called him the "warrior who ran away in the night." Under Demere's supervision, work on the fort was speeded up, and the name was changed from Fort Semintorium to Fort Loudoun, in honor of the Earl of Loudoun, commander-in-chief of British troops in America.

On June 26, 1757, Demere wrote Governor Lyttelton that the fort was entirely done according to De Brahm's specifications. Work was continued for several months more, however, inside the fort, in the construction of a guardhouse and other buildings. In contrast to the small, ungarrisoned Virginia fort, Fort Loudoun covered approximately two acres of ground. In August, Raymond Demere was relieved by his brother, Captain Paul Demere, as commander of the garrison. As the fort approached completion the disposition of the Cherokee improved, except at Great Tellico, where news of French victories in the North encouraged the pro-French faction. It is probable that if Fort Loudoun had not been built when it was, the Cherokee would have severed relations with the English and gone to war against them on the side of the French several years before that actually occurred. Had it happened in 1757 instead of 1760, British success in the French and Indian War would have been many times more difficult.

The Cherokee War ⧉ During the spring and summer of 1757 more than 250 Cherokee participated in the defense of the Virginia frontier, and in 1758 there were four or five hundred so engaged. Ironically, the incidents occurring in connection with this warfare on behalf of the English contributed to the breach which developed between these allies. On the way to or from the Virginia theater of war, many of the Cherokee, annoyed because their extravagant desires for gifts and equipment, especially paint, were not fulfilled, conducted themselves like freebooters. The white settlers naturally retaliated, and the dissension which resulted led the Virginia government to fail to keep its promises to garrison the Virginia fort and resume trade relations. In August, 1758, several Cherokee scalps taken by Virginia militia on New River were turned in as Shawnee for the Virginia bounty for scalps of pro-French Indians. About the same time a group of Cherokee was attacked and several killed by western Virginia settlers angry because of Indian horse-stealing, even though in this case the Indians were retaliating for the loss of their own horses.

The Little Carpenter, on his way to Williamsburg to try to forestall the imminent war between the Cherokee and Virginia, was induced to join General John Forbes's slow-moving expedition against Fort Duquesne. Learning that the fort was being abandoned by the French, he resumed his peace mission. Forbes had him arrested as a deserter and placed in chains. This humiliation of their beloved leader caused an explosion of anger among the Cherokee; the Little Carpenter eventually made his peace with Governor Francis Fauquier of Virginia, who gave him a tongue-lashing but promised to establish trade relations the next spring.

Delighted with that prospect, the Little Carpenter returned to Chote with the news and then went to Charleston to assure Lyttelton of Cherokee friendship. While he was there, a party of Overhill Cherokee from the town of Great Tellico, incited by a Creek chief named Mortar, took about twenty white scalps in western North Carolina. A short time later several more scalps were taken by a party from the Lower town of Estatoe. Governor Lyttelton cut off the supply of ammunition for the Cherokee Nation, which gave the French agents an opportunity to increase their influence. Open warfare seemed inevitable, and Lyttelton started fitting out an expedition to force the Cherokee to keep the peace.

Before the expedition left Charleston, a delegation of Lower Cherokee, but including also the Great Warrior (Oconostota) and Ostenaco from the Overhill towns, arrived to confer with the governor. Their overtures were rejected and they were taken along, virtually as prisoners, as Lyttelton and the army marched to Fort Prince George. The Indians were reminded of the treaty promise of 1730 that if a Cherokee killed an Englishman, he should be turned over to the governor for punishment according to English law; and when most of the Cherokee delegates were released, twenty-eight of the leading chieftains were retained as hostages. Also, the Cherokee were forced to sign a new treaty, agreeing that a hostage should be kept at Fort Prince George for each guilty Indian not immediately surrendered. Disregarded was the fact that the chiefs who were kept as hostages had gone to Charleston under a guarantee of safe return; thus, the Indians justifiably accused the English of bad faith. Also, they pointed out that most of the guilty Indians had already escaped across the mountains. Nevertheless, a few Indians were found and surrendered. It might have been better if Lyttelton had followed Glen's earlier policy of requiring an Indian who had killed an Englishman to go on the warpath against the French and bring in a French scalp.

The Cherokee reaction to the keeping of the hostages was very unfavorable, and they repeatedly demanded their release. Fort Prince George was besieged, and scalpings along the frontier became prevalent. On February 16, 1760, Oconostota lured the commander of the fort, Lieutenant Richard Coytmore, outside for another conversation. Suddenly he waved a bridle in the air as a signal and Indians in ambush opened fire, mortally wounding Coytmore. The soldiers in the fort quickly massacred the twenty-one hostages when they resisted being put in irons. This action brought the whole Cherokee Nation into war against the English, except the Little Carpenter, who had done his best to preserve the peace; having failed, he retired to the woods and refused to participate in the war.

For some time Fort Loudoun had been practically in a state of siege. Located far out on the frontier, its garrison was in great peril. Measures were taken to relieve it, but they were unsuccessful. Governor Lyttelton called on the governors of North Carolina and Virginia for help and sent an appeal for troops to General Jeffrey Amherst, the British commander in New York. Amherst sent 1,200 men, under the command of Colonel Archibald Montgomery, who arrived in Charleston April 1. North Carolina did nothing, but Virginia organized a force under William Byrd to send supplies to Fort Loudoun and to cooperate with Montgomery; however, the force arrived in southwest Virginia too late for either purpose.

Montgomery's army, with the aid of South Carolina troops, ravaged the Lower Cherokee towns and then sent overtures of peace to the other branches of the Cherokee. Had not those Indians been so fearful that their emissaries would be seized and slaughtered as Lyttelton's hostages had been, they probably would have responded to the overtures. Instead, Montgomery marched to the Middle towns, where he battled a large force of Indians on June 27 and suffered such heavy casualties (though not as many as the Cherokee) that he decided to return to Charleston. He had been ordered by Amherst to chastise the Cherokee and return to New York. Having fulfilled the first part of the order, he claimed that he was now bound to fulfill the second. The army departed, and Fort Loudoun was left to its fate.

Unable to take the fort by assault, the Indians hoped to starve the garrison into submission, but those plans were frustrated for a time by Indian women. Some of the women who had husbands among the garrison smuggled food into the fort. Also, the new governor of South Carolina, William Bull, slipped some ribbon and paint into the fort,[7] which was traded for food. When news arrived of the relief expeditions, hopes were raised and then dashed as the Indians exultantly told the garrison that they had defeated Montgomery's army and "killed and scalp'd so many that their hands were sore." As Oconostota succeeded in sealing off the fort with an effective guard, supplies dwindled until the garrison subsisted mainly on horseflesh. Many soldiers became ill and others deserted. Therefore, the fort was surrendered on August 7.

The soldiers were allowed to march out with arms and baggage and with an escort to Virginia or Fort Prince George. After one day's march toward South Carolina, however, the escort disappeared and Indians attacked from ambush. Captain Paul Demere and all the other officers except John Stuart were killed, as were more than twenty others, including three women. Apparently the Indians intended to kill as many soldiers as the number of hostages massacred at Fort Prince George. Survivors were taken as prisoners and tortured as they were marched back toward the fort. Eventually, most of the prisoners were returned to the British as a part of the fitful negotiations for peace which later developed.

The life of John Stuart was spared partly because he was well liked by the Indians and partly because they intended to force him to fire the captured cannon from the fort in an attack planned against Fort Prince George. The Little Carpenter, however, purchased Stuart from his captor and then helped him escape to Byrd's camp in Virginia. The aid expected from the French and the Creek Indians failed to materialize, so the Cherokee were forced to carry on the war alone. When the Cherokee War began, the French and Indian War had practically come to an end, as a result of British victories in the St. Lawrence Valley. The French did attempt to send the Cherokee some ammunition, but the boats were unable to get past the obstructions in the Tennessee River.

It was not long before the Cherokee were inclined to sue for peace, but another army under Colonel James Grant was sent from New York by Amherst to punish the Indians. Grant therefore destroyed many of the Middle and Valley towns before he accepted any peace overtures. After considerable delay, a peace treaty was signed by

[7] The messenger was a Negro slave, Abraham, who was given his freedom because of his courage exhibited on this and other occasions.

a delegation headed by the Little Carpenter. Meanwhile, the Cherokee sent their emperor, Standing Turkey, to negotiate peace with
the Virginia expedition, now under the command of Adam Stephen,
which had built Fort Robinson on the Long Island of the Holston,
at the site of Kingsport. There his army was augmented by 250
North Carolinians under Colonel Hugh Waddell.

After the peace one of Stephen's officers, Ensign (later Lieutenant) Henry Timberlake, was induced to visit the Overhill Cherokee
country. Timberlake made careful notes concerning Cherokee customs and drew a very accurate map of the Overhill towns. When
published in London in 1765, his *Memoirs* became an invaluable
source of information about the Cherokee Indians. Timberlake also
took a Cherokee chief named Ostenaco (Judd's Friend) and two
other Indians to England with him; like the Little Carpenter's
earlier visit, this move helped improve Anglo-Cherokee relations.

The Cherokee, however, had lost 2,500 warriors of their original
5,000 during the war; so they were less able than before to resist
English encroachments on their lands. Many English soldiers acquainted with the rich western country longed to return as settlers,
and although the British authorities attempted to protect the Indians' rights, the tide of the westward movement was too strong.
The next few years were to see the beginnings of permanent settlement of Tennessee.

SUGGESTED READINGS

General Accounts
John A. Caruso,*The Appalachian Frontier* (Indianapolis, 1959), 13–
63; Davidson, *The Tennessee*, I, Chs. 1–9; Folmsbee, Corlew, and Mitchell, *Tennessee*, I, Chs. 3–4; Gipson, *British Empire*, IV, VII, IX; Gilbert
E. Govan and James W. Livingood, *The Chattanooga Country* (New
York, 1952; reprinted, Chapel Hill, 1963), 11–27; Hamer, *Tennessee*, I,
Chs. 2–5; J. G. M. Ramsey, *Annals of Tennessee* (Charleston, S. C., 1853;
reprinted, Kingsport, Tenn., 1926, Knoxville, 1967), 13–66; Constance
L. Skinner, *Pioneers of the Old Southwest* (New Haven, 1919), Chs. 3–
4; Samuel C. Williams, *The Dawn of the Tennessee Valley and Ten-
nessee History* (Johnson City, Tenn., 1937), Chs. 1–21; Woodward,
Cherokees, 17–82.

Specialized Accounts

John Richard Alden, *John Stuart and the Southern Colonial Frontier* (Ann Arbor, 1944); Charles W. Alvord and Lee Bidgood, *The First Exploration of the Trans-Allegheny Region by the Virginians* (Cleveland, 1912); Brown, *Old Frontiers*, 41–122; David H. Corkran, *The Cherokee Frontier, 1740–1763* (Norman, 1962); Vernon W. Crane, *The Southern Frontier* (Durham, 1928); Crane, "The Tennessee River as a Road to Carolina," *MVHR*, III (March, 1916), 3–18; William P. Cumming, *The Southeast in Early Maps* (Princeton, 1958); Stanley J. Folmsbee and Madeline Kneberg Lewis (eds.) and Gerald W. Wade (trans.), "Journals of the Juan Pardo Expeditions, 1566–1567," *ETHS Publ.*, No. 37 (1965), 106–21; W. Neil Franklin, "Virginia and the Cherokee Indian Trade," *ETHS Publ.*, No. 4 (1932), 3–21, No. 5 (1933), 22–38; Philip M. Hamer, *Fort Loudoun on the Little Tennessee* (Raleigh, N. C., n. d.), reprinted from "Anglo-French Rivalry in the Cherokee Country, 1754–1757" and "Fort Loudoun in the Cherokee War, 1758–1761," *NCHR*, II (July, Oct., 1925); Archibald Henderson, *The Conquest of the Old Southwest* (New York, 1920), 46–95; Paul Kelley, *Historic Fort Loudoun* (Vonore, Tenn., 1958); Kelley, "Fort Loudoun: The After Years, 1760–1960," *THQ*, XX (Dec., 1961), 303–22, reprinted in William T. Alderson and Robert M. McBride, *Landmarks of Tennessee History* (Nashville, 1965), 219–38; William A. Klutts, "Fort Prudhomme, Its Location," *WTHS Papers*, No. IV (1950), 28–40; Chapman J. Milling, *Red Carolinians* (Chapel Hill, 1940), Ch. 15; Charles H. Nash and Rodney Gates, Jr., "Chucalissa Indian Town," *THQ*, XXI (June, 1962), 103–21, reprinted in Alderson and McBride, *Landmarks*, 115–33; Nash, "Human Continuum of Shelby County," *WTHS Papers*, No. XIV (1960), 5–31; Mary U. Rothrock, "Carolina Traders in the Overhill Country," *ETHS Publ.*, No. 1 (1929), 3–18, reprinted in Robert H. White *et al.* (eds.), *Tennessee: Old and New* (2 vols., Nashville, 1946), I, 69–83; Williams, *Early Travels*, 3–194; Williams, *Beginnings of West Tennessee in the Land of the Chickasaws* (Johnson City, Tenn., 1930), 20–31.

4. &ve; *Beginnings of Settlement and Revolution*

M OST OF THE FIRST SETTLERS of what is now Tennessee
came from the back country of Virginia and North
Carolina. There were two waves of settlement into those areas: one
westward from the coast region and the other southward from
Pennsylvania. Included were many people of non-English nationali-
ties. From the Tidewater came some Scotch Highlanders and a few
French Protestants (Huguenots) who had found refuge in the
English colonies. More numerous were the Scotch-Irish (Ulster-
Scots) and Germans from Pennsylvania. The former were largely
Presbyterian and were described as "greedy after land." The Ger-
mans were of various religious sects and were usually skilled farmers
and mechanics. Both groups left their imprints upon life in the
Southern Appalachians.

The Westward Movement and British Western Policies
&ve; Before the French and Indian War began the westward movement had progressed to the headwaters of the Holston River in
southwestern Virginia, where Samuel Stalnaker, along with others,
had settled near the site of Abingdon by 1750. To forestall occupation by the French, the Virginia colony made large grants of land
to James Patton and also to the Loyal Land Company, organized by
Dr. Thomas Walker. Since the Peter Jefferson survey in 1749 of
the Virginia-North Carolina boundary stopped near the northeastern corner of the present Tennessee, the activities of the Virginia

speculators extended south of the unknown boundary line. The Walker expeditions of both 1748 and 1750 visited the site of Kingsport, and land titles to that site (actually under the Patton grant) and to Bristol, Tennessee, were recorded in the Virginia land office.

Actual settlement was prevented by the outbreak of the French and Indian War. But when that war ended in 1763 and the French claims were entirely removed from the mainland of North America, and the nearest foreign flag was that of Spain at New Orleans and west of the Mississippi River, the back country people and the speculators were ready to occupy the eastern valley of the Mississippi. The British government, however, held up a restraining hand and by the Proclamation of 1763 prohibited settlement and the granting of land west of the Appalachian divide, except in the newly acquired colonies of East and West Florida and Quebec. The aim was to preserve peace and trade with the Indians by assuring them that their hunting grounds would not be settled without their freely given consent. The "Proclamation Line," however, was not to be permanent. Two superintendents of Indian affairs in cooperation with the colonial governors were authorized to negotiate for cessions of land by the Indian tribes. The two superintendents in 1763 were Sir William Johnson, for the region north of the Ohio River, and John Stuart, a survivor of the Fort Loudoun massacre, for the South. By 1768, Stuart had obtained Cherokee consent in the Treaty of Hard Labour to a line running from Reedy River in South Carolina by way of Tryon Mountain to Chiswell's Mine (at the site of Wytheville, Virginia), and thence in a direct line to the mouth of the Kanawha River. In the same year Johnson at the Treaty of Fort Stanwix permitted the Iroquois to relinquish all claims to the region south of the Ohio River as far west as the mouth of the Tennessee, even though they had only a shadowy claim to that territory. Superior titles to that "No Man's Land" were held by the Cherokee and Chickasaw, who had driven the Shawnee out of the Cumberland Valley early in the eighteenth century.

Land-hungry speculators and settlers naturally assumed that the Treaty of Fort Stanwix had opened to legal settlement all of southwest Virginia, West Virginia, and much of Kentucky and Tennessee. At the Treaty of Lochaber in 1770, however, John Stuart, with the reluctant acquiescence of the governor of Virginia, confirmed the Cherokee title to much of that country but acquired from those

Indians a new cession of land north and east of a line running along the 36°30′ parallel to the Holston River near the Long Island (site of Kingsport) and thence northward to the mouth of the Kanawha. When that line was surveyed in 1771 by John Donelson and Alexander Cameron, the Cherokee accepted two important modifications. As the Little Carpenter explained it, the Indians "pitied" some settlers they found north of the South Fork of the Holston but south of the 36°30′ parallel and allowed the South Fork to be considered the boundary line to the vicinity of Long Island. Since the 36°30′ parallel was supposed to be the Virginia-North Carolina boundary, the Donelson line of 1771 following the South Fork of the Holston was accepted temporarily as the line dividing those colonies, and the portion of Tennessee lying "north of the Holston" (South Fork) was governed by Virginia until the boundary was surveyed in 1779. The other modification of the Lochaber line accepted in 1771 was to have the new boundary run northwestward from the vicinity of the Long Island to the Kentucky River and along that stream to the Ohio, rather than northward to the mouth of the Kanawha.

After the ending of hostilities in the French and Indian War, the people of the back country of Virginia and North Carolina were intrigued by the glowing reports of the richness of the Western lands brought back by hunters, traders, and agents of land companies. Thus, the ban against settlement could not hold for long. The hunters were a peculiar breed: independent, inured to hardship, and unwilling to live "cooped up" in any civilized community. They remained in the wilderness for such long periods of time that they were called "long hunters." One of the most famous was Daniel Boone, who was born in Pennsylvania in 1734 to a Quaker family but was brought while a youth to the Yadkin Valley in North Carolina. As game became scarce in the Piedmont, he extended his hunting expeditions farther to the west and by 1760 had found his way into East Tennessee. For many years there was on the bank of Boone's Creek in Washington County a beech tree on which was inscribed: "D. Boon cilled a Bar on tree in the year 1760."

The next year a party of eighteen or twenty hunters led by Elisha Walden, after whom a mountain range was named, came into Tennessee from Virginia and went on through Cumberland Gap into

Kentucky. By 1766 the Cumberland Valley, as well as East Tennessee, was being explored. Among the hunters were Isaac Lindsey, James Harrod, Michael Stoner, James Smith, and Uriah Stone, after whom Stone River was named. A large party of Virginians led by Abram Bledsoe and Kasper Mansker came into the Cumberland country in 1769 and broke up into smaller groups, operating from station camps, such as the one in Sumner County after which Station Camp Creek was named. The hunters would follow buffalo trails to salt licks, such as Bledsoe's Lick and Mansker's Lick (now Castalian Springs), where buffaloes and other animals came in large numbers to lick the salt and were easy prey.

By 1769 the packing industry had been brought to Tennessee. A trading house in Philadelphia employed Joseph Hollingshed to superintend the operations of hunters and packers in the Tennessee and Kentucky country. Hollingshed's parties came up the Tennessee and Cumberland rivers in boats in the spring. During the wait for the cold season to arrive, when the buffalo beef and venison could be safely cured and casked, time was spent in gathering deerskins and rendering tallow from buffalo fat. When cold weather arrived, the buffalo meat and venison were packed in casks and sent either to New Orleans or to Fort Chartres in the Illinois country.

All of this hunting was possible because there were no Indian towns in the region. But there were several Indian tribes whose hunters were roaming that country, and they all resented the white competition. Therefore, the white hunters were in frequent danger of losing their lives or possessions. In 1770 a detachment of a large party led by Henry Scaggs and Joseph Drake was attacked by Indians, and two hunters were captured or killed. The survivors carved on a tree: "2300 Deer Skins lost Ruination by God."

The long hunters frequently served as agents of land companies in locating good lands for settlement. As early as 1764 the impecunious Daniel Boone was working in such a capacity for his lawyer friend and creditor, Richard Henderson, a judge of a North Carolina district court. Soon Henry Scaggs was employed in a similar manner. It was the urging of these two hunters which eventually led the judge to organize the land company which purchased an immense tract of land in Kentucky and Tennessee from the Cherokee Indians in 1775.

The First Settlements and the Watauga Compact 🙣
The first settlers in what is now Tennessee came mainly from Virginia and North Carolina, although a few came directly from Pennsylvania. The migration from Virginia was largely the result of a gradual pushing of settlement down the Holston Valley across an unmarked boundary, but some settlers came from areas farther to the east. The motivating forces for migration included a venturesome spirit, the lure of Western lands, and the erroneous belief that the Treaty of Fort Stanwix had opened the region to settlement.

The name of the first permanent settler is impossible to determine, particularly since it is difficult to distinguish between temporary occupants such as traders or hunters and permanent residents. Traditionally, the first permanent settler was William Bean, of Pittsylvania County, Virginia, who with a group of relatives and friends settled along the Watauga branch of the Holston in 1769, after visiting the region the previous year. Bean may have been preceded, however, by some of the "Regulators" who lived just across the line from Pittsylvania in Orange and adjacent counties of North Carolina. These people, when they moved into the Holston Valley, hoped they were settling on Virginia's Western lands, but they did not go far enough to the north and were still within the bounds of North Carolina.

Why did they wish to leave North Carolina? One reason was their dissatisfaction with conditions in the Granville District of that colony. When North Carolina became a royal province in 1729, one of the original proprietors, the Earl of Granville, refused to return to the crown his share of the original grant of 1663. Therefore, until the American Revolution he retained title to the section of North Carolina north of the 35°34′ parallel, which included, incidentally, that portion of the present Tennessee north of a line running near the towns of Sweetwater and Covington.[1] The land agents of that English lord were notoriously corrupt; they charged exorbitant fees and sometimes sold the same tract to more than one person.

Dissatisfaction with government under North Carolina also contributed to the desire to move. The Western counties were discriminated against in representation in the colonial assembly, but

---

[1] The eastern section of the only part of North Carolina's Western claim outside the Granville District included the towns of the Cherokee Indians, from which they could not be easily moved. This explains the colony's lack of interest in Western lands.

the people were required to pay high taxes to finance, among other things, the building of "Tryon's Palace," an elegant mansion for the governor. Local government was controlled by corrupt court-house "rings" that profited from a pernicious fee system. It was difficult to get justice in the courts, and the aroused citizenry, calling

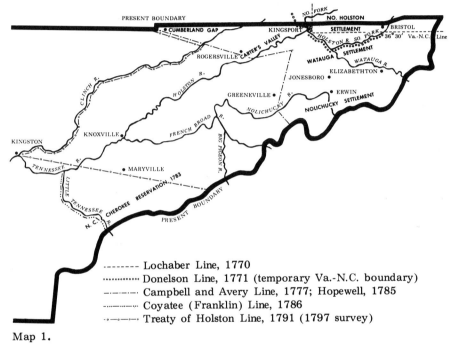

Map 1.

EARLY EAST TENNESSEE SETTLEMENTS AND TREATIES

themselves "Regulators," eventually took the law into their own hands. They broke up several courts, including one presided over by Richard Henderson, and subjected some corrupt officials to mob treatment. Governor William Tryon finally led an army into the Western counties and defeated the Regulators at Alamance in May, 1771, and forced them to submit to royal authority.

There is no doubt that some people of "regulating principles" moved to the Tennessee country before the Battle of Alamance, and probably after that engagement. As early as August, 1768, the

German settlement of Moravians at the site of Winston-Salem included in its records the notation: "A party of men from Orange County passed through our village [Bethabara]. They were Regulators, and said they were going to Holston River to look for land." On September 21, 1770, it was recorded, "There were unusually many strangers in our town today, especially a number who do not wish to be under the law, and are moving to Holston River."[2]

Among the Regulators who came to the Holston area was James Robertson, who has been called the "Father of Tennessee" and also, because he later led the migration to the Cumberland Valley, the "Father of Middle Tennessee." Born in Brunswick County, Virginia, of Scotch-Irish ancestry, he became "a firm believer in the basic principles of civil liberty and the right of self-government." After residing for years in Orange County, North Carolina, Robertson journeyed westward in the spring of 1770 looking for a place to settle. He stayed with John Honeycut on the Watauga River (near the site of Elizabethton and the home of the Beans) long enough to plant and "lay by" a crop of corn and then started his return journey. Robertson became lost in the mountains, but was saved from starvation by two hunters before he finally reached his home on the Yadkin. The part he played in the Regulator movement is not very clear, but it is very probable that he moved with his family to the Watauga before the Battle of Alamance.[3]

Some Regulators settled farther south, near the site of Erwin on the Nolichucky River, a branch of the French Broad. One settler was John Ryan, who probably arrived in 1768, but in 1771 he sold his preemption claim to Jacob Brown, who became the real leader of the Nolichucky settlement. Because of Indian hostility, however, he moved temporarily to the Watauga.

In 1770 two Virginians, John Carter and William Parker, estab-

---

[2] Quoted in Williams, Dawn, 337, 343.

[3] According to J. W. L. Matlock, "John Cotten: Reluctant Pioneer," 277–86, Robertson participated in the battle before moving west with his family and supposedly was soon followed by two other participants with their families, John Donelson and John Cotten (an alleged deserter from Tryon's army), but the manuscript journal of John Cotten, on which the article is based, is of very doubtful authenticity. See Stanley J. Folmsbee, "The Journal of John Cotten," THQ, XXVIII (Spring, 1969). There is no other evidence of any residence of Donelson or Cotten in the Watauga Valley until shortly before their voyage to Nashville in 1779–80. Also although Mr. Matlock claims that this Donelson was a son of Colonel John Donelson, the Virginia surveyor, it is practically certain that it was the same man, who was engaged in surveying "Donelson's line" at the time of the Battle of Alamance.

lished a store near the site of Church Hill in Hawkins County to supply travelers coming down the Holston on the way to Natchez in British West Florida, as well as to trade with the Indians. The Cherokee objected to their presence and forced them to move to Watauga. The area lying west of the Holston between Kingsport and Rogersville became known as Carter's Valley.

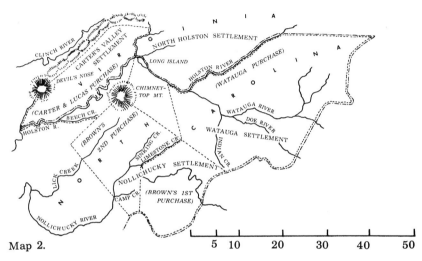

Map 2.

5 10 20 30 40 50

EARLY SETTLEMENTS, ADAPTED FROM MAP IN
GARRETT AND GOODPASTURE, *HISTORY OF TENNESSEE*

"Map showing the supposed line between Virginia and the Western Territory of North Carolina, from 1772 to 1779, and the two Tennessee settlements on either side of said line in 1772; and also the limits of the several private purchases from the Indians, by the Watauga settlers, Jacob Brown, and Carter and Lucas, in 1775."

A fourth area of settlement was developed north of the South Fork of the Holston near the site of Bristol, where the surveyors of Donelson's line found some settlers in 1771. The leaders in this "North Holston" settlement were Evan Shelby and his son Isaac, who came from Maryland and established a store at Sapling Grove, an early name for Bristol. Among their customers and neighbors in 1772 were Daniel Boone and Valentine Sevier. The latter's more famous son John also lived in the North Holston settlement before moving to Watauga in 1775, which he had previously visited in 1771 and 1772. This future governor of Franklin and of Tennessee was of French Huguenot-English descent and had grown up in the Shenandoah Valley of Virginia.

The North Holston settlement was the only one of the four in the Tennessee country whose residents were not ordered to move by Alexander Cameron, Stuart's deputy among the Cherokee, after the Donelson survey of 1771. Since the Donelson line followed the South Fork of the Holston, those settlers were outside the Indian country. Although the other three settlements temporarily consolidated along the Watauga, they refused to move any farther, preferring to make their own arrangements with the Cherokee. As they explained in their petition to North Carolina in 1776, quoted by Ramsey,

> to their great disappointment, when the line was run they were (contrary to their expectation) left out; . . . and feeling an unwillingness to loose [sic] the labour bestowed on their plantations, they applied to the Cherokee Indians, and leased the land for a term of ten years. . . .

James Robertson and John Bean (a son of William) negotiated the lease; and Jacob Brown, who later claimed that he was asked to do so by the Indians, negotiated a similar lease to land on the Nolichucky and reestablished that settlement.

The Cherokee version was quite different. The settlers, when ordered by Cameron to move, "begged as their crops were then on the ground that they might be allowed to reap them and they would certainly remove the Spring following." Later they "brought goods and prevailed on some of their people to give leases." Many Indians were opposed, but the whites said that "they would stay on the land whether they took the goods or not."[4]

In contrast to the North Holston settlement, which was being governed by Virginia, the settlers on the Watauga and Nolichucky were outside the bounds of any organized government. Following the example of the signers of the Mayflower Compact of 1620, they created a homespun-government, which they called the Watauga Association. This document, signed in May, 1772, has been lost, but the government was described in the petition to North Carolina of 1776:

[4] Hamer, *Tennessee*, I, 68.

Finding ourselves on the Frontiers, and being apprehensive that, for the want of a proper legislature, we might become a shelter for such as endeavoured to defraud their creditors; considering also the necessity of recording Deeds, Wills, and doing other public business; we, by consent of the people, formed a court for the purposes above mentioned, taking (by desire of our constituents) the Virginia laws for our guide . . . this was intended for ourselves, and was done by the consent of every individual . . . .

The government apparently consisted of a court of five members, which exercised both legislative and judicial powers, a sheriff, and a clerk. The judges probably were John Carter, who served as chairman, James Robertson, Charles Robertson (a cousin), Zachariah Isbell, and Jacob Brown (until he moved back to the Nolichucky). Probably the first clerk was James Smith, a long hunter of the 1760's, who was succeeded by John Sevier, who in turn, when he became a member of the court, was succeeded by Felix Walker. The name of the first sheriff is unknown, but a later one may have been Valentine Sevier, who preceded his son John in coming to the Watauga country.

Although this government was described by the current governor of Virginia, Lord Dunmore, as "an inconsiderable yet a Separate State," independence was not its design. Beyond the bounds of the government of North Carolina, within whose charter limits the Wataugans were located, and in the Indian country, they designed their association to meet a temporary emergency, and they expressed an intent not to "intrude on the legislatures of the colonies." Nevertheless, as Theodore Roosevelt said, "they exercised the rights of full statehood for a number of years; establishing in American style a purely democratic government with representative institutions, in which, under certain restrictions, the will of the majority was supreme . . . ."[5]

5 *Winning of the West*, I, 213. Like many other writers, Roosevelt (p. 212) repeated Ramsey's error in stating that there was also a committee of thirteen from which the five judges were chosen. That committee did not come into existence until after the Revolutionary War had begun and the Provisional Congress of North Carolina had recommended, September 9, 1775, that each district create a committee of public safety of a president and twelve other members. Evidence of Ramsey's confusion is the fact that the list of the thirteen "Commissioners" of the Watauga Association of 1772, given on page 107 of the *Annals*, is exactly the same as the "Members of the Committee" appended to the petition of the Washington District of 1776, given on

Dunmore's War and the Treaty of Sycamore Shoals ࿗
For several years the Wataugans lived at peace with their neighbors and landlords, the Cherokee, despite the killing of one of the tribe by a Virginian named William Crabtree during a horse race at Watauga in 1774. James Robertson went to the Cherokee towns on the Little Tennessee and succeeded in pacifying the Indians. That same year, "Dunmore's War" developed between Virginia and the Indians of the Ohio River region, but fortunately the Cherokee remained quiet. During the war, King's Mill Fort and Eaton's Station were built near the site of Kingsport for the protection of settlers who were moving into that area, and Shelby's Fort, named for Captain Evan Shelby, was constructed at Sapling Grove. A raid led by a Mingo chief named Logan actually occurred while many of the men of both areas, and some from Watauga, were participating in the Battle of Point Pleasant at the mouth of the Kanawha, at which General Andrew Lewis crushed the Northern Indians.

That victory stimulated the activities of land speculators as the Virginia governor had expected, but companies organized in other colonies besides Virginia sought to participate. One of the most important was the Transylvania Company, organized by Judge Richard Henderson of North Carolina, who planned to establish a colony west of the mountains on land to be purchased privately from Cherokee Indians. Early in 1775 a treaty conference was held between Henderson and other members of the company and about 1,200 Indians at Sycamore Shoals of the Watauga River. For ten thousand pounds' worth of goods, the Transylvania Company purchased on March 19 from the Cherokee an immense tract bounded on the north and east by the Ohio and Kentucky rivers and on the south by the ridge dividing the waters of the Tennessee and the Cumberland. During the negotiations, a young chief named Dragging Canoe, a son of the Little Carpenter, objected to the sale in a brilliant speech in which he warned his fellow Cherokee that they

---

page 138. Both lists include the names of John Sevier and William Tatham, who did not settle on the Watauga until 1775 and 1776, respectively. One unfortunate result of Ramsey's error is the statement by practically every writer about John Sevier that he was one of the original judges of the Watauga Association (he was listed as both a commissioner and a judge by Ramsey), whereas it is practically certain he could not have been. Also, the Cotten Journal, as described by Matlock, is even more suspect, since it lists "twelve Commissioners" and "four Judges," of the Watauga Association of 1772, even though the names of Sevier and Tatham are omitted.

were paving the way for the ultimate extinction of their race. After being overruled by the older chiefs, he dramatically pointed to the west and declared that a dark cloud hung over that land.

The Wataugans were interested spectators at this treaty negotiated in the midst of their settlement. Three years before, knowing that the Proclamation of 1763 and other British laws prohibited private purchases of land from the Indians, they had merely leased from the Cherokee the lands they were occupying. If a big land company was willing to flout the law,[6] they saw no reason why they should not try to transform their lease into an outright purchase. This they proceeded to do, and Jacob Brown did the same for the lands along the Nolichucky. Both purchases included more land than had been leased. Meanwhile, Henderson had negotiated a separate "Path Deed" with the Cherokee; to avoid walking on the Indians' land, he acquired for an additional quantity of goods a tract connecting his original purchase with the Donelson line of 1771 and the area being acquired by the Wataugans. This tract included much of Carter's Valley, west of the Holston, which in accordance with a prior arrangement was turned over to John Carter and a new partner named Robert Lucas. These partners immediately began to convey lands in the area to prospective settlers.

Before the treaties were concluded, Henderson sent Daniel Boone and a party of axe-wielders to mark a trail (later called the Wilderness Road) through Cumberland Gap into Kentucky, and he followed a little later with a group of settlers. Although at first primarily interested in the Kentucky settlement, when Virginia refused to recognize the company's title, Henderson turned his attention to the Tennessee portion of his purchase and sponsored the settlement of the Cumberland Valley in 1779–80. This will be discussed in the next chapter.

Revolution and Governmental Reorganization ह्र~ The beginning of the Revolutionary War in April, 1775, led to some

---

[6] Judge Henderson claimed that the Camden-Yorke opinion handed down by royal law officers had legalized private purchases of land from native Indians. Archibald Henderson (a descendant), *Conquest of the Old Southwest,* 201–3. W. S. Lester, *The Transylvania Colony,* 26–28, points out that the opinion dealt with the Indians of India and not North American Indians and did not legalize the Sycamore Shoals treaty.

governmental changes on the Tennessee frontier. The provisional governments of North Carolina and Virginia, which replaced the royal authorities, authorized the creation of committees of safety in the several districts and counties into which those colonies had been divided. For several reasons most of the Tennessee frontiersmen were inclined to favor the Revolutionary cause. They desired to be free from such British restrictions as the Proclamation of 1763 and from the authority of Superintendent John Stuart, who had ordered the settlers outside the Donelson line to move off of the Indians' lands and who had fulminated against the leases and purchases (at Sycamore Shoals) of land from Cherokee.

To participate in the Revolution, all the future Tennesseans living north of the South Fork of the Holston had to do was to join the activity of Fincastle County, Virginia, of which they were considered an integral part because they were located north of the Donelson line. The newer settlers in the vicinity of the Long Island of the Holston (the site of Kingsport) and in Carter's Valley, west of the Holston, also desired to be under Virginia's government but doubted their eligibility because they were beyond the Donelson line. Nevertheless, they organized Pendleton District, named after the Virginia leader, Edmund Pendleton, and in January, 1776, petitioned Fincastle County for recognition, saying, in part, that the

> Petitioners, being deeply impressed with the Sense of the tyranical & oppresive Measures agitated by the British Ministry against his Majesty's loyal Subjects in America; . . . think it unnatural that they, tho' few, being equally interested in the common Cause should be intirely inactive, while their Brethren are brave bleeding in the Field.

They explained that in order to "contribute their Mite to support the glorious Cause," they had formed themselves "into a Society" and had chosen a committee to superintend their affairs. Finally, they asked to be "incorporated into" the Virginia colony and promised obedience to its laws and "a Cheerful Contribution of their Quota of the general Exigencies."[7] The petitioners' request was granted and they became citizens of Fincastle County. In December, 1776, when that county was divided, the Carter's Valley and

---

[7] Williams, *Revolutionary War*, 15–17.

Long Island area residents were included, along with North Holston settlers, in the new Virginia county of Washington.

Before the Pendleton District was created, the people south of the Holston on the Watauga River also adhered to the Revolutionary cause and revised the government of the Watauga Association to provide for a committee of safety of thirteen members, with John Carter as chairman. The new government took the name Washington District. When the change was made is uncertain, but it must have been in 1775. The Pendleton District petition of January, 1776, mentions the neighboring Washington District, and the Wataugans' petition to North Carolina of July 5, 1776, says the action was taken soon after the purchase of their lands at Sycamore Shoals. Although irregular in form, Washington District was the first governmental subdivision to be named for the commander-in-chief of the Revolutionary armies.

Because of the danger of Indian attack, the new district appealed first to Virginia and then, on July 5, 1776, to North Carolina for annexation. The latter petition was received on August 22 by the North Carolina committee of public safety, which recommended that the people elect delegates to the convention scheduled to meet at Halifax in November to frame a constitution for the now independent state of North Carolina. Five delegates were chosen, but only four, including John Sevier, attended and became signers of North Carolina's first constitution. That constitution asserted the state's title to the Tennessee country, although left open was the question of establishing in the future one or more new governments west of the mountains.

Appended to the constitution was an ordinance naming twenty-one justices of peace for the "District of Washington," as if it were a county rather than a "district." At an election of members of the first general assembly of the state of North Carolina, John Carter was chosen as a senator, and John Sevier and Jacob Womack were elected to the lower house, called the house of commons, to represent the Washington District. The legislature, in 1777, created Washington County, which was to include practically all of present Tennessee. The exceptions were the North Holston settlement and Pendleton District sections of Washington County, Virginia, which were finally restored to North Carolina and included in a new county named Sullivan after the North Carolina-Virginia boundary was surveyed in 1779.

SUGGESTED READINGS

General Accounts

Thomas P. Abernethy, *From Frontier to Plantation in Tennessee* (Chapel Hill, 1932; reprinted, Memphis, 1955, University, Ala., 1967), Ch. 1; Brown, *Old Frontiers*, 3–13, 122–33; Caruso, *Appalachian Frontier*, 61–113, 120–62; Folmsbee, Corlew, and Mitchell, *Tennessee*, I, 95–123; William R. Garrett and Albert V. Goodpasture, *History of Tennessee* (Nashville, 1905), 38–57; Gipson, *British Empire*, IX, *passim*, XI, Ch. 12; Hamer, *Tennessee*, I, Ch. 6, 89–90; Henderson, *Conquest of Old Southwest*, 3–41, 96–226; Ramsey, *Annals*, 92–143; Roosevelt, *Winning of the West*, I, Part 1, Chs. 5–8, Part 2, "In the Current of the Revolution," Ch. 2; Skinner, *Pioneers of Old Southwest*, 1–51, 104–34, 157–72; Williams, *Dawn*, Chs. 22–34; Williams, *Tennessee During the Revolutionary War* (Nashville, 1944), Chs. 2, 7; Williams, *William Tatham: Wataugan* (Johnson City, Tenn., 1947).

Specialized Accounts

Alden, *John Stuart*; Alden, *The South in the Revolution* (Baton Rouge, 1957), Ch. 8; Ben Allen and Dennis T. Lawson, "The Wataugans and the 'Dangerous Example,'" *THQ*, XXVI (Summer, 1967), 137–41; Clarence W. Alvord, *The Mississippi Valley in British Politics* (2 vols., Cleveland, 1916–17); John Bakeless, *Master of the Wilderness: Daniel Boone* (New York, 1939); E. Merton Coulter, "The Granville District," *James Sprunt Historical Papers*, XIII, No. 1 (Chapel Hill, 1913); Louis De Vorsey, Jr., "The Virginia-Cherokee Boundary of 1771," *ETHS Publ.*, No. 32 (1961), 17–31; De Vorsey, *The Indian Boundary in the Southern Colonies, 1763–1775* (Chapel Hill, 1966); Carl Driver, *John Sevier: Pioneer of the Old Southwest* (Chapel Hill, 1932), Ch. 1; Paul M. Fink, "Jacob Brown of Nolichucky," *THQ*, XXI (Sept., 1962), 235–50; William B. Hesseltine, *Pioneer's Mission: The Story of Lyman Copeland Draper* (Madison, Wis., 1954); William S. Lester, *The Transylvania Colony* (Spencer, Ind., 1935); J. W. L. Matlock, "John Cotten: Reluctant Pioneer," *THQ*, XXVII (Fall, 1968), 277–86; A. W. Putnam, *History of Middle Tennessee; or, Life and Times of Gen. James Robertson* (Nashville, 1859; rpt. Knoxville, 1971), 1–65; J. M. Sosin, *Whitehall and the Wilderness* (Lincoln, Neb., 1961); Samuel C. Williams, "Shelby's Fort," *ETHS Publ.*, No. 7 (1935), 28–37;

Williams, "The First Volunteers from the Volunteer State," THM,
VIII (July, 1924), 132–39; Williams, "The First Territorial Division
Named for Washington," *THM,* Ser. 2, II (April, 1932), 153–59, re-
printed in White, *Tennessee: Old and New,* I, 201–21.

5. &➤ Tennessee in the Revolution

A MAJOR PURPOSE of the creation of Washington District in 1775 was to allow the Wataugans to participate more effectively in the Revolutionary War. Therefore, as stated in the petition to North Carolina of 1776, a "company of fine riflemen were accordingly enlisted, and put under Capt. James Robertson." A part of the company, commanded by Felix Walker, was sent in May, 1776, to help repulse the British at Charleston, South Carolina. More men would have been sent had not the Wataugans at that time been seriously threatened by hostile Indians.

The Cherokee War of 1776 &➤ During the summer of 1776 the Cherokee carried out a determined invasion of the settlements in upper East Tennessee. Virginians and Carolinians believed that the primary cause of the invasion was incitement by British agents. Until 1930 the historians of Tennessee and the Old Southwest, almost without exception, accepted this viewpoint and denounced Superintendent John Stuart and his deputies for arousing the savages to wage indiscriminate warfare against the frontier. Recent scholars, however, have discovered evidence which largely clears the British agents of complicity in the beginning of the war and indicates that they tried to restrain the Indians from making their initial attacks.

When the Revolutionary War began, John Stuart, who had been forced to flee to St. Augustine, at first told the several tribes of Southern Indians that the differences between the white people of

England and America did not concern them. Later, he received orders from General Thomas Gage in Boston, who claimed the Americans were using Indians in that area, that he should induce the Southern Indians to "take up arms against his Majesty's Enemies, and to distress them all in their power." Stuart replied that he could not construe the orders to mean an "indiscriminate attack" because he knew that some of the inhabitants on the frontier were loyal to the Crown, and such a war would involve the "innocent & defenceless in ruin." Stuart therefore instructed his agents to "dispose the Indians to Act under their directions when required, but not to take any step except in the Execution of some concerted plan jointly" with Loyalist or British troops.[1]

To put the new policy into effect, John Stuart sent his brother Henry as a special agent to the Southern Indians and sent with him thirty horseloads of ammunition, because the Revolutionists had cut off the Indians' supplies from the usual sources. From Dragging Canoe, who met him at Mobile, Henry Stuart soon learned that the chief problem would be to restrain the Cherokee from making an immediate and indiscriminate attack without waiting for the development of some concerted plan. Dragging Canoe complained bitterly about white encroachments on Cherokee land west of the Donelson line. Stuart reminded him that those settlements were the results of the Indians' own "private bargains" at Sycamore Shoals against his brother's advice. Dragging Canoe replied that those treaties had been made by some men "too old to hunt," and that he and a "great many young fellows" were determined to recover possession of that land.

By the time Henry Stuart's party reached the Overhill towns, "nothing was talked of but War." Henry, as he reported to his brother, protested at a meeting of chiefs against the proposed attack, saying that "there were many poor ignorant people on their Lands who were made to believe that the Lands were legally purchased. . . ." He promised to write to the settlers to try to induce them to move. When the Indians agreed, he and his brother's deputy, Alexander Cameron, on May 7, 1776, drafted a letter which was sent by a trader to the Watauga and Nolichucky settlers. "Humanity and a sincere desire to preserve innocent and wrong informed

---

[1] Hamer, "John Stuart's Indian Policy," 351–62; Hamer, "Wataugans and the Cherokee Indians," 108–9.

people from the great danger that seems to threaten them," Stuart and Cameron explained, were their only motives. The Indians, they said, were greatly discontented because of new settlements in the Indian country and would already have attacked had it not been for the writers' restraining influence. Stuart and Cameron offered those people who were willing to be "good and peaceable subjects" land in West Florida, and added that they had induced the Indians to allow them twenty days in which to move. Enclosed in the letter was a "talk" from the Cherokee.

Although there was consternation among the settlers, the majority determined to hold on to their lands. What was needed was more time in which to prepare their defenses and get aid. Therefore they sent the trader back to Stuart and Cameron with replies which expressed amazement that their "Brothers," the Cherokee, should now wish to destroy them. They had made a "Contract" for their land, but if it was not binding, they were "willing to give it up" when "legally called upon." The settlers asked for a longer period than twenty days in which to move; and to assure British aid in getting additional time they pretended loyalty to the British government. "Subjects must Obey Their Sovereign," they declared; and they asked for an immediate reply designating an asylum, "for We, (some of us at least,) are determined to support His Majesty's Crown & Dignity . . . ."

The ruse was successful and the Indians granted them twenty additional days in which to move. Stuart and Cameron, however, explained in their letter of May 23 that their warning "was intended for the Inhabitants in general without any regard to their Political Principles," for they could never have forgiven themselves if they "had suffered innocent women and Children to fall a Sacrifice."[2]

Meanwhile, the Wataugans were attempting to get aid from Virginia, but to their disappointment the Fincastle County committee advised them to avoid hostilities by moving quickly to the white side of the Donelson line of 1771. Thus it became evident that if they were to obtain aid from the Revolutionary authorities, it would be necessary to create the impression that the only reason why they were in danger was because of their adherence to the Revolutionary cause. Accordingly, they caused to be circulated

2 *Ibid.*, 109–18; Hamer, "Correspondence of Henry Stuart and Alexander Cameron," 452–57.

widely in Virginia and the Carolinas a letter signed with Henry Stuart's name which appeared mysteriously at Charles Robertson's gate on May 18. The contents are so much at variance with the Stuart-Cameron letters of May 7 and 23 that it is impossible to believe that the letter was actually written by the British agent. Stuart later denied that he had anything to do with the letter and submitted testimony given by the trader Isaac Thomas under oath that it had actually been forged by a Wataugan named Jessy (Jesse) Benton.[3]

The allegedly forged letter stated that it was not "the desire of his Majesty to set his friends and allies, the Indians, on his liege subjects," and therefore urged those settlers to make a written pledge of loyalty to the Crown. A British army, it declared, was about to march from West Florida to the Overhill Cherokee country, and with Creek, Chickasaw, and Cherokee Indians invade the frontiers of Virginia and North Carolina while other British forces were attacking the sea coasts of those colonies.[4] Whether forged or not, the letter enabled the frontiersmen to obtain aid for their defense.

Meanwhile, the war spirit was rising rapidly in the Cherokee country. A delegation of Northern Indians arrived and advocated a general Indian war. Dragging Canoe and other young chiefs responded enthusiastically, but when the war belt was passed, Henry Stuart and Cameron refused to touch it, saying they would not sanction a war until John Stuart authorized it. The issue was left in doubt, but at this critical juncture a message arrived from the Fincastle County committee warning the Cherokee against evil and designing men who sought to involve them in the contest between the Americans and servants of the King who wanted to take money from the Americans without their consent. If the Indians had any complaints they should submit them to Virginia or to the Continental Congress. The letter demanded punishment of some Indians who had killed some whites in Kentucky and threatened an invasion which would result in the "destruction and perhaps the utter extirpation of the Cherokee Nation."

This letter, reported Henry Stuart, "so exasperated the Indians that we had little hopes after this of being able to restrain them." Also, Isaac Thomas had brought reports that an army of six thou-

---

[3] *Ibid.*, 458–59.
[4] Ramsey, *Annals*, 147–48.

sand men, which had been raised in Virginia and North Carolina to fight the British, would be used against the Indians instead. It seemed obvious that any invasion to be successful would have to be started very quickly; therefore, plans were made for an attack. Stuart and Cameron departed after giving ineffectual orders that the line of 1771 was not to be passed. The Indians, however, were willing to give the considerable number of Tories residing in the Nolichucky settlement an opportunity to save themselves by joining the invasion or by putting up a white flag. The Indians arranged to have Nathaniel Gist, who was then supporting the British, and four traders deliver the word to the Loyalists; but the traders rushed instead to the forts of the Revolutionists and told the Patriots not only about the time of the attack but also Dragging Canoe's entire plan for the campaign, which had been given to them, according to tradition, by Nancy Ward, the "Beloved Woman" of the Cherokee.

The Indians' plan of campaign was to divide their force of about seven hundred into three commands. One group under Dragging Canoe was to attack the settlers in the vicinity of the Long Island; the second, under Old Abram, was to invade the Nolichucky and Watauga country; and a smaller group, under the Raven, was to deal with the scattered settlers in Carter's Valley. Most of these settlers fled at the approach of the Indians, and the Raven continued his burning and pillaging on up into southwestern Virginia. Dragging Canoe's force approached Eaton's Station by way of the Long Island and camped there. The garrison moved out to attack and in the important Battle of Island Flats on July 20 defeated the Indians and seriously wounded Dragging Canoe.

The next day after Island Flats, Old Abram subjected Fort Caswell on the Watauga, in which the Nolichucky as well as the Watauga settlers had gathered for defense, to a vigorous but unsuccessful assault. He then besieged the fort for about two weeks and resorted to various strategems in attempts to capture it. One nearly successful effort was frustrated when Ann Robertson, the sister of James Robertson, organized a "bucket brigade" among the women to pour boiling water down upon the nearly naked Indians. According to tradition, it was also during this siege that John Sevier helped Catherine Sherrill, who had been caught outside the fort milking cows, over the stockade to safety. Four years later, in 1780, after his first wife, Sarah Hawkins, died, Sevier married Catherine

("Bonny Kate"); she assumed the care of his ten children, and in due time provided him with eight more.

Even before the Cherokee invasion occurred the Revolutionary authorities of Virginia and the Carolinas began to develop plans for concerted attacks upon the several groups of Cherokee towns. The expedition to the Overhill Cherokee country was led by Colonel William Christian of Virginia and included not only the Virginia and Watauga troops, but also a small force from North Carolina commanded by Joseph Williams (whose son John was to become a senator from Tennessee). The rendezvous of 1,800 men was held at the recently constructed Fort Patrick Henry on the Long Island of the Holston in late September, 1776. Overawed by the superior force, the Indians abandoned their towns and sent their older chiefs to Colonel Christian with overtures of peace, which led eventually to peace conferences at the Long Island of the Holston. Dragging Canoe, however, refused to participate and led a secession of the most unruly element to Chickamauga Creek near the site of Chattanooga to become the core of the "Chickamauga Indians."

The leading chiefs of the remainder of the Cherokee Nation met with representatives of Virginia and North Carolina at the Long Island in June and July, 1777. The Virginia commissioners were headed by Colonel Christian and those of North Carolina by Waightstill Avery. To induce the Indians to include in the cessions all of the land already occupied in southwestern Virginia and East Tennessee, the commissioners had to promise that the new line would be forever inviolate. Avery said, "We are about to fix a line that is to remain through all generations, and be kept by our Children's children."[5] Separate treaties were signed with the Virginia and North Carolina commissioners on July 20, the first anniversary of the Battle of Island Flats and a few days after the Indians and the whites had joined in celebrating the first anniversary of the Declaration of Independence.

To Virginia the Cherokee ceded the land north of a line beginning at the "lower corner" of the Donelson line (a point on the Holston six miles above the Long Island), following the river to the mouth of Cloud's Creek (a few miles from the site of Rogersville), and then running in a straight line to a point between three and five miles

[5] Hamer, *Tennessee*, I, 87.

west of Cumberland Gap. Included was a considerable stretch of country south of the 36°30′ parallel which technically belonged to North Carolina but over which Virginia had been exercising jurisdiction. To North Carolina they ceded the country north and east of a line running from the mouth of Cloud's Creek northeastward to the highest point on a mountain called Chimney Top, thence southward to the Nolichucky River at the mouth of Camp Creek (a few miles southeast of the site of Greeneville), and from there in a southwestward direction to the mountains dividing the hunting grounds of the Overhill and Middle Cherokee. Although Judge Henderson was present and protested, the treaties made no mention of his Transylvania Purchase of 1775, but the Virginia treaty did cover most of the territory included in his "Path Deed" of that date.

The defeat of the Indians in the Cherokee War and the negotiation of peace with them had considerable significance in the history of the Revolution. The continued occupation of the East Tennessee country kept the road open to Kentucky, without which the settlements in that area could not have been maintained. And if the settlements had not been held, it is extremely doubtful that there would have been any conquest of the Illinois country by George Rogers Clark or that the frontier would have been pushed westward to the Cumberland while the war was in progress; and it is unlikely that there would have been any battle at King's Mountain.

The King's Mountain Campaign   Before being in a position to participate effectively in campaigns east of the Unaka Mountains, it was necessary for the Westerners to chastise the Chickamauga Indians, whose raids had become increasingly annoying. In April, 1779, an expedition commanded by Colonel Evan Shelby went down the Holston and Tennessee rivers and, meeting no resistance, destroyed several Chickamauga towns and collected a large amount of booty. One part of the army, commanded by Captain John Montgomery, was on the way to join Clark in the Illinois country, but the remainder of the expedition returned home overland. They stopped a short distance above the site of Chattanooga and held a sale of the captured booty on the bank of a creek which became known as Sale Creek. Evan Shelby was honored by appointment as brigadier general by Virginia.

Meanwhile, the East Tennessee country received a new tide of immigration from the east. Some immigrants—the refugee Tories—were not desirable, however. The newly organized (February, 1778) court of Washington County, North Carolina, had to devote much of its time to considering cases of persons charged with being Loyalists or harboring Loyalists. The latter were usually imprisoned, but the Tories frequently were subjected to exile and confiscation of property.

In 1780 the Patriots of the Carolinas instead of the Tories sought refuge west of the mountains. The British had finally captured Charleston, and a large army under Lord Cornwallis soon invaded North Carolina. Subordinate commanders, Colonel Banastre Tarleton and Major Patrick Ferguson, scoured the Piedmont. In response to a call from Colonel Charles McDowell, about four hundred men from Sullivan County (created in 1779) and Washington County, under the command of Colonel Isaac Shelby and Major Charles Robertson, went across the mountains and helped defeat detachments of Ferguson's troops in a number of small engagements, the most important of which was at Musgrove's Mill, August 18. As a result of Cornwallis' victory at Camden, however, both the Westerners and McDowell's troops were forced to retreat across the mountains to Watauga.

Learning apparently for the first time of the Western settlements, Ferguson sent a warning to them that if they "did not desist from their opposition to the British arms," he would "march his army over the mountains, hang their leaders, and lay their country waste with fire and sword."[6] Colonels Shelby and Sevier of Sullivan and Washington counties, respectively, decided not to wait for such an attack but to move against Ferguson first, hoping to surprise and defeat him. With the cooperation of Colonel William Campbell of southwestern Virginia and Colonel McDowell and his refugees, they organized an army of about one thousand men. Sevier induced John Adair, entry taker of Sullivan County, to release funds to obtain supplies. The soldiers of this motley army, dressed in hunting costumes and carrying their own hunting rifles, assembled at Sycamore Shoals, September 25, 1780, and received, according to tradition, the blessing of the Presbyterian preacher, Samuel Doak. East

---

[6] Draper, *King's Mountain*, 562.

of the mountains they were joined by other Patriots of the Carolinas and Georgia. Ferguson, apprised of the Westerners' advance
by two American deserters, retreated eastward to King's Mountain,
a narrow ridge about sixty feet high located in the northeastern
corner of South Carolina. Boasting that "the Almighty" could not
drive him from that height, he awaited expected reinforcements
from Cornwallis. His army, mostly Tories, numbered nearly a thousand men.

The Americans, on October 7, under the general command of
Colonel Campbell, assaulted the enemy's position on the mountain
from both sides. The Westerners fought in Indian fashion, using
trees and rocks for shelter, as they advanced up the mountain side,
retreated before the Tory bayonets, and then advanced again when
the Tories returned to the mountain top to contend with Patriots
coming up on the other side. At length Ferguson was killed, and
Abraham de Peyster, who assumed command, raised the white flag.
Apparently some of the Patriots did not know of the meaning of a
white flag or in the bitterness of their hatred chose not to, and the
American commanders had difficulty in getting them to cease firing.
Reports of the casualties are conflicting. With a very few exceptions,
all of Ferguson's force were killed, wounded, or captured. According
to Shelby's personal account, less exaggerated than the official report, the British and Tories lost 157 killed, 153 wounded, and 706
prisoners. The Americans lost 28 killed and 62 wounded.

The victory was of great significance. It justifiably has been called
the turning point of the Revolution in the South. It greatly encouraged the Southern Patriots and correspondingly discouraged the
Loyalists. It caused Cornwallis to abandon his campaign in North
Carolina and retreat. After receiving reinforcements, however,
Cornwallis renewed the campaign the next year, but was successfully checked by General Nathanael Greene at Guilford Courthouse in March, 1781. Although technically victorious, Cornwallis
moved his army to Wilmington and from there to Yorktown, where
its surrender on October 19 brought hostilities practically to an end.
In Greene's army at Guilford Courthouse there was a small force
from the East Tennessee country under the command of Major
Charles Robertson. Another group of about six hundred Westerners,
under Colonels Shelby and Sevier, aided General Francis Marion in
"mopping up" operations in South Carolina.

The reason the Westerners did not participate more actively in campaigns east of the mountains was the continuing Indian danger. The Overhill Cherokee had planned to take advantage of the departure of the able-bodied men of the Western country to the King's Mountain campaign, but the army returned before they were ready. Colonel Sevier organized an expedition which defeated the Cherokee at Boyd's Creek (in what is now Sevier County) on December 16. Early in 1781 Sevier led an expedition against the Middle Cherokee and in 1782 another against the Chickamauga. A Cherokee guide, John Watts, succeeded in diverting Sevier away from five new Chickamauga towns, including Running Water and Nickajack, along the river below the site of Chattanooga. From those towns the Chickamaugans continued to raid the settlements in what is now Middle Tennessee.

The Cumberland Settlements ঌ When the organized settlement of the Cumberland Valley began in 1779, under the sponsorship of the Transylvania Company, a few scattered settlers were already living in that region. Some were temporary residents, such as Timothy Demonbreun who lived at Kaskaskia in the Illinois country but who spent the major portion of each winter from about 1769 at his trading post at the site of Nashville; also temporary was a hunter named Thomas ("Big Foot") Spencer, who is said to have resided in a hollow tree in Sumner County and to have spread his mammoth footprints over a wide area. But some of the "long hunters," such as Kasper Mansker and Michael Stoner, were returning to become permanent settlers.

When the Virginia legislature in 1778 nullified the Transylvania Company's title to land in Kentucky, Judge Henderson turned his attention more avidly to the North Carolina part of his purchase. In the spring of 1779 he sent James Robertson and eight companions into the Cumberland Valley "with instruments" to determine the latitude of "French Lick" and, if it should prove to be in North Carolina, to plant a crop of corn and make other preparations for the arrival of settlers. Since the "instruments" revealed that the site of Nashville was south of the 36°30′ parallel, Robertson's side trip to Kentucky was merely to explore the country rather than to purchase "cabin rights" from George Rogers Clark, as Theodore Roosevelt and many other writers have said. Also in 1779 Judge Henderson and two other members of the Transylvania Company served as North Carolina's representatives on the boundary commission, along with the Virginia representatives—Dr. Thomas Walker of the Loyal Land Company and Daniel Smith—that surveyed the boundary line between the two states. As noted in Chapter 1, the two groups separated and surveyed parallel lines for a considerable distance; however, when Henderson became convinced that even the Walker line would run considerably north of French Lick, he abandoned his survey and arrived at the Cumberland settlement in time to take the lead in setting up a form of government.

The migration of the settlers to the Cumberland Valley followed two routes, one overland and the other by water. James Robertson led the former group, which followed the Wilderness Road through Cumberland Gap into Kentucky and then turned southwest and reached the vicinity of French Lick late in December, 1779. On New Year's Day these settlers, with their horses, cattle, and sheep, crossed over the Cumberland River on the ice to the southern bank. There they built Fort Nashborough, named for General Francis Nash of North Carolina, and a few cabins while waiting for the other settlers to arrive.

Meanwhile, a flotilla of flatboats under the command of John Donelson assembled at Fort Patrick Henry to carry the remainder of the settlers, including the families of those who went overland, to the Cumberland. Donelson kept a journal of the "Voyage . . . in the good boat Adventure," in which he recounted the departure on December 22, 1779, the delay of two months only three miles from the fort because of weather conditions, and the harrowing experiences during the journey. Other boats joined the expedition at Cloud's Creek and at the mouth of the Clinch. There were several casualties when the boats were attacked by Indians at the "Suck," below the site of Chattanooga. One boat, separated from the others because several passengers had smallpox, was captured by the Chickamaugans, whose population was soon decimated as a result. The passage over the Muscle Shoals, where the voyagers expected at any moment to be dashed to pieces, left them breathless; but the journey across Tennessee and Kentucky to the Ohio was comparatively uneventful. Some boats left for Natchez, but the others made the difficult passage up the Ohio and Cumberland either to the

mouth of the Red River (at the site of Clarksville) or to Fort Nashborough, where Donelson made his final entry in the journal on
April 24, 1780.

By the spring of that year there were two or three hundred settlers
along the Cumberland, scattered among several stations. They were
within the bounds of Washington County, North Carolina, but
separated by more than two hundred miles of wilderness from the
county seat. Therefore, they organized a temporary government
under the "Cumberland Compact," which was written by Judge
Henderson but was probably drafted with the aid of Robertson,
Donelson, and others. Government was vested in a group of twelve
judges, or "Triers," apportioned among the eight stations, and subject to recall in case of dereliction of duty—a very modern concept.
An integral part of the compact was the provision for a land office
where the settlers could purchase their land from the Transylvania
Company; however, no payment was to be made unless North
Carolina should recognize the company's title to the land.

During the first years the settlements were almost destroyed by
raids made by several Indian tribes from both sides of the Ohio
River. It became necessary to concentrate in two or three of the
strongest forts, such as Nashborough, and abandon some of the
other stations. In addition, it was practically impossible to harvest
crops, and dependence on hunting for food led to a scarcity of ammunition. Therefore, Robertson had to go to Kentucky for more
powder. In April, 1781, even Nashborough was invested by Chickamaugans under Dragging Canoe. Robertson and a party of twenty
mounted men were ambushed and cut off from retreat to the fort.
Fortunately, the attention of the Indians was distracted by a pack
of dogs Mrs. Robertson released from the fort, and most of the men
were able to get back safely.

Because of Indian difficulties many of the settlers departed for
safer country. Even John Donelson moved with his family to Kentucky. It was mainly due to James Robertson's influence that enough
settlers remained to keep the settlement in existence. Robertson
was also able to negotiate peace with the Chickasaw, after the
evacuation by the Virginians of Fort Jefferson, the building of which
near the mouth of the Ohio had antagonized that tribe. Later, this
peace was formalized by a treaty between Virginia, represented
by Joseph Martin and John Donelson, and the Chickasaw signed at

Nashborough in November, 1783. That nation accepted the watershed between the Tennessee and Cumberland rivers as the new boundary line.

After the government was suspended for some time because of Indian difficulties, it was resumed under the compact in January, 1783, with Robertson as chairman, Andrew Ewin as clerk, and John Montgomery as sheriff. In addition to trying ordinary cases, opening roads, and fixing the price of liquor, the judges sought the establishment of county government under North Carolina and the regulation of land titles.

The first land law of the state of North Carolina was passed in 1777. For the price of fifty shillings per hundred acres any adult male could acquire 640 acres, and if he had a family one hundred additional acres for his wife and each child. More land could be purchased at a higher price. Since entry of land on the Indian side of the boundary line of 1777 was not prohibited until a year later, speculators had time to acquire title to more than a million acres of land in the Indian country. At the same time Lord Granville's title was declared null and void unless he should become a citizen of the state before October, 1778. Later, the Granville heirs attempted to recover their title by court action, but without success.

Land titles in the Cumberland country also depended on North Carolina's action regarding the claims of the Transylvania Company, based on the Treaty of Sycamore Shoals of 1775. In 1780 and 1782–83 the state, in providing for a military reservation for the location of land bounties for soldiers, ignored the company's claim. As finally determined and surveyed, the reservation covered approximately the upper half of Middle Tennessee. The bounties ranged from 640 acres for a private to 12,000 acres for a brigadier general. General Nathanael Greene was given a special grant of 25,000 acres. Preemption rights to 640 acres were granted to each head of a family or single man who had settled on the land before June 1, 1780. Following the example set by Virginia, North Carolina compensated the Transylvania stockholders with a grant of 200,000 acres in the Clinch and Powell valleys, 10,000 acres of which were to be set aside for the heirs of Carter and Lucas, the beneficiaries of Henderson's "Path Deed" of 1775.

In response to a petition from the Cumberland Association presented by James Robertson, the North Carolina legislature in April,

1783, created Davidson County in the Cumberland country. It was named for General William Davidson and was carved out of another new county created about the same time and named for General Greene, which was to include all of the rest of the state's claim west of Washington and Sullivan counties. The first meeting of the Davidson County court was held on October 6. The next year the name of the county seat was changed from Nashborough to Nashville. Thus, the Cumberland settlement acquired reasonable prospects of security and permanence.

SUGGESTED READINGS

General Accounts

Alden, *South in the Revolution*, 247–52, 268–74; Brown, *Old Frontiers*, 137–224; Joshua W. Caldwell, *Studies in Constitutional History of Tennessee* (Cincinnati, 1895), Ch. 2; Caruso, *Appalachian Frontier*, 111–19, 235–70; Davidson, *The Tennessee*, I, 133–72; Folmsbee, Corlew, and Mitchell, *Tennessee*, I, 123–47; Govan and Livingood, *Chattanooga Country*, 27–50; Hamer, *Tennessee*, I, 73–111; Henderson, *Conquest of Old Southwest*, 259–310; Thomas E. Matthews, *General James Robertson* (Nashville, 1934), Chs. 18–36; William H. McRaven, *Life and Times of Edward Swanson* (Nashville, 1937), Chs. 1–12; Ramsey, *Annals*, 143–277; Roosevelt, *Winning of the West*, I, Part 2, Ch. 3, II, Part 3, "The War in the Northwest," Chs. 4–6, III, Part 3, Chs. 7–9; Skinner, *Pioneers of Old Southwest*, 172–230; Williams, *Revolutionary War*, Chs. 3–33; Williams, *Early Travels*, 231–79.

Specialized Accounts

Jesse C. Burt, Jr., *Nashville: Its Life and Times* (Nashville, 1959), 1–18; Wirt A. Cate, "Timothy Demonbreun," *THQ*, XVI (Sept., 1957), 214–17; Cotterill, *Southern Indians*, Ch. 3; Randolph C. Downes, "Cherokee-American Relations in the Upper Tennessee Valley, 1776–1791," *ETHS Publ.*, No. 8 (1936), 35–53; Lyman C. Draper, *King's Mountain and Its Heroes* (Cincinnati, 1881; reprinted, New York, 1929, Spartanburg, S. C., 1967); Driver, *Sevier*, 16–28, 39–64; Robert L. Ganyard, "Threat from the West: North Carolina and the Cherokee," *NCHR*, XLV (Jan., 1968), 47–66; Philip M. Hamer, "John Stuart's Indian Policy During the Early Months of the American Revolution," *MVHR*, XVII (Dec., 1930), 351–66; Hamer, "Correspondence of Henry Stuart and Alexander Cameron with the Wataugans," *MVHR*, XVII (Dec., 1930), 451–59; Hamer, "The Wataugans and the Cherokee Indians in 1776," ETHS *Publ.*, No. 3 (1931), 108–26; Archibald Henderson, "Richard Henderson: The Authorship of the Cumberland Compact and the Founding of Nashville," *THM*, II (Sept., 1916), 159–67, reprinted in White, *Tennessee: Old and New*, I, 93–111; Henderson, "The Treaty of the Long Island of the Holston, 1777," *NCHR*, VIII (Jan., 1931), 51–116; Lester, *Transylvania Colony*, 258–74; Ben H. McClary, "Nancy Ward," *THQ*, XXI (Dec., 1962), 262–64; Mary H. McCown, "A King's Mountain Diary," ETHS *Publ.*, No. 14 (1942), 102–5; J.W.L. Matlock (ed.), "The Battle of the Bluffs: From the Journal of John Cotten," *THQ*, XVIII (Sept., 1959), 252–65; James H. O'Donnell, "The Virginia Expedition Against the Overhill Cherokee, 1776," ETHS *Publ.*, No. 39 (1967), 13–25; Putnam, *Middle Tennessee*, 65–214; Robert T. Quarles and R. H. White (eds.), *Three Pioneer Tennessee Documents: Donelson's Journal, Cumberland Compact, Minutes of the Cumberland Court* (Nashville, 1964); Helen L. Shaw, *British Administration of the Southern Indians, 1756–1783* (Lancaster, Pa., 1931), 91–116; Woodward, *Cherokees*, 84–101; Carol F. Young, "A Study of Some Developing Interpretations of the History of Revolutionary Tennessee," ETHS *Publ.*, No. 25 (1953), 24–36.

6. ❧ *The State of Franklin and the Spanish Intrigue*

A s THE Revolutionary War ended, Congress asked states with Western claims to cede their lands to the nation. The cession by Virginia of land north of the Ohio River brought pressure on North Carolina to cede the Tennessee country, but before ceding that area, including all "unappropriated" land in June, 1784, the North Carolina legislature made certain that very little land was left unappropriated. Even so, the legislature repealed that cession a few months later and did not make it again until 1789. In the meantime, the people in the eastern part of the region formed a separate state, which they called Franklin.

Beginnings of the State of Franklin ❧ Important in the background of the Franklin movement was the "Land Grab Act" of 1783 pushed through the North Carolina legislature by William Blount and other land speculators. This law offered for sale at a price of ten pounds (about five dollars in view of the depreciation of the currency) per hundred acres all unappropriated land in the Tennessee country, which was soon to be ceded to the United States, with the exception of the Military Reservation in the Cumberland Valley (for the location of military bounties) and a Cherokee Reservation east of the Tennessee River and south of the French Broad and Big Pigeon.[1] Although the land office remained open

---

[1] North Carolina claimed that the Indians had forfeited their title by joining the British during the Revolution but could not ignore the fact that the Cherokee were still living in southeastern Tennessee.

only seven months, nearly four million acres of land were entered, thus creating the foundations for large fortunes of several future Tennesseans.

Before the North Carolina cession in 1784, a separate statehood movement developed in East Tennessee, stimulated by a similar agitation led by Arthur Campbell in what is now southwestern Virginia. Even so, the Western representatives in North Carolina's assembly were about evenly divided on the cession bill, probably because some were irritated by the argument that the country being ceded was inhabited by "offscourings of the earth" and "fugitives from justice."

When the news of the cession law arrived, and also news of the passage by Congress of Jefferson's ordinance providing for the admission of new states into the Union, delegates representing the militia companies of Washington, Sullivan, and Greene counties (but not Davidson) met at Jonesborough (now Jonesboro) August 24, 1784. They chose John Sevier as president and urged the formation of a new state, which should include (as a gesture to Arthur Campbell) any contiguous part of Virginia legally permitted to join. After a second convention in November had broken up in confusion, a third convention met on December 14 and adopted, 28 to 15, a motion by William Cocke in favor of a new state. The third convention also approved for the "State of Franklin" a provisional constitution which was closely modeled after North Carolina's constitution, but which was prefaced by a declaration of independence stating five reasons for separation: (1) North Carolina's constitution and the cession act, which had "reduced us to a state of anarchy," gave implied consent to separation; (2) the withholding of goods from the Indians for the purchase of lands had provoked them to hostile acts; (3) congressional resolutions regarding new states supplied "ample encouragement"; (4) "almost every sensible disinterested traveller" had declared that it was incompatible with the region's interest to be united with the eastern part of the state, from which it was "separated . . . by high and almost impassable mountains"; and (5) the Westerners' lives, liberty, and property would be better protected by separation.

Meanwhile, although the Westerners were unaware of it because of slow communications, the North Carolina legislature on November 20 repealed the cession law, mainly because the act failed to give North Carolina credit for the expenses of Indian expeditions in determining the state's obligations to the federal government, but also because the law would permit the "aggrandizement of a few land jobbers" at the expense, presumably, of the many who had not benefited from the "land grab" of 1783. On the other hand, there were a few of those land speculators, like Hugh Williamson, who favored repeal in order to keep the control of the land system in the hands of the state. Others, however, under the leadership of William Blount, opposed the repeal and continued to work for a renewal of the cession, because they wanted the federal government to protect their titles under the land grab.

After the repeal, the legislature attempted to conciliate the Westerners by organizing the Tennessee country into a new district named Washington. The district had its own superior court judge, David Campbell, so litigants no longer needed to travel over the mountains for important cases. Also, the district had its own militia brigade, with John Sevier as brigadier general. Finally, Richard Caswell and William Blount were appointed as commissioners to negotiate with the Cherokee Indians.

At first, Sevier was proud to "have the honour to command, as general," the new district and believed that the concessions would "satisfy the people with the old state." When Sevier had originally joined the Franklin project, he had done so reluctantly because he feared that the project would interfere with land speculation at the Muscle Shoals by himself, William Blount, Richard Caswell, and others. At that time, following a private purchase from the Cherokee of land at the Shoals (the headwaters of navigation of the Tennessee) by Joseph Martin and John Donelson in 1783, the state of Georgia was induced to create a new county for that region and to give the North Carolina company a large grant of land. The land office was conveniently located at the Long Island of the Holston. Soon after his early opposition to the separate state movement, Sevier seemed to reconsider it as a means of advancing the Muscle Shoals speculation, because the fluid boundaries of Franklin might be extended far enough down the Tennessee to include the Shoals area. One week after the provisional Franklin constitution was adopted, a suspicious Virginian wrote that the new state was controlled by "a few crafty landjobbers" interested in land at the "great bent [bend]" of the Tennessee, who planned if necessary to "drive the natives (Cortez-like) out by force."[2]

Nevertheless, Sevier was willing to give up the separate state movement after the cession law was repealed, but he was soon, as he expressed it, "dragged with the Franklin measures by a large number of people."[3] Since he was unable to stop the movement, the separatist sentiment must have been very strong on the frontier; the West desired to free itself both governmentally and economically from the East.

The first general assembly of Franklin met in March, 1785, at Jonesboro and elected John Sevier as governor, Landon Carter as secretary of state, David Campbell as chief justice of the superior court, and Stockley Donelson as surveyor general. It also confirmed land titles under North Carolina statutes; reincorporated Samuel Doak's Martin Academy, previously chartered in 1783; established a militia with Daniel Kennedy and William Cocke as brigadier generals; created four new counties (Spencer, Caswell, Sevier, and Wayne); and provided for the levying of taxes and the payment of salaries. Because of the scarcity of money of any type and the prevalence of barter in ordinary trade, taxes were made payable in the produce of the country, including flax linen, woolen and cotten linsey, beaver, otter, raccoon, fox, and deer skins, woolen cloth, tallow, beeswax, sugar, rye whiskey, peach and apple brandy, and tobacco. Salaries were to be paid in these "specific articles as collected" or in "current money of the State of Franklin."

In reply to an inquiry from the governor of North Carolina, the Franklin legislators admitted that they had declared themselves "a free and independent state," but they expressed the hope that North Carolina would facilitate their "reception into the Federal Union." If those "sanguine hopes" were disappointed, they were determined never to desert their independence. Finally, they asked "the impartial world" to decide whether they had "deserted North Carolina or North Carolina deserted us."

Governor Alexander Martin responded with a "manifesto" of April 25 asking the people to return to their allegiance to North Carolina. Any implied consent to separation had been rescinded,

2 Whitaker, "Muscle Shoals Speculation," 371.
3 Driver, Sevier, 87.

he claimed, by the repeal of the cession law. He closed with a threat that North Carolina would "regain her government over the revolted territory or render it not worth possessing." On May 14 Governor Sevier issued a counter proclamation enjoining the people to be loyal to the state of Franklin and wrote a letter to the newly elected governor of North Carolina, his friend and fellow-speculator, Richard Caswell. Caswell's reply, however, was noncommital; he said that inasmuch as the special session of the legislature called by Governor Martin had not met because of the lack of a quorum, Franklin's case would have to await the next regular meeting in the fall. Caswell entreated Sevier not to consider his letter "as giving countenance" to the Franklin measures.

Relations with Congress and with North Carolina 〰
The Franklin legislature at its first session had adopted a memorial to the Congress of the United States and sent it to New York by its commissioner, William Cocke, who presented the memorial on May 16, 1785. Cocke also took with him a petition drafted by the people of Washington County, Virginia, asking that they be included in the proposed new state and that its boundaries be drawn so as to include not only East Tennessee but also adjoining portions of Virginia and Kentucky, much of Middle Tennessee, and enough of northern Alabama to take in the Muscle Shoals. The efforts of southwestern Virginians to join the state of Franklin came to a sudden end, however, when Governor Patrick Henry induced the Virginia legislature to declare such activity "high treason."

The congressional committee to which the Franklin memorial was submitted reported that Congress had the right to accept North Carolina's cession at any time within the time limit of one year included in the cession law. It therefore recommended that Congress accept the cession, an action which would pave the way for the admission of Franklin into the Union. Seven states voted in favor of a resolution that North Carolina's repeal of the cession was illegal (two short of the nine votes necessary for passage), but then only four states were willing to vote for accepting the cession in spite of the repeal. Thus, Franklin's hopes of federal approval were blasted.

Some time later William Cocke wrote to Benjamin Franklin,

who had been honored with the name of the state, asking his advice. Franklin advised the state to submit its disputes to Congress. In 1787, however, when the constitutional convention in Philadelphia included in the new Constitution a clause providing that no state can be divided without its consent, Franklin then advised Sevier to apply to North Carolina for a satisfactory compromise.

At a second session of the Franklin legislature in August, 1785, Thomas Stuart was appointed a commissioner to seek North Carolina's consent to separation. Unfortunately, the North Carolina assembly was controlled by the Radical party rather than by Governor Caswell, the Muscle Shoals speculator, so Stuart's mission was fruitless. In an effort to stir up sedition in Franklin, the North Carolina assembly offered pardons to those Franklinites willing to return to their allegiance to the mother state and encouraged elections to the North Carolina general assembly.

Almost as soon as the new state was organized, dissension arose under the leadership of a jealous rival of Sevier's, John Tipton, who perhaps may have belonged to a different group of land speculators. As early as the time of Martin's "manifesto," Tipton had secretly assured the governor of his loyalty to North Carolina. A bitter controversy also arose in the constitutional convention in November at Greeneville, the new capital of Franklin. The committee appointed to draft a frame of government, headed by the Reverend Samuel Houston (a cousin of the Tennessee and Texas hero), submitted a constitution for the "state of Frankland" so radical in character that it was rejected. At Sevier's suggestion, the provisional constitution was continued in force. The contending factions, however, carried on their debate in a "pamphlet war" that left many wounds. Among the supporters of Houston were John Tipton and Chief Justice Campbell.

Although Houston's constitution was criticized as being too religious in character, it was not much more so than the fundamental law of North Carolina, the model for the provisional constitution. Its democratic features were much more notable by the inclusion of universal manhood suffrage, then almost unknown in America; a single legislative house instead of the customary bicameral system; the popular election of the governor, executive council, and county officials instead of election by the legislature; the exclusion of attorneys from the assembly; election by ballot following a registration of voters; and the requirement of a popular referendum before enactment of a general law. One historian has said that in the rejection of this constitution, democracy was defeated on the frontier. On the other hand, the fact that these democratic features were even seriously proposed is ample testimony as to the democratic sentiments of the Westerners.

In August, 1786, the "Tiptonites" held elections in Washington and Sullivan counties for members to the North Carolina legislature. Although in Washington County the Franklinites held a similar election on the same day and cast more votes, the Tiptonite candidates were seated by the North Carolina assembly. Tiptonites, and especially Tipton in the senate, were able to use their influence against William Cocke's eloquent appeal for the recognition of Franklin. The legislature again offered pardons to those Franklinites who returned to North Carolina allegiance, remitted taxes for the past two years in the disaffected region, and created a new county of Hawkins. Declaring vacant the offices of those who had accepted positions under Franklin, it appointed Evan Shelby to replace Sevier as brigadier general of the Washington District. The legislature also granted an extension of time for the making of surveys of Western lands. One Radical leader wrote that he was opposed to any new cession of the lands to the United States until every possible benefit from them could be secured for the state of North Carolina.

Meanwhile, utmost confusion had developed in the Franklin area, with the two rival factions attempting to control the government. The feud between Sevier and Tipton erupted into personal combat, and they had to be separated by friends. The policy of the North Carolina legislature led many supporters of Franklin to conclude that separation could be attained only by prior submission to North Carolina, so they returned to their allegiance to that state. Others, however, became enraged at North Carolina and therefore were more ardent Franklinites. Since Governor Caswell had suggested that agreement among the Westerners was necessary, some Franklin leaders proposed that it be achieved by exterminating the opposition. Outright hostilities between the militia of the two governments were temporarily forestalled by a strange agreement on March 20 between Governor Sevier and General Shelby. The agreement provided that civil suits should not be carried to a "final determination" unless the parties were "mutually agreed thereto," that taxes were to be paid either to North Carolina or to Franklin, that any person convicted of a felony by a North Carolina justice of the peace could be imprisoned in a Franklin jail, and that the question of separation be referred to the next general assembly of North Carolina.

In the state elections of August, 1787, held by the North Carolina faction, the Franklinites ran their own candidates. Two of them, Daniel Kennedy and David Campbell of Greene County, not only won but were seated. John Sevier claimed election from Washington County, but did not attend. His enemy, John Tipton, whose election was contested by Landon Carter, was denied his seat in the senate. But North Carolina's conciliatory policy of offering pardons to Franklinites continued to bear fruit. Even David Campbell was induced to assume his office as judge of the Washington District of North Carolina, to which he was again elected. By the spring of 1788 support of the separate state had almost died out except in the region south of the French Broad River, which North Carolina recognized as Indian country. It was the Indian policy of Franklin which placed its most ardent supporters in a desperate plight and was to have far-reaching consequences.

Indian Relations and the Collapse of the State of Franklin ੩ The first assembly of Franklin authorized the governor to negotiate with the Cherokee Indians, and in June, 1785, several prominent chiefs signed the Treaty of Dumplin Creek, which permitted settlement south of the French Broad River as far as the ridge dividing the Little River from the Little Tennessee. Although this region was within the "Cherokee Reservation" set aside by North Carolina in 1783, Franklinites moved in so rapidly that by 1786 a new county, named Blount, was created for that area.[4]

This southwestern migration was not confined to the region opened by the Dumplin Creek Treaty. Lands outside the reservation, north of the French Broad River and also west of the Tennessee and Holston, were occupied. James White, speaker of the Franklin senate, Francis Ramsey, and others settled in 1785 in the forks

[4] Ramsey's famous map as the frontispiece of his *Annals*, showing the Franklin counties, fails to show this Blount County. See Folmsbee, "Annotations" (in 1967 edition), 747, *et passim* for other errors regarding Franklin's history.

of the French Broad and Holston rivers; the next year White established a settlement called White's Fort at the site of Knoxville,
west of the Holston (now Tennessee River), where he purchased
a tract of land under North Carolina's "Land Grab Act" of 1783.
A settlement was also attempted in the Muscle Shoals region, but
it was abandoned because of the hostile attitude of the Indians.

A major reason for the stiffening of the Cherokee resistance was
the signing by four United States commissioners, led by Benjamin
Hawkins, of the very lenient Treaty of Hopewell in November,
1785. Despite the vigorous protest of the Muscle Shoals speculator,
William Blount, who attended as a representative of North Carolina, those commissioners allowed the Indians to make their own
terms. The Indians reluctantly confirmed the Transylvania Purchase of 1775, but insisted that the treaty lines of 1777 be followed
on the east, including the Avery line running a few miles east of
Greeneville, which placed the capital of Franklin in Indian country. The only exception to the return to the 1777 boundary was an
agreement that the status of the "three thousand" inhabitants in
the forks of the French Broad and Holston rivers should be determined by Congress.[5] Specifically repudiated were the Franklin
Treaty of Dumplin Creek and the Martin-Donelson purchase of the
Muscle Shoals region. The Treaty of Hopewell also nullified North
Carolina's contention that the Revolutionary War had ended the
Indians' title to land except for the temporary right of the Cherokee
to occupy the region south of the French Broad River. In January,
1786, the same commissioners negotiated another Treaty of Hopewell with the Chickasaw, which confirmed the Nashborough Treaty
line of 1783 (the watershed between the Tennessee and Cumberland rivers) and obtained from those Indians the right to establish
a trading post at the foot of the Muscle Shoals.

The Indians were blindly confident that the United States government which had "conquered the King of England" would be
able to enforce the treaties, but the Confederation government was
powerless to do so. When the whites failed to move off the Indian
lands, the Cherokee went on the warpath. The Franklinites retaliated and forced the Cherokee to sign, obviously under duress,

---

[5] Presumably the same consideration would be given to the settlers between the
Avery line and the Tennessee and Holston rivers, including those at White's Fort
(Knoxville), and they may have been "counted" in the "three thousand."

a new Treaty of Coyatee in August, 1786, permitting settlement as far south as the Little Tennessee River.

Franklin's attempt to push its boundary as far as possible down the Tennessee toward the Muscle Shoals was bolstered by the outbreak of war early in 1786 between Georgia and the Creek Indians, who actually had the best claim to the Muscle Shoals area. The prospect of a joint expedition by Georgia and Franklin against the Creeks revived the hope that both the declining state of Franklin and the fortunes of the Muscle Shoals speculators might be saved. Even Governor Caswell of North Carolina, while issuing proclamations against the Franklinites, wrote privately to Sevier in July, 1786, that "The Bent [Bend] of Tennessee is still an Object with me of an Interesting Nature."[6] After vacillating for two years, however, the Georgians finally abandoned their war plans early in 1788, thus extinguishing the last flickering hope for the state of Franklin.

Meanwhile, an especially unfortunate incident, the Kirk episode, precipitated a new war between the Franklinites and the Cherokee, who quickly repudiated the Treaty of Coyatee. A Cherokee party massacred the family of John Kirk, who lived within nine miles of the Little Tennessee River. One son, John Kirk, Jr., was away at the time and escaped death. He joined a retaliatory expedition headed by John Sevier which, after destroying the towns along the Hiwassee River, returned to the Little Tennessee and invited the Cherokee chiefs to negotiate. The peacefully inclined Old Tassel and several other chiefs came in under a flag of truce for that purpose, but while Sevier was absent they were brutally tomahawked by John Kirk, Jr. Although Sevier was not directly responsible, the general reaction throughout the country was extremely unfavorable to him and to the state of Franklin. Also, in the ensuing general war with the Cherokee, the white settlements south of the French Broad narrowly escaped destruction.

While the Indian war raged, the state of Franklin was gradually dying. In August, 1787, the Franklin legislature, instead of reelecting Sevier governor, elected General Evan Shelby, hoping his influence with North Carolina would bring about a reconciliation. Shelby declined, but also resigned as brigadier general of the Washington District and recommended that Sevier be elected in his place. The North Carolina legislature, however, named Joseph Martin.

---

[6] Whitaker, "Muscle Shoals Speculation," 375–76.

Early in 1788 the feud between Sevier and Tipton almost flared into civil war. The North Carolina sheriff, Jonathan Pugh, under orders from Tipton, seized some of Sevier's slaves to satisfy a court judgment and took them to Tipton's home. Sevier organized a force of about fifty men to recover the slaves, and in a consequent skirmish Sheriff Pugh was killed and two of Sevier's sons were captured, but later released. Hostilities ceased after General Martin and the North Carolina militia intervened.

In the spring of 1788 Sevier was nearly ready to make his peace with North Carolina, but he was reluctant to desert his ardent supporters south of the French Broad. On July 29 the new governor of North Carolina, Samuel Johnston, ordered Sevier's arrest for high treason. Therefore, it is understandable why Sevier responded to the overtures of the agent of the Spanish envoy to the United States to engage in the Spanish intrigue. But on October 10 John Tipton, acting for the North Carolina judge, arrested Sevier and took him across the mountains to Morganton for trial, where General Charles McDowell, one of Sevier's fellow commanders at King's Mountain, signed his bail bond and obtained his release from custody. When Sevier's sons and friends came to rescue him, they were apparently allowed to escort him home without interference, and the trial was never held.

By this time the state of Franklin was dead except in the region of the Cherokee Reservation south of the French Broad, where a "lesser Franklin" existed for a few months. In contrast to the many Franklinites who had settled outside the reservation, where land titles could be obtained under North Carolina's laws, the settlers south of the French Broad had title to their lands only from the state of Franklin, because North Carolina had prohibited settlement in that area. The settlers' status under the federal Indian policy was even worse, for the Treaty of Hopewell line ran far to the northeast, on the other side of Greeneville.

The people south of the French Broad, like the Wataugans in 1772, attempted to solve their problem by drafting in January, 1789, "Articles of Association" similar to the Watauga Compact. Instead of adopting the laws of Virginia, however, they adopted those of North Carolina and agreed to ask the next general assembly of that state "to receive us into their protection." Although they recognized John Sevier as their commander and Indian commissioner, the

extent to which he was connected with the "Association" is unknown. At the February term of the Greene County court Sevier
took an oath of allegiance to North Carolina and in August was
elected to the state senate. Not only was he allowed to take his seat,
but he was declared by the assembly to be the brigadier general of
Washington District under his original appointment of 1784.

Thus the conciliatory policy of North Carolina, so successful in
destroying the state of Franklin, was finally extended to its leader,
who was permitted to assume a position of power in the same government he had tried to disrupt. After North Carolina ratified the
Constitution later in 1789, Sevier was elected as a representative in
Congress from the state's most western district. Although the state
of Franklin failed because of its inability to gain recognition and
because of dissension within its own ranks, the idea of a separate
state for what is now East Tennessee did not die.

The Franklin Intrigue with Spain ᗌᕁ According to some
writers, the aim of the Franklin movement from the beginning was
separation from the United States as well as from North Carolina.
It is doubtful that such was the original purpose, but by 1786 dissatisfaction with the government under the Articles of Confederation had led to a consideration of the idea. That secession tendency,
which characterized the Kentucky and Cumberland settlements as
well as Franklin, was accompanied by intrigues with the Spaniards,
who occupied the territory along the Gulf of Mexico and west of the
Mississippi River.

The chief aim of Spain's American policy after the Revolution
was to protect her colonial possessions from the aggressive and
expansive American frontiersmen. To achieve this, Spain took four
steps: (1) claimed the exaggerated boundary of the Tennessee and
Ohio rivers instead of the American contention of the 31st parallel;
(2) closed the Mississippi to navigation to stifle the growth of the
American settlements which were dependent on the river as an
outlet to market; (3) negotiated treaties of alliance with the Creek,
Choctaw, and Chickasaw Indians; and (4) encouraged secession
movements which arose in the American West.

Two actions inflaming the secession movements and the intrigues with Spain were the conciliatory policy of Congress regarding the Southern Indians (illustrated by the Hopewell treaties of 1785 and 1786) and the request by Secretary of Foreign Affairs John Jay in 1786 that he negotiate with Spain a treaty by which the United States would waive for twenty-five or thirty years the right to navigate the Mississippi River, in exchange for commercial concessions. Although this treaty failed to materialize, the West exploded with anger that such an idea should even have been proposed. One Westerner wrote: "To sell us & make us vassals to the merciless Spaniards, is a grievance not to be borne. The parliamentary acts which occasioned our revolt from Great Britain were not so barefaced and intolerable."[7]

Shortly after Jay's proposal, Dr. James White, a congressman from North Carolina who owned land in the Cumberland region (but not the James White who founded Knoxville), told the Spanish representative to the United States that the Western settlements, because of their fear that the Mississippi would remain closed, would surely separate from the Union and would be willing to ally themselves with either England or Spain. White added that by opening the river to the Westerners, Spain could win their allegiance forever. Although Gardoqui gave White a letter of introduction to a Spanish officer in Louisiana, he did nothing further to encourage the intrigue.

After serving for some time as superintendent of Indian affairs in the South, White had an opportunity to renew his conversations with Gardoqui early in 1788. Governor Johnston of North Carolina instructed White to take to and discuss with Gardoqui the letters from James Robertson and Anthony Bledsoe, and also from John Sevier, charging the Spaniards with inciting the Indians to attack the American settlements. Having learned of Sevier's military defeat by Tipton, White suggested that the Franklin governor would be susceptible to Spanish overtures. Gardoqui responded by sending White as a Spanish agent to the Franklin country with a denial of Sevier's charges that the Spaniards were responsible for the Indian outrages; on the contrary, Spain was "much disposed" to give the inhabitants of Franklin "all the protection they ask." Sevier's reply of July 18, 1788, has been lost, but White summarized it later to

---

[7] Hamer, *Tennessee*, I, 134.

the Spanish governor at Havana as saying the Franklinites "wished to place themselves under the protection of the King [of Spain]."[8]

After White had returned to New York, Sevier dispatched his son James with two other letters to Gardoqui, dated September 12, which have been found in the Spanish archives. In the longer of the two letters, Sevier said that the "principal men" of Franklin were as "well disposed and willing" as he was with respect to Gardoqui's "proposals and guarantees" and were "very ardent" regarding the "future probability of an alliance and a concession of commerce." The people of Franklin, Sevier wrote, "have come to realize truly upon what part of the world and upon which nation depend their future happiness and security." After complaining about the inability of the people to "make use of our rivers to the ports below," and referring to the scarcity of money, he appealed for a loan of a few thousand pounds, which he promised would be repaid by means of the export of produce down the rivers to the Spanish ports, if permitted. Finally, Sevier asked for a passport to enable him to go to New Orleans, if deemed necessary.[9]

The shorter of the two letters reveals Sevier's motives even more. He implied that the Franklinites were planning to establish a settlement near the Muscle Shoals, and he hoped that the Spaniards would be "gratiously [sic] disposed to reconcile the minds" of the Indians under their dominion and keep them at peace. Obviously, a major reason for Sevier's entering into the intrigue, besides the near collapse of the state of Franklin and the warrant out for his arrest, was the hope that the Spaniards would facilitate the revival of the Muscle Shoals speculation. Gardoqui sent Sevier a passport by his son James, but neglected to send him any money. That may have been one reason why Sevier abandoned the intrigue and made his peace with North Carolina.

Gardoqui sent Dr. White to New Orleans by way of Havana, Cuba. In a memorandum to the Spanish officials, White tried unsuccessfully to solicit support for a "Greater Franklin." What Franklin wanted, he explained, was an alliance, commercial concessions, and with Spanish protection the opportunity to expand its territory down the Tennessee River past the Muscle Shoals to the headwaters

---

[8] Whitaker, "Muscle Shoals Speculation," 379; Corbitt and Corbitt, "Papers from Spanish Archives," No. 18, p. 144.
[9] Henderson, "Spanish Conspiracy," 234–35.

of the Alabama and Yazoo rivers. In return, the Franklinites would pledge allegiance to Spain, provided they could retain for the time being complete control of their domestic affairs. Spain would gain an advantage in prosecuting the boundary dispute with the United States, profitable trade relations, and increased security for Spanish colonies, since the other settlements west of the mountains would follow Franklin's example.

The Spanish officials were interested but suspicious. One of them wrote: "Don Diego White is thoroughly republican at heart. The movement that is taking place in the state of Franklin has as its object the establishment of independence rather than a *rapprochement* with Spain."[10] When White reached New Orleans, he discovered that the leaders of the Cumberland settlement already had begun correspondence with Governor Don Estevan Miró of Louisiana, and White tried to claim credit for it; for the first time he included Cumberland along with Franklin in his memorial to a Spanish official.

Miró had just received a royal order from Spain in reply to the memorial of General James Wilkinson, the Kentucky intriguer who had offered his services to Miró in bringing about the secession of the American West as early as 1787. Therefore, Miró replied to White in the spirit of that order by a "Memorandum of Concessions to Westerners," dated April 20, 1789. Since Spain and the United States were at peace, Miró could not promote a separation, but if it should happen that the Westerners did obtain their independence, then "His Majesty" would grant them such favors as were "compatible with the interests of the Crown." As an alternative, the memorandum encouraged the immigration of the Westerners into Spanish Louisiana, where they would be granted land and some measure of religious freedom, but would be required to take an oath of allegiance to Spain. Also, the Americans were to be allowed to use the Mississippi River, subject to the payment of a 15 per cent duty, but reduced to 6 per cent for certain individuals. Of course, those who migrated to Spanish territory would be allowed to navigate the river without paying any duties.

White was disappointed, for the reply destroyed his dream of a "Greater Franklin." Nevertheless, he did agree to go at Spain's

10 Whitaker, "Muscle Shoals Speculation," 384.

expense to Cumberland and Franklin with the memorandum. But after reaching the Cumberland settlements he strongly advised against the continuance of the intrigue or migration to Spanish territory. Apparently White did not return to the Franklin area, where Sevier had already abandoned the intrigue.

The Cumberland Intrigue ৯৬ The leaders of the Cumberland settlements had begun their correspondence with the Spaniards, it seems, without any direct involvement of Dr. James White. The chief reason, in addition to a desire for free navigation of the Mississippi River, was the danger that the small population in the area would be wiped out by Indian attacks. Separated by great stretches of wilderness from their nearest neighbors, those settlements were almost defenseless against the raids of the Creeks and the Chickamauga. The Creek chieftain, Alexander McGillivray, claiming to speak for both tribes, had protested against the Cumberland settlements as early as 1785 and had begun a savage war against them by 1786. Although there was a temporary truce, during which the Chickamauga element of the Cherokee took up the slack, the Creek raids were resumed in 1787. It was the belief that the Indians were being incited by the Spaniards which led Robertson and Bledsoe to write to Governor Caswell the letters that were delivered to Gardoqui, along with Sevier's protest, by way of Governor Johnston and Dr. James White early in 1788, thus giving White the opportunity to instigate the intrigue with Sevier and the Franklinites. Gardoqui also sent denials of Spanish incitement to Robertson and Bledsoe, but apparently the letters did not reach the Cumberland until February or March, 1789, because White, it seems, did not go to Cumberland when he made his journey to Franklin in the summer of 1788.

Meanwhile, after his son had been killed and a neighbor's son captured, James Robertson in March, 1788, appealed directly to McGillivray and through him to the Spaniards. McGillivray reported to a Spanish official that the deputies from Cumberland represented their people to be in such distress from the raids that they were willing to submit to any conditions to obtain peace, even to becoming "Subjects of the King [of Spain]." They "were determined," they said, "to free themselves from a dependence on Congress" because that body was unable to protect their persons and property or encourage their commerce.[11] When the raids continued, Robertson attempted to bribe McGillivray with the offer of a gun and a tract of land, but also hinted that the Westerners might join the British in an attack on New Orleans.

Before appealing directly to Miró, Robertson induced the North Carolina legislature to honor the Spanish governor by naming the new district created in November, 1788, for the Cumberland region the "Mero District." Robertson and Brigadier General Daniel Smith of the new district wrote to Miró early in 1789 appealing for peace with the Indians and improved commercial relations. The courier who carried Smith's letter, a Spanish militia officer named Don Antonio Fagot, reported to Miró that the Cumberland people planned to ask the North Carolina legislature for permission to separate from the state; the Cumberland people would then offer allegiance to Spain. Although the same impression was given by Robertson's correspondence with Miró, the Mero legislators actually were instructed to work for a cession of Western lands to the United States. Smith learned from Dr. White early in 1789 the nature of Fagot's report to Miró, but waited until September 19 to tell Miró that Fagot was mistaken. "The people here," he wrote, "wish to be in the closest friendship tho' not subject to his Catholic Majesty." By that time the partial opening of the river and the influence of Miró in the lessening of the Indian raids had greatly improved the situation, for which the Cumberland leaders profusely thanked the Spanish governor.[12]

Obviously, the Cumberland leaders negotiated with the Spaniards mainly to obtain concessions, especially cessation of Indian raids and the right to navigate the Mississippi, and some material benefits were secured by the Westerners. They had no desire, as Smith admitted, to become subjects of the Spanish ruler, except as a last resort. Another major purpose of the intrigue was to frighten North Carolina into ratifying the Constitution and ceding the Western lands to the United States. While the leaders were writing to Miró, they were also writing to the North Carolina governor warning him of the separatist feeling and its encouragement by the Spaniards, and warning also that the population of the Western districts might

11 Caughey, *McGillivray*, 178–79.
12 Corbitt and Corbitt, "Papers from Spanish Archives," No. 21, pp. 89, 93.

be reduced by Spain's new immigration policy. As one writer has said, "A conspirator who advertises his conspiracy is a veritable marplot new to the annals of intrigue."[13] One of Smith's letters to Governor Johnston of North Carolina hinted very strongly that ratification of the Constitution and the cession of the Western lands would bring the intrigue to an end. Thus, the passage of those measures late in 1789 may be considered a fulfillment of the intrigue rather than merely an obstacle to it. After the Tennessee country became the "Territory of the United States South of the River Ohio" and later a new state, its inhabitants no longer considered intrigue with Spain.

SUGGESTED READINGS

General Accounts

Abernethy, *Frontier to Plantation*, 45–102; Brown, *Old Frontiers*, 239–80; Caruso, *Appalachian Frontier*, 271–310; Driver, *Sevier*, 28–33, 64–98; Folmsbee, Corlew, and Mitchell, *Tennessee*, I, Chs. 8–9; Hamer, *Tennessee*, I, Chs. 10–11; Haywood, *Civil and Political History*, 147–259; Henderson, *Conquest of Old Southwest*, 306–49; William H. Masterson, *William Blount* (Baton Rouge, 1954), 75–169; Ramsey, *Annals*, 282–444; Roosevelt, *Winning of the West*, Part 4, "Indian Wars, 1784–1787," Chs. 1–4; Arthur P. Whitaker, *The Spanish-American Frontier* (Boston, 1927), Ch. 6; Samuel C. Williams, *History of the Lost State of Franklin* (Johnson City, Tenn., 1924).

Specialized Accounts

G. H. Alden, "The State of Franklin," *AHR*, VIII (Jan., 1903), 271–89; John Allison, "The Mero District," *AHM*, I (April, 1896), 115–27, reprinted in White, *Tennessee: Old and New*, I, 145–54; Walter F. Cannon, "Four Interpretations of the History of the State of Franklin," *ETHS Publ.*, No. 22 (1950), 3–18; J. W. Caughey, *McGillivray of the Creeks* (Norman, 1938); D. C. and Roberta Corbitt (trans. and eds.), "Papers from the Spanish Archives Relating to Tennessee and the Old Southwest," *ETHS Publ.*, No. 9 (1937), Nos. 16–22 (1944–50); Downes, "Cherokee-American Relations," *ETHS Publ.*, No. 8, pp. 35–53; Rev. Samuel Houston, "The Provisional Constitution of Frankland," *AHM*, I (Jan., 1896), 48–63, reprinted in White, *Tennessee: Old and New*, I, 13–26; Paul M. Fink, "Some Phases of the History of the State of

---

[13] Whitaker, "Spanish Intrigue," 175.

Franklin," *THQ*, XVI (Sept., 1957), 195–213; Archibald Henderson, "The Spanish Conspiracy in Tennessee," *THM*, III (Dec., 1917), 229–43; Thomas B. Jones, "The Public Lands of Tennessee," *THQ*, XXVII (Spring, 1968), 13–36; J. T. McGill, "Franklin and Frankland: Names and Boundaries," *THM*, VIII (Jan., 1925), 248–57; A. W. Putnam (ed.), "Correspondence of James Robertson," *AHM*, I–IV (1896–1900); Putnam, *Middle Tennessee*, 265–333; Frederick J. Turner, "Western State Making in the Revolutionary Era," *AHR*, I (Oct., 1896), 70–87; Arthur P. Whitaker, "The Muscle Shoals Speculation, 1783–1789," *MVHR*, XIII (Dec., 1926), 365–86; Whitaker, "Spanish Intrigue in the Old Southwest: An Episode, 1788–1789," *MVHR*, XII (Sept., 1925), 155–76.

7. ❧ Southwest Territory and Statehood

NORTH CAROLINA'S CONVENTION of November, 1789, finally ratified the United States Constitution, with only two delegates from the Western counties voting against that action; in contrast, the July, 1788, convention had postponed ratification, with only two Western delegates voting against the postponement. The important difference was the representation of the Western counties by Tiptonites in 1788 and by John Sevier and other supporters of the Franklin movement in 1789. Similarly, only two members of the legislature from the Tennessee country in December, 1789, voted against the law ceding that area to the United States. Congress accepted the second cession by North Carolina in 1790, and thus Tennessee became a federal territory.

Government of the Territory ❧ The provisions of the cession law of 1789 were very similar to those of the act of 1784 which was repealed. Under the directing hands of William Blount and other land speculators, all land claims under North Carolina laws were to remain valid. If there was not enough good land in the Military Reservation to satisfy the soldiers' claims, the remaining warrants could be located elsewhere in the region ceded. The law also provided that one or more states should ultimately be made out of the ceded country, but in the meantime the territory was to be governed under the provisions of the Northwest Ordinance of 1787, with an important exception—the clause prohibiting slavery in the Northwest Territory should not apply to the North Carolina cession. That exception was confirmed in the brief act of Congress creating the "Territory of the United States South of the River Ohio," passed on May 26, 1790.

This official name has led some writers to assume erroneously that the territory included at least Kentucky, and possibly also the country extending southward as far as the southern boundary of the nation. Actually, the Southwest Territory, as it was usually called, included only the North Carolina cession—present-day Tennessee. Since Virginia's cession of 1784 included no land south of the Ohio, the Kentucky country was an integral part of the Old Dominion until admitted as a separate state in 1792. Until 1802 the region south of the Tennessee line was claimed by Georgia, which had acquired South Carolina's geographically nonexistent Western claim in 1787.

The Northwest Ordinance provided that a territory should pass through three stages of government on the way to statehood. After being governed by appointed officials—a governor, a secretary, and three judges—a territory was to be eligible for a representative system when the population included 5,000 free male inhabitants of voting age. When the free population reached 60,000, the territory was to be eligible for statehood. President Washington appointed William Blount as governor and General Daniel Smith of the Mero District as secretary. The three judges were David Campbell, John McNairy, and Joseph Anderson. The governorship carried with it the position of superintendent of Indian affairs south of the Ohio.

Governor Blount was a distinguished North Carolinian who had served as paymaster of troops during the Revolution, as a legislator, and as a member of the Confederation Congress and of the constitutional convention. An aristocratic Easterner, he was a businessman who had entered politics not merely to serve the public but also to advance his own pecuniary interests. Together with his partner-brothers, Blount had acquired more than a million acres of Western lands. After learning of his appointment, he admitted to a friend: "... my Western Lands had become so great an object to me that it had become absolutely necessary that I should go to the Western Country, to secure them."[1] Despite these personal aims, he proved to be a capable governor.

Blount first set up headquarters in the home of William Cobb in

[1] Masterson, *Blount*, 178.

the forks of the Holston and Watauga rivers. This house, called "Rocky Mount," the first capitol of the Southwest Territory, has recently been restored. In the summer of 1791 Blount negotiated a treaty with the Cherokee Indians at White's Fort, and he selected that place as the permanent capital of the territory. This small settlement four miles below the junction of the French Broad and Holston rivers had been started by James White only five years earlier. White, after purchasing the land under the "Land Grab Act" of 1783, employed Charles McClung to mark off the area adjoining the river into sixty-four lots, which were then disposed of at a lottery held on October 3, 1791, when the settlement was established as a town. The three individuals who conducted White's lottery were designated as town commissioners.

An astute politician, Blount named the town Knoxville, in honor of his immediate superior in the conduct of Indian affairs, Secretary of War Henry Knox. Blount moved to Knoxville in 1792 and built a two-story frame house, which is now restored and called "Blount Mansion." Also in 1792 George Roulstone moved to Knoxville the Tennessee country's first newspaper, which had started publication on November 5, 1791, at "Hawkins Court House" (now Rogersville), although it was already using the name "Knoxville Gazette."

Governor Blount appointed all the subordinate civil and military officials in his administration, except that President Washington appointed the secretary and the judges and named John Sevier and James Robertson as brigadier generals of the Washington and Mero districts. Blount, in June, 1792, created two new counties, Knox and Jefferson, within the area acquired by the Cherokee treaty, and on March 1, 1793, he organized them into a new district named Hamilton. Thus he honored Secretary Knox a second time and also two other members of Washington's cabinet.

A census taken in September, 1791, revealed a territorial population of 35,691 (including 3,417 slaves and an estimated 6,400 free, adult males). Although the territory was therefore eligible for representative government, Blount, probably wishing to retain the unlimited power in his own hands, took no step in that direction until 1793. As a result of the popular clamor for an elected assembly, he then ordered the election in December, 1793, of thirteen members of a house of representatives. Under the Northwest Ordinance a voter was required to own fifty acres of land, and a representative had to own two hundred acres. This elected house met in Knoxville on February 18, 1794, and nominated ten men (who had to own at least five hundred acres), from whom President Washington subsequently appointed five[2] to serve as members of the council, the upper house of the legislative body.

The first meeting of the two houses of the territorial assembly was held in August. Among its legislative acts were the incorporation of the town of Knoxville, the creation of Sevier County, and the chartering of two colleges: Greeneville, the beginning of Tusculum College, and Blount, the forerunner of The University of Tennessee. The assembly also authorized lotteries to raise funds for public purposes and fixed the tax rate at 25 cents on each one hundred acres of land. Finally, the assembly sent Congress a petition demanding a more aggressive Indian policy and a memorial from the people south of the French Broad River asking for preemption rights and validation of land titles. Since the territory in its representative period was entitled to have a nonvoting delegate in the United States Congress, the assembly elected Dr. James White. A second session of the assembly met on June 29, 1795, to take action for statehood, which will be treated later. At the same time, this session created Blount County, chartered several towns, and gave Samuel Doak's Martin Academy a charter as Washington College.

Indian Relations ⟨⟩ The most serious problem faced by Blount as superintendent of Indian affairs was the resentment of the Cherokee Indians over the failure of the United States to enforce the Treaty of Hopewell of 1785. In addition to the great number of settlers between the French Broad River and the Avery line of 1777 (whose status had been left undecided in 1785), there were more than 3,500 people south of the French Broad, who had moved in under the treaties of the now defunct state of Franklin, and also people in the new settlements west of the Holston and Tennessee rivers. Although the Cherokee in the Hopewell treaty had confirmed the Transylvania Purchase of 1775, the Chickamauga Indians, now returned to the Cherokee fold and known as "Lower Cherokee," joined with the Creeks in demanding the evacuation of the Cumber-

[2] Griffith Rutherford, John Sevier, James Winchester, Stockley Donelson, and Parmenas Taylor.

land Valley, the common hunting grounds of many tribes.

Secretary Knox, on August 11, 1790, instructed Blount to nego-tiate with the Cherokee for the cession of the occupied territory in exchange for an annuity of $1,000. Indian apprehensions concerning the activities of the so-called Yazoo companies, which had obtained huge grants of land from Georgia, caused delay. Zachariah Cox, head of the Tennessee Company, actually led a group of settlers, including some from the territory, to the Muscle Shoals in March, 1791, but the settlement was broken up by the Indians. Blount, an old Muscle Shoals speculator himself, opposed the project because it was certain to interfere with his negotiations with the Cherokee.

Those Indians, including some chiefs of the Chickamauga faction, eventually met Blount at White's Fort (soon to be named Knox-ville) late in June and signed the Treaty of the Holston[3] on July 2, 1791. The cession in the eastern region was bounded on the west by the Clinch River and on the south by a line running from near the mouth of the Clinch to the North Carolina border, passing a few miles south of the site of Maryville. The Transylvania Purchase of Middle Tennessee was again confirmed but in such a manner that the survey of 1797 allowed the addition of some more territory. Other provisions of the treaty placed the Cherokee and their trade under the protection of the United States and gave the whites the privilege of navigating the Tennessee River and using a road connecting the Washington and Mero districts. Finally, with a view to advancing the civilization of the Cherokee, the Indians were to be supplied with "useful implements of husbandry" and instruction in their use.

The peaceful relations expected as a result of the Holston treaty and the Treaty of New York of 1790 with the Creek Indians failed to materialize. One reason for the renewal of Indian warfare in the Southwest was the crushing defeat in November, 1791, of the army of Governor Arthur St. Clair of the Northwest Territory by the Northern Indians, who then urged the Southern tribes to help in recovering lost lands. That defeat also ruined Blount's hopes that federal troops would be sent into the Southwest, and it led to the sending of firm orders by Knox that even the local militia should be used only in defense against attacks and not in any offensive opera-tions. Thus, with less fear of white retaliation, the Indians were en-

---

[3] At that time the name Holston was applied to what later, about 1880, was called the Tennessee, between the mouths of the French Broad and Little Tennessee rivers.

couraged to renew their raids. Two Englishmen, William Augustus Bowles among the Creeks and George Welbank among the Lower Cherokee, also were disruptive influences.

One of the most important causes of the warfare was the aggressive Spanish policy under Hector, Baron de Carondelet, who succeeded Miró on December 30, 1791, as governor at New Orleans. Carondelet immediately revitalized the coalition under Spanish protection of the Creek, Choctaw, and Chickasaw Indians but also now included the Cherokee. According to one authority (A. P. Whitaker), "if Carondelet had had his way, he would have precipitated a general Indian war to compel the United States to relinquish the territory ceded by the Cherokee in the treaty of Holston."

The Cherokee, greatly dissatisfied with the Holston treaty, sent a delegation to the national capital in January, 1792, to persuade Secretary Knox that the Cumberland Valley, the "joint lands" of several tribes, should be evacuated. However, Knox merely increased the Cherokee annuity to $1,500 and showered them with presents. Then, hopes for peace were destroyed by the Spanish influence. John Watts, who had become the war chief of the Chickamauga (or Lower Cherokee) after Dragging Canoe's death in March, 1792, visited William Panton, an English trader at the Spanish post of Pensacola, and was assured that the Spaniards would supply unlimited ammunition and would help to recover the lands. Watts led an army of six hundred Cherokee, Creek, and Shawnee warriors against Buchanan's Station, four miles from Nashville, but was repulsed by Robertson's militia. Carondelet on November 28, 1792, wrote the Spanish prime minister that he had told the Cherokee to suspend hostilities while the Spanish monarch attempted by mediation to restore their lost hunting grounds. Carondelet added, however, that since those Indians had been forced to renew their war against the Americans it would be necessary to support them. He planned "underhandedly [to] Supply the Cherokees and Creeks with sufficient arms and munitions to maintain themselves. . . ."[4]

Under the circumstances, Governor Blount's task of maintaining peace was an extremely difficult one. Although Hanging Maw was able to keep the Upper Cherokee relatively quiet, the raids of the Lower Cherokee and Creeks became so serious in the spring and

4 Corbitt and Corbitt, "Papers from Spanish Archives," No. 28, pp. 139–41.

summer of 1793 that the settlers throughout the Southwest Territory were forced to crowd within the walls of various stations. It was
increasingly difficult to enforce the federal order against offensive
operations, and the fury of the settlers was expressed in several
ambushes of friendly Indians. The most serious of these outrages
occurred in June, soon after Blount left for Philadelphia to urge
the government to adopt a war policy. Captain Hugh Beard and a
group of militia slaughtered the family of Hanging Maw, and thus
brought on a general war with the Cherokee. When the news
reached Philadelphia, Blount's mission became quite fruitless; he
was ordered to return to his post immediately to bring Beard and
his companions to trial. Subsequently, Beard was tried but acquitted
by a partisan jury.

During the next two years a gradual quieting of the Indians resulted from a combination of factors. One of the most important
was the offensive measures taken in disregard of federal orders. Late
in September an army of six or seven hundred Cherokee and Creek
warriors under John Watts approached Knoxville. Discord and
confusion among the Indian leaders diverted the attack to Cavet's
Station, about eight miles distant, where a brutal massacre occurred. Secretary Smith ordered General Sevier to pursue the Indians, with several hundred men. Sevier soundly defeated them at
the Battle of Etowah (near present Rome, Georgia) and destroyed
several Cherokee and Creek towns.

Although this quieted the Indians for a time, complications soon
arose as a result of the intrigues of Edmond Genêt, the French
minister to the United States. France was at war with Spain, so
Genêt was instructed to induce the disgruntled American Revolutionary hero, George Rogers Clark, to organize an expedition of
American frontiersmen and Indians for an attack against Spanish
Louisiana. Clark attempted to comply; one of his wartime associates,
Colonel John Montgomery, raised a force in the Mero District to
join him, but the troops were dispersed by the Chickasaw Indians.
Clark's expedition failed to materialize. Blount, who was later to
engage in a similar intrigue with the British, wrote Robertson that
he was "surprised and mortified" by Montgomery's activities.

Meanwhile, Blount continued his efforts to induce the federal
government to adopt a war policy in the Southwest. In February,

1794, the territorial house of representatives sent a memorial to Congress detailing the two hundred murders by Indians and the loss of more than $100,000 worth of property since 1791. The government, so heavily involved in General Anthony Wayne's campaign against the Northern Indians, could do little more, however, than authorize a few garrisoned posts along the Little Tennessee and Clinch rivers and increase the Cherokee annuity to $5,000.

The Chickamauga faction, living in the "five lower towns" below the site of Chattanooga, continued to join the Creeks in raids against the Cumberland settlements. Therefore, Blount and Robertson worked out a plan to evade the federal orders against offensive operations. Major James Ore was sent with a company of men from Hamilton District to Mero, and Blount gave Robertson explicit orders that those troops and others being organized should be used only for defense. But Robertson, probably with the governor's approval, sent the troops, under Ore's command, on a surprise attack against the Chickamauga towns. Robertson then resigned his commission as brigadier general and assumed full responsibility. This "Nickajack Expedition" was highly successful; two of the lower towns were completely destroyed, and the warlike tendencies of the Chickamauga were greatly reduced.

The crushing defeat of the Northern Indians at Fallen Timbers by General Wayne in the summer of 1794 also had a quieting effect on the Southern tribes, and the Spanish policy became less aggressive. Carondelet devoted himself to trying to heal the breach between the Chickasaw and the Creeks, but because of Robertson's continuing efforts to establish a trading post on the Chickasaw Bluffs, the Spaniards built Fort San Fernando at the site of Memphis in 1795. Also in 1795 the Spanish government in the Treaty of San Lorenzo (Pinckney's Treaty) with the United States accepted the 31st parallel as the boundary between the United States and Spanish Florida and granted the Americans free navigation of the Mississippi River. Although the evacuation of Fort San Fernando was delayed until the spring of 1797, Spain long before that time had abandoned its alliances with the Southern Indians. Denied Spanish support, those Indians were forced to make the best arrangements they could with the Americans. Thus, a more peaceful era dawned as the Southwest Territory advanced from territorial status to statehood. The federal government, meanwhile, as a means of protecting the Indians from the aggressive frontiersmen, took over the control of the Indians by the adoption of the factory system. Trading factories were established at Tellico Blockhouse on the Little Tennessee River in 1795, and at the site of Memphis in 1802.

The Statehood Movement and Constitutional Convention ૬ Although Governor Blount had been responsible for the postponement of representative government for the territory, he assumed the leadership of the movement for statehood. Unable to induce the federal government to adopt an aggressive Indian policy, Blount had become convinced that only as a state in the Union could the people of the Tennessee country protect their vital interests. Incidentally, his own land speculation designs would be advanced by a lessening of the Indians' resistance to white settlement. Also, he was aware that the popular John Sevier was restless in his subordinate position, and statehood would make the governorship available for Sevier; Blount himself had long desired to go to the United States Senate.

Since Tennessee was to be the first state to be admitted from a territorial status, there was no precedent to follow. Learning from the territorial delegate, Dr. James White, that Congress was unlikely to take the initiative, Blount called the territorial assembly into special session on June 29 to take the necessary actions. The assembly provided for the taking of a census to determine if the free population of the territory had reached 60,000 and also for a poll on the question of statehood even if the population should prove to be less than the required number. The Northwest Ordinance allowed a state to be admitted with less than 60,000 people if "consistent with the general interest of the Confederacy."

The census revealed a total population of 77,262 of whom 10,613 were slaves; thus 66,649 were free inhabitants, including 973 free Negroes. The total in the eight eastern counties was 65,338, whereas in the three counties west of the Cumberland Plateau there were only 11,924. The referendum resulted in a vote of 6,504 in favor of statehood even if the population were inadequate and 2,562 against. Most of the opposing votes were cast by Cumberland settlers, who probably feared domination by the more populous eastern section. If statehood should be delayed, the settlers might consider a separate state by themselves.

Governor Blount issued a proclamation for the election on December 18 and 19 of delegates to a constitutional convention to be held in Knoxville in January, 1796. James White made the arrangements for the meeting and was later reimbursed for his expenditures, which included $10.00 for seats, $2.62 for oil cloth, and $22.50 for firewood, candles, and stands. When the convention adjourned, the delegates voted to reduce their own pay from $2.50 to $1.50 per day.

The outstanding personnel of the convention included several territorial officials (Governor Blount, who presided, Secretary Smith, Judges Anderson and McNairy, Dr. James White, the territorial delegate, and General James Robertson), a future President (Andrew Jackson), and several future governors and congressmen (William C. C. Claiborne, Archibald Roane, Joseph McMinn, John Rhea, and William Cocke). There is a tradition that Jackson proposed the name Tennessee for the new state, but that name was already in general use as a result of Daniel Smith's *Short Description of the Tennessee Government*, published in 1793 and re-issued in 1795, with its famous accompanying map.

Although the Blount faction was usually in control, an opposition group led by two Pennsylvanians, Joseph McMinn and Judge Anderson, and the father-in-law of the latter, Alexander Outlaw, advocated a unicameral, or one-house, legislature and more successfully took the initiative in proposing a declaration of rights. The convention naturally used the constitution of the mother-state, North Carolina, as a model, but recent research has shown that the convention copied several features from the constitution of Pennsylvania. There were nearly as many former Pennsylvanians in the convention as North Carolinians.

The preamble of the constitution expresses the familiar doctrine that government originates as a result of a mutual compact, using the phrase, "We the people of the Territory . . . do mutually agree with each other to form ourselves into a free and independent state." This language implied that if Congress did not admit the new state, Tennessee would attempt to function as an independent commonwealth. The influence of the Watauga Compact and the state of Franklin was still present.

Under this first constitution, legislative power was vested in a "General Assembly" consisting of a senate and a house of representatives, the members elected for terms of two years. Representation was to be proportional to taxable inhabitants. In addition to fulfilling age and residence qualifications, a member of either house had to own at least two hundred acres of land. Ministers of the gospel were (and still are) ineligible to membership. The powers of the legislature were extensive and unfettered by any gubernatorial veto. There were constitutional limitations regarding salaries, size of counties, and taxation. Taxes on land had to be "equal and uniform" with "no one hundred acres . . . taxed higher than another, except town lots, which shall not be taxed higher than two hundred acres each." In addition to the customary power of impeachment, the legislature had the power of appointment of all officers except as otherwise directed by the constitution.

The supreme executive authority was vested in a governor elected by the people for a term of two years, but he could not serve more than three consecutive terms; he had to be twenty-five years of age and the owner of five hundred acres of land. The governor was to be commander-in-chief of the militia, except when in federal service, and could grant pardons and reprieves; but he had no veto power and could only appoint the adjutant general and fill vacancies. Since no provision was made for a lieutenant governor, the speaker of the senate succeeded to the governorship in case of the death, resignation, or removal of the governor. A treasurer or treasurers and a secretary of state were to be elected by the legislature.

The judicial branch was to be comprised of "such superior and inferior courts" as the legislature should create, and judges were to be elected by the General Assembly to serve "during their good behavior." County government was to be in charge of justices of the peace named by the legislature. The justices, serving as a county court, appointed the sheriff, trustee, and other county officials.

The suffrage clause of this first constitution is difficult to understand:

Every freeman of the age of twenty-one years and upwards, possessing a freehold in the county wherein he may vote, and being an inhabitant of this state, and every freeman being an inhabitant of any one county in the state six months preceding the day of election, shall be entitled to vote for members of the general assembly, for the county in which he shall reside.

Although some writers have concluded that only property holders— of a freehold—could vote, actually the constitution provided for universal manhood suffrage, including free Negroes, subject only to six months' residence in the county. In addition, freeholders could vote in any county in which they owned a freehold without fulfilling the county residence requirement. According to a member of the constitutional convention of 1834, the clause was designed to exclude "travellers and strolling foreigners" from participating in the right of suffrage, while permitting a freeholder to vote as soon as he became a resident of the state.

The constitution could not be amended except by calling another convention which required a two-thirds vote of the General Assembly and subsequent approval by a majority of those voting for representatives in a general election. Not subject to amendment, however, was the "declaration of rights hereto annexed," which was to remain forever "inviolate."

This declaration asserts that "all power is inherent in the people . . . [who] have, at all times, an unalienable and indefeasible right to alter, reform or abolish the government in such manner as they may think proper." Thus the philosophy of the American Revolution was still influential in 1796. The difficulties with Spain are reflected in the statement that one of the inherent rights of the citizens of the state is "an equal participation in the free navigation of the Mississippi," which cannot be "conceded to any prince, potentate, power, person, or persons whatever." Among the other rights guaranteed are religious freedom, trial by jury, security of persons, houses, and possessions, the privilege of the writ of habeas corpus, and freedom of speech, press, and assembly. The declaration also states that "no religious test shall ever be required as a qualification to any office . . ."; yet, elsewhere in the constitution there was included (and it is still there) the inconsistent clause: "No person who denies the being of God or a future state of rewards and punishments, shall hold any office in the civil department of this state." Actually, during the convention, Andrew Jackson and other leaders

of the Blount faction succeeded in deleting from the original phrase-
ology (borrowed from North Carolina) the additional phrase, "divine authority of the old and new testaments."

Admission into the Union ૭ঌ The people of Tennessee
activated their new constitution immediately, without waiting for
congressional approval. Members of the legislature, and John Sevier
as the first governor of the state, were elected in March, and the
first meeting of the legislature occurred at the end of the month. In
addition to passing laws necessary for a new state, the legislature
also created several new counties. Two of them, Montgomery and
Robertson, were to replace Tennessee County, which went out of
existence, thus allowing its name to be applied to the whole state.
William Blount and William Cocke were elected as Tennessee's
first members of the United States Senate, and provision was made
for the popular election of two members of the House of Representatives. The legislature also elected four presidential electors to
participate in the election of 1796.

Actually, the election of 1796 presented a serious obstacle to the
state's admission. The opposing presidential candidates were John
Adams of the Federalist party and Thomas Jefferson of the Republicans (ancestors of the present Democrats). The Federalists, knowing the popularity of Jefferson and his party in the West, naturally
feared that if Tennessee were admitted in time to participate in the
election, her electoral votes would go to Jefferson. There was also a
sectional angle, since Adams was a New Englander and Jefferson a
Southerner.

In the House of Representatives the opponents of Tennessee's
admission argued that the initiative in creating a new state should
have been taken by Congress; that the territorial census was unauthorized and also unreliable, since many persons merely passing
through the territory had been counted; and that the constitution
was hastily drawn and in some respects was in conflict with the
Constitution of the United States. Also, the opponents contended
that it was illogical to assume that the whole Southwest Territory
should become one state; if it should be divided into more than
one, each state would have to have 60,000 free people to be eligible.

The advocates of admission pointed out that the territorial government was a federal instrument and had the authority to provide for the census. They insisted that the returns were accurate, but even if not accurate, the error would be quickly corrected by rapid immigration into that country. It was evident the people desired statehood and they were entitled to it as a matter of right. They should be relieved as soon as possible from their "degraded situation," subjected to laws "made without their consent."

Since the Republicans had a majority in the House, the bill providing for the immediate admission of Tennessee passed by a vote of 43 to 30. The partisan nature of the issue was evident in the casting of only three affirmative votes by avowed Federalists and only two negative votes by the Republicans. The division was also sectional. Only one representative who lived south of the Potomac River voted against admission, whereas seventeen of the twenty New England votes were on that side. There was some support of the Tennessee cause, on the other hand, in the Middle Atlantic states; the members from Pennsylvania, which had supplied so many settlers for the territory, divided 6 to 2 in favor of admission, and those from Maryland were evenly divided.

The Federalists had a majority in the Senate, however, and they almost succeeded in postponing the admission of Tennessee until after the election. The majority report of the committee to which the bill was referred was a concise restatement of the House arguments against admission, but the report did approve the idea that the territory might be admitted as one state. The committee insisted, however, that a more satisfactory census should first be taken under the authority of Congress, which would naturally postpone admission until after the election. Although there was a minority report emphasizing the anarchy which would result from the overthrow of the state government, the majority report was adopted, 14 to 11, strictly along party lines except that a Kentucky Federalist, Humphrey Marshall, voted against and three Southerners in favor of the majority report. Subsequently, a bill in accordance with the majority report was passed, 15 to 8, with two admissionists voting in favor, apparently in the belief that there was no hope for anything better.

The House of Representatives, however, refused to accept the Senate bill and proposed as a compromise the immediate admission of the state, but with the right to have only one representative instead of two until the next federal census in 1800. This would reduce Tennessee's electoral votes from four to three, since electoral votes are based on the number of senators and representatives combined. The compromise was approved by a conference committee and by the two houses, and President Washington signed the bill admitting Tennessee into the Union on June 1, 1796, the last day of the session of Congress.

While the debate was in progress, William Blount and William Cocke were denied seats in the Senate. It was therefore necessary to elect them a second time, which was done at a special session of the legislature. At that session provision was made for the election of one representative, and Andrew Jackson was later elected to that position. Also, the three electors chosen by a rather cumbersome system set up at that special session cast their votes as expected for Thomas Jefferson and Aaron Burr for President and Vice President of the United States.

SUGGESTED READINGS

General Accounts

Abernethy, *Frontier to Plantation*, Chs. 7–8; Brown, *Old Frontiers*, 281–441; Caldwell, *Constitutional History*, Chs. 5–6; Caruso, *Appalachian Frontier*, Ch. 16; Folmsbee, Corlew, and Mitchell, *Tennessee*, I, Chs. 10–11; Hamer, *Tennessee*, I, Chs. 12–13; Haywood, *Civil and Political History*, 260–485; Masterson, *Blount*, 163–298; Matthews, *General Robertson*, Chs. 1–17, 37–57; McRaven, *Edward Swanson*, Chs. 13–14; Putnam, *Middle Tennessee*, Chs. 20–34; Ramsey, *Annals*, 533–676; Roosevelt, *Winning of the West*, IV, Part 5, "St. Clair and Wayne," Ch. 3, Part 6, "Louisiana and Burr," Chs. 1–2.

Specialized Accounts

John D. Barnhart, "The Tennessee Constitution of 1796: A Product of the Old West," *JSH*, IX (Nov., 1943), 532–48, reprinted in Barnhart, *Valley of Democracy* (Bloomington, Ind., 1953); Clarence E. Carter (ed.), *The Territorial Papers of the United States*, IV, *The Territory South of the River Ohio*, 1790–1796 (Washington, D. C., 1936); Corbitt and Corbitt, "Papers from Spanish Archives," *ETHS Publ.*, Nos. 23–39 (1951–67); Cotterill, *Southern Indians*, Ch. 4; Randolph C. Downes, "Indian Affairs in the Southwest Territory," *THM*, Ser. 2, III

(Jan., 1937), 240–68; Driver, *Sevier*, 32–38, 73–78, 99–119; David E. Harrell, "James Winchester, Patriot," *THQ*, XVII (Dec., 1958), 301–17; Jack D. L. Holmes, "Spanish American Rivalry Over the Chickasaw Bluffs, 1780–1795," ETHS *Publ.*, No. 34 (1962), 26–67; Holmes, "The Ebb-Tide of Spanish Military Power on the Mississippi: Fort San Fernando de las Barrancas, 1795–1798," ETHS *Publ.*, No. 36 (1964), 23–44; Holmes, "Fort Ferdinand on the Bluffs: Life on the Spanish-American Frontier, 1795–1797," WTHS *Papers*, No. XIII (1959), 38–54; Malone, *Cherokees*, Chs. 3–4; Putnam, "Correspondence of James Robertson," *AHM*, I–IV; Robert H. White (ed.), *Messages of the Governors of Tennessee* (7 vols. to date, Nashville, 1952–), I, 1–24, 663–75; Charlotte Williams, "Congressional Action on the Admission of Tennessee into the Union," *THQ*, II (Dec., 1943), 291–315, reprinted in White, *Tennessee: Old and New*, I, 27–50; Samuel C. Williams, "French and Other Intrigues in the Southwest Territory," ETHS *Publ.*, No. 13 (1941), 21–35; Williams, *Phases of Southwest Territory History* (Johnson City, Tenn., 1940); Williams, *West Tennessee*, Chs. 7–8; Williams, "The Admission of Tennessee into the Union," *THQ*, IV (Dec., 1945), 291–319; Woodward, *Cherokees*, 102–22.

GOVERNORS OF TENNESSEE

Tennessee's honor roll of governors dates back to 1790 when William Blount governed the territory that later became the state of Tennessee. On the following pages the governors of Tennessee are pictured and their terms of office given.

William Blount (territorial governor), 1790–1796

Top left: John Sevier (the first governor of the state), 1796–1801, 1803–1809; *top right*: Archibald Roane, 1801–1803; *lower left*: Willie Blount, 1809–1815; *lower right*: Joseph McMinn, 1815–1821.

Top left: William Carroll, 1821–1827, 1829–1835; *top right*: Sam Houston, 1827–1829; *lower left*: William Hall, 1829; *lower right*: Newton Cannon, 1835–1839.

Top left: James K. Polk, 1839–1841; *top right*: James C. Jones, 1841–1845; *lower left*: Aaron V. Brown, 1845–1847; *lower right*: Neill S. Brown, 1847–1849.

Top left: William Trousdale, 1849–1851; *top right*: William B. Campbell, 1851–1853; *lower left*: Andrew Johnson, 1853–1857, 1862–1865 (military governor); *lower right*: Isham G. Harris, 1857–1862.

Top left: William G. Brownlow, 1865–1869; *top right*: DeWitt Clinton Senter, 1869–1871; *lower left*: John C. Brown, 1871–1875; *lower right*: James D. Porter, 1875–1879.

Top left: Albert S. Marks, 1879–1881; *top right*: Alvin Hawkins, 1881–1883; *lower left*: William B. Bate, 1883–1887; *lower right*: Robert Love Taylor, 1887–1891, 1897–1899.

Top left: John P. Buchanan, 1891–1893; *top right*: Peter Turney, 1893–1897; *lower left*: Benton McMillin, 1899–1903; *lower right*: James B. Frazier, 1903–1905.

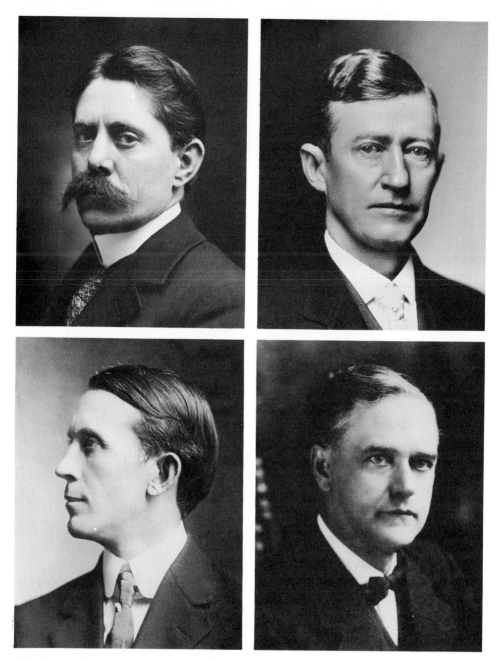

Top left: John I. Cox, 1905–1907; *top right*: Malcolm R. Patterson, 1907–1911; *lower left*: Ben W. Hooper, 1911–1915; *lower right*: Tom C. Rye, 1915–1919.

Top left: A. H. Roberts, 1919–1921; *top right*: Alfred A. Taylor, 1921–1923; *lower left*: Austin Peay, 1923–1927; *lower right*: Henry H. Horton, 1927–1933.

Top left: Hill McAlister, 1933–1937; *top right*: Gordon Browning, 1937–1939, 1949–1953; *lower left*: Prentice Cooper, 1939–1945; *lower right*: Jim McCord, 1945–1949.

Top left: Frank G. Clement, 1953–1959, 1963–1967; *top right:* Buford
Ellington, 1959–1963, 1967–1971; *below:* Winfield Dunn, 1971–.

8. ৯ Social and Economic Developments

TENNESSEE was on the frontier when it entered the Union in 1796. Only about twenty-eight years had elapsed since the first settlements had been made in the Holston Valley and only sixteen years since the settlement on the Cumberland. The population of the state in 1800 was 105,602, of whom 13,893 were black (mostly Negro slaves). The English nationality predominated, but according to the estimate of one expert, the proportion of Scotch-Irish (Ulster Scots) at the time of the Revolution was 25 per cent. There were smaller percentages of Germans, Irish, and French.

In what is now East Tennessee, the area of settlement in 1796 extended from the Virginia line to the Little Tennessee River and as far west as the Clinch River. Most of the settlers west of the Cumberland Plateau, fewer in number than in East Tennessee, were scattered along the Cumberland River between the sites of present-day Carthage and Clarksville. Most of the remainder of the state was still unsettled Indian country.

Pioneer Life ৯ On the Tennessee frontier, two waves of settlers—transient herdsmen and hunters followed by agriculturalists—came very close together. Actually, the farmers were also herdsmen throughout the ante bellum period. Their existence in the back country was dedicated to securing the necessities of life. Their cattle, sheep, and hogs were permitted to graze at will on the "range" and were regularly driven in large droves along the trails to eastern markets. Clearing the land of trees to grow crops was an extremely difficult task; in pioneer days land frequently could be rented merely for the clearing of it.

The typical frontier home was a one-room log cabin with a loft where the boys of the family slept. The floor was of earth or of puncheons, that is, logs split in two and laid with the flat side up. The roof usually was made of long, white oak clapboards, held in place by ridgepoles and by wooden pegs, since in the early days nails were lacking. After the walls were finished, doors and windows were sawed out, and the windows were covered by glazed paper and wooden shutters. On one side of the room was a huge fireplace, for cooking as well as for heat.

The furnishings were primitive. Early bed frames were slabs of wood supported at one end by wooden pegs driven into the wall; mattresses were bed ticks filled with straw or pine needles and covered with animal skins. A large clapboard set on wooden legs provided a table, and chairs were short sections sawed from the trunk of a tree. Spoons whittled out of horn or of wood and hunting knives served for table use; plates were of pewter or wood. The humble gourd served many purposes. Rifles and powder horns rested on wooden pegs inserted in the walls, and the clothing of the family was suspended from pegs or the antlers of a deer.

The dress of the early pioneers was supplied locally and was similar to that of the Indians. The hunting shirt, generally of dressed deerskin, fitted loosely and reached half way down the thighs and was fringed at the bottom. Trousers were of similar material, and moccasins were of dressed buckskin or buffalo hide. Leggings, wide strips of deerskin wound around the ankles, provided protection against briars and snakes. Pioneer women wore dresses of linsey or osnaburg, a coarse linen, dyed in different colors to produce variety. Jewels and other objects of adornment usually were lacking.

Food was simple. Corn, the "staff of life," was made into johnny-cakes or cooked as hominy or mush. Some, of course, was distilled into spirituous liquor. Wild animals supplied most of the meat, but as herds and flocks increased, domestic animals were slaughtered. Meat was preserved by salting (whenever salt was available) or jerking, that is, by stringing meat over strips of wood to dry over a slow fire. Vegetables, fruits, nuts, maple sugar, and honey augmented the diet.

By the end of the eighteenth century the standard of living had been greatly improved, even in the isolated Cumberland settlements. Houses of the more prosperous inhabitants were larger and better furnished than before, and even log houses, usually two stories in height, were better constructed with hewn logs. In the towns there were some frame houses and others of brick or stone. Shingled roofs were customary, some glass windows were to be seen, and puncheon floors had been replaced with planks. Furniture and furnishings had been brought in from the East. An example of the better type of log house was "Rocky Mount," the home of William Cobb near Johnson City used by Governor William Blount of the Southwest Territory as his headquarters before he moved to Knoxville and built the "Blount Mansion" in 1792, one of the first frame houses west of the Blue Ridge. Two early stone houses were "Swan Pond," the home of Francis A. Ramsey (the father of the historian, James G. M.), near Knoxville, and "Cragfont," the home of General James Winchester, near Gallatin. All of the above houses have been restored and supplied with furnishings dating from around 1800.

Agriculture, Manufacturing, and Commerce ♘ Agriculture was devoted chiefly to grazing livestock and growing of corn, the leading crop in both areas of settlement, but some wheat, rye, oats, and barley also were produced. Each home usually had a vegetable garden and cotton, flax, and tobacco patches. At first, these patches produced for home consumption, but by 1799 the legislature had to regulate the export of tobacco, requiring packing in a prescribed manner and inspection to see that no trash was included. Inspection places were established in four counties in Middle Tennessee and in Greene County in the eastern division. Cotton also became an important article for export in Middle Tennessee after Whitney's cotton gin came into use in this region about 1800.

Agricultural implements were quite primitive. Plows were commonly made of wood, except for an iron point, called a "bull tongue," which was bolted on. Mouldboards and iron shares, however, were beginning to come into use by the nineteenth century. Hoes and harrows also were used. Grain was cut with a reap hook or cradle and was separated from the straw by the use of a flail or the feet of horses. In 1795 the average yield of corn per acre was sixty bushels, but on the best land seventy bushels could be raised. The price of corn in Knoxville at that time ranged from 25 to 33⅓ cents per bushel, whereas in Nashville it sold for only 16⅔ cents, the price differential probably being due to the greater isolation of Nashville. Wheat sold at both places for 66⅔ cents per bushel. Whiskey sold for 50 cents a gallon in Knoxville and 75 cents to $1.00 in Nashville. The price of pork in Knoxville was $3.33 per hundred pounds and in Nashville $3.00.

Counterbalancing somewhat the higher prices received for produce in East Tennessee was the greater fertility of the land in the Nashville Basin. Consequently, the plantation system of agriculture had an early beginning in Middle Tennessee, with a greater use of slave labor. As early as 1795 more than 20 per cent of the population of that region were Negro slaves, as compared with 12½ per cent in the eastern division. In 1800 the population of Knoxville was 387, including 146 slaves; of Nashville, 345, including 151 slaves. But Davidson County had 2,936 slaves out of a total population of 9,618, whereas Knox County had only 1,122 slaves out of a total population of 11,981.

Because of the isolation of the Tennessee settlements, the settlers had to make their own supplies, thus contributing to the development of manufacturing. Much of this activity took place in the homes, with the women making clothing at the spinning wheels and hand looms and making soap, candles, and many other necessities. The men in the early days made their own farm implements and furniture and built, with the aid of neighbors, their own houses. The first manufacturing establishments outside the homes were grist mills for the grinding of grain, then tanneries and blacksmith shops.

The development of the iron industry was especially significant. Although the credit for starting the first iron works in the Tennessee country has frequently been given to Colonel James King, for his works near Blountville, the date of 1784 on which this priority is based obviously is erroneous. Before starting out on his own, King was employed at the iron works established by David Ross on the North Fork of the Holston near the site of Kingsport in 1789 or 1790. It is probable that the Blountville enterprise did not get under way until Governor William Blount became interested in the undertaking in 1795. In that year Moses Cavitt sold the iron works he had started on the South Fork near the site of Kingsport to Walter King and John Sevier, Sr. and Jr. Meanwhile, exploitation had begun of the rich Bumpass Cove mines in Washington County; Nicholas Tate Perkins by 1792 had started an iron works on Mossy Creek near the site of Jefferson City; and James Robertson had established the first iron foundry in Middle Tennessee in what is now Dickson County in 1793 or soon thereafter.

The iron industry had become sufficiently important by 1794 for the territorial legislature to consider a resolution to exempt from militia duty a certain number of artisans working at furnaces or bloomeries. Bloomeries were small forges at which rough wrought iron could be produced. Cast iron came from the larger furnaces, and by the turn of the century there were some refinery forges where the pigs of cast iron could be hammered into a finer grade of wrought iron and a few crude rolling mills to produce the flat strips required for the making of cut nails. Water power was necessary for the heavy machinery, and charcoal was the fuel for furnaces and forges. By 1807 the Tennessee legislature had passed a law to encourage the iron industry.

Cotton manufacturing also had an early beginning but very little growth in Tennessee. The first cotton factory in the South, and probably the third in the nation, was established in 1791 in the vicinity of Nashville by John Hague, who smuggled designs of cotton manufacturing machinery out of England. Learning of the cultivation of cotton in the Cumberland Valley, Hague built his factory at a place he called Manchester and advertised for weavers in the December 17, 1791, issue of the Knoxville *Gazette*. Because of Indian raids, however, Hague abandoned his factory and moved to Virginia in 1793. Following the arrival of the cotton gin, George Poyzer established a small cotton factory in Nashville in 1802, and soon thereafter other factories were started in Rutherford and Williamson counties.

For many years wagon trains from Baltimore or Richmond brought various commodities to stock the stores which sprang up in each little town in Tennessee, and especially in the eastern region. The wagons carried back the produce of the country taken in the customary bartering process. A store in Hawkins Court House (Rogersville) advertised in the Knoxville *Gazette*, January 14, 1792:

Clothes, superfine and second and coarse; plain and striped coatings; spotted swan skin; velvets, all colors; buff denim; green plush; poplins; calicoes; muslins; cambricks; lawn and muslin handkerchiefs; men's and women's stockings, cotton and silk; Irish linen; blankets; bed ticks; hats, men's and women's.

Powder, lead and flints; queensware; pewter; playing cards; copperas; madder; brimstone; allspice; pepper and ginger; coffee and chocolate; Bohea and Hyson tea. Bibles and Testaments; tinware of all kinds; knives, pen, pocket and cutting; scissors; needles, thimbles; shoe and knee buckles; stirrup irons, bridle bits; and articles too numerous to mention.

As evidence that these goods could be obtained in exchange for produce, another storekeeper advertised that "The highest price will be allowed for bear, deer, otter, wildcat, muskrat, mink, fox, and raccoon skins, and for all kinds of fur whatever." He also offered generous prices for beeswax, linsey and linen, rye, corn, and fodder. Although much of the produce was carried back east by the wagons on their return journeys, some use was made of the Tennessee River for export despite the obstructions to navigation. The Knoxville *Gazette*, June 17, 1795, reported the departure of five flatboats down the river.

Some of the wagons went on across the mountains to Nashville, but most of Middle Tennessee's imports came by wagon from Philadelphia to Pittsburgh, then either by river down the Ohio and up the Cumberland, or by water from Pittsburgh to Kentucky and then by wagon to Nashville. After the Americans obtained the right to navigate the Mississippi River, some of Nashville's imports came from New Orleans, but that was difficult before the coming of the steamboat. Most of Middle Tennessee's exports went down the Cumberland, Ohio, and Mississippi to New Orleans by flatboat or keelboat. There the boats as well as the cargoes were sold, and the boatmen returned over the Natchez Trace (after it was opened in 1802) to Nashville or took passage on sailing vessels to Philadelphia or Baltimore and from there returned to Tennessee.

Religious Developments ह•• Very soon after the first permanent settlers came into the Tennessee country they were joined by Presbyterian and Baptist preachers, who were needed to counteract the debasing influences of the frontier environment.

Along with the holding of religious services and baptizing converts, the preachers legalized common law marriages.

The first Presbyterian preachers to serve the future Tennesseans actually lived in southwestern Virginia. The Reverend Charles Cummings established a church at the site of Abingdon as early as 1772, and he naturally considered the people of North Holston settlement (of North Carolina, but governed by Virginia) as his religious responsibility. Possibly for his convenience, a "Meeting House," mentioned in deed records as early as March, 1774, was built near the site of Blountville, but it probably was used by any preacher of any denomination who happened to come along. Both Cummings and the Reverend Joseph Rhea, another Presbyterian, accompanied the Christian expedition of 1776 as chaplains. The most noted of the early Presbyterian preachers of the Tennessee country was the Reverend Samuel Doak, who moved from the North Holston settlement to the vicinity of Jonesboro in 1780 and organized the "Salem Congregation" and also established a school which later was to become Washington College.

Because of the large number of Scotch-Irish Presbyterians on the frontier, the Abingdon Presbytery was formed in 1785, and the next year it was divided, with the new presbytery, Transylvania, assuming jurisdiction over the churches in the Cumberland Valley as well as in the Kentucky region. The first Presbyterian preacher in the Cumberland settlements was the Reverend Thomas Craighead, who was induced by James Robertson in 1785 to come to Davidson County to establish a church and also a school, Davidson Academy. In the East Tennessee country there were twenty-six congregations by 1797, and Abingdon Presbytery was again divided, with the more western of those congregations being organized as Union Presbytery.

The insistence of the Presbyterian church upon having an educated ministry made it difficult to supply the growing demand for qualified preachers, but also among the several outstanding Presbyterian divines responsible for the dominant position of Presbyterianism on the early Tennessee frontier were James and Hezekiah Balch, Samuel Henderson, Samuel C. Carrick, and Gideon Blackburn. One of them, however, Hezekiah Balch, illustrated the tendency toward disagreements by being converted to Hopkinsianism,[1]

---

[1] The belief, as taught by Samuel Hopkins, that one must be willing to be damned if the glory of God requires it.

for which he was censured by the general assembly of the church in 1798.

Almost simultaneously with the Presbyterians, preachers of the Baptist faith became active in the Tennessee country. The first two known to have settled there were Matthew Talbot and Jonathan Mulkey, who came to the Watauga settlement and Carter's Valley, respectively, as early as 1775. Mulkey was wounded in Abram's raid of 1776. Whether or not they did much preaching is unknown, but it is probable that they did, for the typical Baptist minister of the early days was a farmer-preacher, who would leave his plow in the field and travel many miles on Sundays to preach to scattered congregations. Some Baptist historians contend that Talbot organized in 1775 or 1776 a Watauga River Church that was the forerunner of the Sinking Spring Church of Carter County. Others claim that the Buffalo Ridge Church of Washington County, organized by the Reverend Tidence Lane in 1778 or 1779, was the first organized Baptist church in the Tennessee country.

Seven Baptist churches in the East Tennessee region were organized into the Holston Association in 1786, the same year that the first Baptist church in the Middle Tennessee country was organized by the Reverend John Grammer. Ten years later five churches in Middle Tennessee were organized as the Mero Association. By 1803 there were about forty-six churches in East Tennessee, divided between two associations, Holston and Tennessee, in addition to an unknown number of churches which were not represented in any association—a result of the Baptist policy of emphasizing the independence of individual congregations. Another reason for the rapid growth of the Baptists on the frontier was the willingness to ordain ministers who had little formal education. A special "call" to preach, together with the inspiration of the Spirit, was considered an adequate qualification. Actually, the unlettered frontiersmen felt more at home with the uneducated preachers than with the learned Presbyterian divines.

Another type of preacher who could talk on the level of the illiterate pioneers was the sturdy Methodist circuit rider. The first of these in Tennessee was Jeremiah Lambert, who was assigned by the Annual Conference of 1783 to the newly formed Holston Circuit in what is now southwestern Virginia and northeastern Tennessee. The Holston Circuit had about sixty members, and Lambert preached to them—and seventeen more by the end of the year—in their scattered homes. In 1786, the first Methodist church in Tennessee, Acuff's Chapel, was built near Blountville. The next year Holston became a district, composed of two circuits, and in 1788 it held the first conference west of the mountains, at Keywood in Virginia. For that occasion the famous Methodist leader, Bishop Francis Asbury, made the first of his sixty-two trips across the Appalachians. While traveling over the district he commented in his *Journal* on the disorders in the state of Franklin. In 1787 a new circuit, as a part of Kentucky District, was created for the Cumberland settlements, with Benjamin Ogden as its preacher. Methodism expanded rapidly in that area as well as in East Tennessee. Although the Methodist circuit system was well suited to the frontier, many circuit riders died of consumption or other lingering diseases from the hardships involved in covering regularly circuits extending 400–500 miles in length.

The churches of all three denominations attempted to regulate the conduct of their members, and the records of individual churches are replete with references to admonitions and sometimes exclusion from fellowship of members for drunkenness, fighting, dishonesty, and other offenses. But the period following the Revolutionary War was characterized by extreme moral laxity, and the work of the churches, supplementing that of the courts, had relatively little effect. The period was one of outlawry, which made travel extremely dangerous. The notorious Harpe brothers (Micajah and Wiley) were only two of the many outlaws who robbed and murdered in Tennessee and the Old Southwest around the turn of the century.

The times were ripe for a spiritual awakening, and a "Great Revival," which began in the West about 1799, had a profound influence. Beginning in Kentucky under the leadership of a Presbyterian preacher named James McGready, the revival spread rapidly to other denominations and into Tennessee. The extreme emotionalism characterizing this movement was especially manifested at the extended camp meetings to which the lonely pioneers flocked in immense numbers. At these meetings, the effect of mob psychology and the intense excitement created by the emotional fervor of the preachers resulted in mass hysteria and strange bodily exercises such as falling, jerking, barking, and rolling. According to one eyewitness, a person afflicted with the "jerks" acted as if he were being goaded "alternately on every side, with a red-hot iron." The head "would fly backward and forward, and from side to side" with quick jolts, and the afflicted would dash violently to the ground and "bounce from place to place like a foot-ball, or hop round with head, limbs and trunk twitching and jolting in every direction, as if it must inevitably fly asunder."

The results of the Great Revival, especially in regard to sectarianism, will be treated in another chapter, but there is no doubt that it greatly stimulated the religious life of the country. Although the extremes of emotionalism subsided, the camp meeting remained a religious feature of some denominations, particularly the Methodists, for many years.

Educational Developments ੨✒ Although the first settlers in Tennessee were surprisingly literate, as shown by the almost complete absence of "marks" among the signatures on the Washington District petition of 1776 and the Cumberland Compact of 1780, the same could not be said of the next generation. Schools were scarce on the frontier, and those which were established usually were started by Presbyterian ministers and attended by the children of the well-to-do, who were able to pay the tuition. The first Presbyterian preachers to establish schools along with their churches in the Tennessee country were Samuel Doak and Thomas Craighead. Doak's school was incorporated as Martin Academy by North Carolina in 1783, reincorporated by the Franklin legislature in 1785, and chartered as Washington College by the Territory of the United States South of the River Ohio in 1795. The next year Washington College conferred its first two A.B. degrees—almost certainly the first two west of the Blue Ridge Mountains—to James Witherspoon and John W. Doak. Today, however, the institution is Washington College High School and is a part of the secondary school system of Washington County.

Craighead's Davidson Academy, chartered in 1785 and opened the next year, near Nashville, became Cumberland College in 1806 and the recipient of Middle Tennessee's share of the college grant under the land compact of that year. Reincorporated as the University of Nashville in 1826, it became the leading institution of higher learning in the state by the time of the Civil War. Today, its assets are included in George Peabody College for Teachers.

Several months before the incorporation of Washington College, the legislature of the Southwest Territory chartered Greeneville College and Blount College. The president of Greeneville, Hezekiah Balch, was the third alumnus, along with Doak and Craighead, of the training school of Presbyterian ministers, New Jersey College (now Princeton University), to come to Tennessee and combine the professions of preaching and teaching. Chartered on September 3, 1794, Greeneville College had nearly one hundred "scholars" in 1799; in the post-Civil War period Greeneville combined with Tusculum under the latter's name.

Blount College was originally a "Seminary" opened in 1793 by the Reverend Samuel C. Carrick, at his home near Knoxville. After being chartered on September 10, 1794, Blount College continued to operate at that place for a few years before the construction of a building on Gay Street in Knoxville. In 1803, however, Blount College was in such a depressed state that one of the trustees proposed that it be abandoned and that the Presbyterians of Knox County respond to the appeals of Dr. Charles C. Coffin of Greeneville College to shift their support to that institution. Governor Archibald Roane and President Carrick objected, and at a meeting of the trustees the amount of $1,000 was subscribed to prevent the future state university from dying in its infancy. Blount College was noted for two unique features, a nonsectarian charter and co-education. Nonsectarianism was difficult to enforce, with a Presbyterian president. The evidence of co-education was the listing of the names of five "co-eds" by the first historian of the institution gleaned from an early record book no longer extant. It is probable that these five girls were enrolled in elementary rather than college courses. The only A.B. degree granted by Blount College was conferred on William E. Parker in 1806. The next year the institution became East Tennessee College and received a land grant under the Compact of 1806. It was re-named East Tennessee University in 1840 and The University of Tennessee in 1879.

The only other schools known to have existed in Tennessee before 1806 were Ebenezer Academy and Union Academy started by Presbyterians in 1801 and 1802 in Knox County, and Valladolid

Academy, opened near Nashville in 1805. There was not much difference between academies and colleges in pioneer Tennessee, except that colleges were authorized to confer degrees. Since there were no public schools, the colleges and academies supplied practically all the education available beyond that given at the mother's knee or by an occasional tutor employed by a wealthy family. Following rudimentary instruction in the "3 R's" came the usual type of classical learning, with the emphasis upon Greek and Latin.

SUGGESTED READINGS

General Accounts

Abernethy, *Frontier to Plantation*, Chs. 9, 12, 13; Harriette Arnow, *Seedtime on the Cumberland* (New York, 1960), *passim*; Arnow, *Flowering of the Cumberland* (New York, 1963), *passim*; Caruso, *Appalachian Frontier*, Ch. 11; Robert E. Corlew, *A History of Dickson County* (Dickson, 1956), Chs. 1–4; Folmsbee, Corlew, and Mitchell, *Tennessee*, I, Ch. 12; Garrett and Goodpasture, *Tennessee*, Ch. 22; Hamer, *Tennessee*, I, Ch. 14; Albert C. Holt, *The Economic and Social Beginnings of Tennessee* (Nashville, 1924), reprinted from *THM*, VII (1921–22), 194–230,252–94, VIII (1924), 24–86; McRaven, *Edward Swanson*, Chs. 15–17; Ramsey, *Annals*, 713–37; Roosevelt, *Winning of the West*, IV, Part 6, Ch. 3; Williams, *Revolutionary War*, Chs. 1, 18.

Specialized Accounts

Theron Alexander, Jr., "The Covenanters Come to Tennessee," ETHS *Publ.*, No. 13 (1941), 36–46; Ward Allen, "Cragfont: Grandeur on the Tennessee Frontier," *THQ*, XXIII (June, 1964), 103–20, reprinted in Alderson and McBride, *Landmarks*, 137–54; Elizabeth Skaggs Bowman and Stanley J. Folmsbee, "The Ramsey House: Home of Francis Alexander Ramsey," *THQ*, XXIV (Fall, 1965), 3–18; Howard E. Carr, *Washington College* (Knoxville, 1935), 1–14; Catharine C. Cleveland, *The Great Revival in the West, 1797–1805* (Chicago, 1916); Pauline Massengill DeFriece and Frank B. Williams, Jr., "Rocky Mount: The Cobb-Massengill Home: First Capitol of the Territory of the United States South of the River Ohio," *THQ*, XXV (Summer, 1966), 119–34; Margaret Burr DesChamps, "Early Days in the Cumberland Country," *THQ*, VI (Sept., 1947), 195–204; Stanley J. Folmsbee and Susan Hill Dillon, "The Blount Mansion: Tennessee's Territorial Capitol," *THQ*,

XXII (June, 1963), 103–22, reprinted in Alderson and McBride, *Landmarks*, 47–66; Folmsbee, "Blount College and East Tennessee College, 1794–1840: The First Predecessors of The University of Tennessee," ETHS *Publ.*, No. 17 (1945), 1–28, reprinted in The University of Tennessee *Record*, Vol. 49, No. 1 (Knoxville, 1946); Raymond F. Hunt, Jr., "The Pactolus Ironworks," *THQ*, XXV (Summer, 1966), 176–96; Isaac P. Martin, *Methodism in Holston* (Knoxville, 1945), 11–33; Walter B. Posey, *The Presbyterian Church in the Old Southwest* (Richmond, 1952), Chs. 1–2; Posey, *The Baptist Church in the Lower Mississippi Valley* (Lexington, Ky., 1957), Chs. 1–4; Posey, *The Development of Methodism in the Old Southwest, 1783–1824* (Tuscaloosa, 1933), Chs. 1–3; Posey (ed.), "Bishop Asbury Visits Tennessee, 1788–1815: Extracts from His Journal," *THQ*, XV (Sept., 1956), 253–68; Allen E. Ragan, A *History of Tusculum College, 1794–1944* (Bristol, 1945), 1–35; William Flinn Rogers, "Life in East Tennessee Near the End of the Eighteenth Century," ETHS *Publ.*, No. 1 (1929), 27–42; O. W. Taylor, *Early Tennessee Baptists* (Nashville, 1957), Chs. 1–8; Ernest T. Thompson, *Presbyterians in the South, 1607–1861* (Richmond, 1963), Chs. 9–11; Stephen B. Weeks, "Tennessee: A Discussion on the Sources of its Population and Lines of Immigration," *THM*, II (Dec., 1916), 246–49; Samuel C. Williams, "Early Iron Works in the Tennessee Country," *THQ*, VI (March, 1947), 39–46; Williams, "The South's First Cotton Factory," *THQ*, V (Sept., 1946); Williams, "Tidence Lane—Tennessee's First Pastor," *THM*, Ser. 2, I (Dec., 1930), reprinted in White, *Tennessee: Old and New*, I, 222–30.

9. ⮑ Politics, War, Boom, and Panic, 1796–1821

PROBABLY ONE REASON Governor William Blount led the movement to bring the Southwest Territory into the Union as the state of Tennessee was to escape dependence upon a Federalist administration in the national capital for continuance in office as governor of a territory where a large majority of the people were Democratic-Republicans. The Federalist opposition to the admission of Tennessee destroyed most of what was left of Federalist influence in the state, and ex-Governor, now Senator, Blount quickly shifted his attachment from the Federalists to the party of Thomas Jefferson and Aaron Burr.

Politics and the Blount Conspiracy ⮑ With only one party active within the state, political contests for several years were based largely upon sectional and personal differences rather than partisanship. The heads of the two leading political factions were William Blount and John Sevier, but a young lawyer named Andrew Jackson was rising rapidly as a Blount lieutenant, and Jackson was ultimately to succeed him. The Blount faction was the better organized of the two, but Governor Sevier had the advantage of immense personal popularity. That popularity, however, was not as strong in the Mero District as it was in East Tennessee, partly because many people in Middle Tennessee were jealous of the more populous and wealthy eastern division of the state.

William Blount's career in the United States Senate was cut short suddenly in 1797 by the exposure of his connection with a conspiracy designed to promote British conquest of Louisiana and the Floridas from Spain. The occasion for the intrigue was the prevalence in the West of rumors that Spain had been induced to return to France the port of New Orleans and the territory west of the Mississippi which France had given her in 1763. France would not be bound by the United States treaty with Spain of 1795; it was also believed that if such a return occurred, Napoleon would close the river to the Americans and attempt to incite revolution in the American West. British occupation of New Orleans would be much less dangerous because the treaty of peace of 1783 with Britain included a guarantee of free navigation of the Mississippi.

The originator of the conspiracy was John Chisholm, a tavern keeper of Knoxville who was still a British subject, but William Blount also played an important role. As unfolded by Chisholm to the British minister, Robert Liston, in November, 1796, the plan proposed that the British, who were at war with Spain and France, should finance expeditions of Americans and Indians against the Spanish Floridas and Louisiana to take possession of them on behalf of Great Britain. As compensation the British would grant land to members of the expeditions, make Chisholm superintendent of Indian affairs, make Pensacola and New Orleans free ports, and guarantee free navigation of the Mississippi. Liston was very evasive, but finally agreed to send Chisholm to London to deal directly with the British authorities; the British, however, flatly rejected the plan.

Meanwhile, Blount had assumed the leadership of the conspiracy and promoted it under the misconception that the British government would be certain to cooperate. Blount's motives were economic. He and his brothers and their associates had greatly over-expanded their land speculations and faced financial bankruptcy because land values were seriously depressed by rumors that the French would soon occupy New Orleans. Success of the Blount scheme would restore land values in the West and thereby provide opportunities for immense profits. Since Western interests would be promoted, Blount would also be a hero, with infinite possibilities for political advancement. Blount conferred in New York with a fellow speculator, Nicholas Romayne, who then went to England to talk with the British while Blount returned to the Southwest to take preliminary steps for putting the plan in operation.

Blount's activities were interrupted, however, by the calling of a special session of Congress; thus he resorted to the dangerous expedient of writing letters; one letter, dated April 21, 1797, and addressed to James Carey, an interpreter in the employ of the federal government, fell into the hands of public officials. The letter said that the plan mentioned by Chisholm to the British minister might be attempted in the fall, and if so, Blount probably would be "at the head of the business on the part of the British." Further, Carey was warned not to let the plan be discovered by Benjamin Hawkins, agent to the Creek Indians and acting-superintendent of Indian affairs, or any of several other specified federal employees; Carey also was to try to reduce the influence of Hawkins with the Indians and increase that of Blount. If the Cherokee were dissatisfied with the treaty Blount had negotiated, the boundary line of which had recently been surveyed, the letter continued, Carey was to shift the blame for the treaty to President Washington who was "now out of office." Finally, Carey was told to "read this letter over three times, then burn it."

Carey, possibly while under the influence of liquor, permitted one of the individuals against whom he had been warned, James Byers, the factor in charge of the trading post at Tellico Blockhouse, to see the letter; Byers seized it and turned it over to one of Blount's personal enemies, Colonel David Henley, agent of the War Department at Knoxville. Henley sent it to Philadelphia, where President Adams submitted it to Congress. When asked in the Senate if he had written the letter, Blount was evasive, but there is no doubt of his authorship. Two senators testified that the letter was in Blount's handwriting, and Blount himself in effect admitted it in correspondence with friends in Tennessee:

> In a few days you will see published, by order of Congress a letter said to have been written by me to James Carey. It makes a damnable fuss here. I hope, however, the people upon the Western Waters will see nothing but good in it, for so *I intended it*—especially for Tennessee.[1]

The House of Representatives adopted impeachment charges and asked that Blount's Senate seat be "sequestered." The Senate, however, expelled Blount and thereby placed a serious obstacle in the way of successful impeachment. Pending trial, the ex-senator was

---

[1] Masterson, *Blount*, 320–21. Italics added.

released on bond and he journeyed along back roads to North Carolina. When he returned to Tennessee, Blount found that Andrew Jackson, James White, and other loyal friends were engaged in successful efforts toward his rehabilitation. The Adams administration was very unpopular in the state, especially when it sent in federal troops to remove two or three hundred settlers living on the wrong side of the Indian boundary line as surveyed by one of Blount's leading critics, Benjamin Hawkins. Blount was depicted as the victim of partisan prejudice, and the legislature meeting in the fall of 1797 was evidently willing to reelect him to the Senate position from which he had been expelled. Blount, however, refused to be a candidate. Instead, two of his friends, Andrew Jackson and Joseph Anderson, were elected to the Senate.

For more than a year Blount was out of office, with impeachment charges hanging over his head, and his enemies were certain that his political career was at an end. Except for a quirk of fate, however, Blount would have become governor of Tennessee in December, 1798. The speaker of the state senate, James White, was appointed by Sevier as Indian commissioner, and Blount was elected to succeed him both as senator and speaker. From this position Blount would automatically succeed to the governorship in case Sevier should resign, as he was expected to do because he had been appointed a brigadier general of the provisional army which was being recruited for the anticipated war with France. President Adams, however, was able to resume relations with the French, and since the war did not occur Sevier continued in office as governor.

The articles of impeachment of William Blount were presented to the Senate early in 1798, but the trial did not begin until December 17. Blount did not attend—incidentally, he was presiding at the same time over the impeachment of a state judge in Tennessee—but was represented by counsel. The Blount defense was mainly on the question of jurisdiction rather than his guilt or innocence of the charges that he had conspired to violate American neutrality, to reduce the influence of American representatives with the Indians, to seduce Carey from his duty and trust, and to diminish the confidence of the Cherokee Indians in the United States. His lawyers contended that senators were not civil officers in the meaning of the impeachment clause of the Constitution and therefore were not subject to impeachment; and even if they were, Blount, having been expelled, was no longer a senator. The Senate decided on January 11, 1799, that it had no jurisdiction in the case and dismissed the impeachment.

There is no doubt that Blount was guilty of the charges, but his provocation was great. Not only was his personal fortune in jeopardy, but the interests of the West were also involved. The Spaniards used the conspiracy as a pretext for their delay in evacuating Natchez, north of the treaty line of 1795, but it seems that the fears aroused by Blount's activities actually led them to evacuate sooner than they might have done otherwise. Also, the United States government was led to pay more attention to the needs of the West than had been the custom—a trend brought to a climax by the Louisiana Purchase, which among other benefits placed the Mississippi River entirely in American territory. Whether Blount's own efforts to recoup his political fortunes would have been successful can never be known; his sudden death on March 21, 1800, removed him from the political scene.

The Jackson-Sevier Feud Even before Blount passed away, Andrew Jackson, his lieutenant, had differences with Sevier which eventually developed into a feud of considerable political significance. Jackson, of Scotch-Irish descent, was born in 1767 near the boundary between North and South Carolina, and both states claim his birthplace. Orphaned at the age of fifteen, he had little opportunity to gain a formal education, and his legal training was based on a short period of reading law in the office of a North Carolina lawyer. Jackson came to the Tennessee country in 1788 with John McNairy, who had been appointed a judge for the Mero District; Jackson soon became attorney general for the district.

Jackson boarded with the widow of John Donelson, one of the founders of Nashville, and became interested in her daughter Rachel, who was separated from her husband, Lewis Robards. After a temporary reconciliation and return to the Kentucky country with her husband, Rachel again insisted upon a separation. Jackson as a family friend escorted her through the dangerous wilderness back to Nashville—a journey which Robards later described as an elopement. Jackson also went along as a protector when Rachel fled to Natchez after Robards threatened to force her to return to his home.

Some time later Jackson, seeing a newspaper report that Robards had obtained a divorce by legislative action, rushed down to Natchez and brought Rachel back to Nashville as his bride. To their great consternation they discovered two years later that the report was in error; the Virginia legislature had merely granted Robards the right to bring suit for a divorce in the courts. Robards now obtained a divorce without any difficulty, and Rachel and Andrew made their marriage legal by a second ceremony. Although Rachel's technical bigamy was the result of a misunderstanding, it was used frequently by Jackson's political opponents to embarrass him. The impetuous Jackson, according to a biographer, kept his pistol in perfect condition for thirty-three years for use against anyone who dared to breathe the name of his beloved Rachel in anything but honor.

One man who acquired Jackson's enmity by such a statement was John Sevier. The origin of the Sevier-Jackson feud appears to have been disputes regarding technicalities in connection with militia elections in 1796. Nevertheless, Sevier appointed Jackson, who had resigned from the Senate, to the superior court, then the highest court in the state. In 1801 Sevier, having reached the constitutional limit of three consecutive terms as governor, ran against Jackson for major general of the state militia. The result was a tie vote, February 16, 1802, which was broken in favor of Jackson by Governor Archibald Roane. Jackson then made available to Roane some evidence Jackson had uncovered which indicated that Sevier had been guilty of land frauds. Two years later, when Sevier was running against Roane for governor, Roane and Jackson publicized the land fraud charge in an unsuccessful effort to defeat Sevier. Before retiring from office, Roane submitted the evidence to the legislature and recommended an investigation.

These developments brought the feud between Jackson and Sevier to a bitter climax. During a name-calling contest in front of the courthouse in Knoxville, Sevier in the heat of anger declared that he knew of no service which Jackson had rendered the country except to take a "trip to Natchez with another man's wife." Jackson exploded: "Great God, do you mention *her* sacred name?" Had Jackson not been armed merely with a sword cane, whereas Sevier had a cutlass, there probably would have been a bloody encounter. Instead, Jackson the next day challenged Sevier to a duel. Sevier accepted but, since the state law prohibited dueling, insisted that they meet outside the state. Jackson replied: "In the town of Knoxville did you take the name of a Lady into your polluted lips . . . and in the Neighborhood of Knoxville you shall atone for it or I will publish you as a coward and a poltroon."[2]

The subsequent letters and interviews are rather confusing and leave the impression that neither antagonist desired to risk his career by fighting a duel, but each hoped to be able to cast the stigma of refusing to fight on the other. Finally, Sevier wrote to Jackson: "I shall not receive another letter from you, as I deem you a coward." Jackson then sent a definite challenge to fight where Sevier had suggested—in Virginia. Sevier refused to receive the letter, and Jackson advertised him in the press as a "base coward and poltroon—he will basely insult but has not the courage to repair the Wound."[3]

A few days later Sevier and Jackson happened to meet at Southwest Point (Kingston) in the Indian country, where Jackson had once suggested their duel might be fought. The reports of eyewitnesses are conflicting, but according to one report, while Jackson was brandishing a gun Sevier had to hide behind a tree because his horse wandered off with his pistols in the saddle-holsters. Finally, the governor and the judge were induced by friends to remount and resume their journeys. In the eyes of contemporaries, Jackson, whose reputation was yet to be made, came out second best in the controversy; the people were unwilling to believe that Sevier, the hero of King's Mountain and of thirty-five Indian campaigns, was a coward.

Also, most of the people were willing to give Sevier the benefit of the doubt in regard to his land dealings. His friends in the legislature were able to remove from the report of the committee which investigated the Jackson-Roane charges any implication that Sevier was guilty. Modern historians have disagreed on Sevier's involvement in land frauds. One distinguished historian, Thomas P. Abernethy, insists that "there is not a flaw in the evidence as presented in 1803"; but according to Sevier's leading biographer, Carl Driver, his innocence or guilt "is not possible of determination."

The main charge dealt with an arrangement Sevier had made in 1795 with North Carolina's Secretary of State James Glasgow to void a serious monetary loss which Sevier had suffered through no

2 Driver, *Sevier*, 176–80; Clayton, *History of Davidson County*, 142–43.
3 *Ibid.*, 144–45.

fault of his own. Sevier still had in his possession a great number of land warrants acquired under the Confiscation Act of 1779; he had purchased land confiscated from alleged Tories, but some of these Tories were able to retain the land by proving that they were unjustly charged. Although Sevier then was entitled to the same number of acres of substitute lands, there was practically no unappropriated land of value in Washington County. Therefore, he arranged with Glasgow to shift the warrants (changing the "consideration" from fifty shillings to ten pounds) to the virgin country west of the Cumberland Plateau. For this favor Sevier gave Glasgow three of the warrants, saying in his letter that he hoped they would be sufficient to pay the fees to which Glasgow was entitled. Jackson, however, claimed that the three warrants, which he said were worth at least $960, constituted a bribe to Glasgow for performing an illegal act. Sevier and his friends insisted that Glasgow had committed no crime—that the payment was no more than a reasonable compensation for services rendered. Although there were some irregularities in Sevier's conduct, the people apparently condoned them and ignored the remainder of Jackson's charges; it was Andrew Jackson rather than John Sevier who suffered the greater loss of popularity as a result of the controversy.[4]

In 1806 two events occurred which further injured Jackson's prestige—the Dickinson duel and the Burr conspiracy. The former grew out of a trifling dispute regarding a horse race, but Dickinson had aroused Jackson's anger by making remarks about Rachel's matrimonial difficulties. To avoid a violation of Tennessee law, the duel was held in Kentucky, and a rule was adopted allowing each contestant only one shot. Jackson, fearing that Dickinson's bullet might deflect his own aim, held his fire. Then, although seriously wounded, Jackson took careful aim at his helpless opponent and pulled the trigger, but the hammer stopped at half-cock. Jackson aimed again and this time mortally wounded Dickinson. Jackson's apologists claim that his lack of magnanimity was due to his fear that he would not survive Dickinson's bullet, and he did not want to die and leave

[4] Glasgow was later convicted of graft, though not on the basis of his dealings with Sevier. One of those implicated was Jackson's brother-in-law, Stockley Donelson. Land frauds were very prevalent in that era, and very few speculators operated strictly within the law. Even Driver admits that Sevier's payment to Glasgow, though not necessarily a bribe, might have been "hush" money. *Sevier*, 165.

his enemy alive. Critics, however, considered his killing of a defenseless opponent practically the same as murder.

Although historians concede that Jackson's connections with the Burr conspiracy involved no treasonable intentions on his part, many of the general's contemporaries were inclined to be suspicious. Aaron Burr's career in the East was ruined by his killing of Alexander Hamilton in a duel, but he was still popular in the West. On two occasions Jackson entertained former Vice President Burr at the Hermitage and presented him at formal dinners in Nashville. Burr apparently told Jackson that he planned to lead an expedition into Spanish Mexico as soon as the anticipated war with Spain occurred, but he failed to mention his alleged plan to separate the Western states from the nation. Jackson (and associates) contracted to build some boats for the project and indirectly encouraged the recruitment of soldiers.

Having received information from a visitor that Burr was involved in some treasonable design with the notorious Kentucky conspirator, General James Wilkinson, now in command of American troops in the Southwest, Jackson demanded an explanation when Burr returned to Nashville. Again assured by Burr that he had no treasonable purpose, Jackson allowed him to depart with two boats that had been completed. Soon thereafter the news arrived in Nashville of President Jefferson's proclamation calling for Burr's arrest, and Jackson immediately put two of his militia brigades under arms and called for the recruitment of volunteers. Although his purpose undoubtedly was to defend the Union, the widespread rumors concerning the Burr intrigue included the story that Jackson was organizing an army to support Burr's projected attack on New Orleans, a report which was accepted by some newspapers and which aroused the suspicions of Secretary of War Henry Dearborn.

After Burr had been arrested and taken to Richmond for trial, Jackson apparently became convinced that Burr was innocent and that his betrayer, Wilkinson, was the real culprit. Because of Jackson's haranguing the crowds around the courthouse in Richmond, many of his critics concluded that he and Burr were tarred with the same brush. Burr was acquitted, but his career was ruined, and some of the condemnation rubbed off on Jackson, although he was guilty of no treasonable intent. Jackson, relegated to a position of political impotence, held no public office except major general of the militia until the War of 1812 gave him the opportunity to retrieve his fortunes.

Meanwhile, Jackson's enemy, John Sevier, was reelected governor without significant opposition in 1805 and 1807. Willie (pronounced Wylie) Blount, William's half-brother, defeated William Cocke for the governorship in 1809 and was reelected in 1811 and 1813. Although again eligible in 1811, Sevier preferred not to oppose the Middle Tennessean, Blount, for governor, since that section had grown so rapidly it was now the most populous area in the state. Instead, Sevier was elected to Congress in his East Tennessee district and served until his death in 1815; his death occurred while he was surveying an Indian boundary line in the Alabama country. During his tenure in Congress in 1811–12, Sevier was closely identified with the "War Hawks" who desired war with Great Britain, as were the other members of the Tennessee delegation—an illustration of the popularity of the War of 1812 in Tennessee.

Tennessee and the War of 1812 ?? There were several reasons for the warlike tendencies of Tennesseans. Like other Westerners, Tennesseans were very nationalistic and patriotic, and they resented the numerous infringements by the British on American rights on the high seas, such as impressment of seamen. Although very few Tennesseans were directly involved, the interruption of trade by European blockades and the Jeffersonian policy of peaceable coercion seriously injured the economy by reducing the markets for surplus products. Tennesseans, like other Westerners, were also ardent expansionists and looked hungrily toward British Canada and the Florida possessions of Britain's ally, Spain. As prices paid for their cargoes declined at New Orleans because of trade interruptions, the Tennesseans desired to use a short-cut to the Gulf at Mobile, which was made possible by the proximity of the Coosa and Tombigbee rivers to branches of the Tennessee. Although claimed by the United States as a part of the Louisiana Purchase, Mobile, however, was still occupied by Spain. When the War of 1812 began, General Jackson proclaimed to his militia that the rivers and harbors (especially Mobile) of West Florida were "indispensable to the prosperity" of the people of Tennessee. He also claimed that the Indians of that region were being incited to ravage the white settlements.

By 1811 many Tennesseans had become convinced that there was a giant conspiracy, engineered by the British in Canada and aided by Spaniards in the Floridas, to unite the Northern and Southern Indians in a war on the American frontier. Creek raids on Tennessee settlements and a visit by Tecumseh to the Southern Indians as an emissary of Northern tribes which were about to engage an American army at Tippecanoe were cited as proof. Although evidence of the Europeans' complicity was lacking, the only way to peace with the Indians, and incidentally to easier acquisition of their lands by the whites, Tennesseans argued, was to drive the British out of Canada, and the logical moment was when Britain was involved in a life-and-death struggle with Napoleon. Felix Grundy, the congressman from the Nashville district, declared in 1811: "I therefore feel anxious not only to add the Floridas to the South, but the Canadas to the North of this empire."[5] Nevertheless, it is probable that the issues of neutral rights and national honor were more important than expansionism; Tennessee and other Western congressmen supported unanimously the declaration of war.[6] The news of the declaration, passed on June 18, reached Tennessee in time to make the celebration of Independence Day a riotous occasion. At a banquet in Rogersville one of the toasts was: "The 18th of June, 1812—May future ages be proud to celebrate the day on which a virtuous Congress Declared War against imperial Britain."[7]

Although Governor Blount and the legislature promised support and General Jackson offered 2,500 volunteers, very little use was made of Tennessee troops during the early part of the war. A small contingent under General James Winchester participated in the ineffectual effort to invade Canada. General Jackson led 2,000 volunteers to Natchez, but upon arrival he was ordered to disband them since Congress had refused to sanction an invasion of the Spanish Floridas. Refusing to throw his men adrift many miles from home, Jackson led them back to Nashville along the Natchez Trace before dismissing them from service. A soldier's comment

[5] Parks, *Grundy*, 42.
[6] Risjord, "1812: Conservatives, War Hawks and the National Honor," 196–200.
[7] Hamer, *Tennessee*, I, 220–21.

that he was as "tough as hickory" seems to have been the origin of his nickname, "Old Hickory." Meanwhile, a small group of East Tennesseans under the command of Colonel John Williams of Knoxville made an unauthorized expedition to join a force of United States troops in an attack upon the Seminole Indians of East Florida (December, 1812), but Congress refused to permit any occupation of Spanish territory. It was not until a year later that General Wilkinson, without the aid of Tennesseans, was permitted to occupy the West Florida post of Mobile to prevent seizure by the British.

A major part of Tennesseans' military activity during the War of 1812 was against the Creek Indians, following the massacre of Americans at Fort Mims in the southern Alabama country in August, 1813, by a faction of the Creeks called the "Red Sticks." Although the attack probably was due more to a civil war among the Creeks —between the primitive "Red Sticks" and the more civilized mixed-breeds—than incitement by the British, the warlike faction became British allies, and thus the Creek War was a phase of the War of 1812.

Without waiting for federal authorization, the Tennessee legislature called for 3,500 volunteers, and in accord with the tradition which was to give Tennessee the name, "Volunteer State," recruitment was enthusiastic. Two armies were organized, one under the command of General Jackson in Middle Tennessee and the other under General John Cocke in East Tennessee. Jackson had been seriously wounded in an affray with the Benton brothers, Jesse and Thomas H., following his serving as William Carroll's second in a duel with Jesse, but he got out of bed to assume command. After establishing a supply base called Fort Deposit, at the "bend" of the Tennessee River, Jackson cut a road to the Coosa, where he built Fort Strother only thirteen miles from the Creek town of Tallushatchee. This town was destroyed by a force, under General John Coffee, which included a bear-hunting scout named Davy Crockett. Jackson marched to the relief of a friendly Creek town of Talladega besieged by the "Red Sticks." A quick end to the war, however, was prevented by the unfortunate attack by a portion of Cocke's army upon a Creek faction which was attempting to sue for peace.

Jackson also had trouble because of the mutinous disposition of his troops; this mutiny was caused first by the lack of supplies and later by disputes regarding terms of service. Although he dealt vigorously with the mutineers, on one occasion putting a gun across the back of a horse and promising to shoot the first soldier who took another step toward home, Jackson finally had to release his troops and wait for another army to be recruited. When that was accomplished, he was able to crush the Creeks at the Battle of Tohopeka, or Horseshoe Bend, March 27, 1814. In this bloody engagement not only Jackson but other Tennesseans, including William Carroll, John Williams, and Sam Houston, achieved reputations which were to pave their roads to political success.

Jackson was appointed a major general in the United States army and given command of the Seventh Military District. Carroll succeeded him as major general of the Middle Tennessee militia. These generals and other Tennesseans soon engaged the British along the Gulf coast. After successfully defending Mobile and driving the British out of Pensacola, Jackson assumed command at New Orleans. It was his successful repulse, with considerable aid from a pirate named Jean Lafitte, on January 8, 1815, of the British effort to take New Orleans which was the high watermark of his military career and a steppingstone toward the presidency. Although the battle was fought after the treaty of peace had been signed at Ghent, the Battle of New Orleans contributed greatly to the rise of a spirit of nationalism in the United States and increased respect for the nation abroad. It has been argued that if the British had taken New Orleans, they would have refused to execute the treaty, still not ratified, and would have attempted to restore the Louisiana country to Spain. Although there is evidence that such a plan was under consideration, it is highly improbable that the British would have carried it out, in view of Napoleon's return from Elba and the resumption of the European war.

Jackson's popularity was further increased in 1818 by his invasion of Spanish East Florida, a region long desired by the United States. Jackson was instructed to chase the marauding Seminole Indians back into Spanish territory, if necessary, but he also took possession of the forts at St. Marks and Pensacola and seized and executed two British subjects who had been aiding the Indians. Although Jackson claimed he had received authorization from President Monroe, his actions became the subject of a congressional investigation, which merely increased his stature as a national hero. After the region invaded was subsequently acquired by a treaty with Spain, Jackson served for several months as its territorial governor.

Banking Problems and the Panic of 1819 ᎒᎒ The War of 1812 was followed in Tennessee and the West by a speculative boom and a financial panic. These developments occurred during the three administrations of Joseph McMinn, a Hawkins Countian who defeated four Middle Tennesseans for the governorship in 1815 and was reelected in 1817 and 1819. Born in Pennsylvania, McMinn had moved to the Tennessee country in 1786 and had served in the territorial assembly, the constitutional convention of 1796, and repeatedly thereafter in the state legislature, including three terms as speaker of the senate.

Closely related to the boom and the panic was the history of banking in the state. During the early years there was little need for banks because trade was carried on largely by means of barter. With the acquisition of large tracts of land from the Indians (to be described later), the growth of the state's population was phenomenal —from 105,602 in 1800 to 261,727 in 1810 and 422,823 in 1820. The resulting growth of trade and commerce led to the establishment of banks. The first was the Bank of Nashville, chartered in 1807, soon after much of Middle Tennessee had been opened to white settlement by the Indian treaties of 1805 and 1806. In 1811 the Bank of the State of Tennessee was established in Knoxville with the state as a minority stockholder and Hugh Lawson White as its very capable president. Three more banks, located in Fayetteville, Franklin, and Jonesboro, were chartered in 1815.

By that year, because of the War of 1812 and the ending of the First Bank of the United States with the expiration of its charter in 1811, a trend toward "wild cat" banking had developed, and most of the banks in the West and the South suspended specie payments.[8] The chartering of the Second Bank of the United States by Congress in 1816 placed some restraint on the "wild cat" tendencies of state

[8] One of the functions of banks during this period was the issuance of paper money backed merely by the credit of the bank but redeemable on demand in specie (gold or silver coins). The "wild cat" banks neglected to keep adequate supplies of specie on hand and frequently were forced to suspend specie payment. Consequently, their notes would depreciate in value.

banks, but the Second Bank's effectiveness was reduced by the fact that no branch was established in Tennessee until 1827. An effort was made in 1817 by Felix Grundy, William Carroll, and others[9] to establish a branch, but the legislature passed a law subjecting any bank not chartered by the state to a special tax of $50,000 a year. At the same session the legislature chartered nine state banks to be located in various small towns, but permitted them to become branches of either the Nashville or the Knoxville bank. White, the president of the latter, was a leading proponent of this legislation; but if he planned to absorb most of the small banks and create a strong state banking interest, the boom times following the war prevented its achievement.

The unhealthy business expansion and the orgy of land speculation, encouraged by the state banks, led to the inevitable crash in 1819. The Farmers and Mechanics Bank of Nashville, also chartered in 1817, was the first to suspend specie payment, but all the others soon followed suit, with the exception of White's bank in Knoxville. Prices fell rapidly, business enterprises failed, mortgages were foreclosed, and the oppressed debtors called on the legislature for help. During the 1819 session an Endorsement Act, or "stay law," was passed which postponed the execution of judgments for two years unless the creditor agreed to accept depreciated paper money. This was helpful mainly in enabling merchants to hold off their eastern creditors.

The depression was most serious in Middle Tennessee, where the boom had reached greater heights than in the eastern division. Although an East Tennessean, McMinn yielded to the popular clamor and called a special session in 1820 and joined forces with the architect of the stay law, Felix Grundy of Nashville, in providing additional relief. Grundy's plan was to create a new Bank of the State of Tennessee (generally called the "new state bank" to avoid confusion with White's "old state bank" in Knoxville), which was to be completely state-owned. Through its loan offices in Nashville and Knoxville and agencies in all the counties, the new bank was authorized to lend at 6 per cent interest a maximum of one million dollars to the hard-pressed citizens. The paper money issued for this purpose was to be backed by the proceeds of the sale of the state's

---

[9] Jackson made recommendations for its officers, but it is doubtful that he really favored its establishment.

public lands. Andrew Jackson condemned the measure, and the old banks reduced the bill's effectiveness by limiting their circulation of paper money in proportion to the amount issued by the loan offices.

The financial situation supplied the major issues in the state election of 1821, in which William Carroll and Edward Ward were the opposing candidates for governor. General Carroll had come out of the war with a military reputation second only to Jackson's, but he was suspected of feeling that Old Hickory had monopolized the glory. A native of Pennsylvania, Carroll was a Nashville merchant and part owner of the first steamboat to reach Nashville. His business enterprises failed in the panic of 1819, a factor which helped him win the election of 1821 because the poor debtors believed he could sympathize with them in their difficulties. Ward, on the other hand, was a conservative, wealthy planter and a neighbor and friend of Jackson, who supported Ward because of his opposition to the new state bank. Even so, Carroll's victory was overwhelming, and he went on to serve as the chief executive for a longer period of time[10] than any other governor of Tennessee.

Despite the nature of the campaign, Carroll opposed inflation of the currency and induced the legislature to require the banks to resume specie payment by 1824. At a special session of 1822, however, it re-enacted the stay law of 1819, which the state supreme court had declared unconstitutional. Even though Grundy, suddenly turning conservative, secured a postponement of forced resumption to 1826, most of the banks of the state had gone out of existence by that time. Therefore, in 1827, the legislature repealed the law against the Bank of the United States, and that institution established a branch in Nashville. The war against that bank waged by Jackson after he became President in 1829 will be treated in another chapter.

SUGGESTED READINGS

General Accounts

Abernethy, *Frontier to Plantation*, Chs. 10, 14; Abernethy, *The South in the New Nation* (Baton Rouge, 1961), Chs. 7, 11, 14; Folmsbee, Corlew, and Mitchell, *Tennessee*, I, Chs. 13–14; Garrett and Goodpasture, *Tennessee*, Chs. 19, 24; Hamer, *Tennessee*, I, Chs. 15–17; Eric Russell Lacy, *Vanquished Volunteers: East Tennessee Sectionalism from*

[10] Although Sevier also served six terms, his first term was for less than two years.

Statehood to Secession (Johnson City, Tenn., 1965), Chs. 1–3; Remini, R. V., *Andrew Jackson* (New York, 1966); White, *Messages*, I–II.

Specialized Accounts
   Thomas P. Abernethy, *The Burr Conspiracy* (New York, 1954); Abernethy, "Andrew Jackson and the Rise of Southwestern Democracy," *AHR*, XXXIII (Oct., 1927), 64–77; Abernethy, "The Early Development of Commerce and Banking in Tennessee," *MVHR*, XIV (Dec., 1927), 311–25; John S. Bassett, *Life of Andrew Jackson* (2 vols., New York, 1911), I; William E. Beard, "Joseph McMinn, Tennessee's Fourth Governor," *THQ*, IV (June, 1945), 154–66; Aaron Boom, "John Coffee, Citizen Soldier," *THQ*, XXII (Sept., 1963), 223–37; Claude A. Campbell, *The Development of Banking in Tennessee* (Nashville, 1932), 1–55; William N. Chambers, "Thwarted Warrior: The Last Years of Thomas Hart Benton in Tennessee," *ETHS Publ.*, No. 22 (1950), 19–44; Chambers, *Old Bullion Benton: Senator from the New West* (New York, 1956); W. W. Clayton, *History of Davidson County* (Philadelphia, 1880), 137–59; Cotterill, *Southern Indians*, 166–90; David Crockett, *Autobiography of David Crockett* (New York, 1923), 51–111; Driver, *Sevier*, Chs. 7–11; Paul M. Fink, "Russell Bean, Tennessee's First Native Son," *ETHS Publ.*, No. 37 (1965), 31–48; R. E. Folk, *Battle of New Orleans: Its Real Meaning* (Nashville, 1935); Stanley J. Folmsbee and Anna Grace Catron, "The Early Career of David Crockett," *ETHS Publ.*, No. 28 (1956), 58–85; Albert V. Goodpasture, "Genesis of the Jackson-Sevier Feud," *AHM*, V (April, 1900), 115–23, reprinted in White, *Tennessee: Old and New*, I, 167–75; Lunia Paul Gresham, "Hugh Lawson White as a Tennessee Politician and Banker, 1807–1827," *ETHS Publ.*, No. 18 (1946), 25–46; Harrell, "James Winchester," *THQ*, XVII (Dec., 1958), 301–17; Joseph T. Hatfield, "William C. C. Claiborne, Congress and Republicanism," *THQ*, XXIV (Summer, 1965), 157–80; Reginald Horsman, *The Causes of the War of 1812* (Philadelphia, 1962); Marquis James, *The Life of Andrew Jackson* (2 vols., New York, 1933–37), I, Chs. 1–20; James, *The Raven: A Biography of Sam Houston* (New York, 1929), 27–46; Leota D. Maiden, "Colonel John Williams," *ETHS Publ.*, No. 30 (1958), 7–46; Masterson, *Blount*, Chs. 10–11; Mary H. McCown (ed.), "The 'J. Hartsell Memora': The Journal of a Tennessee Captain in the War of 1812," *ETHS Publ.*, No. 11 (1939), 93–115, No. 12 (1940), 118–46; McRaven, *Edward Swanson*, Chs. 18–19; Parks, *Felix Grundy*, Chs. 3–8; James Parton, *Life of Andrew Jackson* (3 vols., New York, 1860), I; James S. Ranck, "Andrew Jackson and the Burr Conspiracy," *THM*, Ser. 2, Vol. I (Oct., 1930), 17–28, reprinted in White, *Tennessee: Old*

and New, I; N. K. Risjord, "1812: Conservatives, War Hawks and the National Honor," *William and Mary Quarterly,* Ser. 3, XVIII (1961), 196–200; J. E. Roper, "Isaac Rawlings, Frontier Merchant," *THQ,* XX (Sept., 1961), 262–81; C. G. Sellers, Jr., "Banking and Finance in Jackson's Tennessee," *MVHR,* XLI (June, 1954), 61–84; James A. Shackford, *David Crockett: The Man and the Legend,* ed. John B. Shackford (Chapel Hill, 1956); Joe Gray Taylor, "Andrew Jackson and the Aaron Burr Conspiracy," WTHS *Papers,* No. I (1947), 81–90; Isabel Thompson, "The Blount Conspiracy," ETHS *Publ.,* No. 2 (1930), 3–21; W. A. Walker, Jr., "Martial Sons: Tennessee Enthusiasm for the War of 1812," *THQ,* XX (March, 1961), 20–37; Arthur P. Whitaker, *The Mississippi Question, 1795–1803* (New York, 1934), 101–15; White, *Messages,* I–II; Samuel C. Williams, "A Forgotten Campaign," *THM,* VIII (Jan., 1925), 266–76.

THE NORTH CAROLINA GOVERNMENT at the time of the Revolution not only asserted its title to the Tennessee country, but also claimed that the Indians had forfeited their title by their adherence to the British cause. Therefore, the state in 1783 opened the entire area to acquisition by land speculators, with the exceptions of a section of upper Middle Tennessee (the Military Reservation), which was reserved for the location of land bounties to soldiers, and the Cherokee Reservation, south of the French Broad and Big Pigeon rivers and east of the Tennessee, where the Indian towns were actually located. Five years later, North Carolina ceded her Western claim to the United States, but gave up only such lands as might be left over after all the claims of her Revolutionary War veterans and land speculators had been satisfied. As will be pointed out later, this meant in the final analysis that the United States never acquired any revenue whatsoever from the sale of land in Tennessee.

The federal government was more successful, however, in reversing North Carolina's nullification of the Indian title. Although for some time it was impossible to keep the promises made to the Indians in the Hopewell treaties of 1785 and 1786, ultimately the stronger national government under the Constitution was able to insist that white occupation was illegal until the land had been formally ceded to the United States by the Indian claimants. When Tennessee entered the Union in 1796, approximately three-fourths of the area was still claimed by the Cherokee and Chickasaw Indians, but outside the Cherokee Reservation most of the area was blanketed with land warrants issued by North Carolina. Consequently, the United States was under continuous and heavy pressure from thousands of land claimants and prospective settlers to clear the Tennessee land of the Indian title as quickly as possible.

Indian Cessions, 1791–1819 ࿐ During the territorial period, Governor William Blount as superintendent of Indian Affairs had negotiated the Treaty of the Holston of 1791 which extinguished the Cherokee title to all lands east of the Clinch River and north of a line from near the site of Kingston to the North Carolina boundary. This line, as surveyed by Benjamin Hawkins in 1797, ran just to the south of the site of Maryville. The Cherokee also again confirmed, as they had previously done at Hopewell, their relinquishment of title to the Cumberland Valley in Middle Tennessee, first sold to the Transylvania Company in 1775.

The Holston cession of 1791, however, had failed to include some lands occupied under the Treaty of Coyatee of 1786 by which the state of Franklin, it will be recalled, had forced the Cherokee to permit settlement as far south as the Little Tennessee River. After the survey of 1797, federal troops began to remove by force settlers who were located on the wrong side of the line; the family of the prominent Judge David Campbell was among those forced to move. The Tennessee legislature sent a vigorous remonstrance to Congress, and the government responded with the appointment of commissioners who, with the aid of Governor Sevier and James White of Knoxville, induced the Cherokee to cede two tracts of land in Tennessee. One tract lay between the Hawkins line (east of Chilhowee Mountain) and the Tennessee and Little Tennessee rivers and the other between the Clinch River and the eastern edge of the Cumberland Plateau. This "First Treaty of Tellico" was signed at Tellico Blockhouse, October 2, 1798.

Tennesseans, disappointed by the smallness of the cession, continued to exert pressure on the government to acquire more land. In 1805–6 the agent to the Cherokee, Return Jonathan Meigs, resorted to the customary bribing of individual chiefs and thus obtained a series of important cessions. By the Third[1] Treaty of

---

[1] The Second Treaty of Tellico did not include any Tennessee land. Bribery of the chiefs was made under direct orders from Secretary of War Henry Dearborn, who

Tellico, October 25, 1805, the Indians ceded all their claims north of the Duck River and a line from its source to the mouth of the Hiwassee. In addition to the customary down payment and annuity

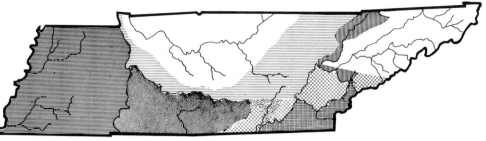

Map 3.

INDIAN TREATY CESSIONS

Pre-Statehood Treaties, 1770-91

First Treaty of Tellico, 1798

Third Treaty of Tellico, 1805

Dearborn's Treaty, 1806

Jackson and McMinn Treaty, 1817

Chickasaw Purchase, 1818

Calhoun's Treaty, 1819

Treaty of Removal, 1836

Conflicting Chickasaw claims with the Cherokee east of the Tennessee River had been removed by treaties of 1805 and 1816.

to the tribe, the treaty included secret articles reserving two tracts of land for Chief Doublehead at the mouth of the Clinch and two tracts elsewhere for another chief. Two days later, by the Fourth Treaty of Tellico, the Indians were induced to cede the valuable land occupied by the United States garrison at Southwest Point (Kingston); they were assured that the land was considered a "desirable place" for the legislature to meet. The Tennessee legislature cooperated at the close of the 1805 session by providing that its next meeting would be held at Southwest Point. It did meet there for one day, September 21, 1807, but merely adopted a resolution moving the capital back to Knoxville.[2] Meanwhile, the negotiations had been shifted to Washington because the Indians were becoming

---

earlier had insisted on it as a means of obtaining Cherokee consent in 1803 to the opening of a road from Tennessee into the Cherokee country in Georgia. Horsman, *Expansion and Indian Policy*, 125–26.

[2] This enabled Kingston (along with Knoxville and Murfreesboro) to acquire a monument proclaiming that it was once the capital of Tennessee.

suspicious of the perfidy of their chiefs, and by Dearborn's Treaty of January 7, 1806, most of the remainder of Middle Tennessee was acquired.[3] Not long after Doublehead returned home with his bribe he was assassinated, presumably under orders of the tribal council.

As a result of these Indian cessions, migration to Tennessee increased enormously. Between 1800 and 1810 the free white population increased 137 per cent and the slave population 238 per cent, making necessary the creation of many new counties. In the first eleven years after admission the number of counties in East Tennessee increased from eight to seventeen. The growth of Middle Tennessee was even greater, from three counties in 1796 to twenty in 1809. Some of this immigration, of course, came from the eastern division.

Meanwhile, Tennesseans had become greatly interested in Jefferson's suggestion in July, 1803, to remove all the Indians living east of the Mississippi to the recently acquired Louisiana Purchase. As a matter of fact, a memorial to Congress by the Tennessee legislature in October, 1803, suggesting the same idea almost antedated the President's proposal. Agent Meigs was instructed to spread the removal idea among the Cherokee, and he was so successful that he had to undo some of his work because Congress had not appropriated enough money to remove all who were willing to go. Of those who did move, the largest number seems to have been from the Tennessee part of the Cherokee country. Not having any specific lands assigned to them, they became involved in difficulties with their new neighbors in the West. In 1817 these Indians sent a delegation to a conference of the eastern Cherokee and a federal commission headed by Andrew Jackson and Governor McMinn of Tennessee. As a result, the Upper Cherokee obtained an assignment of lands along the Arkansas and White rivers in exchange for a Cherokee cession of land in Georgia and the Sequatchie Valley in Tennessee. The United States promised to pay the removal expenses for any Indians who wished to migrate west.

Governor McMinn was appointed as a federal agent to arrange for the general removal of the Cherokee, but that nation as a whole continued to reject all proposals, including an offer of $200,000 for all their lands in the East. Most opposed to removal were the mixed-

[3] A small portion of the conflicting Chickasaw claim to land east of the northward-flowing Tennessee was removed in 1805 and the remainder in 1816.

bloods and others who had adopted much of the white man's civilization. They did not wish to abandon the considerable amounts of property they had acquired and revert to their former primitive ways of living. A group of missionaries reported the typical reaction as follows:

> The Indians say they don't know how to understand their Father the President. A few years ago he sent them a plough & a hoe—said it was not good for his red children to hunt—they must cultivate the earth. Now he tells them there is good hunting at the Arkansas, if they go there he will give them rifles.[4]

Less unwilling to move were the uncivilized Indians of the hilly country, and McMinn induced about 3,500 to go west despite the tribal policy of persecuting those who enrolled for removal. The Cherokee council sent a delegation to Washington to protest against the pressure for removal, but Secretary of War Calhoun countered with a demand that the Indians make another large cession of land to compensate for the additional territory necessary for the Cherokee who had already moved or were about to move west. The delegation finally agreed and in Calhoun's Treaty of February 27, 1819, ceded three tracts of land, including first the remainder of the Cherokee claim north of the Tennessee River lying east and west of the Sequatchie Valley cession by the Jackson-McMinn Treaty of 1817. Also ceded was the Hiwassee District, which included a large tract between the Hiwassee and Little Tennessee and a smaller tract north of the latter river. Four new counties were created in the areas ceded in 1817 and 1819, and one county was enlarged.

Meanwhile, the last claims of the Chickasaw in Tennessee had been extinguished. It will be recalled that in 1783 by the Treaty of Nashborough the Chickasaw had agreed to a boundary running along the watershed between the Tennessee and Cumberland rivers, and in 1805 and 1816 had relinquished the remainder of their conflicting claims to the Cherokee cessions in Middle Tennessee. In 1818 Andrew Jackson and former Governor Isaac Shelby of Kentucky were appointed as commissioners to negotiate with the Chickasaw for West Tennessee and western Kentucky. The land in those areas, they told the Indians, had been given by North Carolina and Virginia to Revolutionary War soldiers thirty-five years

[4] Malone, *Cherokees*, 69.

before, and the United States could not guarantee any longer to keep settlers out of the region. Actually, North Carolina had sold much of the West Tennessee land to land speculators. The area was not opened to soldiers' warrants until a few months before the treaty was signed.

Following the acquisition of this "Jackson Purchase" on October 19, 1818, West Tennessee, or the Western District as it was known for several years, received a large migration from other parts of Tennessee and from neighboring states. Whether the settlement was accelerated or hindered by the panic of 1819 is a subject of dispute, but probably the settlement was hindered. The first county created entirely in the Western District was Shelby, where the fellow speculators Judge John Overton, General James Winchester, and General Andrew Jackson established the town of Memphis. Since the evacuation of Fort San Fernando by the Spaniards in 1797, Americans had used the bluff as a site for a trading post and a fort, but it had only a handful of settlers. Isaac Rawlings ran the trading post from 1814 to 1818, when he was sent to the Arkansas River to establish a "factory" (trading post) for the Western Cherokee. He did not return to Memphis until 1820; Rawlings then became a rival merchant of Marcus Winchester (a son of one of the founders of Memphis and later the town's first mayor). Following the Chickasaw treaty, Jackson was able to turn a neat profit in disposing of his remaining land interests at the site of Memphis to Winchester and John C. McLemore. In 1820 the proprietors advertised Memphis in a prospectus as "destined to become a populous city" because it was "the only site for a town of any magnitude on the Mississippi between the mouth of the Ohio and Natchez." Nevertheless, its growth was slow, and for a few years it had a serious rival—Randolph—at the mouth of the Hatchie. Also, until after 1830 the largest population in the Western District was in the eastern section. The plantation type of agriculture is indicated by the total slave population of 26,161 in the fourteen district counties in 1830.

Tennessee and the Removal of the Cherokee 〰 As a result of the treaties of 1791–1819, all of Tennessee had been cleared of the Indian title except the southeastern corner of the state, which was still held by the Cherokee. Sixteen years were to pass before those Indians could be induced to surrender that territory and their extensive holdings in neighboring North Carolina, Alabama, and especially Georgia, where the Indians had become largely concentrated by 1819. The people of Tennessee, who previously had been the chief advocates of removal, were content to let the Georgians complete the task, but they gave them valuable moral support.

The stubbornness with which the Cherokee resisted the federal removal policy was due largely to their progress in civilization, which was considerably greater than that of other Southern tribes. Especially noteworthy was the agricultural development, in the growing of cotton, tobacco, corn, and other crops. There was also a considerable amount of domestic manufacturing. According to an official census published in 1828, the total population was about 15,000. The Cherokee owned about 1,000 slaves, 22,400 cattle, 7,600 horses, 1,800 spinning wheels, 700 looms, and had 12 saw mills, 55 blacksmith shops, and 6 cotton gins. The aggregate value of their property was estimated at $2,000,000.

Practically all the mixed-bloods could speak English and many could read and write, as could a considerable number of the full-blooded Cherokee. After the great Sequoyah in the 1820's had invented his syllabary, which made possible the writing and printing of the Cherokee language, a large number of the Indians learned to read and write in their native tongue. It is probable that there was less illiteracy among the Cherokee than among the whites living in the same states. A printing press was obtained and a newspaper, the *Cherokee Phoenix,* was published from 1828 to 1832 in the two languages, English and Cherokee. As early as 1817 the Cherokee had set up a republican form of government with an elected council. In 1827 they adopted a constitution modeled after that of the United States and hoped for admission into the Union as a state—a proposal which aroused indignation in the states where they resided.

There were two main causes of the rapid progress of the Cherokee in civilization: (1) the policy of the United States of supplying seeds, farm implements, and some training in agriculture, and (2) the work of Christian missionaries. The former seems to have originated in a provision of the Holston Treaty stating that the United States would supply the Cherokee with "useful instruments of husbandry." The federal agents to those Indians, particularly R. J.

Meigs, worked earnestly, and in cooperation with the missionaries, to make the civilizing program effective.

Attempts to Christianize the Cherokee were made during the colonial period, but it was not until the early years of the nineteenth century that any real success was achieved. Then the Moravians, Presbyterians, Methodists, Baptists, and an interdenominational American Board of Commissioners for Foreign Missions established mission schools in the Cherokee country. Several were located in East Tennessee, including two Presbyterian schools started by the Reverend Gideon Blackburn in 1804–6; Blackburn claimed four or five hundred young Cherokee had learned to read and write before the schools were closed in 1810. John Ross was converted at a Methodist Mission at Ross's Landing (Chattanooga).

The most noted and successful school in the Cherokee country was the Brainerd Mission, which was started in 1817 by the American Board, then under Congregational-Presbyterian control, on Chickamauga Creek near the site of Chattanooga. The mission had the advantage of outstanding leadership, first under its organizer, Cyrus Kingsbury, and later under the capable and highly educated Samuel Austin Worcester.[5] Worcester arrived when large numbers of the Cherokee were learning to read and write their own language, and he was instrumental in starting their newspaper and translating the Bible and other types of religious literature into Cherokee. In recognition of his services the Indians called him "The Messenger." Several of the most intelligent of the Brainerd pupils continued their studies at the more advanced school operated by the American Board at Cornwall, Connecticut. Two of them, however, Elias Boudinot and John Ridge, married white girls of the community, and the resulting furor led to the closing of the Cornwall school.

Also contributing to the refusal of the Cherokee to move west was the encouragement of most of the missionaries. Near the end of the controversy, however, some missionaries concluded that the combination of Jackson and Georgia was too strong to resist and advised yielding to the inevitable. Georgia's insistence on Indian removal was based on a number of factors: the claim that the United States in the so-called Compact of 1802 had promised to clear the state of Indian title; cupidity, aroused by the discovery of gold in

---

[5] His name became historic because of the *Worcester v. Georgia* case.

the Cherokee country and the sight of the fine farms and homes owned by the more wealthy Indians; and the resentment caused by the petition of the Cherokee for admission into the Union as a separate state.

Following the election to the presidency of the old Indian fighter, Andrew Jackson, Georgia in December, 1828, disregarding previous constitutional interpretations, passed an act extending the jurisdiction of the state over the Indian country, effective in 1830. When a Cherokee delegation came to Washington to protest against the law, they were told that the federal government had no authority to interfere and that the Indians would have to submit to Georgia's jurisdiction or move west. Dissatisfied with the piecemeal removal policy, Jackson asked Congress for a general removal law which would give him more expressed authority. Such a measure, which also appropriated $500,000 for removal purposes, was passed in May, 1830, with Hugh Lawson White and John Bell of Tennessee acting as chief sponsors in the two houses. The only member of the Tennessee delegation to vote against the bill, David Crockett, was defeated for reelection. In 1832 the Supreme Court in the *Worcester* v. *Georgia* case declared the Georgia law unconstitutional, on the grounds that the Constitution gave the United States exclusive jurisdiction in Indian affairs. Jackson, however, refused to enforce the decision and permitted Georgia to continue to exercise its unconstitutional authority. He seems to have believed that the Indians would be better off in the West and that under the combined federal and Georgia pressure they would be forced to accept the removal policy.

Georgia's oppressive jurisdiction was now applied with the utmost severity. The Cherokee lands were surveyed and disposed of by means of a lottery, and laws were passed providing that no Indian could bring suit or testify in a Georgia court and prohibiting the holding of any Indian assemblies. It became necessary to move the Cherokee capital and the meetings of the council across the state line to Red Clay, Tennessee. But Georgia refused to respect the boundary. Chief John Ross, the leader of the anti-removal faction, and his visitor, the celebrated author-composer John Howard Payne, were arrested at Red Clay and taken back into Georgia. After being released, Payne wrote a bitter denunciation of Georgia's policy, but it failed to restrain that state.

Under continued pressure from Georgia, the Tennessee legislature, after three previous failures, finally passed, on November 8, 1833, a law extending Tennessee jurisdiction over the Indian country. The Tennessee legislation, however, was more lenient than Georgia's. The law protected the property rights of the Indians and limited the criminal jurisdiction of the state courts in the Indian country to cases involving murder, rape, and larceny. An interesting court case resulted. In 1835 an Indian named James Foreman was brought to trial for murder but was acquitted on the ground that the Tennessee law was unconstitutional in view of the decision in the *Worcester* v. *Georgia* case. The Foreman decision was reversed by the state supreme court. Judge John Catron, in delivering the court's opinion, stated that the Indians were "mere wandering savages" and might even "deserve to be exterminated as savage and pernicious beasts."[6] He also contended that no treaty or act of Congress could deprive a state of its undelegated sovereignty. When the case finally reached the United States Supreme Court, a minority faction of the Cherokee had signed a removal treaty and the trial was never held.

The signing of that removal treaty was due to the growing conviction of Elias Boudinot, the editor of the *Cherokee Phoenix*, and of John Ridge, especially after Jackson had been reelected in 1832, that the only intelligent course for the Indians to follow was to get the best terms possible from the government and move west. The only alternative would be the acceptance of the intolerable jurisdiction of Georgia and the loss of independence as a nation. Boudinot and Ridge converted the elder chieftain, "Major" Ridge (John's father), to their viewpoint, and he became the leader of the faction. The beloved principal chief, John Ross, however, retained the support of the overwhelming majority for his anti-removal policy, in the vain hope that Northern and Whig pressure would force the Jackson administration to abide by existing treaties and the Supreme Court's decision. The Ridges and Boudinot resorted to unethical tactics, and by working hand in glove with the Georgia authorities attempted to reduce the influence of Ross and the other leaders of

[6] Nine years earlier in a dissenting opinion in another case Catron had stated that the "earlier notions . . . 'that the Indians were *mere savage beasts without rights of any kind,*' have long since been exploded." Two years after his change of heart Catron was appointed by Jackson to the United States Supreme Court. Gass, "Constitutional Opinions of Catron," 54–59.

the anti-removal faction and to block their efforts at every turn. In exchange, the Ridges and Boudinot were leniently treated by Georgia and given large payments for their lands and other properties, but they were in violation of the Cherokee constitution and therefore subject to the death penalty. Major Ridge in signing the removal treaty commented prophetically that he was signing his death warrant. After the removal of 1838 the Cherokee council, without the knowledge of John Ross, executed that death penalty on the Major, his son, and Boudinot.

The Treaty of Removal was signed December 29, 1835, at an assembly of the Indians at New Echota called by the government agents William Carroll and John F. Schermerhorn. Of the three hundred Indians who signed only seventy-nine were legal voters. The Ross faction had boycotted the assembly, and Ross, now realizing that removal was inevitable, had departed for Washington at the head of a delegation to negotiate a more satisfactory and legal treaty. Jackson ignored the Ross group, accepted instead the New Echota treaty, and submitted it to the Senate. Although the treaty was repudiated by all but a small minority of the Cherokee, the Senate approved it on May 23, 1836.

By the treaty the Cherokee ceded all their lands east of the Mississippi for $5,000,000 and agreed to move west within two years. But when that time expired in 1838, only a small number of the Cherokee had removed; so the United States army ejected the remainder by force, and thousands of Indians died on their so-called "Trail of Tears." Many Tennesseans were involved in the removal; most of the camps in which the Indians were concentrated were in Tennessee, and one of the steamboats used in the removal was commanded by George Washington Harris, the author of the "Sut Lovingood" stories. The latest migrants, under the supervision of John Ross despite Jackson's violent protest, followed the overland route, passing near the Nashville home of the retired President who had been responsible for their expulsion from their homes. Many of the Indians, however, escaped removal by hiding out in the Great Smoky Mountains. They were aided by a friendly North Carolinian, Will Thomas, in later obtaining possession of the Qualla Reservation at Cherokee, North Carolina, where many Indians still live.[7]

[7] At Cherokee, *Unto These Hills,* the very popular outdoor historical drama depicting the removal story, has been presented each summer since 1950.

The Tennessee territory ceded by the Treaty of New Echota was the region south of the Hiwassee River and east of the Tennessee, together with a strip along the North Carolina border between the Hiwassee and the Little Tennessee rivers. Two new counties were created, and two others, one of them Hamilton, were greatly enlarged. In Hamilton County, Ross's Landing, soon to be renamed Chattanooga, already was an important shipping point in 1838, and it was expected to be the terminus of a railroad. In that year F. A. Parham began the publication of the *Hamilton Gazette*. Lots in the town were sold at auction in 1839, and in December of that year Chattanooga was incorporated. In advertising the sale of lots the commissioners not only called attention to the economic possibilities of the area but pointed out that the town was "surrounded by scenery the most grand and picturesque."

Public Land Policy ౾౿ When Tennessee entered the Union in 1796, she became involved in a triangular dispute with North Carolina and the United States over title to land in the state. North Carolina claimed that on the basis of her cession act of 1789 holders of land warrants under her land laws of 1780–83 were entitled to land as soon as the Indian title was extinguished. North Carolina insisted that her Revolutionary War soldiers, even if they had not obtained their warrants, still were entitled to the number of acres allowed them, which varied according to rank, under her military bounty laws. It will be recalled that the cession act provided that if there was not enough good land in the Military Reservation, the warrants could be located elsewhere in the region ceded —outside of the Cherokee Reservation. The United States claimed title to any land which remained after all of North Carolina's claims had been satisfied. Tennessee argued that North Carolina had set a deadline date of 1792 for the filing of entries and that the extensions of time North Carolina had granted were illegal. The United States claim, Tennessee contended, was weakened by the failure to assert it during the territorial period[8] or at the time of Tennessee's admission to the Union.

---

[8] Congress had made no provisions for survey or sale of land in the Southwest Territory because Secretary of State Jefferson had reported that there were no unappropriated lands available which were cleared of Indian title.

After a bitter controversy, during which Tennessee threatened to set up her own land offices, the three-cornered dispute was eventually settled by Congress in the Compact of 1806. By this compromise Tennessee recognized the title of the United States to all ungranted lands in the "Congressional Reservation," which included all of West Tennessee and the southwestern corner of Middle Tennessee. In return, the United States surrendered to Tennessee all claims to land in the remainder of the state, subject to the following conditions: (1) Tennessee should satisfy all future North Carolina grants in that area, outside the Cherokee Reservation; (2) where existing claims permitted, Tennessee was to reserve 640 acres in each township of 36 square miles for the support of public schools; (3) Tennessee was to appropriate two 100,000-acre tracts of land in the Cherokee Reservation—one for the support of two colleges (to be located in East and Middle Tennessee) and the other for the support of an academy in each county of the state; and (4) Tennessee was not to sell land for less than the national minimum land price (then $2.00 an acre), except that occupants in the Cherokee Reservation should be permitted to purchase up to 640 acres, at $1.00 an acre.

Governor Sevier predicted that this legislation would make any increase in taxation unnecessary, but he underestimated both the extent and subsequent increase of North Carolina's claims. Since many warrants were held by Tennesseans, the people of the state insisted upon the rapid removal of the Indian title so that their grants could be located. Considerable objection was raised, however, when Tennessee, in accord with the compact, used the rectangular,[9] township method of survey rather than North Carolina's "crazy-quilt" pattern. Also, speculators were annoyed because Tennessee permitted occupants to acquire up to 200 acres of land, even in conflict with a North Carolina survey, if North Carolina warrants were presented for that amount. The squatters in Middle Tennessee and in the Cherokee Reservation joined forces in securing the passage of this Tennessee law allowing ownership of 200 acres, thus effecting a political alliance which was to last indefinitely.

Outside the Cherokee Reservation the desirable lands were taken

---

[9] Tennessee, however, surveyed townships five miles square (instead of the six of the federal system), thus making it difficult to set aside the 640 acres in each township for common schools.

by the holders of North Carolina warrants as rapidly as the Indian title was extinguished. Therefore, it became necessary for Congress in 1818 to open the Congressional Reservation to take care of the military warrants. In that year Jackson's Chickasaw Purchase opened West Tennessee to settlement, and the holders of North Carolina warrants flocked to that region and soon secured title to much of the best land, using either warrants and surveys under North Carolina's "Land Grab Act" of 1783 or military bounties. Also, at about that time, the North Carolina government published the muster rolls of her Revolutionary companies so that the soldiers or their heirs who had not secured warrants would be able to do so. Previously, land bounties to soldiers who died without heirs were transferred to the University of North Carolina, which therefore received a great number of warrants; the institution desired land in the West Tennessee region, but Tennessee refused to recognize those warrants until 1822 when two agents of the University worked out an arrangement with Felix Grundy whereby the land grants would be shared with two Tennessee colleges. In 1825 a similar division of some additional warrants included Tennessee's common schools as well as the colleges.

According to the Compact of 1806, any lands in the Congressional Reservation left over after North Carolina's claims were satisfied belonged to the United States, but as warrants continued to pour forth, it became evident that there would not be much good land remaining. A movement then developed in Tennessee to ask the United States to cede that land to the state for educational purposes. In 1823 the legislature made such a request of Congress in a memorial which had been drafted by James K. Polk. Polk's main argument was that only 22,705 acres of land could be set aside for common schools instead of the 400,000 acres envisioned under the Compact of 1806. When he became a member of Congress, Polk sponsored legislation to cede this United States land to Tennessee but was frustrated first by Northerners and then by his colleague, David Crockett, who feared that the land revenue would be used for a college, as John Bell was advocating, instead of common schools. Crockett, who represented many West Tennessee squatters, also wished to donate 160 acres to every occupant in that area or at least safeguard their right to buy their holdings at a nominal price. This defense of the squatters in their contest with the land speculators was the real cause of Crockett's break with the Jacksonians, rather than his opposition to Jackson's Indian policy. Congress eventually, in 1841, authorized Tennessee to sell the waste land in the Congressional Reservation for the federal government's benefit, but granted occupants pre-emption rights to 200 acres at 12½

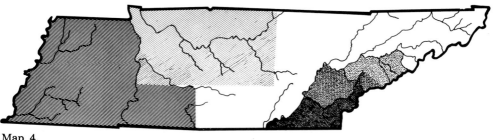

Map 4.

PUBLIC LANDS OF TENNESSEE

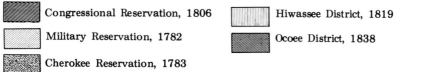

Congressional Reservation, 1806		Hiwassee District, 1819	
Military Reservation, 1782		Ocoee District, 1838	
Cherokee Reservation, 1783			

cents an acre. In 1846 Congress ceded the remaining lands, together with the revenue obtained since 1841, to Tennessee on condition that $40,000 of the proceeds be used for the establishment of a college in West Tennessee.[10] The remainder was added to the common school fund.

Not only in the Congressional Reservation but also in the rest of the state, except in the area reserved for the Cherokee, all of the desirable lands were taken by holders of North Carolina warrants. Since Tennessee was prohibited from selling land at less than the national price, the remaining waste land could not be sold until that restriction was removed by an act of Congress in 1823. In that year the legislature provided for the sale of that waste land at 12½ cents an acre, the receipts to go into the common school fund which was created by the same law.

[10] West Tennessee College (now Union University) was the recipient of this grant. Thomas B. Jones, in "The Public Lands of Tennessee," has shown that Polk and other Tennesseans greatly underestimated the total acreage in the Congressional Reservation. Thus the United States cession amounted to much more than is generally believed.

It was from the sale of land in the Cherokee Reservation that Tennessee received the largest part of its land revenue, because that region was not available for the location of North Carolina warrants. At the time of the Compact of 1806 only about one-third of the reservation—north of the Little Tennessee River—had been cleared of the Indian title. Most of the good land, including the college and academy tracts, was occupied by squatters who were allowed pre-emption rights at $1.00 an acre. However, the state was unable to collect even that amount from those people, as will be discussed in a subsequent chapter; thus the revenue was relatively small. From the proceeds of the sales of land outside the college and academy tracts about $12,000 was used for the improvement of the Holston (portion now called Tennessee) and Tennessee rivers.

By Calhoun's Treaty of 1819 another section of the Cherokee Reservation was acquired. It included the area between the Little Tennessee and Hiwassee rivers (except for the mountainous country along the eastern border) plus a small tract north of the Little Tennessee along the foothills of the Great Smokies which had not been included in the 1798 cession. When surveyed into townships and sections, this region became known as the Hiwassee District. Since the district was relatively free of squatters and was closed to North Carolina warrant holders, the state had great expectations of revenue from the sale of land there, but the economic depression which began in 1819 interfered. It will be recalled that the proceeds from sales were used as a backing for the paper money issued by Grundy's loan office (Bank of the State of Tennessee) established in 1820. At first the land, except for the sections reserved for schools,[11] was sold at auction at a minimum of $2.00 an acre, with pre-emption rights granted to occupants at one-half that price. When Congress in 1823 allowed Tennessee to sell land at less than national minimum price, the legislature introduced a graduation system for the sale of the remaining lands in the district. An occupant was given six months to purchase 160 acres for $1.25 an acre; then for the next three months any one could buy the land at that price. Subsequently, the price was lowered to $1.00 an acre, then

[11] In 1825 the legislature provided that these and other school lands be sold and the revenue added to the school fund, but the state supreme court declared the law in violation of the Compact of 1806. After Congress in 1843 permitted their sale, practically all of the school lands were sold except for one tract in Polk County, which is still owned by the state.

50 cents, then 25 cents, and finally 12½ cents. The inventor of this graduation scheme was J. C. Mitchell, who seems also to have been the source of Senator Thomas H. Benton's similar proposal for the national land system.

The remaining portion of the Cherokee Reservation, called the Ocoee District, between the Hiwassee and Tennessee rivers and the southern boundary of the state, plus the foothills region between the Hiwassee and the Little Tennessee rivers, became available for white settlement when the Cherokee were moved west in 1838. This area also, after being surveyed into townships and sections, was sold under a graduation system, with the prices ranging from $7.50 to one cent an acre. Ultimately, the revenue from the sales of land in the Hiwassee and Ocoee districts, except for $150,000 appropriated for internal improvements in 1830, became the major part of the common school fund of the state, which contained about $1,500,000 at the time of the outbreak of the Civil War.

SUGGESTED READINGS

General Accounts

Annie H. Abel, "The History of Events Resulting in Indian Consolidation West of the Mississippi," *American Historical Association, Annual Report*, 1906 (2 vols., Washington, D. C., 1908), I, 241–45, 278–82, 370–81; Abernethy, *Frontier to Plantation*, Ch. 11; Gerald M. Capers, Jr., *The Biography of a River Town—Memphis: Its Heroic Age* (Chapel Hill, 1939; New Orleans, 1966), 17–74; Cotterill, *Southern Indians*, Chs. 7, 10–13; Folmsbee, Corlew, and Mitchell, *Tennessee*, I, Ch. 15; Grant Foreman, *Indian Removal* (Norman, 1932), 229–314; Garrett and Goodpasture, *Tennessee*, 130–54; Govan and Livingood, *Chattanooga Country*, Chs. 4–6; Hamer, *Tennessee*, I, Ch. 18; Reginald Horsman, *Expansion and American Indian Policy, 1789–1812* (East Lansing, Michigan, 1967); Francis P. Prucha, *American Indian Policy in the Formative Years* (Cambridge, 1962); White, *Messages*, I, 50–51, 110–11, 148–52, 193–204, 227–30, 245–55, 291–93, 354–56; Williams, *West Tennessee*, 84–93, 283–306.

Specialized Accounts

Althea Bass, *Cherokee Messenger* (Norman, 1936); Guy B. Braden, "The Colberts and the Chickasaw Nation," *THQ*, XVII (Sept.–Dec.,

1958), 237–47, 318–35; Brown, *Old Frontiers*, Chs. 27–36; Stanley J. Folmsbee and Anna Grace Catron, "David Crockett: Congressman," ETHS *Publ.*, No. 29 (1957), 40–78; Grant Foreman, *Sequoyah* (Norman, 1938); Ralph H. Gabriel, *Elias Boudinot, Cherokee, and His America* (Norman, 1941); Edmund C. Gass, "The Constitutional Opinions of Justice John Catron," ETHS *Publ.*, No. 8 (1936), 54–73; Jones, "Public Lands of Tennessee," *THQ*, XXVII, 13–36; Henry T. Malone, "Return Jonathan Meigs: Indian Agent, Extraordinary," ETHS *Publ.*, No. 28 (1956), 3–22; Malone, *Cherokees*, Chs. 5–11; O. B. Peake, *A History of the United States Indian Factory System, 1795–1822* (Denver, 1954); James E. Roper, "Marcus Winchester and the Earliest Years of Memphis," *THQ*, XXI (Dec., 1962), 326–51; Charles C. Royce, "Indian Land Cessions in the United States," U. S. Bureau of American Ethnology, *18th Annual Report* (Washington, D. C., 1899), Pt. II, 600–754; Royce, "Cherokee Nation," *5th Annual Report*, 212–28, 254–94; Charles G. Sellers, Jr., *James K. Polk, Jacksonian, 1795–1843* (Princeton, 1957); Sellers, *James K. Polk, Continentalist, 1843–1846* (Princeton, 1966); Sellers, "James K. Polk's Political Apprenticeship," ETHS *Publ.*, No. 25 (1953), 37–53; St. George L. Sioussat, "Tennessee and the Removal of the Cherokee," *Sewanee Review*, XVI (July, 1908), 337–44; Marion L. Starkey, *The Cherokee Nation* (New York, 1946); Joseph Tracy, *History of the American Board of Commissioners for Foreign Missions* (Worcester, Mass., 1940); Robert S. Walker, *Torchlights to the Cherokees: The Brainerd Mission* (New York, 1931); Woodward, *Cherokees*, Chs. 6–10.

The "First Tennesseans" were the Indians. Pictured above are Indian burial grounds at Chucalissa in Shelby County.

David Crockett, frontiersman and hero of the Battle of the Alamo, was a humorist and writer as well as a congressman.

This typical pioneer woman was the wife of James Robertson, sometimes called the "Father of Tennessee."

Top: Fort Nashborough, existing now in partial replica, was the site of the "Battle of the Bluffs"; *below*: Rocky Mount, near Johnson City, was the first capitol of the Southwest Territory.

op: Blount Mansion, home of the territorial governor, was one of the first frame ouses west of the Blue Ridge; *below*: This block house at Benton guarded the supply nes to Andrew Jackson at the Battle of New Orleans.

The Dean Cornwell murals, depicting the history of Tennessee, are on the walls of the State Office Building at Nashville. The mural above shows some of the explorers and pioneers who figured prominently in the early history of the state.

The panel above represents later historical figures who contributed to the further development of the state.

Fiery Indian fighter and hero of the Battle of New Orleans, Andrew Jackson was the nation's seventh President.

Jackson's home, The Hermitage, is a National Historic Landmark.

Howard Pyle painted this view of the charge of Minnesota troops in the Battle of Nashville.

11. ࿔ Jacksonian Domination of Tennessee Politics

WHEN CONSTITUTIONAL LIMITATIONS prevented Governor McMinn from seeking another term in 1821, a lively contest developed between Edward Ward and William Carroll. Ward, supported by Andrew Jackson, had many qualifications for the governorship, but he lacked knowledge of frontier campaign methods, and without this knowledge he could not be elected. Although he was a man of wealth, education, and stately bearing, Ward's enemies described him only as a Federalist whose "Virginia bearing," affluence, and social position made him unacceptable to frontiersmen. Carroll, however, was a military hero whose Tennessee troops had withstood the heaviest shock of the British attack at New Orleans. Furthermore, the failure of his business establishment in Nashville after the panic of 1819 had left him "a poor man." These "qualifications" seemed unbeatable on the American frontier, and Carroll surprised no one when he overwhelmed the Virginian by one of the largest majorities received by a candidate in all the gubernatorial elections of the nineteenth century.

Carroll was an able governor, and he served longer in that office than any other man. He was exceedingly popular during his twelve years of service. With no opposition in 1823, 1825, and 1829, Carroll had little difficulty in achieving reelection in 1831 and 1833. Carroll's accomplishments—internal improvements, sound fiscal policy, educational development, reform measures, and constitutional revision—were many. Important as Carroll's administration was, Tennesseans were concerned even more with Andrew Jackson's

exciting demonstration of political strength in the presidential election of 1824, his four-year political war with John Quincy Adams,
and his elevation to the White House in 1829.

Presidential Elections of 1824 and 1828 ᗉᔌ Perhaps no
more controversial figure than Andrew Jackson has performed on
the American political stage. Contemporaries seldom were neutral
where he was concerned; they either loved him or despised him.
Some of the great state and national leaders of the times became
his bitter enemies; yet, to thousands of laborers and yeoman farmers
he was the "Old Hero"—the "Hero of the Common Man."[1]

Jackson emerged from the Battle of New Orleans (1815) as a
national hero, and his friends immediately attached political significance to his victory. Carroll, who had served as second in command under him at New Orleans, approached him on the question
of becoming a presidential candidate. On a recent visit with political leaders in nearby states, Carroll reported, he had talked with
many who expressed a distinct interest in seeing the Old Hero's
name on the ballot in 1820. Jackson said little, but John Overton,
John Eaton, and other state leaders also urged him to run.

While Jackson said little, events in Florida three years after the
Battle of New Orleans again brought him into the national lime-
light. A group of Seminole Indians, escaped slaves, freebooters, and
smugglers, using the Spanish-owned peninsula as a base of operations, for several years had robbed and terrified American settlements in Georgia, South Carolina, and Alabama. In 1818, Secretary
of War John C. Calhoun had dispatched Jackson to the Florida
frontier with orders to "adopt the necessary measures" to end the
border troubles. Jackson later claimed that Congressman John Rhea
of Blountville also had indicated to him that the administration

---

[1] Both contemporaries and historians of a later period have described Jackson as a
complex figure. James Parton, writing little more than a decade after Jackson's death,
despaired at the conflicting sources which his research uncovered and concluded that
his subject was both a patriot and a traitor. Old Hickory, wrote Parton, "was one of
the greatest generals, and wholly ignorant of the art of war; . . . a writer brilliant,
elegant, eloquent, without being able to compose a correct sentence, or spell words
of four syllables. The first statesman, he never devised, he never framed a measure. He
was the most candid of men, and was capable of the profoundest dissimulation. [He
was] a most law-defying, law-obeying citizen. A stickler for discipline, he never hesitated to disobey his superior. [He was] a democratic autocrat . . . [an] urbane
savage . . . [and an] atrocious saint." *Andrew Jackson*, I, vii.

would not object if he invaded the peninsula and, "without implicating the Government," took possession of it on behalf of the United States. Accordingly, when a band of renegades appeared in Georgia, Jackson chased them back into Florida. Not content with that, he destroyed several Spanish posts, drove the governor and garrison out of Pensacola, executed two British subjects, and returned to United States territory. The episode caused President Monroe considerable embarrassment as he tried to explain the action to Spanish and British authorities, and it required the skillful diplomacy of Secretary of State John Quincy Adams to smooth over the international quarrel. To the Western frontiersmen, however, Jackson now was even a greater hero. Thousands of Tennesseans hailed him in Nashville when he arrived from Florida and unanimously agreed that his conduct was "marked with energy, valor, skill and patriotism, not surpassed in the annals of our country."

Although Jackson's raid interrupted negotiations with Spain for the purchase of Florida and the adjustment of the disputed boundaries of the Louisiana Purchase, in the long run the raid facilitated the completion of the Adams-Onís Treaty of 1819 by which those aims were achieved. After the treaty was ratified in 1821, Jackson was named governor of the Territory of Florida, but he resigned and returned to Nashville after serving for only a few months.

In the meantime, remnants of the old Blount faction in Tennessee politics fought for their political lives. Although Tennessee had entered the Union as a strong Republican state, factions within the party had developed soon after statehood. One, tracing its origins to the leadership of Territorial Governor William Blount, numbered among its leaders John Overton, Pleasant M. Miller, and former governors Willie Blount and Joseph McMinn. Overton and Jackson had become fast friends as early as 1789 when they found lodging together in the home of Jackson's future mother-in-law, the widow of Colonel John Donelson. Overton became a lawyer, bank president, planter, and land speculator—pursuits which made him known later as "the wealthiest man in Tennessee." Miller, a Knoxville businessman, politician, and son-in-law of the late William Blount, became identified with Overton as the master strategists for Jackson.

The other group in the Republican party was known as the John Sevier faction. This group, still potent by 1820, had lacked a strong leader after Sevier's death in 1815. They looked to Andrew Erwin, a planter and land speculator of Bedford County, as their leader and numbered Senator John Williams and Congressmen John Cocke and Newton Cannon among their members. They recently had discovered a champion in William Carroll who by 1821 no longer considered Jackson as his friend and who soundly defeated the Jackson-Overton backed candidacy of Edward Ward. Jackson's display of political strength in 1824 and 1828 quieted leaders of this group for several years, but shortly after his second term began they appeared again at the forefront and weakened the Chief's grip on the state.

The remnants of the old Blount faction considered running Jackson for the presidency in 1820 but became discouraged by the apparent popularity of President Monroe. Soon after the Virginian's second inauguration, however, they pushed Jackson forward as a presidential contender for 1824. They received considerable encouragement in July, 1822, when members of the state legislature unanimously endorsed him. Describing Jackson as one who was "calm in deliberation, cautious in decision, and efficient in action," the legislators concluded that "the welfare of the country may be safely entrusted to the hands of him who has experienced every privation, and encountered every danger to promote its safety, its honor, and its glory." Jackson said little, but he encouraged his supporters a few months later by declining President Monroe's offer of an appointment as minister to Mexico.

Serious debate ensued within the Jackson ranks early in 1823. The three-pronged question among the leaders was whether to run Jackson for governor in 1823 against Carroll, whether to have him oppose incumbent John Williams for the United States Senate, or whether to let him appear untested in the presidential race in 1824.[2] A vigorous minority feared that the Hero might suffer defeat in a state contest which would destroy his chances for the presidency; therefore, the minority insisted that he not become involved at all until 1824. Pleasant M. Miller, however, entreated Jackson to run for governor; he contended that the General could purge the state administration of the Carroll-Erwin men, enhance his own prestige

[2] Jackson and Williams had been enemies since 1814, when Colonel Williams refused to comply with Jackson's request to release some arms in his possession for use by another commander in the Gulf campaign.

in time for the presidential contest of 1824, and, incidentally, help elect a legislature which would send Miller instead of Williams to the United States Senate. The majority, however, was convinced that Jackson could defeat Williams in the Senate race and that the victory would increase Jackson's prestige and make him a viable presidential candidate. On the day before the contest, this group hastened to the Hermitage to urge the Old Hero to go to Murfreesboro and appear before the legislators. Jackson rode all night in order to arrive in time. His personal appearance was sufficient to win the undecided voters, and, accordingly, he was elected by a vote of 35 to 25. The General apparently had little ambition to go to the Senate, but his supporters attached great significance to the victory and openly boasted that it would elect him President in 1824.

People across the country viewed the approaching presidential election with great interest. In each of the earlier contests the party nominee had been selected by a congressional caucus, that is, by the party members serving in Congress. Because only the Republican party was active (the Federalists did not nominate a candidate after 1816), many people believed that nomination by caucus would be unfair. Opponents of "King Caucus" found vociferous support in the West where seeds of democracy were germinating rapidly and where the settlers, deprived of much influence in the nation's capital, hoped to ride into power on the shoulders of Jackson or Henry Clay. Therefore, when the caucus nominated William Crawford of Georgia (who, incidentally, had quarreled earlier with Jackson), Western Republicans vowed that they would not support the nominee. When Western politicians could not agree on a single candidate, both Jackson and Clay were pushed forward. John Quincy Adams, son of the second President, was selected by party stalwarts in the East. John C. Calhoun, whose supporters urged him to run, compromised by agreeing to accept the vice presidency.

The outcome of the election exceeded the dreams of even Jackson's most sanguine supporters, although Adams and not Jackson became President. Jackson carried eleven states and received 99 electoral votes to Adams's 84, Crawford's 41, and Clay's 37. Of the popular votes, he polled 152,901 to 114,023 for Adams. Because Jackson did not have a majority of the electoral votes, it became the duty of the House of Representatives to choose the President from the top three candidates. Crawford during the campaign had suffered a stroke of paralysis and thus was not given serious consideration. Adams was elected, thanks to the powerful influence of Clay, whose years of service in Washington enabled him to know personally most of the members of the lower house.

The Old Hero accepted his defeat graciously until he heard that Adams had appointed Clay as secretary of state. The apparent "bargain and corruption" caused Jackson to fly into a rage. He vowed he would get even with the "conniving" Adams and his chief Cabinet official, "The Judas of the West." Shortly after the inauguration Jackson resigned his Senate seat and returned to Tennessee determined to devote much time to plans for the campaign in 1828; Jackson swore that he would unseat those who had been guilty of such "barefaced corruption." He was succeeded in the Senate by Hugh Lawson White of Knoxville.

Jackson remained in relative quietude during the next three years, but he kept up a voluminous correspondence with many of the leading politicians of the time. His work made easier the task of John Eaton of Nashville who took the lead in strengthening the Jackson faction and who was especially pleased with the consummation of an alliance with some of the supporters of Vice President Calhoun. Eaton urged the old-line Jackson men, including Overton, John Coffee, William B. Lewis, Felix Grundy, and Sam Houston, to work amicably with Duff Green, Thomas Hart Benton, Martin Van Buren, and other converts. Van Buren, a Crawford supporter in 1824, was viewed as the most valuable of the new men because it was believed that he could control the vote in New York. Benton, then in Missouri, had fired a bullet into Jackson's shoulder several decades before in Nashville but had become reconciled to the Chief shortly after Jackson's election to the Senate in 1823. Duff Green was editor of the *United States Telegraph*, a Washington daily, and became one of Jackson's foremost supporters.

The General opened the campaign of 1828 on the same note that he had closed the one of four years earlier—the charge of a "corrupt bargain" between Adams and Clay. The campaign scarcely had begun when it degenerated into one of mudslinging in which supporters of each candidate sought to outdo the other in propagating malicious charges. The Adams men found plenty of ammunition. After Jackson and Rachel Donelson Robards had married in the mistaken belief that the Virginia legislature had granted her a divorce from her first husband, Jackson's enemies widely publicized this unfortunate happening in addition to representing Rachel as a woman unfit by refinement or talent to become the First Lady. Critics also condemned the Hero for executing six deserters in the Creek campaign of 1814; animadversions ran the gamut from slave peddling to dueling, and from associating with Aaron Burr to misconduct in Florida.

Adams's public career did not offer so fertile a field for political propagandists, but the Jackson press did not hesitate to stretch the truth or to fabricate new stories. They accused the President of misuse of funds, "wasteful extravagance," and misconduct while minister to Russia; they claimed he was a Federalist masquerading in Republican clothing, a "Sabbath breaker," and a menace to the country's most sacred religious and political institutions. Tennessee legislators added to the abuse. Unanimously they resolved that "many of the measures" of the Adams administration were "injurious to the interests and dangerous to the liberties" of the nation. The "surest remedy for these evils," the legislators resolved, "is the election of Andrew Jackson to the Presidency of this Union."

Careful political observers conceded a Jackson victory several weeks before the election. Backwoodsmen of the West and factory workers of the East may not have comprehended Clay's American system and Adams's nationalism, but they had no trouble understanding the Old Hero's simple message of corruption and aristocracy in Washington. Jackson embodied their conceptions of democracy, and they readily united with him to expel the "aristocratic rascals" from the nation's capital. Jackson carried the West and the South solidly and received all of the electoral votes of Pennsylvania and part of those of New York, Maryland, and Maine; his margin was 178 to Adams's 83. In Tennessee, where he received 44,193 votes to 2,240 for Adams, Jackson appeared to have few enemies.

The contest had captured the imagination of the people and had brought out thousands of voters, many of whom had not voted before. Twice as many Tennesseans went to the polls as had voted in 1824. The yeoman farmers and frontiersmen of the West, joined by laborers and mechanics of the East, had selected one of their own as the nation's Chief Executive and had therefore proved that the Virginia dynasty and aristocratic East were not invincible at the polls.

Sam Houston Elected Governor ఇ Governor Carroll, having served for three consecutive terms, was constitutionally ineligible for reelection in 1827. He hoped to replace John Eaton, who had been in the Senate since his appointment to succeed George W. Campbell in 1818, but Carroll did not have the support of Jackson, and even the most casual observer readily perceived that the Chief had the legislature of 1825–26 firmly in his grasp. Everyone knew that Eaton was one of Old Hickory's strongest supporters and closest friends, and tales of the governor's jealousy and lack of admiration for Jackson were widely repeated. Rumors that the governor was "Henry Clay's confidential correspondent and . . . Adams' secret well wisher" were not abated by his letters of denial to legislators and his public statement that he would support the General in 1828. Consequently, in November, 1826, Eaton was reelected to another term, and Carroll applied his political talents to the gubernatorial campaign of Sam Houston.

Houston won easily with Jackson's and Carroll's support. Former Governor Willie Blount failed miserably in an attempt at a political comeback, and Newton Cannon, a wealthy Williamson County planter who was handicapped by the charge that he was unfriendly to Jackson, did not offer substantial opposition. Houston was inaugurated on October 1, 1827.

The colorful and dramatic Houston was born in Virginia, in 1793, but moved at the age of fourteen with his widowed mother and eight brothers and sisters to Blount County. The "wild and impetuous" youth (as Houston later described himself) soon ran away from home and took up abode with the Cherokee Indians for three years; the Cherokee named him "The Raven." Enlisting in the United States army in 1813, he served under Jackson in the Creek campaign and received a wound at Horseshoe Bend which was to plague him for the rest of his life. During the campaign he developed great admiration for Jackson, and the two became fast friends.

For a decade after the war Houston followed a varied career, including the study and practice of law at Lebanon and Nashville, election to the office of district attorney general, and service as major general of the Tennessee militia. In August, 1823, he was elected to Congress, with the support of Carroll and Jackson, and remained in Washington until 1827. He was an active supporter of Old Hickory in 1824 and again in 1828.

Houston's term was but an interlude in the Carroll administrations. The Raven continued the sound fiscal policies and the reforms instituted by Carroll and was considered as a protégé of his predecessor.

Fortune for Houston began to turn soon after his inauguration. Charges were brought against him by the Masonic Lodge at Nashville for dueling, and in 1828 he was expelled from the order. At the same time, a noticeable coolness developed between him and his erstwhile mentor, Carroll. The former governor, chagrined at not being chosen for the United States Senate, and somewhat miffed at Houston for openly accepting support from both himself and Jackson, made plans to return to the governor's chair in 1829. Houston denied that he had agreed to serve but one term. He exhibited considerable independence and, no doubt with Jackson's encouragement, promptly announced that he would oppose Carroll's attempt to perpetuate his control of the state administration by seeking reelection.

A contest between the two was settled when Houston suddenly surprised everyone by resigning the gubernatorial office, withdrawing from the race for reelection, and taking up temporary residence again with a group of Cherokee Indians who had moved to the West. He became the first governor in the history of the state not to serve out the term for which he was elected.

Houston's strange conduct generally has been attributed to domestic troubles. The romantically inclined chieftain (his Indian friends had referred to him as "Squaw's Man") had decided after his election as governor to "settle down." Consequently, on January 22, 1829, Houston, then thirty-five, married eighteen-year-old Eliza Allen, whose father, Colonel John Allen of Gallatin, was his close friend and admirer. The young bride remained with him for only a short while before she returned to her parents in Gallatin. Houston refused to issue a public statement about his marital affairs, but he wrote to Colonel Allen that Eliza had been "cold" to him and that he did not believe she loved him. After a brief sojourn with the Indians Houston headed for Texas. He secured a divorce, was married again, and reared a family. His claim to greatness rests more with his accomplishments in the Lone Star State than in Tennessee.

Houston's resignation elevated William Hall, speaker of the senate, to the governorship. Born in North Carolina in 1775, Hall had moved with his parents to Castalian Springs in Sumner County when he was only ten years old. At the age of twenty-two he was elected to the house of representatives, and later served four terms in the senate. During the War of 1812 he fought under Jackson and rose to the rank of brigadier general. Hall's term of office as governor was only five and one-half months. No attempt apparently was made to push him into the race in 1829, but he was elected to Congress two years after he retired from the gubernatorial chair. Carroll, therefore, was elected to a fourth term without opposition.

Constitutional Convention of 1834 › Perhaps the most important accomplishment of Carroll's long tenure in the governor's office was the revision of the state's fundamental law, in 1834. For three decades legislators and interested citizens had expressed interest in a constitutional convention. A legislative move in 1806 to submit the question to the people was defeated by one vote. In 1819 the question was submitted to the qualified voters. Those wanting a convention argued that the time had come to dispossess the large landholders in the rich valleys of East Tennessee and the Cumberland Basin of their special tax privileges which makers of the constitution of 1796 had given them by declaring that all land should be taxed equally regardless of its value. Opponents, however, perhaps remembering the Philadelphia convention of 1787, argued that it was too dangerous to place such unlimited powers in the hands of a small group of convention delegates. At any rate, the proposal was defeated. A move for a convention also was defeated in 1821 and again a few years later. The democratic trend ushered in by Andrew Jackson, however, accentuated the need for a reevaluation of the organic law. Considerably more interest was shown in 1831 when the question again was submitted to the people, but the efforts of the revisionists fell short by about 2,000 votes. Two years later when the question came up again, the people voted for a convention by more than 8,000 votes. The outcome represented a culmination of efforts of many years toward constitutional democracy. The pressure for reform had come principally from rural West and Middle Tennessee, while opposition came largely from the old established counties such as Carter, Davidson, Greene, Jefferson, Sullivan, and Washington.

The leaven of Jacksonian Democracy, unlike anything before it, had inspired the underprivileged to seek to wrest some of the powers and privileges from "the lords of the soil." They wanted, as might have been expected from the rising common men, tax relief and more equitable representation. Therefore, it was only natural that these issues should become the principal ones at the convention.

Sixty delegates—18 from East Tennessee, 30 from the middle division, and 12 from the west—assembled on May 19, 1834, at Nashville. Few of them had claim to distinction, but former Governor Willie Blount, Newton Cannon, Adam Huntsman, Robert J. McKinney, Terry H. Cahal, William B. Carter, and Francis B. Fogg were exceptions. Blount acted as temporary chairman until Carter, of Carter County, was elected president.

The people as a whole apparently had confidence in the delegates, and it is highly doubtful whether at anytime in 1833 or 1834 very many, if any, people seriously feared that a group of "radicals" would gain control and grossly upset the status quo. The editor of the Knoxville *Register*, one of the more conservative newspapers, voiced no profound fears, and the editor of a Nashville paper thought that the "sterling integrity and patriotism" of the delegates would insure Tennesseans of a revision devoid of extremes. The editor of another mid-state paper found "little to invite our censure," and "A Farmer," writing in the Nashville *Whig*, pointed to the growth of American democracy since 1796 and urged that confidence be placed in the delegates. Carter and Cahal were known as strong conservatives who had expressed fears of extremism, but Carter's election as president of the convention must have quieted the fears of both.

Taxation and representation were the most important matters at the convention. For many years the taxation clause—which provided for equal taxation of all land (except town lots which could be taxed as high as two hundred acres of land)—had been a thorn in the flesh of small farmers who occupied land less valuable than that of others, especially in the valley and basin areas. When people asked why the constitution-makers of 1796 had imposed this restriction upon the taxing power of the legislature, they were told that in 1796 there were few improvements on the land anyway, that it was done to encourage persons to invest in Tennessee lands, and that the founding fathers wanted to encourage landowners to improve their lands by guaranteeing that improvements would not increase taxes. Changing economic conditions had modified things, said the delegates from the rural counties, and Adam Huntsman of Madison County and John A. McKinney led the fight for a change. They showed how "the poor man" might pay twenty-five times more tax money than "the rich man." They condemned a system whereby a town lot worth $10,000 and earning an annual rent of $600 should be taxed for the same amount as one worth $20. By a vote of 43 to 13 the delegates adopted a provision stating that "all property should be taxed according to its value; that value to be ascertained in such manner as the Legislature shall direct . . . ."

Legislative representation also was debated extensively. Conservatives wanted to retain unamended the provision which apportioned representation on the basis of free taxable inhabitants and limited the assembly to forty representatives and twenty senators. Especially objectionable to them was a movement led by Adam Huntsman, James Scott (representing Perry, Hardin, and McNairy counties), and others from other rural districts, to secure equal representation for the counties. Robert M. Burton of Lebanon believed that such a scheme would return Tennessee to the "rotten borough system of England," and asked, "Shall hills, mountains and rocks . . . be the basis of representation?" Cahal agreed. "Why [should] four hundred . . . voters in one county," he asked rhetorically, "possess as much political power . . . as four thousand in another . . . ?" After several days of debate delegates compromised by agreeing to apportion representation according to the number of qualified voters and to increase the number of representatives to a maximum of ninety-nine (seventy-five until the population reached one and one-half million) and of senators to one-third the number of representatives.

Another change reflecting the democratic spirit of the times was a provision which gave voters the right to elect county officials. Under the existing constitution, members of the county courts, chosen by the legislature for life, elected sheriffs, trustees, coroners, and other officials. Such a practice had bred many abuses. West H. Humphreys of Fayette County believed that the popular election of all officials would "call forth the best talents" and improve the quality of office holders. Delegates agreed and gave voters the right to select justices of the peace, sheriffs, trustees, registers, and other public officials for specified terms of office.

The slavery question had developed into a burning issue by 1834 and had been debated thoroughly in Virginia and other Southern states. Scores of memorials reached the convention, many of them asking for gradual emancipation. Tennesseans, however, like Virginians, decided not to tamper with the troublesome question. By a close vote of 30 to 27 they wrote into the constitution that the legislature could pass no laws for the emancipation of slaves without the consent of their owners. Free Negroes had voted under the old constitution, but under the new one they were denied that privilege.

Other changes were made. The legislature of 1843 was commanded to select a permanent location for the state's capital within the first week of its session. Duelists were disqualified from holding office, divorces could be granted only by the courts, and lotteries were prohibited. Judges could no longer hold office for life but were to be selected by the legislature for terms of twelve years.[3] Property qualifications were removed as a condition for office holding.

A significant change involved the amending process. Under the constitution of 1796, two-thirds of the legislators were given authority to submit to voters the question of a convention. If a majority of citizens voting for representatives wanted a convention at which revision would be considered, then the next General Assembly was commanded to call one. Under the constitutional provision of 1834, an assembly might propose amendments by a simple majority. The next legislature, to meet two years later, was required to act on the proposed changes; if members accepted the amendments by a two-thirds vote, the matter was to be submitted to the people for acceptance or rejection, but a majority of the number of votes for representatives was required for approval. Amendments could not be considered more often than once in six years. Interest-

---

[3] An amendment providing for the popular election of judges and district attorneys was approved in 1853. Efforts in 1858 to call another constitutional convention to limit the size of the state debt failed. No additional efforts to amend were made until after the Civil War.

ingly, the delegates retained a provision prohibiting ministers of the gospel from accepting seats in the legislature, but defeated efforts of prohibitionists to exclude alcoholics.

Unlike the delegates to the convention of 1796, those of 1834 directed that their work be submitted to the voters for rejection or approval. Consequently, on the first Thursday of March, 1835, the people went to the polls and accepted the revised constitution by a vote of 42,666 to 17,691. Only four counties—Davidson, Smith, Williamson, and Robertson—showed majorities against ratification. On March 27, Governor Carroll proclaimed the revised document to be the fundamental law of the state.

The decade of the 1820's was a highly significant one for Tennessee. Andrew Jackson, the pride of Tennessee and the West, in 1824 became the state's first presidential candidate, and four years later, the first president from the West. Jackson's election was of great importance for the people west of the mountains. During most of the decade and part of the succeeding one he was quite powerful in state politics. Tennessee produced other leaders of prominence. Governor William Carroll was one of the ablest and most successful governors ever to serve. He suggested many reforms, some of which were enacted into law during the 1820's and others during the decade that followed. Sam Houston represented the state in Congress and presided from the gubernatorial chair during the period. Felix Grundy and John Bell were among a half dozen other Tennesseans who were active on the national scene. Agitation for a revision of the state's fundamental law bore fruit in 1833 when Tennesseans voted favorably for the first constitutional convention since the organic law had been framed in 1796. The approval given by the people to the work of the delegates was indicative of their belief that convention members had accomplished well the task assigned to them.

During the 1830's Tennesseans joined in the reaction against the Hero of the Hermitage; Jackson lived for almost a decade after he vacated the White House in 1837, but at no time during this period did a Democratic presidential candidate win the electoral votes of Tennessee. This seemingly anomalous conduct on the part of the voters of the Volunteer State is discussed in the next chapter.

SUGGESTED READINGS

General Accounts
Abernethy, *Frontier to Plantation*, Chs. 15–16; Bassett, *Jackson*; Claude C. Bowers, *The Party Battles of the Jackson Period* (Boston, 1929); Chambers, *Old Bullion Benton*; Clement Eaton, *Henry Clay and the Art of American Politics* (Boston, 1957); Folmsbee, Corlew, and Mitchell, *Tennessee*, I, Ch. 26; Llerena Friend, *Sam Houston, The Great Designer* (Austin, 1954); Hamer, *Tennessee*, I, Ch. 19; James, *Life of Jackson*; James, *The Raven*; Arthur M. Schlesinger, Jr., *The Age of Jackson* (Boston, 1945); Glyndon G. Van Deusen, *The Jacksonian Era, 1828–1848* (New York, 1959); John W. Ward, *Andrew Jackson, Symbol of an Age* (Oxford, 1955); White, *Messages*, II–III.

Specialized Accounts
Abernethy, "Andrew Jackson," *AHR*, XXXIII (Oct., 1927), 64–77; Louis R. Harlan, "Public Career of William Berkeley Lewis," *THQ*, VII (March, June, 1948), 3–37, 118–51; Isabel Thompson Kelsay, "The Presidential Campaign of 1828," *ETHS Publ.*, No. 5 (1933), 69–80; Richard P. McCormick, "New Perspectives on Jacksonian Politics," *AHR*, LXV (Jan., 1960), 288–301; Chase C. Mooney, "The Question of Slavery and the Free Negro in the Tennessee Constitutional Convention of 1834," *JSH*, XII (Nov., 1946), 487–509; Charles Grier Sellers, Jr., "Jackson Men with Feet of Clay," *AHR*, LXII (April, 1957), 537–51; Culver H. Smith, "Propaganda Technique in the Jackson Campaign of 1828," *ETHS Publ.*, No. 6 (1934), 44–66; Florence Weston, *The Presidential Election of 1828* (Washington, D. C., 1938).

12. ࣿ *The Rise of the Whig Party*

For two decades after Jackson's brilliant victory at New Orleans in 1815, the political vocabulary of the people of Tennessee could be summed up in the words, "Andrew Jackson." While there is probably little truth in the legend that Tennessee backwoodsmen still wrote in the Old Hero's name on their ballots ten years after his death, the story does serve to illustrate the tenacious hold which Jackson had on the popular imagination. The masses viewed him as one of their own, one who shared their opinions of government, their suspicions, and their credulities. When Tennesseans gave Jackson a tremendous majority in 1824, 1828, and 1832, few dreamed that before the ballots had been counted in 1836 a reaction against the Chief would develop and that Tennessee, where first were planted the seeds of Jacksonian Democracy, would become a hotbed of Whiggery.

Few people ever were neutral where Jackson was concerned. The strong-willed descendant of Scotch-Irish parentage took a vigorous stand on most public issues and either won or repulsed people by his strong words and actions. Able leaders, such as Sam Houston and James K. Polk, and thousands of "common men" in the Southwest and much of the East were attracted to him personally. Some men, including Hugh Lawson White, John Bell, Ephraim Foster, and Balie Peyton, were not personally attracted to Jackson but supported the broadening of the country's democratic base which the Jackson program sought to accomplish. Others supported Jackson because they were opportunists and wished to ride the bandwagon. On the other hand, there were those who for various personal reasons disliked the Chief and watched carefully for an opportunity to dislodge him from power and from the affections of the people. This group, which included Senator John Williams of Knoxville, Congressman Newton Cannon of Williamson County, Congressman David Crockett of West Tennessee, and Andrew Erwin, a wealthy planter and politician from Bedford County—not to mention many leaders outside the state such as Henry Clay, John Q. Adams, and Daniel Webster—formed the nucleus of the opposition which blossomed into the Whig party late in Jackson's second term.

John Williams, a brother-in-law of Senator Hugh Lawson White, had considered Jackson his friend until the Creek War of 1813–14. Animosity developed, however, after Jackson threatened to court-martial Williams for disobeying an order to turn over his arms and ammunition to an East Tennessee militia leader, General Nathaniel W. Taylor. The Knoxvillian was elected to the United States Senate in 1815 and, as a senator during the Seminole investigation in 1819, vigorously attacked the Old Chief for his invasion of Florida. In 1823 Jackson defeated Williams for the Senate by only ten votes, thus embittering the senator and his supporters.

Newton Cannon had incurred the enmity of Jackson in 1812 when, as a youthful juror in the case of *State of Tennessee* v. *Magness*, he had voted for the acquittal of David Magness who was on trial for the murder of Jackson's close friend, Patton Anderson. Cannon further incurred the wrath of the Hero during the Creek campaign when, after leading a regiment to Jackson's aid, he brought the regiment back to Tennessee immediately upon the expiration of the soldiers' three months' enlistment period, despite vigorous objection from Jackson. Cannon subsequently was elected to Congress where on many issues he voted in a manner which incurred additional disapproval of Old Hickory.

Crockett had acquired a large following in West Tennessee, and became the spokesman against Jackson in the frontier region. He had been a member of the General Assembly in 1823 and had voted for Williams instead of Jackson in the contest for senator. Crockett entered Congress in 1827 as a supporter of Jackson's candidacy for President, but cooled toward the Hero soon after the election and opposed both Jackson's public land policy and his stand on removing the Cherokee Indians. The President turned the full force of his political machine against Crockett's bid for reelection in 1831 and defeated him. Crockett returned to Congress in 1833 but was defeated in 1835 when the Jackson forces brought out Adam Huntsman of Jackson.

Andrew Erwin was the Chief's bitter enemy of long standing, the quarrel having stemmed from the Dickinson-Jackson duel of 1806. The widow and small children that Dickinson left when Old Hickory's fatal bullet struck him in the chest were Erwin's daughter and grandchildren, and Erwin never forgave him. He became a master strategist of the anti-Jackson faction after James Knox Polk, with Jackson's support, defeated him in a bid for Congress in 1825. In the meantime, Erwin and Jackson became engaged in litigation which brought Erwin to the brink of financial ruin. He therefore hated the Chief with a passion but bided his time for revenge.

The sparks of dissent, kept glowing by this nucleus of anti-Jackson men, probably would not have burst into open flame had not disagreements within the Jackson fold itself developed. John Bell, for example, never forgot that the Hero supported Felix Grundy when Bell ran for Congress from the Nashville district in 1827. Hugh Lawson White, Pleasant M. Miller, and William Carroll—the last named was no admirer of Jackson after 1821, but as governor Carroll kept up appearances by not criticizing him openly—were offended when Jackson named John Eaton to his Cabinet. Miller in disgust and anger wrote a blistering attack on the President because of the appointment. Others within the Jackson fold became offended when it appeared that John Overton, William B. Lewis, and Eaton influenced the Chief to the exclusion of all others. When in 1832 Jackson vetoed the bank bill and subsequently removed the funds from the bank, the commercial classes in the cities were aroused. Hundreds gathered in Nashville in April of 1833, for example, to defend Western credit and denounce as "unfortunate," "unwise," and "most unjust" a report prepared by Congressman Polk upholding Jackson. Supporters of Henry Clay's American System, especially in isolated East Tennessee and the recently opened Western District, were disappointed at the Chief's opposition to internal improvements. Also, admirers of John C. Calhoun, including many cotton planters, thought that Jackson unwisely had condemned the South Carolinian's theories of nullification and condemned the Chief for signing one of the protective tariff laws which South Carolina had nullified.

Despite the rumblings of unrest, both within and without the Jackson ranks in Tennessee, the Old General's national popularity still would have enabled him to remain in control at home had he not been resolute in his determination to name Martin Van Buren as his successor. The "Little Magician" (as Van Buren was called) was never popular in Tennessee. He had supported Crawford in 1824, but moved into the Jackson orbit after Jackson's manifestation of strength and Crawford's serious illness, and delivered to the Chief in 1828 a majority of the electoral votes of New York. For this and other patronizing deeds, Jackson had appointed Van Buren Secretary of State in 1829 and had arranged his nomination for Vice President on the Democratic ticket in 1832. Van Buren, however, had never won the confidence of the masses in Tennessee; they thought that he had mesmerized Jackson and they refused to consider Van Buren a suitable choice to carry on the banner of Jacksonian Democracy. Many people of the Volunteer State hoped that Hugh Lawson White could succeed the Old Hero. Knowing that the President's nod was tantamount to nomination, they turned the full impact of their wrath against Van Buren in an effort to dissuade the Chief. As events developed, John Bell and White became the leaders of the anti-Jackson faction in Tennessee, and concomitantly, the nemesis of the Van Buren-Jackson group.

John Bell Leads the Opposition ैॐ John Bell often is considered the "creator" of the Whig Party in Tennessee, although when his break with Jackson became apparent Bell had no intention of leaving the Democratic party. He had had little reason to support Jackson—on many issues he silently disagreed with the Chief's policies and was displeased at his coolness toward him—but Bell avoided an open break because of the President's political power. On the nullification issue, for example, Bell had been sympathetic to Calhoun. To friends, Bell conceded his concern about Jackson's Force Bill which he thought unwise and unconstitutional; yet, as chairman of the House Judiciary Committee, he felt that political expediency required his open support of the bill. That Bell was sympathetic to the United States Bank was well known and was pleasing to many of his Nashville constituents, although he voted in 1832 with the Administration forces against rechartering it.

A factor which greatly affected Bell's relations with Jackson was the rivalry between himself and Polk for the speakership of the House of Representatives in 1834. Polk had served in the House since 1825, and Bell had been elected two years later; both were able men and both wanted Jackson's support. The Chief did not endorse either candidate, but all members of Congress knew that Jackson favored Polk. Bell emerged the victor[1] after ten ballots, but his support came largely from those who had opposed Jackson on the bank and other issues. Both Jackson and Polk then proceeded to denounce Bell. Jackson hinted to friends that the new speaker was exhibiting too much independence and was "politically gone" unless he lent greater moral support to Jackson's anti-bank policy. Polk condemned him for alleged "treachery."

Although the breach between the President and the speaker widened daily, both hesitated to move in a manner which would bring an irreparable breach. Bell, in selecting committee chairmen, for example, named Polk to head the Ways and Means Committee and placed other Jackson men in high posts. On other matters Bell tried to be equally circumspect. Not long after he became speaker, however, it became known generally that he would not support Van Buren for the Democratic nomination in 1836, but that he might support Richard M. Johnson of Kentucky or Hugh Lawson White.

The possibility of White's candidacy had become a topic for political gossip as early as the constitutional convention of 1834. In December of that year the Tennessee congressional delegation, with the exception of Grundy, Polk, and Cave Johnson, met informally at the Washington residence of Congressman Balie Peyton and endorsed White for the nomination. The meeting at Peyton's was widely discussed. The legislature of Alabama endorsed White two weeks later, and leaders in other states discussed him as a possible nominee. Democratic leaders close to Jackson worried little about White's candidacy in a Democratic convention, for they were confident that he would be overwhelmed by Jackson's choice. They did, of course, fear a split in party ranks should White emerge as an opposition candidate.

[1] Late in the next year Polk again contested the speakership with Bell and, with Jackson's support, defeated him. Bell unsuccessfully challenged him in 1837, and Polk continued as speaker until his resignation in 1839 to become a candidate for governor.

White at first discouraged the movement to endorse him. He had entered the Senate in 1825 as a supporter of Old Hickory's candidacy for the presidency; after Jackson became Chief Executive, White supported him in matters regarding the bank and Indian removal, and Jackson in turn spoke of him as an "upright and incorruptible patriot." White was determined, however, not to be intimidated by either Jackson or Jackson men. White's supporters were encouraged considerably, then, when he stated publicly, after being told that Jackson had threatened to ruin him politically if he ran for President, that "despotic power" had never controlled him and that he would not "be the slave of any man or set of men."

When Congress adjourned in the spring of 1835 the struggle for political possession of Tennessee reached major proportions. Bell returned to Nashville in May and was asked by friends to deliver a major address at the city's fashionable Vauxhall Gardens. There, in a stirring oration on May 23, Bell "lighted the torch of revolt against the Democratic party." He strongly defended White's record, declared that White was an able and deserving friend of Jacksonian Democracy, and claimed that the Knoxvillian had been far more consistent in his support of the Chief's policies than had Van Buren. When Bell finished the two-hour address, none could question his open declaration of war on Jackson's choice for the White House. Bell left no stone unturned in his efforts to further the cause of Hugh Lawson White.

Jackson realized now that the supporters of White were serious and intended to press for the Democratic nomination regardless of what he might say about the matter. For Bell, he expressed words of scorn; it was he who had the Knoxvillian mesmerized and in the process had committed political suicide. For White, instead of indignation, Jackson expressed only sympathy. If the senator could be shaken free from his lethargy and the polluting grip of John Bell's "cunning and management," the Chief said, he could be induced to stop the revolt and thus save himself from political ruin. Especially disturbing to the President was the fact that many of the leading newspapers and local politicians in the state supported White and Bell, while the Jacksonians said little. "How is it," Jackson wrote Polk, "that there is no man in the . . . [Democratic] ranks to take the stump, and relieve Tennessee from her degraded attitude of abandoning principle to sustain men who have apostatised [*sic*] from the republican fold for the sake of office?" If he were free to do it, Jackson admonished Polk, he would set the state firmly upon its democratic legs and hurl "Mr. Bell, Davy Crockett and Company . . . from the confidence of the people." Their only object, Jackson believed, was to destroy him politically and to hand him "down to posterity as an old dotard, ruled by corrupt office holders . . . ."

In the meantime, Jackson had determined that the Democratic candidate should be chosen by a convention in which all the states were represented. (The caucus system had been discarded after the election of 1824.) Consequently, the Jacksonians proclaimed that in May, 1835, a free and open convention would be held in Baltimore. Accordingly, three days before Bell's Vauxhall Gardens speech, Democrats assembled as scheduled and nominated Van Buren as Jackson had planned. The White supporters made no effort to nominate their man, so convinced were they that the Jackson faction completely controlled the convention, which they called a "packed jury," and would secure the nomination of Van Buren. Tennessee Democrats sent no delegation, but a spectator from Murfreesboro, Edmund Rucker, was picked from the crowd, seated as the Tennessee "delegation," and permitted to cast all of the state's votes. The White-Bell group back home made much fun of the "Ruckerized convention," and the Jackson-Van Buren faction was mortified.

Newton Cannon Elected Governor ᕽᕁ In the meantime, although national issues obscured local ones, the Jackson forces could not ignore the gubernatorial campaign of 1835 in which Newton Cannon of Williamson County had challenged Governor Carroll. Cannon for many years had been a personal and political enemy of the Old General. During the early 1820's Cannon favored Crawford for the presidency; in 1827 Cannon had been an unsuccessful candidate for governor against Sam Houston, Jackson's choice; Cannon had flaunted the Chief by championing the United States Bank; and when Jackson successfully led the Democrats out of the old Republican party, Cannon became not a Democrat but a National Republican. The Bell-White revolt was the culmination of his dreams, and his announcement for governor contained a strongly worded endorsement of White for President.

Governor Carroll meanwhile permitted the word to circulate that he would be responsive to a movement for a seventh term. He received an endorsement from Jackson, who certainly preferred him to Cannon, and Carroll immediately became a forthright supporter of Van Buren. Carroll, it will be remembered, had served in the gubernatorial chair from 1821 to 1827 and again from 1829 to 1835. Because he had been a successful governor, generally beloved by the people, he probably would have been elected again had not a major constitutional issue been involved. The constitution clearly specified that no person should serve as governor for more than six years in any term of eight. Carroll argued, however, that a "new" constitution had been framed by the convention of 1834; therefore, he said, he should be able to serve another three consecutive terms under the "new" fundamental law. Flimsy argument that it was, Carroll ran in the expectation of establishing this interpretation of the constitutional revision and capitalizing upon his general popularity.

Cannon, although admittedly a man of mediocre talents, campaigned well on several good issues. The main one was the dubious constitutionality of a fourth term sought by his opponent, and Cannon kept it constantly before the people. Also very important, of course, was the claim that he had been among the first to push forward the candidacy of Hugh Lawson White for President against that of the Little Magician from New York whose cause Carroll espoused in order to win the Jackson support. Cannon also spoke out for internal improvements and public schools, and his stand favoring a national bank gained him status among the rising commercial classes in the cities.

The election results were not surprising. Cannon received 41,970 votes, Carroll polled 31,205, and a third candidate, West H. Humphreys, also a White supporter, received 8,054. Cannon's strength had come mainly from East Tennessee where White was most popular, and from the urban areas, particularly Nashville, where the Whig party soon was to reflect strength. The opposition victories did not end with Cannon. The White-Bell party captured the state legislature and elected to the house speakership an outspoken White supporter, Ephraim H. Foster. The Jackson-Van Buren men claimed that Carroll had been defeated on the constitutional question, but the White supporters insisted that the chief issue had been that of White against Van Buren.

The developments over the past few months stung the Old Chief to the quick, and he returned to Washington after the gubernatorial contest determined to crush the White movement and to destroy politically those associated with it. Jackson's chief lieutenants in Tennessee—Polk, Grundy, and Cave Johnson of Clarksville—were urged to work night and day to stop the revolt and win the bolters back to the fold.

In the meantime the Whig party was formed in other states. It consisted of a variety of dissatisfied groups, including the National Republicans, who followed John Quincy Adams and Henry Clay; the states rights Democrats, who had broken with Jackson when he threatened to use force against the nullifiers; the Anti-Masons, who had formed in a protest against all secret orders; and the pro-bank and pro-internal improvement Democrats. In brief, these groups had one thing in common; their dislike for Jackson. The Chief had acted in such a dictatorial manner, they said, that he resembled King George III of colonial days. Therefore, they called themselves "Whigs" to remind people of an earlier group of patriots who had resisted dictatorship. The coalescence of the group was no surprise to a seasoned politician like Jackson, but opposition to him in Tennessee was a thing which caught him completely off guard. Each new development cut him to the quick, and his reactions sometimes were in anger and sometimes in pain.

Highly distressing to the Old Chief was a resolution adopted in the United States Senate in March, 1834, censuring him for assuming "power not conferred by the constitution and the laws" after he ordered the removal of deposits from the United States Bank and dismissed a Cabinet member without the Senate's consent. Jackson's friends sought immediately to have the resolution repealed, or, as they said, "expunged." In Tennessee, the Chief's friends introduced resolutions in the house and senate to "instruct" Tennessee's senators in Washington to vote for expunging the censure. (Before the adoption of the Seventeenth Amendment in 1913, senators were of course elected by the state legislatures. Because of this, the legislative bodies from time to time enacted resolutions instructing their senators to vote for or against controversial legislation in Washington.) The legislators hoped also to embarrass White, who, as senator, opposed expunging but was expected to obey the instruction or resign.

White said little during the debate in Nashville and hid behind the cover of semantics. He had not been in favor of censuring the President in the first place, he said, but now that it had been written into the records he did not want to expunge it. To expunge, he said, would be to "obliterate" and "mutilate" the record and thus take away from those senators who had ruled on the matter earlier their right to vote. He would not object to "repealing," "rescinding," or "reversing" the resolution, but he would resign before he would vote to expunge.

Senator James L. Totten of West Tennessee and Representative Joseph C. Guild of Sumner County, both Jacksonians, sponsored resolutions instructing Tennessee's senators to vote to expunge the resolution. "To expunge from the journals" of the Senate, Guild said, was the only "rightful" and "adequate" remedy which could be adopted. They were answered ably by Representative Addison A. Anderson of Jefferson County. Tracing the word "expunge" to its Latin origin and its eventual adoption into the Anglo-Saxon language, Anderson said that it could mean only to "erase," "efface," and "obliterate." He opposed such action and he praised Senator White for his stand to maintain the integrity of the congressional journals. The resolution to instruct then was tabled and all efforts later to remove it failed, despite the fact that on more than one occasion Jackson sent the legislators free issues of the Washington *Globe* containing speeches by Thomas Hart Benton favoring expunging. This action probably hurt Jackson's cause more than it helped because he promptly was accused of trying to interfere with legislative proceedings.[2]

Hugh Lawson White Nominated for President ষ্ব Even before a vote could be taken on the resolution to instruct, the White group had forced to the floor the question of the senator's reelection.[3] He was chosen without a dissenting vote. Soon thereafter the

2 The censure was not expunged until 1837. With Thomas Hart Benton taking the lead, and Daniel Webster, Henry Clay, and John C. Calhoun vainly objecting, the Jacksonians had the satisfaction of seeing the Senate secretary draw lines around the resolution condemning the Chief and write across it, "Expunged by order of the Senate, this 16th day of January, 1837."

3 White had been elected in 1825 to fill out Jackson's unexpired term and was reelected in 1829.

legislators endorsed the Knoxvillian for President by a vote of 60 to 12 in the house and 23 to 2 in the senate. They also had a word to say about Jackson. While expressing general approval of the policies of the "distinguished Chief Magistrate" who was "qualified by his principles, energy and great popularity," the lawmakers condemned the "tendency to a usurpation of the rights and powers of the people" in the Baltimore convention and made a plea for freedom of elections.

White accepted the legislative endorsement, and Jackson promptly read him out of the party. A vigorous campaign ensued. The President spent the summer at the Hermitage, but his stay became a political campaign for Van Buren rather than a vacation. At several places Jackson denounced White as a "red hot Federalist." Bell, Jackson said, was an "apostate." In Nashville, the President was feted at a barbecue given at the Hermitage, and hundreds of guests heard him again denounce the senator as a "red hot Federalist" and a sympathizer with Whigs, nullifiers, and bank men.

The White forces were not idle. They made the chief issue that of White against Van Buren and not one of White versus Jackson. They presented the senator as the true wearer of the mantle of Jacksonian Democracy and not Van Buren. The White forces shunned any appearance of adhering to another party, although outside the state they generally were considered as Whigs. White on several occasions emphasized that he was not "in the confidence of any party" and stoutly maintained that the only matter of disagreement between him and the President was Jackson's officious and inexcusable determination to choose Van Buren as his successor.

Whigs over the nation considered White as one of their own. Realizing their lack of strength against an established party such as the Democrats and against a hero such as Jackson, the Whigs believed that their best chance for success lay in nominating several candidates in the hope that the choice of a President eventually would have to be made in the House of Representatives. Consequently, Daniel Webster of Massachusetts and William Henry Harrison of Ohio also became candidates.

The Jacksonians in Tennessee argued that a Jackson-controlled Democrat such as Van Buren would be better than running the risk of electing Harrison or Webster. The Nashville *Union*, which supported Van Buren, presented damaging statistics just before the election. White's name would appear on the ballot in only eleven of the twenty-six states; those eleven states had only 133 electoral votes, whereas 148 votes were necessary for election. Therefore, White's only hope was his selection by members of the House of Representatives, where Webster and Harrison men predominated.

Tennesseans voted for White despite the fact that his chances of being elected were slim indeed. The vote was 35,962 to 26,120. Even Old Hickory's Hermitage precinct was in the White fold, 61 to 20. It was a stunning blow to the Democratic party in Tennessee, and to the Old Hero himself, despite the fact that Van Buren won the presidency by a comfortable electoral majority.[4] White's strength came mainly from the eastern and western sections of the state. In the Jackson stronghold of Middle Tennessee, where Polk, Grundy, and Cave Johnson waged a hard battle, each candidate carried twelve counties.

The victory was more than a personal one for Bell and White. It was the birth pangs of the Whig party in Tennessee, although the White men had carefully avoided that label. For the next twenty years Tennessee was to be a two-party state, and Jackson, who died nine years later, was not to see his state again in the Democratic fold in a presidential contest.

Tennesseans in Texas ε While Tennesseans in Washington and at home fought political battles, others in Texas sought to cast aside the Mexican yoke. Tennesseans had been among the first Anglo-Americans to migrate to Texas. The Panic of 1819 served as an impetus for a westward movement. The establishment of Mexican independence in 1821 left Americans free to negotiate with the new government instead of the Spanish, and, therefore, Stephen F. Austin in that year negotiated a contract to establish a settlement of three hundred families, among whom were some Tennesseans. Within the next three years many others from Tennessee joined the exodus to Texas.

Foremost among Tennesseans who migrated westward was Sam Houston. After his unfortunate marriage he had resigned the gov-

---

[4] White carried only one other state—Georgia—but he did receive 40 per cent or more of the votes in Mississippi, North Carolina, Alabama, Virginia, and Missouri.

ernorship of the state and had moved west. A few years later Houston became active in Texas affairs and served as chairman of a committee which wrote a Texas constitution. By November, 1835, he was commander-in-chief of the Texas forces, and soon became the first president of the Lone Star Republic.

Others from Tennessee also became prominent in Texas affairs. George Campbell Childress wrote the Texas Declaration of Independence. He had been editor of the *National Banner and Nashville Advertiser* before his departure for Texas early in 1836. Childress applied for a grant of land in a colony headed by another Tennessean, Sterling C. Robertson, and immediately became important in public affairs. Two brothers, William H. and John A. Wharton, migrated several years before Childress. In 1836 William H. Wharton and Stephen Austin visited many cities, including Nashville, New York, and Philadelphia, in search of aid for the new republic. John A. Wharton was editor of a Texas paper called *The Advocate of the People's Rights*. Several men from Davidson County, including Sterling Robertson, organized a company known as "The Texas Association," and expressed the intention of leading hundreds of Tennesseans to Texas.

Although Mexican officials at first welcomed the Americans into Texas, the officials soon cooled toward them when they heard ambitious Yankees talk of annexing Texas and noted increasing trouble between them and the natives. Finally, in 1830, the Mexicans enacted a colonization law which forbade further immigration into Texas from the United States. Stephen Austin presented demands before Mexican officials, including one to repeal the ban on immigration, but he was arrested and imprisoned. Actual hostilities began in October, 1835, at Gonzales, and Houston was named commander-in-chief of the army.

Tennesseans viewed these events with alarm. Soon after news of the outbreak was received, meetings were held across the state designed to arouse interest in helping the Texans. Hundreds of young men departed immediately by land and sea to shoulder arms in the cause of Texas liberty. General Richard G. Dunlap boasted that he would raise a force of more than two thousand men if the Texans would furnish transportation. Early in the following year, the ill-fated David Crockett arrived with a few friends to join, as he said, "the volunteers from the United States."

When armed bands left Tennessee and other states to fight in the cause for Texas independence, the Mexican *chargé d'affaires* in Washington complained bitterly. Finally, Mexican officials issued a circular in which they threatened to punish as pirates all armed foreigners entering Texas. Men from the Volunteer State were not intimidated, however, and continued to fight against Mexican oppression.

In the meantime, Texans were winning on the field of battle. On April 21, Houston defeated and captured Santa Anna at San Jacinto in what turned out to be the last major battle of the war. Interest in the welfare of Texans did not subside, however. Meetings were held throughout Tennessee to consider sending food, clothing, and other relief to the destitute. Tennesseans appointed themselves personal guardians of Texas liberty and independence, and stood ready to strike when the need arose. John A. Rogers of East Tennessee, for example, wrote Austin that in his opinion "thirty or forty thousand" men would volunteer to repel the invader should he attack again.

Many Tennesseans gave their lives in the cause for Texas independence, but none was better known than David Crockett. Drama and fiction have been kind to the memory of the "King of the Wild Frontier." He joined Colonel William B. Travis at the Alamo in February, 1836, and was with him when the Mexicans slaughtered the small band of defenders on March 6. Stories differ about the last hours of Crockett and the other defenders of the Alamo, but if the Frontier King was not among the last five or six survivors, slaying scores of hapless Mexicans on all sides, it should not detract from his glory. He was one of Tennessee's great fighting men—a person of indomitable bravery and intrepid courage, whose life was dedicated to the frontier ideals of liberty and freedom.

In Washington, President Jackson was reluctant to push the matter of annexation. Representative John Bell presented a memorial from a Nashville delegation requesting recognition of the new republic, and Hugh Lawson White presented the same memorial in the Senate. On the last day of his presidential term, Jackson appointed a *chargé d'affaires* to Texas and received a Texas minister. Texans had expressed their desire for annexation soon after the Battle of San Jacinto, but it was not until 1845 that the American Congress acted favorably.

A Supreme Court Established &~ Although the Texas Revolution and the revolt against Jackson overshadowed everything else during Cannon's first term, at least one important law, enacted in December, 1835, should be mentioned. This measure established a new Supreme Court in accordance with the constitutional provision of 1835. Legislators were in agreement that the judicial body should be composed of three members, and, in order that all sections of the state might be equally represented, that not more than one justice should reside in any one of the three grand divisions of the state. The salary was fixed at $1,800 per annum, and the term was set at twelve years. William B. Turley, William B. Reese, and Nathan Green were selected as justices.

Cannon Reelected Governor &~ The White-Bell forces had avoided the Whig label in 1836, but within a year it was evident that they had assumed the principles of the party. Not until 1839 did White reluctantly accept the Whig classification, although others by that time had embraced the new party both in name and in principle. From the beginning there had been no hesitancy on the part of Governor Cannon, who boldly announced for reelection in 1837 as a Whig. Democrats had difficulty finding a candidate to oppose Cannon, so pessimistic were they about their chances of victory. Finally, however, General Robert Armstrong, a successful military leader but poor political campaigner, agreed to run. Cannon's chief issue was the financial Panic of 1837, which he carefully blamed on Jackson and Van Buren. The governor won by a majority of over 17,000, and his party also gained control of both houses of the legislature.

The Panic of 1837 caused economic issues to loom large during Cannon's second term. Farm prices were depressed, many merchants were bankrupt, and some of the principal banks were near financial ruin. Legislators, after considerable debate, decided upon sweeping "new deal" legislation which included establishing a state bank with broad powers and authorizing the issuance of internal improvement bonds to the amount of four million dollars, largely in payment of state subscriptions of 50 per cent of the stock of railroad and turnpike companies. The bank was to have a capital stock of five million dollars, and was required to set aside from its profits annually $100,000 for common schools and $18,000 for academies. This legislation consolidated the commercial classes and for a time relieved pressures on debtors, but it was not until after Cannon had left the gubernatorial chair that prosperity returned.

In the meantime, ambitious and impetuous Whigs became embarrassed by the fact that both of the state's senators were Democrats. The Whigs therefore determined upon a bold course designed to replace Felix Grundy, whose term would expire in 1839, with a man of their own party. On December 15, 1837—some fifteen months before the term expired—Whigs chose Ephraim H. Foster as Grundy's successor. Grundy, realizing that he could not defeat the Whig coalition, had refused to run, and William Carroll, backed by Democrats, was soundly defeated. Grundy, of course, had the right to remain in the Senate until March, 1839, when his term expired, but Whigs—thinking that he would rather resign than comply—tried to remove him earlier by passing a resolution instructing him to vote against the Van Buren-sponsored sub-treasury plan then before Congress. He surprised the Whigs by obeying the instruction, but his refusal to quit was a keen disappointment to them. Within a few months Grundy resigned to become attorney general in Van Buren's Cabinet, however, and Governor Cannon appointed Foster to fill out the remaining months of the unexpired term.

The period of 1834–39 constituted a stormy half-decade in Tennessee politics. The Whig party was established, not originally as a segment of the national Whig group, but as a faction opposed to Jackson's arbitrary conduct in selecting his successor. The Tennessee group gained momentum with the gubernatorial election of 1835, enhanced its power and increased its membership with the presidential election of 1836, and by 1837 had gained strength equal to that of its rival. By that time the political map of the state had jelled, and party members remained loyal through the election of 1852. Of the 65 counties making returns in 1836, 53 continued to support the same party for the next sixteen years. Of the remaining 12, 6 supported White in 1836 but voted for Democratic candidates thereafter, and the other 6 wavered from one party to the other.

Shortly after the election of 1836 a newspaper editor in West Tennessee described the campaign as having been a contest between the rural folk and the urban dwellers. The Whigs were said to have been largely of the wealthy city group, with some of the planter class scattered among the rural population; the Democrats were thought to be mainly of the poor, agrarian group. The tendency among writers has been to apply that interpretation to the parties during the twenty years of Whig-Democratic competition, and especially to emphasize that Whigs were a class of aristocrats who distrusted "that scene of wild impulse, and . . . pure democracy." More recent studies, however, have modified this point of view and have shown that, while large planter and commercial interests may have been exceedingly strong, they did not dominate the party to the exclusion of all others.

The two decades following the election of 1836 have been described as a period of "partisan fury" in Tennessee politics. Certainly never before nor since has Tennessee had two political parties so nearly evenly matched.

SUGGESTED READINGS

General Accounts

Abernethy, *Frontier to Plantation*, Ch. 19; Thomas B. Alexander, *Thomas A. R. Nelson of East Tennessee* (Nashville, 1956); E. Malcolm Carroll, *Origins of the Whig Party* (Durham, 1925); Arthur C. Cole, *The Whig Party in the South* (Washington, D. C., 1913); Crockett, *Autobiography*; Folmsbee, Corlew, and Mitchell, *Tennessee*, I, Ch. 27; Hamer, *Tennessee*, I, Ch. 20; Eugene I. McCormac, *James K. Polk: A Political Biography* (Berkeley, 1922); Parks, *Felix Grundy*; Parks, *John Bell of Tennessee* (Baton Rouge, 1950); Ulrich B. Phillips, "The Southern Whigs, 1834–1854," in *Essays in American History Dedicated to Frederick Jackson Turner*, ed. Guy S. Ford (New York, 1910), 203–9; George R. Poage, *Henry Clay of the Whig Party* (New York, 1936); George L. Rives, *The United States and Mexico* (2 vols., New York, 1913); Sellers, *Polk, Jacksonian*; Shackford, *David Crockett*; Glyndon G. Van Deusen, *The Life of Henry Clay* (Boston, 1937).

Specialized Accounts

Thomas P. Abernethy, "The Origin of the Whig Party in Tennessee," *MVHR*, XII (March, 1926), 504–22; Eugene C. Barker, "The United States and Mexico, 1835–1837," *MVHR*, I (June, 1914), 3–30; Robert Cassell, "Newton Cannon and State Politics, 1835–1839," *THQ*, XV

(Dec., 1956), 306–21; Folmsbee and Catron, "David Crockett: Congressman," ETHS *Publ.*, No. 29, pp. 49–78; Folmsbee and Catron, "David Crockett in Texas," ETHS *Publ.*, No. 30 (1958), 48–74; Clement L. Grant, "The Public Career of Cave Johnson," *THQ*, X (Sept., 1951), 195–223; Gresham, "Hugh Lawson White as a Politician and Banker," ETHS *Publ.*, No. 18, pp. 25–46; Gresham, "Hugh Lawson White: Frontiersman, Lawyer, and Judge," ETHS *Publ.*, No. 19 (1947), 3–24; Gresham, "The Public Career of Hugh Lawson White," *THQ*, III (Dec., 1944), 291–318; Maiden, "Colonel John Williams," ETHS *Publ.*, No. 30, pp. 7–46: Walter Lord, *A Time to Stand: The Epic of the Alamo* (New York, 1961); Chase C. Mooney, "The Political Career of Adam Huntsman," *THQ*, X (June, 1951), 99–126; Powell Moore, "The Political Background of the Revolt against Jackson in Tennessee," ETHS *Publ.*, No. 4 (1932), 45–66; Moore, "The Revolt Against Jackson in Tennessee," *JSH*, II (Aug., 1936), 335–59; Norman L. Parks, "The Career of John Bell as Congressman from Tennessee," *THQ*, I (Sept., 1942), 229–49; Charles Grier Sellers, Jr., "Who Were the Southern Whigs?" AHR, LIX (Jan., 1954), 335–46; Glyndon G. Van Deusen, "Some Aspects of Whig Thought and Theory in the Jacksonian Period," AHR, LXIII (Jan., 1958), 305–22.

13. &❧ Party Politics, 1839–1849

THE POLITICAL REVOLUTION of 1835 was like a knife
thrust at the heart of the Democratic party in Tennessee, and the losses of 1836 and 1837 were like salt rubbed in raw
wounds. So disorganized was the party of Jacksonian Democracy
and so discouraged were its leaders that some seriously considered
leaving the state or withdrawing from politics entirely. Cave Johnson, the Jackson stalwart from Clarksville, was so perturbed over
the losses (which included his own congressional seat) that he considered moving to Mississippi. Jackson, in humiliation, retired to
the Hermitage where he bitterly assailed the people's "damnable
apostacy," and Felix Grundy could not understand how voters could
dishonor the Old Hero who had brought the highest civil and military honors to his state. Only Polk, the distinguished speaker of the
House of Representatives, emerged unscathed. The Maury Countian now was the acknowledged head of the party, and the Elder
Statesman of the Hermitage and other Democrats looked to Polk
as the one who might rescue the party from the doldrums.

Polk Elected Governor &❧ Shortly after the election of
1837, discouraged Democrats met in Nashville to reorganize and
lay plans for wresting such power as they might from the opposition.
Speaker after speaker denounced the Whigs, and the Democrats
shouted approval when Polk described the opposition as Hamil-
tonian Federalists in disguise. Polk, urged on by demonstrations of
approbation, censured the new Whigs for shamefully deserting the
standards of Andrew Jackson and declared war on Henry Clay and

Daniel Webster. Democrats, encouraged by the fighting spirit exhibited by Polk, vowed support when the congressman urged them all to cast off their lethargy and join him in thoroughly reorganizing the party down to the county and precinct levels.

Polk, only 43 at the time, hoped eventually to become Vice President, and many Democrats thought that he should be Van Buren's running mate in the next election. Polk had to decide whether he could accomplish this aim and restore his party to power in Tennessee by running for governor or by remaining in Congress. If he decided upon the gubernatorial race, William Carroll, who remained potent in state politics and whose friends wanted him to run in 1839, would have to be considered. If he ran for Congress, opposition was sure to arise because he had made some firm enemies in his district and Whig leaders were sure to fan the flames of dissent. The governor's office was viewed by many as a better stepping-stone to the executive branch in Washington than membership in Congress, and Polk's closest friends believed that with a little persuasion he would agree to run for governor.

The Polk supporters were highly desirous of getting him committed to the gubernatorial race as early as possible. Accordingly, they planned a rally in Murfreesboro on August 30, 1838, and invited him to deliver the principal address. On the appointed day some 2,000 Middle Tennesseans gathered at the Rutherford County seat to consume hundreds of pounds of ham, barbecue, beef and mutton—to say nothing of gallons of wine and whiskey—and to hear Polk denounce Whig policies, which in modern terminology he might have called "creeping socialism." He condemned the Whigs for their insistence upon a national bank and internal improvements at federal expense; their plan of "building up a splendid and extravagant government," he said, would tax the farmers of the South and the poor generally in a discriminatory manner.

After the speech the crowd rushed to the tables and helped themselves to the refreshments. After an hour of eating and drinking, most of them returned with some difficulty to the speaker's stand where, to their pleasant surprise, they heard William Carroll, who had arrived while Polk was speaking, disclaim any intention of seeking the gubernatorial chair. Deteriorating health and "other reasons," the former chief executive said, would prevent his being a candidate in 1839. Jubilant Polk men then pushed the Maury

Countian to the platform and swelled with pride when he announced his candidacy for governor. Party leaders proclaimed Polk as their Moses and boldly predicted that the people would rally *en masse* to him who would lead the state out of a Whig wilderness and back into the folds of Democratic control. The editor of the Nashville *Union* predicted that his majority would be no less than 20,000 votes.

James Knox Polk was descended from one of Middle Tennessee's prominent families. His elder cousin, Colonel William Polk, had been highly successful as a land speculator, and his father, Sam Polk, had grown wealthy as manager of Colonel Polk's holdings. Sam Polk had done well on his own as a land speculator, army contractor, merchant, and bank director. After graduating in 1818 from the University of North Carolina at the head of his class, young Polk studied law with Felix Grundy, and became a practicing attorney at Columbia. Through Grundy's influence he obtained a clerkship in the state senate in 1819, and was elected to the lower house in 1823. There he voted for Jackson in the Chief's successful bid for the United States Senate seat held by John Williams, and two years later Polk followed the Old Hero to Washington and served in the House of Representatives until he was chosen governor in 1839.

Whigs, needless to say, made light of Polk's candidacy. They accused him of seeking the governorship only as a steppingstone to the vice presidency and boldly asserted that he would have been defeated had he sought reelection to Congress. Behind the scenes, however, Whig leaders were worried and scouted about for a strong candidate to oppose Polk. When none other could be found, they agreed somewhat reluctantly upon Governor Cannon.

The campaign opened officially at Murfreesboro on April 11, 1839. Polk spoke for two hours; then Cannon was heard. Polk's speech followed closely the platform which he had outlined in a twenty-eight page pamphlet and circulated several weeks before. He contrasted the virtues of Jackson with the alleged iniquities of Henry Clay and John Quincy Adams, and charged that Cannon and Tennessee Whigs were mere tools in the hands of the Kentuckian. Polk devoted little time to state issues but traced the genealogy of "Federal-Whiggery" to the federalism of Adams and Hamilton and excoriated Cannon for jeopardizing the rights of the people by his insistence upon his national and state banks. Governor Cannon followed Polk, and for ninety minutes described the congressman as a "tool of Jackson," defended Henry Clay, blamed the Democrats for the depression of 1837, and spoke highly of a national and state banking system. A few days later they moved on to Lebanon where Polk spoke for four hours, Cannon for nearly two, and John Bell for one hour. From Lebanon they went to Carthage, and from there to towns in the Cumberland Plateau. Large crowds attended the debates, and from the beginning the people saw that Polk was master of the situation. Skillful in the use of sarcasm and abuse, the Maury Countian poked fun at the ponderous but self-confident Cannon and became a favorite with the people early in the series of debates.

Verbal fireworks did not provide the only attraction for the audiences. Bloody street fights broke out among belligerent Democrats and Whigs in several towns, and many people, including local candidates and speakers, carried weapons. After several of the joint meetings, Cannon, apparently sensing that he was no match for the skilled debater, pleaded that the press of state business required his attention more than did participation on the hustings. John Bell, Congressman William B. Campbell, Senator Ephraim Foster, and other Whigs were left to defend the governor as best they could.

Polk was elected, but the results were so close that for several days the outcome was in doubt. He lost the eastern and western sections, but his majority in Middle Tennessee was sufficient to enable him to win by about 2,500 votes. His party also captured control of both houses of the legislature and gained three additional congressional seats, which gave Democrats a total of six out of thirteen. Party leaders across the state hailed the victory as a "great and glorious triumph."

The Whigs, although disheartened, did not despair. Bell called a convention to meet in Nashville, where Whig leaders mapped strategy for recapturing control of the state. They blamed their defeat upon the unprecedented efforts of Polk, made plans to reorganize down to the precinct level, and predicted victory in 1841.

The legislature assembled in October, and before the governor's message could be received, eager Democrats pushed through a resolution recommending Polk for Vice President. After receiving Polk's message, legislators turned their attention to such matters as the Bank of Tennessee, internal improvements, public education, and construction of an asylum for the insane, all of which are discussed in other chapters.

United States Senators Elected 𝆑 One of the most important matters which the legislators took up was that of selecting replacements for the two Whig United States senators. Democrats found themselves in a position similar to that occupied by Whigs two years before. They controlled the gubernatorial chair and the legislature, but the United States senators, as well as a majority of the congressmen, were of the opposing party. Senator White's term would expire in 1841, and that of Ephraim Foster, who had replaced Felix Grundy in 1838, would expire in 1845. Victorious Democrats, unwilling to wait until the terms ended, unfolded a plan whereby the two senators would be forced to resign. They knew that both White and Foster would quit before they would vote for Van Buren's measures then before the Senate in Washington. They therefore prepared resolutions of instruction on vital issues.

On November 14, 1839, the Democratic legislators passed a series of resolutions which, in part, instructed senators to vote for Van Buren's sub-treasury bill and to "support in good faith, the leading measures . . . advocated by the present President . . . ." Foster resigned on the following day, and victorious Democrats promptly restored Grundy to the Senate. White, however, did not resign at once, and indicated that he would wait until the measure came up for a vote before deciding whether to obey the instruction or quit. At Polk's insistence, Senator Thomas Hart Benton had the measure brought up in the Senate on January 13, 1840, and White promptly resigned. He returned immediately to Knoxville where within a few months he died and soon became a martyr to his party's cause. The selection of a Knox County Democrat, Alexander Anderson, as his replacement did not ameliorate the situation, and astute observers in Democratic ranks realized that they had made a mistake of grave proportions when they forced the resignation of the popular Hugh Lawson White.

Presidential Election of 1840 ❧ The simple duties of the governor's office of Polk's day gave the Maury Countian ample time to plan his political future. Legislative resolutions in Tennessee and elsewhere nominating him for the vice presidency pleased him, and he wrote letters to acquaintances indicating his availability for the post. Close friends such as Jackson wrote to Van Buren, Francis Blair, Thomas Hart Benton, and others. A delegation of Tennessee Democrats, including such stalwarts as Grundy, Carroll, Aaron Brown, Cave Johnson, and Samuel H. Laughlin, departed for the Baltimore convention in May, 1840, with the intention of pushing Polk's candidacy to the utmost. Vice President Richard M. Johnson appeared to be stronger than Tennessee Democrats had realized, however, and Polk, upon advice of friends, went along with the plan of having the convention decide not to nominate any vice presidential candidate. Previously, Polk had indicated his intention of seeking a second term as governor.

Whigs in the meantime had held a convention in Harrisburg, Pennsylvania, and nominated William Henry Harrison, a clerk of an Ohio court who a quarter of a century earlier had defeated on the battlefield a coalition of Indians in the Northwest and had emerged a hero. Party leaders in Tennessee had supported Henry Clay and General Winfield Scott and were amazed at Harrison's nomination. They agreed, nevertheless, to support the nominee, and assembled in Nashville early in January to make plans for a statewide canvass.

Leaders of both parties had organized completely down to the county and precinct level where they vied for grassroots support. Whigs surprised even themselves in the amount of noise and ballyhoo they engendered; brass bands, free barbecue and whiskey, pet raccoons, and log cabins—the last two named items, especially, being symbolic of the party—were always on hand. Excitement ran high. Typical of the many Whig rallies was one held in Clarksville in late May where more than 7,000 people assembled, made merry, partook of the refreshments, and praised Whig candidates. Few issues were stressed, and ribaldry and cheers of "Tippecanoe and Tyler, too" replaced sobriety and common sense. One politician, pleased with the enthusiasm, wrote that "there never had been anything to compare with it. . . . The very children are as deeply imbued with the party Spirit as the grown people."

The Democrats were not idle; even the ailing and infirm Hero of the Hermitage appeared at some of the hustings, and Polk left gubernatorial duties unattended while he excoriated Whig "Claptraps" who emphasized no issues other than "the log cabin, hard cider, and raccoon humbuggery." The combined efforts of Jackson, Polk, Grundy, Cave Johnson, and others were unavailing, however, and stunned Democrats witnessed the first presidential defeat in the history of their party. Harrison carried Tennessee by 12,000 votes and defeated Van Buren by an electoral majority of 234 to 60. Polk's failure to receive the vice presidential nomination had been one reason for Van Buren's loss of the Volunteer State, but the "Little Magician" had never been popular in Tennessee, and the Whig barbecue and whiskey could not be totally discounted. In the minds of some Democrats the hopes engendered by Polk's victory in 1839 were shattered, and faith in the people's ability to distinguish sound issues and principles from "coonery and foolery" was destroyed.

James Chamberlain Jones Defeats Polk ๏๛ Democrats were yet to reach the depths of despair in the gubernatorial contests of 1841 and 1843. Polk had announced for reelection on July 4, 1840, even though the election still was more than a year off. He had used satire, ridicule, and effective debate against the slow-witted Cannon in 1839; Whigs, still smarting from that defeat, sought a man who could beat him at his own game. After rejecting John Bell's brother-in-law, David W. Dickinson, they decided upon James C. (Lean Jimmy) Jones, whose political experience had been limited to one term in the legislature and brief service as a presidential elector in 1840.

Jones, Whigs believed, could match Polk with his stock of anecdotes and mimicry and even add a bit of the folksy common touch which the distinguished and austere congressman lacked. Jones was an odd-looking man of only thirty-one years; he stood six feet or more and weighed only 125 pounds, and his solemn, almost grotesque, countenance soon became a favorite among the people regardless of whether he told stories from the platform or walked among the crowds shaking hands and telling yarns without the least implication of condescension. The Whig press described him as able, efficient, and "a true Whig." Democrats did not appear at all worried and rejoiced that Bell or some other well-known person was not selected. Even Jackson wrote Polk that Jones's nomination was "well for the Democratic cause" and that Polk need have no fear.

On March 18, 1841, Polk published a list of speaking engagements and invited the Whig candidate to join him in debate. Jones accepted, and they met first in Murfreesboro on March 27, where a large crowd heard them for nearly five hours. Throughout the campaign Jones went down the line in his support of national Whig policies, including a national bank, but his stock-in-trade was his anecdotes. Polk discussed state and national issues with dignity and sobriety, and his experience and broad understanding of government enabled him to deliver learned and convincing arguments in favor of the sub-treasury system, of marketing unsold Tennessee bonds then in the hands of British brokers, and other issues. Jones's limited knowledge and experience handicapped him, but he refused to permit ignorance of the issues to embarrass him. His friendly and simple manner appealed to the rural folk, and he had only to appear before them stroking a raccoon fur to send them into gales of laughter. His aggressive nature worried Polk, and the Democratic press complained that Jones substituted bold assertion for knowledge and brazenly discussed any subject Polk brought up simply by refuting it vigorously and denying it was true.

The crowds gave Polk a respectful hearing, but they voted for Jones. The Whig majority was a little more than 3,000 votes, and the party also gained control of the house of representatives. The senate, however, was won by the Democrats who gained thirteen of the twenty-five seats. The thirteen Democrats remained steadfastly together on important issues, especially on the election of senators, and soon became known as "The Immortal Thirteen." The defeat was Polk's first before the people of Tennessee.

In his first message to the legislators, Governor Jones recommended that the school system be improved and that internal improvements, sound currency, encouragement to manufacturing interests, and completion of the insane asylum be given attention. The immediate question before the legislature, however, was that of electing two United States senators. Both seats were vacant. Alexander Anderson had replaced White in 1840, and his term expired on March 3, 1841. Senator Felix Grundy had died in December, 1840, and A. O. P. Nicholson had been appointed in his place until the legislature could choose a successor. The Whigs were not in as covetous a position as they had been in 1837, or as the Democrats were in 1839. Although the Whigs controlled the house by a majority of three, the Democrats held the senate by a majority of one—a majority made precarious in that Senator Sam Turney, Democrat from the Cumberland Plateau district where Whigs were equally strong, could not be counted upon to hold steadfastly to the Democratic ranks.

Whigs were confident that they could elect both senators, because the customary method of electing such officials was by a joint convention composed of the entire legislature. Democrats realized that they would be outvoted by the Whig majority in the house if they accepted the conventional method; they therefore concluded that each house should vote separately and hoped that the Whigs would compromise by naming one senator and permitting them to select the other. Whigs remained adamant, however, and those in the senate became known as the "Twelve Destructives." The Democratic majority was called the "Immortal Thirteen." The result was that no agreement was reached, no senators were elected, and Tennessee was unrepresented in the upper house of Congress for the next two years. Blame was heaped generally upon the "Immortal Thirteen," but Jackson, watching carefully from the Hermitage, thought that Democrats had protected "the fundamental principles of our Republican system."

Successful in blocking the election of senators, the thirteen Democrats then resolved to obstruct other Whig legislation. They rejected the governor's nominations of bank directors on two occasions, and blocked an attempt to investigate the Bank of Tennessee, despite a Whig allegation that an investigation would bring forth "some awful disclosures." Jones disgustedly referred to the assembly as a "do-nothing" body.

Jones Defeats Polk Again ❧ For some time Democratic leaders assumed that Polk—now referred to by the Democratic press as "the Goliath of Modern Democracy"—would seek to avenge his defeat of 1841. Therefore, no other candidate was even suggested. Whigs, fearful that the magic of Jones's oratory might not again have its mesmerizing effect, were hesitant to choose Jones. Even the governor, himself, expressed pessimism. Ephraim H. Foster, however, assumed leadership of the party, and dictated that Jones should run. Foster convinced local leaders, who were organized even at the precinct level, and party members that Tennessee now truly was a Whig state.

Polk, with an eye not only to the governorship but also to the vice presidency in 1844, announced the longest list of speaking engagements ever published by a gubernatorial aspirant and laid the ground work for an extensive campaign. Jones promptly promised to meet the challenger wherever he went. Thus began the most thorough campaign the people had yet witnessed. Polk tried to ignore the work of the "Immortal Thirteen," and spent much of his time denouncing Henry Clay inasmuch as it generally was assumed that Clay would be a presidential candidate in 1844. Jones, however, kept the Thirteen before the people. He chided Polk because of the obstructionist tactics of the Democratic legislators—and told jokes and tall tales. Polk's efforts to keep the campaign on a high plane of issues were ineffective, and Jones defeated the Maury Countian by nearly 4,000 votes. Whigs won both houses of the legislature and five of the eleven congressional seats. Polk's defeat was the darkest hour of his career; Whigs, however, hailed their victory as "one of the greatest triumphs" in the history of the party.

The two major issues before the Twenty-fifth General Assembly were the election of two United States senators and the selection of a permanent location for the state capital. With a majority of two in the senate and of five in the house, the Whigs had no difficulty in electing two senators from their own party. They promptly chose Ephraim H. Foster and Spencer Jarnigan—the men they had planned to elect two years before, but the "Immortal Thirteen" blocked the attempt. The Whigs then proceeded to enact into law a method for electing senators so that there would be no repeat performance of the events of 1841. Henceforth senators were to be chosen by the "two Houses assembled in Convention."

Deciding upon a permanent location of the capital was not so simple a matter. Members of the constitutional convention of 1834 had commanded the legislature of 1843 to select a permanent location within the first week of its session, the location not to be changed except by a two-thirds vote of both houses. During the state's brief history the capital had been located at four separate towns. Territorial Governor William Blount had established the seat of government in Knoxville. When Tennesseans drafted a constitution preparatory to becoming a state, they provided that the Knox County seat should continue as the capital until at least 1802. When the constitutional limit expired, legislators continued to meet in Knoxville for an indefinite period. In 1807 they met in Kingston for one day, in order to fulfill the terms of a treaty with the Cherokee Indians, but promptly returned to Knoxville. During the next decade the peripatetic legislature met in three different cities. Knoxville remained the seat of government until 1812, at which time the lawmakers moved to Nashville, but they returned to Knoxville in 1817. In the following year they moved to Murfreesboro. Legislative sessions were held in the county courthouse until fire destroyed the building in 1822; the following year legislators met in the First Presbyterian Church. The capital remained at Murfreesboro until 1826, at which time it was returned to Nashville.

Dozens of towns had been suggested both before and after the legislators convened. During the week-long debate, at least the following were considered: Nashville, Kingston, Lebanon, Hamilton (Sumner County), Sparta, Knoxville, Clarksville, McMinnville, Shelbyville, Chattanooga, Murfreesboro, Franklin, Harrison (Hamilton County), Woodbury, Columbia, Charlotte, Reynoldsburg (Humphreys County), Carrollsville (Wayne County), Carthage, Smithville, Jackson, Manchester, Monticello (Putnam County), and Taylorsville (Johnson County). Representative John W. Richardson of Rutherford County finally proposed that the capital be established "at the county town in the county of which the geographical center of the state may fall." A professor at the University of Nashville was employed to make a survey. His study revealed that the exact center was one and one-half miles east of Murfreesboro—Richardson's home town! Those preferring Nashville prevailed, however, and seven days after sessions began Nashville had been chosen as the permanent seat of government. Plans were made immediately to construct a capitol on Campbell's Hill, near the center of town, which the city council of Nashville transferred to the state. A board of building commissioners was appointed, and William Strickland was engaged as architect.

The Whigs next turned their attention to the election of bank commissioners, an investigation of the state bank, and other measures advocated by Jones during his first term but blocked by the "Immortal Thirteen." Since the Whigs controlled both houses, they had little difficulty in passing the legislation they wanted. The bank investigation, however, proved disappointing because it revealed no wrong doing.

James Knox Polk Elected President &~ An even more important development affecting Tennessee during Jones's second term was the nomination and election of James Knox Polk as the eleventh President of the United States. After Polk's second defeat, he had returned to Columbia to practice law. His interest in politics continued unabated, however, and he kept up a wide correspondence with party leaders.

While plans were being made for the Democratic convention in May, 1844, various names were mentioned, but Van Buren, with Jackson's support, had an advantage over the others. Polk was seldom mentioned in connection with the presidency, but he received prominent attention as a vice presidential possibility. In April, Van Buren weakened his chances considerably by taking a stand against the annexation of Texas. Polk, who had been outspoken in favor of Texas, soon gained support, including an endorsement from Jackson. The able work of Gideon J. Pillow and others on the floor of the convention brought a strong movement for the Tennessean on the eighth ballot, and on the ninth vote Polk was chosen as the standard bearer for his party. Whigs, meanwhile, had nominated Henry Clay.

Polk made the principal issue that of expansion—"re-annexation of Texas and the re-occupation of Oregon." At the beginning of the campaign Clay spoke against annexation of Texas because such was against the wishes, he said, of "a considerable and respectable portion" of the people. Instead, he talked in favor of the regular Whig policies of a protective tariff, a national bank, and internal improvements. Eventually, he was forced to hedge on the Texas issue.

In Tennessee the fact that voters were evenly divided between Whigs and Democrats made it evident that the contest would be close. Not only did pride in carrying his home state motivate Polk to action in Tennessee, but also the state's thirteen electoral votes caused him to urge leaders to organize and campaign extensively on the local level. Oddly enough, the home state of Houston and Crockett voted against their son who promised annexation of Texas, and in favor of a Kentuckian who hedged on the issue. Although Polk won the presidency by an electoral vote of 170 to 105, he failed to carry Tennessee by 113 votes. The explanation was of course that Whigs outnumbered Democrats, as indicated in the gubernatorial elections of 1841 and 1843, and they remained loyal to their party in 1844.

Death of Jackson ತಿ❧ Polk's elation over his victory was offset by sadness when Andrew Jackson, his political mentor and friend of many years, died shortly after the inauguration. The Hero of the Hermitage had watched political events with unflagging interest after his retirement in 1837. During the campaign of 1844 he had published commendations of Polk and had been overjoyed when the Tennessean defeated Clay, whom Jackson earlier had called "that Judas of the West." Jackson had suffered from the effects of malaria and acute dysentery since the Indian wars, and at the time of Van Buren's inauguration many feared that Jackson would not reach the Hermitage alive. He had regained his health, temporarily, but during the winter and spring of 1845 his condition grew increasingly worse. He died on June 8, and was buried beside his beloved Rachel at the Hermitage.

Flags were flown at half mast, and ceremonies in his honor were held throughout the state. Typical was a memorial service at Charlotte on July 18, where Jeremiah George Harris, editor of the Nashville *Union*, was the principal speaker. In a two-hour eulogy, Harris compared Jackson with Washington. He "was to the American people," Harris said,

> as the sun to the mariner. Like the father of his country, he descended to the grave loaded with all the civil and military honors of his countrymen . . . . The mother shall teach her infant to lisp their names [Washington's and Jackson's] in unison—the father shall teach him to emulate their sterling virtues.

Aaron V. Brown Elected Governor ❧ While Jackson lay dying, Democrats perfected plans to regain the gubernatorial chair. Aaron V. (Fat) Brown, of Pulaski, a Democratic stalwart of long standing, had served ably in Congress and in both branches of the legislature, and he became his party's unanimous choice. Whigs discussed the names of Neill S. Brown, Gustavus A. Henry, and Ephraim Foster, and in the convention on March 20 nominated Foster. The Whig nominee had served in the United States Senate and in both houses of the state legislature. Foster had been with Jackson during the Creek War and had supported the Chief for several years before deserting him in favor of Bell and White. The two experienced men began their joint debates in Clarksville, and the speeches gave promise of another colorful campaign.

Neither candidate espoused a major issue, but each defended the policies of his party. Brown praised Polk for his stand on Texas and Oregon and condemned Foster for voting against annexation while a member of the Senate. The Whig candidate naturally advocated a national bank, protective tariff, and internal improvements at federal expense. Both were gifted orators and thrilled the crowds with their references to the Bible, motherhood, the Constitution, the flag, and classical literature.

Once again the election was close, and the decision was in doubt for several days. The final and official count gave Brown the victory by a majority of a little over 1,500 votes. Democrats also gained control of the legislature, and jubilant leaders boasted that Tennessee had been "redeemed, regenerated, and disenthralled from the dominion of Whiggism."

The most important matter to come before the legislature during Brown's administration was the election of a United States senator to replace Foster, who had resigned to make the gubernatorial race. The Democratic caucus had expressed a preference for A. O. P. Nicholson, but W. C. Dunlap, Hopkins Turney, and General William Trousdale also were contenders. The Whigs, outnumbered in both house and senate, did not hope to elect a senator from their own party, but they sought to block the election of Nicholson. For two weeks legislators debated and voted but were unable to unite behind one candidate. Nicholson, who led on most of the early ballots, finally withdrew in exasperation, and his friends then supported Dunlap. At this point, the Whigs concentrated their strength on Turney, and, with the help of six Democrats, elected him. The disgusted Democratic majority termed Turney a traitor and turned him out of the party.

Neill S. (Lean) Brown Defeats Aaron V. (Fat) Brown ᢒᢧ Democrats were pleased with Brown's conduct of state affairs, so they nominated him for a second term. Whigs had begun to plan for his defeat shortly after his election in 1845, and Foster, Meredith P. Gentry, Gustavus A. Henry, and Neill S. Brown received consideration as candidates. Several months before the election, Whig leaders decided upon Brown.

Again, national issues dominated the campaign, and the race between the two Browns was close. Whigs condemned Polk for his stand on the Oregon question and for his prosecution of the Mexican War. The people, weary of war, elected Neill Brown by a thousand votes and gave the Whigs a majority in both houses of the legislature. Once again the political pendulum had swung to the Whig side.

The legislature now faced the new election of a United States senator, and Whig party leaders were determined not to reelect Spencer Jarnigan because he had supported the Democrat-sponsored Walker tariff (which reduced the levy on most items). Among Whigs considered were Governor Jones, Ephraim Foster, John Bell, Robertson Topp, John Netherland, and others, all of whom spent long hours in the legislative halls, in the lobby, and in the tavern taprooms wooing legislators. Bell, a member of the House of Representatives, finally was chosen on the fifty-fourth ballot after a month of debate. The competent Nashvillian served in the Senate until 1859, and became a candidate for President in the following year.

Texas, Oregon, and the Mexican War ᢒᢧ While Whigs and Democrats, almost equally divided, struggled for control of the state, national affairs held the attention of the people. As observed earlier, Polk was elected on a platform which obligated him to settle the Oregon dispute and annex Texas. In his inaugural address he had stated the acquisition of California as an additional goal.

Texans sought annexation to the United States soon after they gained independence. Jackson had closed his political career by granting recognition to the republic, and William H. Wharton, a Tennessean who played an important role in the war for Texas independence, was named minister to the United States with instructions to "effect annexation." Many people, especially those north of the Mason-Dixon line, opposed adding Texas. They claimed that it would saddle the country with a huge debt, extend slavery, and lead to a war with Mexico. Former President John Quincy Adams, then a congressman from Massachusetts, spoke for three weeks against annexation, and a Boston editor wrote that all proper Bostonians would oppose it "with the last drop of our blood."

The matter was quieted for a few years; then in 1842 the legislatures of several states, including Tennessee, passed resolutions insisting upon annexation. Tennesseans urged representatives in Washington to "use every exertion in their power to procure the admission of Texas into the Union . . . ." In the following year, Aaron V. Brown, a member of the House of Representatives, wrote Jackson for advice. The Old Hero urged him to press for annexation at once.

President Tyler, encouraged by Brown, Jackson, and especially by Polk's mandate in the presidential election of November, 1844, sought to have Texas annexed by joint resolution of Congress before his term expired on March 4, 1845. Previous efforts to annex Texas by treaty had failed, largely because of opposition from the Whigs— including Whigs from Tennessee. After considerable debate a joint resolution providing for annexation passed by a close vote in the House, where it obviously was known that such unilateral action would be defeated in the Senate;[1] Senator Thomas Hart Benton (then from Missouri) proposed that the President be authorized to accomplish annexation by negotiation between the United States and Texas, should it be preferred. With this amendment the joint resolution passed the Senate by a vote of 27 to 25, with Tennessee's two Whig senators voting against it. This measure then was returned to the House, which on February 28, 1845, concurred in the Senate amendment, but all Tennessee Whigs (except John Dickinson of

[1] This enabled the Tennessee Whigs in the House to go on record in favor of annexation as their constituents wanted but to vote against annexation, as their party required, on final passage of the measure.

Murfreesboro who was ill and could not attend) voted against annexation. The acceptance of the measure, obviously, made annexation possible, and on March 3 President Tyler forwarded an invitation to Texas to enter the Union. By late December, 1845, Texans had drafted a new constitution and accepted the American proposal, and the Lone Star State had become the twenty-eighth state of the Union.

The Oregon question was resolved with less difficulty. For more than three decades American and British interests in Oregon had been a subject for diplomatic negotiation. Joint occupation had been decided upon in 1818, and nine years later the two countries agreed to continue the arrangement indefinitely. In the early 1840's, as Americans swarmed westward, increased interest was manifested in Oregon, and a few expansionists insisted that the United States should assert its claim to all the territory; that is, to the line of 50°40'. The Oregon question became an issue in the campaign of 1844, and Polk declared in his inaugural address that Americans should take all of Oregon. A vociferous minority of Democrats even insisted that we should make war on Britain rather than surrender one inch of the claim.

Polk, however, in the quietude of White House conferences with party leaders, questioned whether the country should risk war to acquire the disputed territory. Senators Thomas Hart Benton and John C. Calhoun refused to support the claims of the extremists and insisted upon compromise at the forty-ninth parallel. Senator Hopkins Turney, also supporting compromise, wrote Polk that to insist upon all of Oregon would create an irreparable breach in the Democratic party. When British officials offered settlement at the forty-ninth parallel, Polk submitted the matter to the Senate with his recommendation of acceptance. Consequently, the Senate voted 37 to 12 in favor of such a compromise. The final treaty was concluded on June 15, 1846.

California was not so easily acquired. On the contrary, only after war with Mexico could the Bear Flag State be added to the Union. Tennesseans had developed an intense hatred of Mexico after the Texas Revolution; therefore, the declaration of war, passed in May, 1846, met with general approval in Tennessee. The same enthusiasm which had inspired Americans to action in 1812 was renewed, and thousands of Tennesseans rushed forward to volunteer.

Nearly a week elapsed after the declaration of war before Governor Brown received orders from Washington to mobilize men for action. Tennesseans were mortified when they heard that the War Department wanted only one regiment of cavalry and two regiments of infantry from Tennessee—about 2,800 men—and some went to other states to volunteer. Because more than ten times the number needed offered their services, the "privilege" of being taken into military service was determined by lottery. According to one Nashville newspaper, some disappointed volunteers offered to give as much as $250 for the right to fight in Mexico. Once organized, Tennessee troops were dispatched with haste across the border where they fought bravely and played important roles in the battles of Cerro Gordo, Monterrey, and Chapultepec.

Tennesseans, like many others, were overconfident; they believed that the war would be brief and that the Mexicans would surrender after a few skirmishes. General Zachary Taylor, a Knoxville editor boldly declared, was only awaiting the arrival of troops from Tennessee before he undertook what surely would be a hasty and triumphal march into Mexico City. As the war continued without victory, and as the stubborn resistance of the Mexican army brought loss of life to many who had marched proudly to war only a few months earlier, Tennessee Whigs became caustic in their denunciation of the administration's war policy. When dysentery, measles, and other illnesses took more lives than did Mexican bullets, Polk was described as a butcher who had brought on an "unwanted war," and General Gideon J. Pillow was denounced for the "terrible carnage."

The conduct of the war became the main issue in the gubernatorial contest of 1847. Neill S. Brown denounced President Polk for his "unconstitutional acts" and accused him of favoring Democratic generals over those of Whig persuasion, of interfering with the commands of Generals Winfield Scott and Zachary Taylor, and of destroying the morale of the men in the field by appointing his "Democratic friends" to positions of command instead of abiding by the time-honored custom of letting volunteer troops elect their own commanders. Aaron Brown defended Polk and the conduct of the war but, as observed earlier, he was defeated by his Whig opponent.

In Washington, John Bell became the spokesman for Tennes-

seans opposed to the war. On February 2, 1848—the same day
Mexican officials met Nicholas P. Trist at Guadalupe Hidalgo and
signed a treaty of peace—Bell denounced the conduct of the war,
blamed the President for it, and opposed the raising of more troops.
When Trist's treaty was presented to the Senate, in which the vast
area known as the "Mexican Cession" was added to the United
States, both Bell and Turney voted with the majority to accept it.
Although Bell pronounced the acquisition of California and New
Mexico "a curse," he felt justified in voting for the treaty because
it would mean a cessation of hostilities.

Polk's term ended on March 4, 1849. Although many of his
friends insisted that he become a candidate for a second term, Polk
remained true to his pledge made in 1844 that he would serve only
four years. His had been a successful administration, although not
devoid of strife. He had led his country in the accomplishment of
those things most desired by his party, including the annexation of
Texas, the reduction of the tariff, the reestablishment of the independent treasury plan, the settlement of the Oregon dispute, and
the acquisition of California and New Mexico. After his term expired, Polk returned to Middle Tennessee and took up residence in
the home formerly belonging to Felix Grundy; Polk died a few
months later.

Polk's death marked the passing of fifteen years of partisan fury
in the Volunteer State. Whigs and Democrats had been evenly
matched during the period and practically every gubernatorial election was decided by a relatively few votes. Tennesseans could view
their military record with satisfaction. Jackson's men who served in
the War of 1812 had earned the title of the "Volunteer State" for
their homeland, and their sons and grandsons enhanced the state's
reputation in the Mexican War. During the period some of Tennessee's ablest men had performed on the state and national stages,
and Polk had become one of the strongest Presidents to hold office.

SUGGESTED READINGS

General Accounts
   Alexander, *Thomas A. R. Nelson*; Thomas Hart Benton, *Thirty
Years' View; or a History of the Working of the American Government*

for *Thirty Years, from 1820 to 1850* (2 vols., New York, 1856), II; Folmsbee, Corlew, and Mitchell, *Tennessee*, I, Ch. 18; Hamer, *Tennessee*, I, Ch. 21; Parks, *John Bell*; Sellers, *Polk, Continentalist*; Sellers, *Polk, Jacksonian*; White, *Messages*, III.

Specialized Accounts

Thomas B. Alexander, "The Presidential Campaign of 1840 in Tennessee," *THQ*, I (March, 1942), 21–43; Clement Eaton, "Southern Senators and the Right of Instruction, 1789–1860," *JSH*, XVIII (Aug., 1952), 303–19; Turner J. Fakes, Jr., "Memphis and the Mexican War," WTHS *Papers*, II (1948), 119–44; John Hope Franklin, "The Southern Expansionists of 1846," *JSH*, XXV (Aug., 1959), 323–38; Billy H. Gilley, "Tennessee Opinion of the Mexican War as Reflected in the State Press," ETHS *Publ.*, No. 26 (1954), 7–26; Norman A. Graebner, "James K. Polk's Wartime Expansionist Policy," ETHS *Publ.*, No. 23 (1951), 32–45; LeRoy P. Graf and Ralph W. Haskins (eds.), *The Papers of Andrew Johnson, Volume 1, 1822–1851* (3 vols. to date, Knoxville, 1967—); Clement L. Grant, "Cave Johnson and the Presidential Campaign of 1844," ETHS *Publ.*, No. 25 (1953), 54–73; Ralph W. Haskins, "Internecine Strife in Tennessee: Andrew Johnson Versus Parson Brownlow," *THQ*, XXIV (Winter, 1965), 321–40; Robert Selph Henry, "Tennesseans and Territory," *THQ*, XII (Sept., 1953), 195–203; Robert S. Lambert, "The Democratic National Convention of 1844," *THQ*, XIV (March, 1955), 3–23; Powell Moore, "James K. Polk and Tennessee Politics, 1839–1841," ETHS *Publ.*, No. 9 (1937), 31–52; Moore, "James K. Polk and the 'Immortal Thirteen,'" ETHS *Publ.*, No. 11 (1939), 20–30; Moore, "James K. Polk: Tennessee Politician," *JSH*, XVII (Nov., 1951), 493–516; Ray Gregg Osborne, "Political Career of James Chamberlain Jones," *THQ*, VII (Sept., Dec., 1948), 195–228, 322–34; Parks, *Felix Grundy*; Sellers, "James K. Polk's Apprenticeship," ETHS *Publ.*, No. 25, pp. 37–53; Justin H. Smith, *The Annexation of Texas* (New York, 1941); Clara B. Washburn, "Some Aspects of the Campaign of 1844 in Tennessee," *THQ*, IV (March, 1945), 58–74; Robert H. White, "The Volunteer State," *THQ*, XV (March, 1956), 53–56; White, "Tennessee's Four Capitals," ETHS *Publ.*, No. 6 (1934), 29–43; Frank B. Williams, Jr., "Samuel Hervey Laughlin, Polk's Political Handyman," *THQ*, XXIV (Winter, 1965), 356–92.

14. ৡ Slavery and Politics, 1849–1859

POLITICS CONTINUED TO EXCITE the hopes and imagina-
tions of Whigs and Democrats alike at mid-century.
Although Jackson, Polk, White, and Grundy were dead, John Bell,
Aaron Brown, and Andrew Johnson kept major issues before the
people. National developments continued to command the attention of all Tennesseans, but the partisan fury between the two
evenly matched parties showed no signs of abatement, whether
on the state or national levels. Within the decade of the 1850's,
however, the Whigs, as such, ceased to function and new parties
developed. Slavery loomed as the major issue of controversy.

Slaves were brought into Tennessee by some of the first pioneers
from Virginia and North Carolina and by James Robertson and
others who came later to establish Fort Nashborough in the Central
Basin. Tennessee had entered the Union as a slaveholding state,
and slavery remained legal until after the Civil War. On the eve of
the war, more than 25 per cent of the total population was Negro.

Expansion of Slavery ৡ A few years after permanent
settlements were built on the Cumberland, the first federal census
was taken and revealed that the Negro population was 3,417—a little
less than one-tenth that of the white population. Both races increased rapidly after Tennessee's admission to the Union in 1796
and especially after West Tennessee was opened to settlement
(1818); cotton growers flocked there to occupy and till the warm
and fertile soil. By 1820, Negroes numbered 80,107, which was

almost one-fifth of the total. On the eve of the Civil War, the slave population of 283,019 was more than one-fourth the total population.

Although slaveowners lived in all sections of the state, there were more slaves in Middle Tennessee than in the other two divisions combined; the blacks were concentrated more heavily in the Cumberland Basin than elsewhere in Middle Tennessee. In 1860 more than 25 per cent of the Middle Tennesseans were Negroes. In the hill lands of East Tennessee, where many tillers of the soil pursued bare subsistence farming, there were comparatively few slaves; yet, in the rich river valleys of the Watauga, Holston, French Broad, Tennessee, and the Little Tennessee from Bristol to Chattanooga many farmers held slaves in small numbers. For the section as a whole, however, less than 15 per cent of the families were slaveowners, and Negroes constituted only about 8 per cent of the population in 1860. In the southwest corner of the state, where cotton predominated, the slave population was concentrated to a greater degree than anywhere else. On the eve of the Civil War several of the counties had more blacks than whites, and the Negroes of all the western section together consisted of about 40 per cent of the whole population of West Tennessee in 1860.

Only a minority of Tennesseans were slaveholders; the vast majority of those who did own slaves held only a few. Owners such as Montgomery Bell of Dickson County who held over 300 slaves in 1850, G. A. Washington of Robertson County who held 274 in 1860, and John W. Jones who owned 235 slaves in 1850 were indeed rare. Even in the cotton counties of the southwest most owners held only a comparatively few slaves.[1] A typical slaveowning farmer worked side by side with his Negroes in fields of corn, cotton, and tobacco, and supervised their labor himself. The result was that he had more personal contacts with his Negroes and came to understand their weaknesses and infirmities. James Stirling, an English traveler who toured the Southern states in the mid-1850's, observed that not infrequently slaves lived with the master's family and that

[1] Numbers of slaveholders holding varying numbers of slaves in Tennessee in 1860 are as follows:

1 Slave	2 Slaves	3 Slaves	4–6 Slaves	7–9 Slaves	10–20 Slaves	21–40 Slaves	41–99 Slaves	100–500 Slaves
7,820	4,738	3,609	7,614	4,608	5,523	2,266	619	47

owners worked in the fields alongside their slaves and were respected by them.

Treatment of Slaves ৯৯ As a general rule, slaves were treated well. If slaves were old or had performed meritorious service, owners often emancipated them (as long as state law permitted) and otherwise provided for their well-being. Elias W. Napier, a Middle Tennessee planter and iron producer, gave his "negro man Ephraim" his freedom "in consequence of his faithfulness, honesty, and industry in attending to [Napier's] business . . . ." Ephraim also received Napier's "best wagon" and eight mules and gear. William Dickson and John Humphries of Dickson County, James Currin of Fayette County, and William L. Lambert of Haywood County were concerned especially about their old slaves. Dickson provided that his "old Negro fellow called Harry" could choose between one of Dickson's sons with whom to live his remaining days. Humphries, a justice of the peace and affluent farmer, provided that his "old woman Amy . . . is to be permitted to live with which of my children she pleases but not as a slave, and which ever she chooses to live with shall be bound to maintain her as long as she lives but she shall be compelled to live with some of them." Currin wrote that his "old woman Ditty" should have the right to "select from among [his] children such one as she may wish to live with and the one so selected is to . . . receive . . . thirty dollars to be used in supporting comfortably said old Negro woman." Lambert wanted his old slaves kept together until death.

In many cases Negroes were buried alongside whites in both public and private cemeteries. Andrew Jackson's servant, Alf, was buried at the Hermitage near the body of his master, and Colonel James Tubb of DeKalb County requested in his will that his servant, Caleb, be buried next to him. Samuel Henderson, who buried his servant, Tom, in the family plot, wrote of Tom that "a more faithful and constant Christian either white or black I have seldom known." John Houston Bills's old servant, Sam, died in the 1870's, and was buried in the family plot beside the body of Bills's only son. Sam "was a faithful Honest man," Bills wrote, who "refused to leave me when free, and was true to my interest during the war of the rebellion—peace to his ashes." By 1860 nearly 4,000 Negroes had been buried in the old Nashville Cemetery, located on Fourth Avenue South, along with 7,000 whites.

Not all masters treated their slaves humanely. Loafers and trouble-makers often were flogged, ironed, and denied privileges extended to others whose work and conduct were satisfactory. The frequent appearance of newspaper advertisements for fugitives, especially in the 1840's and 1850's, indicates that all Negroes were not happy in bondage. Montgomery Bell, for example, advertised several times for his fugitive, Billey. Bell described the slave as a man whose coun-tenance showed "discontent, unless when he affects a smile," and who "was guilty of crimes previous to his elopement." Bell requested anyone apprehending Billey to "iron him in the most secure manner, paying no regard to any promises he may make," lodge him in jail, and notify his master. On other occasions Bell offered substantial rewards for "an engineer called Tom" and "a blacksmith named Jim." Nathan Bedford Forrest in 1856 offered $300 for the return of a skilled carpenter. William B. Robertson offered a substantial reward in 1820 for "Clem," whom he described as being over six feet tall and who had never been "thrown down by black or white and seldom beat at running or jumping." John Eubank of Charlotte wrote in 1846 that a "slave boy Jack" had fled because he feared that Eubank "would flog him."

Even before Tennessee became a state, legislators of North Caro-lina had devised a system to recapture fugitives. This system pro-vided for "searchers," or "patrols," as they usually were called, to search slave quarters periodically for weapons and to return runaway slaves to their rightful owners. A Negro not on his master's property could be searched for a "pass" signed by his owner, but if the slave had no "pass" the patroller could chastise him with not more than fifteen lashes and commit him to jail until his owner could be located.

Tennessee was an agricultural state, and most of the Negroes were employed on the farms and plantations. Some Negroes, however, worked in industry, especially at the iron furnaces in Middle and East Tennessee. Others worked at barbering, carpentering, and blacksmithing. Many of the women were house servants but some worked along with the men in fields of corn, cotton, and tobacco.

Iron manufacturers during busy seasons depended upon hired slaves from neighborhood farms in order to produce at maximum capacity. Hiring was beneficial to both parties, since the persons hiring would not have to maintain a full corps of slaves at all times, and owners during lax periods could have their Negroes employed in remunerative work. Prices paid for hired slaves varied with the supply and demand of labor and the skill of the worker. An unskilled slave could earn for his master no more than $80 to $100 for a full year's work. The ironmongers of Middle Tennessee, however, occasionally paid as high as $200 per year for skilled workers, and a blacksmith belonging to Samuel P. Polk earned nearly $500 for his master in 1852. Montgomery Bell promised to pay a "generous price" for Negroes hired and to supply them with a weekly ration of seven pounds of pork, a peck of meal, and a quantity of molasses, in addition to necessary clothing.

Tennessee's location made it one of the leading slave trading states. John Overton, Isaac Bolton, Nathan Bedford Forrest, John Armfield, E. S. Hawkins, Will Boyd, and Isaac Franklin were only a few of those who engaged in the trade. Overton was buying and selling slaves in Middle Tennessee before 1800. Armfield joined Franklin in Sumner County in 1824, and they formed a highly successful team on the Natchez Trace and throughout the South. One observer described the pair as men who had "a positive genius for speculating in slaves." Bolton and Forrest confined their activity largely to Memphis where they made fortunes, and Hawkins and Boyd worked in Nashville.

Nashville and Memphis were the slave trading centers of the state. Memphis, because of its accessibility to the lower South, soon outstripped the state's capital as a center for Negro sales and later became the largest slave trading city of the central South. The newspapers contained many advertisements of sales and auctions. Forrest, Bolton, Hawkins, and the others frequently announced that they had cooks, washers, ironers, plow boys, carpenters, brick layers, and men and women of other skills. Forrest, who in the 1860's was to demonstrate his true genius and courage, had graduated at midcentury from horse swapping to slave trading, and made a fortune during the decade.

The prices of slaves depended upon many factors, including the age, quality, and skill of the Negroes. Prices rose rapidly after the invention of the cotton gin and the industrialization of New England and Great Britain. Except for a dip in prices during the depressions of the late 1830's and mid-1840's, the average price for slaves in the state rose steadily until 1860.[2] The highest valuation, generally, was in the cotton country of West Tennessee.

Slaves were encouraged to go to church, and many were taught to read and write. At church services they were seated in the rear of the sanctuary or, if the church had a balcony, they were seated there. In some cases, slaves had their own preachers and services on Sunday afternoons; in other cases, especially in the cities, slaves had separate churches. Probably the first separate Negro church of any consequence was the First Baptist Church, Colored, of Nashville, established in 1848 by several interested whites and 500 Negroes. The Reverend Nelson Merry was the first pastor, serving until his death in 1884. Other churches were established during the 1850's in Nashville, Memphis, and in some rural communities.

Although the Methodist bodies with their emphasis upon a heartfelt religion appealed greatly to emotional slaves, the Baptist Church with its simple and democratic polity and dogma made even a greater appeal. Too, the method of baptizing, differing as it did from that of other churches, held an especial attraction for the Negroes. To be dipped beneath a cleansing flood, even though it was a muddy creek, or, in Memphis, the rolling Mississippi, was enough to bring shouts of joy from the person being baptized, to say nothing of the well-wishers who watched from the banks. When the Civil War began, the Methodist Episcopal Church claimed a Negro membership of over 200,000, but Southern Baptists claimed more than twice that number.

Hundreds of recorded wills and other records attest to the owners' interest in education for their slaves. Elihu Embree, for example, wrote that money should be provided from his estate for schooling "each of Nancy's children" to "the best advantage that conveniently offers." George R. Witt of Fayette County provided that his wife "be allowed a reasonable compensation from year to year" to school

[2] The following table indicates the average value for the two and one-half decades before the war:

Year	Average Value	Year	Average Value
1836	$584	1852	$547
1840	543	1856	689
1848	467	1860	855

Negroes. Christopher Strong of Dickson County commanded his wife and the administrators of his estate to "have those [slave] children, John Wesley and Tennessee, taught to read the Bible . . . ."

Free Negroes constituted a problem which could not be solved entirely by legislation. Although never large in number, they were considered by whites to be shiftless, depraved, and dangerous to the maintenance of a satisfactory relationship between slave and master. Most of the free Negroes lived in Memphis, Nashville, and Knoxville, but a few could be found in nearly all of the counties. Until 1835, Tennessee was considered the most lenient of all Southern states toward Negroes of that class and under the constitution of 1796 had permitted them to vote. During the first three decades of the nineteenth century the free colored population increased from 309 to 4,555; in 1860 it numbered 7,300.

The free Negro came from several sources, including immigration, emancipation, self-purchase, and natural increase from free women. Migration from other states was prohibited after 1831, but in 1842 the right of entry was restored if the court of the county where the Negro expected to reside would give bond guaranteeing good behavior. All of the Negroes were kept under careful surveillance. In 1806 a statute was written providing for the registration and numbering of each free Negro or Mulatto. Age, name, "color," "any apparent mark or scar," and an explanation of how freedom was attained were recorded. A law was passed in 1860 permitting them to enter slavery at their own volition.

The lot of the free Negro was a hard one. Most were in dire poverty and received little help or encouragement from whites and slaves. Some were shiftless and others pursued whatever jobs they could find. One, called "Black Bob," ran a tavern in Nashville, and John Brown and Joseph Clauston were Memphis barbers. Many worked as cooks, domestic servants, stonemasons, bricklayers, carpenters, and painters, but the vast majority were farm laborers. Acts of raucous troublemakers usually were heralded in the press, but seldom did the good works of the less pugnacious ones get into print. Justice John Catron wrote that free Negroes were "a very dangerous and most objectionable population," and Senator Spencer Jarnigan said in 1833 that they corrupted the slave population. Senator E. B. Littlefield called the free Negro "a curse to society."

Antislavery Sentiment ट्कॎ Until the last three decades before the Civil War, strong manumission sentiment was present in every slaveholding state, and prominent citizens in Tennessee frequently spoke out against the "peculiar institution." According to a tradition unsustained by documentary evidence, members of the constitutional convention of 1796 defeated by a very small majority a proposal to abolish slavery.

Thomas Embree and his sons, Elijah and Elihu—iron manufacturers of East Tennessee—were some of the earliest exponents of emancipation. Thomas was outspoken. Shortly after Tennessee became a state, he called upon legislators to make possible "a gradual abolition of slavery of every kind" and urged the people of Washington and Greene counties to form antislavery societies. Elihu Embree began the publication of *The Manumission Intelligencer* at Jonesboro in 1819. The Quaker editor had a sincere conviction that slavery was inhuman and denounced it as "one of the blackest" of crimes. Embree suspended publication of the weekly after one year and founded *The Emancipator* as a monthly. His untimely death at the age of thirty-eight brought an end to the journal after only seven issues had been published. Embree's papers were the first antislavery journals in the country, antedating Benjamin Lundy's first efforts in Ohio in 1821.

Shortly after Elihu Embree's death, Benjamin Lundy brought his *The Genius of Universal Emancipation* to Greeneville, Tennessee. The publication appeared regularly from April, 1822, to August, 1824. Lundy's departure from the state later in that year left Tennessee manumissionists without an outlet for propaganda. All of these papers were organs of the "Manumission Society of Tennessee," which was formed with an expressed goal of accomplishing the gradual abolition of slavery. The members of the society pledged themselves to urge legislators to declare that all Negroes born after "some fixed time" would be free at "some reasonable age." As a qualification for freedom, the society insisted that slaves be instructed in the Holy Scriptures and be taught some gainful occupation. Members of the society were confined primarily to the eastern counties. In 1824 a group of Middle Tennesseans met at Columbia and formed the "Moral Religious Manumission Society of West [now Middle] Tennessee." They denounced slavery as "the greatest act of practical infidelity," and described it as being "absolutely incompatible with the spirit of Christianity."

The manumission societies in Tennessee were a part of the reform movement which swept the state and nation soon after the turn of the century; they reached their zenith in the late 1820's when twenty-five societies boasted of a membership of 1,000. Their influence, however, was a salutary one in Tennessee. Few, if any, members expressed interest in radical movements, but all members favored gradual abolition, humane treatment of slaves, and training and education for the slaves. The Tennessee societies were short lived—practically all had ceased to exist by the mid-1830's. The advent of radical self-seekers who advocated immediate, uncompensated abolition, by violent means if necessary, was a factor in causing many people to lose interest in emancipation.

Colonization was discussed by many slaveowners, but it was too expensive to be practical. The American Colonization Society was formed in Washington in 1817, and a chapter with sixteen members was organized in Nashville twelve years later. The members purchased land in Africa, and established Liberia as a haven for liberated slaves. Phillip Lindsley, president of the University of Nashville, was named president of the state Colonization Society, and at his insistence the state legislature in 1833 provided for a payment of ten dollars to the American Colonization Society for the removal of each free Negro from the state.

Few Tennesseans had the necessary funds to colonize slaves. Three who did were General Logan Douglas of Williamson County, Montgomery Bell, who owned iron works throughout Middle Tennessee, and Christopher Strong of Dickson County. They found the cost of sending each Negro to be about $180. Slaves belonging to Douglas and Strong were sent in 1852. In the following year, Bell offered to free his slaves if they would agree to go to Liberia. He would pay their transportation costs and furnish them with six months' provisions. Ninety accepted the offer, and departed Savannah, Georgia, in December, 1853.

Some reformers talked of colonization within the United States; Texas frequently was mentioned after she gained her independence from Mexico in 1821. Frances Wright established a colony near Memphis in the mid-1820's, and her experiment became a subject of controversy for several years among Tennesseans.

The radical Scot reformer visited the United States in 1818 and termed slavery a "sin against humanity." She believed that slaves should undergo a period of education and training and then be freed. She proposed to purchase Negroes and establish them in a colony where they might be educated and trained and where they might also work and earn the costs of their purchase and transportation to some place outside the United States. Accordingly, in the autumn of 1825 Miss Wright purchased 1,940 acres on both sides of the Wolf River a dozen miles northeast of Memphis, named the estate "Nashoba" (a Chickasaw word for "wolf"), and sought a small group of slaves on which she could perform her experiment. Eight were purchased in Nashville. A planter in South Carolina gave her a Negro mother and five small children. Others were bought in the vicinity of the colony. In the following spring, land was cleared for corn and cotton, and an apple orchard was planted. Before crops could be harvested, however, Miss Wright became ill and returned to Europe. The colony was left in charge of her sister, Camilla Wright, and others.

The colony had little chance of success. As stories of free love, loose morals, and racial mixing became known, West Tennesseans threatened fire and destruction. The Nashoba group, always verbose, defended themselves eloquently, and Frances Wright returned to add her voice to their support. Finally, however, in frustration she determined to abandon her project, and resolved to take the Negroes to Haiti. Chartering her own ship, she accompanied them to the Haitian shores where they were given land by the governor.

Before 1831 antislavery sentiment in the country had been mild and restrained with leaders such as Daniel Webster, William Ellery Channing, and James Russell Lowell directing their appeal for emancipation to the slaveholder instead of railing against him. With the first issue of William Lloyd Garrison's *Liberator* (January 1, 1831), however, a new leader with a new theory appeared. Garrison wanted immediate, uncompensated emancipation, to be accomplished by violence if necessary. Because the Constitution sanctioned slavery, Garrison denounced the organic law as "a covenant with death and an agreement with hell." The extremism expressed by him and his followers nullified efforts at peaceful emancipation and caused many Southerners to defend slavery rather than to consider it as an evil which in due course must be eradicated.

Fear caused Tennesseans to tighten their grip on slavery during the three decades before the Civil War. The Nat Turner Insurrections of 1831 in Virginia recalled the horrors of earlier slave revolts in Santo Domingo and South Carolina. Next came reports in the early 1830's of revolts in North Carolina, Delaware, and Georgia. From Lincoln County came rumors that slaves planned to burn buildings, seize weapons, and terrorize the whites. Legislators, apparently influenced by the reports, took stern measures. In 1831 they forbade all unlawful assemblages of slaves "in unusual numbers" or at "suspicious times and places," and expanded the powers and responsibilities of the patrols. The legislators also forbade free Negroes to enter Tennessee and prohibited emancipation unless freedmen were taken outside the state.

When delegates to the constitutional convention of 1834 assembled, slavery was a principal topic for discussion. Hundreds of memorials were received which asked that slavery be constitutionally abolished, and John A. McKinney of Hawkins County was named chairman of a committee to draft replies to petitioners. McKinney believed that a clause emancipating slaves would cause many masters to move to other slaveholding states. The "wisest heads and the most benevolent hearts," he wrote, had not been able to solve the slavery problem satisfactorily. He had faith, however, that it could be resolved in time if only "misguided fanatics, in those parts of the United States where slavery does not now exist, will only refrain from intermeddling in a matter in which they have no concern and in which their interference can do no possible good . . . ." Slavery, McKinney said, "with all its ills," would be abolished by slaveholders themselves "as certainly and as speedily as the friends of humanity have any reason to expect." Delegates, like the Virginians in 1831–32, agreed that slavery was the only practical solution to the race problem as long as the Negro was a part of the social order.

Much uneasiness was aroused in the minds of slaveholders during the late 1850's, when additional rumors of slave insurrections spread. Unrest throughout the South caused all states to strengthen their patrols. In 1856, especially, rumors of revolts accentuated the fears. A Fayette County owner overheard a group of his slaves plotting insurrection, and promptly had fifty-five of them thrown in jail. Two kegs of gunpowder were found in possession of slaves in Maury County. Uprisings were reported in Franklin and Perry counties. In

Nashville the patrol was strengthened, Negro schools and churches were temporarily forbidden to operate, and all Negro assemblages after sundown were prohibited. The people of Montgomery and Stewart counties were reported in the press to be "perhaps the most terror-stricken community of the entire South." Slaves in those counties were said to be planning a general uprising on Christmas Day, 1856, at which time they would march on Clarksville, capture the town, plunder its banks, and flee to free territory. Several Negroes were slain and many others were imprisoned in the confusion which followed. By 1860 exaggerated tales of uprisings were heard in every Southern state.

By the 1850's the voices of the abolitionists such as Ezekial Birdseye of Newport seldom were heard, and Tennesseans, like many other Southerners, were defending an institution which a few years earlier they had sought to eradicate. Congressman John Savage said as early as 1850 that he was "ready for war, subjugation, or extinction" before he would agree to free slaves and permit them to remain as freedmen in the country. When secession came, many people no doubt viewed the situation as did Parson Brownlow, who described himself as a proslavery man who hated secession and who blamed the abolitionists for the unhappy condition in which the American people found themselves.

The Election of 1849, The Compromise of 1850, and the Nashville (Southern) Convention ह‍ॶ Shortly before negotiations with Mexico began, whereby the United States acquired California and other territory in the West, Congressman David Wilmot of Pennsylvania attached to an appropriations measure a rider stipulating that slavery should be excluded from all territory acquired from Mexico. The Proviso, successful in the House but not in the Senate, was the occasion for bitter controversy both in and out of Congress. Southerners had borne the brunt of the Mexican War, and Wilmot's attempt to exclude slaveholders from the newly gained lands raised a storm of protest. State senators in Tennessee agreed unanimously that they were "opposed to the 'Wilmot Proviso' in every shape and form . . . ." State Whigs and Democrats alike deplored it and shared President Polk's comment that it was a "mischievous and foolish amendment."

When Democrats assembled for a gubernatorial convention in the summer of 1849, passions were aroused. Delegates called for "a firm declaration of our purpose to resist the encroachments of northern fanaticism . . . ." In the event Congress enacted the Proviso, Tennessee Democrats were ready "heart and soul, with a united front," to join with other Southern states, "through a southern convention or otherwise," to plan a course of action. Congress had no mandate, they said, to impair the rights of slaveholders or other property owners. Excoriation of the abolitionists and other "Northern fanatics" accomplished, Democrats turned their attention to the main purpose of the convention. They nominated William Trousdale, "the Warhorse of Sumner County," to oppose incumbent Governor Neill S. Brown.

The campaign was uneventful. The war, Wilmot Proviso, and other national issues were debated. Trousdale, although not as able on the hustings as Brown, was known as a military hero who as a youth had quit school to enlist in the Creek War. He defeated the incumbent by about fourteen hundred votes. Brown was appointed as minister to Russia soon after his retirement from the gubernatorial chair.

A Southern convention, as discussed by the Democrats in 1849, already was in the making. In December, 1848, Senator Hopkins L. Turney and other Southern congressmen under the leadership of John C. Calhoun met in Washington to protest against the Wilmot Proviso and to formulate plans to avert dangers which ominously threatened the South. They published an "Address to the People of the Southern States" in which they voiced hopes for a convention. In October, 1849, a group of Mississippians called on people of the slave states to send delegates to Nashville in the following June to consider "the presentation of a united protest from the South against the attempt to exclude southern men with their slaves from the national territories" recently won from Mexico. Democrats in Tennessee welcomed the proposal but Whigs, asserting that Tennessee should not be a "stamping-ground" for seceders and nullifiers, urged "the plotters to assemble elsewhere."

Before the delegates assembled in Nashville, Congress had begun consideration of measures which were to have an important bearing on North and South alike. In January, 1850, Henry Clay—still an idol of Tennessee Whigs—introduced bills which eventually became the Compromise of 1850. Clay would settle many sectional issues by providing for the admission of California with its free-state constitution, by creating a territorial government for the remainder of the Mexican Cession without restriction as to slavery, by abolishing the slave trade but not slavery in the District of Columbia, and by enacting a more effective fugitive slave law.

All of Tennessee's congressional delegation were heard on the compromise proposals. Bell agreed that California might be admitted as a free state, but he urged that in order to maintain the balance of power between South and North a new slave state be carved from Texas to balance California. Congressman Andrew Johnson urged Southerners to take a "stand against the encroachments of the North . . . upon southern institutions, and thereby save the Constitution from violation . . . ." In the final votes on the various measures Senator Bell favored all of them except the abolition of slave trade in the District of Columbia. Turney supported only the fugitive slave law. In the House, only one Tennessean voted for the District of Columbia bill, but the only other votes against the compromise measures were four votes (out of eleven) against the admission of California.

Meanwhile, delegates from most of the slaveholding states assembled in Nashville for a nine-day "Southern Convention." Langdon Cheves of South Carolina and other fire-eaters from the lower South were in charge. Over one hundred Tennesseans attended after the Whig-dominated legislature defeated efforts of the Democrats to elect "official" delegates. Members denounced Northern abolitionists, declared the Wilmot proposal to be unconstitutional, demanded that a stringent fugitive slave law be enacted, suggested that the Mexican territory be divided along the Missouri Compromise line, and asserted that until some agreement was reached all states had equal rights in the territories.

Following congressional passage of the compromise measures in September, 1850, a second session of the Southern convention was held in November. Interest was shown only by extremists because most Southerners accepted the Compromise of 1850 in good faith and believed that it would stem the rising tide of sectionalism. Gideon J. Pillow and Aaron V. Brown drafted "Tennessee Resolutions" in which they urged that secession talk be ended and the Compromise be accepted. Although Brown vilified Northern extremists who would "beggar" his children, "fire" his dwelling, and spread around him "all the horrors of a servile war," he still urged that "the past can be endured" and forgotten. All Americans, regardless of their sectional feelings, should strive to bind up the nation's wounds and preserve the Union and the Constitution. The Tennesseans were in the minority, however, and the states voted six to one to adopt stronger resolutions, including a recommendation that another convention be held soon to restore, if possible, "the constitutional rights of the South," and if not, "to provide for their safety and independence."

The Compromise of 1850 caused sectional bitterness to subside only for a short while. John Bell understood this well when he said to his constituents in the autumn of 1850 that

> The crisis is not past; nor can perfect harmony be restored to the country until the North shall cease to vex the South upon the subject of slavery. . . . A spirit of conciliation and forbearance is demanded by patriotism and the exigencies of the times, as well on the part of the South, as on that of the North . . . .

Election of 1851 &> With the ghost of sectional strife at least temporarily laid, Tennesseans turned to the gubernatorial contest of 1851. Democrats nominated Trousdale, the incumbent, and Whigs chose Circuit Judge William B. Campbell, himself a hero of the Mexican War. The Compromise of 1850 was the main issue. Trousdale reluctantly accepted the measures, but believed them to be oppressive and unjust to the South. He accused Campbell and the Whigs of being "too favorable to northern views . . . ." The Whig candidate, however, viewed the Compromise as "the work of wisdom" and urged Tennesseans to accept it in good faith. Campbell was elected by a majority of about fifteen hundred votes, and became the last Whig to serve in the gubernatorial chair. Jubilant Whigs also captured control of both houses of the legislature.

In his inaugural address Governor Campbell stressed the need for "moderation and firmness" in regard to sectional matters. "Idle" and "insane" talk about peaceable dissolution of the Union, he said, should cease. He urged legislators to proceed with the business at hand without strife and rancor.

Several matters of importance were disposed of by the General

Assembly. James C. Jones, a Memphis railroad executive and businessman after his retirement as governor, defeated former Governor William Trousdale for United States senator. Because redistricting was necessary after the census of 1850, a committee of ten Whigs and five Democrats was appointed to recommend changes to the assembly, and took pains to gerrymander counties to assure Whig majorities in Congress and in the legislature. A Committee on Federal Relations drafted resolutions defining Tennessee's position in the Union. Committee members described Tennesseans as people who cherished "an abiding devotion to the Union and Constitution," but who distrusted and abhorred Northern "abolitionists and fanatics." Although Democrats wanted to describe the Compromise of 1850 as one which fell "short of that measure of justice to which the South . . . [was] fairly entitled," Whigs prevailed and termed the Compromise as the best "which under the circumstances" could have been adopted. The resolutions stated further that the Constitution did not recognize the right of secession; that the state would aid the President in executing his constitutional powers; that the people of Tennessee recognized the right of revolution when "palpably, intolerably, and unconstitutionally oppressed"; and that in a spirit of "hope and kindness" Tennessee warned "her sister States of the North" that any modification of the fugitive slave law or failure to execute it would bring about "a train of deplorable consequences, from which a dissolution of the Union will be the most probable result."

Election of Andrew Johnson as Governor and the Decline of the Whigs ⮷ Dissension within the Whig party could be observed during the debates on the Compromise; it was evident in the election of 1852, and continued until the party was destroyed. The nomination of Winfield Scott as the Whig presidential candidate in 1852 widened the breach between the Northern and Southern factions. Several Tennesseans, including Congressman Meredith P. Gentry, joined a bloc known as the "Southern Whigs," and William G. Brownlow openly asserted that the national unity of the party was destroyed. Senators Bell and Jones supported the nominee, but Gentry and others refused. Scott lost the election but carried the state by less than 2,000 votes. It was the last presidential election won by the Whigs in Tennessee. The Tennessee victory did little to unify the unhappy party members. Even Bell admitted three months after the election that he saw "signs of a more decisive breaking up" of the party than he ever had observed before.

Whigs assembled in April, 1853, to nominate a gubernatorial candidate and tried to quiet dissension by talking of their achievements during the past two decades. They took pride in the fact that for six consecutive presidential elections they had carried Tennessee, and in six of nine gubernatorial elections they had emerged victorious. The margin of victory in each case had been small, however, and leaders therefore stressed the need for unity. Whigs chose Gustavus A. Henry, a Clarksville lawyer and descendant of Patrick Henry, as their candidate, and assured the rank and file Whigs that not only could he win but that he also could restore party harmony.

Democrats nominated Andrew Johnson. The East Tennessee tailor had enjoyed a phenomenal rise in Tennessee politics. Born in 1808 in Raleigh, North Carolina, of a poor family, he was denied even the rudiments of a formal education. He was bound out to a local tailor at an early age, but ran away from his master who promptly offered a ten-dollar reward for his apprehension. In 1826 the seventeen-year-old youth and his widowed mother resolved to seek a new home across the mountains, and late in that year they arrived in Greeneville, where young Andrew established a tailor shop. Three years later he joined twenty-six others in a race for seven aldermanic positions, and was successful by four votes. Shortly thereafter Johnson became mayor. He was elected to the house of representatives in 1835; defeated in his bid for reelection two years later, he was chosen again in 1839. In 1841 he began a term in the state senate. Two years later, pledging economy and reform in furthering the rights of the laboring classes, Johnson was elected to Congress, and remained in Washington until his nomination for governor.

The doughty warriors conducted a vigorous joint campaign, beginning at Sparta on June 1. Johnson reaffirmed his pride in his plebeian origin and called upon all who earned a living by the sweat of his brow to support him. He took full credit for the Homestead Bill, then pending in Congress, and favored constitutional amendments by which the people might elect directly the President,

Vice President, United States senators, and justices of the Supreme Court. He frequently alluded to Henry's aristocratic origin, asserted that the Clarksvillian had voted when a member of the legislature against the best interests of the laboring classes, and accused him of refusing to honor Jackson and the heroes of New Orleans. Henry, the "Eagle Orator," had few peers as a polished speaker. He criticized Johnson for his participation in the work of the "Immortal Thirteen" during Jones's administration, charged him with being sympathetic to abolitionists, and asserted that his "White Basis Bill" (which Johnson had sponsored in the legislature in 1842 whereby congressional apportionment in Tennessee would be made without regard to the Negro population), was unconstitutional.

A record vote was cast, and for several days the outcome was in doubt. The final count, however, revealed that Johnson had won by a majority of a little more than 2,000 votes. He had lost both the eastern and western sections of the state, but voters of Middle Tennessee had given him the majority necessary for victory. Whigs, however, elected five of the ten congressmen, and won a substantial majority in the house of representatives. Their majority in the legislature assured John Bell of reelection to the United States Senate although two other Whigs, Henry and Thomas A. R. Nelson, received support.

The bitterness resulting from the Kansas-Nebraska Act in the following year destroyed the national unity of the Whigs. The measure, enacted in May, repealed the Missouri Compromise and provided for the organization of Kansas and Nebraska as territories without restriction as to slavery. Southern Democrats for many years had fought congressional intervention in the matter of slavery, and interpreted the measure as a concession to the South. Harsh words were spoken, and Senator Jones excoriated such Northern extremists as Charles Sumner, Benjamin F. Butler, Ben Wade, William H. Seward, and Salmon P. Chase, and declared his independence from the Whig party. Congressman William Cullom, a Whig from Smith County, denounced the measure as the work of Southern politicians who plotted "against the peace and quiet of the Union." His inflammatory words aroused Democratic Congressman William M. Churchwell of Knoxville, and a physical encounter between the two was stopped by the sergeant-at-arms. In the final vote, four of

the six Tennessee Whigs in the House and one of the four Democrats voted against the pro-Southern measure. John Bell was the
only Southern Whig in the Senate to vote against it.

The controversy over the Kansas-Nebraska Act produced ominous
and sweeping changes in the nation's political structure. It sounded
the death knell of the Whig party, and the addition of Jones and
other Southern Whigs to the Democratic fold strengthened that
party and increased the Southern influence within it. Unfortunately,
the strong conservative influence which the Whig party had given
to American politics was removed. Tennessee Democrats took control of the state and retained it, although they did lose the presidential election to Constitutional Unionist John Bell in 1860.

The Know Nothing Movement ➣ The decline of the
Whigs set the stage for the entrance of two new parties upon
the American political stage. The Republican party, organized in the
North as a sectional, antislavery party, aroused little interest in Tennessee. The American, or "Know Nothing,"[3] party, however, drew
a considerable following from Whigs and discontented Democrats,
and for a short time replaced the Whigs as the "other" major party.
The group had had its origin in the Northeast where the wave of
immigration at mid-century had caused much dissatisfaction among
laborers. Many "native Americans" spoke of organizing a political
party, the success of which they believed would give them an opportunity to limit the number of foreign laborers coming into the
country. Because Irishmen were of the Catholic faith, the Catholic
Church became a target. The cardinal principle of the movement
became, therefore, that of suppressing the influence of new immigrants and Catholics. A "Native American" convention called
in Philadelphia in 1848 pledged support to Zachary Taylor for
President.

In Tennessee, William G. Brownlow had attacked foreigners and
Catholics as early as the 1830's, had prayed that the country might
be "saved from the foreign influence and demagoguery of Democ-

---

[3] The organization was formed as a secret oath-bound group, but members could
recognize each other by signs. If a member were asked by an "outsider" what the
organization stood for, he was instructed to answer, "I don't know." Hence, they
came to be designated, derisively, as "Know Nothings."

racy," and had warned the people of East Tennessee against all Catholics. He had criticized President Polk for appointing Catholic chaplains during the Mexican War and had accused the President and his friends of contributing over one thousand dollars for the building of a Catholic church in Washington. The new party was the answer to Brownlow's prayers. He believed that "Divine Providence" had "raised up this new order to purify the land, and to perpetuate the civil and religious liberties of this country." J. R. Graves, a militant Baptist leader and publisher in Nashville, for years had feared "foreign Catholics and German infidels." He embraced the party, urged his readers to be cognizant of the dangers which the Know Nothing party sought to eradicate, and predicted only success for its leaders.

To many Whigs, looking for new persuasions to cast before the electorate, the aura of irresistible attraction surrounding the novel party seemed to meet their needs. Voters in Memphis and Nashville elected Know Nothing mayors, and reports of successful candidates in Murfreesboro, Lawrenceburg, Clarksville, Loudon, and elsewhere filled the newspapers. Party leaders did not hold a gubernatorial nominating convention in 1855, but the Whig press heralded the name of Meredith P. Gentry (who had parted company with Whigs shortly after the nomination of Scott in 1852) as the best candidate. Consequently, Gentry announced from his Bedford County home that the "overwhelming support" expressed in newspapers and private correspondence had convinced him that he should oppose Johnson's bid for reelection.

The campaign opened at Murfreesboro on May 1. Johnson hacked away at his protagonist as with a broadaxe. The Know Nothing party, said the governor, was an ally "of the prince of darkness—the devil, his satanic majesty." When the governor compared party members with the John A. Murrell gang, local leaders shouted in unison, "It's a lie," and they drew weapons when the governor exclaimed, "Show me the dimension of a Know-Nothing, and I will show you a huge reptile, upon whose neck the foot of every honest man ought to be placed." Johnson paused only when he heard the cocking of pistols, but he was permitted to conclude his two-hour speech unharmed. Gentry, although an able orator and politician, did not defend the Know Nothing party and was a disappointment to his supporters. Johnson won by about 2,000 votes. As in 1853,

Johnson failed to win the eastern and western sections but received sufficient majorities in the Middle Tennessee counties to bring victory.

Although they lost the gubernatorial race, the Know Nothings elected six of the ten congressmen and gained control of the General Assembly. They elected Edward S. Cheatham as speaker of the senate and former Governor Neill S. Brown as speaker of the house of representatives.

Johnson's support of education, agriculture, better penitentiary conditions, and better working conditions for mechanics and laborers will be discussed later. Other legislative accomplishments included appropriations to increase the number of volumes in the state library and to create the office of state librarian. The Hermitage property, consisting of Jackson's residence and 500 acres, was purchased for $48,000 and was promptly tendered to the federal government on the condition that a military academy similar to the one at West Point was established there. Although the offer was never accepted, when Johnson delivered his last message to the legislature in 1857 he reported that "the proposition . . . seemed to be favorably entertained by both houses of Congress."

The Career of William Walker ೩✷ The colorful career of William Walker, the "grey-eyed man of destiny" who sought to carve for himself an empire in Central America, reached a high point during Johnson's second administration, and the former Nashville physician was honored in both the state and nation. As a young man the filibusterer had been educated at the University of Nashville and at the University of Pennsylvania School of Medicine. Dissatisfied with the practice of his profession, Walker turned to the country south of the United States as a fertile field for conquest. When the Mexican government refused to grant him permission to settle in Lower California, he nevertheless invaded the peninsula with a band of forty-five men, and on November 8, 1853, he proclaimed himself president of a new "Republic of Lower California." A Mexican army soon appeared, however, and chased him across the border. He was arrested for violation of the neutrality laws but soon was acquitted.

Walker's attention next fell upon the Central American republics, which he considered as nothing more than pawns of imperial interests of Great Britain and the United States. He determined to secure one or more of them as slaveholding territory for the United States. Therefore, Walker appeared in Nicaragua in 1855, placed himself at the head of the Liberal party by sheer force of personality, and soon defeated the conservative opposition. In May, 1856, he secured recognition from the United States, and a few months later was officially inaugurated President of the Republic of Nicaragua. As head of the new regime, Walker visited his home state and was received with enthusiasm. Thousands of Nashvillians cheered him in a parade and at a reception given in his honor. He also was well received in Memphis and elsewhere, and many people pledged money for his support in Nicaragua.

Walker's career as a Central American executive soon was terminated, partly by the influence of another American. When Walker assumed control of Nicaragua he discovered that Commodore Cornelius Vanderbilt's Accessory Transit Company, established in 1854, had a monopoly on transportation and was making a fortune on it. Once in power, Walker cancelled Vanderbilt's concessions and gave the business to a company in which he and other Americans who had financed his filibustering campaigns had a large interest. Vanderbilt countered by encouraging the President of Costa Rica, who resented Walker's intrusion into Central American affairs, to make war on the Nashvillian. Walker was expelled from Nicaragua in 1857. He tried twice to regain his power but was unsuccessful. In his last attempt Walker waged war on Honduras, whose conservative government had joined his Nacaraguan and Costa Rican enemies. He finally was captured in 1860 by a contingent of British sailors, and turned over to his enemies. On September 16, 1860, Walker was executed by a firing squad of Hondurans.

Presidential Election of 1856 ?❧ Tennessee Democrats looked forward to the presidential election of 1856 with more assurance than they had mustered since Jackson swept to victory in 1828 and 1832. They had hoped to place either Andrew Johnson or Aaron V. Brown on the ticket as Vice President, but they agreed readily to support the party nominees, James Buchanan and John C.

Breckinridge. Andrew Jackson Donelson, Jackson's nephew and former personal secretary, led Tennessee Know Nothings to the Philadelphia convention where he won the vice presidential nomination under Millard Fillmore, who had served as President for the remainder of Zachary Taylor's term after Taylor died in 1850. Republicans had organized in the North in 1854 in opposition to the extension of slavery, and in 1856 they nominated John C. Fremont for President. Naturally, they received no significant support in Tennessee or in any other slave state.

In the campaign in Tennessee, two Whigs of long standing—John Bell and James C. Jones—took opposite sides. Bell denied that he was a member of the Know Nothing party, but he endorsed the "great and leading principles" of it and spoke out for Fillmore and Donelson. Jones, however, believed that Southern states would be justified in seceding if Fremont were elected. Jones said that he would vote for Buchanan not because he cherished the Democratic party, but because he hated "Black Republicanism."

The November election brought victory to the Democrats, both in the state and nation. For the first time since 1832 the party of Andrew Jackson won a presidential contest in the Volunteer State. For the first time since the Whig party was organized, West Tennesseans deserted their political alliance with voters in the eastern section and joined with those of the middle division to give the Democrats a majority of nearly 7,500. Brownlow, greatly discouraged, believed that his party was "utterly vanquished."

Gubernatorial Elections of 1857 and 1859 ∽ The defeat in 1856 left the Know Nothings with little enthusiasm for a gubernatorial contest in 1857. Nevertheless, they chose Robert Hatton of Wilson County—the "Demosthenes of the great American Whig-Know Nothing party"—to oppose Isham G. Harris of Shelby County, whom the Democrats already had nominated. The campaign opened at Camden on May 25, and closed two months later when Harris and Hatton spoke in Nashville. Slavery and sectional equality in the territories were the principal issues. Much rancor characterized the campaign; fist fights developed in the audience at several towns, and on one occasion even between the two candidates. Harris's resounding majority of over 11,000 votes brought an end to the

Know Nothing party in Tennessee. Democrats also had a clear majority in the house and senate.

The victorious party of Jackson made plans at once to take both United States Senate seats. Jones's term expired; as his replacement, legislators chose Governor Johnson over Neill S. Brown by a solid majority. Jubilant Democrats observed that Bell's term would expire in 1859, and they proceeded to elect A. O. P. Nicholson to replace him when his term was over. Brownlow, who never had kind words for Democrats, was humiliated to think that Nicholson would replace the distinguished John Bell. His bitterness knew no bounds when he heard that Johnson—"that unmitigated liar and villainous coward"—also had won a Senate seat.

Two years later, remnants of Whigs, Know Nothings, and anti-administration Democrats united to form what they called the "Opposition Party." They chose John Netherland of Hawkins County as their gubernatorial candidate and Democrats nominated Harris. The impending national crisis overshadowed all state issues, and sixty-five debates were heard by audiences tense with excitement. Harris tried to link the new party with the Republicans and abolitionists of the North, and told listeners that a vote for Netherland was a vote against the South. The Opposition candidate, however, disclaimed any connection with the radical elements of the North, and pledged "unwavering firmness" in maintaining slavery under the Constitution. The rights and interests of the people of all sections, he said, should be carefully guarded.

Harris was victorious again, but his majority of 8,000 was considerably less than what it had been two years earlier. Although the Opposition party failed to gain majorities in the legislature, its congressional candidates won seven of the ten seats. Bell and Brownlow took heart, and both predicted that their party would meet with success in 1861.

SUGGESTED READINGS

General Accounts
Abernethy, *Frontier to Plantation*, Ch. 20; Frederic Bancroft, *Slave Trading in the Old South* (Baltimore, 1931); Mary R. Campbell, *The Attitude of Tennesseans Toward the Union, 1847–1861* (New York, 1961); Corlew, *Dickson County*; Avery O. Craven, *The Coming of the*

Civil War (Chicago, 1957); Folmsbee, Corlew, and Mitchell, *Tennessee*, I–II, Chs. 22, 24–25; Hamer, *Tennessee*, I, Chs. 30–32; Arthur Y. Lloyd, *The Slavery Controversy, 1831–1860* (Chapel Hill, 1939); Chase Mooney, *Slavery in Tennessee* (Bloomington, Ind., 1957); Ulrich B. Phillips, *American Negro Slavery* (New York, 1918).

Specialized Accounts

Thomas B. Alexander, "Thomas A. R. Nelson as an Example of Whig Conservatism in Tennessee," *THQ*, XV (March, 1956), 17–29; Mary R. Campbell, "Tennessee and the Union, 1847–1861," ETHS *Publ.*, No. 10 (1938), 71–90; W. M. Caskey, "First Administration of Governor Andrew Johnson," ETHS *Publ.*, No. 1 (1929), 43–59; Caskey, "The Second Administration of Governor Andrew Johnson," ETHS *Publ.*, No. 2 (1930), 34–54; Robert E. Corlew, "Some Aspects of Slavery in Dickson County," *THQ*, X (Sept., 1951), 224–48, 344–65; J. Merton England, "The Free Negro in Ante-Bellum Tennessee," *JSH*, IX (Feb., 1943), 37–58; O. B. Emerson, "Frances Wright and Her Nashoba Experiment," *THQ*, VI (Dec., 1947), 219–314; Sister Mary de Lourdes Gohmann, *Political Nativism in Tennessee to 1860* (Washington, D. C. 1938); Graf and Haskins, *Papers of Andrew Johnson*, I; William B. Hesseltine, "Some New Aspects of the Pro-slavery Argument," *JNH*, XXI (Jan., 1936), 1–15; Isabel Howell, "John Armfield, Slave-trader," *THQ*, II (March, 1943), 3–29; William L. Imes, "Legal Status of Free Negroes and Slaves in Tennessee," *JNH*, IV (July, 1919), 254–72; Asa E. Martin, "Anti-Slavery Societies of Tennessee," *THM*, I (Dec., 1915), 261–81; Martin, "Pioneer Anti-Slavery Press," *MVHR*, II (March, 1916), 509–28; George Fort Milton, *Age of Hate: Andrew Johnson and the Radicals* (New York, 1930); Chase C. Mooney, "Some Institutional and Statistical Aspects of Slavery in Tennessee," *THQ*, I (Sept., 1942), 195–228; Edd Winfield Parks, "Dreamer's Vision: Frances Wright at Nashoba, 1825–1830," *THM*, Ser. 2, II (Jan., 1932), 75–86, reprinted in White, *Tennessee: Old and New*, I, 299–319; J. W. Patton, "Progress of Emancipation in Tennessee," *JNH*, XVII (Jan., 1932), 67–102; William Pease and Jane H. Pease, "A New View of Nashoba," *THQ*, XIX (June, 1960), 99–109; William O. Scroggs, *Filibusters and Financiers: The Story of William Walker and His Associates* (New York, 1916); William O. Scroggs (ed.), "With Walker in Nicaragua: The Reminiscences of Elleanore (Callaghan) Ratterman," *THM*, I (Dec., 1915), 315–30; St. George L. Sioussat, "Tennessee, The Compromise of 1850, and the Nashville Convention," *MVHR*, II (Dec., 1915), 313–47; Henry Lee Swint, "Ezekiel Birdseye and the Free State of Frankland," *THQ*, III (Sept., 1944), 226–36.

15. ᷀ *Transportation and Internal Improvements*

T HE DEVELOPMENT of adequate means of transportation, so necessary for the commerce and well-being of any society, has been a problem of vital importance to Tennesseans. Before railroads were constructed, the people were dependent on roads and rivers, and since the navigation of the principal rivers, especially the Tennessee, was seriously obstructed, the opening and maintenance of roads were matters of great concern. The roads first used by the pioneers usually followed Indian trails, which in turn were frequently former buffalo paths. Later, these buffalo-Indian-pioneer trails became turnpikes and eventually modern highways; until modern earth-moving machinery made possible the improvement and straightening of these highways, travelers needed very little imagination to believe that they were following routes originally marked by a wandering buffalo.

Early Travel by Road and River ᷀ One of the earliest and most noted trails was the Wilderness Road marked by Daniel Boone from the Long Island of the Holston along the southern border of Virginia through Cumberland Gap into Kentucky following the Treaty of Sycamore Shoals in 1775. Actually this trail was an extension of a road down the Holston Valley through southwestern Virginia over which early hunters and settlers had passed. The trail later became a wagon road and one of the most important routes of migration in our national history. In the late 1770's a wagon road was opened from Burke County, North Carolina, across the mountains to Jonesboro. As settlement progressed down the Holston Valley, roads were opened along that river and also along the Nolichucky and French Broad as far as Knoxville. From a point on the Holston Road called Bean's Station (now inundated by Cherokee Lake), an alternate route of the Wilderness Road was opened about 1785 across Clinch Mountain to Cumberland Gap.

For many years the only overland connection between the East and Middle Tennessee settlements was by the Wilderness Road into Kentucky and through the Cumberland Valley to Nashville. In 1788, however, a road was cut from Campbell's Station, a few miles west of Knoxville, across the Cumberlands to the Middle Tennessee settlements. Since it was originally opened by the North Carolina militia, it was called the North Carolina Road, or occasionally Avery's Trace, after Peter Avery, who guided the expedition. As a result of a provision in the Holston Treaty for "free and unmolested use of a Road" between the East and Middle Tennessee settlements, the Walton Road was eventually opened from Southwest Point (Kingston) to Nashville. Its construction involved an unsuccessful lottery of 1794, a state appropriation of $1,000 in 1799, and the incorporation of the Cumberland Turnpike Company (Tennessee's first) in 1801, with authority to collect prescribed tolls. The road was named for William Walton, the most active of the commissioners appointed for its construction.

In 1802 the Chickasaw Indians consented to the opening of a road through their country, and the federal government built the famous Natchez Trace (now a national parkway) from Nashville to Natchez. Extended northward by the Tennessee Path to Lexington, Kentucky, the trace became the highway by which boatmen returned from New Orleans to the Cumberland and Kentucky settlements. In 1804 the Tennessee legislature appropriated $750 for the cutting of a road from Southwest Point (Kingston) and Tellico to connect with a Georgia road in the Cherokee Nation. The state contracted with Adam Peck for the construction of this so-called "Federal Road."

Local roads were maintained by the county governments. As early as 1801, specific counties were authorized to open roads, to put turnpikes (turnstiles) on them, and to collect tolls. By 1804 a general law was passed authorizing county courts to lay out public roads, build bridges, and establish ferries. All white males between the ages of 18 and 50 were required to work on the roads or pay 75 cents a day in lieu of such work. In 1821 the legislature directed that all public roads be divided into three classes: stage roads, second-class wagon roads, and horse paths. Sometimes individuals were authorized to open roads and collect tolls for keeping them in repair, but as time passed it became customary to charter turnpike companies for the building and maintenance of through roads. A perennial problem, later necessitating legislative action, was the evasion of payment of tolls by travelers striking out across country around the toll gates.

As detailed in earlier chapters, the Indians and then the white settlers made considerable use of the rivers for commerce and travel. The Indians used mainly "dugout" canoes, but the whites built flatboats and keelboats. The flatboats varied from primitive rafts to large, flat-bottomed boats with cabins for passengers. It was almost impossible to propel these boats upstream, so after the destination was reached, the boats usually were broken up and sold, and their navigators returned home overland. The keelboat, lighter and narrower than the largest flatboats, was framed about a long, stout piece of timber called a "keel" which made steering easier. The keelboat could be propelled upstream; although sails were used if there was wind, chief reliance was placed on poles. The members of the crew, on each side of the boat, would place the ends of their poles on the bottom of the river and propel the vessel upstream as they walked from prow to stern. Where the current was too deep or swift for "poling," the crew would put a rope around a tree on the bank and literally pull the boat upstream. Both methods involved backbreaking labor. In 1819, it required 67 days to propel a keelboat from New Orleans to Nashville.

Various devices were resorted to for improving the navigability of rivers. One was the incorporation of navigation companies, such as those for the Nolichucky and Harpeth, respectively, in 1801 and 1813, with authority to remove obstruction and collect specified tolls from the users of the river. Lotteries and special taxes also were imposed, and a small amount of revenue from the sale of land south of the French Broad was appropriated in 1817 for the improvement of what is now the Tennessee River between Knoxville and the Alabama line. After the Hiwassee District had been acquired in 1819, a bill was introduced in the legislature for the appropriation of $500,000 from the anticipated receipts from the sale of land in that area for the improvement of the rivers of the state; but the onset of the economic depression, together with a natural reluctance to appropriate funds before they were in the treasury, prevented its enactment.

The inhabitants of the Cumberland Valley had a reasonably direct access by river to the Gulf of Mexico at New Orleans, even though the Cumberland does follow a northward course for some distance before reaching the Ohio. But the much greater bend of the Tennessee down into Alabama and its longer northward course across Tennessee and Kentucky to the Ohio, together with the serious obstructions at the Muscle Shoals and elsewhere, meant that the inhabitants of the upper Tennessee Valley had a long and hazardous journey to reach the mouth of the Mississippi. Consequently, they were greatly interested in the possibility of a short cut to the Gulf at Mobile, made feasible by the proximity of branches of the Mobile River to branches of the Tennessee. Residents of lower Middle Tennessee were interested in the proposal, made as early as 1807, that a road or canal could be built to connect the Tombigbee, the western branch of the Mobile River, with Bear Creek, which flows into the Tennessee below the Muscle Shoals.[1] East Tennesseans were more partial to a connection between the eastern tributaries of the Mobile—the Alabama and its branch, the Coosa—with the Hiwassee River, which would not only provide a shorter route to the Gulf but also would bypass the obstructions at the Muscle Shoals. A modification of this idea seems to have been used to some extent, beginning in 1821. The Cherokee Indians objected to the practice, however, and when a company was chartered by Tennessee in 1826 to build a Hiwassee-Coosa canal, the Indians absolutely refused to permit its construction. By the time the Indians were moved west, the railroad era had arrived, and the canal idea was considered obsolete.

The canal fever in the West which was aroused by the building of the Erie Canal in New York led to several other Tennessee pro-

---

[1] A variation of this canal proposal, actually to connect the Tennessee itself with the Tombigbee, has been before Congress continuously since TVA developed the Tennessee as a navigable waterway to Knoxville. If actually carried out, it would result in a direct connection of the Tennessee with the Gulf of Mexico.

posals; however, only one waterway was built, and it was located outside the bounds of the state. Tennesseans, as well as the residents of Alabama, proposed the construction of a canal around the Muscle Shoals, and a canal, built with the aid of a federal land grant around the middle part of the Shoals, actually was completed in 1836. It was almost useless, however, and was largely superseded by a railroad.

Steamboats on Tennessee Waters The first steamboat on the Mississippi, the *New Orleans*, commanded by Captain Nicholas Roosevelt, met with an unusual reception. The steamboat arrived at the border of Tennessee in December, 1811, just in time to encounter the first shock of the New Madrid earthquakes which created Reelfoot Lake. Nevertheless, within the next few years steamboats were regularly plying the "Father of Waters" and the Ohio. The first steamboat to reach Nashville—the *General Jackson*, owned in part by William Carroll—did not arrive until March 11, 1819. The Nashville *Whig* reported briefly: "A sight so novel, at this place, has attracted large crowds of spectators." Within a few days the boat departed for New Orleans with passengers and a cargo of tobacco. The development of steamboat navigation on the Cumberland,[2] when the necessary river improvements were made, greatly benefited Nashville, which became a distributing point for a large area. Even Knoxville merchants profited by obtaining some of their goods from New Orleans by way of Nashville. Exports from Middle Tennessee—including cotton, tobacco, other farm produce, and the iron products of the furnaces of Dickson, Stewart, and Humphreys counties—also could be moved more profitably to market. Clarksville in Montgomery County became an important shipping center for tobacco, exporting 7,000 to 8,000 hogsheads annually by the middle 1840's.

Soon after steamers appeared on the Cumberland, steamboat navigation began on the Tennessee, as far as the foot of the Muscle Shoals. The *Rocket* arrived at Florence, Alabama, from New Or-

2 Most of the boats ran to New Orleans, but some went to Louisville, Pittsburgh, St. Louis, Florence, and other river ports. In a typical week in 1846 fifteen steamboats arrived at Nashville and thirteen departed.

leans and Nashville in 1822. It was not until 1828, however, that a steamboat succeeded in getting over the Shoals, conquering the dangerous hazards of the "Suck" and the "Boiling Pot" below the site of Chattanooga, and finally reaching Knoxville. This boat, appropriately named the *Atlas,* arrived at the East Tennessee metropolis on the evening of March 3, but then dropped back down the river and waited until the next morning, when it "sailed up in handsome style to the great gratification of a numerous concourse of citizens." Despite its enthusiastic reception, the *Atlas,* after returning to the Muscle Shoals, never again ventured a trip to Knoxville. Her arrival, however, had stimulated Knoxvillians. A company organized by W. B. A. Ramsey promptly acquired a steamboat and christened it the *Knoxville;* the boat reached the place after which it was named on April 25, 1831. When a few improvements were made in the navigability of the river, the boat gave intermittent service between Knoxville and Decatur, Alabama, at the head of the Muscle Shoals. The obstructions to the navigation of the Tennessee were so great, however, that it required the TVA ultimately to surmount them.

The coming of the steamboat to Tennessee waters greatly stimulated interest in internal improvements, with major attention being given to the removal of obstructions to steamboat navigation of the principal rivers. Interest also was stimulated in the use of keelboats on the smaller streams and in turnpike building, so that outlying farmers might have more ready access to steamboat shipping points. Effective measures for internal improvements were postponed, however, by a prolonged debate over whether the state or the federal government should supply the funds. In 1827 the legislature summarily closed the door to the major source of state funds for internal improvements—the proceeds from the sale of public lands. With the exception of one-half of the funds already received (about $175,000), the legislature assigned all past and future receipts from that source to the common school fund. Even the appropriation of the unassigned $175,000 was postponed until the next session.

At this next session of 1829–30, the legislators enacted Tennessee's first comprehensive system of state aid; yet, inconsistently, they also sent three memorials to Congress asking federal assistance in making internal improvements. One memorial requested aid in removing obstructions from the Cumberland River at Harpeth Shoals; another asked that the federal government promote the building of a national road from Buffalo by way of Washington to New Orleans; and the third memorial asked for aid in the building of a canal or a railroad between the Hiwassee and Coosa rivers. When President Jackson in 1830 revealed his opposition to federal aid by vetoing the Maysville Road Bill, the Tennessee legislators swallowed the words of these memorials by adopting in 1831 without a dissenting vote a resolution approving the presidential veto. Nevertheless, there was considerable sentiment in Tennessee, especially in the eastern and western divisions, in favor of federal aid;[3] this sentiment contributed to the anti-Jackson movement which soon developed within the state. Ironically, Middle Tennesseans, who most loyally supported Jackson's anti-federal aid policy, were the only citizens of the state to benefit materially from federal appropriations made while he was President. Jackson's interpretation of the Constitution was characterized by some "hair-splitting"; he was willing to approve appropriations for river improvement up to the highest port of entry from the ocean, since such rivers were related to foreign commerce. Nashville was declared a port of entry, and between 1832 and 1837 Jackson signed bills providing a total of $135,000 for the improvement of the Cumberland River below the Middle Tennessee metropolis near which was located his own home and plantation, the Hermitage.

Just before Tennesseans' hopes for federal aid were largely blasted by Jackson, the state legislature on January 2, 1830, made its first substantial appropriation for internal improvement: $150,000 from the unassigned land revenue, with East and Middle Tennessee being allocated $60,000 each and the remaining $30,000 going to the Western District. Under the administration of a special board of internal improvement for East Tennessee, that section's share was used rather effectively for the improvement of the Tennessee River between Knoxville and the Alabama line, making possible the ir-

---

[3] Three East Tennesseans in Congress and the West Tennessee representative, David Crockett, voted for the Hemphill Bill for the Buffalo-Washington-New Orleans road (which failed to pass) and also to override Jackson's veto of the Maysville Road Bill. Crockett, however, expressed his disappointment that the Washington road was not to terminate at Memphis, and he explained his support of the measure on the ground that Tennesseans should "share in the snacks" of public funds which apparently were going to be spent.

regular navigation mentioned above. In the other two divisions, the funds were scattered among numerous local projects without much benefit to the state as a whole.

The Early Railroad Movement ॐ Locomotives were operated by horse power in the eastern United States as early as 1826, and in 1829 the first steam locomotive was imported from England. The railroad fever rapidly spread to Tennessee, with the suggestion being made in 1827 that a railroad instead of a canal be used to connect the Hiwassee and Coosa rivers. In 1831, the Tennessee legislature granted six railroad charters; obviously, some of the companies receiving charters intended to build merely short lines as alternatives to canals or turnpikes, but still as adjuncts to river navigation. This was true, for example, with respect to the first company chartered, the Franklin Railroad, which actually built a turnpike instead of a railroad from Nashville to Franklin. Some of the companies, however, had more grandiose designs, involving the establishment of rail connections with the Atlantic seaboard, which were in response to railroad activities currently developing in the Eastern states. East Tennessee, the most isolated of the three grand divisions but the nearest to the Atlantic Ocean, was the first to be afflicted—and also the most violently—with the railroad fever.

The first East Tennessean to be affected was the Knoxville physician-historian, Dr. James G. M. Ramsey. When the steamboat *Atlas* came to Knoxville in 1828, he welcomed it with a rather tactless speech, stating that regular steamboat navigation to New Orleans, even if practicable, would not benefit East Tennessee and further would subject the farmers and manufacturers of that section to the ruinous competition of the producers in the upper Mississippi Valley. The most logical market for East Tennessee was the Atlantic seaboard, at Charleston or Savannah. Ramsey journeyed to Charleston and was able to convince the promoters of South Carolina Canal and Railroad Company, chartered in 1827 to build a railroad from Charleston to the Savannah River at Hamburg (opposite Augusta, Georgia), that it would be to their interest to extend their line to the Tennessee River. Although he developed that thesis through letters to the Charleston *Mercury* which were reprinted in the Knoxville *Register*, the plan did not have much immediate success.

Meanwhile, the residents of upper East Tennessee were becoming excited about the prospects of a rail and water connection northeastward through Virginia to the Atlantic. In 1831 the Virginia legislature chartered the Lynchburg and New River Railroad to provide a continuation of the James River Canal by rail to the New River, a branch of the Ohio in southwestern Virginia. East Tennesseans immediately began an agitation in favor of an extension of this proposed line through their section to Knoxville. From July 4, 1831, to June 14, 1832, a newspaper called the *Rail-Road Advocate* was published in the little town of Rogersville to exploit that idea. This probably was the first railroad newspaper to be published in the United States. The states of Virginia and Tennessee, however, refused to grant financial aid for the extension and the project collapsed. The *Rail-Road Advocate* also suspended publication, still proclaiming (June 14, 1832) that "Rail-Roads are the *only hope* of East Tennessee." The editor advised the people again to look in the direction of Charleston, which was standing with "outstretched arms" toward the West.

Meanwhile, the residents of Memphis had become interested in Charleston's westward designs. The South Carolina Railroad was completed to Hamburg in 1833, and for several years it was the longest railroad in the world. As early as 1831, consideration was given to an extension of this line to the Tennessee River at the head of the Muscle Shoals, because the Tuscumbia, Courtland and Decatur Railroad Company had been organized in Alabama to build a railroad around those obstructions, which was completed in 1834. Thus, when the Memphis Railroad Company was chartered in 1831, its immediate aim was to relieve nearby planters from their dependence on miry West Tennessee roads leading to the Mississippi, but the company's ultimate dream was a rail connection with Charleston. This design was made clear by the new name of the company acquired in 1833—the Atlantic and Mississippi Railroad. A resident of Memphis who was most active in promoting this abortive dream was Major General Edmund Pendleton Gaines, who had grandiose ideas of an extensive system of internal improvements as an aid to national defense. Gaines also became a sponsor of another grand scheme—a railroad from Memphis to Baltimore, which like Charleston was the terminus of a pioneer American railroad, the Baltimore and Ohio. Through his connections with the War Department,

Gaines was able to secure the services of Major Stephen H. Long for the survey of both routes. Towns in the interior of Tennessee, such as Jackson and Columbia, became excited over the prospect of being stations on a railroad from the Mississippi to Chesapeake Bay. Congressman James K. Polk received enthusiastic letters in 1834 from friends predicting that his home town of Columbia was destined to become the metropolis of Middle Tennessee, succeeding Nashville, which would be left with its steamboats high and dry on the banks of the Cumberland River.

In 1835, Dr. Ramsey's idea of a rail connection between Knoxville and Charleston was revived as a part of a much larger project—a railroad from Charleston to Cincinnati. The initiative this time came from the "Queen City of the West," but the South Carolinians responded enthusiastically. Within a few months the Louisville, Cincinnati and Charleston Railroad was incorporated in the two Carolinas, Tennessee, and Kentucky.[4] To promote the undertaking, a convention of nearly four hundred delegates representing nine states convened in Knoxville on July 4, 1836. When the convention selected the difficult route over the mountains from North Carolina along the French Broad River to Knoxville and thence through Cumberland Gap into Kentucky, the delegates from Georgia and lower East Tennessee were disappointed. The easier route they had proposed, south of the mountain barrier, had been accepted merely as a possible branch road rather than as the main line. The Georgians were informed by the delegates from McMinn County, Tennessee, of the existence of a charter of the Hiwassee Railroad Company, granted in January, 1836, to build a railroad from Knoxville to the Georgia line to connect with the projected extension of the South Carolina Railroad to the Tennessee River. Consequently, Georgia initiated a project independent of the Cincinnati and Charleston undertaking. Under Georgia's plan, the road already under construction by the Georgia Railroad Company westward from the Savannah River at Augusta (opposite the terminus of the Charleston and Hamburg line) would be extended to the Chattahoochee River (at Atlanta), where the road would meet other projected lines from Savannah, Milledgeville, and Columbus. The state

---

[4] The Kentucky legislature insisted on the inclusion of branches to Louisville and Maysville, in addition to the main line to Covington (opposite Cincinnati), and also the adding of Louisville to the corporate name.

of Georgia was to build a road from Atlanta to Ross's Landing (Chattanooga) to be called the Western and Atlantic. The Hiwassee Railroad was to be built from Knoxville to a junction with the Western and Atlantic at Dalton, Georgia. Thus, Knoxville would be supplied with two separate rail connections with Charleston.

The State-Stock System of 1836–38 The development of interest throughout the state in railroad building led to the enactment of the second general law providing for state action for the improvement of transportation facilities. In February, 1836, several months before the Knoxville convention, the legislature, following the injunction placed upon it by the constitutional convention of 1834 to encourage internal improvements, passed an act providing that the state should subscribe for one-third of the stock of all companies engaged in the construction of railroads or macadamized turnpikes. The inclusion of turnpikes was due to the insistence of the Middle Tennessee legislators. In this section, except for the temporary excitement in Columbia and a short flurry of interest in a proposal of a railroad from New Orleans to Nashville, the railroad fever was not as fervid as in East and West Tennessee. More adequately supplied with steamboat navigation, Middle Tennesseans were chiefly interested in the building of highways to the shipping points on the major rivers. Even so, the law was passed by East and West Tennessee votes overcoming the opposition of a majority of the Middle Tennessee legislators, who feared the creation of a large state debt and a consequent increase in taxes. Somewhat less evident, though still noticeable, was the tendency of future Whigs to support the measure more wholeheartedly than the Democrats, who were in the minority in this legislature. Also, the anti-Jackson governor, Newton Cannon, strongly recommended the legislation. Equally significant was the influence of General Gaines, who came to Nashville to lobby for state aid for the building of a network of railroads.

It soon became evident that the one-third system was inadequate. Only one railroad and three Middle Tennessee turnpike companies were able to obtain the "well secured" private subscriptions of the remaining two-thirds of the stock necessary to qualify for state aid. The railroad was the LaGrange and Memphis, chartered in 1835 as a successor of the Memphis and the Atlantic and Mississippi companies mentioned above. The limiting of its immediate aims to the building of a road from LaGrange to Memphis and a branch line to Somerville reduced its capitalization sufficiently to make it possible to obtain the necessary amount of private subscriptions. But to get these subscribers actually to pay for their stock was much more difficult. West Tennessee was still so young and poor that there arose in Madison County a movement in favor of the construction entirely at the expense of the state of a "Central Railroad" from the Mississippi to Bristol. The legislature appropriated $15,000 for a survey of the route, but this intersectional railroad never was constructed. The Hiwassee Railroad, under the presidency of Solomon D. Jacobs, although unable to qualify for the state subscription, did begin construction work in August, 1837, near Athens. According to one authority, this was "the first lick ever made in the state in the construction of a railroad." The Louisville, Cincinnati and Charleston Railroad resorted to a banking scheme to keep the project alive. Under the authority of an amendment to its charter, the railroad established a bank at Charleston and a branch, called the Southwestern Railroad Bank, at Knoxville. Dr. James G. M. Ramsey quite appropriately was made president of the branch.

As a consequence of the Panic of 1837, the legislature at its next session was bombarded with appeals for help from railroad and turnpike companies, and the legislators responded by increasing the amount of state subscriptions from one-third to one-half. This result was achieved by a remarkable example of log-rolling on the part of the rival interests of internal improvements, banking, and education. The Bank and Improvement Act of 1838, as the law was called, satisfied the depression-caused need for increased banking facilities by creating the completely state-owned Bank of Tennessee. The bank's capital stock was to be raised mainly by the sale of state bonds, but also the entire common school fund of the state was to be included, plus all future receipts from the sale of public lands, as already promised in 1827. The bank was required to set aside from its profits $100,000 annually for the support of common schools and $18,000 for academies. To satisfy the advocates of river improvement, which had been ignored in the 1836 law, $300,000 in state bonds were to be issued for that improvement, to be divided equally among the three grand divisions of the state. In contrast to the previous law, under which the "sky was the limit," the act of 1838 provided that the maximum amount of state funds available for internal improvements was to be four million dollars, including the river bonds. The remaining amount of $3,700,000 was to be made available for the state subscriptions for one-half of the stock of railroad and turnpike companies, to be apportioned as follows: $1,300,000 to East Tennessee, $1,500,000 to Middle Tennessee, and $900,000 to West Tennessee. At the request of the East Tennessee legislators, however, the whole of that section's share was to be divided equally between the Louisville, Cincinnati and Charleston and the Hiwassee railroad companies. East Tennessee turnpike companies were not to be eligible for aid unless one of the railroads failed to qualify. The state subscriptions, instead of being paid in one lump sum when called for by the directors as under the previous law, were to be paid in proportion to the payments actually made by the private subscribers. As was the case in 1836, the act was passed by East and West Tennessee votes over the strenuous opposition of Middle Tennessee legislators. Although the legislature was controlled by the Whigs, the members of both parties supported the bill by small majorities.

Because of the seriousness of the economic depression, the state aid laws of 1836 and 1838 were almost complete failures. The only tangible benefit was the construction of a number of turnpikes, most of them located in Middle Tennessee, which, ironically, had been most opposed to the legislation. The credit of the state also suffered severely. Only one million of the $2,500,000 of 6 per cent state bonds for the capital of the bank could be sold; and the 5 per cent bonds for river improvement, which, like the bank bonds under the law could not be sold at less than par, could not be sold at all. The bonds issued to the railroad and turnpike companies in payment of the state subscriptions could be sold by those companies only at ruinous discounts. The bonds were hawked in the markets of the world and sold for whatever they would bring, in some cases as little as 50 cents on the dollar. Consequently, in 1840, during the administration of Governor James K. Polk, the state aid laws were repealed insofar as it was possible. Where state subscriptions had been made, the companies involved were still entitled to receive the bonds due from the state if the companies complied with the law. The repeal was carried by a large majority of both parties in this Democratic-controlled legislature.

The railroad enterprises were the chief casualties of the depression. The Cincinnati and Charleston project was the first to collapse. The LC&C company, weakened by internal dissension following the death of its inspired president, Robert Y. Hayne, in 1839 and by a bitter controversy with the Hiwassee Railroad, surrendered its charter and returned the small amount of state bonds it had received. Both the Hiwassee Railroad and East Tennessee turnpike companies hoped to inherit the $650,000 state subscription to the Louisville, Cincinnati, and Charleston Railroad, but the legislature cancelled the subscription. The Hiwassee Railroad, which after fighting the LC&C had attempted to consolidate with it before its demise, managed to struggle on alone until 1842, when it also succumbed. The Hiwassee Railroad had succeeded, however, with the aid of $357,000 in state bonds (sold for $279,282.72), in grading about sixty-five miles of the road, building a bridge over the Hiwassee River, and in starting an iron works at Charleston, Tennessee, for the manufacture of rails. The railroad's work on a road from Dalton to Knoxville was later resumed by a successor company (the East Tennessee and Georgia) and was eventually completed in 1855.

The LaGrange and Memphis Railroad at first refused to accept the state-aid law of 1838 because of the requirement of actual payments by private subscribers as a precedent to the issuance of state bonds. Later the railroad obtained a state subscription to one-half of its stock on its own terms and eventually received a total of $216,250 in state bonds. Nevertheless, as a Memphis historian expressed it, "With a hamlet at one end, and an Indian trading station [LaGrange] of 240 inhabitants at the other, and an unsettled country intervening, what was to be expected but failure?" Under the leadership of its energetic president, Eastin Morris of LaGrange, the LaGrange and Memphis Railroad was able, however, to make a name for itself as the first company to operate a railroad train in Tennessee. By the end of 1841, the major portion of the road had been graded and rails laid for a distance of about ten miles at the Memphis end. The railroad acquired several cars and a locomotive which early in 1842 transported a handful of frightened passengers on a round trip to a turntable about six miles from Memphis. A few months later the sheriff of Shelby County took possession of the property because of unsatisfied court judgments. After several years' delay, a new company, the Memphis and Charleston, absorbed the

LaGrange and Memphis and with the aid of connecting lines brought to reality in 1857 the dream of General Gaines and John C. Calhoun of a rail connection between the Atlantic Ocean and the Mississippi River.

As mentioned above, the only immediate benefits from the state-aid system of 1836–38 came from turnpike construction. Twenty-four turnpike companies—nineteen in Middle Tennessee and five in West Tennessee—succeeded in qualifying for state subscriptions and eventually received a total of $1,245,357 in state aid. A few of the companies failed, but the others managed to build more than four hundred miles of turnpikes. A state investigation revealed, however, that a considerable amount of fraud and corruption characterized their operations, and the dividends paid on the state stock were very insignificant. The most important of the turnpikes were those radiating from Nashville to neighboring towns, because the turnpikes contributed greatly to the rise of the capital city, with its steamboat facilities, to a dominant economic position and to the blooming prosperity of the whole Nashville Basin. An unfortunate result was the accentuation of sectional antagonisms, since East and West Tennessee had received little or no benefit from the state subsidies. In 1841–42, separate statehood movements[5] arose in both of these sections, and although other issues were involved, the disparity of benefits in internal improvement was a contributing factor. This is well illustrated by a speech delivered by a West Tennessee representative, David Fentress, during the debate in January–February, 1842, on a bill which cancelled the unsold river bonds issued in 1838:

> Yes, it may now be said, with propriety, what was said of old Rome, "every road leads to Nashville." Yet the people of the most remote parts of the State have to pay their proportion of the taxes, raised to build these fine roads, though they may never have seen the *beautiful* city of Nashville. . . .

Fentress ventured a prophecy that if the selfish Middle Tennesseans denied the "provinces" their paltry river funds, there would appear in the Western District a "Peter, the Hermit" and in East Tennes-

---

[5] Andrew Johnson introduced a resolution, similar to one proposed by Alfred Martin in 1840, for a new state of "Frankland" in East Tennessee, and John A. Gardner of Weakley County introduced one for a new state to be called "Jacksoniana" in West Tennessee.

see an "Attila, the Hun" who would "preach a crusade" and lead an avenging host that would "devastate and waste your Palestine!"[6] The Middle Tennesseans were sufficiently frightened that they permitted the appropriation from the treasury of $200,000 for river improvement, to be divided equally between East and West Tennessee.

It should be kept in mind that many other states expanded recklessly in the fields of banking and internal improvements during the same period; several states defaulted on the payment of the interest on their bonds, and a few states even repudiated their debts entirely. It is to the credit of Tennessee that she courageously increased taxes and maintained the payment of the interest on the two-million-dollar debt incurred and eventually retired the bonds.

State Loans and Railroad Construction — For several years after the collapse of the railroad enterprises aided under the state-stock system, Tennesseans were not interested in that new type of transportation. During the latter part of the 1840's, however, interest rapidly revived. This was largely because of the progress being made in railroad construction in neighboring states, especially in Georgia. With the recovery from the economic depression, work was resumed on the Georgia lines leading to Chattanooga whose initiation had earlier aroused interest in East and West Tennessee. The Georgia Railroad was completed from Augusta to Atlanta in the fall of 1845, thus completing the rail connection from Charleston[7] to Atlanta. A railroad from the seaport of Savannah reached Atlanta early the next year. By the end of 1849 the Western and Atlantic was completed from Atlanta to Chattanooga, except for a tunnel near Dalton which was opened in May, 1850. Meanwhile, a locomotive and cars had been hauled in wagons around the uncompleted tunnel, and the first train chugged into Chattanooga on December 1, 1849, to be received by a rousing welcome. As the rails approached Chattanooga, the hope of connecting with them was revived in Knoxville and Memphis, and a similar hope arose in Nashville, where earlier little interest had been

[6] Folmsbee, *Sectionalism*, 219–20.
[7] It will be recalled that the South Carolina Railroad from Charleston to Hamburg (across the Savannah River from Augusta) had been completed in 1833.

shown. State pride was also involved. In 1850 a national publication, the *Railroad Gazette*, published some statistics giving the estimated mileage of Southern railroads in operation on January 1 of that year: Georgia, 631 miles; Alabama, 111; Mississippi, 98; Kentucky, 28; and Tennessee, 0. The two sessions of the Southern and Western Convention held in Memphis in July and November of 1845 also greatly stimulated interest in railroad building in the South and West. The second session, presided over by John C. Calhoun, attracted six or seven hundred delegates from sixteen states and territories. Within the next three or four years the Tennessee legislature had chartered the Nashville and Chattanooga, the Memphis and Charleston, and the East Tennessee and Georgia railroad companies, designed to connect Nashville, Memphis, and Knoxville, respectively, with the Georgia and South Carolina roads leading to the Atlantic Coast at Charleston and Savannah.

At first the railroad promoters argued that the roads could be built by private enterprise without resort to governmental assistance, but it was not long before appeals were being made for state aid. This was especially true after the federal government in 1850 inaugurated a system of granting to public-land states generous grants of federal land in aid of railroad construction. Tennessee, however, had no federal lands, and the burden therefore fell more heavily upon the state government. The legislature began slowly and hesitatingly in 1848 with the offer to endorse company bonds issued by the Nashville and Chattanooga and the East Tennessee and Georgia companies to the amounts of $500,000 and $350,000, respectively. It was expected that the state endorsement would enable the companies to sell their bonds at par, whereas without it they would not be able to dispose of them except at ruinous discounts. This was the case with the Nashville and Chattanooga company, which built its road without obtaining any other type of direct aid from the state. The East Tennessee and Georgia, however, refused the state's endorsement and two years later succeeded in obtaining a direct loan in state bonds of the same amount, thus providing a precedent for the general system of state aid enacted two years later.

After the General Assembly of 1849–50, controlled by Democrats, refused to pass that type of a general law, the question of state aid became a major issue in the election of 1851. By that time a great number of railroad enterprises were being projected in many parts of the state, and this fact contributed to the election of a legislature more friendly to the idea of granting governmental assistance. The General Internal Improvement Law of 1852 provided for state loans to railroad companies in the form of 6 per cent bonds at the rate of $8,000 per mile (increased to $10,000 in 1854) to be used exclusively for acquiring and putting down the rails and obtaining necessary equipment. To be eligible for a loan a company had to show that it had bona fide subscriptions of stock sufficient to grade and bridge the whole line and that one section of thirty (later ten) miles, beginning at one terminus, was ready for the laying of the rails. It could then obtain the bonds for that section, and as other sections were completed additional allotments of bonds would be available. The companies were required to pay the interest on the loan semiannually, and beginning five years after the road was completed to make annual payments into a sinking fund to enable the state to retire the bonds at maturity. The state also was to have a lien on the property of the railroads until the loans were repaid. In 1854 the legislature authorized additional loans to assist in the construction of bridges over any of the major rivers in the state. With the exception of the Nashville and Chattanooga, practically every railroad incorporated in Tennessee before the Civil War was granted aid under this system. Indirect aid was provided by authorizing counties and municipalities to subscribe for stock of railroad companies, subject to a referendum, and by exemption from taxation of state, county, and municipal bonds issued to aid railroad construction.

The first railroad completed in Tennessee was the Nashville and Chattanooga. The incorporation of the company, in December, 1845, was the result of a vigorous campaign waged by Dr. James Overton and A. O. P. Nicholson of Nashville to overcome the indifference of a city apparently wedded to steamboat navigation. They were aided by the state geologist, Dr. Gerard Troost, who made a report concerning the feasibility of the road and the abundance of mineral resources, especially coal, along the route. The Memphis conventions of 1845 also created a fear that the establishment of a rail connection between Memphis and Charleston would take much of the trade of lower Middle Tennessee away from Nashville. From the organization of the company until long after the road's completion, Vernon K. Stevenson served as president, and he was the real builder of the road. He and ex-Governor James C. ("Lean Jimmy") Jones were adept stock salesmen, obtaining subscriptions from the city of Charleston, the Georgia Railroad Company, as well as from Nashville and many towns and counties along the route. To avoid much of the mountain barrier, the route chosen dipped down into Alabama and approached Chattanooga along the Tennessee River. The road was completed to the river at Bridgeport, Alabama, by the beginning of 1853 and to Chattanooga in January, 1854, and the only aid received from the state to build this road was the endorsement of the company's bonds, to the total amount of $1,500,000. With the aid of booming business during the Civil War, the company was able to pay off the bonds when they became due. Thus, the Nashville and Chattanooga was not only the first Tennessee road completed but also the only one which the state aided without suffering any financial loss.

Before the war the Nashville and Chattanooga became closely associated with some branch lines, most of which it later absorbed. One was the McMinnville and Manchester, which was completed from Tullahoma to McMinnville in 1857. The extension to Sparta was not made until after the war. The original aim of the Winchester and Alabama, as the name indicates, was a connection with the projected Memphis and Charleston Railroad at Huntsville, Alabama. But when the road reached the Alabama line from Decherd and Winchester, it was diverted northwestward to Fayetteville, and the connection with Huntsville was not made until after the war. Another important branch, to the coal mines of the Sewanee Mining Company near Tracy City, when completed in 1855 provided Nashville with a more regular and cheap supply of coal.[8]

Very closely associated with the Nashville and Chattanooga was the Nashville and Northwestern Railroad, which after 1856 had the same president, V. K. Stevenson. Projected to run from Nashville to the Mississippi River at Hickman, Kentucky, the road had been built eastward from Hickman as far as McKenzie in Carroll County before the war began. But at the eastern end, the road had been built only a few miles from Nashville before the Union army took over and continued it to the Tennessee River at Johnsonville as a war

[8] To satisfy the terms of the subscription by the town of Shelbyville to the stock of the Nashville and Chattanooga Railroad, the company built a short branch to it from Wartrace.

measure. Shortly after the gap between the river and McKenzie was filled during the postwar years, the Nashville and Northwestern was absorbed by the Nashville and Chattanooga in 1872, and the combination assumed its modern name, the Nashville, Chattanooga and St. Louis Railroad, usually abbreviated to N.C. & St. L. It is now a part of the Louisville and Nashville system to be discussed later.

Although incorporated February 2, 1846, the Memphis and Charleston Railroad did not make much progress until another railroad convention was held in Memphis in 1849 and "Lean Jimmy" Jones helped to get the project off the ground. As the first president of the company, he did for the Memphis and Charleston what he had helped Stevenson do for the Nashville and Chattanooga—sell stock in widely separated places. In New Orleans, Jones argued that the building of the road would greatly increase the amount of cotton which would be shipped down the Mississippi. In Charleston, however, he confidently predicted that a rail connection with the Atlantic Ocean would divert most of the Mississippi River trade to Charleston.[9] When the Memphis and Charleston absorbed the old LaGrange and Memphis company, good use was made of the construction work the latter company had done. The Memphis and Charleston also took over the railroad which had been built around the Muscle Shoals. For some time Mississippi held up the work by refusing to grant a charter except on the terms that the road should go through Holly Springs. Eventually, this restriction was removed, and the original route was followed, cutting across merely the northeast corner of Mississippi by way of Corinth. The road was completed to Stevenson, Alabama, in March, 1857, and since arrangements had been made to use the tracks of the Nashville and Chattanooga for the remainder of the distance to Chattanooga, the rail connection between Memphis and the Atlantic seaboard was now complete. On May 1, a "marriage" ceremony was performed at Memphis, with the mayors of Charleston and Memphis serving as proxies in the betrothal of the "Old Ocean" and the "Father of Waters." Then a barrel of ocean water was pumped into the Mississippi River, to the cheers of 25,000 spectators. Some time later the ceremony was repeated at Charleston, where the fresh water of the Mississippi River was mingled with the salt water of the Atlantic

[9] Actually, as soon as the Western and Atlantic Railroad was completed, it began to carry large amounts of cotton toward the seaboard.

Ocean. Eventually (1892), the Memphis and Charleston Railroad, since it came under the control of the East Tennessee, Virginia, and Georgia after the war, became a part of the Southern Railway system.

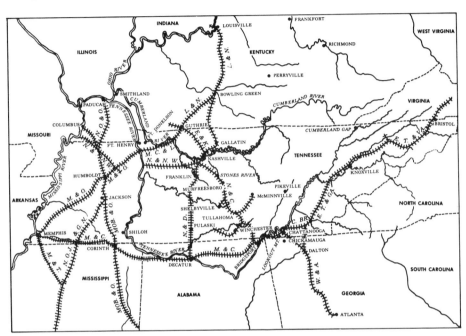

Map 5.

RAILROADS IN TENNESSEE
AT THE TIME OF THE CIVIL WAR
KEY TO RAILROAD NAMES

C. Br. Cleveland Branch, East
   Tennessee and Georgia
E.&K. Edgefield and Kentucky
E.T.&Ga. East Tennessee and Georgia
E.T.&Va. East Tennessee and Virginia
L.&N. Louisville and Nashville
M.&C. Memphis and Charleston
M.C.&L. Memphis, Clarksville,
   and Louisville

M.&O. Memphis and Ohio
M.&T. Mississippi and Tennessee
Mob.&O. Mobile and Ohio
N.&C. Nashville and Chattanooga
N.&N.W. Nashville and Northwestern
N.O.J.&G.N. New Orleans, Jackson,
   and Great Northern
N.O.&O. New Orleans and Ohio
N. & D. Nashville and Decatur
W.&A. Western and Atlantic

Another part of the present Southern which was built before the Civil War brought to reality the early (1831) dream of East Tennesseans of seeing a railroad through their section which would connect at each end with lines leading to the Atlantic seaboard—through

Georgia and Virginia, respectively. This aim was achieved by two companies, the East Tennessee and Georgia and the East Tennessee and Virginia (meeting at Knoxville), which were consolidated in 1869 under the name East Tennessee, Virginia, and Georgia (E.T., Va. & Ga.). The East Tennessee and Georgia was a revival of the Hiwassee Railroad, which before its collapse in 1842 had made a good beginning in the effort to build a railroad from Dalton, Georgia (on the route of the Western and Atlantic from Atlanta to Chattanooga) to Knoxville. Following the successful termination in 1846 of a suit brought against the Hiwassee by the state, the company was reorganized with T. Nixon Van Dyke as president and obtained its new name and a new charter in 1848. With the aid of new subscriptions and state loans, the East Tennessee and Georgia was able to complete the construction of the road from Dalton by way of Athens and Blair's Ferry (Loudon) to Knoxville in June, 1855.[10] Thus, under the presidency of the energetic Campbell Wallace, the line became the second railroad completed in Tennessee. In 1858 a "branch road" (now the main line of the Southern) from Cleveland to Chattanooga was completed, which avoided the roundabout route from Knoxville to Dalton and then back to Chattanooga on the Western and Atlantic.

The incorporation of the East Tennessee and Virginia Railroad on January 27, 1848, resulted from a convention at Greeneville in 1847 which became involved in a dispute between railroad and river improvement interests. The legislature, however, failed to carry out the compromise recommendations of the convention—a state subscription to the railroad company and an appropriation of $250,000 for the improvement of the Holston and French Broad rivers. With great difficulty the supporters of the railroad succeeded in getting enough subscriptions to organize the company in 1849, and Dr. Samuel B. Cunningham of Jonesboro was elected president. To advance the project a group of Jonesboro citizens began the publication of the *Rail Road Journal* in 1850. Jonesboro and Greeneville became involved in a bitter controversy with Rogersville (the home of the earlier paper, the *Rail-Road Advocate*) and other communities on the other side of Bay's Mountain over the location of the

[10] In August, 1855, after the completion of both the Nashville and Chattanooga and the East Tennessee and Georgia, 150,000 bushels of wheat were shipped over the Western and Atlantic, some of it destined for Northern markets.

route. The eastern route won, and the Carter's Valley people had to be satisfied with a branch line, built by a separate company from Bull's Gap to Rogersville, which was not completed until after the war.[11] When the East Tennessee and Virginia was opened throughout its entire length from Knoxville to Bristol in May, 1858, it filled a gap in completed rail lines extending from such Eastern cities as Boston, New York, and Washington all the way to Atlanta, Charleston, Savannah, Montgomery, Nashville, New Orleans, and Mobile. East Tennessee's "isolated condition" at last had been ended.

Another railroad system of great importance in Tennessee is the Louisville and Nashville, familiarly known as the L. & N. A considerable portion of this line was constructed before the Civil War. The initiative for the construction of the main line, between the cities in its name, came from Louisville, which feared that other cities would capture its Southern markets. The company, first incorporated in Kentucky on March 5, 1850, had some difficulty in obtaining a Tennessee charter. The L. & N. was financed largely by a subscription of a million dollars by the city of Louisville and by state aid under Tennessee's general laws. Its route in Tennessee was determined by the amounts subscribed by local governments along the alternative routes, and Gallatin and Sumner County won the contest. Completed on the eve of secession (October, 1859), the road was viewed as a link binding the North and South together. The legislatures of Tennessee and Kentucky met in Louisville and then joined in a Union-saving excursion to Columbus, Ohio. Eloquent Unionist speeches were made by political leaders of Tennessee who not long thereafter were to be identified with the Confederate States of America.

[11] Before the war some other East Tennessee companies had made some slight beginnings in railroad construction with the aid of state loans. The companies were absorbed and some work completed by the E.T., Va. & Ga. in the postwar years. Included was the ultimate achievement of the "grand design" of the Louisville, Cincinnati and Charleston. The Knoxville and Charleston, designed to connect with the Rabun Gap Railroad of South Carolina, stopped after reaching Maryville, sixteen miles from Knoxville; but the Cincinnati, Cumberland Gap and Charleston, which was nearly completed from Morristown, on the E.T. & Va., to the North Carolina line before the war, eventually attained a connection by way of Asheville with the Atlantic seaboard in 1881. The Knoxville and Kentucky, nearly completed to Clinton before the war, after troublous postwar years eventually was completed as a part of the E.T., Va. and Ga. to a connection with a branch of the L. & N. at Jellico in 1883. Meanwhile, Cincinnati had already achieved a rail connection with Charleston, and also with a network of southwestern lines, by the completion of the Cincinnati Southern Railway to Chattanooga in December, 1879.

Other parts of the present L. & N. system were built by other companies, which were absorbed by the L. & N. after the Tennessee state-aid system collapsed during the Reconstruction period. Before the war, one line, generally known as the Nashville and Decatur Railroad and built by two companies, the Tennessee and Alabama[12] and the Central Southern, connecting at Columbia, was completed from Nashville southward to the southern boundary of the state, where the line met an Alabama road from Decatur on the Memphis and Charleston Railroad. Another road later acquired by the L. & N. in which Middle Tennessee was greatly interested was the Edgefield and Kentucky. It was completed from Edgefield, a suburb of Nashville across the Cumberland River, northwestward to the Kentucky line at Guthrie early in 1860. There the Edgefield and Kentucky was to meet a Kentucky road from Henderson, but this line through western Kentucky coal fields was not finished until after the war. The Edgefield and Kentucky, however, did connect at Guthrie with another part of the future L. & N. system which was completed just as the war was beginning—the so-called "air-line" route from Memphis to Louisville. It was built by the Memphis and Ohio from Memphis to Paris, by the Memphis, Clarksville, and Louisville from Paris to Guthrie, and by the L. & N. itself, which built a branch line from Bowling Green to Guthrie.

Before the Civil War, West Tennesseans had also acquired rail connections with Mobile, New Orleans, and Columbus (Kentucky) as a result of the work of the Mobile and Ohio Railroad (now the Gulf, Mobile and Ohio) and a group of companies which are now included in the Illinois Central system. Involved was a race between Mobile and New Orleans in their efforts to achieve a connection by railroad with the mouth of the Ohio River. The aim of Mobile was to divert to its port much of the traffic going down the Mississippi River to New Orleans. The citizens of the "Crescent City," however, were determined not only to counteract that effort but also to negate the influence of the Memphis and Charleston and other railroads in diverting traffic from "Old Man River." As finally located, the Mobile and Ohio entered Tennessee just north of Corinth, Mississippi, where it connected with the Memphis and Charleston

---

[12] This line was extended also in a southwestern direction from Columbia to Mt. Pleasant, and was completed after the war by the L. & N. to Sheffield, Alabama, on the Memphis and Charleston line.

Railroad, and proceeded northwardly through Jackson and Trenton in the direction of Columbus, Kentucky, below the mouth of the Ohio. There, the Mobile and Ohio made connection by ferry with Cairo, the terminus of the Illinois Central Railroad from Chicago. The section from Columbus to Jackson, Tennessee, was completed by the end of 1858, but the longer portion between Jackson and Mobile was not finished until April 22, 1861, ten days after the Civil War had begun.

Meanwhile, the New Orleans, Jackson, and Great Northern Railroad had been completed through Jackson, Mississippi, to Canton; and the line was continued by Mississippi Central Railroad to Grand Junction, where the Memphis and Charleston crossed the Tennessee-Mississippi state line, and by the Mississippi Central and Tennessee Railroad to a connection with the Mobile and Ohio at Jackson, Tennessee. The line was completed in January, 1860. Thus, by using the completed section of the Mobile and Ohio from Jackson to Columbus, New Orleans had the benefit of rail communication with the Northwest more than a year before its rival, Mobile. Also, the Mississippi and Tennessee Railroad built a line from Memphis to Grenada, Mississippi, on the Mississippi Central, which as it progressed southeastward gave the planters of northwestern Mississippi easier access to the river port of Memphis; when completed in July, 1861, the line gave Memphis a direct rail connection with New Orleans. The Illinois Central, which came into possession of this whole system of roads after the war, in December, 1873, completed the building of the "Cairo Extension," from Jackson, Tennessee, to Cairo; thus, that city and the Illinois Central were released from their dependence on the Mobile and Ohio.[13]

The people of Memphis and West Tennessee, and even other parts of the state, became very much interested in the Pacific railroad movement, which aroused a great amount of national attention in the years following Asa Whitney's proposal of the idea in the 1840's. During the next decade the claims of Memphis as the most logical point for the crossing of the Mississippi River were advanced with enthusiasm. In 1855–56, the Tennessee legislature instructed the

[13] A Kentucky company, the New Orleans and Ohio Railroad, had built by 1858 a road from Paducah to the connection with the Nashville and Northwestern Railroad three miles east of Union City, Tennessee. The road was extended to Memphis by 1873 and was acquired by the Illinois Central in 1897.

state's members of Congress to vote to support a route by way of Memphis, Little Rock, and El Paso, and the legislature authorized the state's endorsement of $350,000 in bonds issued by the city of Memphis in aid of the Memphis and Little Rock Railroad, not one mile of which was located in Tennessee. In 1859 a convention in Memphis adopted a resolution in favor of the same route, but the Civil War ruined any chances it may have had of being selected. In that war, however, the approximately twelve hundred miles of railroads which had been built in Tennessee during the decade of 1850's played a very significant role in military strategy. The railroads also had great potentialities for improvement and expansion of the state's economy, but those results, only partially realized before the war, were postponed by that struggle and by the difficulties of Reconstruction.

SUGGESTED READINGS

General Accounts

Capers, *River Town—Memphis*; Davidson, *The Tennessee*, I, Chs. 14–16, 18–19; Byrd Douglas, *Steamboatin' on the Cumberland* (Nashville, 1961); Folmsbee, Corlew, and Mitchell, *Tennessee*, I, Ch. 19; Stanley J. Folmsbee, *Sectionalism and Internal Improvements in Tennessee, 1796–1845* (Knoxville, 1939); Govan and Livingood, *Chattanooga Country*; Hamer, *Tennessee*, I, Chs. 25–28; Holt, *Economic and Social Beginnings*; Lacy, *Vanquished Volunteers*, Ch. 5; Ulrich B. Phillips, *A History of Transportation in the Eastern Cotton Belt to 1860* (New York, 1908); Mary U. Rothrock (ed.), *The French Broad-Holston Country: A History of Knox County, Tennessee* (Knoxville, 1946), Chs. 9, 19; White, *Messages*, I–V, *passim*; Williams, *West Tennessee*, Ch. 22.

Specialized Accounts

L. R. Ahern and R. F. Hunt, Jr., "The Boatyard Store, 1814–1825," *THQ*, XIV (Sept., 1955), 257–77; William E. Beard, "A Saga of the Western Waters," *THQ*, II (Dec., 1943), 316–60; Madison Bratton, "The Unionist Junket of the Tennessee and Kentucky Legislatures in January, 1860," ETHS *Publ.*, No. 7 (1935), 64–80; Addie Lou Brooks, "The Building of Trunk Line Railroads in West Tennessee," *THQ*, I (June, 1942), 99–124, reprinted in White, *Tennessee: Old and New*, II, 188–211; Brooks, "Early Plans for Railroads in West Tennessee," *THM*, Ser. 2, III (Oct., 1932), 20–39; Jesse C. Burt, "The Nashville and Chattanooga Railroad, 1854–1872: The Era of Transition," ETHS *Publ.*, No. 23 (1951), 58–76; T. J. Campbell, *The Upper Tennessee* (Chattanooga, 1932); Thomas D. Clark, "Development of the Nashville and Chattanooga Railroad," THM, Ser. 2, III (April, 1935), 160–68; Clark, *The Beginning of the L & N* (Louisville, 1933); Clark, *A Pioneer Southern Railroad, from New Orleans to Cairo* (Chapel Hill, 1936); Clark, "The Building of the Memphis and Charleston Railroad," ETHS *Publ.*, No. 8 (1936), 9–25; Jonathan Daniels, *Devil's Backbone: The Story of the Natchez Trace* (New York, 1961); David L. Eubanks, "J. G. M. Ramsey As a Bond Agent: Selections From the Ramsey Papers," ETHS *Publ.*, No. 36 (1964), 81–99; Stanley J. Folmsbee, "The Beginnings of the Railroad Movement in East Tennessee," ETHS *Publ.*, No. 5 (1933), 81–104, reprinted in White, *Tennessee: Old and New*, II, 164–87; Folmsbee, "The Origins of the Nashville and Chattanooga Railroad," ETHS *Publ.*, No. 6 (1934), 81–95; Folmsbee, "The Turnpike Phase of Tennessee's Internal Improvement System of 1836–1838," JSH, III (Nov., 1937), 453–77; Kincaid A. Herr, *The Louisville and Nashville Railroad* (Louisville, 1943); William B. Hesseltine (ed.), *Dr. J. G. M. Ramsey: Autobiography and Letters* (Nashville, 1954); James W. Holland, "The East Tennessee and Georgia Railroad, 1836–1860," ETHS *Publ.*, No. 3 (1931), 89–107; Holland, "The Building of the East Tennessee and Virginia Railroad," ETHS *Publ.*, No. 4 (1932), 83–101; Robert L. Kincaid, *The Wilderness Road* (Indianapolis, 1947), Chs. 7, 13–15; Kincaid, "The Wilderness Road in Tennessee," ETHS *Publ.*, No. 20 (1948), 37–48; James W. Livingood, "Chattanooga: A Rail Junction of the Old South," THQ, VI (Sept., 1947), 230–50; John C. Mehrling, "The Memphis and Charleston Railroad," WTHS *Papers*, XIX (1965), 21–35; Dawson A. Phelps, "The Natchez Trace in Tennessee History," THQ, XIII (Sept., 1954), 195–203; Phelps, "Genesis of the Natchez Trace Parkway," WTHS *Papers*, XIX (1965), 58–68, reprinted in Alderson and McBride, *Landmarks*, 241–56; James W. Silver, "Edmund Pendleton Gaines: Railroad Propagandist," ETHS *Publ.*, No. 9 (1937), 3–18; St. George L. Sioussat, "Memphis as a Gateway to the West," THM, Ser. 1, III (March, June, 1917), 1–27, 77–114.

Top: This was the Columbia home of James K. Polk until he was inaugurated as the eleventh President of the United States; *lower*: Near Smyrna stands the birthplace of Sam Davis, "The Boy Hero of the Confederacy" who was hanged by the Federals in 1863.

Top: Nathan Bedford Forrest led his Confederate cavalry on campaigns still studied by military experts; *lower*: The remains of the earthworks fort and abandoned cannon from the Civil War can still be seen at Fort Donelson on the Cumberland River.

Andrew Johnson, who became the seventeenth President of the United States, practiced his early trade as a tailor in this shop at Greeneville.

William Jennings Bryan was well known in Tennessee before he became embroiled in its famous "monkey trial." Here he is, second from left, during an earlier visit (1900) on one of his three campaigns for President. He carried Tennessee each time.

Top left: Although once called "The Rich Uncle" of TVA, Senator Kenneth D. McKellar fought the Authority over the patronage issue; *top right*: Cordell Hull, secretary of state under FDR, was an outstanding statesman of the twentieth century; *below*: TVA's Norris Dam created the first of the man-made "Great Lakes of the South."

Top: Ed Crump, "the Red Snapper," was a powerful Tennessee political boss for over forty years; *lower*: In 1948, Estes Kefauver successfully challenged the Crump machine's domination of Tennessee politics.

Top: Memphis serves mid-America as the trade center of a seven-state region; *lower*: Chattanooga, historic Civil War battleground, is now a thriving industrial city.

The wind tunnel at the Space Center in Tullahoma provides essential information for the exploration of outer space.

16. &~ *Educational and Religious Development*

THEODORE ROOSEVELT, according to his own testimony, examined numerous original documents when he wrote *The Winning of the West* and was amazed that so many Tennessee backwoodsmen could sign their names. Education, as the cowboy-President learned, was by no means confined to the East. The majority of Tennesseans cherished learning and many acquired at least a working knowledge of the rudiments. It is probably true, nevertheless, that opportunities for education were much less available during the pioneer period than they were to become later, after the use of public land revenue and state and local taxes had provided greater support.

Public Lands and Public Education &~ A nineteenth-century historian commented that "The history of the common schools is in the main, the history of public lands in Tennessee, and the history of public lands in this State is the history of confusion." In Chapter 10, it was pointed out that the educational provisions of the Compact of 1806 authorized the state: (1) where existing claims permitted, to set aside 640 acres in each township of 36 square miles for the support of common schools; (2) to designate two tracts of 100,000 acres each, one tract for the support of two colleges in East and Middle Tennessee and one for academies in each county; and (3) to sell no land at less than $2.00 an acre, except to squatters in the Cherokee Reservation.

The legislature in 1806 appointed commissioners for the several county academies and selected Davidson Academy of Nashville (rechartered as Cumberland College) to be the recipient of the half of the college grant stipulated for Middle Tennessee. The next year the legislature accepted the offer of Blount College of Knoxville, instead of the proposals of other East Tennessee institutions, and gave the school a new charter and a new name, East Tennessee College, along with the eastern section's half of the land grant. Most of the good land in the Cherokee Reservation which had been cleared of the Indian title at that time was already occupied by squatters, and this was true of the college and academy tracts, which were laid off in Blount and Sevier counties. Thus the value of the endowments to these educational institutions was cut in half, since the squatters could not be charged more than $1.00 an acre. Actually, the state in most instances was unable to collect even that amount. The squatters had moved into the area during the period of the "lost state" of Franklin, and they claimed that by holding their lands against Indian assaults they had "bought every acre with drops of blood" and should not be required to pay anything to the state.

Even the hesitant efforts of the government to force the occupants to pay for their lands for the benefit of colleges and academies created public opposition to institutions of higher learning which lasted for many years. To make it easier for the squatters, the state allowed them to pay on the installment plan and later forgave some of the unpaid installments and interest. In 1823, as a result of the protests of the colleges and academies, the legislature finally ordered the sale of the lands of any squatters who defaulted on the payments, but because of the outcries of the people south of the French Broad River, legislators soon were forced to suspend this stringent policy.

Politicians also took advantage of the situation. Among those were Dr. J. C. Gunn, a candidate for the legislature from Knox County. When East Tennessee College, with the aid of funds obtained from the sale of squatters' lands, built its first building on College Hill in Knoxville, Gunn violently attacked the institution in a speech on the courthouse steps.

> Behold the great rotunda—that monument of folly, the College [he said]. That building for the rich man's son—that building which closes its doors against the poor man's child; . . . Why, do they forget that the south-of-the-river people paid drop by drop of sweat,

to erect this tomb of extravagance . . . this melancholy building, raising its proud front on an isolated hill, until you become exhausted to reach the summit?

As a consequence, timid legislators despaired of foreclosing on the squatters' claims and cast about for substitutions which might satisfy all concerned. The colleges reluctantly agreed to accept a half-township each in the Ocoee District after the Cherokee Indians were removed from that area in 1838; the academies did likewise, but soon surrendered the land in exchange for a grant of $18,000 annually from the profits of the common school fund in the Bank of Tennessee. Meanwhile, in 1822 and 1825 the University of North Carolina shared with the two Tennessee land-grant colleges (and in 1825 the common schools also) its warrants to land in Tennessee, in exchange for the exemption of the University's lands from taxation. These substitutions, however, fell far short of giving the colleges and academies the amount of revenue they had anticipated when the Compact of 1806 had been enacted.

The Compact had made no provision for aiding an institution in the Western District, because that area was in Indian hands at that time. Consequently, when in 1846 Congress ceded to the state its claim to unappropriated lands in the Congressional Reservation, it was stipulated that $40,000 of the revenue should be used to support a college in West Tennessee. West Tennessee College at Jackson became the recipient of the grant.

The setting aside of 640 acres of each township posed a difficult problem, because before 1806 Tennessee lands had not been surveyed into townships. In 1823 Representative James K. Polk, in a memorial to Congress, reported that only 22,705 acres had been set aside instead of the 450,000 acres anticipated under the Compact of 1806. In the same year, however, Congress amended the Compact to allow Tennessee to sell land for less than $2.00 per acre; the state therefore sold the waste land north and east of the Congressional Reservation line (but outside the Cherokee Reservation) for 12½ cents per acre. Both the revenue obtained and subsequent taxes on the school lands were placed in the common school fund created by the same law. In this area, and later in the Hiwassee and Ocoee districts, where the number of prior surveys was relatively few, it was possible to set aside 640 acres in many of the townships. Therefore, the amount of school lands increased greatly. In 1843, after another amendment to the Compact, the legislature provided that all of the school lands be sold and the revenue placed in the common school fund. Consequently, all of the school lands were sold except one tract in Polk County, which is still owned by the state.

There were other additions to the common school fund made from time to time, including the state's profits on stock held in various banks. The most important addition, however, was the major portion of the revenue from the sale of land in the Hiwassee and Ocoee districts, where North Carolina warrants were not to be located. Some federal money also went into the fund, including all but a small portion of Tennessee's share of the surplus revenue distributed among the states in 1837. Also, when Tennessee acquired in 1846 the remaining lands in the Congressional Reservation, all but the $40,000 assigned to West Tennessee College went into the school fund. According to the State Code of 1858 the total fund amounted to $1,500,000.

Although the constitution of 1835 made the common school fund a "perpetual fund" which should "never be diminished," some of the money was lost as a result of poor administration. In 1830, when the legislature made its first real attempt to establish a public school system, the entire principal of the fund was distributed among the counties in proportion to free, white population, to be managed by county commissioners who were to lend it out and use the interest for the support of common schools. Six years later the legislature decided to bring the fund back to Nashville, where it was placed in the hands of the state's first superintendent of public instruction. That official was made a member, along with the treasurer and comptroller, of the state board of commissioners of common schools which was required by the new constitution of 1835. To get the fund back from the county commissioners was a difficult task and some of it never was collected, leading the superintendent to say that the school fund had been "plundered by a thousand hands." Even back at the capital, it was not safe, for the first superintendent, Robert H. McEwen, was charged with mismanagement. Therefore, when the Bank of Tennessee was created by the Bank and Improvement Act of 1838, the entire school fund, actual and prospective, was made a part of the capital of the bank. The bank, in turn, was required to set aside annually $100,000 from its profits to be distributed among the counties for the support of common schools and $18,000 for the county academies. This amount was the chief support of public education until it was supplemented by state and local taxes authorized by legislation in 1854.

Andrew Johnson assumed the governor's chair in 1853 and tried to improve the educational framework. A man to whom circumstance had denied the advantages of a formal education, Johnson as governor was zealous in his efforts to provide free public education for all. He no doubt had observed with dissatisfaction the census reports at mid-century which indicated that from a total white population of 316,409 persons over twenty years of age, 77,522 could neither read nor write. In his first message to the legislature, he decried the fact that the school system "falls very far short" of the goal set at the constitutional convention of 1834, and sought legislative support of a program of educational improvement.

The legislators responded to the governor's plea and passed what Robert H. White has described as "the most important act for common schools . . . in Tennessee before the Civil War." The measure provided for a poll tax of 25 cents on free males and a property tax of 2½ cents on each $100 of taxable property. Efforts to revive the office of state superintendent were defeated (the state treasurer functioning in that capacity instead), but the tax, small as it was, practically doubled the amount of funds available for the public school program. Educators were encouraged and used their influence to expand facilities for public education across the state.

City systems were established in Nashville and Memphis during the 1850's. In 1852, Alfred Hume (later known as "the father of the Nashville public schools") examined urban educational facilities in the North and East. After visiting Cleveland, Boston, Providence, Philadelphia, and Baltimore, Hume presented to the city council a report which became the basis of Nashville's system. The city was to be zoned, at least one plant located in each zone, and taxes consisting of a poll tax of $2.00 on free white males between the ages of twenty-one and fifty and a property tax of 20 cents on each $100 of taxable real estate were to be levied to provide funds for operation. By 1860, the Nashville system boasted of 35 teachers and a total enrollment of 1,892 pupils. The Memphis system was established in 1858 and patterned after the one in Nashville.

By 1860, nearly 140,000 pupils attended public schools of the state and more than 15,000 were enrolled in "academies and other schools." More attended academies than in any other state in the South except Kentucky. The contrast in the amount of financial support for the two systems is significant. The funds available for the public schools totaled only $402,904, whereas for the much smaller number of pupils in the academies, $581,561 was available, mainly from tuition payments.

Private Schools and Academies 8⤳ Private schools and academies, the first educational establishments in the state, became the foundation of the educational superstructure. High hopes were raised at the acceptance of the Compact of 1806, by which 100,000 acres were appropriated for the support of academies, and the state legislature promptly authorized the establishment of an academy in each of the twenty-seven counties. Because very little financial aid was realized from the land, some of the academies, such as Tracy of Dickson County, did not open until a quarter of a century after the chartering act was passed, and some never opened. Finally, in 1838 the academies agreed to accept $18,000 per year from dividends on the school fund deposited in the Bank of Tennessee in lieu of land claims which they had under the Compact of 1806. Although small, the money did supplement endowment, tuition, and other funds which most of the academies had. Lotteries, interestingly, served as an important source of revenue for many of the schools. Typical was one held in Nashville in 1833 for the Harpeth Male and Female Academies, in which tickets sold for five dollars. The first prize was $5,000, and other prizes were awarded amounting in all to $33,660. A lottery of $8,000 was authorized for Somerville Academy in 1830, and several years later one planned for Lexington Male Academy offered a first prize of 121 acres, complete with a sawmill and gristmill.

A variety of courses was offered at the academies. The faculty of Manhattan School in Maury County announced in 1821 that their offerings included English grammar, trigonometry, navigation, logic, and natural philosophy. Students at Bolivar Male Academy could study astronomy, higher mathematics, Latin, Greek, French, and Hebrew. Jacob Voorhies' "classical academy" at Charlotte offered chiefly the classical languages. Joseph Estabrook, president of East Tennessee College, in 1838 pointed to the high quality of work done at most academies, and termed their demand for able teachers a "cheering circumstance."

Most of the academies admitted only men, but a few were established exclusively for women. Fisk Female Academy, chartered in Overton County in 1806 after Sampson Williams and Moses Fisk each gave 1,000 acres of land, was claimed to have been the first chartered academy for girls in the South. Others were established, principally by religious or fraternal groups, in Knoxville, Memphis, Nashville, Gallatin, Rogersville, Murfreesboro, McMinnville, Paris, Lebanon, and other towns.

One of the best known schools for girls in the South was the Nashville Female Academy, a nonsectarian institution established in Nashville in 1816. It was successful from the beginning. When President James Monroe visited Nashville in 1819, city officials proudly displayed the school and presented the President for an address before the 200 students and faculty members.

The Nashville academy reached its peak during the administration of the Reverend Collins D. Elliott, who served as its principal from 1844 to 1866. A strict disciplinarian and a strong believer in education for women, Elliott administered a sound program. As early as 1833, students of the French language were placed under the supervision of their professor, a native of France, who required them to converse only in French. Able music instructors were brought in from Europe. A variety of subjects was taught, but the "Ornamental Department"—vocal music, instrumental music, painting, and fancy needle work—was the most popular. Elliott demanded long hours of study from his students. He firmly announced to parents concerned about their daughters that the "young ladies see no [male] company; never visit but with our approbation; read no novels [and] never leave the yard but in company with a teacher." The tuition in 1857 was $275, which defrayed all expenses. A Nashville newspaper at that time described the school as "the most extensive in the United States devoted to female education."

Colleges ?❧ The Compact of 1806, it will be recalled, provided a gift of 100,000 acres for the benefit of two colleges, one to be located in East Tennessee and the other in the Cumberland settlements. Davidson Academy in Nashville was designated as the

Western recipient of the grant; a new institution, to be called "East Tennessee College" and located at Knoxville, was to receive the funds and property of Blount College in addition to the share of the land grant. Officials were empowered to offer the degrees of bachelor of arts, master of arts, and "any other degree known and used in any college or university of the United States."

Davidson Academy was reincorporated as Cumberland College in 1806. Financial problems plagued the school, and it was closed from 1816 to 1822. Two years after the reopening, trustees called to the presidency an able executive, Dr. Philip Lindsley, who served for nearly thirty years and developed the school into one of the best in the South. The new administrator was graduated from the College of New Jersey (Princeton), and was an ordained minister in the Presbyterian Church. He added new faculty members who were recognized scholars, and expanded the curriculum. In 1826, he asked the legislature to change the name to "The University of the State of Tennessee." The senate voted as requested, but house members substituted "Nashville" for "State of Tennessee," and the senate concurred. In 1850, Lindsley resigned to become a professor in the New Albany Theological Seminary, but returned three years later to Nashville where he died in 1855. Trustees closed the school temporarily in 1850 and, except for a medical department which began operation in 1851, did not reopen it until the year of Lindsley's death. By 1855, more than 2,000 students had been enrolled in the University, and nearly 400 bachelor's degrees and 60 master's degrees had been conferred.

The University of Nashville was reopened in 1855, with Lindsley's son, John Berrien Lindsley, as chancellor. A person of remarkable talents, young Lindsley reorganized the university and within a few years helped to make it a well-recognized institution. A part of his program was to merge Western Military Institute, headed by Colonel Bushrod Johnson, with the university. On the eve of the Civil War the enrollment was 648—a sizable increase from the 154 students enrolled in 1855.

East Tennessee College (formerly Blount College) opened in 1807, but closed two years later when the president, the Reverend Samuel Carrick, died. When reopened in 1820, it was merged for a short time with Hampden-Sydney Academy, which had been organized several years before as a school to be subsidized by expected land sales from the Compact of 1806. A few years later, trustees decided to change the location of the college, and in 1826 they purchased from Pleasant M. Miller the present site of the main campus of The University of Tennessee—a forty-acre hill located one mile west of the Knox County courthouse. A large building, with a spire, clock and ornaments, was constructed.

In 1834, Joseph Estabrook, a Dartmouth College graduate then principal of Knoxville Female Academy, was elected president. He served for nearly two decades and did much to advance the college to a position of academic respectability. During his administration, the physical plant was expanded considerably, but he was more than a "brick and mortar" president. High academic quality was demanded, and an able faculty employed. Applicants for admission were examined in Virgil, Cicero's *Orations*, arithmetic, English grammar, and geography. The name was changed in 1840 to "East Tennessee University" in recognition of Estabrook's program of expansion. A military department was added in 1860.

Cumberland University, at Lebanon, was founded in 1842 under the auspices of the Cumberland Presbyterian Church. Its department of law, established in 1847, soon built a national reputation for the school. On the eve of the Civil War the institution had an enrollment of nearly 500, 188 of which were enrolled in the law department.

The forerunner of Southwestern at Memphis was Stewart College at Clarksville. In 1848 the Masonic Order acquired title to the property of Clarksville Academy, but met with little success in its efforts to operate an institution of higher learning. In 1855 the property was purchased by the Presbyterian Synod of Nashville, and in the autumn of that year a school was opened under the name of "Stewart College." Emphasis was placed upon classical language and literature.

Many other colleges, most of them small in enrollment, were established during the ante bellum period. Greeneville College, chartered in 1794 (a few days before Blount), had a precarious existence during its early years. After the Civil War, Greeneville was consolidated with Tusculum College, which in 1844 had been organized from Tusculum Academy. Samuel Doak, who established the first school in the Tennessee country, in 1783 had received from

North Carolina a charter for Martin Academy which later in 1795 became Washington College. Maryville College was begun in 1819 as Southern and Western Theological Seminary to train Presbyterian ministers. Among other colleges organized during the ante bellum period were: Jackson (Maury County, 1832), West Tennessee College (Jackson, 1844), Union University (Murfreesboro, 1845),[1] Bethel College (McLemoresville, 1842, but later moved to McKenzie), Mossy Creek Baptist Seminary, a forerunner of Carson-Newman College (Jefferson County, 1851); and Lambuth, established by Presbyterians but taken over by Methodists (Jackson, 1842). One of the most promising institutions established before the war was the University of the South, at Sewanee. The trustees received a charter in 1858 and proposed to offer an extensive program in arts and sciences. English, French, German, Spanish, Italian, and Oriental languages were to be taught, in addition to civil engineering, natural science, chemistry, and agriculture. Bishop Leonidas Polk laid the cornerstone in 1860 and dedicated the institution "for the cultivation of true religion, learning, and virtues." Because of the Civil War, the school did not function until 1865.

Literary societies flourished at all of the colleges, and students vied with one another for honors in composition and oratory. At the University of Nashville students debated such subjects as the justification of the execution of Mary, Queen of Scots; whether slavery as practiced in the United States was an evil; the relative merits of secession; and whether male students should "cultivate the acquaintance of the ladies." At East Tennessee University, students also debated a variety of subjects, but rejected in 1860 the subject "Should the South secede if a Black Republican is elected President?" because of its inflammatory nature.

Disciplinary problems faced most of the college executives from time to time. In 1821 rules and regulations were prepared at East Tennessee College. Students could be expelled if they did not show "reverence and obedience" to the faculty or if they were guilty of blasphemy, fornication, robbery, dueling, or striking the president

---

[1] This institution at Murfreesboro was closed shortly after the Civil War, and in 1907 the name Union University was given to the school which had once been West Tennessee College, at Jackson, but which had used the name Southwestern Baptist University, 1875 to 1907.

or one of the instructors. Fighting, wearing women's apparel, lying, defamation, and playing "at billiards, cards, dice or any other unlawful game" were punishable only by firm admonition. Similar rules were enforced at the other colleges. In 1844 a student at the University of Nashville was suspended for visiting "a house of dissipation." Another was dismissed two years earlier, not for moral turpitude but for poor scholarship, which, one faculty member recorded, was "about nothing."

Adult Education ⧽ Little attention was given to adult education during the first few decades after Tennessee's admission to the Union. By the 1830's, however, lyceums, libraries, and organizations "for literary, intellectual and moral improvement" were formed. Probably the first lyceum in the state was organized in Nashville in 1830 at the insistence of William G. Hunt, editor of a local newspaper. Hunt proposed weekly meetings to study and discuss geography, history, natural philosophy, chemistry, and other branches of science and literature. Two years later the books of the Nashville Library, consisting of 830 volumes, were transferred to the lyceum committee. The Knoxville Lyceum was formed in 1831. It had thirty members whose goals were similar to those of the Nashville group.

Catering to a more select membership was "A Society for the Advancement of Literature and Science in the State of Tennessee," which was organized in Nashville in 1835. A similar group was formed in Knoxville in 1838 "for the purpose of literary, intellectual and moral improvement." Two years earlier, the "Tennessee Society for the Diffusion of Knowledge," with Return Jonathan Meigs, II, as president, was formed in Nashville.

Groups of adults were organized periodically for the study and preservation of history and historical artifacts. In 1820 the "Tennessee Antiquarian Society" was formed at Nashville. A decade later Dr. James G. M. Ramsey and other citizens organized a historical society in Knoxville. The East Tennessee Historical Antiquarian Society was chartered in 1848, and the Tennessee Historical Society was formed one year later.

Libraries, most of them small, were organized in various parts of the state. The first reference to a library in the public acts is the incorporation of the Nashville Library Company, in 1813. Two years later the Dickson Library Company was formed at Charlotte. Others were organized in Knoxville, Columbia, and Memphis.

Professional Education ε‌‌ Little progress was made during the ante bellum years toward developing professional schools. The licensing system was lax and many people practiced a profession without the advantages of a formal education.

Perhaps the outstanding professional school of the period was the medical department of the University of Nashville, which opened in 1851 with twenty-eight-year-old John Berrien Lindsley as dean. Included in the professorial staff of seven was Paul Fitzsimmons Eve, a Georgia-born physician who had studied in the clinics of Paris and London and who had ministered to the wounded in Paris at the time of the July Revolution (1830) and in Warsaw in the Polish Revolution of 1831. Known as one of the ablest surgeons in America, Eve frequently performed difficult operations before medical students. Among the first to anesthetize his patients, Eve used both chloroform and sulfuric ether, although some of his colleagues were skeptical of both. Lindsley required of all candidates for graduation two full years' attendance at the professorial lectures, three years' service in the office of a practicing physician, composition of a thesis, good moral character, and attainment of twenty-one years of age. At the time of the Civil War, the medical school had 456 students and ranked second among the schools of the nation in enrollment.

Three schools of medicine had been established during the 1840's. The Memphis Medical College and the Botanico-Medical College of Memphis began operation in 1846; a medical division of the Memphis Institute began in 1849. The Shelby Medical College was established in Nashville in 1858 by the Methodist Episcopal Church, South. All failed to survive the war. For twenty years concerted efforts were made to establish a medical school at East Tennessee University, and in 1858 a faculty was appointed, but lack of funds caused failure.

All church-controlled colleges offered courses in theology. Perhaps the best known department was at Cumberland University, which began operation in 1854. Richard Beard, professor of systematic theology, was the ablest of the instructors. Cumberland also opened a department of civil engineering in 1852. Surveying and construction were taught. Courses in surveying and civil engineering were suggested to the trustees at the University of Nashville in 1851, but apparently little attention was given to the proposal when the school reopened in 1855.

Young men who wished to enter the legal profession usually "read law" in the offices of a judge or an established practitioner, not infrequently performing clerical work in exchange for room and board. No particular period of study was required. The first law school of significance was at Cumberland University, which began operation in 1847 with six students, but by 1860 had nearly 200. Professor Abram Caruthers and other distinguished faculty members maintained high standards of scholarship. A law department opened at the University of Nashville a few years after the one at Cumberland, and in 1856 the West Tennessee Law School of the City of Memphis was chartered.

The English and scientific department at East Tennessee University had as one of its aims that of qualifying "young men to become teachers in the common schools and academies." Beginning in 1844, free tuition was provided for two men from each county in East Tennessee who would agree to devote three years to teaching after they completed a course of study. In 1855 a bill was introduced providing for the establishment of a normal school for training teachers, but the measure was defeated.

By 1860, nearly 3,000 short-term public schools were in operation, not to mention academies and private schools. Even so, Tennessee had one of the highest rates of illiteracy in the country. According to the census reports of 1860, more than 27,000 men and 43,000 women over twenty years of age could neither read nor write. Even when compared with neighboring states, especially with such educationally progressive states as Mississippi and South Carolina, Tennessee ranked poor indeed. Tennessee's educational position as compared with other states is shown in the table on page 281.

Although there was a high rate of illiteracy, interestingly, more Tennesseans could read and write than could the people in many European countries. In 1846 in England and Wales, for example, of the couples securing marriage licenses, over one-third affixed their marks instead of their signatures to their applications. In the French

State	Total White Population	Number Illiterate	Per Cent Illiterate
Alabama	526,271	37,605	7.14
Georgia	591,550	43,684	7.38
Kentucky	919,484	67,577	7.34
Massachusetts	1,221,432	46,262	3.78
Mississippi	353,899	15,526	4.39
New York	3,831,590	115,965	3.02
North Carolina	629,942	68,128	10.81
South Carolina	291,300	14,792	5.07
Tennessee	826,722	70,359	8.51
Virginia	1,047,299	74,055	7.07

army in 1851, more than one-third of the 311,218 conscripts could neither read nor write, and in parts of Spain, Portugal, Italy, the Balkans, Poland, and Russia, illiteracy was more than 90 per cent. At mid-century, indeed, there were more people in colleges from the Southern states, in proportion to population, than in any other section of the country. The disastrous Civil War then interrupted all educational progress, but once that fratricidal struggle was over, a workable public school program was formulated.

Early Development of Churches ཡ Some of the outstanding educators were ministers of the gospel, and by the beginning of the eighteenth century such leaders as Gideon Blackburn, Samuel Doak, Thomas Craighead, and James McGready had preached and taught in Tennessee. The Presbyterian Church was the strongest on the frontier, but soon after the turn of the century Methodists and Baptists made such gains that they soon dominated the religious scene. Other churches, such as the Catholic, Disciples of Christ, Episcopal, Lutheran, and Judaic, also had membership in Tennessee.

Presbyterians ཡ Presbyterians were first on the frontier, but a variety of factors curtailed their growth during and after the Great Revival of 1800. A strict interpretation of Calvinism and insistence that ministers should be well educated hindered Presbyterian leaders from the beginning. People whose self-reliance had enabled them to clear the frontier and hold it against Indian assaults were reluctant to embrace a Calvinistic God who cared only for the "elect." In 1814, when Gideon Blackburn organized the First Church in Nashville, Presbyterians had seventy-nine congregations in Tennessee. Despite dissension and the organization of new Presbyterian groups, still the mother church grew. By 1860 nearly 200 churches had been established in the state. Presbyterians at mid-century ranked fourth in the number of members—behind Methodists, Baptists, and Cumberland Presbyterians.

Cumberland Presbyterians ⊱ The Cumberland Presbyterians developed from a schism within the Presbyterian Church. Many prominent leaders had been reluctant to participate in the Great Revival of 1800 because they questioned the sincerity of both the leaders and the converts. Ministers interested in the revival, however, soon secured control of the Cumberland Presbytery (which after 1802 embraced Middle Tennessee and part of Kentucky) and ordained or licensed for the ministry men whom Presbyterian authorities contended were unsound both educationally and doctrinally. The Cumberland group wished to reject the doctrines of predestination and foreordination because to them such was synonymous with "fatality." For several years both laymen and clergymen debated the subject. By 1810 only three ordained members of the revival group—Finis Ewing, Samuel King, and Samuel McAdow—remained; the others had returned to the Presbyterian fold without further argument. These determined men, however, met on February 3–4, 1810, in McAdow's home (now embraced within the Montgomery Bell State Park, in Dickson County) and organized an independent presbytery, but agreed to make sincere efforts to effect a reconciliation with the mother church. By 1813, when efforts both to re-unite with the Presbyterians and to join the Methodists had failed, the group considered that they had formed a separate Christian body and called themselves "Cumberland Presbyterians." Within five years new congregations had been formed in Alabama, Arkansas, Illinois, Kentucky, Mississippi, and Missouri.

Four reasons may be given for the formation of the Cumberland Presbyterian Church. First, Presbyterian ministers were unable to accommodate the inflexible tenets of Calvinism to the self-reliant frontier mind. As Methodists, "New Lights," Stoneites, and Campbellites preached an Arminian doctrine of "whosoever will," the Presbyterian insistence upon election and limited atonement could not compete. The Great Revival was a second cause. As physical demonstrations—contortions of the body, shakings, and barkings—became popular forms of emotional release, most of the Presbyterian leaders refused to participate, but those who organized the Cumberland Presbyterians were of the revival party. Educational requirements for the ministry were a third factor. Because of the need for ministers, Presbyterian leaders in the Cumberland area ordained several men who were learned in the Scriptures but who did not have a classical education and who did not meet the standards set by the Presbyterian Church for ordination. A fourth cause was the inability of the Cumberland leaders to distinguish theologically between "fatality" and predestination. They referred to their dogma as "medium theology" which to them represented a half-way point between Calvinism and Arminianism. After West Tennessee was opened for settlement, the faith grew rapidly, so that at mid-century it was the largest of the Presbyterian bodies in Tennessee.

Disciples of Christ ৡ৵ The Disciples of Christ developed out of the teachings of Alexander Campbell and Barton W. Stone, and emerged at about the same time as did the Cumberland Presbyterians. Both men had been Presbyterian ministers but, like the Cumberlands, they rejected the rigidity of Calvinism. Their cry for a return to pristine purity of Christianity, their insistence that the Bible was the supreme authority in the church, and their persuasion that not merely ministers of the Gospel but all men are commissioned to proclaim the truths of God were reminiscent of Peter Waldo of the twelfth century and some of the Reformation leaders of four hundred years later. Stone began his ministry in East Tennessee and Kentucky before 1800, but Campbell did not come to America (from Scotland) until 1809. By that time Stone had expressed the basic tenets of his faith: that the Bible was "the only sure guide to heaven," that ministers of the Gospel should be treated like everyone else and not distinguished by a " 'Reverend' title," and that his (Springfield) presbytery might be dissolved—as indeed should all denominational bodies—and merged "into union with the Body of Christ."

Campbell was the embodiment of dissent. His great-grandfather had been a Roman Catholic, but his grandfather had rejected Romanism and united with the Church of England. Thomas, his father, had been an ordained minister in the Seceder Presbyterian Church, which had been formed from a schism in the Church of Scotland in 1733. Thomas Campbell came to Pennsylvania in 1807 and was followed by his twenty-one-year-old son two years later. There they issued a document called "The Declaration and Address" which condemned human creeds, urged all Christian groups toward an ecumenical movement, and emphasized conformity to the letter of the law as laid down in the New Testament. Three years later, in determining that immersion was the only proper mode of baptism, they affiliated with the Baptist Church for awhile. Campbell became known as a "reforming Baptist," and his followers generally were known as "Reformers" and "Disciples." He preached and debated leaders of other churches in all sections of Tennessee, but his principal following was in Nashville.

In 1832 the Stone and Campbell forces were united. They became variously known as Disciples, Churches of Christ, Christians, and Reformers. By 1842, the leaders were publishing *The Bible Advocate* in Paris, and a few years later the *Christian Review* in Nashville. At mid-century the Campbell and Stone forces, ranking fifth among the religious bodies in Tennessee, had 106 churches with a membership of over 12,000 in the state. The congregations were concentrated chiefly in Middle and West Tennessee.

Baptists ৵ Frontier Baptist preachers were in East Tennessee almost as early as were Presbyterians, and by 1800 they had gained a foothold in the Cumberland country. While the Baptists did not draw as many followers from the Great Revival of 1800 as did the Methodists and Cumberland Presbyterians, they did boast of more than eleven thousand by 1812. By that time the Holston and Tennessee associations had been formed in East Tennessee and the Cumberland and Concord associations in the central division. Soon after the purchase of the area between the Tennessee and Mississippi rivers, the Western District Association and Forked Deer Association were formed.

Like the Presbyterians, the Tennessee Baptists suffered from controversies and schisms within the church. When in 1835 Robert B. C. Howell came to Nashville from Virginia to pastor the First Baptist Church, he found at least ten distinct Baptist sects whose members refused to take communion even with one another. Among the many discordant elements within the church was one known as "Old Landmarkism" and led by James R. Graves of Nashville. Graves had come to Nashville from Ohio in 1845, and at mid-century was editor of the *Tennessee Baptist*; in this journal he condemned the regular Baptists and urged all to "return" to "the old landmarks" of New Testament Christianity. Like Campbell and Stone, Graves believed that emphasis upon human creeds had corrupted mankind, and he traced Baptists to the apostles. His influence was limited to Nashville and Middle Tennessee until after the Civil War, when he moved to Memphis to continue his struggle for a return to the original "landmarks."

Most of the Baptist churches in Tennessee became affiliated with the Southern Baptist Convention after its formation in 1845. By 1842, the slavery question had become an issue which involved ministers in both North and South, and Robert T. Daniel and others had preached throughout the state in favor of a Southern convention which would meet the peculiar needs of the South and Southwest. When the Foreign Mission Board in 1844 refused to recommend a Georgia slaveholder for appointment as missionary to the Cherokee Indians, Southern Baptists formed the Southern Baptist Convention. In 1849 the First Church in Nashville became the meeting place for the annual convention.

Despite the various disruptive factors, Tennessee Baptists ranked second only to the Methodists during the ante bellum period. In 1860, the Baptists had nearly 700 churches and over 35,000 members well distributed throughout the state; at least one church was located in every county. There were 21 congregations established in Sevier County, 19 in Wilson, and 18 in Carroll.

Methodists ફ No religious body exerted more leadership in Tennessee church affairs during the ante bellum period than did the Methodists. As has been observed earlier, Bishop Francis Asbury, Benjamin Ogden, Jeremiah Lambert and others had labored over the circuits before 1800, but it was not until the Great Revival of that year that the church began to show decided growth. In 1812, when the Tennessee Conference was formed, membership in the state was estimated at about 17,000. The Holston Conference was formed east of the mountains in 1824, and the Memphis Conference west of the mountains in 1840.

Tennessee Methodists were fortunate in that divisive forces did not impede their growth as in the Presbyterian and Baptist churches. Although Methodist Protestants had withdrawn in 1830 after a dispute over lay participation in church government and the powers of bishops, although zealots had formed the Wesleyan Connection in 1843 over slavery, and although the Free Methodists had coalesced a few years later over "holiness," none of these divisions affected the church in Tennessee. It was only in the sectional controversy of 1844–45, when two distinct branches of Methodism—North and South—were formed, that Tennessee Methodists participated actively. Some Tennesseans, including Dr. Alexander L. P. Green and John B. McFerrin, joined other Southerners in signing a "Declaration of the Southern Delegates," which resolved that "the continued jurisdiction of the General Conference over the ministry in the slaveholding states would be inconsistent with success." Leaders from the Holston, Tennessee, and Memphis conferences met with other Southern leaders in Louisville in 1845 and formed the Methodist Episcopal Church, South.

By 1860, the Southern Methodist Church exceeded all other groups in membership in Tennessee. Several factors were responsible. First, the church did not have to contend with controversies as did the Presbyterians and Baptists. (The Free and Wesleyan divisions did not materially affect Methodism in Tennessee, and the formation of the Northern and Southern divisions in 1845 was along sectional lines.) Second, the Arminian doctrine of free grace, free will, and individual responsibility fitted well into the rising democratic spirit of the new West. Third, the courageous nature of the circuit-riding preacher enabled the gospel to be preached over a wide area. Bishop Asbury, for example, may have slept in "filthy houses and filthy beds" and have "taken the itch," but he also crossed the Appalachians sixty-two times and preached over 15,000 sermons.

Fourth, like the Baptists, the Methodists placed little emphasis upon a college-trained ministry. The sermons of the Methodist itinerants were simple, but forceful, direct, and unfettered by manuscripts. Finally, Methodist leaders entered vigorously into the Great Revival of 1800 and continued the spirit of the revival and camp meeting. Leaders at mid-century claimed nearly 1,000 churches located from Memphis to Bristol. At least one church was in every county, and Madison had 33, Giles and Maury 26 each, and Davidson 20.

Episcopalians, Catholics, Lutherans, and Jews ১৬ Episcopalians in Tennessee were unorganized during the first two decades of the nineteenth century. Their church had lost considerable membership after the Revolutionary War, and Tennessee frontiersmen looked askance at the church when they learned of its former connection with the Church of England and its formal liturgy and similarity to Catholic polity. St. Paul's Church, in Franklin, organized in 1827 by the Right Reverend James H. Otey, was probably the first to be formed in the state. Much of ante bellum Episcopal history centers upon Otey. He came to Williamson County in 1825 to establish a school, but soon sought also to organize a congregation of Episcopalians. Shortly after St. Paul's was formed, Otey was called to Nashville, where he organized a congregation. In 1829 the Right Reverend John S. Ravenscroft, Bishop of North Carolina, visited the Nashville congregation and stirred "up the minds of the people by his bold and eloquent sermons." Construction work on Christ Church began soon thereafter, and services were held in the new building in 1831. By that time, St. John's had been built in Knoxville and St. Peter's in Columbia. Otey became the first bishop of the Protestant Episcopal Church in Tennessee in 1833, at which time the communicants numbered 117. Although he threatened in 1853 to resign unless the diocese were more punctual in the payment of his salary, Otey continued to work among Middle Tennessee Episcopalians and probably deserved more credit than anyone else for the success of the church in Tennessee.

By the time of the Civil War, twenty-seven Episcopal clergymen and 1,500 communicants were in the state. Episcopalians concentrated in the larger towns such as Nashville and Memphis. Among the clergymen of note other than Otey were Leonidas Polk, Charles Tomes (who married Otey's daughter and became pastor of a Nashville congregation in 1848), and Thomas Wright of Memphis.

Few Catholics came into the state before the War of 1812, but in the early 1820's members came in large numbers, chiefly to perform construction work on Nashville's first bridge across the Cumberland River. In later years others came in to build railroads. In 1820 the Right Reverend Bishop David and Father Robert Abell offered the first mass in Nashville. Some years later the Right Reverend Richard Pius Miles became the first resident bishop of Tennessee. He was a man of ability and experience, and established parishes, built churches, and founded seminaries. One of the churches was organized in north Nashville in 1853 to serve German families. John Anthony Vogel was ordained in 1858 by Miles, and was placed in charge of the church. Upon Miles's death in 1860, Bishop James Whelan succeeded him.

Not until some years later did Catholicism become established in Memphis. Father John R. Clary held services in the city at mid-century and shortly before the Civil War moved his congregation into the new St. Peter's Church. As in Nashville, railroad building aided in establishing a Catholic population in Memphis. In 1854 a large influx of Irishmen arrived from St. Louis for railroad work. By 1860 more than one-fifth of the 18,000 people in Memphis were Irish, most of whom were ardent Catholics.

Catholics were hindered by nativistic sentiment aroused by the Know Nothing party. "Parson" Brownlow always was in the forefront of the attack. In 1854, when a speaker from the American and Foreign Christian Union lectured in Presbyterian and Methodist churches of Nashville on "Romanism, or The Man of Sin," Brownlow characterized his anti-Catholic outbursts as "good work, and we say Amen to every blow they strike." The editor of the Nashville *Union and American*, however, termed it "persecution" and "a disgrace to the intelligence of the age."

The German Lutherans, relatively few in number, centered largely in Sullivan County in East Tennessee, and some settled in nearby Greene and Cocke counties. Shortly after 1800, the Reverend William Jenkins organized the Shofner Church near Shelbyville in Middle Tennessee. Paul Henkel, a remarkably versatile author and preacher, was an early missionary in the state, and in 1820 two of his sons organized the Tennessee Synod as an independent body. Reminiscent of other frontier schisms, leaders sought fundamentals and believed that their congregation was based upon "the Holy Bible . . . and the Augsburg Confession of Faith as a pure emanation from the Bible." In 1855, J. C. Beyer organized a congregation in Memphis. It was not until 1859 that a church was organized in Nashville, and the Reverend Herman Eggers, a Pennsylvanian, became the first pastor. In 1860 the Holston Synod was formed from the Tennessee Synod and became much the stronger of the two, since most of the churches were in East Tennessee. When the Civil War began, Lutherans had only eighteen churches in the state, and fourteen of them were in the eastern division. It was not until twenty years after the war ended that the Tennessee and Holston synods agreed to join with the General Synod of the South, to form the United Synod in the South.

People of the Judaic faith lived mainly in the cities. A congregation was organized in 1851 in Nashville. Three years later, when Rabbi Alexander Iser, a Russian-Pole, arrived, the congregation was reorganized and chartered as "Khal Kodesh Mogen David," which meant a "Holy Congregation—and Shield of David." A congregation was formed in Memphis in 1853, although by that time Jews had been in that city for at least a decade. In the following year, a congregation called "Children of Israel" was formed and chartered by the legislature. Also in that year, a Ladies Benevolent Society was organized. By 1860 the Memphis synagogue had a membership of approximately seventy-five, and the Nashville group had about the same number. A smaller congregation, Beth El, House of God, was organized in Knoxville during the war.

By 1860 sectarianism had wrought its worst in Tennessee and the various religious bodies had assumed a less controversial nature. Although the Disciples were to divide later into the conservative (Church of Christ) and progressive groups, no other serious division was to result, and Methodists were later (1939) to re-unite. The frontier had been won by 1860 by the Methodists and Baptists; Presbyterians finished a poor third. Methodists claimed more members than Baptists, but the margin was slender, and Baptist leaders whittled it away soon after Appomattox.

SUGGESTED READINGS

General Accounts

Peter Cartwright, *Autobiography of Peter Cartwright, the Backwoods Preacher* (Nashville, 1946); H. E. Carr, *Washington College*; I. N. Carr, *History of Carson-Newman College* (Jefferson City, Tenn., 1959); Cleveland, *The Great Revival in the West*; F. Garvin Davenport, *Cultural Life in Nashville on the Eve of the Civil War* (Chapel Hill, 1941); Stanley J. Folmsbee, *Blount College and East Tennessee College, 1794–1840* (Knoxville, 1946); Folmsbee, *East Tennessee University, 1840–1879, Predecessor of the University of Tennessee* (Knoxville, 1959); Folmsbee, Corlew, and Mitchell, *Tennessee*, I, Chs. 20–21; Hamer, *Tennessee*, I, 799–827; B. W. McDonnold, *History of the Cumberland Presbyterian Church* (Nashville, 1899); Posey, *Baptist Church in the Lower Mississippi Valley*; Posey, *Methodism in Old Southwest*; Posey, *Presbyterian Church in Old Southwest*; Taylor, *East Tennessee Baptists*; Arthur P. Whitaker, "The Public School System of Tennessee, 1834–1860," *THM*, II (March, 1916), 1–30, reprinted in White, *Tennessee: Old and New*, II, 45–75; Robert H. White, *Development of the Tennessee State Education Organization, 1796–1929* (Nashville, 1929).

Specialized Accounts

Milton L. Baughm, "An Early Experiment in Adult Education: The Nashville Lyceum, 1830–32," *THQ*, XI (Sept., 1952), 235–45; F. Garvin Davenport, "Culture Versus Frontier in Tennessee, 1825–1850," *JSH*, V (Feb., 1939), 18–33; Paul M. Fink, "Methodism in Jonesboro, Tennessee," ETHS *Publ.*, No. 21 (1949), 45–59; Stanley J. Folmsbee, "East Tennessee University: Pre-War Years, 1840–1861," ETHS *Publ.*, No. 22 (1950), 60–93; David Edwin Harrell, Jr., "Disciples of Christ Pacifism in Nineteenth Century Tennessee," *THQ*, XXI (Sept., 1962), 263–74; Richard H. Haunton, "Education and Democracy: The Views of Philip Lindsley," *THQ*, XXI (June, 1962), 131–39; W. W. Herron, "A History of Lambuth College," WTHS *Papers*, No. X (1956), 20–37; Laura E. Luttrell, "One Hundred Years of a Female Academy: The Knoxville Female Academy, 1811–1846 [and] The East Tennessee Female Institute, 1846–1911," ETHS *Publ.*, No. 17 (1945), 71–83; Frank L. and Harriet C. Owsley, "The Economic Structure of Rural Tennessee, 1850–1860," *JSH*, VIII (May, 1942), 161–82; Verton M. Queener, "Gideon Blackburn," ETHS *Publ.*, No. 6 (1934), 12–28; Rosa Dyer Rutledge, "Union University Through the Century, 1834–1950," WTHS *Papers*, No. IV (1950), 83–96; Rufus B. Spain, "R. B. C. Howell: Nashville Baptist Leader in the Civil War Period," *THQ*, XIV (Dec., 1955), 323–

40; Spain, "R. B. C. Howell: Progressive Baptist Minister of the Old Southwest," *THQ*, XIV (Sept., 1955), 195–226; Spain, "R. B. C. Howell: Virginia Baptist Tradition Comes to the Old Southwest," *THQ*, XIV (June, 1955), 99–119; Buford C. Utley, "The Early Academies of West Tennessee," WTHS *Papers*, No. VIII (1954), 5–38; Harry C. Wagner, "The Beginnings of the Christian Church in East Tennessee," ETHS *Publ.*, No. 20 (1948), 49–58; Rabbi James A. Wax, "The Jews of Memphis, 1860–1865," WTHS *Papers*, No. III (1949), 39–89; Virginia Williams, "Tennessee's Public School Lands," *THQ*, III (Dec., 1944), 335–48; John F. Woolverton, "Philip Lindsley and the Cause of Education in the Old Southwest," *THQ*, XIX (March, 1960), 3–22.

Tennesseans at mid-century boasted of rapidly growing towns, developing industry, expanding agriculture,
and of a total population of 1,002,717. Agrarian reforms resulted in
a more efficient use of land and labor. Within the towns, infant
industry brought a measure of wealth; wealth was partly responsible
for a growing awareness of cultural deprivation and a desire to share
in the refinement which characterized larger urban areas. People
for decades had been conscious of a need for social reform, and they
initiated movements which culminated in better treatment and
better living conditions for the unfortunate elements of society.

Agricultural Development ह&ण्ण In a legislative message
delivered in 1799, Governor John Sevier spoke of the great agricultural advantages enjoyed by Tennesseans. "Providence," he asserted, "has blessed this State with a soil peculiarly calculated for
the production of wheat, hemp, flax, cotton, tobacco, and indigo."
During the next half century, Tennesseans cultivated the soil in-
tensively and produced in abundance all of the crops which the
governor enumerated except indigo. Corn was king, but much cotton was raised in the southwestern and south central counties, and
millions of pounds of tobacco were produced in the north central
counties. Wheat, oats, and a variety of other crops, including
vegetables, were raised in great quantities. Agriculture was unquestionably the main economic pursuit during the first half of the

nineteenth century. In 1850, the state had nearly 120,000 farmers, but only 66 iron workers and only 26 industrial weavers.

East Tennessee was the first section to be settled, but at mid-century it was the poorest in agricultural production. Although the counties of the river valleys were fertile and productive, much of the remaining land was hilly and farmers there were compelled to follow subsistence agriculture. East Tennesseans had a greater diversification of crops than did the farmers of the other two sections; they raised tobacco, wheat, cotton, flax, hemp, and also fruits and vegetables. As a whole, however, the eastern counties were unable to compete favorably with those of the central and western divisions.

Middle Tennessee consists of long mountain slopes, plateaus, and undulating lands, and includes the rich Central Basin and fertile bottoms of the Cumberland, Harpeth, and Tennessee rivers. A variety of crops, including cotton, corn, tobacco, and many vegetables, was produced in the Basin and also on the peripheral Highland Rim. Tobacco was the principal money crop in the northern counties of Montgomery, Sumner, Robertson, Stewart, and Dickson. In 1840 the state's yield was exceeded only by that of Kentucky and Virginia. Ten years later Maryland also had surpassed the Volunteer State in tobacco production; by 1860, however, Tennessee had regained her spot just behind Kentucky and Virginia. Cotton was grown by John Donelson in Davidson County as early as 1780, but until the invention of the cotton gin cotton was not an important money crop in the central division.

West Tennessee was the last section to be settled, but it soon surpassed the rest of the state in production because of its fertile soil, particularly in the southwestern counties. At mid-century, this comparatively small area produced more than four-fifths of the state's cotton crop, and Colonel John Pope of Shelby County received a medal at the London Exposition in 1851 for "the best cotton known to the world." In 1810 (before West Tennessee was opened for settlement), the Volunteer State had an annual production of less than 3,000 bales, but by 1820, 50,000 bales were sold. At mid-century, the state's production of 194,532 bales was exceeded only by that of Alabama, Georgia, Mississippi, and South Carolina. On the eve of the Civil War, production had been increased 50 per cent over that of 1850.

Farmers in all sections of the state raised livestock and poultry. The earliest settlers had brought beef and milch cattle into the wilderness, and James Robertson drove stock overland into the Cumberland area in 1780. In the raising of horses, mules, oxen, sheep, and swine, the state compared favorably with the other Southern states, and in number of mules and swine Tennessee ranked at the top. Poultry—both turkeys and chickens—were raised not only for home consumption but also for the market. Middle Tennessee producers often drove flocks of 750 or more overland to Nashville and then put them on steamboats bound for New Orleans. Merino sheep, Berkshire hogs, and Shorthorn cattle were of especial interest to Tennessee farmers. One of the most successful breeders was Mark Cockrill, who for several decades owned and farmed 5,000 acres of Davidson County land located on the Charlotte Pike. He raised only choice cattle, horses and mules, Berkshire hogs, and sheep. In 1854 at the World's Fair in London, Cockrill received a premium for the finest wool in the world. Upon his return, Tennessee legislators presented him a medal for his "devotion of a long life to the advancement . . . of agricultural resources," and a later assembly placed his bust in a position of honor in the capitol. Lucius Julius Polk and Ben Harlan of Maury County, Woods S. Miller of Gallatin, and L. C. Coleman of Nashville were other well-known breeders. Animals produced by these men brought high prices, and Miller in 1840 wagered $500 that in any contest his would be judged superior to any in the state.

During a forty-year period before the Civil War, agricultural specialists not infrequently were critical of agriculture practices in the Volunteer State. Enlightened leaders such as Dr. Henry Brooks of Smith County, and Tolbert Fanning, editor of *The Agriculturist*, urged farmers to diversify and practice crop rotation, contour plowing, and terracing. Gideon J. Pillow, in speaking at a Middle Tennessee fair in Maury County in 1855, urged farmers to grow less cotton and to raise more corn, oats, wheat, hay, and livestock.

Dr. Brooks was one of the many reformers who insisted that Tennessee cotton raisers and tobacco growers should turn to silk production. In 1829, Brooks told legislators of his own experiments with silk worms, of the small amount of labor necessary for their culture, and of expected profits. He urged the assembly to appropriate $200 per annum for silk worm eggs and mulberry seed which would be distributed free among interested farmers. Many editors of newspapers took up the cry, and soon a "Tennessee Silk Company and Agriculture School" was incorporated "to teach the art of the culture and manufacture of silk." A Nashvillian was convinced that silk could make Middle Tennessee "equal to the valley of the Piedmont or any region in the Chinese Empire." Governor Jones appeared for his second inauguration dressed in a suit manufactured by the Tennessee Silk Company from material produced in the state. In 1840, silkmen sold nearly 1,100 pounds; more than 90 per cent of this was produced in the eastern and middle divisions. By 1850, the output had doubled that of ten years earlier, and Tennessee then ranked first in production among the states. During the 1850's, however, the dream of an Oriental Empire of silk all but vanished, as farmer after farmer told of losses of his cocoons. Production in 1860 amounted to only 71 pounds, and was limited almost entirely to the counties of Humphreys, Lincoln, and Sevier.

The interest in agricultural reform could not have been sustained had it not been for the State Agricultural Bureau, created in 1854. Its chief duties were to sponsor county agricultural organizations and to supervise county, division, and state fairs. Under the bureau, county organizations complying with certain regulations received a bounty of $200, which could be spent in any way beneficial to the agricultural interests of the county. The act of 1854 also provided $10,000 for fairs, where farmers could exhibit their produce and compete with one another for premiums. Governor Johnson showed much interest, and in 1855, at his insistence, the legislature authorized the issuance of $30,000 in state bonds to purchase a permanent location for fair grounds near Nashville and to construct the necessary buildings and fixtures.

Reformers continued their agitation until Southern economic life was paralyzed by the effects of the Civil War. Many of their ideas had been carried out, however, and much progress had been made. Values of land had increased considerably, and thousands of acres had been improved for cultivation.

Ante Bellum Industry ⧉ Comparatively little industrial development had taken place in Tennessee at mid-century. Social and economic prestige was associated with tillers of the soil and not with mechanics and laborers—this association no doubt made it difficult to lure Tennessee yeomen from the plow to the factory. Iron had been the principal industry; cotton, silk, and wool manufacture existed largely in the minds of a few who dreamed of industrial development in the Volunteer State.

Even before Tennessee became a state, iron forges and furnaces had been built by David Ross, James King, Moses Cavitt, Walter King, John Sevier, and Nicholas Perkins along the Holston, and by James Robertson in Middle Tennessee. Montgomery Bell purchased Robertson's interests in 1804, and soon became one of the state's greatest industrialists of the time. His advertisement in a Nashville paper in 1808 for 5,000 cords of wood is indicative of his operations; indeed, at one time Bell owned or had an interest in more than a dozen furnaces and forges. Iron works were opened by other capitalists from time to time, especially in Washington, Unicoi, Greene, Hickman, Montgomery, Stewart, and Lewis counties. In 1850, the Chattanooga Foundry and Machine Shop was established; after the Civil War, the shop was to exhibit dynamic growth in iron and steel. Also in Chattanooga, the Vulcan Iron Works was opened in 1860. By this time, Tennessee ranked third in bloomery output, and was excelled only by Pennsylvania and New York. The Civil War brought renewed interest in the lead mines of East Tennessee, and in the 1860's much interest was shown in the Bumpass Cove area in Washington County which had been productive earlier.

Copper and coal also were mined in East Tennessee at mid-century. Early settlers found copper, next to iron, to be the most useful metal. During the 1850's, large quantities of copper were taken from mines in Polk County. The Hiwassee mine was opened in August, 1850, and by 1854 at least fourteen mines produced several million pounds of copper annually; owners sold the copper in the markets of London, New York, and Boston. Charcoal was used generally instead of coal, but during the 1850's New York capitalists opened the Sewanee Mining Company and exploited rich coal veins in the eastern part of the Cumberland Plateau.

Efforts to arouse interest in textiles met with little success. A joint committee, appointed by state legislators in 1845, was one of several groups which from time to time studied manufacturing possibilities. The committee told of successes in Alabama and elsewhere, pointed to Tennessee's natural resources, and contended that both slaves and free workers could be used profitably in textile manufacture. Mark R. Cockrill believed that every county where cotton was grown in abundance could have one or two cotton mills. He proposed that fifteen planters in each county might invest $4,000 each to get the project started, and then small blocks of stock could be sold to interested citizens. This, Cockrill believed, would "render the South magnificiently rich, and gloriously independent." Talk of industrial reform, however, fell upon deaf ears. Although at mid-century factories had been established in at least Knoxville, Paris, Athens, Gallatin, Nashville, Murfreesboro, and Franklin, the state's output was small. Less than $700,000 worth of manufactured goods was produced in 1860, but adjacent Georgia made goods valued at $2,371,207, and Massachusetts at over $38,000,000. In the same year, only one wool factory was in operation, and the state's total output was worth only $8,100. Virginia's output of woolen goods, however, was valued at $717,827, Georgia's at $464,420, and North Carolina's at $291,000.

Probably the main reason for the sparcity of industrial development at mid-century was the people's lack of interest. Politicians, realizing that major political decisions lay with farmers, seldom advocated industrial development. European immigrants from industrial centers rarely came South; nativists such as William G. Brownlow had even urged them to settle in the North instead of Tennessee. Landowners and men of capital turned their attention increasingly to cotton which at mid-century continued to spiral upward in price.

Towns and Cities ?? The large metropolitan centers which we know today did not exist in the mid-1800's; in fact, there were few cities in the entire country which were as large as Memphis and Nashville are today. The state's capital, a sprawling town on the banks of the Cumberland River, was the largest in the state and was primarily an agricultural and commercial center. Its 10,165 people pursued a variety of occupations, including flour-milling and saw-milling, and other small manufactures. By 1850, fifteen toll roads radiated from Nashville, making it the hub of some of the best roads in the state. The Nashville and Chattanooga Railway was almost completed, and the first steam locomotive began operation in 1851.

Memphis, with a population of 8,841, was the next largest city in 1850. From its incorporation in 1826, Memphis grew rapidly; the census of 1830 indicated a population of only a few hundred, but ten years later nearly 2,000 persons had settled there. Memphis was an outstanding cotton center. At mid-century, factors handled 150,000 bales valued at $7,520,000, and by 1860 the figures were tripled. The river traffic, coupled with the promise of increased trade when railroad construction was completed, caused a New Orleans editor in 1850 to predict that Memphis soon would be "the most important town in the Southwest after New Orleans."

The oldest of the major towns, Knoxville, had a population of 2,076 at mid-century and led the cultural and commercial life of East Tennessee. The Bank of the State of Tennessee was established there in 1811, and Knoxville continued as a town of strong financial interests. Steamboat transportation caused considerable growth during the 1830's, and the opening of rail facilities during the 1850's brought further expansion. As in Nashville, flour-milling and saw-milling were the chief industries.

Chattanooga was not incorporated until 1839, and at mid-century its population numbered only a few hundred families. Earlier, Chattanooga had been a stopping place for river traffic, and was known as "Ross's Landing." In 1850, the Western and Atlantic Railroad, which reached northward from Atlanta to Chattanooga and had connections with lines to Charleston and Savannah, began operation. A decade later, Chattanooga was a focal point of all the railroads in the Southeast. It was not until after the war that the town began a great period of growth, and not until 1870 that Chattanooga became the county seat of Hamilton County.

At mid-century, other towns in all sections of the state grew rapidly, and several had populations in excess of those claimed by Knoxvillians and Chattanoogans. Columbia, established in the first decade of the nineteenth century and later the county seat of Maury County, was the third largest town, with 2,977 people in 1850. Murfreesboro, county seat of Rutherford County, boasted of 1,917, and nearby Lebanon, county seat of Wilson County, had 1,554. Pulaski, the Giles County seat, had 1,137, and Franklin, county seat of Williamson County, 891. In West Tennessee, Jackson, with a population of 1,006, and Brownsville with 971, ranked next behind Memphis. The migration from East Tennessee into the middle and western division—to say nothing of Arkansas and Texas—kept towns in that section small. Greeneville, with 660 and Kingsport, with 320, ranked next behind Knoxville and Chattanooga.

Ante Bellum Society ⥤ The picture of Southern society as created by ante bellum writers and travelers from Europe and the Northeast became a stereotype widely accepted for many years. This picture showed a threefold class society consisting of the lazy but well-to-do, mint julip-drinking planters at the top and the equally lazy but more degenerate, shiftless, and hopeless poor whites—"that lawless and idle rabble"—near the bottom. It was the worthy but imposed-upon slave, however, who composed the "mud sill" upon which the superstructure was built. Those at the top were arrogant; those at the bottom, surly. It was not until comparatively recently that Frank L. Owsley and others working under him at Vanderbilt University produced a preponderance of evidence of a strong middle class. The absence of a middle, or "yeomen," class, as shown in the stereotype, was disproved by Owsley, and an accurate picture of the social structure presented. The planter class, the poor white, and the slaves actually were minorities; the vast majority of Southern people were middle-class farmers who composed the backbone of the social and economic structure of the South.

As middle-class people, the yeomen enjoyed middle-class pleasures. The house raisings, corn huskings, and quilting parties did not expire with the early pioneers but continued through the ante bellum days. After a log rolling or house raising invariably came an all-night dance and frolic, at which refreshments flowed in large quantities. By the light of the moon or the burning embers, the "Virginia Reel" and the "Kentucky Hoe-Down" were executed with such fervor that people from miles around came to observe and to participate.

Fist fights and wrestling matches often accompanied gatherings of all kinds. David Crockett once told of attending a wedding party at which the bride and groom staged a wrestling match; to the amusement of all and the amazement of some, the buxom female, said Crockett, threw her husband-to-be three times in a row. At times, the fights became gory struggles in which participants gouged, kicked, bit, clawed, and otherwise fought with "no holds barred." James Flint, a Scot traveler who was nauseated by what he beheld, wrote of "gouging or putting out the antagonist's eyes by thrusting the thumbs in the sockets," and noses and ears being mutilated by "canine modes of fighting." Spectators, "rooting" for one or the other, often became embroiled. In 1816, at Elkton, for example, the champion of the Price family fought the best man of the McKinneys; even as the principals, James Price and James McKinney, squared off, half the crowd stripped to fight, and for several hours the hills and valleys of the Giles County community echoed with the sounds of the struggle.

Tobacco and whiskey were indulged in frequently. That Rachel Donelson Jackson smoked a corncob pipe and many other women dipped snuff profusely was by no means unique among frontier women. Most of the men smoked and chewed—whether at home, on the streets, in court, or in church. Dr. Phillip Lindsley, president of the University of Nashville, told of standing for prayer one Sunday morning, and immediately a tobacco-chewing parishioner behind him let loose such a salvo of tobacco juice into Lindsley's pew that he was unable to find a dry spot on the seat after the prayer had been concluded. Peter Cartwright, a Methodist circuit rider, told of seeing ministers and laymen alike drink whiskey to keep off the winter chills, to ease the pains of rheumatism, or simply to drink for "old times' sake."

European writers who traveled through Tennessee and the South supplied their readers with many interesting tales of frontier life. James Flint, for example, wrote that he had never seen such noisy and ill-mannered people as those west of the Unakas. On one occasion (in 1818) shortly after Flint had seated himself in an East Tennessee tavern, a group of boisterous youths entered. The group engaged in "noisy gabbing, drinking, and swearing" the like of which Flint vowed he had never seen or heard before. Mrs. Frances Trollope, an English traveler who came several years later, found manners in West Tennessee to be even worse than that. She was amazed at the eating habits of people who dined in the Memphis hotels. On one occasion she watched horror-stricken as fifty diners rushed to the table and swallowed potatoes, meat, and bread with little or no mastication. Not a word was spoken; she heard only the sounds of smacking, chomping, and an "unceasing chorus of coughing." James E. Alexander, another English visitor, came to Nashville in the 1830's in hopes of finding people with better manners, but he could write only of his disappointment. At the sound of the dinner bell, Alexander watched scores of men rush into hotels and boarding houses, spitting chewing tobacco in one direction and blowing their noses in the other, to devour chunks of roast beef and loaves of bread like party sandwiches. He was horrified as men reached completely across the table, knives and forks in hand, to stab biscuits and steaks even before a blessing had been said. Hot coffee poured into saucers to cool, Alexander wrote, would be blown with such vigor as to send a spray across the room. Plates overflowing with food would be licked clean seconds later. Every person, he wrote, ate "as if it were [his] last meal . . . ."

Such stories as the travelers wrote were amusing and, if true, were exceptions rather than the rule. Many Tennesseans, especially in the towns and cities, had acceptable table manners and had an appreciation of refinement and culture which was not unlike the tastes of the people of the East and of Europe. Many artists coming to Nashville, Knoxville, and Memphis during the ante bellum period charmed audiences with their superb performances. Perhaps the most widely heralded artistic performances in ante bellum Tennessee were those of the 1850's, when Jenny Lind was heard in Nashville and Memphis, Signor Luigi Arditi's Italian Opera Company performed in Nashville, Edwin Booth introduced Nashvillians to Shakespeare, and when Christy's Minstrels thrilled audiences in Memphis. Nashville was described as being in "one wild uproar" on March 29, 1851, when Miss Lind arrived. From the presentation of her first selection, an aria from *Lucia di Lammermoor,* to her closing rendition of *Home, Sweet Home,* the Swedish Nightingale enthralled her audience and held it spellbound. Standing room at $3.00 was considered cheap in the newly constructed Adelphi Theater; in Memphis a capacity crowd paid $5.00 each to hear her, even though the performance was at eleven o'clock in the morning.

Nashville was the cultural center of the state, and others besides Miss Lind were seen and heard. In 1854, Arditi presented the Italian Opera Company with Madame Rosa DeVries as prima donna. Miss Lind had introduced Nashvillians to Gaetano Donizetti, and Arditi opened with the Italian composer's tragic *Lucia di Lammermoor.* On succeeding evenings he presented Antonio Rossini's *Barber of Seville,* Vincenzo Bellini's *Norma* and *La Sonnambula,* and Giuseppe Verdi's *Ernani.* Although Miss DeVries could not reach the high notes of Jenny Lind, many believed her to be a greater artist. Her warm interpretation of *Norma* sent her audience into rapture, and they permitted her to retire only "under a perfect deluge of bouquets." In March, 1859, Edwin Booth appeared in Nashville and was billed as "the distinguished young tragedian." A man of melancholy and romantic countenance, graceful carriage, and poetic temperament, whom nature had cast as a nineteenth-century Hamlet, Booth for two weeks interpreted Shakespeare before capacity crowds. Although he probably was the most polished Hamlet Nashville audiences had seen, Booth played Macbeth equally well.

Memphis, a rapidly growing frontier town at mid-century, presented many cultural features. During the 1840's and 1850's, many of those who performed in Nashville, including Miss Lind, Booth, and Ole Bull (a self-taught Norwegian violin virtuoso), also performed in Memphis. Others included Boston-born soprana Signora Elisa Biscaccianti, a baritone named Signor Belletti, and Joseph Burke, a violinist. The 1850's was a decade of minstrelsy in Memphis, and a half dozen groups—including Christy's—gave public performances.

Although Knoxville was not visited by Jenny Lind or Edwin Booth, Knoxvillians heard able artists of perhaps less renown. The faculties of East Tennessee University and East Tennessee Female Institute provided leadership for many home talent productions in both music and drama. A group known as the Swiss Bell Ringers appeared before a capacity crowd in 1854; a few years later Anna Vail, accompanied by Theodore Schreiner, performed for Knoxvillians before returning to Europe. As in Memphis, minstrel groups were popular.

Humanitarian Reform—Prisons and the Penal Code ᜒᜒ
Tennessee's criminal code and constitution were taken from several sources, principally those in use in Pennsylvania and North Carolina. Both states had harsh criminal codes, and local legislators adopted them with little modification. Horse thieves and murderers usually suffered death on the gallows; a perjurer might be sentenced to stand in the pillory for hours with his ears nailed, and afterwards both ears were severed from his body and left nailed on the pillory. In actual cases on record, a Stewart County man wounded another

and was sentenced to be whipped publicly, cropped on both ears, and branded on the arms with hot wine. A Madison County man, convicted of manslaughter, was sentenced to be branded with the letter M. In Washington County, Elias Pybourn was convicted of horse stealing; he escaped the death penalty, but his sentence included confinement in the pillory for one hour, having both ears nailed to the pillory and severed at the end of the hour, thirty-nine lashes "well laid on," and branding with the letter H on the right cheek and the letter T on the other. Counterfeiters, according to an 1811 statute, received as punishment:

> 39 stripes on his, her, or their bare back, be imprisoned not less than six months, nor more than two years, shall sit in the pillory two hours on three different days, and shall be rendered infamous, and pay the costs of the prosecution, and shall also be branded on . . . the left thumb with the letter T.

Penalties were so severe that jurors sometimes refused to return a verdict of guilty, not because they were convinced of the innocence of the defendent but because of the severity of the punishment. John Sevier gave attention to the need for revision of the penal code as early as 1807, but little was done until shortly after William Carroll became governor.

In the meantime, reformers across the country talked of better treatment for those convicted of crime. Many believed that if the convict could be incarcerated for a time in a "penitentiary house" and accorded humane treatment, he would have the opportunity for the first time to contemplate the enormity of his crime and thereafter live an exemplary life. By the time Carroll became governor in 1821, several Northern and Eastern states had constructed modern penitentiaries.

In his initial message to the legislature, Carroll suggested a revision of the penal code and the construction of a penitentiary. Legislators should establish a scale of punishment bearing a just proportion to the magnitude of each offense, he said, and should construct a prison where solitary confinement, coarse food, and hard labor might afford the criminal ample opportunity to repent of his crimes. In 1825, Governor Carroll, at the suggestion of the General Assembly, procured information about costs and operations of prisons in Kentucky, Virginia, Ohio, New Jersey, New Hampshire, and Maryland. It was not until 1829, however, that legislators acted favorably upon his suggestions.

The law of 1829 made sweeping changes. It abolished the whipping post and the practices of cropping and confinement in the pillory and stocks. For some felonies formerly punishable by death, offenders would be confined in a new penitentiary at hard labor. Equally important was a provision for an elaborate penitentiary. Work was begun immediately, and the new prison was ready for use on January 1, 1831. A contemporary writer described it as a

> beautiful and substantial Prison. . . . It presents a front of three hundred and ten feet, and is three hundred and fifty in depth. The wings of the front building contain two hundred cells, and half of the center building is occupied by the Keeper, and the other half is used for a hospital, guard rooms, etc. The yard walls are four and a half feet thick at the bottom, and three at the top, and have an average height of twenty feet.

During the next three decades the penitentiary increased in size as plant facilities expanded, more land was bought, and the number of criminals housed at state expense increased. By 1860, the state prison had 352 cells, measuring six and one-half feet in length, three feet in width, and seven feet in height, and housed more than 300 prisoners.

Contemporaneous with the movement for a revision of the criminal code was a growing demand for repeal of laws which provided for capital punishment and for imprisonment of debtors. Continued agitation for the former failed to reap success, but in 1842 imprisonment for debt was abolished entirely.

Care of the Insane ?☙ The movement for better care of the insane did not begin as early as did the agitation for revision of the criminal code. Many Tennesseans, not unlike people of other parts of the country, clung to the medieval idea that mental illness was a visitation of divine displeasure; thus the afflicted and his family should be ashamed. In some cases, people of unsound mind were mistreated by being chained in a cellar or attic, flogged into obedience, or slowly starved by an inadequate diet. Dorothea Lynde Dix, a Massachusetts woman who devoted her life to the improvement of prisons and hospitals for the insane and who had visited and studied almshouses and hospitals in practically every state as well as Europe, visited Tennessee in 1847 and was shocked to find so many insane people "pining in cells and dungeons," and bound with ropes and chains.

Before Miss Dix visited the state, some attention had been given to the problem of the insane. Soon after Tennessee was admitted to the Union, county courts were authorized to appoint guardians for mental defectives who owned property. Those without property were "let out" for maintenance to the lowest bidder, and those violently insane could be confined in the county jails. State officials gave little attention to these unfortunate people during the first three decades of the century.

The first significant act came in 1832, when the legislature appropriated $10,000 for a hospital for the insane, to be located at Nashville. Funds were inadequate, however, and for fifteen years reformers were disappointed at the lack of progress. A legislative committee appointed in 1837 to investigate the hospital work, for example, found a half-built structure "in bad order" and "daily and hourly injuring" from exposure to rain and weather. Not until two years later was the hospital, consisting of sixty beds, ready for operation.

Reformers were far from satisfied with Tennessee's efforts to minister to the insane. Governor Polk in 1841 pointed to statistics which showed that the state had approximately 800 people who were mentally defective, and urged that hospital facilities be expanded. Governor Jones observed with regret what he characterized as public indifference to the "unfortunate class of our fellow-citizens." A legislative committee was appointed to study plans for enlarging facilities, but little had been done when Miss Dix arrived in Nashville in December, 1847.

The Massachusetts reformer inspected the hospital for the insane as well as such county jails and poor houses as her time permitted. She found jails and poor houses to be as inadequate as the hospital. At the State Hospital, she found heating facilities to be "a complete failure" and expressed amazement at finding no bathrooms and neither cisterns nor wells sufficient to afford an adequate water supply. In urging legislators to start anew, Miss Dix suggested the purchase of at least 100 acres of land readily accessible to all parts of the state and the erection of a new hospital large enough to house at least 250 patients.

Legislators acted favorably upon her suggestions. The governor was authorized to appoint seven commissioners to purchase a tract of land and supervise the construction of a new hospital with the features Miss Dix had suggested. A site on the Murfreesboro Road, six miles from Nashville, was purchased, and construction was begun in the autumn of 1848. Work moved slowly, however, because of inadequate funds. Governor William Trousdale in his final legislative message (October, 1851) observed that the hospital was ready at last for occupancy and a few months later patients were transferred. Not until 1857, however, was the structure finished according to original specifications.

Training for the Blind and the Deaf-Mutes ୧୬ The humanitarian spirit of the period also gave rise to a demand for public assistance for the blind and for deaf-mutes. Newspaper editorialists wrote of unfortunates in these categories, albeit much less frequently than they did of the insane. The first legislation on behalf of the blind came at the insistence of James Champlin, a blind son of an Overton County merchant, who in 1842 after a period of training established a school for the blind in Nashville. In the following year he asked legislators to appropriate money for a state-supported school. The lawmakers set aside only $3,000 for the biennium, but they authorized the solicitation of private contributions. A few wealthy individuals gave generously, and within a short time after the passage of the act, Champlin's school was opened with expanded facilities—the seventh state-supported school in the nation.

The institution, laboring under the difficulties of small enrollment and inadequate operating capital, progressed slowly. Although it was estimated that there were more than 400 blind persons in the state, only twenty had been admitted to the school by 1847. Three years later, legislators set aside $4,000 for a new school, and in 1852 appropriated an additional $8,000. Trustees purchased one and one-half acres on the Lebanon Road where construction began immediately on a three-story brick building. In 1858, the school was placed on a per capita basis, with $200 being apportioned for each student. Provisions were made for thirty students, who would be taught arithmetic, chemistry, history, geography, spelling, grammar, and other subjects.

Similar attention was focused upon help for deaf-mutes during the two decades before the Civil War. Tennessee became the seventh state to establish a school for the deaf when, in 1844, the legislature appropriated money for a school at Knoxville. As in the case of education for the blind, interest in an institution for the deaf and dumb developed slowly. The school began operation with only six pupils, and by 1853 trustees reported that not more than twenty-five persons had availed themselves of the opportunities which the school afforded, although there were over 500 deaf-mutes in the state, about one-fourth of them of school age.

In 1854, an agent was employed by the state to search for pupils and to convince parents of the advantages of the school. By the time of the Civil War, the school had eighty pupils, who studied a variety of subjects, including pantomime, Bible, arithmetic, and manual training such as shoemaking and cabinet work.

The Poor, Orphans, and Other Unfortunates Humanitarians of the pre-Civil War period also sought to improve the living conditions of the dependent poor. As early as 1797, legislators empowered justices of the peace to "take cognizance" of all the poor and adjudge which should receive public aid. For their support, county courts were authorized to levy a tax, the amount of which could not exceed six cents on each 100 acres of land, six cents on each slave, and three cents on each free person. A few counties maintained "poor houses," but the majority lodged paupers with individuals who provided subsistence for minimum fees. Some improvement resulted from an enactment in 1826 which permitted county courts to levy additional taxes and appoint building commissioners for the construction of necessary buildings for the accommodation of the poor. As a result, counties purchased farm land on which they built poor houses and employed the able-bodied poor to cultivate the land.

The reform spirit also was manifested by the development of privately established benevolent institutions. The sympathies of many, but most notably socially prominent matrons, were stirred particularly by the unfortunate conditions of destitute orphans. In

1845 several ladies of Nashville, including Mrs. John Bell and Mrs. Boyd McNairy, purchased a dwelling house which they converted into an orphanage for girls, and, by October of that year, had admitted a dozen children. In the same year the Nashville Protestant School of Industry was incorporated for the support and education of destitute girls. Mrs. Aaron V. Brown, Mrs. Francis B. Fogg, and other prominent Nashville ladies were named as trustees. In 1856 a group known as the Robertson Association was organized for the purpose of apprenticing orphans to learn suitable trades, and three years later the Nashville Orphan Asylum was chartered to care for indigent males.

The Temperance Movement ॐ Throughout the colonial, Revolutionary, and early republic periods drinking was quite common. Little thought was given to the moral issue. Nevertheless, a temperance movement developed soon after Tennessee became a state, and leaders pointed to considerable success during the first half of the nineteenth century. The first anti-liquor law affecting the state was enacted by North Carolina in 1779. The law restricted drinking to homes and establishments for travelers and made illegal the retailing of intoxicants in quantities of less than a quart, except in taverns and hotels. Legislators had intended, of course, to eliminate saloons whose sole business was the sale of liquor which could be consumed on the premises. Many "tippling houses" (as the saloons were called) existed in open violation of the law, however, and state legislators in 1831, apparently despairing of the enforcement of the enactment, legalized saloons. Proprietors were required to procure licenses from the clerks of the county courts and to give bond that they would keep peaceful and orderly houses and not permit gambling. It was called the general license system because any establishment, saloons as well as taverns, could be licensed to retail liquor.

In the meantime, prominent temperance leaders organized to combat demon rum. Some leaders formed temperance societies to dissuade people from the consumption of alcoholic beverages, others established temperance journals, and still others memorialized the legislature for stricter liquor laws. Two societies, probably the first in the state, were organized in 1829. One was at Kingsport, where members condemned intemperance and pledged themselves neither to vote for candidates who sought support with liquor nor to employ persons who drank while at work. The other society was at Nashville, where William Hume, Philip Lindsley, Robert Whyte, and other prominent citizens organized the "Nashville and Davidson County Temperance Society, Auxiliary to the American Temperance Society." They met quarterly, evangelized to procure additional members, and subscribed to the following pledge:

> We, the undersigned, do hereby agree that we will abstain wholly from the use of distilled spirits (except for medicinal purposes); that we will discourage the use of them in our families, not provide them for the entertainment of our friends, or for persons in our employment; that we will abstain from the business of making them or selling them by large or small, and that in all suitable ways we will discountenance the use of them in the community.

Four years later, the Reverend James Smith published the Nashville *Western Philanthropist*, which he described as being "Devoted to Temperance and general Benevolence." In 1837 the Reverend Darius Hoyt published in Maryville a paper called the *Temperance Banner*. He sought to focus attention upon domestic difficulties caused by drunken fathers and pledged to save them "from the ignominy and horrors of a drunkard's life and a drunkard's grave." Scores of petitions were sent to legislators after the law of 1831. Typical was one presented in 1837 by 374 Nashville women, who described intemperance as "the hot bed in which nine tenths of the crimes daily perpetrated are engendered."

Many legislators assembled in 1837 with instructions from their constituents to abolish tippling houses. Consequently, a measure was enacted early in the next year to repeal laws which licensed saloons and to prohibit the sale of intoxicants in quantities of less than a quart. The law was poorly enforced, and eight years later the "Quart Law" was repealed. Legislators returned to the licensing system, under which anyone might retail liquors who secured a license, provided he took an oath that he would not sell on Sunday, would not permit gambling, and would not sell to minors without written permission from their parents or sell to slaves without permission from their masters. This law remained on the statute books until after the Civil War, except for two years (1856–57) when the Quart Law of 1838 was resurrected.

Other efforts were made to regulate public morals during the ante bellum period. Newspapermen not infrequently editorialized upon the large amount of vice and misconduct, especially in the cities. Horse racing frequently was condemned; one correspondent described the track as a place of "noise and dust; hard drinking; profane cursing and swearing; quarrelling; fighting; bloody noses; black eyes; fractured noses; [and] ragged citizens who can not give bread to their wives and children . . . ." Card playing also was condemned by some, and in 1815 legislators placed a heavy tax on vendors of cards. Two years later, Senator William C. Roadman, of East Tennessee, led a legislative battle to abolish billiard tables. The senator described the game as one which encouraged "the vice of gambling which will eventually be attended with pernicious consequences to society, by corrupting the morals of the youth of our country . . . ."

The continued agitation for reform evidenced a growing awareness of social evil on the part of at least some of the people. Much crime and vice continued, however, especially in the cities. The river town of Memphis teemed with robbers and gamblers, and Old Bell Tavern was a dive where confidence games were common and liquor could be had day or night. Sections of Nashville offered little by way of improvement. The river front, known as "The Jungle," was especially notorious for its cheap saloons, brothels, and hideouts for criminals.

Considerable good had been accomplished, however, by the end of the ante bellum period. The Civil War, on the other hand, added crime and depredation and counteracted much of the good which had been brought about during the several decades before. The reform movement in Tennessee, which was only a small part of a great current of liberal and humanitarian sentiment then sweeping the country, was largely experimental in nature, but gains were made upon which future generations were to build.

SUGGESTED READINGS

General Accounts
Folmsbee, Corlew, and Mitchell, *Tennessee*, I, Chs. 22–23; Hamer, *Tennessee*, II, Chs. 48–49, 51–52; Blake McKelvey, *American Prisons: A Study in American Social History Prior to 1915* (Chicago, 1936); Frank

L. Owsley, *Plain Folk of the Old South* (Baton Rouge, 1949); White, *Messages*, I–IV.

Specialized Accounts

R. E. Barclay, *Ducktown: Back in Raht's Time* (Chapel Hill, 1946); Barnhart, "Tennessee Constitution of 1796," *JSH*, IX (Nov., 1943), 532–48; Constantine G. Belissary, "Industry and Industrial Philosophy in Tennessee, 1850–1860," ETHS *Publ.*, No. 23 (1951), 46–57; Capers, *River Town—Memphis*; Blanche Henry Clark, *The Tennessee Yeoman* (Nashville, 1942); E. Katherine Crews, "Early Musical Activities in Knoxville, Tennessee, 1791–1861," ETHS *Publ.*, No. 32 (1960), 3–17; Jesse C. Crowe, "The Origin and Development of Tennessee's Prison Problem, 1831–1871," *THQ*, XV (June, 1956), 111–35; F. Garvin Davenport, "Cultural Life in Nashville on the Eve of the Civil War," *JSH*, III (Aug., 1937), 326–47; Harry R. Edwall, "Some Famous Musicians on the Memphis Concert Stage Prior to 1860," WTHS *Papers*, No. V (1951), 90–105; Edwall, "The Golden Era of Minstrelsy in Memphis: A Reconstruction," WTHS *Papers*, No. IX (1955), 29–47; Paul M. Fink, "The Bumpass Cove Mines and Embreeville," ETHS *Publ.*, No. 16 (1944), 48–64; Gilbert E. Govan, "Some Sidelights on the History of Chattanooga," *THQ*, VI (June, 1947), 148–60; Hunt, "Pactolus Ironworks," *THQ*, XXV (Summer, 1966), 176–96; Holt, *Economic and Social Beginnings*; Paul E. Isaac, *Prohibition and Politics: Turbulent Decades in Tennessee, 1885–1920* (Knoxville, 1965), Ch. 1; Shields McIlwaine, *Memphis Down in Dixie* (New York, 1948); Owsley and Owsley, "Economic Structure of Rural Tennessee," *JSH*, VIII (May, 1942), 24–45; Charles C. Ritter, " 'The Drama in our Midst,' The History of the Theater in Memphis," WTHS *Papers*, No. XI (1957), 5–35; James I. Robertson, Jr., "Frolics, Fights, and Firewater in Frontier Tennessee," *THQ*, XVII (June, 1958), 97–111; Kenneth Rose, "A Nashville Musical Decade, 1830–1840," *THQ*, II (Sept., 1943), 216–31; Rose, "Jenny Lind, Diva," *THQ*, VIII (March, 1949), 34–48; E. Bruce Thompson, "An Early Temperance Society at Nashville," *THM*, V (Oct., 1919), 142–44; Thompson, "Reforms in the Care of the Insane in Tennessee, 1830–1850," *THQ*, III (Dec., 1944), 319–34; Thompson, "Reforms in the Penal System of Tennessee, 1820–1850," *THQ*, I (Dec., 1942), 291–309; Charles P. White, "Early Experiments with Prison Labor in Tennessee," ETHS *Publ.*, No. 12 (1940), 45–69; Williams, "South's First Cotton Factory," *THQ*, V (Sept., 1946), 212–21;·Williams, "Early Iron Works," *THQ*, VI (March, 1947), 39–46.

18. 🐦 War Clouds

Dr. James G. M. Ramsey, eminent East Tennessee physician and historian, wrote as early as 1858 that he could "conceal from no one" his "deep conviction that the days of . . . [the] present Union are . . . numbered." Northern people had degenerated, he believed; in place of the once "high toned New-England spirit" only corruption, covetousness, and selfishness remained. On the other hand, in the South the "proud Cavalier spirit," the "virtue and integrity of the Huguenot," and the "probity and honor of the Presbyterian" had been intensified. "We are essentially two people," Ramsey said, as he concluded that a nation so different in refinement, tastes, and character could not stand.

The majority of Tennesseans, however, did not share Ramsey's pessimism. Except for a few extremists, they accepted the Compromise of 1850 in good faith and, while few if any acquiesced in Daniel Webster's theory of an "indissoluble union," saw no imminent danger of secession. The majority believed that although the reins of government temporarily were in unfriendly hands the ultimate victory lay with the "real" Union of constitutional government and equality among states. Disunion was not seriously considered, and Tennessee remained virtually free of secession propaganda until 1860.

The fear of "Black Republicanism" and its concomitant threats to slavery of course were present before the sixties. Tennessee was a slave state whose slaveholders had millions of dollars invested in Negroes, and slaveholders distrusted the party which encouraged operation of the "Underground Railroad." To most Tennesseans, the Republican party was synonymous with abolitionism, and to describe another as an "abolitionist" was an insult. Allen A. Hall, for example, editor of the Nashville *News*, in November, 1859, shot and killed George G. Poindexter, editor of the *Union and American*, because Poindexter had accused him of abolitionist leanings. Another editor asserted that Republican leaders were political opportunists who would foment sectional strife, even to the point of destroying the republic, if such appeared expedient in their quest for power.

William H. Seward, a Republican leader in New York who seemed to Southern spokesmen to typify their conception of Republican abolitionists, became the target for abuse because of his scathing and persistent verbal attacks on slavery. In October, 1858, he had asserted that war between the two sections was inevitable—an idea which became known as Seward's "irrepressible conflict doctrine" and which was taken up by other Northern Republicans. To Tennesseans, the vast majority of whom believed coexistence was possible and desirable, the statement was a "bomb-shell fired by a fanatic." It caused the few East Tennessee Republicans to repudiate their newly adopted party, and inspired Democrats to make slavery one of the major issues in the gubernatorial campaign of 1859. The Tennessee legislature branded the doctrine "infamous," and called upon "national men of all parties throughout the Union" to do their duty by uniting to crush it.

Many people blamed Seward for John Brown's raid at Harper's Ferry (October, 1859)—an event which a Nashville editor described as "one of the most daring and reckless affairs which ever took place in this country." Andrew Johnson, then in the United States Senate, placed full blame for the incident upon Republican leaders. He ridiculed contentions by Republicans that Thomas Jefferson had considered Negroes and whites as equals, pointed to inequalities of opportunities between the races in the North, and urged Republicans to cease their agitation of the slavery question. The state legislature deplored the raid, and placed the blame upon "the head of the Black Republican party, William H. Seward," whose "treasonable policy" might yet sound the death knell of the Union. A group of medical students from Tennessee, enrolled at the University of Pennsylvania, transferred to the University of Nashville when a professor remarked that the death penalty for Brown might be too

severe. Beyond question, the defense of Brown by Northern abolitionists weakened the case of the strong Unionists in Tennessee and
brought into the open rabid secession talk by extremists.

Although as late as 1860 the vast majority of Tennesseans still
abhorred the idea of secession, a militant minority coalesced early
in that year in despair of reconciliation with the North; Governor
Isham G. Harris became the nominal head of that minority. With
aroused emotions, Harris told legislators early in January that, although he hoped "wise, temperate, and calm, firm counsel may avert
the impending evils," he believed nevertheless in the right of revolution and feared that the right would have to be exercised "in case
the reckless fanatics of the North should secure control of the government." Before the year had ended, others not infrequently echoed
Harris's talk of disunion.

The Election of 1860   When Democrats met in Nashville in January to prepare for the national convention to be held in
Charleston in April, their mood was not a conciliatory one. They
condemned Seward's irrepressible conflict doctrine, indicted the
Republican party for "its hostility to slavery . . . and its war upon the
Constitution and upon the rights of the States," and warned that "if
this war upon the Constitutional rights of the South is persisted in it
must soon cease to be a war of words." They endorsed the Dred Scott
decision and the administration of President Buchanan, and suggested Andrew Johnson for the presidency.

The Opposition group met one month later, on Washington's
birthday and, in the state's capital, "Know Nothing, American,
Whig, and Opposition Friends" formed a "Grand National Union
party." They did not draft a formal platform, but pledged themselves to support the Constitution and the Union. The group deplored the agitation of the slavery controversy and, nominating John
Bell, proclaimed that Bell's "superior qualifications . . . broad and
expansive patriotism," and "unswerving devotion to the Union and
the Constitution" rendered him the man best suited for the presidency. Neither Democrats nor Republicans could be entrusted to
lead the country safely through the perilous days ahead, the group
contended, and they urged people of conservative temperament
throughout the nation to rally to the support of the Tennessee

Unionist. Balie Peyton, Thomas A. R. Nelson, Horace Maynard, and others talked with politicians across the country in Bell's behalf, and newspapers in Philadelphia, Cincinnati, Baltimore, New Orleans, and other leading cities raised their standard for him. Three months later, Conservatives met at Baltimore, formed the Constitutional Union party, and formally nominated Bell. Their simple platform called for support of "the Constitution of the Country, the Union of the States, and the enforcement of the laws."

In the meantime, Democrats assembled at Charleston, South Carolina. After considerable debate, Northern Democrats refused to write into the platform the demands of Southern party members that slavery should be protected in the territories. After many delegates from the lower South had walked out in disgust, the convention adjourned with no one being nominated. A few weeks later, Northern Democrats met in Baltimore and selected Stephen A. Douglas of Illinois; Southern Democrats convened in Richmond and chose John C. Breckinridge. None of Tennessee's twenty-four delegates had bolted at Charleston, and they therefore reassembled with the "regulars" at Baltimore. When efforts at compromise proved unavailing and the Douglas men refused to make any overtures whatsoever to the Southerners, delegates from Virginia withdrew and those from Tennessee retired "for consultation." Only five Tennesseans decided to remain and participate in the nomination of Douglas. The other nineteen assembled at Richmond with the group nominating Breckinridge; there Andrew Ewing "thanked God that he was now on a floor where he could speak without being hissed . . . or compelled to listen to nauseating speeches."

Republicans in the meantime confidently assembled in Chicago. Seward led on the first two ballots, but his supporters, apparently believing that he could not win in a national contest, cast him aside on the third ballot for Abraham Lincoln of Illinois. Republicans denied that Congress or a territorial legislature had the right to establish slavery in any of the territories, and described secession as a "treasonous doctrine." No Tennessean took part in that party's deliberations, and no attempt was made to organize the party within the state. The party of John Bell rightly claimed to be the only one of national organization.

All candidates except Lincoln had organized support in Tennessee. Supporters of Douglas were limited largely to West Tennessee where the Memphis *Appeal* kept his name before the public. Weeks before the election it was apparent to all that the contest in Tennessee was between Bell and Breckinridge. Supporters of the former included the old Whig hierarchy, including Oliver P. Temple, William G. Brownlow, Neill S. Brown, Balie Peyton, Gustavus A. Henry, and Thomas A. R. Nelson. They disliked secession, but they also were opposed to any attempt by the federal government to "coerce" the states. Breckinridge supporters included Andrew Johnson, Governor Harris, Landon C. Haynes, Gideon J. Pillow, and John H. Crozier. Supporters of Breckinridge called for congressional protection of slavery in the territories, as did some Constitutional Unionists, but most of the latter attempted to avoid the slavery issue.

Lincoln, although he received less than 40 per cent of the popular vote, carried the Northern states where the electoral vote was large, and thus was elected President. In Tennessee, where Lincoln received no support, John Bell defeated Breckinridge by less than 5,000 votes. Voters in the three divisions of the state balloted as follows:

	Bell	Breckinridge	Douglas
East Tennessee	22,320	18,904	1,659
Middle Tennessee	29,006	34,452	2,187
West Tennessee	18,384	11,697	7,548
TOTALS	69,710	65,053	11,394

These results are from the Nashville *Patriot*, November 26, 1860. Other newspapers give only slightly different results. Official returns cannot be located in the state Archives.

Despite his initial popularity in West Tennessee, Douglas's support was negligible when compared with that of his two opponents. He carried only one county (Tipton), but lacked only 89 votes of defeating Bell in Shelby County. Bell's support was a straight Whig vote, and differed in no important respect from the Whig votes of the preceding twenty years. Breckinridge carried the traditionally Democratic counties in Middle Tennessee, and received a respectable vote in the cotton counties of West Tennessee.

Secession ॐ The election of Lincoln—by one section and by a minority vote—precipitated secession among the states of the Deep South. Two days after the election the legislature of South Carolina called a convention, and on December 20 the delegates by unanimous vote adopted an ordinance of secession. Within a few weeks six other states—Georgia, Alabama, Florida, Mississippi, Louisiana, and Texas—joined the Palmetto State, and early in February set up a provisional government in Montgomery.

Tennesseans, like other Southerners, were distressed at the success of a sectional candidate. Unlike the people of the cotton states, however, they were not ready to secede, and editors and spokesmen in the three sections deplored the hasty action of the Deep South. The editor of the Memphis *Appeal*, for example, pointed to the profits made from the distribution of Northern-made goods, declared that the people of many of the Northern states were "as sound on the negro question as the secessionists themselves," and advised that loyalty to the Union would pay dividends in the years to come. The editor of the Nashville *Union and American* condemned the Deep South for leaving the border states "on a sinking ship."

Many Tennesseans believed that a "General Convention of the Slave States" should be held to discuss relations with the federal government. Soon after Lincoln's election, prominent members of both the Democratic and Constitutional Union parties issued a joint statement to local politicians throughout the state urging them to request the governor to call an extra session of the legislature, which, once assembled, would be implored to aid in bringing "about a convention of the Southern states." Shortly thereafter, Governor Harris called the legislature into special session, and members convened on January 7, 1861.

The legislators assembled as requested and heard Governor Harris deliver a message strongly pro-Southern in tone. The slaveholding states had suffered many grievances, he said, which resulted from the "systematic, wanton, and long continued agitation of the slavery question." Now, Harris pointed out, the presidency was in the hands of a sectional party which had sworn undying enmity to slavery and the South. Although he had no doubt as to the necessity and propriety of calling a state convention to determine whether Tennessee should secede, he proposed that the lawmakers submit the question to the people. The legislators complied and set February 9, 1861, as the date for the referendum. The people were to vote for "Convention" or for "No Convention," and also were to select delegates so that a second poll might not be necessary if the convention were authorized.

In the meantime, leaders discussed compromises and ways of averting civil war. In the Senate, Andrew Johnson proposed a constitutional amendment calling for sectional alternation of the presidency and membership on the Supreme Court, and a permanent division of the territories into free and slave sections. In Tennessee, Governor Harris suggested the establishment of a dividing line between free and slave territories and further proposed that authorities in such Northern states as refused to return fugitive slaves to their rightful owners should be required to pay double the value of the slave. Slaveowners should be guaranteed protection of their slave property while passing through or temporarily residing in any state, Harris claimed, and slavery should never be abolished in the District of Columbia or any other area in the slave states over which the United States had jurisdiction.

The only compromise proposal which was considered seriously by congressional leaders was Senator John Crittenden's measure, which was similar in some respects to the proposals made by Governor Harris. Although Tennesseans supported the Crittenden measure, little interest in compromise could be aroused among Republican leaders; therefore, all congressional attempts at compromise failed.

Tennessee sent delegates to the Washington Peace Conference held in the nation's capital on February 4, 1861. The meeting, called at the request of the Virginia legislature and presided over by former President John Tyler, was attended by delegates from twenty-one states. Eleven of Tennessee's twelve delegates stood staunchly for moderation, but their attempts at compromise, like the others, resulted in failure.

Preparatory to the February referendum in Tennessee, secessionists and Unionists strove to win victory at the polls. Union meetings were held throughout the state, and Gustavus A. Henry, Brownlow, and others urged the people not to act precipitately, but to give the Republicans "a fair trial." Prominent Democrats, however, including the editors of the Memphis *Avalanche* and the Nashville *Union and American*, urged the people to approve the holding of a convention, and to elect "states rights, anticoercion men."

On election day, the people rejected the convention by a substantial majority. The total vote of the Union candidates was nearly four times that amassed by the disunion candidates. The people of West Tennessee favored the convention, those of the eastern section opposed it, and people in Middle Tennessee were almost equally divided, but with a small majority against it. The election did not end the controversy. The Unionists of East Tennessee hailed the vote as a great victory, and many believed that the state was destined to remain permanently within the Union. Although the danger of precipitate action had been removed, secessionists did not despair. They excoriated Bell and other Unionists, claimed that the victory had given Lincoln new determination to "wage an irrepressible conflict," and resolved to continue their agitation. Governor Harris, now considered the leader of the pro-Southern forces in the state, was reminded by a friend that "eternal vigilance is the price of liberty." Extremists in Middle and West Tennessee urged friends to aid the cause of the seceded states, and hundreds in Franklin County, under the leadership of Peter Turney, signed petitions requesting that Franklin County be annexed to Alabama.

Tennesseans next turned their attention to Lincoln's inauguration, and John Bell and others hastened to Washington to be present for the ceremonies. In his inaugural address, the new President adopted a conciliatory tone but made clear that he considered secession illegal and would enforce the laws in all the states. People saw in the address whatever they wished to see, depending upon whether they were secessionists or Unionists. The editor of the Democratic *Union and American* called it "a declaration of war against the seceded states," and prophesied that "in less than thirty days . . . we shall have the clangor of resounding arms, with all its concomitants of death, carnage, and woe." The editor of the *Republican Banner*, however, considered the address "mild and conservative" and believed that Lincoln had dispelled the fear of "coercion." If war came, the editor wrote, it would not be the responsibility of the President.

A problem of immediate concern to Lincoln was what to do about Fort Sumter, a United States fort and arsenal lying within the borders of South Carolina. A symbol of federal authority in the state, the fort lay at the mercy of the Confederates. President Buchanan had tried in January without success to send provisions to the small force of eighty-four men, but when a ship bearing supplies entered the harbor it was fired upon by South Carolina artillery. Although Lincoln had been warned by Confederate authorities that any attempt to send in fresh provisions would precipitate war, in April he gave formal orders for an expedition to proceed. When Confederate authorities became aware of the move, they called on the officer in charge of the fort, Major Robert Anderson, to surrender. His refusal brought the fire of the Confederate batteries, and on April 13 Anderson surrendered. The war thus had begun, and two days later President Lincoln issued a call for 75,000 volunteers.

When Governor Harris received Lincoln's call for troops, he answered the message with characteristic vigor. "Tennessee will not furnish a single man for purposes of coercion," he telegraphed, "but 50,000 if necessary for the defense of our rights and those of our Southern brothers." Announcing that "in such an unholy crusade no gallant son of Tennessee will ever draw his sword," Harris issued a call for a second extra session of the legislature to convene in Nashville on April 25.

As legislators began to arrive for the extra session, they found sentiment in Middle Tennessee to be considerably different from what it had been only a few weeks earlier. In no other section of the state had people changed so rapidly from a Unionist to a secession position. Major Campbell Brown of Spring Hill, for example, was amazed at the transformation. Brown had returned to Tennessee in March after a trip to England. Before his departure he had found "the union feeling . . . very strong" in Nashville, so strong, indeed, that he "had a sufficiently disagreeable time in defending . . . [his] opinion." He was bitter because of "the villainous" way in which "the abolition journals and speakers of the North misrepresented . . . [the South] abroad." Immediately after the fall of Fort Sumter, however, he returned to Nashville from Spring Hill. To his "perfect surprise" he "found secession . . . at every corner." Confederate flags and secession parades were constantly in the streets and everybody was "ripe for joining the Confederacy."

The legislators found Governor Harris in no mood for compromise. He blamed the President for having "wantonly inaugurated an internecine war upon the people of the slave and nonslaveholding states," and he described the "real" Union (as "established by our fathers") as no longer existent. Harris recommended the immediate enactment of a measure declaring that Tennessee had resumed her sovereignty, after which she should declare her independence from the United States. Accordingly, the lawmakers on May 6 drafted "A Declaration of Independence . . . Dissolving the Federal Relations between the State of Tennessee and the United States," and stipulated that it should be submitted to the people for ratification or rejection on June 8.

As the time for the referendum approached, prominent leaders of church, state, and press in Middle and West Tennessee urged ratification of the declaration of independence, while those of East Tennessee demanded that it be rejected. The Reverend James H. Otey and the Reverend Leonidas Polk, Episcopal bishops, declared themselves to be strongly in favor of secession, and Bishop Polk soon exchanged his clerical robes for a Confederate uniform. John Bell, Neill S. Brown, Cave Johnson, Return J. Meigs, E. H. Ewing, and Balie Peyton, all erstwhile prominent Unionists, issued a joint statement urging that coercion of the Southern states be resisted. The editors of the five Nashville newspapers, who often had been bitter rivals and had advocated diverse policies, joined forces to urge that Tennessee be declared "independent forever of the United States Government." The editor of the Nashville *Republican Banner*, who vehemently opposed secession earlier, now urged the people to vote for "the best interests of the state," and declared that "the rapidly developing policy [of the North] of . . . subjugation of the South . . . must serve to convince every patriotic and fair-minded man . . . that all hopes of a reconstruction of the Union" had been abandoned. One week later the editor, angered by what he saw in newspapers published in Northern cities, wrote:

> *People of Tennessee!* If you could sit here in our offices and read all the journals of the North as we do, there would be little Northern sentiment left.

On election day the editor had nothing but contempt for those who wanted a "union with a people . . . dead to all moral and constitutional obligations."

Although Brownlow and Thomas A. R. Nelson branded the referendum as "unconstitutional," Tennesseans voted by a substantial majority in favor of "Separation" from the Union and "Representation" in the Confederacy. Only in East Tennessee, and in a few isolated areas elsewhere, did strong Unionist sentiment prevail. People in both the central and western divisions voted overwhelmingly for secession, indicating that there had been many defections from Unionist ranks within recent weeks. The vote was as follows:

	For Separation	Against Separation
East Tennessee	14,780	32,923
Middle Tennessee	58,265	8,198
West Tennessee	29,127	6,117
Military Camps	2,741	0
TOTALS	104,913	47,238

A careful analysis of the returns shows that the people of the old Whig districts in East Tennessee, with Knoxville at the center, strongly opposed separation just as they had voted four months earlier against holding a convention. Democratic Sullivan and Meigs counties, which had voted for a convention, were for separation; they were joined by four other East Tennessee counties—Sequatchie,[1] Rhea, Polk, and Monroe. The Middle Tennessee counties of Bedford, Cannon, DeKalb, Rutherford, Smith, Jackson, Overton, White, Wilson, Williamson, and Van Buren, which had opposed a convention in February, now favored separation. The Middle and West Tennessee counties voted solidly for secession except for Fentress and Macon, in Middle Tennessee, and for those in a strip of territory running north and south at the junction of the two sections composed of the counties of Weakley, Carroll, Henderson, and Decatur, of West Tennessee, and Hardin[2] and Wayne of the middle division.

Even before the referendum, Governor Harris made preparations to join the Confederacy. As authorized by the legislature, he entered on May 7 into a military league with the Confederate states, gave them permission to erect a battery at Memphis as a part of the Mississippi River fortifications, and encouraged volunteers to join the Southern forces. On May 24, Harris wrote Major General Gideon J. Pillow that he was "making every possible effort to organize and procure such military force as may be necessary to protect the state from invasion." On the following day, Harris ordered from a New Orleans firm "at any reasonable price," a "ten thousand stand

[1] Now a Middle Tennessee county, Sequatchie was in 1861 considered to be in East Tennessee. The towns of Knoxville and Chattanooga favored secession.
[2] Now a West Tennessee county, but then considered to be in Middle Tennessee.

of arms," with the "Endfield [*sic*] saber rifle bayonett [*sic*] or rifle musket" preferred.

Immediately after the referendum, United States Senator A. O. P. Nicholson resigned and wrote Harris that he would "acquiesce cheerfully" in the result of the referendum. As Nicholson saw it, the people had declared their independence of the United States government and he no longer had a right to a place in its Senate. He had not been a rabid secessionist—when South Carolina seceded he stated in Congress that he could not recognize the "*de jure*" secession of the state, although he did admit the "*de facto*" separation from the Union—but now he followed his state. Andrew Johnson, however, decided to retain his seat in the federal Senate.

John Bell, one of the state's outstanding Unionists until soon after Sumter, despaired of any concessions from the Lincoln administration and joined the ranks of the secessionists. A change of heart so pronounced by so able a leader deserves more than passing consideration. Soon after the Republican victory in November, 1860, Bell openly expressed confidence in the President-elect and believed that Lincoln was sincere and courageous. Bell was confident that only one-third of the Republicans could be considered as "dangerous," and that the rest had no desire to make war on Southern interests. Preparatory to the referendum of February 9, Bell made speeches in which he expressed confidence in the new administration, interpreted Lincoln's policy as one of conciliation, and criticized Harris for his strong stand on secession.

Bell had hurried to Washington for Lincoln's inauguration. As the recognized leader of the Tennessee Unionists, and one who had been mentioned prominently for a seat in Lincoln's Cabinet, Bell was the logical person to dispense the patronage in the state. While in Washington, Bell had urged the new President to exercise care so that "no opportunity for a collision between the troops of the seceding States and those of the Government" might take place. Bell insisted that the bayonet could accomplish nothing of lasting value, and he suggested that if the seceding states rejected conciliation, "the wisest course would be to let them go in peace." The Tennessean left Washington confident that the policy of the new administration would be one of conciliation.

Various historians have disputed the influence of Bell, and some have expressed the belief that had he remained faithful to his Unionist convictions, Tennessee might not have seceded. Although Bell was powerful, such is to attribute to him a degree of influence which probably no one in the state possessed. An important factor in Bell's change of heart was Lincoln's selection of Andrew Johnson—who had been in the Breckinridge camp in November, 1860, and had been a lifelong Democrat—as the chief patronage dispenser in the state instead of Bell or some other ex-Whig. Apparently Bell was in agreement with William G. Brownlow and was ready to carry to its logical conclusion the sentiment expressed by the Knoxville editor, who wrote that he had little desire to remain in the Union if Johnson and Emerson Etheridge were permitted "to monopolize the power and patronage of the Union party in Tennessee." Brownlow believed that such action on Lincoln's part merited "the scorn and condemnation of every honest man in the Union ranks." Bell and his Unionist friends in Tennessee had labored long and faithfully in their devotion to the letter and spirit of the Constitution; at last they became convinced that not only did Lincoln and the Republicans have little veneration for constitutional principles, but they connived with Johnson to build an allied political group in Tennessee from the elements that had proved in the past to be the least devoted to the defense of the Constitution.

On April 18, 1861, Bell and ten other Tennessee conservatives issued a statement in which they commended Harris and condemned Lincoln. Thenceforth, John Bell of Tennessee was in the ranks of the secessionists. He remained in Nashville until the approach of the Union forces and then joined his children in Rutherford County. Later, during the war, he lived in Alabama and Georgia, but returned to Tennessee in 1865.

Tennesseans Prepare for War 𐑫 The second six months of 1861 was a period of hasty preparation for war. Harris appointed Gideon J. Pillow as commander of the Tennessee forces, with three subordinates in charge of each of the grand divisions of the state. On July 2, Governor Harris tendered to the Confederate President 22 regiments of infantry, 2 regiments of cavalry, 10 companies of artillery, an engineering corps, and an ordinance bureau. The infantry, Harris wrote, was "fully armed and equipped ready for the field," and the cavalry was armed with sabers and double-barrelled shotguns. All cavalrymen were mounted. The tender was made with the hope that the Confederate states "at all times" would defend Tennessee from invasion. Davis of course accepted the troops, and on July 4 replaced Pillow with General Leonidas Polk, a West Point graduate and Episcopal bishop.

Unionists of East Tennessee, in the meantime, posed a major problem. They had voted 2 to 1 against secession and now entertained strong sentiments about establishing a separate state. Meetings of prominent Unionists were held in Knoxville, Greeneville, and perhaps elsewhere, and plans for separation were freely discussed. Finally, at the meeting in Greeneville, a committee consisting of John Netherland, Oliver P. Temple, and James P. McDowell prepared and presented a memorial to the legislature asking that the counties of East Tennessee and "such counties in Middle Tennessee as desire to co-operate with them" be permitted to form a separate state. The memorial was referred to a legislative committee, which doubted that the request represented the true opinion of East Tennesseans and recommended that no action be taken on it during that session. Governor Harris viewed the situation with alarm. Many East Tennesseans "are bent on rebellion," he wrote General Pillow on June 20, and "I can't tell at what moment there will be an onslaught of Union men upon the southern rights men . . . ." The situation, the governor concluded, required that a considerable force be dispatched to the scene. Two weeks later, Landon C. Haynes advised that it would take six regiments to keep the eastern Unionists in line, since "moral power" could "no longer be relied on to crush the rebellion [against Tennessee]."

Harris confidently gave little attention to reelection. Secessionists, now referring to themselves as the "Southern Rights Party" and supported by all the principal newspapers except the Nashville *Republican Banner* and Brownlow's Knoxville *Whig*, assured the governor of a landslide victory. Brownlow had announced in March that he would carry the banner of the Unionists, but withdrew several weeks later in favor of William H. Polk, a brother of the late President.

The gubernatorial contest was subordinated to the military developments. Polk accused Harris of trying to become a military dictator, blamed him for the state's secession, charged that he had exceeded his rights under the constitution, and predicted that Harris would go to the Confederate Senate rather than serve out his term as governor even if he were reelected. Polk's supporters claimed that their candidate was acceptable to East Tennesseans and alleged that the election of Harris would drive all Unionists from the state. Supporters of Harris, however, pointed to the threat of invasion from the North and to Harris's determined efforts to defend the state against aggression. The editor of the Memphis *Appeal* wrote that all who even dared vote against Harris were committing treason. Mass hysteria prevailed, and Harris was elected by a vote of 75,300 to 43,495.

The secessionists secured large majorities also in both house and senate. Legislators, convening in October, 1861, redistricted the state into eleven Confederate congressional divisions. They chose Landon C. Haynes and Gustavus A. Henry as Confederate senators; Haynes was a Breckinridge fire-eater and Henry a John Bell Whig. Although the two had been bitter enemies in days past, they now pledged "their whole souls, energies, and talents to the cause of Southern rights." Legislators met from October to December, before adjourning for Christmas, and enjoyed their last undisturbed session. When they resumed deliberations in January, the federal military command was making plans to take Forts Henry and Donelson, and the legislators soon fled to Memphis.

Loyalists in the four congressional districts of East Tennessee and northeastern Middle Tennessee in the August election had selected congressmen and sent them to Washington. Three—Horace Maynard, George W. Bridges, and Dr. A. J. Clements—were seated but the other, Thomas A. R. Nelson, was captured by Confederate authorities while seeking to pass through Virginia. After a brief imprisonment, Nelson took the oath of allegiance to the Confederate government and was returned to his home. Following the redistricting, another congressional election was held and a full complement of representatives sent to the new Confederate capital, Richmond.

Whether Tennesseans, in view of the circumstances, were justified in their declaration of separation from the federal Union always will of course remain an academic question. Had there been no invasion by federal troops—had Lincoln taken John Bell's advice about the use of force—Tennessee beyond any question would not have left the Union. Professor J. Milton Henry has contended that had the Tennessee conservatives, who were deeply devoted to the Union, remained faithful to their original principles after the fall of Sumter secession might have been prevented. The conservatives, however, as Professor Henry has shown, had many reasons to lose confidence in the Lincoln administration. At length, they became convinced that not only did Republicans have little veneration for constitutional principles, but that party leaders were engaged in building an allied political group in Tennessee (with Andrew Johnson at the head) from people who were not devoted to the defense of the Union. Once having become convinced that they had little to fear and perhaps more to gain from an alliance with the Confederates, they gave up their struggle for the Union. Historians who have blamed Bell and other conservatives for the state's secession may have overstated their case; the minds of the Middle and West Tennessee slaveholders were made up, and it is highly speculative whether Bell or anyone else could have dissuaded them. The determination of President-elect Lincoln to oppose all efforts at compromise, the precipitant secession of the deep Southern states without so much as first calling a convention of slave states, and the strong secession leanings of Governor Harris were decisive factors in the state's secession.

The vast majority of Tennesseans were Unionists until the fateful April days. The fall of Fort Sumter and Lincoln's call for troops convinced them that a search for a peaceful solution was futile. Being a border state, they could not remain neutral but must join one side or the other. Perhaps many people, at least in Middle and West Tennessee, must have shared the sentiments of a West Tennessee farmer named B. W. Binkley, who wrote during the war: "I was for the Union so long as there was any hope of our remaining in it with peace and honor. When Lincoln issued his proclamation calling for 75,000 troops to whip . . . the Seceded States, I was satisfied that day had passed, and now—though not what you'd term a regular Secessionist—I am the most uncompromising *rebel* you ever knew."

SUGGESTED READINGS

General Accounts
   Abernethy, *Frontier to Plantation*, Ch. 21; Campbell, *Attitude of Tennesseans Toward the Union*; E. Merton Coulter, *William G. Brownlow:*

Fighting Parson of the Southern Highlands (Knoxville, 1971); Dwight Dumond, *The Secession Movement, 1860–61* (New York, 1931); Folmsbee, Corlew, and Mitchell, *Tennessee*, II, Ch. 26; Hamer, *Tennessee*, I, Chs. 32–33; Milton, *Age of Hate*; Parks, *John Bell*.

Specialized Accounts

James W. Bellamy, "The Political Career of Landon Carter Haynes," ETHS *Publ.*, No. 28 (1956), 102–26; James B. Campbell, "East Tennessee During the Federal Occupation, 1863–1865," ETHS *Publ.*, No. 19 (1947), 64–80; Mary R. Campbell, "Tennessee's Congressional Delegation in the Sectional Crisis of 1859–1860," *THQ*, XIX (Dec., 1960), 348–71; Campbell, "The Significance of the Unionist Victory in the Election of February 9, 1861, in Tennessee," ETHS *Publ.*, No. 14 (1942), 11–30; LeRoy P. Graf, "Andrew Johnson and the Coming of the War," *THQ*, XIX (Sept., 1960), 208–21; Howard Hall, "Franklin County in the Secession Crisis," *THQ*, XVII (March, 1958), 37–44; Marguerite Bartlett Hamer, "The Presidential Campaign of 1860 in Tennessee," ETHS *Publ.*, No. 3 (1931), 3–22; J. Milton Henry, "The Revolution in Tennessee, February, 1861, to June, 1861," *THQ*, XVIII (June, 1959), 99–119; Hesseltine, *Ramsey*; Stanley F. Horn, "Isham G. Harris in the Pre-War Years," *THQ*, XIX (Sept., 1960), 195–207; Eric Russell Lacy, "The Persistent State of Franklin," *THQ*, XXIII (Dec., 1964), 321–32; Joseph H. Parks, "John Bell and Secession," ETHS *Publ.*, No. 16 (1944), 30–47; James W. Patton, *Unionism and Reconstruction in Tennessee, 1860–1869* (Chapel Hill, 1934); Verton M. Queener, "East Tennessee Sentiment and the Secession Movement, November, 1860–June, 1861," ETHS *Publ.*, No. 20 (1948), 59–83; Oliver H. Temple, *East Tennessee and the Civil War* (Cincinnati, 1899).

THE CONFEDERATE STATES embarked upon a war for independence with few advantages over their enemy. The disadvantages far outweighed the advantages. The Southerners, for example, were faced by an enemy whose white population outnumbered their own by nearly four to one and which had 90 per cent of the country's industry, a standing army and navy, and a superior transportation system. By no means least of the disadvantages was the Confederate's problem of defense, made difficult by the natural barriers which impeded effective communication. The Blue Ridge Mountains split the South into east and west, and the west was divided by the Mississippi River. The Tennessee and Cumberland rivers were highways into Tennessee and the Confederacy. On the other hand, the Confederates had some advantages. They had a superior fighting force commanded by competent officers, and they would wage war—if at all—on home soil.

Tennesseans Prepare for War ☙ General Leonidas Polk was assigned command in the west on July 4, 1861, and he arrived in Memphis a few days later to take up his tasks with characteristic vigor. General Gideon J. Pillow already had begun the fortification of Memphis and Island Number 10 (located a few miles west of the extreme northwest corner of the state), and had undertaken an ambitious work seventy-five miles north of Memphis at a place later called Fort Pillow. Polk continued Pillow's work and also gave attention to the pressing problems in East Tennessee. Upon Polk's recommendation, Felix Zollicoffer was commissioned brigadier general and dispatched to Knoxville with a motley force of less than 4,000 recruits to keep the rebellious malcontents in line.

Polk clearly saw the strategic importance of the area assigned to him, and he urged President Davis to combine all Confederate operations "west to east across the Mississippi Valley" under one commander. He suggested Albert Sidney Johnston as the man most likely to effect satisfactory coordination. Accordingly, on September 10, Johnston was assigned to the command of Department Number 2, a vast area embracing Tennessee and Arkansas, a part of Mississippi, and such sections of Kentucky, Missouri, Kansas, and the Indian territory where military operations were being carried on. Tennesseans were jubilant over the appointment of the tall, muscular general of august appearance, and the Confederate press in Nashville and Memphis hailed him with zealous enthusiasm.

Perhaps the most important task Johnston faced was that of devising an adequate defense for Tennessee. The general proceeded with haste, and soon established the "Line of the Cumberland" which he believed would be sufficient to protect the state and the western Confederacy. The thin line of troops extended from Columbus, Kentucky (on the Mississippi River), through Bowling Green, and to the Cumberland Gap on the east. Although seriously handicapped by lack of manpower, Johnston determined to fortify the strategic points of Henry and Donelson (forts on the Tennessee and Cumberland rivers, respectively, which Governor Isham G. Harris had begun to construct soon after the state seceded), and the Cumberland Gap, where East Tennessee Unionists threatened revolt. His undermanned forces soon were bolstered by a few Tennessee slaves, used in construction work, and regiments from Mississippi, Tennessee, and Arkansas.

Johnston found the people of Nashville generally apathetic about defense. While workers at the Nashville Plow Company beat plowshares into swords at a fairly rapid rate, the more important Nashville Powder Mills in October could provide only 400 pounds of their product per day, although officials of the company earlier had promised 10,000 pounds daily. Requests for slaves for use in construction work brought only scant response. The Nashville warehouses were laden with food, but General Zollicoffer's men in East Tennessee went hungry, so poorly were the transportation facilities coordinated. By November, Johnston had an army of 40,000 men, but they were inadequately clothed and fed, and over one-half were without weapons.

Despite the many vexatious problems, chief of which was inadequate manpower, Johnston realized that time was precious and that defensive measures should be formulated with the manpower and supplies on hand. He recognized that the Tennessee and Cumberland rivers were veritable highways from Ohio into the heart of Tennessee, northern Mississippi, and Alabama, and Johnston ordered that work proceed without delay toward the completion of the strategic positions at Henry and Donelson.

His fear for the safety of Tennessee was shared by Governor Harris, who on October 30 wrote President Jefferson Davis that he believed invasion along "the northern border of this state" was imminent. Harris requested the President to return the Tennessee troops, then stationed in Virginia, to their native state. Should the Federals obtain control of Tennessee then "the whole Confederacy" would face "incalculable mischief," the governor warned. On November 20, Harris sent terse messages to the governors of Alabama, Mississippi, and Louisiana, requesting aid. "Columbus and River definitely threatened by very large force," he wrote; "Have you an armed force that you can possibly send to our aid?"

In the meantime, General Johnston had inspected the works at Fort Henry and Fort Donelson and was appalled at the dilatory manner in which work proceeded. He summarily ordered Brigadier General Lloyd Tilghman, a Kentuckian commanding at Hopkinsville, to assume charge of the two forts and to complete the works at once. "Sloth," Tilghman was told, would not "be tolerated."

Fort Henry and Fort Donelson ॐ The forts had not been completed when Federals attacked in February, 1862. On the morning of February 4, seven gunboats under the command of Captain Andrew H. Foote and 18,000 Federal soldiers under General Ulysses S. Grant arrived in the vicinity of Fort Henry, which was held by less than 2,800 Confederates. A few shots were exchanged, and then on the following day Foote began heavy bombardment with his sixty-five naval guns. The twelve Confederate cannons were no match for Foote's guns, and after sustaining several hours of bombardment, Tilghman climbed to a parapet and raised a flag of surrender. Grant, having landed three miles downstream, had floundered in the slush and mud and had not reached the fort in time to participate in the fighting.

Strengthened by the addition of six new regiments of infantry which increased his command to 30,000 men, Grant moved rapidly toward Fort Donelson where Confederates prepared diligently for defense. His strategy was to be the same as he had planned for Fort Henry; Captain Foote was to batter the garrison into submission with his naval guns while Grant blocked all escape routes and exacted terms of unconditional surrender.

Fort Donelson was commanded by General John B. Floyd, a political officer from Virginia who brought to Donelson an uneasy conscience and little military acumen. While secretary of war under President Buchanan, Floyd allegedly had misappropriated funds and unnecessarily transferred arms and ammunition to Southern forts. He therefore personally feared capture because he believed that he would be executed as a traitor should he fall into Federal hands. Floyd also apparently had little confidence in his staff, which consisted partly of Generals Gideon J. Pillow, Simon B. Buckner, Bushrod Johnson, and Colonel Nathan Bedford Forrest—all men of some ability.

At dawn on February 13, Grant's men appeared about 700 yards from the outer defenses of the fort, but were beaten off when they assaulted the Confederate center. Of far greater importance on the first day of the battle was the sudden change in the weather. A cold front changed the fair and mild afternoon into a cold, rainy evening and a near-zero night. When day dawned on the fourteenth, a two-inch snow blanketed many of the wounded and dying. Despite the cold weather, Confederates seemed to have victory within their grasp on February 14 and 15. On the fourteenth, the gunboats were driven off and Foote was wounded twice. In mid-afternoon of the following day, Floyd, apparently having the enemy on the run, permitted General Pillow to withdraw his men completely from Wynn's Ferry Road, an escape route which led to Nashville. This gave Grant an opportunity to reorganize his assault and to surround the Confederates. On the night of the fifteenth, Floyd called his staff together to discuss surrender. Despite Forrest's assertion that he would get "out of this place . . . or bust hell wide open," Floyd,

Pillow, and Buckner insisted that their men were demoralized, their supply of ammunition exhausted, all avenues of retreat blocked, and that surrender was the only alternative. Floyd, Pillow, Johnson, and Forrest escaped, and Buckner, on the morning of the sixteenth, surrendered unconditionally to Grant.

The fall of Fort Donelson came as a distinct surprise to the people of the South, and was the worst loss the Confederates had suffered. Johnston's line now collapsed, and Nashville was abandoned. Triumphantly, Federals marched into the state's capital a few days later (February 24), and Tennessee and northern Mississippi were at the mercy of the enemy. Tennesseans were dazed by the disastrous events which had taken place so suddenly, but Nashvillians were in panic.

Johnston now determined to evacuate Middle Tennessee and to make a stand at Corinth, Mississippi. In the meantime, General Leonidas Polk, who commanded troops at Columbus, Kentucky, moved southward to defend Island Number 10. Polk believed that if he could hold the island he could prevent the Federals from moving southward toward Vicksburg and New Orleans. Captain Foote moved against the Confederates on March 16 and laid siege. On April 8, he forced Polk to surrender his command of 7,000 men.

Shiloh ॐ Johnston had been reinforced at Corinth by troops under the command of Generals P. G. T. Beauregard and Braxton Bragg. When he learned that the Federals were concentrating around Shiloh Church near Pittsburg Landing, just south of Savannah, Johnston decided to attack them before they could launch an organized assault against him. On April 4, the Confederates arrived near Pittsburg Landing and prepared to attack the troops commanded by Generals Grant and William T. Sherman. Two days later they were ready for battle in a daylight assault and surprised the Federals who were dressing, cooking, and eating in the company streets. Grant, careless and complacent, was at his Savannah headquarters nine miles away, and Sherman, although on the field, also was surprised because he had refused to take seriously the warning of his scouts that Confederate troops were near.

The first day of battle ended with the Confederates in control, but at a fearful price. The gallant Albert Sydney Johnston had been killed when a stray Minie ball struck him in the right thigh and severed a major artery. Governor Isham G. Harris, riding by his side when the mishap occurred, lowered the wounded general to the ground but was unable to stop the profuse bleeding before Johnston expired.

Confusion spread among the Confederates when they learned of Johnston's death. During the night Grant was reinforced with the arrival of nearly 30,000 fresh troops, and early on the next morning he assaulted his enemy with vigor. Beauregard (who assumed command when Johnston fell) decided by afternoon that his weary divisions could not hold the field and by four o'clock began a retreat to Corinth. Both sides suffered tremendous losses in what proved to be one of the bloodiest battles of the war.

Memphis Falls ঌ Middle and West Tennessee now were in the hands of the Federals, except for a small garrison at Memphis. The center for Confederate cotton was one of the most important points on the Mississippi River, and the Federals were eager to take it so that they might proceed further into the heart of the Confederacy. If they could capture Vicksburg and New Orleans (which they did by mid-summer, 1863), the Federals could cut off the Trans-Mississippi West from the rest of the Confederacy. On June 6, a fleet of Federal gunboats, superior in size and number to a small group of boats manned by Confederates, attacked the Southerners and drove them off. Some Memphians, including the editor and publisher of the Memphis *Appeal*, fled southward. The editor, without missing an issue, now published the strong Confederate paper at New Grenada, Mississippi.

In the meantime, John Hunt Morgan and Nathan Bedford Forrest disputed control of Middle Tennessee with the Federals. During the spring and summer, the Confederates made numerous raids on the enemy at Pulaski, Lebanon, Nashville, Gallatin, Hartsville, Murfreesboro, and elsewhere. On July 13, Forrest assaulted one of General Don Carlos Buell's brigades at Murfreesboro and captured the entire force, together with a million dollars' worth of supplies. He moved so close to Nashville that Andrew Johnson, who had been appointed military governor of Tennessee, made plans to evacuate the capital.

Forrest was the most brilliant cavalry leader to fight in Tennessee. Always he moved so silently and swiftly that the enemy could not determine where he would strike next. He disrupted telegraph lines and ripped up railroad tracks faster than the Federals could repair them. Morgan was almost as effective, especially at Gallatin and Hartsville.

Stone's River ஐ After the Battle of Shiloh, the Army of Tennessee had retreated to Corinth where General Bragg was placed in command. In the meantime, General Edmund Kirby Smith had taken charge of Confederate troops in East Tennessee, and he urged Bragg to join him in a campaign into Kentucky. The Blue Grass State, rich in food and supplies, might be won to the Confederacy if a successful invasion was made. On August 16, General Smith marched from Knoxville into Kentucky and won a brilliant victory at Richmond. Two weeks later Bragg moved with nearly 30,000 men up the Sequatchie Valley, through Pikeville, Sparta, and Gainesville, and into Glasgow, Kentucky.

The most vigorous fighting of the Kentucky campaign took place at Perryville on October 8, when Bragg met General Buell who had pursued him from Corinth. Bragg, discouraged by the failure of Kentuckians to join his forces and fearing that Buell would crush him before he could escape, retreated in an orderly manner to Murfreesboro in November, where, joined by Generals John C. Breckinridge and Forrest, he made plans to take Nashville.

General William S. Rosecrans in the meantime had been placed in command of Federal troops at Nashville. When he heard that Bragg was encamped nearby, he made plans at once to dislodge him and on December 26 began a movement toward Murfreesboro. He required four days to make the thirty-mile march because General Joseph Wheeler, a young cavalry leader from Alabama almost as able as Forrest, harassed him day and night and destroyed millions of dollars' worth of supplies.

The battle began at daybreak on December 31 when a detachment of Bragg's men stumbled into a company of Federals a few miles west of Murfreesboro. The day went well for the Confederates and by nightfall Rosecrans' troops had been pushed back a distance of more than four miles. So convinced was Bragg of victory that he hastened into town early the next morning to notify President Davis. "The enemy has yielded his strong position and is falling back," he telegraphed; "God has granted us a happy New Year." Bragg was amazed therefore to find Rosecrans still encamped in the area when daylight came on the morning of January 1, 1863.

The tide of victory escaped the Confederates on January 2 when Rosecrans' men, reinforced by fresh troops, raked Breckinridge's charging infantry with artillery fire when the Confederate leader attempted to take a hill just west of Murfreesboro. On the following day, Bragg ordered a retreat, and the unhappy soldiers began a slow movement through Murfreesboro toward Chattanooga. Both officers and enlisted men complained about Bragg's general ineptitude as a leader and urged that he be removed as commander of the Army of Tennessee. Victorious Federals now occupied Murfreesboro and Bragg went into winter quarters in Bedford and Coffee counties.

Forrest, restless and wishing to harass the enemy, meanwhile spent no time in winter quarters. He provided excitement and hope for Tennessee Confederates when, with fewer than 4,000 men, he attacked Federal outposts at Trenton, Humboldt, Union City, Lexington, and other points in West Tennessee. Forrest rapidly was becoming famous for his ability to take the enemy by complete surprise and destroy large stores of supplies.

Chickamauga and Chattanooga ᘉ General Rosecrans, with 70,000 men, waited until June before he moved toward the Confederates. Bragg retreated orderly in a southeasterly direction; by August, he had reached Chattanooga but soon abandoned the town and retreated into northern Georgia. Rosecrans, believing that the Confederates would not stop until they reached Atlanta, pushed recklessly on and was amazed when on September 13 he found his enemy encamped and ready for battle approximately twenty miles south of Chattanooga near Lafayette.

On the early morning of September 19, the Army of Tennessee crossed the Chickamauga River to meet Rosecrans in what proved to be one of the bloodiest single days of the war. Generals James Longstreet and John B. Hood had arrived on the eighteenth with Confederate armies from the Virginia campaigns and by midafternoon on the nineteenth had ripped Rosecrans' army to shreds.

Only the gallant stand of General George H. Thomas (himself a Virginian but loyal to the Union) prevented a complete massacre of the Federal troops. Charles A. Dana, assistant secretary of war and an observer of the battle, wrote that "Bull Run had nothing more terrible than the rout and flight of these veteran soldiers."

The Federals then encamped at Chattanooga. Grant was sent to take command, and General William T. Sherman hastily moved his troops from Mississippi to join Grant. Bragg, who could have taken Chattanooga had he moved with alacrity after Chickamauga, quarreled with his subordinates, fatuously dispersed his troops, and laid siege to Chattanooga in an effort to starve his enemy. He also failed to prevent the Federals from bringing in supplies and reinforcements by a famous "Cracker Line" up the Tennessee River.

Grant in the meantime had been placed over all operations east of the Mississippi and had moved hastily to Chattanooga to lift the siege. Because the Battle of Chattanooga began on November 23 in a dense fog at the base of Lookout Mountain and General Joseph Hooker drove the Confederates from the mountains the next day, the fight sometimes has been called the "Battle Above the Clouds." The Confederate positions on Missionary Ridge fell on the twenty-fifth before the charging bluecoats of Hooker and Sherman who smashed the gray infantry back in a savage hand-to-hand encounter. The Confederates fled in panic and were regrouped at Dalton, Georgia, where they went into winter quarters. The Battle of Chattanooga was a serious blow to the Confederates and marked the end of Bragg's career as a field commander. Joseph E. Johnston, who held the confidence of enlisted men and officers alike, was chosen to command the Western army.

Federals Take East Tennessee ¿➤ In the meantime, General Ambrose E. Burnside had moved his Federal forces from Cincinnati to Knoxville. After Chickamauga, General Longstreet was sent to dislodge him, but on November 20 the Confederates were defeated at Fort Sanders. A few days later Sherman moved to aid Burnside, and Longstreet retreated into Virginia, leaving practically all of East Tennessee in undisputed control of the Unionists. A majority of the people had been Unionists all along, and viewed Burnside's triumph with wild excitement.

General Sherman moved immediately into Georgia in pursuit of the retreating Confederates. During the next nine months his losses were more than twice those of his enemy; still, by September 6, he had gained control of Atlanta. General Leonidas Polk was among the thousands of Tennesseans who fell in the defense of Georgia.

General John Bell Hood—sometimes called the "Gallant Hood of Texas"—replaced General Johnston as the Confederate commander and planned bold strategy. Hood would surprise Sherman by making a quick dash across Alabama and into Tennessee. If he could cut Sherman's supply lines, he could starve the Federals into submission. Hood dreamed of seizing vast stores of supplies at Nashville for his hungry and barefoot men, and then he might move on to Louisville and Cincinnati, and perhaps even join Lee in Virginia for an assault on Washington. The fact that Hood had lost a leg in Virginia and no longer had the use of one arm did not deter the plucky commander.

Franklin and Nashville &⟩ The first serious engagement of Hood's campaign in Tennessee occurred at Franklin. General John M. Schofield, who had returned from an unsuccessful attempt to capture Forrest in West Tennessee, managed to slip past the Confederates during the night, but was poorly prepared when Hood encountered him on the afternoon of November 30. He was driven from the field after five hours of fierce fighting and retreated during the night to the safety of the fortifications at Nashville where Federal forces were commanded by General Thomas. Hood was left in possession of the field, but he had paid a fearful price. The Federals, fighting behind breastworks, had lost more than two thousand men; Hood's dead and wounded amounted to more than three times that number.

Although Grant feared that Hood might push immediately toward Louisville or even Chicago, the youthful Confederate commander determined to occupy the hills just south of Nashville and force Thomas to fight. Hood did not have long to wait. In a two-day encounter (December 15–16), the Confederate forces were completely defeated. On the first day of battle, Hood retreated two miles to the foot of the Brentwood Hills. On the following afternoon,

Schofield's infantry and cavalry completely broke the Confederate resistance and sent the reeling remnants in hasty retreat southward. Thomas, with about 70,000 men, listed his killed and wounded at slightly less than 4,000; Hood, with about 23,000 men, claimed that his losses did not exceed 1,500.

The Battle of Nashville was the last engagement of significance in the state. The retreating Army of Tennessee stopped at Brentwood long enough to form a semblance of organization and then proceeded southward. At Columbia they were joined by Forrest who had retreated from Murfreesboro. Deaths at Franklin and Nashville, sickness, furloughs, and desertions had reduced the Army of Tennessee to an effective fighting force of only about 5,000 when the men finally joined the Confederate forces in North Carolina where they were surrendered to Sherman at Durham.

War Heroes ⧫ Many Tennesseans fought bravely; both the North and the South had their share of men from the Volunteer State. A fair estimate is that about 100,000 wore the gray and approximately half that number wore the blue.

Many served with particular distinction in the Confederate army. Two officers—Alexander P. Stewart of Lebanon and Nathan Bedford Forrest of Memphis—rose to the rank of lieutenant general. Eight attaining the rank of major general were William B. Bate, John C. Brown, Benjamin F. Cheatham, Daniel S. Donelson, W. Y. C. Humes, Bushrod R. Johnson, John Porter McCown, and Cadmus M. Wilcox. More than thirty attained the rank of brigadier general, including Generals McComb, Pillow, and Zollicoffer. Commodore Matthew Fontaine Maury was the ablest Tennessean in the Confederate navy. Even before the war he was recognized as one of the world's greatest naval scientists.

Several Tennesseans became generals in the Federal army and served with equal valor. Included were James P. Brownlow, William B. Campbell, Samuel P. Carter, Joseph A. Cooper, Alvan C. Gillem, George Spalding, James G. Spears, and William J. Smith. One of the most competent of the Tennessee officers serving in the Federal navy was Admiral David G. Farragut, of Knoxville, who played an important role in the capture of New Orleans, Mobile, and other important points. During the war, Farragut rose to the rank of vice admiral and became the first full admiral in the history of the country in 1866.

Perhaps the real heroes were not the generals and admirals but the enlisted men who fought on the battle lines. All Tennesseans know the story of Sam Davis, the young Confederate who was hanged as a spy on November 27, 1863, near Pulaski. "I would die a thousand deaths before I would betray a friend," the youth exclaimed when Federals offered him his life if he would name the person who had given him detailed information about the movement of Federal troops. No less glory surrounds the memory of DeWitt S. Jobe, and his cousin, DeWitt Smith. Jobe (like Davis, a Coleman scout) carried valuable battle plans when he was seized by the enemy near Murfreesboro. Before the eyes of his captors Jobe tore the documents to shreds and hastily swallowed some of the pieces. The infuriated Federals beat him to death with rifle butts. When DeWitt Smith heard of his cousin's merciless slaughter, he left Bragg's army and returned to Middle Tennessee to wage his own private war of revenge. He killed more than fifty Yankees before being slain by cavalrymen near Nolensville.

Internal Affairs; Unrest in East Tennessee ࢤ⤳ While soldiers fought on the battlefields, the people at home faced hardships which must have seemed to many to be unbearable. An immediate problem of major concern for Governor Harris was the strong Union movement in East Tennessee. The people of that section—most without slaves and without attachment to the "slavocracy" of Middle and West Tennessee, long conscious of themselves as a sectional minority within the state, confident of Federal assistance, and influenced by Union leaders such as Brownlow and Johnson—stood by the national government and thus destroyed the unanimity of the secession sentiment in the state.

Governor Harris, determined upon a policy of conciliation with respect to East Tennessee, sent Felix Zollicoffer, a former Knoxvillian then living in Nashville, to command troops in the eastern section. Zollicoffer sought to carry out Harris's policies, and announced upon his arrival in Knoxville that his sole purpose was to "insure peace."

All who desire peace can have peace [he stated], by quietly and harmlessly pursuing their lawful avocations [*sic*]. But Tennessee, having taken her stand with her sister States of the South, her honor and safety require that no aid shall be given within her borders to the arms of the tyrant Lincoln . . . .

Some East Tennessee Unionists were won to the Confederate side, but Brownlow, Johnson, Horace Maynard, and others steadfastly refused and aggressively championed the cause of the Union. Johnson and Maynard urged Lincoln to send a military force into East Tennessee, and Johnson pleaded with Washington legislators to send aid.

In November, 1861, a small group of East Tennessee Unionists unfolded a daring plan. William Blount Carter, a Presbyterian minister living at Elizabethton, had journeyed to Washington in May to discuss problems with Lincoln, General George B. McClellan, and others. Carter, particularly wanting Federal troops to be sent into East Tennessee immediately, suggested that he and his friends would burn nine key bridges between Alabama and Virginia and that simultaneously Federal forces should move into Knoxville where a general uprising would begin. He apparently thought that he had agreement from the President. On November 8, Carter performed his part of the bargain by destroying five of the bridges (and was paid $20,000 for his trouble), but Federal troops did not arrive. Unknown to Carter, General W. T. Sherman, who had been assigned the task of invading East Tennessee, had decided to hold his men in readiness to strike at Nashville instead of crossing the Cumberland Mountains. Consequently, the Union group in East Tennessee was then without defense against the wrath of the Tennessee Confederates, whose spirit of conciliation was consumed in the fires of the railroad bridges.

Stern measures were demanded. A Nashville editor wrote that East Tennesseans obviously "could not appreciate magnanimity and leniency." General Zollicoffer imposed martial law, and Secretary of War Judah P. Benjamin ordered that all bridge burners be hanged. Some of those implicated, including Carter, escaped the hangman's noose, but others suffered public execution.

For two years Confederate and Unionist neighbors waged a civil war of their own. By the use of martial law Unionists were silenced, but many went into hiding to await the day of deliverance; however, it did not come until 1863 when General Burnside restored them to control. With Burnside came Brownlow who, by pen and tongue, kept the fires of hatred glowing. Trusted implicitly by Federal authorities, Brownlow became the section's journalistic lord and economic dictator. His grasp spread from East Tennessee over the entire state when in March, 1865, he was elected governor.

Federal Occupation of Middle and West Tennessee ↬ While East Tennesseans waged their own civil war, Confederates in the rest of the state tried to fight off the Yankee invader. After General Forrest carried to Nashville news of the fall of Fort Donelson, Governor Harris and other state officials fled to Memphis and eventually to the safety of the Confederate lines in Mississippi, and thus Middle and West Tennessee were in the hands of the Federals after Fort Donelson fell. Grant soon proclaimed martial law for much of West Tennessee.

Immediately after the military successes, President Lincoln determined upon a bold course. He established a "military governorship" for the state and chose as governor Andrew Johnson, who, as a member of the United States Senate at the time, had refused to follow his state into the Confederacy. Lincoln gave the East Tennessean broad powers, including that of suspending the writ of habeas corpus and the right to hold office at the pleasure of the President until "the loyal inhabitants" organized a civil government "in conformity with the Constitution of the United States." Both Lincoln and Johnson contended that none of the seceded states were out of the Union. They believed that the "disloyal" element, if given proper leadership, would follow the "loyal" group into full acceptance of Union control.

Objections to the appointment came from a wide area. The people of Middle and West Tennessee now looked upon Johnson as a traitor, and they viewed his appointment as military governor with disdain. They recalled that in his two gubernatorial contests (1853 and 1855) he had failed to win East Tennessee; the central section had provided the small but necessary margin of victory in both contests. Johnson received hundreds of insulting and threatening letters. Every "dog has his day," one wrote, and "you will have yours. We are preparing a knise [nice] coat of feathers for that orcation [occasion]," the writer continued, "so when we have the chanse [chance] we will turn your black skin read [red], and then andy your black friends will not know you." Others informed Johnson of guerrilla bands which planned to intercept his train and seize him as he journeyed from Washington to Nashville. Assistant Secretary of War Thomas A. Scott, in Nashville at the time the appointment was being considered, telegraphed Washington authorities that Johnson would do more harm than good. Scott urged instead the appointment of General William B. Campbell. General Buell advised General McClellan that such a provisional government with Johnson at the head would be "injudicious."

If Johnson had any misgivings about the situation, he did not show them. He assumed the position of governor with the aggressiveness which characterized his nature. A one-time slaveowner who supported the Southern Democratic ticket in 1860, Johnson horrified Tennesseans by denouncing secession leaders and suggesting that they probably should be executed. Six days after his arrival in Nashville (on March 12), he issued "An Address to the People." The purpose of the military governorship, he said, was to aid in the prompt restoration of the state to its rightful place in the Union. He expressed only contempt for "intelligent and conscious treason in high places," but offered complete amnesty to "the erring and misguided" who would renounce their disloyalty and embrace the Union.

Johnson was disappointed and perhaps surprised when few people responded to his offers of pardon. Adamant public officials, newspaper editors, school teachers, and ministers of the gospel became objects of his vengeance. When Nashville Mayor Richard B. Cheatham and the city council refused to take an oath of allegiance, Johnson turned them out of office and arbitrarily appointed Union sympathizers in their places. Cheatham was imprisoned; former Governor Neill S. Brown, Judge Joseph Guild, and others summarily were arrested. The offices of several secessionist newspapers, including the *Daily Times*, the *Republican Banner*, the *Gazette*, and the *Patriot*, as well as the Baptist and Methodist publishing houses, were ordered closed for alleged disloyalty. Clergymen were jailed because of their "Confederate sermons," which Johnson believed were preached in every church in Nashville. His policies stirred the people to indignation and earned for him the sobriquet,

"Johnson the Tyrant," but he did not flinch from his avowed purposes. The failure of the native population to support his reconstruction program and the frequent threats to his authority by the Southern cavalry leaders, Morgan and Forrest, only made him more resolute. His frequent embroilment in quarrels with Generals Buell, Henry W. Halleck, and Rosecrans, who earnestly sought his removal, added to his worries.

The threat to Johnson's reign as military governor was removed as an immediate possibility in January, 1863, when Rosecrans drove Bragg from Murfreesboro, and was removed entirely in the autumn of that year when the Confederates withdrew southward from Chattanooga and General Burnside freed East Tennessee. After that, his rule, if contested at all, was disputed only by roving bands of guerrillas, until Hood's invasion in 1864. The success of the Federal armies in Tennessee proved an invigorating tonic to the Union cause, and President Lincoln urged Johnson to prepare the state for reconstruction. "The whole struggle for Tennessee will have been profitless . . . if it so ends that Governor Johnson is put down and Governor Harris put up," the President wrote; "Let the reconstruction be the work of such men only as can be trusted for the Union."

By December, 1863, Federal armies had achieved widespread successes, and Lincoln therefore issued his "proclamation of amnesty and reconstruction." Lincoln's plan was designed to heal the nation's wounds as quickly and painlessly as possible. Amnesty and pardon, he said, would be accorded (with a few exceptions) to all who took an oath of allegiance to the federal government. When the number taking the oath equaled one-tenth of the voting population of 1860, they should organize a government which would be recognized in Washington and accorded all the privileges and immunities the state had enjoyed before the war.

Lincoln's talk of leniency aroused little sympathy among Radicals such as Johnson. "The intelligent and influential leaders must suffer; the tall poppies must be struck down," he told a group of followers. Lincoln's oath might absolve one from treason, but something more stringent—"a hard oath, a tight oath," Johnson said—must be used for those who wished to vote. Accordingly, when Johnson issued a proclamation calling for an election of county officers on March 5, he prescribed an oath, referred to by many as Johnson's "Damnesty oath," which all—Confederate sympathizers and ardent

Unionists alike—must take. Prospective voters not only must agree to support the Constitution and the government, but must agree ardently to "desire the suppression of the present insurrection" and the extension to Tennessee of the Emancipation Proclamation. East Tennessee Unionists were humiliated at having to take an oath at all, and many conservative Unionists, in disgust, resolved not to take it. Johnson's prestige suffered and the election proved, as one editor predicted, "a farce." Only Johnson's nomination for Vice President at the Republican convention (called by Republicans "The National Union Convention") enabled him to regain respect among a large segment of Tennessee Unionists.

The presidential election created much interest in the state. The Lincoln-Johnson ticket was supported of course by the Johnson followers but opposed by both the secessionists and the Union Peace party, the latter consisting of loyal Unionists not of the Johnson persuasion and who favored a cessation of hostilities. The secessionists, though large in number, posed no problem because they were excluded by Johnson's test oath. Members of the Union Peace party presented more formidable opposition, and included such prominent Unionists as Emerson Etheridge, Thomas A. R. Nelson, and General William B. Campbell. They supported General George B. McClellan, commander-in-chief of the Federal armies in 1862, who had received the Democratic nomination on a platform declaring that "justice, humanity, liberty, and the public welfare demand that immediate efforts be made for a cessation of hostilities." Johnson now prescribed a new "Damnesty oath," requiring voters to "cordially oppose all armistices or negotiations for peace with rebels in arms . . . ."

Violence and allegations of corrupt politics marred the campaign. Johnson pleased some people by denouncing the "Tennessee aristocrats" who "sneer at Negro equality," and by advocating that the estates of the rich be seized and divided among free farmers. He angered many Unionists, however, by his high-handed conduct. Violence flared not infrequently, and armed forces dispersed at least one group which had assembled for a McClellan rally. Only a small minority of Tennesseans voted and, as expected, they supported the Lincoln-Johnson ticket. Congress, however, rejected Tennessee's electoral votes on the grounds that the state was in rebellion and that no valid election had been held.

Unionists, encouraged by the reelection of Lincoln, immediately formed plans for reconstruction of Tennessee. Five hundred of them assembled in Nashville on January 9, 1865, to amend the constitution and provide for the restoration of civil government. They submitted to "the people" on February 22 a constitutional amendment abolishing slavery and a "schedule" accompanying the amendment which repudiated the ordinance of separation and the military league with the Confederacy and which declared null and void all acts of the state government after May 6, 1861. The schedule further ratified Johnson's appointments to civil and military office, gave to the first legislature which assembled under the revised constitution the power to determine the qualifications of voters, and provided for the election of a governor and General Assembly on March 4. As a final act, the Unionists nominated for governor William G. Brownlow—a man who in 1861 could not interest even East Tennessee Unionists in his candidacy, but who now appeared as a hero and a martyr of Tennessee Unionism. Also, they nominated candidates for every seat in both houses of the legislature to be elected on a general ticket along with the governor. The amendment and schedule were adopted, and Johnson departed for Washington to take the oath as Vice President. On the same day that Lincoln and Johnson were sworn in, Brownlow was elected governor with barely 10 per cent of the number of voters of 1860 participating. He was inaugurated on April 5.

Johnson was a controversial figure throughout his stay in the military governor's chair. That he was sincere and earnest few questioned, but his prejudices and personal dislikes,[1] never concealed, often were so violent and biased that he drove otherwise loyal people into the camps of rebellion. His lack of gentleness, broad sympathy, and deep understanding of humanity—qualities which characterized Lincoln—caused him often to be misunderstood. Johnson has been criticized for arbitrarily delaying reconstruction in the state, for employing methods which were "arbitrary, unconstitutional, and permanently injurious," and for excluding by his "Damnesty oath" many unquestionably loyal men from participating in reconstruc-

---

[1] "If Johnson were a snake," well-born Governor Isham G. Harris once observed, "he would lie in the grass to bite the heels of rich men's children." Hall, *Andrew Johnson, Military Governor,* 22.

tion and thus destroying their interest in the work and losing their counsel, influence, and cooperation. Johnson unquestionably made mistakes, but he gave fearlessly and unsparingly of what he had for the Union cause in Tennessee. There were of course no precedents for him to follow; often without the advice and cooperation of the Federal military authorities, he had to make the rules as he went. He was loyal, self-sacrificing, and steadfastly devoted to a cause which he believed was just.

Conditions at Home ₰ Destruction followed in the wake of the marching armies, and the deprivations which the people suffered only added to the anguish they experienced under Johnson. Diaries and letters described the hardships of war. Dr. James G. M. Ramsey told of the burning of his spacious home at the confluence of the Holston and French Broad rivers.

> I had the honor of a correspondence with the elite and distin-guished [he wrote] . . . with A. Jackson, Calhoun, Polk, . . . [and] Democratic leaders and editors everywhere. . . . All my historical and antiquarian manuscripts—some of them containing the sub-stance of my second volume of the History of Tennessee . . . un-published biographies of the leading master spirits of their day in Tennessee and elsewhere, . . . my library—medical, miscellaneous, . . . historical and literary, I had for many years been collecting from Europe and America, and which was, I believe, the best in the west-ern states—was stolen, destroyed, or burned."[2]

In Middle Tennessee, Mark Cockrill, who had won world renown during the 1850's as a cotton and wool producer, watched helplessly as Federal soldiers took from his Davidson County farm 20,000 bushels of corn, 26 horses, 60 head of cattle, 220 sheep, 200 tons of hay, 2,000 bushels of oats, and 2,000 pounds of cured bacon. At Murfreesboro, Mrs. Bettie Ridley Blackmore wrote of her people being "surrounded by a desperate, insolent, unscrupulous, but vic-torious foe" which burned her home and destroyed her father's

---

[2] Hesseltine (ed.), Ramsey, *Autobiography and Letters*, 55–56. David L. Eubanks, however, in his Ph.D. dissertation, "Dr. J. G. M. Ramsey of East Tennessee" (Uni-versity of Tennessee, 1965), doubts that Ramsey had actually written much, if any, of the proposed second volume of his *Annals*.

property after General Bragg was driven out in January, 1863. In West Tennessee, one writer compared some of the west-state area to an Arkansas town where thousands of "old men, women, and children had been reduced to poverty."

Shortages of food and manpower became acute throughout the state by 1863. Coffee, sugar, and salt, if available at all, sold at prices many times those before the war. Both men and women smuggled food and medicines through the lines. One Nashville woman, affecting great sorrow, carried a coffin packed with valuables through Federal lines at Nashville, and others concealed under their flowing skirts and spacious bustles coffee, quinine, sewing thread, and even bolts of cloth and boots. Most of the men were in uniform, and many slaves refused to work. Although many Southern military authorities gave furloughs at planting and harvest time, still much land formerly cultivated went unworked.

Urban dwellers suffered more than did their rural neighbors. News of the fall of Fort Donelson threw Nashvillians into a panic. Within an hour after the news was received, the roads leading out of Nashville were crowded with people seeking residence elsewhere. Many others robbed and looted stores and shops. Prices soared. The editor of the *Daily Press* commented on May 3, 1864, that "the city is filled with thugs, highwaymen, robbers and assassins. Murder stalks throughout the city almost every night." More whiskey was drunk in Nashville than in Boston, he asserted. On August 4, 1864, a day which President Lincoln had set aside for fasting and prayer, sixty persons went before the recorder's court on charges of drunkenness. The population swelled with undesirables. Memphis was occupied by Federal forces soon after Nashville. There also the population and prices soared. By early 1863, the population was estimated at 11,000 original whites, 5,000 slaves, and 19,000 newcomers. The latter, according to press reports, consisted of a "crowd of sharks, cormorants, sharpers, gamblers, speculators, and anxious relatives seeking for sick soldiers . . . ." During and after the siege of Chattanooga, the town was ravaged to such an extent that the residents were in dire want. Knoxville, said William G. Brownlow on an extensive speaking tour in the North in 1862, was a city of destitution; not even a spool of thread, he told a Cincinnati audience, could be bought there. Throughout much of East Tennessee a wave of murders, whippings, and threats drove out a substantial portion of the population which wanted only peace.

Tenneseee indeed had been a major battlefield of the Civil War. While the sufferings of the people are not to be compared with those of the people of South Carolina or northern Virginia, they had been intense. Donald Davidson has written that "not since the Duke of Alva ravaged the Netherlands, or Cromwell . . . harried Ireland, has a civilized country so felt the brunt of invasion . . . ."[3] The state also had been the subject of an experiment in government, headed by one whose temperament was not suited to such a task. In East Tennessee, four years of bitterness left some old wounds which to this day have not been completely healed. The end of the war did not mean that the time of troubles had ended, however; the people yet were to suffer through four years of reconstruction under Governor Brownlow.

SUGGESTED READINGS

General Accounts

Thomas B. Alexander, *Political Reconstruction in Tennessee* (Nashville, 1950); Freeman Cleaves, *Rock of Chickamauga: The Life of General George H. Thomas* (Norman, 1948); Davidson, *The Tennessee*, II; Jonathan T. Dorris, *Pardon and Amnesty under Lincoln and Johnson* (Chapel Hill, 1953); John P. Dyer, *The Gallant Hood* (Indianapolis, 1950); Folmsbee, Corlew, and Mitchell, *Tennessee*, I, Chs. 27–28; Govan and Livingood, *Chattanooga Country*; Clifton R. Hall, *Andrew Johnson: Military Governor of Tennessee* (Princeton, 1916); Hamer, *Tennessee*, I, Chs. 35–37; Robert S. Henry, *The Story of the Confederacy* (Indianapolis, 1931); Milton, *Age of Hate*; Joseph H. Parks, *General Edmund Kirby Smith, CSA* (Baton Rouge, 1954); Parks, *General Leonidas Polk, C. S. A.* (Baton Rouge, 1962); Digby Gordon Seymour, *Divided Loyalties: Fort Sanders and the Civil War in East Tennessee* (Knoxville, 1963).

Specialized Accounts

Thomas H. Baker, "Refugee Newspaper: The Memphis *Daily Appeal*, 1862–65," *JSH*, XXIX (Aug., 1963), 326–44; Edwin C. Bearss, "Cavalry

[3] *The Tennessee*, II, 108.

Operations in the Battle of Stones River," *THQ*, XIX (March, June, 1960), 23–53, 110–44; Bearss, "Unconditional Surrender: The Fall of Fort Donelson," *THQ*, XXI (March, June, 1962), 47–65, 140–61; Jesse Burt, "East Tennessee, Lincoln, and Sherman," ETHS *Publ.*, Nos. 34, 35 (1962, 1963), 3–25; Burt, "Sherman's Logistics and Andrew Johnson," *THQ*, XV (Sept., 1956), 195–216; Thomas Lawrence Connelly, *Army of the Heartland: The Army of Tennessee, 1861–1862* (Baton Rouge, 1967); E. Merton Coulter, "Parson Brownlow's Tour of the North During the Civil War," ETHS *Publ.*, No. 7 (1935), 3–27; Alfred Leland Crabb, "The Twilight of the Nashville Gods," *THQ*, XV (Dec., 1956), 291–305; Sims Crownover, "The Battle of Franklin," *THQ*, XIV (Dec., 1955), 291–322; Fairfax Downey, *Storming the Gateway: Chattanooga, 1863* (New York, 1960); Eugene G. Feistman, "Radical Disfranchisement and the Restoration of Tennessee, 1865–1866," *THQ*, XII (June, 1953), 135–51; Harold S. Fink, "The East Tennessee Campaign and the Battle of Knoxville," ETHS *Publ.*, No. 29 (1957), 79–117; Gilbert E. Govan and James W. Livingood, "Chattanooga Under Military Occupation, 1863–1865," *JSH*, XVII (Feb., 1951), 23–47; James J. Hamilton, *The Battle of Fort Donelson* (New York, 1968); Ralph W. Haskins, "Andrew Johnson and the Preservation of the Union," ETHS *Publ.*, No. 33 (1961), 43–60; Robert S. Henry, *"First with the Most" Forrest* (New York, 1944); Stanley F. Horn, "Nashville During the Civil War," *THQ*, IV (March, 1945), 3–22; Horn, *The Army of Tennessee* (Indianapolis, 1941); Horn, *The Decisive Battle of Nashville* (Knoxville, 1968); James W. Livingood, "Chattanooga, Tennessee: Its Economic History in the Years Immediately Following Appomattox," ETHS *Publ.*, No. 15 (1943), 35–48; Livingood, "The Chattanooga *Rebel*," ETHS *Publ.*, No. 39 (1967), 42–55; Franklyn McCord, "J. E. Bailey: A Gentleman of Clarksville," *THQ*, XXIII (Sept., 1964), 246–68; Grady McWhiney, "Braxton Bragg at Shiloh," *THQ*, XXI (March, 1962), 19–30; Harriet Chappell Owsley, "Peace and the Presidential Election of 1864," *THQ*, XVIII (March, 1959), 3–19; Joseph H. Parks, "A Confederate Trade Center Under Federal Occupation: Memphis, 1862–1865," *JSH*, VII (1941), 289–314; Parks, "Memphis Under Military Rule, 1862 to 1865," ETHS *Publ.*, No. 14 (1942), 31–58; Edgar L. Pennington, "The Battle at Sewanee," *THQ*, IX (Sept., 1950), 217–43; Sarah Ridley Trimble (ed.), "Behind the Lines in Middle Tennessee, 1863–1865: The Journal of Bettie Ridley Blackmore," *THQ*, XII (March, 1953), 48–80; Peter F. Walker, "Building a Tennessee Army: Autumn, 1861," *THQ*, XVI (June, 1957), 99–116; Walker, "Holding the Tennessee Line," *THQ*, XVI (Sept., 1957), 228–49; Walker, "Command Failure: The Fall of

Forts Henry and Donelson," *THQ*, XVI (Dec., 1957), 335–60; T. Harry Williams, "Beauregard at Shiloh," *Civil War History*, I (March, 1955), 17–34; Williams, "Andrew Johnson as a Member of the Committee on the Conduct of the War," ETHS *Publ.*, No. 12 (1940), 70–83.

20. ⇘ Reconstruction

ALTHOUGH TENNESSEE CEASED to be a battlefield after the army commanded by General Hood was defeated at Nashville in December, 1864, Tennesseans endured for several years thereafter conditions which have been described as "neither peace nor war." The sufferings of East Tennesseans, so pronounced during hostilities, became more intense with the return of the blue and the gray, and street fights and rural feuds and ambushes became common. In many parts of the state men returned to a land of waste and barrenness. Much of the state was "the womb of desolation," one newsman observed; "Government mules and horses are occupying the homes . . . in which . . . [Tennessee's] chivalric sons so often slumbered." Another wrote with some degree of romantic imagination:

> Go from Memphis to Chattanooga, and it is like the march of Moscow in olden times. . . . Whether you go on the Salem, the Shelbyville, the Manchester, or any other pike [from Murfreesboro] for a distance of thirty miles either way, what do we behold? One wide wild, and dreary waste . . . . The fences are all burned down; the apple, the pear, and the plum trees burned in ashes long ago; the torch applied to . . . splendid mansions, the walls of which alone remain.

The death toll of Tennesseans in both armies was high. For others survival was but a reprieve, because men weakened and diseased from years of military service soon filled premature graves. Amputation had been the only defense against gangrene and infection; therefore, many men hobbled back maimed or otherwise unfit for the heavy physical labor demanded by agricultural readjustment. The distress and destruction caused by the battling armies were augmented by problems posed by many freed Negroes who had to be oriented to a new and, to many, a bewildering status.

Such gaping wounds in the economic and social order would heal—if at all—very slowly; only then could recovery reasonably be expected if the affairs of state were administered with tender care in a spirit of understanding and charity. Unfortunately, however, such would not be the case. A militant oligarchy had selected William Gannaway Brownlow as governor on March 4, 1865, and for four years the vengeful crusader imposed his will upon the people of the state.[1]

Brownlow assumed office on April 5, 1865, two days after the General Assembly convened, and urged legislators to enact harsh measures to punish the former Confederates. Brownlow recommended that the criminal code be strengthened to crush the guerrilla menace and the state militia reestablished and reorganized; that the franchise be restricted to Union men only; that freedmen be protected from "those who fought to perpetuate slavery"; and that Confederate officers and bank directors should be held personally responsible for bank and railroad losses. The governor further called for ratification of the Thirteenth Amendment and for the prompt election of United States senators and representatives.

The legislature which acted on these recommendations consisted of Union men, most of whom had had little or no political experience. The overwhelming majority were farmers, with a sprinkling of merchants and lawyers. Most had been Whigs before the war. No clear-cut party alignment had developed when they convened, and all were known simply as "Unionists." Soon after they began work, however, a division developed between those who accepted completely the governor's proposals and those who objected to his proscriptive recommendations. The former group had a working majority, and Samuel R. Rodgers, Brownlow's speaker of the senate, defined their chief aim as being that of keeping the loyal people from ever being "governed by rebels." This group became known

---

[1] Brownlow's biographer has written of his election: "It was a strange and dangerous act to set a person of Brownlow's record to rule over a million people. In peaceful times it would have been perilous; in the confusion incident to the closing of a civil war, it might seem preposterous. . . . For the promoting of the orderly progress of peace, it would have been impossible to make a worse choice." Coulter, *Brownlow*, 262.

as "Radicals," and they followed the leadership of the Washington Radicals who favored a harsh reconstruction program for the South. The others were called "Conservatives"; they followed the leadership of President Johnson and the Washington Conservatives who wished to put into effect the Lincoln-Johnson plan of leniency in reconstruction.

The Radicals made horse stealing, housebreaking, burglary, and house or bridge burning capital offenses, and prescribed the gallows for guerrillas and armed prowlers. Sedition laws were enacted which made a mockery of the Bill of Rights, and the Thirteenth Amendment was ratified by a unanimous vote. Other measures, aimed at former Confederates, were passed. A joint resolution authorized the governor to respond to the "cries of the wounded and dying, the wail of the widow, [and] the weeping of the orphan" by proclaiming a reward of $5,000 for the arrest of former Governor Isham G. Harris. Harris, who had joined other Confederates in Mexico after the war to develop a "new South," was described as one who was "responsible to a great extent for the war . . . ." The reward was never claimed, however, and Harris, who had gone to England after a brief stay in Mexico, returned to Tennessee in 1867 after the legislature repealed the reward offer.

The culmination of the efforts of the Radicals was the enactment of two franchise laws designed to perpetuate their control of the state government. The laws were worded clearly to exclude former Confederates (the leaders for fifteen years and others for five) and to permit only those of "unconditional Union sentiments"[2] to vote. County court clerks were required to administer the test oath to registrants except in cases of persons of "publicly known Union sentiments." When, after several months, it was observed that some clerks were registering people of questionable loyalty, as shown by the election on the basis of the returns of five out of eight Conservative congressmen, the Radicals reconsidered the law of 1865. From February to May, 1866, they wrangled. Finally, disfranchisement of ex-Confederates was made perpetual, and the right of registration was taken from the county court clerks and placed in the hands of "Commissioners of Registration" to be appointed by the governor. This measure, of course, gave Brownlow complete

---

[2] This Arnell Franchise Law of 1865 even went so far as to designate six separate categories of persons permitted to vote.

power to decide who could vote. Conservatives filed suits to have the law declared unconstitutional, but their efforts resulted in failure, and the law remained on the statute books until the Radicals were driven from power.

Tennessee Restored to the Union in 1866 &* Various leaders presented plans for reconstructing the prostrate South. Both Lincoln and Johnson in 1865 contended that the Southern states had not been out of the Union but had existed in a state of suspended animation during their participation in the "rebellion." Now that the war was over, these states needed only to organize loyal governments, recognize Federal authority, and elect representatives and senators to Congress. Radical leaders, however, asserted that the seceded states had committed treason by their acts and must suffer before being restored to their ante bellum status. Thaddeus Stevens, Radical leader in the House of Representatives, had suggested a "conquered province" theory whereby Confederate states would become the property of Congress to be dealt with by that body as the members saw fit. Charles Sumner, equally powerful in the Senate, proposed a "state suicide" theory, in which he argued that the seceding states had lost their positions in the Union and were now territories subject to the exclusive jurisdiction of Congress. Governor Brownlow announced a plan to be used in case Southerners rose in a second civil war. He believed that such a conflict was inevitable and that Andrew "Johnson would, in this second rebellion, take the place of Jeff Davis." After the "second rebellion" was put down, the "loyal masses" should "make the entire Southern Confederacy as God found the earth when he commenced the work of creation, 'Without form and void.' They . . . ought not leave a rebel fence-rail, out-house, or dwelling in the eleven seceded states. And as for the rebel population, let them be exterminated," he said. Still others suggested no plans of their own but opposed the presidential plan for various reasons. Implicit in all the plans was the desire for vengeance against a hated and now conquered foe.

Johnson of course disagreed with the Radicals and sought to have Tennessee immediately restored to its former relations with the federal government. He rejoiced at the state's acceptance of the Thirteenth Amendment and the election of United States senators and representatives. He received gladly a request from the legislature that

> the State of Tennessee be no longer considered in a state of insurrection, and that the loyal people of that state be granted all the rights and privileges that are granted . . . to the loyal citizens of any of the sister states that are not considered in a state of rebellion against the Government of the United States.

The Radical Congress, however, much to the surprise and chagrin of Tennessee Radicals and to the dismay of Johnson, refused on December 4, 1865, to seat the Tennessee delegation. For several months the stalemate was debated both in and out of Congress. A joint committee on reconstruction, consisting of nine members from the House and six from the Senate, then was established to study the situation in all of the Southern states. On April 30 the joint committee suggested to Congress that when a seceded state ratified the proposed Fourteenth Amendment, it should be given representation in Congress and thus, in effect, be readmitted to the Union.

Vigorous opposition to the Fourteenth Amendment already had developed in Tennessee and other Southern states. Some objected to one clause and some to another; to still others all four sections were equally obnoxious. The editor of the Nashville *Union and American* believed that the amendment was far more dangerous to American liberties than the Civil War itself, was "without parallel in American history," and was "aimed at a revolution of the social and political fabric . . . ."

Governor Brownlow called the General Assembly into special session on July 4, and the capitol became the scene of much excitement before the amendment finally was ratified. The senators promptly accepted the amendment, but the Conservatives in the house determined to make a strong fight against it. When, shortly before the session opened, they discovered that they did not have sufficient strength to defeat the proposal, the Conservatives decided to accomplish their aims by absenting themselves and thus prevent the formation of a quorum, which consists of two-thirds of those elected to the house. After convening and promptly adjourning for lack of a quorum for six days, the Radicals decided to issue warrants of arrest for the absent members and thus force the formation of a quorum. On July 16 the sergeant-at-arms, with the assistance of Negro troops, arrested Representatives Pleasant Williams of Carter County and A. J. Martin of Jackson County and forcibly detained them in the capitol. Their applications for writs of habeas corpus were granted by Criminal Judge Thomas N. Frazier of Davidson County, but the legislature denied the court's jurisdiction. Only after the sheriff had formed a *posse comitatus* and stormed the capitol were the two prisoners released. On the day before the prisoners were released (July 19), however, the house ratified the amendment. Williams and Martin were recorded as being present but having "failed and refused" to vote. Brownlow promptly telegraphed Washington authorities that Tennessee Radicals had "fought the battle and won it." On July 23 the President signed a congressional resolution restoring Tennessee to its former relation with the Union, and the state's congressional delegation promptly took its seats in the national assembly. Thus, Tennessee escaped the military program of reconstruction applied by the Radical Congress to the other ten states of the Confederacy.

Negro Suffrage and the Election of 1867 ₰ The Radical oligarchy of Tennessee, realizing that they owed their political life to Governor Brownlow, began in January, 1867, to plan for the August election. Throughout January, county conventions were held at which Radical leaders urged the reelection of their chief. On Washington's birthday, they assembled in Nashville where they warmly praised the governor and strongly condemned President Johnson. Brownlow, the Radicals said, was a man of "firmness, courage, and wisdom" whose "healthy mind . . . bears with like equanimity the throes of pain and the perilous cares of State . . . ." They vowed that they would not even consider any other candidate for governor.

A bill which would give Negroes the privilege of voting was before the legislature when the Radicals assembled, and they strongly recommended its passage. The measure had been written at the insistence of Brownlow who for some time had concluded that the votes of loyal Negroes probably would be necessary to keep his regime in power. Before the war the governor had been a staunch defender of slavery, and, more recently, an opponent of Negro suffrage. Shortly after the war he had suggested that Negroes be colonized in Texas or some other Western state. The goadings of the Northern press and of Negro leaders, however, together with the realization that he might lose the election in 1867, caused Brownlow to change his views. Consequently, on February 26, a measure enfranchising Negro men but excluding them from office holding and jury duty was enacted.

In the meantime, Conservatives held a nominating convention in Nashville in April and selected Emerson Etheridge as their gubernatorial candidate. Because they realized that Negroes would hold the balance of power in the forthcoming election, the Conservatives freely courted them with such expressions as "our colored fellow-citizens." The nomination of Etheridge was ill-advised, however. Although an able man of unquestioned integrity and loyalty to the Union, he had been a slaveholder and was reputed to have declared (although he denied it): "The negroes are no more free than they were forty years ago . . . and these negro troops . . . ought to be shot down." Brownlow Radicals constantly emphasized these inconsistencies during the canvass.

The incumbent governor was too ill to campaign extensively, but he had taken adequate measures to insure his victory even before Etheridge was nominated. During and after the debates on the Negro suffrage bill, the governor pushed through the legislature two measures which would give him more power. One, passed on February 20, provided for the raising of an armed force to be known as the Tennessee State Guard, with Brownlow as commander-in-chief. Troops were necessary, he said, to stop "atrocious murders and numerous outrages" which had been committed by "violent and disloyal men." The second law strengthened the franchise law by giving the governor authority to set aside registrations in any county. Brownlow, his dictatorial powers enhanced, now was ready for the gubernatorial campaign of 1867.

The governor's inability to campaign did not mean that he would not be represented on the hustings throughout the state. Horace Maynard was popular especially among Negroes, and was joined by William B. Stokes (who became the Radical candidate in 1869), Samuel M. Arnell, and others who carried Brownlow's candidacy to the people. At Murfreesboro a picnic was held for 1,500 Negroes, and at Gallatin a Negro preacher told his audience that Brownlow was "a colored man" who deserved the support of every "other" colored man in Sumner County.

Etheridge was an able orator whose skill in the use of vituperative language matched that of Brownlow's, but he must have realized that his chances of victory were indeed slim. Radicals placed many obstacles in his way and even threatened his life. At Greeneville he was forced to defend himself against attackers, and at Elizabethton a Brownlow supporter drew a pistol and pointed it at him as he spoke. Disturbances occurred at Rogersville, Knoxville, Gallatin, Franklin, Fayetteville, Lewisburg, Pulaski, Columbia, and other places. In most counties, contingents of the State Guard stood by menacingly as he spoke.

On election day the Radicals and the Negroes delivered the majority which Brownlow expected and needed. The governor won by a vote of 74,034 to 22,550; all the Radical candidates for Congress and all but three Radical candidates for the state legislature were elected. After some delay, that legislature gave the Negroes the right to hold office and sit on juries.

The Impeachment of President Andrew Johnson ೩ఆ Shortly after the election, Washington Radicals began seriously to consider impeaching President Johnson. Radical legislators in Tennessee were pleased with the movement, and in October, 1867, considered a joint resolution requesting the state's delegation in Washington to vote for the impeachment articles. The Radical press, led by the Knoxville *Whig* and the Nashville *Daily Press and Times*, urged that no mercy be shown the Chief Executive. "Let Johnson be impeached, treason made odious, and the arch-traitor punished," wrote the editor of the Nashville paper.

Tennessee's House delegation did not need encouragement from the Radicals back home; their opinions already had been formed. With the exception of Congressman Isaac R. Hawkins, they voted for impeachment and denounced the President in the process. William B. Stokes charged Johnson with drunkenness while he served as military governor, described him as a man who had "no regard for truth," and denounced him for attempting to "put the rebels in power to again plant their heels upon our necks and crush the colored men into the dust." Congressman James Mullins believed that the President had ambitions to be "the sole legislator, the Nero of our day." "The Czar of Russia has never assumed more despotic power and more absolute sway" than Johnson, Mullins fumed.

Tennessee's two senators who would sit as a court with their fellow solons in judgment of the charges brought against the President were David T. Patterson, a son-in-law of the Chief Executive, and Joseph S. Fowler. Radicals assumed that Patterson would vote for an acquittal, but Fowler, who had sided with the Radicals on many issues, kept both friend and foe in doubt until the final roll call. He received hundreds of visitors—not to mention letters and telegrams —who urged him to vote for conviction. All of Tennessee's Radical delegation in the House of Representatives visited him and insisted that he should resign unless he could vote "what he well knows to be the sentiment of the loyal people of his state." Brownlow, Johnson's enemy of long standing, was alleged to have offered Fowler an appointment to the state supreme court if he would resign.

Upon final roll call both senators voted for acquittal. The Radicals failed by one vote to remove Johnson by impeachment. Needless to say, Senator Fowler was excoriated by his erstwhile Radical cohorts and characterized as a "nineteenth century Judas."

The Ku Klux Klan ह≫ Brownlow's overwhelming victory in 1867 disturbed Conservative Unionists and old Confederates alike; the latter lamented that their cup of woe overflowed and that their situation rapidly was becoming intolerable. Indeed, throughout the Southern states such feeling was more apparent; the South was ripe for an underground movement. The feeling was expressed through many organizations—Knights of the White Camelia, Pale Face League, Shotgun Club, Council of Safety, White Brotherhood, and others—but the best known was the Ku Klux Klan. All had generally the same aims, which were to recover for the whites the control of government and society and to destroy the influence of the carpetbaggers and Northern opportunists among Negroes. The work of the Union League irritated many Southern whites. This organization had been formed by Northern Radicals ostensibly for the purpose of teaching the blacks good citizenship and loyalty to the Union, but the real purpose became that of propagating the cause of the Radical Republicans on election day.

The Klan was organized at Pulaski shortly after the war by a group of young men seeking amusement. By 1867, the Klan had been transformed from a social club to a political organization when its leaders observed that they might frighten Negroes from the polls and Union Leaguers out of the South; if they could do this, then their day of political deliverance would come more quickly. The group grew rapidly and leaders determined upon a state meeting where a greater degree of centralization might be achieved.

Consequently, a secret convention was held at the Maxwell House Hotel[3] in Nashville in April, 1867. So loyal were the leaders that they could assemble under the shadow of the capitol where Brownlow reigned and in the presence of Federal troops and officers actually residing in the hotel. General Forrest was placed at the head of the organization, with the title of "Grand Wizard of the Empire." Each state constituted a Realm headed by a Grand Dragon, each congressional district a Dominion under a Grand Titan, and each county a Province governed by a Grand Giant. Local units were called Dens, headed by a Grand Cyclops. A constitution, or prescript, set forth the various duties of the officials. A revised prescript was issued the following year and stated the purposes of the Klan. These included protection of "the weak, the innocent and the defenseless, from the indignities, wrongs, and outrages of the lawless, the violent, and the brutal"; aid to the suffering, especially "widows and orphans of Confederate soldiers"; protection and defense of the Constitution of the United States; and "aid in the execution of all constitutional laws."

For the next two years, activities of the Klan were reported widely. Disguised men staged numerous night parades in cities and towns throughout Middle and West Tennessee and in some counties of East Tennessee. Activity was reported in most of the counties, but especially in Maury, Lincoln, Giles, Marshall, and Humphreys (in Middle Tennessee), and in Obion, Hardeman, Fayette, Gibson, and Dyer (in West Tennessee). Leaders in Negro affairs were abused and threatened. Even Brownlow reported having received threatening letters "accompanied with pictures of coffins, daggers, pistols

---

[3] The Maxwell House, later to become a nationally known establishment, had just been completed when the meeting took place. Construction was begun by Colonel John Overton in 1859 and the half-built structure was used by the Federals during the war as a hospital.

and the gallows." Alleged depredations included murders, rapes, and whippings.

To meet the new emergency Brownlow called the legislature into an extraordinary session. He described the Klan as a "dangerous organization of ex-rebels" which had "grown into a political engine of oppression." He forcefully recommended that "these organized bands of assassins and robbers be declared outlaws by special legislation, and punished with death wherever found."

The inflammatory message was received with both fear and anger by many Tennesseans. The editor of one Nashville paper described it as "the gauge of battle thrown to an exasperated people," while the editor of the Gallatin *Examiner* thought it was a declaration of war upon the Southern veterans. "If he [Brownlow] wishes war, he will find our entire population ready for it . . . . If war is the decision we can promise to make it short and sharp," he concluded. Cooler heads prevailed, however, and Conservatives insisted that the people wanted only peace. A group of former Confederate generals, including Benjamin F. Cheatham, W. B. Bate, Nathan Bedford Forrest, John C. Brown, Gideon J. Pillow, Bushrod R. Johnson, and seven others assembled in Nashville on August 1 and urged that peace and harmony should replace threats of war. They denied that they were hostile to the state government or that they or any organization desired the overthrow of the government by violence and illegal means—they wanted only peace. The depredations of "armed men roving through portions of the country" was regrettable, they said, but that would cease "as soon as the determination of the leaders to have peace was made known."

The legislators in special session formed a committee to study Ku Klux Klan activity soon after they convened. Committee members took testimony of "a great many" witnesses and reported that they found that "a perfect reign of terror" existed in many of the counties of West and Middle Tennessee. Armed and disguised men, they said, were

> going abroad . . . robbing poor Negroes . . . taking them out of their houses at night, hanging, shooting and whipping them in a most cruel manner, and driving them from their houses. . . . Women and children . . . [were] subjected to the torture of the lash, and brutal assaults . . . committed upon them by these night prowlers. . . . In

many instances the persons of females . . . [were] violated, and when the husband or father complained, he had been obliged to flee to save his own life.

The committee report supplied the motivation Brownlow desired. He recommended that two comprehensive measures be enacted. The first reestablished the state militia (the earlier act having expired) and gave the governor authority to declare martial law in any county where the law could not be enforced. The second, commonly called the Ku Klux Klan Act, provided severe penalties for persons who "unite with, associate with, promote or encourage, any secret organization of persons that shall prowl through the country or towns . . . by day or night, disguised or otherwise, for the purpose of disturbing the peace." Violators were to be fined $500, imprisoned for not less than five years, and "rendered infamous." The same punishment was provided for persons who impeded the prosecution of the guilty. All citizens were authorized to arrest violators of the law.

When several months elapsed with no prominent ex-Confederate having been charged with violating the Klan law, Brownlow employed Captain Seymour Barmore of Cincinnati to spy upon prominent citizens in an effort to obtain names for exemplary trials. The purpose of the ostentatious Barmore—who described himself as "the greatest detective in the world"—was soon discovered by Nashville Klansmen who warned him to return to Cincinnati. He refused; instead he immediately caught a train to Pulaski, the center of Klan activity. There, dressed as a Klansman, he attended a meeting of the Pulaski Klan and obtained the names of many of its members. The ruse was not discovered until Barmore had boarded a train for Nashville. At Columbia, however, Klansmen forcibly removed him. Six weeks later, on February 20, 1869, his body was recovered from the Duck River. A rope was about his neck and a bullet had pierced his skull.

On the same day that Barmore's body was recovered from the murky waters, Brownlow declared martial law in the counties of Gibson, Giles, Haywood, Jackson, Lawrence, Madison, Marshall, Maury, and Overton, where he believed lawlessness abounded and where the Klan still operated unimpeded. A few weeks earlier the governor after much difficulty had raised the desired number of men to constitute the new state militia, and he placed General Joseph A. Cooper in command.

On February 25, 1869, Brownlow resigned in order to accept a seat in the United States Senate, and shortly thereafter General Forrest commanded that Klan masks and costumes be destroyed. Forrest believed that the Klan in large measure had accomplished its objectives, and he regretted that many acts of violence, not committed by Klan members, were blamed upon the organization.

Freedmen's Bureau in Tennessee ৡ Leaders of the Radical Congress entertained no idea of allowing Southerners to assume political control over Negroes; on the contrary, Stevens, Sumner, and other Radicals determined at an early date to influence and manipulate the Negroes in the conquered provinces and thus insure Republican control. The major role in the operation was to be performed by the Freedmen's Bureau.

Bureau officials were given considerable power. They distributed relief funds to needy whites as well as to Negroes. Bureau officials supervised Negroes' contracts with white landowners, Negro education, and certainly their ballots after the franchise was conferred upon them. Bureau officials also set aside for use of the freedmen such tracts of land as were declared "abandoned," or which might be acquired by the government by sale or confiscation. Not more than forty acres could be leased to a freedman or refugee.

General O. O. Howard, who recently had been in command of the Army of the Tennessee, was named bureau commissioner, and General Clinton B. Fisk was named assistant commissioner in charge of a district embracing Kentucky and Tennessee. Sub-districts in Tennessee were formed, with headquarters at Nashville, Memphis, Chattanooga, Pulaski, and Knoxville. Fisk announced at the beginning that Negroes would be expected to work. "Do not expect us to do all, nor half, but put your shoulders to the wheel and do for yourselves," he told a group of Negroes soon after his arrival in Nashville. Thousands of rations were issued to the destitute, and four orphanages and two hospitals were established.

The Educational Division performed one of the most important functions of the bureau. Hundreds of teachers from the North, with a variety of motives, attitudes, and intentions, poured into the South. Most considered themselves the spiritual and intellectual successors to Grant and Sherman; the blue-coats merely had conquered armies, but the teachers had the more important task of conquering and enlightening the Southern mind. The "political rights of the blackest man" must be "put on a level with the whitest," they announced, and the South must be made safe for "the reddest Republican" or the "blackest Abolitionist." By September, 1866, more than 9,000 Negroes had been enrolled in forty-one schools. A few months later the legislature provided for the maintenance of Negro education, and soon many of the schools were being maintained by the state.

Many native whites did not sympathize with the purposes or methods of the bureau in educating the Negro; one writer (Henry L. Swint) has written, "The Southern reaction to the presence of the Yankee teacher was definite, decided, and violent."[4] The majority of Southerners did not condemn Negro education, but to the contrary had approved of it both before and after the war. However, they resented and feared the "typical Yankee teacher," who they believed would do more to foment racial unrest than to help the Negroes develop intellectually and economically; and the majority feared racially mixed schools.

Bureau officials received many reports of violence against schools and teachers. School buildings at Wartrace, Carthage, Decherd, Shelbyville, Brentwood, Athens, and other places were burned. Teachers at Carthage received advice to "go North where they belonged," and many elsewhere were threatened. M. M. Hiland, a Cheatham County white man who conducted a Negro school, reported in 1868 that he had received a note signed "By order of the Grand Cyclops" as follows:

M. M. Hiland, alias Nigro [sic] Hiland:—
You are hereby notified to disband the school of which you are in charge at Jackson Chapel as it is contrary to the wishes of every respectable man in the vicinity and an insult to the refinement of the community. If this notice fails to effect its purpose, you may expect to find yourself suspended by a rope with your feet about six feet from terra firma. We hope you will give the same consideration;

4 *Northern Teacher in the South,* 94.

and in case of failure on your part, we intend to carry into execution
the above mentioned plan.

BEWARE!   BEWARE!!   BEWARE!!!⁵

Despite discouragement, officials continued to operate the
schools. J. H. Barnum, assistant superintendent of the Educational
Division of the bureau, toured Middle Tennessee in 1868 and found
many people who "manifested a great interest in the subject of
schools." Shortly thereafter a reporter for the Nashville *Daily Press
and Times* toured many of the counties and corroborated Barnum's
report. The editor of the Nashville *Republican Banner* argued that
the South should assume the burden of educating the Negroes instead of waiting for the Northern people to do it.

While teachers taught Negroes reading, writing, and arithmetic,
bureau officials taught them to vote the Republican ticket. In many
of the Southern states, the bureau became little more than a political
propaganda machine designed to perpetuate the Radicals in power,
but in Tennessee the officials probably were less active than elsewhere.

The Radicals and the Railroads ᚵ᙮ The Radicals found
several ways to enrich themselves at the expense of the state treasury.
None, however, was more fantastic than that involving the railroads
of the state; indeed, one historian (Robert H. White) has described
the situation as "the most putrid mess perhaps to be found in the
annals of Tennessee history."

The decade of the 1850's had been an era of railroad expansion.
Tennessee, like other states, had loaned money to companies which
would build railroads in or through the state. By 1861 a fairly satisfactory system of transportation had been built by companies which
at that time showed no danger of financial disaster.

The wanton destruction of railroads and bridges during the war
left the roads in disrepair and the companies in poor financial condition, although the federal government did build several hundred
miles of lines and repaired others. After Appomattox, the Brownlow
administration attempted to rebuild the entire system. By 1869 the
legislature had appropriated nearly $14,000,000 for the relief of the

⁵ Corlew, *Dickson County,* 112.

railroad companies; this, of course, was at a time when the people struggled for the bare necessities of life and could scarcely afford increased taxes.

In view of the unprecedented generosity, it would appear that the railroad companies could have become completely reconstructed, financially rehabilitated, and free of debt. The generosity of the state, however, was matched only by unprecedented corruption on the part of the legislators and railroad officials; the latter used the money for private speculation or for bribing legislators to grant additional amounts of money instead of for repairing the railroads and maintaining efficient operations. These practices were carried on to such an extent that the railroads could not (or would not) pay even the interest on the bonds, which further impaired the unstable credit of the commonwealth. When the state defaulted on bonds maturing in 1867–68, the price of Tennessee securities dropped sharply. Several of the railroad officials who were able to pay interest refused to do so, in hope that the state would default so that they then might buy up past due coupons at a low rate and cash them later at full value. The railroad men, able to manipulate the price of state securities, freely speculated in Tennessee bonds. When in 1868 a bill was proposed which would appropriate an additional $3,000,000 for the railroads, State Comptroller G. W. Blackburn told legislators that such a measure would force the state to the brink of bankruptcy.

Committees were formed from time to time to investigate the conduct of railroad officials. At the suggestion of Governor Brownlow, one was formed in 1868, but the members surprised no one when they discovered nothing. Another, formed in 1869 after Brownlow had accepted a seat in the Senate, reported that considerable fraud had transpired. The Mineral Home Railroad, for example, which existed entirely on paper—"not a shovel of dirt was ever dug, nor even a survey of the route attempted," the committee said—received $100,000 in state bonds. Talk of repudiating some of the bonds hastily was quieted, however, when Washington Radicals threatened military reconstruction.

It remained for the legislature of 1879 to uncover the sordid details of the amazing and flagrant conduct of the railroad and government officials. Legislators had been bought and sold, and even former Governor Brownlow—although perhaps innocently—profited handsomely. Governor Albert S. Marks told legislators in 1879 that efforts of "honest men" in the Radical-dominated legislatures "were unavailing." According to Marks and the legislative committee appointed to investigate the situation, the legislatures refused to make appropriations unless the members were paid by railroad officials to make them. "Fine brandy by the barrel was on hand," the committee reported, "and money was in abundance."

The most amazing testimony in the investigations of 1879 came from General Joseph A. Mabry, the erstwhile "kingpin of the railroad lobbyists," who testified as follows:

> Myself and the other gentlemen . . . were in New York, and engaged in bond speculations. Some of us consulted a celebrated New York Spiritualist, Madame Mansfield, and she told us that bonds would go down and that there would be trouble in Tennessee, . . . but we could control "old scratch," meaning Governor Brownlow, with money. . . . We had speculated in bonds on account of Governor Brownlow, and had made nearly $5,000. We then determined to make the Governor a present of the $5,000, furnishing out of our own private means what we had failed on the $5,000 in our speculating for his benefit. I notified him the day before that we would. Callaway and myself went up to present it; he was lying on a lounge and told us to give it to his wife and we did so . . . .

Mrs. Brownlow, questioned by newsmen during the investigation, admitted taking the money but saw no wrong in it. The railroad men "were under great obligations to Governor Brownlow for many acts of kindness," she said, and when they "begged" her to "accept a present from them" she could not refuse. Such innocence did not extend to Mabry and the other lobbyists, however; they sought more appropriations to fatten their already bulging coffers and they wanted friends in high places who would come to their rescue in case of trouble. The story of the settlement of the tremendous debt, saddled upon the taxpayers of Tennessee by unscrupulous government and railroad officials, is discussed in another chapter.

The Downfall of the Radicals 〰 Brownlow had been elected to succeed United States Senator Patterson, whose term expired March 4, 1869. Consequently, the governor resigned on February 25, 1869, and was succeeded by DeWitt C. Senter, speaker of the senate, whom Brownlow described as "a loyal man, capable, tried, and trusty, who is sound in his principles and who will steadily adhere to them upon the platform of the Union Republican party in Tennessee."

Brownlow based his description of the new governor upon the record. Senter, an East Tennessean, had served three terms in the legislature before the war and had voted against secession in 1861. He had been imprisoned by the Confederates, driven from his home by guerrillas, and had lived in Louisville during the war. In 1865 he returned and was elected to the state senate. There Senter voted for disfranchisement of the Confederates and otherwise supported Brownlow and the Radicals. As a member of the senate in 1867, Senter had taken a leading role in the election of Brownlow to the United States Senate.

Senter proceeded cautiously during his first few weeks as governor and determined upon only slight modification of the Brownlow program. One of his first official acts was to declare the militia subordinate to civil government and to make clear that it did not supersede civil law. Shortly thereafter he mustered out the militia. With the removal of martial law only disfranchisement kept the former Confederates from resuming positions of power, but in this respect Senter gave them little hope for immediate relief. Until the campaign for governor in 1869, Confederates had no reason to consider Senter anything but a "mild" Radical.

When Radicals held a gubernatorial convention in Nashville on May 20, 1869, the field of hopefuls had narrowed to Senter and General William B. Stokes, congressman from the Third District, whom Brownlow had defeated two years earlier in the election to the Senate. Each was supported by a faction determined to nominate its man, and soon the convention became—as one writer described it—"fit only for lunatics." A few days later when the convention broke up in confusion, each faction held its own meeting and claimed its favorite to be the Radical nominee. Therefore, both Stokes and Senter became gubernatorial candidates.

Conservatives declined to nominate a candidate but vowed to support the Radical nominee who appeared most favorable to their cause. At first they leaned toward Stokes. He was a Middle Tennessean, while Senter, endorsed by the governor and considered the "administration candidate," was believed to favor continued disfranchisement. They soon shifted wholeheartedly to Senter, however, when it became apparent that enfranchisement of the Confederate veterans would be the major issue.

On June 5 the campaign opened in Nashville. Stokes favored a gradual return of the ex-Confederates to the ballot box, and suggested that such might be accomplished by a two-thirds vote of the legislators after each disfranchised person could prove that he was peaceful and lawabiding. Senter, however, proposed universal manhood suffrage and promised if elected to remove all restrictions. Brownlow, who always reserved for himself the right to change his mind when not on a popular side, left Radicals dumbfounded by supporting Senter's stand. Brownlow was aware of the trends of the times, however; he also knew that the state supreme court six weeks earlier had rendered a unanimous decision declaring unconstitutional the legislative act which had conferred on the governor the power to set aside registrations of voters of a county where he detected fraud. The decision in effect re-enfranchised about 30,000 ex-Confederates.

The campaign waxed bitter throughout the summer and much strife was aroused wherever the candidates spoke. Although he knew that Stokes had the bulk of the Radical support, Governor Senter believed that he could be elected if enough ex-Confederates were granted the franchise before the election. Consequently, Senter began the wholesale removal of Radical registrars in counties across the state and replaced them with Conservatives. Thousands of former Rebels soon were announcing proudly their intention of carrying the day for Senter. Toward the end of the campaign, Stokes, in Middle and West Tennessee, shifted to a position of universal suffrage. At Memphis he admitted that "suffrage is a dead letter. Any man can get a certificate." At Huntington he promised to "enfranchise every man of God's green earth who will come up and ask for it."

Senter's election became a foregone conclusion. He received a majority of 65,297 out of 175,369 votes cast. Furthermore, the Conservatives ran their own candidates for the legislature and won control of both houses. The next General Assembly would have 20 Conservatives and 5 Radicals in the senate, and 66 Conservatives and 17 Radicals in the house.[6] The election meant that Reconstruction was over in Tennessee and that the power of the Radical minority was broken.

Several reasons may be assigned for Senter's victory. One is the political war of attrition which the Conservatives waged against the Radicals; they harassed their political foes at every turn. They made capital out of Radical mistakes and won even some support from the inner sanctum of Radicalism itself. Second, many of the white Radicals lost confidence in Brownlow and other leaders and refused to go along with them on some measures. Third, the enthusiasm of the Negro began to wane. By 1869, Negroes, hoping to hold lucrative offices, had been disappointed; too, activity of the Klan had discouraged many. Fourth, the supreme court decision rendered in April, 1869, in the case of *State v. William Staten*, had taken from the governor some of his arbitrary disfranchisement powers and had the effect of extending the ballot to his enemies. Finally, the "fatal animosity and dissension" which developed within the ranks of the party itself accounted for the downfall of the Radicals.

Why did Senter desert his Radical friends? Apparently he, like Brownlow, realized that Radicalism was a dying cause in Tennessee. No senatorial position opened as a means of escape as in the case of his predecessor; therefore, he determined to play the role of a Conservative hero rather than that of a Radical goat.

The Conservative legislature began immediately to undo much of the Radical program. The State Guard Act and the "Act to Preserve the Peace" (Ku Klux Klan law) were repealed. Oaths for officeholders were removed. Most important of all, the legislature submitted to the people the question of electing delegates to a constitutional convention in which it was assumed that the fundamental law would be purified of Radicalism. By a 5 to 1 majority, the people voted in favor of the convention, which assembled in January, 1870.

Radicals did not accept the revolution without a struggle. Stokes and others believed that the federal government would declare Senter's election illegal, and urged Congress to place the state under

[6] Conservatives in the General Assembly were primarily men who had been Whigs before the war. It was not until the elections of November, 1870, that the name "Democrat" was used interchangeably with that of "Conservative."

military reconstruction. Their hopes were in vain, however, and their cause proved to be dead in Tennessee.

Thus, after four years of Radicalism, the government of Tennessee again was in the hands of the majority. Within recent years there has been a tendency among scholars to treat the Reconstruction period in the South with greater objectivity than formerly. Certainly the Radicals were in power during a trying time and when the Chief Executive offered little by way of leadership. Certainly they did much to encourage industry, immigration, and education during a time of the state's greatest need. Regardless of whatever accomplishments might be claimed for them, however, it must be admitted that the democratic principle of majority rule was abandoned. Little was seen of charity, forbearance, and compromise, which are such necessary ingredients in the satisfactory workings of a democracy.

SUGGESTED READINGS

General Accounts

Alexander, *Political Reconstruction*; George R. Bentley, *A History of the Freedmen's Bureau* (Philadelphia, 1955); E. Merton Coulter, *The South During Reconstruction, 1865–1877* (Baton Rouge, 1947); Coulter, *Brownlow*; Folmsbee, Corlew, and Mitchell, *Tennessee*, II, Ch. 29; Hamer, *Tennessee*, I, Chs. 37–43; Stanley F. Horn, *The Invisible Empire* (Boston, 1939); Patton, *Unionism and Reconstruction*; Alrutheus A. Taylor, *The Negro in Tennessee, 1865–1880* (Washington, 1941); White, *Messages*, V.

Specialized Accounts

Thomas B. Alexander, "Kukluxism in Tennessee, 1865–1869," *THQ*, VIII (Sept., 1949), 195–219; Alexander, "Whiggery and Reconstruction in Tennessee," *JSH*, XVI (Aug., 1950), 291–305; Howard K. Beale, *The Critical Year: A Study of Andrew Johnson and Reconstruction* (New York, 1930); James B. Campbell, "East Tennessee During the Radical Regime, 1865–1869," ETHS *Publ.*, No. 20 (1948), 84–102; Corlew, *Dickson County*; Feistman, "Radical Disfranchisement," *THQ*, XII (June, 1953), 135–51; Willard Hays, "Andrew Johnson's Reputation," ETHS *Publ.*, No. 31 (1959), 1–31, No. 32 (1960), 18–50; Jack D. L. Holmes, "The Underlying Causes of the Memphis Race Riot of 1866," *THQ*, XVII (Sept., 1958), 195–221; Weymouth T. Jordan, "The Freedmen's

Bureau in Tennessee," ETHS *Publ.*, No. 11 (1939), 47–61; James H. O'Donnell, III, "Taylor Thistle: A Student at the Nashville Institute, 1871–1880," *THQ*, XXVI (Winter, 1967), 387–95; J. W. Patton, "Tennessee's Attitude Toward the Impeachment and Trial of Andrew Johnson," ETHS *Publ.*, No. 9 (1937), 65–76; Paul David Phillips, "White Reaction to the Freedmen's Bureau in Tennessee," *THQ*, XXV (Spring, 1966), 50–62; Verton M. Queener, "Origin of the Republican Party in East Tennessee," ETHS *Publ.*, No. 13 (1941), 68–90; J. A. Sharp, "The Downfall of the Radicals in Tennessee," ETHS *Publ.*, No. 5 (1933), 105–24; J. Reuben Sheeler, "The Development of Unionism in East Tennessee, 1860–1866," *JNH*, XXIX (April, 1944), 166–203; Frank B. Williams, "John Eaton, Jr., Editor, Politician, and School Administrator, 1865–1870," *THQ*, X (Dec., 1951), 291–319.

21. ꝫ∾ Postwar Recovery

WITH THE BROWNLOW ADMINISTRATION behind them, Tennesseans turned to other problems, most of which were legacies of the Reconstruction period. The people had voted for a revision of the fundamental law soon after Governor Senter's election, and early in January delegates convened for the first major constitutional convention in nearly four decades. The state debt, a Civil War-Reconstruction onus which increased at a fearful rate, required settlement, and soon after the convention adjourned attention was focused upon this debt. Another postwar problem which could not be overlooked was that of rehabilitating the state's economic system; this problem was especially acute in agriculture, because declining farm prices had demoralized tillers of the soil. Many Southern leaders thought that industry and immigrants might be the answer to the South's economic problems. Indeed, Tennessee had its share of protagonists of the "New South" philosophy, and through their influence Northern capital and industry were secured for the urban centers. Then, as some of the problems decreased, Negro leaders exhibited an active interest in political matters, and urban areas expanded during the two decades after the war.

Constitutional Convention of 1870 ꝫ∾ Delegates to the constitutional convention assembled according to plan on January 10, 1870. They brought to the assembly an array of political talent and experience. The majority had been slaveholders and were men of property and of conservative temperament. One had been governor; others, including the chairman, were to hold that office later. A few had served in the United States or Confederate congresses, and over half had been members of the state legislature. Most of the delegates had served in Northern or Southern armies, and four had been Confederate generals.

Radicals, both in Tennessee and in Washington, watched the proceedings carefully. Those in Tennessee repeatedly urged Congress to place the state under military rule with other former Confederate states. Congressman Lewis Tillman of Shelbyville, for example, believed that the government in his state consisted entirely of former Confederate leaders who were "trampling underfoot" all semblance of law and order. A large conclave of Negroes, convening in Nashville on January 2, reported to Congress that "the Rebel party" then in power in Tennessee was "unChristian, inhuman and beyond toleration"; Negroes and other Unionists could find relief, they said, only through military reconstruction.

Delegates to the convention, realizing that their actions would be scrutinized carefully by federal officials, wisely chose a moderate as chairman. They elected a Pulaski lawyer and former Confederate general, John C. Brown, who urged delegates to mark their deliberations with "wisdom, prudence, and moderation." The delegates should raise their sights "above the passions of the hour," Brown said, and "accept the situation and not seek to alter circumstances which have passed beyond . . . control." He hoped that Tennesseans could escape the federal military occupation which harassed citizens of some of the other Southern states. Brown promptly appointed committees to study the bill of rights, the legislative department, the executive department, elections and the right of suffrage, finance and internal improvements, and miscellaneous subjects.

The question which caused the most debate was that of suffrage. Should the law giving Negroes the right to vote be written into the constitution? William Blount Carter, the East Tennessean of bridge-burning fame, believed that it would bring about the destruction of "our republican system." John C. Brown and his brother, former Governor Neill S. Brown, expressed widely held fears of federal intervention if Negroes were not given the ballot. After several days of debate, the group voted 56 to 18 in favor of Negro suffrage. The question of making the payment of a poll tax a prerequisite for voting also caused debate. Five delegates prepared a statement in which they alleged that such a measure was "an unjust discrimination against the poor man"; a few others who had championed the cause of Negro suffrage said it would discourage freedmen from voting. Finally, however, the provision was included with the stipulation that money received from the tax would be used to support public education.

Few changes were made in the bill of rights except to prohibit slavery and provide for Negro suffrage. The delegates, learning a lesson from the Brownlow assemblies, prohibited future legislatures from lending the credit of the state in aid of "any person, association, company, corporation, or municipality," and limited the governor's control of the militia. They also provided that legislators could not be paid for more than seventy-five days of a regular session and twenty days of a special session. To prevent hasty action on amendments to the federal Constitution, the delegates provided that no convention or General Assembly should act on any proposed amendment unless that convention or assembly had been elected after the submission of the proposed amendment. Partly to rid the state of Radical domination of the supreme court, the convention enlarged the judicial body to five members and provided that not more than two were to reside in any one grand division of the state. The exceedingly difficult process of amending the basic law as provided in the constitution of 1835 was retained, and long-delayed reforms changed the date of state elections to November of even numbered years and gave the governor veto power.

After a session of six weeks, the delegates adjourned (February 23) and submitted their work to the people for ratification. March 26 was the date set for the referendum. In the meantime, Radicals urged that the new constitution be rejected, and then they hastened to Washington again to ask for military intervention in Tennessee. In fear of federal interference, House Speaker W. O. Perkins and Senate Speaker D. B. Thomas issued a joint statement to Congress in which they refuted "false and mischievous" charges that the legislature and convention had been composed entirely of "rebels," and that the two bodies had enacted laws of discriminatory nature affecting Negroes and Union men. A careful examination of the constitution itself, they wrote, would indicate that delegates secured "equal rights and liberties for all, and discriminations against none . . . ."

On March 26, 1870, the people accepted the new constitution by a vote of 98,128 to 33,872. Although the referendum apparently was a fair expression of the public sentiment, Radicals carried their case to President Ulysses S. Grant and urged that the state be placed under the Reconstruction laws of 1867. The Chief Executive, however, refused to send troops at their behest.

Politics and the State Debt, 1870–83 ঐঙ During the two decades after Appomattox, Tennessee Democrats became well entrenched and Republicans were relegated to a minority status. The Democrats, who controlled West and Middle Tennessee and for a while made serious inroads into Unionist East Tennessee, embodied several distinct elements. Within their ranks were former Whigs, Know Nothings, and of course lifelong Democrats; the vast majority were former Confederates, but some were Union men who had rejected the extremes of Radicalism. The party, which included men of such diverse antecedents as Andrew Johnson, Thomas A. R. Nelson, Isham G. Harris, A. O. P. Nicholson, and Nathan Bedford Forrest, had at least one strong bond of union: their determination that the Radical extremists should not rise to a dominant position within the state. Republican support came chiefly from East Tennessee, but a few of the counties along the Tennessee River in the western part of the state which had voted against secession also were counted within party ranks. The conduct of the Brownlow group had decimated Republican ranks, but the assurance that the leaders could control the Negro vote strengthened flagging Republican morale.

The first gubernatorial election under the new constitution was held in November, 1870, and resulted in a decisive victory for the Democrats. The work of John C. Brown in the constitutional convention led to his nomination as the Democratic standard bearer; Republicans had selected William Wisener of Shelbyville, who also had been a delegate to the convention. Not only was Brown elected by a 2 to 1 majority, but his party captured 20 of the 25 senatorial seats and 60 of the 75 places in the house. Furthermore, they won 6 of the 8 seats in Congress and, still not satisfied, began to make plans to capture at least one of the congressional seats held by Republicans. Democrats were chosen to fill all of the major offices of the state, and vengeful legislators announced plans to gerrymander the state so that Republicans would be excluded from all congressional and legislative seats.

The vindictive policy pursued by the former Confederates within Democratic ranks drove some Conservative Unionists from the fold and resulted in a serious breach in 1872. Thomas A. R. Nelson and other Unionists sought to form a third party in conjunction with the abortive Liberal Republican movement of that year. Andrew Johnson, whose indomitable ambition remained undimmed by unjustified treatment accorded him by Washington Radicals, caused the most serious break. Shortly after his return from the nation's capital, he entered a contest for United States senator. Defeated, he then plunged into a race for congressman-at-large against Democratic nominee Benjamin F. Cheatham and Republican Horace Maynard.

Republicans nominated Alfred A. Freeman of Haywood County as their gubernatorial candidate and Democrats chose Brown for reelection. Maynard and Freeman quietly sought a united Republican front, while Johnson, whose hatred of the privileged class and the Confederate leaders became even more pronounced after the war, was determined to defeat them even at the expense of party harmony. Consequently, Maynard was elected. Although Brown was reelected by a small majority, the Democratic congressional majority was reduced to a minority, and a fusion of Republicans and Johnson Democrats controlled the legislature.

Republican hopes of gaining a larger measure of control through cooperation with the Johnson Democratic wing soon were destroyed by the conduct of Republicans in Washington. In 1874, Charles Sumner, whose animosity toward former Confederates was well known, proposed a civil rights bill which provided that "all persons" should be entitled to "the full and equal" enjoyment of all accommodations of hotels, theaters, common carriers, and the like. The measure, later declared unconstitutional, was sufficient to solidify Democrats for the election of 1874. They nominated James D. Porter of Henry County for governor and charged that Congressman Maynard, now the Republican nominee, was an ardent integrationist. Maynard vigorously denied the charge and repeatedly asserted his belief that while Negroes should have equal rights, legislation upon the matter was not necessary. He did not, however, convince either Republicans or Democrats in any part of the state. Porter, thanks to the Civil Rights Bill, carried even the Republican stronghold of East Tennessee and defeated the congressman by a 2 to 1 majority. Republican stock fell so low that even Parson Brownlow was reported to have voted the Democratic ticket in a Knoxville election in 1875. His son, John B. Brownlow, wrote of the "fearful demoralization" within the party caused by "Sumner's legacy."

The legislature which assembled in 1875 elected Andrew Johnson to the United States Senate to replace Brownlow, whose term soon would expire. The former President had returned to Greeneville in March, 1869, and had begun immediately to rebuild political fences. In April, 1869, he told a Knoxville audience that he would devote the rest of his life to a vindication of his public career. When Johnson spoke to Negro groups, he not infrequently reminded them that it was he, not Lincoln, who had freed the slaves in Tennessee. Before farmer and debtor groups, he denounced the rich bondholders and implied that the legislators should repudiate the public debt. He had been nominated for the Senate soon after his return from Washington, but had been defeated. In 1872 he was mentioned as a candidate for governor, but ran instead for congressman-at-large. In the autumn of 1874, Johnson launched a statewide campaign in the interest of his senatorial candidacy. When the legislature convened in January, 1875, nearly a dozen names were presented for consideration, but the voting soon narrowed to a contest among Johnson, John C. Brown, and General William B. Bate. President Grant sent word that if Johnson were elected he would consider it a "personal insult." Despite Grant's influence (whether real or imagined), Johnson won on the fifty-fifth ballot after several days of voting. He considered the victory a great personal triumph because it would enable him to return to the body which had tried his impeachment. He took his seat on March 4, 1875, and promptly denounced President Grant as a charlatan. He suffered a stroke a few weeks later, however, and died on July 31. David M. Key of Chattanooga was appointed to fill the vacancy.

Tennessee Republicans were demoralized in 1876 from the effects of "Sumner's legacy" and "Grantism." They refused even to nominate a candidate for governor but divided their support among Dorsey B. Thomas, an independent who formerly was speaker of the senate, George Maney, a former Confederate general and railroad official, and William F. Yardley, a Knoxville Negro lawyer and justice of the peace. Porter was reelected by a decisive majority. In the same year, Democratic presidential candidate Samuel J. Tilden carried Tennessee, but later was "counted out" by a special electoral commission formed by the federal Congress to determine the results of the disputed election. The successful candidate, Rutherford B. Hayes, appointed Senator David M. Key of Chattanooga as postmaster-general.

Governor Porter refused a third term in 1878, and Democratic leaders nominated Albert S. Marks of Winchester. Republicans chose E. M. Wight, a medical doctor from Chattanooga. The National Greenback party, which had made a national appearance in 1876, nominated R. M. Edwards of Cleveland. The question of the state debt became the major issue, and solutions to the problem were offered in the platforms of the three parties.

For more than a decade after the Democratic restoration, the dominating issue in state politics was the question of the state debt. As has been observed in earlier chapters, the state had pursued a very liberal policy in promoting the development of railroads during the three decades before the election of Governor Brown. Although some of the Southern states had established state-owned railroads, Tennessee had loaned its credit to private railroad corporations; earlier it had purchased stock in railroad and turnpike companies, which proved generally unproductive. Before Brownlow's election, state funds had been invested generally in sound bank stock and in loans to railroad companies which were required to make semiannual interest payments on the state bonds and to contribute to a sinking fund for their retirement at maturity. Tennessee first issued bonds in 1832 in order to purchase $500,000 of stock in the Union Bank of Tennessee. More bond issues were authorized in 1836 and 1838 to aid internal improvements and to provide one million dollars' worth of stock for the state-owned Bank of Tennessee. None of the Bank of Tennessee bonds had been retired by the time of the Civil War, but three-fourths of the Union Bank bonds had been paid off. Other bonds were issued to complete the state capitol, to purchase the Hermitage property, and to aid the Agriculture Bureau in erecting buildings at the Fair Grounds. The destruction occasioned by the Civil War weakened the railroad companies to such an extent that after 1865 many of them could no longer make payments; the state, however, still was liable for the debt and the accruing interest. The Brownlow policy of free-spending, in which reckless and fraudulent loans were made even to hopelessly bankrupt lines, has been discussed in an earlier chapter. At the time of Brownlow's election, the principal of the "state debt proper"—which included obligations for the banks, the internal improvement companies, the capitol, and the Hermitage property—totaled $3,894,600; the principal on the railroad debt was $16,213,000. The total debt, principal and interest, amounted to over $25,277,000. By the time of Brown's election, the debt exceeded $43,000,000, much of which was the "railroad debt."

Republicans agreed that the debt should be repaid; if the debt were scaled down, however, it should be done only with the consent of the creditors. Democrats were divided on the matter. Although all Democrats blamed Republicans for the debt and accused them of bad judgment and fraud, the industrial—or "state credit"—wing favored full payment and demanded that the state's credit be maintained. Talk of default, they believed, would frighten away Northern capital and consign Tennessee to an agrarian grave. Opinions among other elements in the party varied. Some people advocated outright repudiation of the debt; they said that the Brownlow administration, which issued many of the bonds, was a revolutionary government by usurpation and did not represent the whole people. Others recommended negotiation with bondholders to arrive at a fair but realistic figure consistent with the state's ability to pay. The latter group generally was known as "low tax" Democrats.

The debt question did not become acute until after the Panic of 1873. During the administration of John C. Brown the debt was reduced to nearly one-third, but the depression which followed made further payment difficult. A funding act (at par value), passed in 1873, authorized the issuance of more 6 per cent bonds to take care of the unpaid interest on the debt, but two years later the state defaulted in the payment of interest on the bonds. During Porter's administration, bondholders became increasingly uneasy as talk of repudiation became rife. Bonds which in 1873 sold on the market at 79 cents on the dollar declined to an all-time low of 35 cents in

1878. Early in December, the governor called the legislature into extra session and announced that bondholders had agreed to accept a settlement whereby they would be paid 60 cents on the dollar. This was rejected by the legislature. At a second extra session, legislators were unable to agree when a proposal of 50 cents on the dollar was made, and the session adjourned with nothing accomplished.

Albert S. Marks defeated his two gubernatorial opponents in 1878 and pledged to the voters that he would settle the debt question by means of a popular referendum. He formed a legislative committee to study the question and make recommendations. The ensuing report showed that during the Brownlow administration railroad officials had conspired to defraud the state, had not complied with the terms of the appropriation measures, and had given a generous present to the Brownlow family in order to insure protection. This evidence strengthened the demand that the "Brownlow debt" be repudiated and caused interest to mount in favor of repudiating the entire "railroad" debt. Legislators then enacted a measure providing that, subject to the will of the people, some of the debt (the Mineral Home Railroad bonds) would be repudiated, and some would be paid at 30 per cent, some at 50 per cent, and some at 60 per cent. Voters, however, defeated the proposal by a vote of 76,333 to 49,772.

Division within the Democratic party in 1880 enabled a Republican to win as governor. The state credit faction chose John V. Wright of Columbia as its candidate; the low tax group (or repudiationists, as they were sometimes called) nominated S. F. Wilson of Sumner County. Republicans selected Alvin Hawkins of Huntingdon, and the Greenback-Labor party chose R. M. Edwards. Last minute efforts by Democrats to restore party harmony were unavailing, and Hawkins was elected by more than 25,000 votes. The Republicans, like the Democrats, were unable to solve the problem of the state debt, although legislators were called into extra session. One attempted settlement was declared unconstitutional by the supreme court and another was rejected by the creditors.

It remained for Governor William B. Bate, Hawkins's successor, to solve the debt problem. Democrats in 1882 united behind the former Confederate general in fear that Republicans would continue in control, and Bate defeated Hawkins by more than 27,000 votes.

In March, 1883, legislators arrived at a settlement suitable to the creditors. Some of the debt, particularly bonds held by Mrs. James K. Polk and by educational, literary, and charitable institutions, were paid in full. The railroad debt, except for the repudiated Mineral Home bonds, were paid at 50 cents on the dollar and 3 per cent interest. The remainder of the debt was divided into three parts, and some of it was paid off at 76 cents, some at 79 cents, and some at 80 cents on the dollar. The creditors, weary from the years of turmoil, accepted the offer. Thus, the troublesome debt question had come to an end and party harmony—albeit ephemeral—was restored within Democratic ranks.

Negroes Enter Politics ই Negroes became active in Tennessee politics soon after gaining the right to vote in 1867 and to hold office in 1868. Leaders entered many local political contests and one ran for governor; few, however, were successful. The first Negro to serve in the house of representatives was elected in 1872, but during the 1880's nearly a dozen were elected. None served in the state senate, federal Congress, or as governor. Practically all voted the Republican ticket, but some became discouraged when they received little support from the white party leaders.

One of the first Negroes to achieve political success was Sampson W. Keeble, a Nashville barber and bank director, who was elected to the house of representatives in 1872. He attended Governor Brown's banquet for the legislators at the Maxwell House Hotel and sat (according to one account) "side by side with his fellow members and with them drank champagne, and said afterwards he was treated with utmost courtesy." Keeble served only one term and introduced only three bills, none of which passed beyond first reading. On practically all issues he followed the lead of L. C. Houk, Knox County representative and Republican leader.

No other Negro served in the legislature during the decade, but William Francis Yardley became a candidate for governor in 1876. An intelligent, well-trained, and affluent Knoxville lawyer and businessman, Yardley had held several local offices in Knoxville and Knox County before 1876. His race for governor caused white Republicans considerable embarrassment, especially when Democratic leaders encouraged him and publicized his campaign in the leading newspapers. He polled few votes, however, and soon retired from state politics.

During the 1880's, other Negroes served in the house of representatives. T. F. Cassels and I. F. Norris of Shelby County, J. W. Boyd of Tipton County, and Thomas A. Sykes of Davidson County were elected in 1880. They considered Cassels to be their spokesman, and he introduced several measures, one of which would repeal the segregation act of 1875. The law had given innkeepers, carriers of passengers, and operators of places of amusement the right to admit or exclude persons from their places of business in the same manner as might the owner of a private home. When the measure to repeal the segregation law failed, the four Negroes issued a protest in which they asserted that "four hundred thousand citizens are citizens *de jure,* but are aliens *de facto* and entitled to no rights that the railroads, hotels, and theaters are bound to respect." Later in the session a compromise measure was passed which provided that all railroads should furnish separate but equal facilities for Negroes. Specifically, the law required "separate cars, or portions of cars cut off by partition walls, in which all colored passengers who pay first class passenger rates of fare, may have the privilege to enter and occupy . . . ." Negroes objected to colored passengers, including women, being forced to ride in smoking cars.

In 1883, Representative Boyd, together with Samuel A. McElwee of Haywood County, Leon Howard of Shelby County, and D. F. Rivers of Fayette County, fought an unsuccessful battle to end segregation on the railroads. McElwee, a Fisk graduate and a lawyer, was the most capable of the four and returned to the house in 1885 and 1887. In 1885 he was joined by Greene E. Evans and W. A. Fields of Shelby County, and William C. Hodge of Hamilton County. McElwee became a candidate for speaker of the house and polled thirty-two votes out of ninety-three. In 1885 Evans sought to end segregation in the public carriers, but his proposal did not get beyond the committee room. McElwee was joined by S. L. Hutchins of Hamilton and M. W. Gooden of Fayette in 1887, and they were the last Negroes to serve in the General Assembly until 1965.[1] In 1891 an all-white legislature passed a more effective law requiring "Jim Crow" cars in the railroads.

[1] J. M. H. Graham, a Clarksville Negro, was elected from Montgomery County in

Industry and Agriculture ॐ After the Civil War many pragmatic captains of industry came to regard the great struggle of 1861–65 as but a clash of economic systems and Appomattox as but a symbol of defeat for a decaying economic order. To them, the Old South of slavery and secession was dead, and upon its grave a New South of industry and commerce was destined to be constructed. Weaving together the humanitarian and materialistic motives which characterized American imperialistic ventures in the Pacific at the end of the century, they sought to establish in the South an economic system comparable to that in the victorious North. They were joined by numerous articulate supporters of the New South philosophy in Tennessee and throughout the South.

Although the Volunteer State remained primarily agricultural to the end of the century, proponents of industrialization became very active in the three decades following the war. Scarcely had the noise of battle ceased when the urban press began a campaign for industry and "economic carpetbaggers." Colonel A. S. Colyar of Nashville, Judge James E. Bailey of Clarksville, Joseph B. Killebrew of Nashville, and others proclaimed from the rostrum the virtues of materialism. Typical of the press statements was one appearing in the Chattanooga *Daily Republican*:

> The people of Chattanooga no longer wishing to stay in the background, and feeling the necessity of immediately developing the vast mineral resources surrounding them, . . . extend a general invitation to all carpet-baggers to leave the bleak winds of the North and come to Chattanooga . . . .
>
> Those who wish to come can be assured that they will not be required to renounce their political and religious tenets . . . .

Editors throughout the state frequently admonished their readers for their continuing sectional animosities and urged them to forgive and forget, lest Northern businessmen and skilled laborers be frightened away.

While Northern capital did not flow into the state in the proportions which some Tennesseans hoped, fortune seekers from the North did establish many industries. Within two months after Appomattox, a number of companies received charters. Among them

---

1896, but he was disqualified by the house members when they determined that he had not complied with residence requirements.

were the Tennessee and Kentucky Petroleum, Mining, and Manufacturing Company; the East Tennessee Union Petroleum, Coal, Iron, and Salt Company; the Tennessee Mountain Petroleum and Mining Company; the New York and Tennessee Petroleum and Mining Company; and the Tennessee Mining and Manufacturing Company.

Although small towns became sites for some factories, the urban areas—particularly Knoxville and Chattanooga—attracted most of the money from the North and East. The Knoxville Industrial Association, organized soon after the war, became a vigorous campaigner for industrial establishments. Although in 1868 members of the group complained because Knoxville did not get its "fair share" of Yankee capital, statistics show that by the following year one-sixth of the business properties of Knoxville were owned by Northern businessmen. By that date the Knoxville Iron Company, which included a rolling mill, a foundry, a machine shop, a nail mill, and a railroad spike machine had been established by a federal officer; many other factories produced soap, flour, paper, and a variety of products. According to a Richmond newspaper in 1871, "no city of the South except Atlanta" had "improved more rapidly since the war" than had Knoxville.

Chattanooga grew even more rapidly than Knoxville. Although the main street was described as a "mudhole" as late as 1868, conditions improved immediately after that date. The twenty-two small industries which in 1860 had employed 214 men no longer represented a true picture of industrial Chattanooga; by 1870 fifty-eight industrial establishments employed nearly two thousand workers. By that date J. T. Wilder, often described as "the greatest of the carpetbaggers," and Colonel S. B. Lowe had returned to Chattanooga. Wilder established the Roane Iron Company in Roane County and brought into the thriving business a defunct rolling mill in Chattanooga. In 1878 the Roane company made use of the first open hearth furnace south of the Ohio River. Colonel Lowe established the Vulcan Iron Works. Furniture factories, sawmills, gristmills, and many other types of factories had been established by 1883, but the iron works predominated. The editor of the Chattanooga *Daily Times* noted the progress with pride and wrote that

the frozen fingers of the North have been laid in the warm palms of the South, and a healthful, invigorating temperature pervades them both as one body. They are moving in united thought—united action, placing wherever they tread some monument of their skill, industry, and patriotism, and garlanding the nation with their intelligence and virtue.

Memphians and Nashvillians of course joined in the search for industry. The Memphis Chamber of Commerce reorganized in 1865 to begin a vigorous campaign for industry. Soon such a "rush and roar of business" prompted a visitor from Kentucky to predict that the river town in a short time would surpass St. Louis as a manufacturing and commercial center. By 1870, Memphis had many business establishments and had become the greatest processor of cotton seed in the Union. The yellow fever scourge which threatened to decimate the population during the 1870's hindered the growth of the city considerably and caused it to lag behind the other three major cities in industrial growth. By 1880, however, the worst of the dread disease was over, and Memphis again moved forward industrially. By 1869, Nashvillians could point to new liquor distilleries, sawmills, paper mills, gristmills, stove factories, and an oil refinery. A few years later the Nashville Woolen Mill Company was organized, and the cotton market in the capital was described by a Northern visitor as being "brisk." A Nashville editor in 1883 prophesied industrial greatness for the city, and urged the people to discover the "road to wealth" and happiness through "the workshop, the factory, the foundry, and the iron and coal beds."

Manufacturing plants of various sizes were constructed in other counties and towns. Immediately after the war, Julius Eckhardt Raht returned to his East Tennessee copper mines and opened offices in Cleveland. The Jackson Flouring Mills were built in Jackson in 1868, and the Jackson Woolen Manufacturing Company began operation a few years later. By 1880, one of the largest woolen mills in the state had been established in Tullahoma.

The industrial growth of the state had been rapid in the several years following Appomattox. By 1870 the value of manufactured goods for the state had increased nearly twofold over that of 1860; the number of plant units had increased from 2,500 to 5,300, and the number of industrial workers from 12,500 to 19,400. Development was arrested for a few years after the Panic of 1873. By the end of the decade, however, more people were employed than in 1870. Some plants had been consolidated and others had not reopened so

that only about four thousand factories were in operation in that
year; however, 22,445 people found employment in them. About
one-fourth of the plants were grist and flour mills, but carriage and
wagon shops flourished, as did tobacco and whisky manufacturing
establishments.

As leaders of the New South movement sought industry, many
rural people quietly beat their swords into plowshares and diligently
tilled the soil. Joseph B. Killebrew, secretary of the Bureau of Agriculture of Tennessee, made an extensive study of agriculture and
labor during the early 1870's and found Tennessee farmers to be in
what was termed "fairly good condition." In West Tennessee, people cultivated cotton profitably. Memphis was the thriving cotton
center and experienced in 1870 the greatest volume of sales since
1860. Although cotton sold for fourteen and three-eighths cents per
pound—the lowest since the war—West Tennesseans apparently did
not become discouraged. Middle Tennesseans grew a variety of
crops, including cotton, corn, tobacco, potatoes, and peanuts. East
Tennesseans also grew a variety of crops and livestock.

Hard times, falling prices, and an unsatisfactory credit system
drove many farmers into bankruptcy and tenancy. By the end of the
century, cotton reached an all-time low of four and three-fourths
cents on the New Orleans market, and other crops—corn, tobacco,
and wheat—had declined accordingly. Cotton production declined,
as farmers who remained on the soil shifted to livestock and greater
diversification. Many farmers, however, faced by the stark realities,
lost confidence in the economic god of their fathers, and sought
jobs in the nearby plants and factories.

Immigration ৪৯ Leaders of the New South movement
who saw in the agrarian system an incubus which prevented Tennessee from taking its rightful place in the economic structure of the
nation made a strong bid for immigrants; they sought Yankees and
foreigners with equal enthusiasm. Parson Brownlow, the scourge
of foreigners and Catholics in the 1850's when he championed the
cause of the Know Nothing party, strongly courted immigrants
during his years as governor. Farmers in a state agricultural convention held at Nashville in 1873 deplored "laziness and unreliability" of native laborers and called for Northern immigrants. The

editor of the Knoxville *Daily Press and Herald* observed that both Negroes and native whites made poor industrial workers, and urged that they make way for "intelligent labor" from the North. Editors of newspapers in the four metropolitan centers called for immigrants almost daily. A correspondent for a West Tennessee paper deplored the fact that state officials "were idle" while "hundreds of thrifty immigrants are pouring into other and more uninviting localities."

State officials, however, were not idle. In 1867, Hermann Bokum, an East Tennessee Unionist, was commissioned to compose a "handbook" advertising the economic potentialities of the state. The book, published in 1868, contained messages both to Tennesseans and to prospective residents. European farmers and laborers, Bokum wrote, had constituted the backbone of the world's economic advancement; Tennessee and the South would continue to remain behind other states unless they obtained outside capital, labor, and technical skill. To prospective residents, he depicted Tennessee as an area of virgin timber and minerals, cheap land and fertile soil, and peace-loving and hard-working people. In the same year, William Darby's *Emigrant's Guide*—a small book which presented an exaggerated picture of the industrial and agricultural potentialities of the state—was published. At Brownlow's insistence, legislators appointed standing committees on immigration and established a state board of immigration. Democrats who came into power in 1870 anxiously tried to attract immigrants, and their brochures contained as many exaggerations as did those published by the Radicals. Governor James D. Porter, for example, in 1877 told an audience in Philadelphia that Tennessee had "mountains of iron and coal, with no one to work them; an absence of muscle as well as of capital." He urged the "dissatisfied sons of Pennsylvania" not to go West, "but South."

Although people came from Prussia, France, England, Scotland, Ireland, and other European countries, their number was small. Equally few were the immigrants from Pennsylvania, Indiana, Ohio, New York, Wisconsin, Connecticut, and other Northern states. The state census of 1870, for example, shows that less than 2 per cent of the population was foreign born, and that the number of foreigners in Tennessee in that year was actually less than the number in 1860. Colyar, Bailey, Killebrew, John Moffat (secretary of the

Tennessee Immigration and Labor Association), and other exponents of the New South did not become discouraged; they continued to write and speak of the golden opportunities which awaited
immigrants and captains of industry. When realists pointed to the
small number of immigrants, Colyar and others always offered hope.
Much was made of a letter written by a Minnesotan in 1875 in
which the writer purported to speak for many Northern immigrants:
"We are coming, fifty thousand men. Not in hostile array, but with
plows and spades, . . . and skilled labor and with capital to . . . develop your mighty resources." In 1881, Killebrew answered critics
by asserting that thousands of skilled artisans and workers from
England and Ireland were on the verge of coming to the New World.
He was confident that the British iron and coal deposits were exhausted and that the exodus of workers was imminent.

Although the immigrants did not come in the numbers expected, the influx of Northern capital was of benefit to the state
and offered employment to many Tennesseans. The four urban
centers, especially, were showing definite signs of becoming industrial centers of the future. Despite the destruction caused by the
Civil War, Tennesseans by 1885 were well along the road to
recovery.

SUGGESTED READINGS

General Accounts

Alexander, *Political Reconstruction*; Folmsbee, Corlew, and Mitchell,
Tennessee, II, Ch. 30; Hamer, *Tennessee*, II, Chs. 41–43; White, *Messages*, V, VI.

Specialized Accounts

Clyde Ball, "The Public Career of Colonel A. S. Colyar, 1870–1877,"
THQ, XII (March, June, Sept., 1953), 23–47, 106–28, 213–38; Barclay,
Ducktown; Constantine G. Belissary, "Tennessee and Immigration,
1865–1880," *THQ*, VII (Sept., 1948), 229–48; Belissary, "The Rise of
Industry and the Industrial Spirit in Tennessee, 1865–1885," *JSH*, XIX
(May, 1953), 193–215; Campbell, "East Tennessee During the Radical
Regime," ETHS *Publ.*, No. 20, 84–102; James F. Doster, "The Chattanooga Rolling Mill: An Industrial By-product of the Civil War," ETHS
Publ., No. 36 (1964), 45–55; Folmsbee, *East Tennessee University*;
Folmsbee, "The Origin of the First 'Jim Crow' Law," *JSH*, XV (May,

1949), 235–47; LeRoy P. Graf (ed.), " 'Parson' Brownlow's Fears: A Letter About the Dangerous, Desperate Democrats," ETHS *Publ.*, No. 25 (1953), 111–14; William B. Hesseltine, "Tennessee's Invitation to Carpet-Baggers," ETHS *Publ.*, No. 4 (1932), 102–15; Verton M. Queener, "A Decade of East Tennessee Republicanism, 1867–1876," ETHS *Publ.*, No. 14 (1942), 59–85; Queener, "The East Tennessee Republicans as a Minority Party, 1870–1896," ETHS *Publ.*, No. 15 (1943), 49–73; Samuel Boyd Smith, "Joseph Buckner Killebrew and the New South Movement in Tennessee," ETHS *Publ.*, No. 37 (1965), 5–22; James E. Thorogood, A *Financial History of Tennessee Since 1870* (Sewanee, 1949); Frank B. Williams, "The Poll Tax as a Suffrage Requirement in the South, 1870–1901," *JSH*, XVIII (Nov., 1952), 469–96; Monroe N. Work (comp.), "Some Negro Members of Reconstruction Conventions and Legislatures and of Congress," *JNH*, V (Jan., 1920), 63–119.

THE SETTLEMENT of the state debt was Governor Bate's outstanding accomplishment during his first term. Although the industrial wing of his party blamed him for not paying all off at par and some of the rural Democrats believed that he had honored fraudulent bonds, the majority of Tennesseans were pleased that Bate had settled a question which had plagued the state for over a decade. The former Confederate general's personal popularity enabled him in 1884 to defeat the Republican gubernatorial candidate, Frank T. Reid of Nashville, but the election returns clearly indicated that the breach in the Democratic party had not been healed completely. Despite the Democratic victory in the presidential election, Bate's majority in Tennessee was reduced from nearly 30,000 (in 1882) to 7,000. Also discouraging to Democratic leaders was the election of Republicans to the railroad commission which had been established recently. Industrialists in the Democratic party bitterly resented the law of 1883 which gave the commission power to regulate railroads. The fact that during Bate's second administration industrialists brought about the repeal of the regulatory act (but only after a bitter legislative fight and over the veto of the governor) caused wider rents to appear in the Democratic fabric.

Political Factions ₴ Even after the settlement of the debt question, at least four powerful political groups were evident; three were factions within the Democratic party, and the fourth was the Republican party. In addition, other groups, associated with the agrarian movement, appeared. One of the Democratic factions had formed during the slavery controversy and consisted of those who followed Calhoun's doctrine of state sovereignty. Although the group was evident as early as the 1830's, its influence had been minimized by the nationalism of Jackson and Polk until the gubernatorial accession of Isham G. Harris and the secession movement which followed. During the 1860's, the faction went into eclipse temporarily, but the return of Democrats to power in 1870 brought it again to the forefront. Having within their ranks the vast majority of the former Confederates, and being able generally to control the party machinery, members often were called "the machine crowd" and "the Bourbons." To Andrew Johnson, however, who was able temporarily to interrupt their influence during the early 1870's, the leaders always were the "damned brigadiers." Former Governor Harris, who was elected to the United States Senate in 1877, secured and retained undisputed control of the group until his death two decades later.[1]

A second faction was composed of conservative industrialists who had within its ranks most proponents of the "New South" philosophy. Leaders agreed with Republicans on some matters, especially that of industrialism. Although relatively small in number, this faction exerted an influence disproportionate to their size because of the enormity of their resources. Also, their inclination toward some of the Republican policies enabled them often to bargain with the machine group if their wants went unheeded. During most of the time they looked for leadership to Colonel Arthur S. Colyar, a Nashville industrialist, lawyer, newspaper publisher, and politician who had organized the Tennessee Coal, Iron, and Railroad Company. Over the last two decades, the group, composed almost entirely of old-line Whigs, had been driven into the Democratic party by various factors, including the war policies of Lincoln, the war itself, Reconstruction, and the race question.

The third group, composed of the small-farmer elements—sometimes called the "wool-hat boys"—were descended from the old

[1] Some writers, in discussing reconstruction of the South, place the industrial faction along with the Bourbons. The "redeemers," as they often are called, were a polyglot group which secured control after Reconstruction ended. In Tennessee, however, the three factions appear more pronounced than in the South as a whole and are discussed as such here.

Jackson-Polk-Johnson Democrats of an earlier period. These sons of toil were led by Andrew Johnson, who sought to recoup his political fortunes after his retirement from the White House. His death in 1875, however, left this segment of the party leaderless for a decade despite the fact that it was the oldest and strongest numerically among the factions. The apathy of the agrarian group was such that Harris feared for the future of the party. Finally, in 1886, conditions within the party became favorable for the emergence of a new leader. From Happy Valley in Washington County came Robert Love Taylor, and the rural element united behind him and fondly referred to him as "Our Bob."

The fourth group was the Republican party. It was composed almost entirely of Unionists located in the counties which had voted against secession in 1861. Because of the divisions within Democratic ranks, Republicans showed strength throughout the last third of the century. Although they were divided into two factions over the control of federal patronage, they usually could patch up their differences on election day. The enfranchisement of Negroes increased the number of Republican voters. L. C. Houk of Knoxville and H. Clay Evans of Chattanooga were the leaders of the party.

Other groups—Greenback, Prohibition, Agricultural Wheel, Farmers' Alliance, and Populist—made inroads into both the Democratic and Republican ranks. In 1890 the agricultural wing of the Democratic party, in league with the Alliance men, elected the governor and controlled the legislature. The ingress into Republican ranks was far less serious and at no time threatened to break the party's hold in the eastern section.

"The War of the Roses"—the Election of 1886 ᔆ᠊ Lack of harmony within the party, together with the rising threat of Republicanism, led Democrats urgently to seek a candidate who could unify the three factions in time for the election of 1886. As the Bate administration continued in power, the lack of harmony among followers of Harris and Colyar became more pronounced, and the growing apathy of the rural Democracy alarmed party leaders. "Our party needs reorganization. We have been . . . discordant, belligerent, and . . . rent with feuds" which threatened to destroy the party, Bob Taylor told Nashville Democrats early in

January, 1886. To Taylor and other party leaders, a factional truce appeared necessary if the political lifeblood was to continue to flow in Democratic veins. Fortunately, state and national issues were not of sufficient consequence to cause dissension within the party; should they become ominous, party leaders were determined to compromise or postpone them in the interest of party harmony. The selection of a candidate resulted in compromise. Young men desired more recognition within the party, and rural voters, perhaps inspired by the developing agrarian movements in the South and West, could be awakened from their lethargy if a suitable candidate were nominated. The most satisfactory candidate, therefore, would be one who could satisfy the demands of the younger generation of Democrats, please the rural voters, appeal to Democrats in East Tennessee, and conciliate the industrial and Bourbon wings of the party.

Thirty-six-year-old Bob Taylor, an East Tennessean who captured the imagination of the young Democrats and the rural element, won the nomination on the fifteenth ballot. A man of conciliatory manners who could arouse the enthusiasm of the common people, Taylor understood well that his role as head of the state's majority party would be to unite the party factions. Even during the balloting when the convention seemed deadlocked at one point, he had advised friends that he did "not want the nomination at the cost of bitterness." His nomination not only brought better party relations, but also presaged a decline of the influence of the "brigadiers," continuing influence of the young party leaders, and the beginning in Tennessee of the agrarian revolt which was to loom large in state politics for the next decade.

Interestingly, the Republicans had nominated Taylor's brother, Alfred A. Taylor (usually called "Alf"), seven weeks before the Democratic convention. A man of considerable ability but who lacked his brother's personal magnetism, Alf was selected apparently to forestall the nomination of Bob, whom Republicans feared. Thus, the nomination of the brothers launched the "War of the Roses," a political tradition remembered among the people even to this day.

Tennesseans always have been infatuated with a colorful political campaign; in 1886 they were not to be disappointed. From the first of the forty-one joint debates to the balloting on election day, both Democrats and Republicans enjoyed a campaign which attracted nationwide interest. In the same spirit that Whigs and Democrats had chosen symbols in the campaign of 1844, Democrats and Republicans of 1886 chose the white rose of York and the red rose of Lancaster as their respective emblems. Enormous crowds thronged around the heroes. At Murfreesboro, for example, 3,000 men escorted Bob to his hotel; at Franklin, 8,000 listeners attended the hustings; and at Columbia, 1,000 mounted men met the train which brought the candidates into the city.

The bitterness which had characterized many gubernatorial campaigns in past years was not apparent. On many occasions the brothers traveled, slept, and ate together. On the platform each defended his party with vigor, but elsewhere they were friendly, jovial brothers. Both were skilled "fiddle" players and both told a variety of stories and anecdotes;[2] listeners generally agreed, however, that Bob's "unpruned" rhetoric and droll anecdotes, his fiddle, and his charming manner outshone Alf's. Issues were pushed into the background. Neither candidate advanced profound arguments and discussions, but the brothers did provide a "happy interlude" at a time when party and factional strife, to say nothing of racial and sectional bitterness, still clouded the memories of many people.

Bob's popularity with the rural masses enabled him to defeat Alf by a majority of over 16,000. While the victory was by no means a landslide, the margin was more than twice that of Bate's in 1884, which attested to Taylor's ability as a party conciliator. For the next decade his most useful role in the Democratic party was to be that of pouring oil on the troubled waters of factionalism within his party.

Bob Taylor received the Democratic nomination again in 1888, despite formidable opposition within his party, and defeated Republican candidate Samuel W. Hawkins and Prohibition candidate J. C. Johnson. Taylor's stand on the Blair Bill, a measure which

---

[2] Many stories amused the audiences. Bob on one occasion found Alf's speech (some people claimed that their father, Nathaniel, wrote the addresses for both sons) and committed it to memory. When the brothers met on the platform on the following day, Bob, speaking first, delivered Alf's speech. The embarrassed and chagrined Alf hastily had to construct a new one.

Many stories centered around "fiddle" playing. Still told in Happy Valley is the story of Bob's tale of a paroled convict who returned unexpectedly to his mountain home after a two-year stay in the penitentiary to find his wife tending her three-months-old baby. The parolee said nothing but merely took from beneath his coat a fiddle on which he played the mountain ballad, "Who's Been Here Since I've Been Gone."

would provide federal aid to education, proved to be the major issue in the contest. Although Senator Howell E. Jackson and several members of the House supported the bill, most Tennesseans agreed with other Southerners that federal aid would result in federal-controlled schools. Therefore, when Taylor expressed approbation of the measure, a storm of protest arose. Students at Cumberland University burned him in effigy, and editors across the state decried his alleged apostasy to "Southern Democracy." Consequently, not until after six days of wrangling and forty ballots did Taylor overcome the opposition of the state's rights wing within his party and win the nomination. The campaign was colorless and listless in contrast to the preceding one, and Taylor won handily.

The administrations of Bob Taylor are remembered not for profound and far-reaching legislation but for the stability which he gave to his party and for several laws enacted to facilitate suffrage. Among them were laws designed to preserve the purity of the ballot box, promote honest elections, and to raise revenue for schools. One law, the Dortch Law, specified that in the more populous counties and cities voters should mark printed ballots in secrecy unless blind or otherwise physically disabled. The second, sometimes referred to as Myer's Registration Law, provided for registration of voters in cities, towns, and civil districts having a voting population of 500 or more. A third, the Lea Election Law, was designed to avoid federal interference in state elections. It provided for separate ballot boxes and for election officials in contests for state and federal offices. A fourth law, enacted in a special session held early in 1890, confirmed the payment of a poll tax as a prerequisite for voting, as required by the constitution of 1870.

Governor Taylor did not disappear from the political scene after the expiration of his second term. Party leaders continued to seek his aid and counsel, especially in 1896, when it seemed that once again the Democratic party might be dashed to pieces on the rocks of factionalism. Taylor returned in that year again to mend the torn fabric of his party and to win election to another term as governor.

The Agrarian Movement ৵ As discussed earlier, farmers of the South and West did not relinquish their position of leadership at the nation's economic table willingly. When each year brought rising costs of production but falling prices of farm products, vigorous leaders organized the farmers and complained that among businessmen there existed a conspiracy to discriminate against tillers of the soil. Although Tennessee, with diversified agriculture and a relatively small Negro population, differed somewhat from the Deep South as well as from the West, the effects of the agrarian movement were felt strongly in the state.

The first farm organization of importance was formed soon after the war by Oliver Hudson Kelley. An employee of the Department of Agriculture, Kelley called the new organization "Patrons of Husbandry," but it soon became known simply as the "Grange." "Its grand object is not only general improvement in husbandry," Kelley announced, "but to increase the general happiness, wealth, and prosperity of the country." Soon the organization spread to the South and West, so that by the early 1870's more than one thousand chapters were located in Tennessee.

Other organizations followed closely on the heels of the Grange. The Greenback movement was next to appear in the state. In contrast to the Grange, it was political in nature and advocated inflation of the currency through the issuance of paper money. Greenback leaders nominated a candidate for each gubernatorial election from 1874 to 1884 (except in 1876) but did not muster sufficient strength to affect materially the outcome of the contests. The National Agricultural Wheel appeared in the state in 1884, and three years later the Farmers' Alliance was established. Both groups grew rapidly, especially in the central and western counties. In December, 1888, the national organizations of the Wheel and Southern Alliance united under the name of "Farmers' and Laborers' Union of America." In July, 1889, members of the two groups in Tennessee met in Nashville and united under the name of "Farmers' Alliance." The new organization consisted primarily of farmers, but also included others closely associated with farmers, such as rural mechanics, teachers, physicians, ministers, and editors of agricultural papers. In 1890 Alliance leaders claimed a membership of over 100,000 and openly sought to capture working control of the Democratic party; their voting strength, however, probably was less than one-half the number claimed.

In view of the organization's strength and purpose, it was only natural that the leaders should look with increasing interest to the election of 1890. John P. Buchanan, of Rutherford County, was the first president of the Tennessee Alliance, and in 1889 he became president of the combined Wheel and Alliance. The real power, however, lay with John H. McDowell, of Obion County, who was a vice president of the Southern branch of the Alliance and editor of a Nashville publication called *The Weekly Toiler*, the principal mouthpiece of the Alliance leaders. Before Democrats assembled in convention on July 15, 1890, McDowell had announced that he would not rest until Buchanan was nominated as the Democratic candidate for governor.

Three parties chose candidates. Among the Democrats, the Bourbon wing supported Josiah Patterson of Memphis, and the Colyar faction pushed forward Jere Baxter of Nashville. As in 1886, however, the rural element gained control, and Buchanan was chosen on the twenty-sixth ballot after three days of voting. The nominee assured all that he would maintain the "great principles of Democracy as enunciated by Jackson, Polk, and Johnson." The Republicans chose Lewis T. Baxter, Nashville banker and businessman. Despite the protests of Baxter, they supported the Lodge Force Bill—the spiritual successor of the Sumner Force Bill mentioned earlier—and thus insured the defeat of their candidate. Prohibitionists nominated D. C. Kelly, a Methodist minister who had had a varied career.

Although not vigorously supported by the Bourbons, Buchanan won the election by a substantial majority. His rural supporters—the "hayseeds," as their urban opponents called them—also would control the legislature. In his inaugural address, Buchanan pointed to the spirit of Andrew Jackson which "stalks abroad and lives in the hearts of the people," and promised his hearers that he, like the Old Hero, would champion the cause of the people against the "trusts" and all else.

The farmer-dominated General Assembly under Buchanan surprised critics by avoiding the extremes advocated by Western agrarians and illustrated generally the conservatism of the Tennessee Farmers' Alliance. Several beneficial laws were enacted. One provided for closer regulation of the sale of commercial fertilizers. Another awarded pensions of $25 per month for totally disabled Confederate veterans. Other laws made more effective the poll tax requirement for voting passed during the Taylor administration, made trusts and other combinations in restraint of trade and production unlawful, and restricted foreign corporations which did business in the state.

Buchanan, however, did not possess the personal magnetism of his predecessor and was unable to win nomination in 1892. While the Harris and Colyar factions found nothing to complain about in regard to the administration in general, they never fully accepted Buchanan and they always regarded McDowell with suspicion. The governor's inability to settle the coal miners' insurrections in East Tennessee (to be discussed presently) and his use of state troops in an attempt to handle the situation angered many voters. Other people complained that Buchanan gave lucrative state jobs to Alliance men rather than to old-line Democrats. Especially galling was the fact that McDowell accepted an important position but continued as editor of *The Toiler*. The formation of the new People's (or Populist) party, however, became the wedge which Democrats used to separate Buchanan from his party. National leaders of the new group sought to pull away enough votes from Democrats and Republicans to create a party of sufficient strength to capture the presidential nomination. The thought of leaving the party of the solid South was highly repugnant to old-line Democrats. Although Buchanan asserted that the formation of a third party of agrarians meant "the ruin of the South," none could deny that the movement had a strong appeal to many of the rural leaders, including McDowell. When the governor refused to break with McDowell, leading Democrats shifted their support to Peter Turney, chief justice of the supreme court. Turney's political star rose rapidly. Buchanan, realizing that he could not win the nomination, withdrew from the contest before the Democratic convention was held and left the field to Turney.

Three candidates in addition to Turney made the race. Governor Buchanan still had a respectable following among rural Democrats. In August he was "drafted" by Alliancemen, Populists, and "Buchanan Democrats," and ran as an independent. Republicans chose George W. Winstead of Dresden, and Prohibitionists named Edward H. East. The shadow of McDowell continued to fall across Buchanan's path. The governor was denounced as a tool of the agrarian leader, an advocate of integration, and a destroyer of the Democratic party. Even more damaging to his bid for reelection was the report of a "deal" engineered by McDowell between Populists and Republicans. Buchanan's candidacy, according to the allegation, would take votes from Turney and insure a Republican victory; McDowell would receive $15,000 in cash and Republican support for the United States Senate. Buchanan's vehement denial did not convince the many who detested McDowell. Reports of the "deal," together with other rumors of Populist-Republican coalitions and the repercussions of the "Coal Miners' War" (to be discussed later), caused many erstwhile Buchanan supporters to break with the governor and hold to the party line. Consequently, Turney, although he received less than half of the votes cast, was elected, and the Bourbons were returned to power. The agrarian movement in Tennessee had reached its height during the Buchanan administration and declined rapidly thereafter.

Peter Turney had enjoyed a distinguished career. The son of Senator Hopkins L. Turney, he had been prominent in politics before the war. In 1861 he had urged Tennesseans to secede and had formed a company of volunteers from his native county of Franklin. He served with distinction during the war and actively opposed Brownlow's reconstruction measures after his return to civilian life. Appointed to the supreme court in 1870, Turney became chief justice in 1886, and performed ably until he exchanged the bench for the governor's chair. While his administration offered little of the spectacular, Turney followed a conservative course which in general was satisfactory to party leaders. Consequently, in 1894 he was nominated for a second term because of the relatively little opposition that he aroused and the threat of Republican and Populist fusion.

The Disputed Election of 1894 ॐ The contest, which ended in a dispute and shook the Democratic party to its foundations, got underway late in August after Republicans chose a Chattanooga industrialist, H. Clay Evans, for the nomination. In addition to managing his extensive business interests in East Tennessee, the Pennsylvania-born industrialist had served four terms as alderman of Chattanooga, two terms as mayor, and one term as congressman. His support of the "Force Bill" while in Congress cost him reelection in 1890 and 1892, and weakened his appeal in the gubernatorial race of 1894. Democratic leaders recognized Evans as one of the most formidable opponents Republicans could offer. Populists nominated A. L. Mims, a Davidson County schoolteacher. Prohibitionists failed to choose a candidate, but they adopted a platform in harmony with that of the Populists.

Turney opened his campaign at Murfreesboro on September 13. The sixty-five-year-old governor spoke briefly before lunch and resumed his position on the platform after an hour of rest and refreshments. Within a few minutes he became exhausted, however, and was forced to call upon his brother to read the remainder of his speech. Democratic leaders now realized that Turney was too feeble to make the active and energetic campaign necessary for election; therefore, Edward Ward Carmack, vigorous editor of the Memphis *Commercial Appeal*, carried the governor's campaign from Memphis to Bristol. Turney's only other oratorical effort was an address to a group of workers in Chattanooga on Labor Day.

Evans, young and vigorous, opened his campaign at Huntingdon on September 5. From that time to his final address at Ashland City on November 5, the industrialist-politician eloquently talked his way across the state. He severely indicted President Cleveland for the manner in which he had handled the gold crisis and accused Turney of not knowing how to run the affairs of state "on business principles." In turn, the most serious charges Evans had to face were those alleging that he was a carpetbagger and that he had voted while a member of Congress for Henry Cabot Lodge's "Force Bill" which would establish federal jurisdiction over congressional and presidential elections. His inability to counter these charges adequately became important factors in the campaign. In September, state Republican leaders announced that Governor William McKinley of Ohio, former Speaker of the House Thomas B. ("Czar") Reed of Maine, and other prominent party members would speak in Tennessee in the interest of Evans's candidacy. Only McKinley came; he delivered an address in Chattanooga on October 20. When the campaign closed at the Cheatham County seat on November 5, Republican chances for victory appeared best in over a decade.

Soon after the returns were tabulated, but before the results were announced, Republicans and Democrats agreed that the election was very close. Turney had lost support in the urban-industrial areas of Nashville and Memphis; even in some rural counties he had not polled as many votes as Democrats had expected. Not until December 13, five weeks after the election, did the secretary of state make public the returns. The official count, which showed a small majority for Evans, gave the Republican candidate 105,104 votes; Turney, 104,356; and Mims, 23,088. Republicans claimed the victory, but Democrats contended that fraud could be proved in some of the counties where Evans had polled a majority. Two weeks later Turney issued notice that he would contest the election.

The legislature, dominated by Democrats, assembled on January 5 and promptly selected a "Committee on the Governor's Election," consisting of seven Democrats and five Republicans. After hearing allegations of fraud from both Turney's and Evans's attorneys, the committee in April filed both a majority and a minority report. The former, signed by the seven Democrats, declared that many violations of the poll tax law had taken place in counties which Evans carried, and declared that when the fraudulent votes were taken from the returns the official count should be Turney, 94,620 votes; Evans, 92,266; and Mims, 23,088. In the minority report the five Republicans questioned the authority of the committee, declared that the seven Democrats showed partiality from the beginning, and alleged that the majority did not seek to develop the whole truth. The contest, they believed, was as fair as any ever held in Tennessee and the returns as originally reported should stand. On May 4, the members of the joint assembly voted 70 to 57 to accept the majority report. Consequently, Governor Turney took the oath of office for a second term on May 8.

Although Evans lost the governorship, he emerged as a hero and a martyr to Republican leaders. He enjoyed an Evans-for-Vice President boom, and when convention leaders assembled his nomination seemed probable. Marcus Alonzo Hanna, however, preferred another; therefore, Evans ran second to the choice of the Republican bosses. Evans nevertheless continued to be active in politics. He became commissioner of pensions under McKinley, and consul-general in London under Theodore Roosevelt.

Turney's victory in 1894 had been won at the expense of party harmony. The industrial wing had opposed the contest from the beginning, and Arthur S. Colyar had served as one of Evans's attorneys during the investigation. Also, among the fifty-seven who opposed the acceptance of the majority report were nine Democrats and ten Populists. Many Democratic newspapers termed the action a "steal" second only to the Tilden-Hayes presidential contest of 1876. Thus, Turney began his second term without the support of a large segment of his party. His enemies soon had fresh ammunition for renewing their attacks. Increased state expenditures, the "Paste Pot" affair (in which Turney's enemies alleged that two of Turney's friends received $3,000 for pasting a few coupons on canceled bonds), failure to appropriate necessary funds for the Tennessee Centennial Exposition, expenses involved in calling the legislature into two extra sessions, and failure to assess railroad property at its true value brought increased dissension within the Democratic ranks and made it evident to all that Turney's administration would pass unwept, unhonored, and unsung.

Democratic prospects looked exceedingly dark in the spring of 1896. The older men among the industrialists showed considerable apathy, and some of the young men even joined the Republicans. Doubtless the Democratic party would have been doomed had not the rural constituency pushed forward the candidacy of Bob Taylor, the conciliator, who, as mentioned, returned to carry the Democratic banner to victory.

Convict Leasing and Prison Reform ঌ Tennessee, in comparison with other Southern states, made considerable improvements in penal reform during the ante bellum period. The war, however, disrupted economic progress and left the state with an enormous debt. Furthermore, the penitentiary had been used as a military prison and was in a dilapidated condition. The enormous increase in prison population after the war added to the problems. Freed Negroes, hungry, confused, and ignorant of the white man's rules, and equally hungry and displaced whites, soon ran afoul of the law and were incarcerated. Negroes, who before the war seldom composed more than 5 per cent of the prison population, made up over half of the inmates by 1866.

State prison operations throughout the United States still were in their infancy and were emerging from an experimental stage. The prevailing belief among authorities was that the prisoners should defray their expenses by hard labor. Tennessee authorities before the war had used penitentiary inmates in a variety of ways, including work on the state capitol. Several states, including Kentucky, Missouri, Alabama, Indiana, and Illinois, had experimented with leasing, and had discovered that from a businessman's point of view the system had many advantages. Felons were leased to individuals and companies who exploited them, and thus the state was relieved of the maintenance costs.

Because the economy had reached its nadir, Tennessee—and indeed the South in general—was ripe for a convict lease system. The treasury was empty, the prison population increased daily, and expenses involved in operating the penitentiary mounted. Moreover, businessmen from the Northeast who had settled in Tennessee accentuated concepts of an independent capitalist society where labor was exploited and large gains were reaped by the investor. These ideas, combined with the concepts of a slave economy and mounting racial tensions caused by the war and reconstruction, made Tennessee a fertile field for the lease system. When several proposals to alleviate the prison conditions—including one to erect two additional penal institutions—failed because of the expense involved, legislators turned to leasing in the belief that it would pay prison costs and might even bring profits.

The first convicts were leased in July, 1866, to a Nashville firm which manufactured furniture. The firm built workshops on the penitentiary grounds and agreed to clothe and feed the prisoners and to pay the state forty-three cents per day for each man. State officials rejoiced, and wrote that

> Now, every convict, old or young, skilled or unpracticed, clumsy, indolent, or vicious, is at once turned over, at forty-three cents per day; and it is the lessee's business to provide work profitable or otherwise, without regard to the character, condition or competency of the laborer. Possibly the convict may have been a good field hand, . . . but within the walls of the prison, no such employment is to be had and the laborer may be said to be both green and raw. Hence to instruct and to put mechanical tools into the hands of a novice, and pay forty cents per day, besides, is compensation greater than at first appears.

The prisoners, however, were not in sympathy with the arrangements. Some protested loudly and others refused to work. Finally, in June, 1867, they burned the workshops. The contract was canceled in July, 1869.

State officials promptly sought new lessees. Articulate industrialists, such as Arthur S. Colyar, for several years had urged that convicts could be used effectively in coal mines. Legislators were in agreement, and accordingly established branch penitentiaries at the Tracy City and Battle Creek mines and leased the entire prison population to a Memphis firm having extensive mining interests in the eastern section of the state. In 1884, when the contract expired, a new agreement was made with the Tennessee Coal, Iron, and Railroad Company which had extensive mining interests in Tennessee and wanted to use the prisoners in the mining operations.

In the meantime, opposition to the lease system developed. Scores of miners, many of whom had been lured into Tennessee by immigration propaganda which promised good jobs and high wages, lost their jobs and protested vigorously against the use of convict labor in the mines. An organization known as the "Mechanics and Manufacturers Association of Tennessee" alleged that the leasing system was unfair to labor and that the living conditions of the "honest mechanics" were damaged by the "suicidal" system. Dr. John Berrien Lindsley and other humanitarians condemned the state for permitting the reformatory purposes of the penitentiary to become subservient to the desire for material gain. Leaders of the press indicted the leasing system and charged that lessees mistreated prisoners, fed them inadequately, and created living conditions which were "hells on earth where men are made devils of . . . ." The warden and other prison officials, however, argued that conditions were no worse than those found in other states and pointed to the financial returns which the system brought to the state.

Officials of the Tennessee Coal, Iron, and Railroad Company signed a five-year lease in 1884 and agreed to pay the state $101,000 per year. The contract was renewed from time to time and ultimately expired on December 31, 1895. Since the company had extensive coal and iron mines in East Tennessee, most of the convicts worked there. Others were subleased to other companies.

Criticisms of prison conditions brought legislative investigations. When the General Assembly convened in January, 1885, the editor of the Chattanooga *Times* published a "shocking story" about prison conditions. A convict recently discharged had told of being forced to mine coal "in water a foot deep" and of being whipped with a lash of 23-ply sole leather braid, "applied with all the strength the guards could summon." Prisoners who complained about the rough prison fare, much of which was unpalatable, received only kicks and the lash well laid on. Others confirmed the *Times* story. A legislative committee appointed to investigate the charges filed two reports. The majority found living conditions to be adequate and affirmed that the food was equal in quality to that "used by some of the best families of Nashville." The minority alleged that an objective investigation could not be conducted because prison officials, anticipating the visit of legislators, would not permit the committee to see conditions as they actually were. Additional investigations were made in 1887 and 1889. As before, the committees filed two reports. The minority in 1889 termed the whole system "a horror and shame upon the state," but the majority pointed to the profits which the system brought the state. Officials in the following year pointed to a net profit of $771,400, which was only $176,000 short of the entire cost of penal institutions since their beginning in 1829.

Despite the favorable reports from legislative committees, and regardless of the profits realized from the system, labor and manufacturing groups across the state joined a large segment of newspaper editors, ministers, lawyers, health officials, and public-spirited citizens to advocate abolition of the lease system. They recommended the adoption of a central prison having manufacturing and agricultural facilities at which convicts might work. Agitation on the part of these groups, combined with a series of labor disturbances in East Tennessee, eventually led to the abolition of the lease system.

By 1891, free coal miners could maintain only a bare subsistence living, although the mining industry had grown to a respectable size in Tennessee and owners reaped sizable profits. Miners had objected to the use of convict labor for two decades; especially obnoxious to them was the use of felons as strikebreakers, but they could point to many other grievances. They were paid in "scrip" (which required them to spend their wages at the company store or else have their scrip discounted in other stores), were forced to sign "iron-clad" contracts pledging confidence in company officials, and had to promise not to engage in strikes. The inflamed miners for years had viewed the use of convict labor as a practice which would strip them of their small livelihood. Therefore, the East Tennessee mining communities were like tinderboxes where a spark might set off a conflagration.

Trouble soon developed. Violence first ensued in July, 1891, when convicts were taken to Briceville (in Anderson County) as strike-breakers. Three hundred armed miners entered the stockade and forced convicts, officers, and guards to march to Coal Creek (now called Lake City) and there to entrain for Knoxville. A few days later Governor Buchanan, accompanied by a battalion of state militiamen, journeyed to Briceville. He heard the complaints of the miners, pleaded with them to observe the law, and then returned to Nashville, leaving the convicts and the militia at the mines. A few days later, two thousand miners forced the convicts and soldiers to return to Knoxville. Governor Buchanan again journeyed eastward to hear complaints and ordered fourteen companies of militia to mobilize at Knoxville. After several days of negotiation, the governor and the miners agreed that the militia would be removed from the scene, that the convicts and guards would return to the mines, and the miners would repose "confidence in the governor and general assembly."

The situation was far from settled. The governor called the legislature into special session shortly after his return to Nashville to consider a repeal of the lease law, but the measure was defeated in the house by a 2 to 1 margin. Miners then sought relief in the courts. Failing there, they again resorted to violence. On the night of October 31, 1891, several hundred miners surrounded the Briceville stockade, released the prisoners, burned the stockade and other buildings, and fled into the hills. Two nights later the miners liberated 200 convicts at Oliver Springs, in Roane County, and set fire to the buildings. Most of the convicts were apprehended and returned to the penitentiary at Nashville. In July, 1892, outbreaks occurred at the Tracy City and Inman mines in Grundy County. Buchanan pursued a vacillating course, but he did offer rewards for the apprehension and conviction of the leaders and sought to shift the blame to the legislature and the lessees. Some miners were arrested, but few were convicted.

The four gubernatorial candidates of 1892—Turney, Buchanan,

Winstead, and East—pledged immediate abolition of the lease system. During the campaign, Colonel Colyar stated that the hiring of convicts as strikebreakers was no longer profitable, and Nathaniel Baxter, vice president of the Tennessee Coal, Iron, and Railroad Company, asserted that anti-leasing agitation and the Anderson, Roane, and Grundy trouble had "demoralized convicts" and rendered many of them no longer acceptable to industrialists.

Legislators of 1893 quickly found a substitute for the lease system. They provided for a new penitentiary to be "managed and conducted upon just, humane, and civilized principles" and to be large enough to house 1,500 convicts, and required the state to buy "not more than ten thousand . . . acres" of coal lands on which prisoners would work so that they would not be in competition with free miners. Consequently, state officials purchased 9,000 acres of coal lands in Morgan County where they established the Brushy Mountain Prison, and for the penitentiary grounds they bought the Mark Cockrill farm, a 1,128 acre tract located approximately six miles west of Nashville on the south bank of the Cumberland River. Work on the prison—modern in every respect—was begun immediately. When completed in 1898, the prison had cost more than $800,000 and consisted of an administration building, two wings of four hundred cells each, a hospital, and separate quarters for women. By the end of the century, the state had developed, through trial and error, a prison system comparable to some of the best in the country.

Humanitarians also severely criticized lack of separate facilities for juvenile offenders. The Reverend Collins D. Elliott, for example, in 1881 pointed with shame to more than 400 prisoners twenty-one years of age or under, and urged legislators to establish a separate reformatory. Numerous religious and humanitarian groups petitioned the General Assembly to implement Elliott's suggestions, and Judge John C. Ferriss of Nashville canvassed the state in an effort to arouse public sentiment.

When it appeared that the state would do nothing, Colonel Edmond W. Cole provided money for the establishment of a reformatory for both youthful offenders and "abandoned children." The state accepted the gift and established the Tennessee Industrial School in 1887.

The agricultural revolt and the Populist movement in the nation as a whole came somewhat abruptly to a close in 1896 with the return to power of the business-oriented and industrially minded Republicans. Also coming to an end late in the century was the long period of agricultural depression which farmers had experienced since Reconstruction. The conclusion of the Spanish-American War and the dawn of the new century brought undreamed-of prosperity to Tennessee farmers which was to continue uninterrupted for two decades. With the settlement of the prison problem and the election soon thereafter of the affable Bob Taylor to the governorship, a new day dawned for Tennesseans.

SUGGESTED READINGS

General Accounts

Solon J. Buck, *The Agrarian Crusade* (New Haven, 1921); Folmsbee, Corlew, and Mitchell, *Tennessee*, II, Ch. 31; Hamer, *Tennessee*, II, Ch. 44; John D. Hicks, *The Populist Revolt* (Minneapolis, 1931); Anna Rochester, *The Populist Movement in the United States* (New York, 1943).

Specialized Accounts

Lane L. Boutwell, "The Oratory of Robert Love Taylor," *THQ*, IX (March, 1950), 10–45; Crowe, "Origin and Development of Tennessee's Prison Problem," *THQ*, XV (June, 1956), 111–35; Sarah M. Howell, "The Editorials of Arthur S. Colyar, Nashville Prophet of the New South," *THQ*, XXVII (Fall, 1968), 262–76; A. C. Hutson, Jr., "The Coal Miners' Insurrections of 1891 in Anderson County, Tennessee," ETHS *Publ.*, No. 7 (1935), 103–21; Hutson, "The Overthrow of the Convict Lease System in Tennessee," ETHS *Publ.*, No. 8 (1936), 82–103; J. Eugene Lewis, "The Tennessee Gubernatorial Campaign and Election of 1894," *THQ*, XIII (June, Sept., Dec., 1954), 99–126, 224–43, 301–28; Verton M. Queener, "The East Tennessee Republicans in State and Nation, 1870–1900," *THQ*, II (June, 1943), 99–128; Queener, "East Tennessee Republicans, 1870–1896," ETHS *Publ.*, No. 15, pp. 49–73; Daniel M. Robison, *Bob Taylor and the Agrarian Revolt in Tennessee* (Chapel Hill, 1935); Robison, "Tennessee Politics and the Agrarian Revolt in Tennessee, 1886–1896," *MVHR*, XX (Dec., 1933), 365–80; Robison, "The Political Background of Tennessee's War of the Roses," ETHS *Publ.*, No. 5 (1933), 125–49; J. A. Sharp, "The Entrance of the

Farmers' Alliance into Tennessee Politics," ETHS *Publ.*, No. 9 (1937), 77–92; Sharp, "The Farmers' Alliance and the People's Party in Tennessee," ETHS *Publ.*, No. 10 (1938), 91–113; Alf A., Hugh L., and James P. Taylor, *Life and Career of Senator Robert Love Taylor* (Nashville, 1913); Williams, "Poll Tax as a Suffrage Requirement," *JSH*, XVIII (1952), 469–96.

The Governor's Mansion in Nashville is the official home of the chief executive and his family.

Top left: Albert Gore served in the House of Representatives for fourteen years and in the Senate for eighteen; *top right:* Howard H. Baker, Jr., was the first Tennessee Republican to be elected to the Senate by popular vote; *below:* William E. Brock III ousted Senator Gore in 1970 by 46,344 votes.

Top: Knoxville, where lakes and mountains meet, is the oldest of the major towns in Tennessee and was the state's first capital; *lower*: Tennessee's Capitol and nearby state buildings form the focal point for this view of Nashville.

Top: Manufacturers of chemical and allied products, such as the W. R. Grace Company of Memphis (above), represent Tennessee's leading industry; *lower*: Tennessee is the leading dairy state in the South.

Top: Cotton normally ranks as one of the two principal cash crops in the Volunteer State, the other being tobacco; *lower*: The soils of Tennessee, constituting the state's most important natural resource, provide fertile fields for tobacco growing.

The Tennessee River system of locks and navigable channels has become the "world's most modern waterway."

Now a National Historic Landmark, the Graphite Reactor at Oak Ridge once served as a pilot plant for production of plutonium.

Built in 2½ years, Oak Ridge became Tennessee's fifth largest city and had the world's first Gaseous Diffusion Plant (above).

More tourists travel to the Great Smokies than to any other national park.

Top: Internationally known as "Music City, U.S.A.," Nashville has its own Country Music Hall of Fame and Museum; *lower*: The lakes formed by TVA's dams help make the Tennessee region a prominent center for recreation.

23. ❧ Tennessee in the Gilded Age

A LOW EBB in tastes, refinement, and moral turpitude was reached in America in the several years which followed the Civil War. The extremes of the Reconstruction Era, the rough treatment accorded President Johnson by the Radical Congress, the graft and corruption of the Grant Era, and the increased emphasis upon materialism left their marks upon American civilization. For better or worse, a new order of society was conceived based upon liquid capital and centralization; conformity, not individualism, was the ultimate result. It was an era of millionaires. Captains of industry—some lacking in refinement and cultural background and having little regard for legal sanctions—plied their wares and reaped enormous profits; as these men conspicuously consumed their wealth, millions of less fortunate Americans viewed their machinations with emotions mixed with envy and disgust. The materialistic philosophy, admittedly more apparent in the lusty and confident North and East, also had its exponents and practitioners in Tennessee and the South.

The three decades following Reconstruction were filled with reform movements—and Tennesseans had their share—perhaps because people were anxious to flee from guilty consciences or, on the other hand, perhaps they sincerely desired to reap better things for themselves and their children and believed that the quickest route was to worship at the shrine of Mammon. Although during the four decades after the war only one state registered less religious growth (as evidenced by church membership) than Tennessee, still Tennesseans did enjoy increased emphasis upon education. For the first time in the history of the state, a workable public school system was put into operation, and institutions of higher learning—financed largely by Northern industrialist-philanthropists—flourished. The century closed with the state's greatest display of fact and fancy—the Centennial Exposition of 1897.

Public Schools and Colleges ह्≫ The Civil War disrupted the work of private schools, and Governor Brownlow soon after his election asked legislators to establish a public school system so that "thousands of children" would not "pass the school age hopelessly illiterate." Not until 1867, however, did the legislature comply. The law provided for centralized control; the new system would be headed by a state superintendent of the common schools, under whom county superintendents would work. Increased taxes would support the program. John Eaton, Jr., a New Hampshire-born minister who had served as a chaplain, a Freedmen's Bureau official, and a newspaper editor in Memphis, was named state superintendent. A man of considerable energy, Eaton toured the state to determine school needs. In 1869 he prepared a comprehensive survey of educational needs and published it under the title of *The First Report of the Superintendent of Public Instruction of the State of Tennessee*. Eaton called for increased appropriations to provide better school buildings, outhouses, and playgrounds. Normal schools for teachers should be provided, he said, and equal opportunities should be given Negro pupils and teachers.

Within a few months after Eaton's report was published, the Radicals were swept from power. Iconoclastic Democrats, anxious to destroy the last vestige of Reconstruction and Brownlowism, tossed aside both the good and the evil—the educational program being among the former. They abolished the office of state superintendent and made the counties responsible for establishing schools. No provision was made for educating Negroes, but the Freedmen's Bureau schools remained in operation.

Public-spirited citizens continued, however, to arouse the people to the need for a sound public school system, and soon the legislature was flooded with petitions requesting that changes be made. Both Negroes and whites joined in the clamor. A "State Convention of Colored Men," meeting in Nashville in 1871 under an American flag flanked with pictures of Abraham Lincoln and John Brown (of Harper's Ferry notoriety), petitioned Congress to establish a national system of schools. In the following year, Governor John C. Brown called legislators into special session and recommended that they establish a constructive educational system, but his efforts were in vain. The lawmakers did, however, order several thousand copies printed of a comprehensive study of state educational needs prepared by Joseph B. Killebrew, who in 1872 held the title of "Assistant Superintendent of Public Instruction." This report became the foundation for the educational law of 1873 and the present system of public education. Killebrew, like Eaton, emphasized pragmatic rather than cultural values of learning; he stressed the economic opportunities which stemmed from education. Men who had been trained to make a living would be less inclined to commit crime, he said; therefore, fewer prisoners would have to be maintained at state expense. Killebrew deplored the increasing illiteracy present in the state. Although during the 1860's the population had declined 13 per cent, the increase in illiteracy of whites had increased 50 per cent. A full-time state superintendent was mandatory, he said; adequate legislative appropriations were absolutely necessary. The failure of legislators to act in 1872 only brought additional petitions and condemnation upon state authorities.

When the General Assembly convened in 1873, Governor Brown told legislators that the high illiteracy rate caused Tennessee to rank "third in ignorance" among the states of the Union—a condition he described as "a disgrace to our people." Legislators then passed the school law of 1873, with broad provisions. A state superintendent of public instruction was to be appointed by the governor,[1] and county superintendents—"men of literary and scientific attainments"—were to be elected biennially by the county courts. Three school directors in each civil district also would be chosen by the county courts, and would assist the county superintendent. A permanent school fund of $2,512,000[2] was reestablished, and 6 per cent paid semiannually on the amount was to be used for the support of schools, in addition to the emoluments received from a

---

[1] Governor Brown appointed a young legislator from Knox County, John M. Fleming, who had edited the *Tennessee School Journal*.

[2] The school fund was a legal fiction—the amount existed on paper only, but the interest on it was paid regularly.

poll tax and a property tax. County courts were authorized to levy additional taxes where local needs demanded them.

The decade following the enactment of the public school law was a difficult one for school officials. The state debt seemed to defy settlement and the Panic of 1873 crippled the entire economy. County superintendents outlined tales of woe. The state superintendent reported in 1875 that 60,000 fewer pupils were enrolled than in the previous year. By 1880 slow recovery was being made, but still the state superintendent wrote of "disaster and apprehensions of impoverishment . . . ."

Some of the financial handicaps were overcome by money provided by the Peabody Fund, established during the Reconstruction Era by a New York railroad executive and philanthropist named George Peabody. By 1870, Tennessee schools had received $17,000 and four years later were receiving twice that amount annually. The Peabody Fund became one of the best administered and one of the most beneficial of all the philanthropic ventures by Northern businessmen after the war.

Several school laws were enacted during the next two decades which deserve brief mention. A state board of education was established in 1875. In 1889 a law was passed making women eligible for the office of county superintendent. Two years later the legislature made provision for secondary schools as well as primary schools. Until that time secondary education had been largely a function of academies and private schools. In the same year the state superintendent was named an *ex-officio* member of the State Board of Education, where his influence and knowledge could be used more effectively. In 1895 the board was authorized to specify standards and qualifications for county superintendents; to those who qualified, the board issued certificates which had to be filed with the chairman of the county courts. Two years later a more efficient accounting system was installed by requiring county trustees to make quarterly settlements with the county courts. In 1899 the "Uniform Textbook Law" established a state commission whose function included the adoption of a series of textbooks which could be used in all public schools.

"Teachers' Institutes" did much to remedy the problem of poorly trained and incompetent teachers—a problem of which both county and state superintendents complained biennially. The institutes

were begun in the 1870's but did not become popular until the following decade. They usually continued from one to four weeks and
were conducted by a college professor or a visiting school official.
Not only did the participants discuss methods and share experiences,
but they also studied sorely needed content material, including
spelling, grammar, geography, and history. In 1884, State Superintendent Thomas H. Paine announced that institutes would be conducted in every senatorial district. He was confident that the
sessions would provide "marked improvement . . . in every grade
throughout the state." In 1888 institutes were held in ninety counties and were attended by more than 4,000 teachers.

Of importance equal to the establishment of public schools were
the formation and operation of more than a dozen new colleges
and universities. The old University of Nashville, which had maintained outstanding schools of liberal arts and medicine before the
war, took the lead in training teachers through the use of money
provided by the Peabody Fund. "The Peabody State Normal School
of the University of Nashville" was established in December, 1875.
University authorities, recognizing the need for teacher training in
Tennessee and the South, soon closed the doors of the medical
school and other departments and concentrated entirely upon preparing teachers. In 1878 the name was changed to "State Normal
College," and a few years later, to "Peabody Normal College." In
1881 the state legislature appropriated $10,000 per year for school
maintenance and by 1895 had doubled its annual appropriation.
Not until shortly after the turn of the century did school officials
change the name to "George Peabody College for Teachers."

Vanderbilt University, soon to become one of the foremost institutions of the South, was chartered in 1873. The financial generosity
of Cornelius Vanderbilt and the untiring efforts of leaders in the
Southern Methodist Episcopal Church, particularly Bishop Holland
N. McTyeire and Landon C. Garland, were responsible for the
institution. Garland became the first chancellor. In 1875 the University began full operation with departments of law, medicine,
religion, and arts and science. Despite some difficulties, including
unfavorable publicity associated with the dismissal of Professor
Alexander Winchell whose ideas of evolution were diametrically
opposed to those of the conservative Methodist Board of Trustees,
the new university made solid progress. The election in 1893 of

James Hampton Kirkland, a thirty-three-year-old professor of Latin, as chancellor meant continued advancement and emphasis upon sound scholarship and able teaching.[3] At the turn of the century, Nashvillians hailed the institution as "the pride of Nashville and of the whole South." Academic, theological, pharmaceutical, and engineering departments were maintained on the main campus; law, dental, and medical departments were operated in other parts of town.

The history of The University of Tennessee may be traced to Blount College, founded in 1794, to East Tennessee College, and then to East Tennessee University. In 1879 the institution became The University of Tennessee. With the passage of the Morrill Act in 1862, Congress granted considerable land to the states, the proceeds from which were to be used for the development of agricultural and mechanical colleges. Tennessee, in the Confederacy at the time, could not avail itself of federal aid until 1869, two years after a special act had been passed. The legislature promptly established an Agricultural and Mechanical College as a part of the University and transferred to it the proceeds of the endowment resulting from the Morrill Act. By 1879, when the name was changed, four courses of study described as "agricultural, mechanical, classical, and scientific" were offered. Dr. Charles W. Dabney became president in 1887 and his sixteen years of service represented a period of solid growth for the University. In 1890 the school of law opened with a two-year curriculum, and three years later the University was opened to women.

The origin of the University of Chattanooga may be traced to Chattanooga University, which was organized by the Freedman's Aid Society of the Methodist Episcopal Church. After several years of acrimonious debate, the Chattanooga school was consolidated with East Tennessee Wesleyan University, at Athens, under the name of U. S. Grant University. Dissatisfaction continued, and in the early 1890's a division was effected whereby the College of Liberal Arts was moved to Athens and the professional schools of

---

[3] Kirkland infused into the University a love for truth and a hatred for sham, a spirit which persists to this day. Dr. Edwin Mims, in his *Chancellor Kirkland of Vanderbilt*, 76–77, quotes one student who said of Kirkland, "He put into my soul the love of truth, the hatred of a lie. He made pretense forever a dastardly and damned thing to me. He taught me what thoroughness and genuineness and reality mean in the world. Pretense and hypocrisy had a new meaning for me."

medicine, law, and theology remained at Chattanooga. Not until after the turn of the century was the liberal arts school returned to Chattanooga, the name "University of Chattanooga" adopted, and control taken from the Methodist Church and placed in the hands of a private board of trustees.

The University of the South, at Sewanee, established in 1857 but unable to begin operation until after the war, soon emerged as one of the state's outstanding liberal arts colleges. The school was re-opened in 1866 at Winchester, but in the following year was moved back to "the Mountain" a few miles east of the Franklin County seat. It was reopened largely through the efforts of Bishop Charles T. Quintard and the philanthropy of his brothers, George and Edward. In 1868 only nine students were enrolled, but by 1870 the institution had 125 students. Enrollment fell slightly during the next two decades, but by 1890 it numbered several hundred, and three permanent buildings had been erected. The school also had one of the best libraries in the state.

Other colleges—Cumberland, Maryville, Southwestern, Lincoln Memorial, Tusculum, Bethel, Carson-Newman, Union, Lambuth, Nashville Bible School (David Lipscomb), and others too numerous to name—also made contributions within their own particular spheres of operation. Cumberland University, under the guidance of such teachers as Nathan Green, A. B. Martin, and E. E. Beard, became known throughout the nation for its law school.

Several colleges for Negroes were established during the period. One of the best known, "Fisk School," was founded in Nashville in 1866 through the joint efforts of the American Missionary Association and the Western Freedmen's Aid Commission of Cincinnati. In 1867 the name was changed to "Fisk University." George L. White soon organized the "Fisk Jubilee Singers," a group of students who toured the country and much of Europe and earned for the school more than $150,000. When in 1879 members of the legislature heard the Negro chorus, they described the performance as "remarkable," and commended University officials for the progress in Negro education. By 1900 the buildings and grounds were valued at $350,000. Schools of arts and sciences, religion, and teacher training had been established, from which were graduated 433 students. Among other institutions for Negroes established soon after the war were Nashville Normal and Theological Institute (later

Roger Williams University), founded by Baptist leaders in 1866; Central Tennessee College, Nashville, chartered in 1866 by the Methodist Episcopal Church; Knoxville College, founded in 1875 by the United Presbyterian Church; Lane College, Jackson, established in 1882 by the Methodist Episcopal Church; and LeMoyne Normal and Commercial School, Memphis, founded in 1871 from funds supplied by F. Julius LeMoyne and the American Missionary Society of the Congregational Church.

By the turn of the century, Tennesseans could point to considerable educational progress since the basic law of 1873 was enacted. In the public schools the enrollment had increased more than 100 per cent. The average length of terms now was nearly five months, as compared with a three and one-half month term in 1874. The number of schools had increased from 4,588 to 7,963, the number of institutes held had increased sixfold, and the estimated value of school plant and equipment had increased threefold. Teachers, however, received only a thirteen cents' per month raise during the quarter century; during the quadrennium of 1874–1878, the "average monthly salary" of teachers was $30.74, and twenty-five years later the figure was $30.87. Colleges and universities of high quality had been established.

Religious Development ❧ During the four decades which followed the Civil War, only one state registered less increase in church membership than did Tennessee. Perhaps the war and reconstruction, coupled with the new concepts of Darwinism, pragmatism, and materialism, were partly to blame. Northern bayonets ended the Southern bid for political independence and reunited the country politically, but they did not allay the sectional strife within the churches.

Methodists had divided sectionally in 1845, and were not reunited until 1939. Especially in East Tennessee was the strife bitter between the Northern and Southern wings of the church during the several decades following Federal occupation of that section in 1863. "Parson" Brownlow, who followed the victorious Northern armies into the eastern section, tried to force members of the Southern church into the "loyal" group. When many refused, the preacher-politician urged returning Federal soldiers to try to intimidate ministers of the Southern church. The result was that some preachers were beaten, and many were not permitted to hold services. The Southern group retaliated. They charged that the Northern church was composed of radical politicians, abolitionists, and "grand thieves and rascals," all of whom sought "Negro equality." Members of the Ku Klux Klan took a hand and ordered all "Carpet bag" preachers from the state. Despite the schism and bitterness, Methodist leaders added members to the fold and retained state leadership. Shortly after the turn of the century, nearly 200,000 persons were communicants of the Methodist Episcopal Church, South. The Northern Methodist Episcopal Church, the Methodist Protestant Church, the Wesleyan Methodist Connection, the Free Methodist Church, and the Methodist Episcopal Church of North America claimed another 50,000.

Baptists also made decided gains. Like the Methodists, they had divided sectionally before the war. About 1900, the Southern Baptist Convention claimed 160,000 members and was second only to the Methodists. Other groups, including the Primitive Baptists, the Free Will Baptists, the Northern Baptist Convention, the Regular Baptists, the General Baptists, the Duck River and Kindred Association of Baptists (sometimes called the Baptist Church of Christ), and the Two-Seed-in-the-Spirit Baptists, claimed 22,000 members.

At the beginning of the war, the Presbyterian Church divided into Northern and Southern branches, and the latter adopted the name "Presbyterian Church in the Confederate States of America." After the war, Southerners accepted the name "Presbyterian Church in the United States," as distinguished from the Northern group, which continued to employ the name "Presbyterian Church in the United States of America." The strongest of the Presbyterian bodies in Tennessee was the Cumberland Presbyterian Church, which had seceded from the main Presbyterian branch in 1810. By the turn of the century, Presbyterians of all kinds in the state numbered 75,000, including the United Presbyterian Church of North America and the Associated Reform Synod of the South, in addition to those named. The Cumberland group composed about one-half of that number.

The Church of Christ, the conservative wing of the Disciples of Christ discussed in an earlier chapter, grew rapidly until by the end of the century it rivaled the dominant Methodists, Baptists, and

Presbyterians in all sections of the state. (The Disciples, it will be recalled, had determined to restore Christianity to its pristine pureness. They sought to avoid sectarianism by refusing to accept creeds and dogmas; they would speak only "where the Scriptures speak.") Before the Civil War, factions had developed among the Disciples; their main points of disagreement were the use of instrumental music in the churches, the support of organized missions, and centralization, the ideas held by the liberal Christian Church.

Nashville became a center of the Church of Christ movement. There, David Lipscomb, a gifted writer and spirited preacher, edited the *Gospel Advocate*, a conservative periodical with a wide circulation. Through this publication, Lipscomb and others of like persuasion drew the lines more closely. Various points of disagreement were developed, but basically the quarrel narrowed down to instrumental music and "organizations" or "societies." Instrumental music and organized choirs were believed to discourage congregational participation; one writer referred to the organ as "an instrument of Satan." Missionary and Sunday School organizations were not scripturally approved; Christians should not make such a "departure from New Testament Christianity" by becoming affiliated with the movements. Efforts to bind the churches into one centralized group met with Lipscomb's condemnation. "Decrees of Associations, Conferences, Synods, . . . and Romish councils" were unscriptural; therefore, any "meeting" which attempted to make recommendations to the churches for a centralized organization was "an improper assumption of power and authority" for which Lipscomb found "no authority in the Bible." At the turn of the century, the majority of the membership of the Church of Christ centered in Tennessee, with some 41,411 members in the Volunteer State—more than three times that of Kentucky and Alabama. Of the eight adjacent states—Arkansas, Missouri, Virginia, North Carolina, Kentucky, Georgia, Alabama, and Mississippi—the total membership of all combined did not exceed that of Tennessee.

Many other groups, of various sizes, also were present in the state. Among them were the Protestant Episcopal, Lutheran, Catholic, Disciple or Christian, Church of God, and Church of the Nazarene. The last two named were formed near the end of the nineteenth century.

Separate Negro churches were established soon after the Civil

War. The vast majority of the freedmen became Methodists or Baptists. Before the war the Methodist Episcopal Church, South, claimed a Negro membership of over 200,000. After the war the majority of them became members of the African Methodist Episcopal Church, which was founded before 1845 and had moved into the South with its white counterpart. In 1906 it had the largest Negro membership in the state. The Colored (later Christian) M. E. Church, organized in Jackson in 1870, and the African M. E. Zion Church also had sizable followings. Several Baptist congregations were formed even before the war. In Nashville the First Baptist Church, Colored, was established even before 1850. The Beale Street Baptist Church, Memphis, was one of the largest Negro groups formed after 1865. By the turn of the century several divisions in the Beale congregation had occurred, but the parent group still consisted of several thousand members. By 1906 the National Baptist Convention claimed 759 Negro congregations in Tennessee. In addition, the Primitive Baptists and others claimed Negro churches and missions. Several other denominations, smaller in size, had Negro members. The Colored Cumberland Presbyterian Church was organized at Murfreesboro in 1869. By 1906 seventy-nine Colored Cumberland Presbyterian congregations had been established in the state. Other denominations sponsoring Negro churches included the following: Presbyterian Church in the United States, United Presbyterian Church, Associated Reformed Synod of the South, Churches of Christ, Disciples of Christ, Church of the Living God, Seventh Day Adventist, Adventist Christian, and Roman Catholic.

Women's Rights Movement &ๆ Although American leaders of the women's suffrage movement did not attain rights at the ballot box until August, 1920, when the Tennessee legislature ratified the Nineteenth Amendment, many outstanding women actively had sought equal rights for their sex for over a century. During the first half of the nineteenth century, feminist activity was confined almost entirely to the Northern states. Not until after the Civil War was it introduced into the more conservative South.

The women's rights movement in Tennessee probably had its

beginning in August, 1876, when Mrs. Napoleon Cromwell, of Mississippi, addressed the Democratic gubernatorial convention in Nashville. "Woman is as free by nature as man," Mrs. Cromwell told the Tennesseans, who at first received her with both laughter and applause. Playing upon an issue with which she could reach every Democrat in the convention, she deplored the fact that Negro men could vote, but the mothers, sisters, wives, and daughters of the men assembled could not. She thus urged the unity of the white race by enfranchising women. Even the racial issue could not break the barrier, however, and her request that Democrats endorse woman suffrage met only with laughter and scorn from those assembled.

Mrs. Cromwell's appearance apparently was an isolated incident, and more than a decade elapsed before Tennesseans manifested much interest in women's rights. In 1885 Mrs. Elizabeth Lyle Saxon was appointed by leaders of the National Woman Suffrage Association as state president for Tennessee, but she moved from the state in 1886 before any steps were taken to organize a state chapter. Two years later Memphians organized a women's suffrage league with forty-five members. Mrs. Lide A. Meriwether, who for the next two decades was the state's leading suffragette, was elected president. Other groups soon were formed in Nashville, Maryville, and elsewhere, but leaders met with little encouragement. Although Mrs. Meriwether toured much of the state during the summer of 1895, she could claim in December, 1895, only five organizations with a total membership of 128. She had secured endorsements of her goals by 535 women, however, and had sponsored the appearances in Memphis of Susan B. Anthony and Carrie Chapman Catt, two of the country's leading feminists.

The century closed with a flurry of activity on the part of a few determined leaders. Mrs. Meriwether staged a state suffrage convention in Nashville in May, 1897, where delegates heard leaders from Kentucky, Alabama, and elsewhere. During the convention, Mrs. Meriwether organized a group called the Tennessee Equal Rights Association. Five months later the National Council of Women of the United States met in Nashville and heard Susan B. Anthony pledge that she "would not rest until a woman's name stood for as much as a man's name (and) until a woman's opinion was worth as much as a man's . . . ." In 1900, delegates of the Tennessee Equal Rights Association convened in Memphis. There, they heard Carrie Chapman Catt denounce all who supported the concept of inequality of rights for men and women.

Customs of long standing are not easily overturned and, as was to be expected, the feminists met with considerable opposition. Some of the most caustic critics were newspaper editors, women, and ministers. The editor of the Nashville *American,* for example, in 1887 described feminist agitation as a movement "which proposes . . . a radical and fundamental change in the theory and policy of government." Editors were quick to publish statements by "disloyal" women who contended that "woman's place was in the home." Ministers frequently urged women to remain in their "place" if they did not wish to violate the will of God. Mrs. Meriwether usually countered their arguments—especially those of "disloyal" women—with spirited replies. Mrs. Bettie M. Donelson, of Nashville, wrote in retrospect that "it required a woman of strong purpose and heart to be counted as a suffragist and brave the caricatures from the artists' pencils, and the malicious and undeserved reproach from the pens of editors and literary critics." Despite discouragement, feminists, at the threshold of the twentieth century, could point to some solid achievements during the preceding two decades, and looked with confidence to the future.

The Prohibition Movement, 1870–1900 ❧ For several decades before the Civil War, Tennesseans had joined temperance leaders in other states in seeking the passage of laws which would prohibit or curtail the manufacture, sale, and consumption of intoxicating beverages. The movement subsided during the war but was revived in the first decade after Reconstruction. The Sons of Temperance, the Tennessee Order of Good Templars, and the Prohibition party were among the more vociferous prohibitionists of the various organized groups. A state branch of the Women's Christian Temperance Union was founded in 1882, and soon exceeded all others in zeal for temperance. Stage productions, the most popular of which was "Ten Nights in a Bar Room," and editorial comment and letters to editors kept the question before the people.

On two separate occasions, attempts were made in 1870 to write local option into the constitution, but both failed; three years later legislators enacted local option, but the measure was vetoed by Governor Brown. Still later, in 1885, Senator John H. McDowell of Obion County pushed through the legislature a joint resolution calling for an amendment which would make it unlawful for any person to "sell, or keep for sale as a beverage any intoxicating liquors whatever." As required by the constitution, the proposal was submitted to the legislature two years later and received the constitutionally required majority; then the amendment was submitted to the people. There the measure failed, by a vote of about 145,000 to 118,000.

Earlier, in 1877, a significant law was passed known as the Hamilton Bill but later better known as the "Four Mile Law." With a few exceptions, it made unlawful the marketing of intoxicating beverages within four miles of an incorporated school in rural areas. Violations carried a penalty of a fine not to exceed $250 and imprisonment not to exceed six months. This measure, with amendments, became the bill by which prohibition ultimately was accomplished in the state. In 1887, the first of a series of amendments was added, this one applying the law to all schools whether incorporated or not.

Temperance forces, with leaders of the Protestant churches in the forefront, accelerated their agitation during the final decade of the twentieth century. Efforts to extend the Four Mile Law to the entire state failed in each biennium from 1889 through 1897, but in 1899, although local option was rejected, the provisions of the Four Mile Law were extended to towns of 2,000 or less provided they incorporated after the law was passed. Towns in this population category could, therefore, if they so desired, surrender their charters, reincorporate, and thereby become dry automatically. This, the beginning of the extension of the Four Mile Law which brought prohibition to all cities ten years later, was hailed by leaders as a great step forward toward their ultimate goal.

The Prohibition party, although organized nationally soon after the Civil War, was not established in Tennessee until 1883. Five years later, the Tennessee Temperance Alliance joined forces with the party. The Prohibitionists abandoned their earlier non-partisan position, bitterly attacked Governor Bob Taylor and Senator Isham G. Harris as friends of the liquor interests, and nominated a candidate (J. C. Johnson) for governor. Although Johnson received only about 7,000 votes out of more than 300,000 votes cast, Prohibitionists felt encouraged and promptly made plans for 1890. The Reverend D. C. Kelley, pastor of a Methodist church in Gallatin, became the party's candidate in that year. Kelley had been suspended from his ministerial activities for six months because he had left his pastorate without permission; the Nashville *American* (later merged with the *Tennessean*) condemned Kelley as a "Negro lover" and as one who had described Abraham Lincoln as a great American. Kelley entered vigorously into the race and received nearly twice as many votes as Johnson had in 1888. During the remainder of the decade, the party nominated candidates for governor (except in 1894), but none received more than a token number of votes.

Although not attaining their ultimate goal during the nineteenth century, temperance advocates did lay solid groundwork for themselves and others who carried the fight into the twentieth century. The nineteenth-century leaders deserved considerable credit for the law of 1909 which added Tennessee to the rapidly expanding list of dry states.

Social Experiments 8→ Among other reformers there were those who sought to revise the economy by establishing communistic societies. Indeed, there were so many such experiments in Tennessee that one writer (Grace Sloan) has referred to the Volunteer State as a "social and economic laboratory." The short-lived colony of Nashoba in Shelby County has been discussed in an earlier chapter. Gruetli, Rugby, and Ruskin were three others which thrived in the post bellum days.

Gruetli, indeed, had been established in Grundy County by a handful of Swiss settlers before the war. Natives of Grundy knew them for their industrious manual toil and their skill in cabinet making, woodworking, and gardening. At the turn of the century a newspaper reporter visited the colony and found it to be "like a part of a foreign country" because of the "strange" customs of the people and because French, German, and broken English were spoken by all. He was impressed by the skill of the wood carvers, gardeners, and producers of fine wines.

Rugby has been a subject not infrequently exploited by historians and littérateurs. Thomas Hughes, author of *Tom Brown's School Days* and other books for boys, opened Rugby (in the northern part of Morgan County), in October, 1880. He thought of it as a haven for young British yeomen "with good education and small capital, the class which of all others is most overcrowded in England at this time . . . ." Tired of getting, spending, and wasting their powers, the rising generation would establish a "kingdom" in the virgin forests of America where they would enjoy high thinking and plain living. Hughes, a dreamer, conceived of a society in which the humblest members living by the "labour of their own hands, would be of such strain and culture that they would be able to meet princes in the gate without embarrassment and self-assertion." Within a few years the colony of "enchanted solitude" in the Cumberland Plateau had failed, largely because of lack of business-like methods in administering the affairs of the settlement.

Ruskin Colony originated in the mind of an Indianian named Charles Augustus Wayland—a self-styled "grass roots Socialist" described by one Marxist historian as "the greatest propagandist of Socialism that has ever lived." Wayland already had a sizable following through the wide circulation of his newspaper, *The Coming Nation*, when, in July, 1894, he established in Dickson County the "Ruskin Cooperative Association." Impressed by the writings of John Ruskin (for whom the colony was named), Edward Bellamy, and Henry George, Wayland believed that he could establish an agrarian paradise far from the noise and strife of the complex industrial society.

The Ruskin colony failed in 1899. Although the settlers had tilled the soil and manufactured a variety of items, most of the funds for operation had come from gifts and from subscriptions to *The Coming Nation*. In addition to issuing the newspaper, the settlers published thousands of leaflets and tracts in which they denounced the "wage slavery" of the Northeast and called for "another Lincoln" to lead the common man of the East out of economic bondage. The editors deplored the fact that some corporations and businessmen defied Congress, "the constitution, courts, or any other power." Following the dissolution of the settlement, some of the colonists continued to live in Dickson County, but others carried the remnants of the colony to Georgia. When the movement collapsed a few years later, leaders still proclaimed that only socialism held the key to future happiness in America.

Bob Taylor Returns to the Gubernatorial Chair ठ॰
Many observers thought that Democratic chances for success in 1896 had floundered on the rock of political controversy of 1894. Democrats themselves were disheartened. The older generation of party leaders, although with some degree of guilt after their conduct in 1894, still were loyal to the party; they looked with disbelief at the exodus of young industrially minded Democrats who flocked to the Republican party. Believing that their problems were not dissimilar to those which had faced them in 1886, they readily concluded that their only hope for redemption before the people lay with Robert Love Taylor, whose silver tongue and skillfully maneuvered bow had mesmerized voters and healed the party breach by his performances on the hustings in that year. They therefore pressed "Our Bob" into service and nominated him for governor. On a financially successful lecture tour in the West, Taylor hastily returned to don the Democratic mantle. Chiding party leaders for their "dissension and discord" and admitting that they "had departed from the true policies of old-fashioned Democratic government," the Hero of Happy Valley promised all-out war on Republicans and Populists alike.

The thunder of Populism was little more than an echo now, but Republican leaders, hoping to capitalize upon Democratic dissension, revived cries of the "martyrdom" of H. Clay Evans and pledged a Democratic defeat. Populists again nominated A. L. Mims of Nashville, and Republicans chose George N. Tillman, also of Nashville. An able orator, Tillman pointed to promises of "Republican prosperity" and to the Democratic depression under Cleveland, accused Taylor of running for governor to use the office as a stepping-stone to the United States Senate, and denounced the entire Democratic party for the conduct of its leaders in 1894.

In a close contest, Taylor won by about 7,000 votes.[4] William Jennings Bryan, although he lost the presidency, carried Tennessee.

[4] Taylor, 156,333 votes; Tillman, 149,374; and Mims about 12,000.

In the state legislature, Democrats gained a 4 to 1 majority. The overwhelming success of the party was attributable largely to the magnetism of Bob Taylor. Tillman's allegations of fraud and claims of contesting the election soon disappeared when the Democratic-controlled legislature discouraged him by enacting a law requiring contestants to post penal bonds of $25,000.

Trouble between the United States and Spain already was brewing when Taylor was elected. Many American capitalists by this time had made enormous profits from the development of Cuban sugar and they, supported by the United States government, were angered by Spain's mismanagement of the affairs of the island. In 1895, Cubans staged an insurrection in which much property belonging to American businessmen was destroyed, and the Republican party in the following year elected McKinley on a platform which favored the independence of Cuba.

Conditions became worse after McKinley's inauguration. In January, 1898, the United States sent the battleship *Maine* to Havana to protect American lives. A few weeks later the vessel was blown up and several officers and 258 crewmen were killed. Although guilt was never clearly determined, Americans thought that the Spanish were responsible and therefore prepared for war. On April 28 the United States declared war to make Cuba safe from Spanish treachery and inhumanity and to join in an imperialistic race for colonies in the Pacific.

Four Tennessee regiments were mustered into service, and other Tennesseans served in additional regiments or in the navy or marines. The First Tennessee, originally commanded by Colonel William Crawford Smith, fought heroically at Manila. When Colonel Smith died of heat prostration, Lieutenant Colonel Gracey Childers assumed command and led the regiment admirably for the remainder of the battle. The Second Tennessee Regiment under the command of Colonel Kellar Anderson, the Third Tennessee led by Colonel J. P. Fyffe, and the Fourth Tennessee Regiment commanded by Colonel George Leroy Brown were sent to Cuba, but they saw little if any fighting. When the troops returned late in 1899, Benton McMillin had been elected governor (having defeated the Republican candidate, James A. Fowler, by a vote of 105,640 to 72,611 during the war) and welcomed the veterans in a florid address before a large throng of Middle Tennesseans.

Although Bob Taylor had sought, among other things, greater equity in taxation, and even had called the legislature into extra session for this and other purposes, little of significance was accomplished during his administration. His major function once again had been that of uniting dissident forces within the Democratic party.

The Tennessee Centennial Exposition 8∾ The greatest extravaganza during the Taylor administration—and perhaps the greatest even that Tennesseans had ever witnessed—was the Tennessee Centennial. It began at noon on May 1, 1897, when President William McKinley pressed a button in Washington which officially opened the gates in Nashville to the Tennessee Centennial Exposition. For six months thereafter, people from all parts of the world viewed the real and the fancied. Preparations, proceeding at a torrid pace in 1896, were not complete on the one hundredth anniversary of Tennessee's statehood. All officials could do on June 1, 1896, was to open and dedicate Centennial Park and to announce hopefully that the celebration would begin in the following spring.

The "centennial dream" may have originated in the mind of Douglas Anderson, a prominent Nashvillian. In 1892 Anderson wrote letters to editors of various newspapers and suggested that preparations be made immediately for a celebration to be held in 1896. He proposed that six cities—Nashville, Knoxville, Chattanooga, Memphis, Columbia, and Jackson—compete for the privilege of staging it. For two years the idea "existed on oral wind and printers' puffs," Anderson later wrote, but in 1894 Nashvillians, who in 1880 had staged a successful performance in celebration of the one hundredth anniversary of their city, began to prepare in earnest for the exposition. A "Centennial Association" was organized to arouse interest in Tennessee history and make preliminary plans for an exposition. Educators added Tennessee history to the curriculum of studies in elementary schools, which did much to create interest in the exposition.

Shortly before opening day, Professor R. L. C. White prepared a list of one hundred questions on Tennessee history and called it his "Centennial Dream." He published the questions in newspapers and offered rewards for correct answers. The Association published an *Official Guide to the Tennessee Centennial and International Exposition and City of Nashville,* which described in detail the wonders visitors could see. Readers of the *Guide* had their attention called to a "six-day tour" that featured displays in the Mineral and Forestry Buildings, the Parthenon, Little Egypt, Vanity Fair, and the like. Hotel rates for room and board were quoted at from two to four dollars per day, carfare was five cents, and individual meals cost twenty-five cents.

On opening day, thousands of visitors heard the usual bursts of oratory and cannon; they heard Governor Taylor, in a spirit of levity not uncommon to the Hero of Happy Valley, describe his vision of the world one hundred years hence.

> Who can tell what another century will unfold, [exclaimed Our Bob]. I think I see a vision of the future opening before me. I see triumphs in art, and achievements in science, undreamed of by the artisans and philosophers of the past. I see the sun darkened by clouds of men and women flying in the air. I see throngs of passengers entering electric tubes in New York and emerging in San Francisco two hours before they started. I see the gloved and umbrellaed leaders of the Populist party sitting in their horseless carriages and singing the harvest song, while the self-adjusting automatic reapers sweep unattended through the fields, cutting and binding and shocking the golden grain. I see swarms of foreign pauper dukes and counts kissing American millionaire girls across the ocean, through the kissophone. I see the women marching in bloomers to the ballot box and the men at home singing lullabies to the squalling babies. I see every Republican in America drawing a pension, every Democrat holding an office, and every "cullud pusson" riding on a free pass; and then I think the millennium will be near at hand.

With the speech-making over, visitors entered to view the great and the majestic, the weird and the fantastic. They walked along winding, graveled roads bordered by buildings, beautiful flowers, fountains, and lakes. Most of the buildings were of wood, but plastered in such a manner as to appear to be of pale gray stone. The Parthenon, however, which occupied the most conspicuous site on the grounds, was of permanent construction. A replica of the Athenian building, the Parthenon housed an extensive art exhibit. Nearby stood the Erectheum, another reproduction of a building on the

Acropolis of Athens, which was devoted to historical relics. There, as two historians, Garrett and Goodpasture, wrote in 1905, Robert T. Quarles and G. P. Thruston displayed a collection of state historical relics, maps, and artifacts. In other buildings was exhibited what Gentry R. McGee[5] termed "a marvelous array of almost everything to be found in a civilized country." Laces and various other textiles, jewelry, firearms and ammunition, and the finest specimens of timber, iron, coal, stone, and other minerals were on display. Another building housed vehicles from wooden-wheeled ox carts to "the most elegant and elaborate palace cars."

Vanity Fair, "so replete with strange people, strange sights, and strange noises," could be enjoyed in its entirety for $5.90. Within this section of the exposition were reproductions of the streets of Cairo, a Chinese village, a "Colorado gold mine," and a display designed "to show the progress of the Negro race from the old plantation days to the present." Here and there were side-show men who clamored for all to see "the greatest show on earth."

The musical presentations provided one of the highlights of the exposition. On many occasions the large pipe organ in the auditorium, a novelty to some visitors, could be heard. Vocalists and choruses, including the Fisk Jubilee Singers, entertained thousands. Bands and orchestras attracted large audiences, but the Marine Band of Cincinnati, the "Legion Band," the "Prohibition Band," the Centennial Orchestra, and Victor Herbert and his Twenty-Second Regiment Band of New York were the most popular. The last was wildly cheered; listeners claimed that they played Verdi and Stephen Foster with equal skill and feeling. When the band departed for New York, a group of Nashvillians followed them to the train as though they were reluctant to permit such talent to leave Tennessee.

Hundreds of thousands had viewed the spectacular and the bizarre when the exposition closed on November 1. As Gentry R. McGee[6] wrote two years later,

> When the first blasts of November winds were scattering the fallen leaves the grand exposition closed. It had been one of the most successful and creditable ever undertaken and carried out by a single state. Every department had shown the wonderful progress of the state since her pioneer days, and the creation and manage-

[5] *History of Tennessee*, 259.
[6] *Ibid.*, 259–60.

ment of the great exhibit had shown the genius and energy of the men and women who had charge of its fortunes.

General Albert Sidney Johnston, who thirty-five years earlier had called vainly for a few Nashville-owned slaves to assist him in constructing Forts Donelson and Henry, would not have thought Nashvillians capable of such a display of energy. General John B. Hood's barefoot men who trudged hopelessly into the capital only three decades earlier would not have recognized the Davidson County seat. The Exposition truly was Tennessee's greatest contribution to the gilded age.

SUGGESTED READINGS

General Accounts

Folmsbee, Corlew, and Mitchell, *Tennessee*, II, Ch. 32; Hamer, *Tennessee*, II, Ch. 46; Henry McRaven, *Nashville, Athens of the South* (Chapel Hill, 1949); A. Elizabeth Taylor, *The Woman Suffrage Movement in Tennessee* (New York, 1957); White, *Tennessee Educational Organization*; White, *Messages*, VI, VII.

Specialized Accounts

Douglas Anderson, "The Centennial Idea and the Centennial 'Dream,'" *THM*, Ser. 2, III (Jan., 1935), 107–10; W. H. G. Armytage, "New Light on the English Background of Thomas Hughes' Rugby Colony in Tennessee," ETHS *Publ.*, No. 21 (1949), 69–84; Francelia Butler, "The Ruskin Commonwealth: A Unique Experiment," *THQ*, XXIII (Dec., 1964), 33–42; Arthur B. Chitty, Jr., *Reconstruction at Sewanee* (Sewanee, 1954); Corlew, *Dickson County*, Ch. 10; E. Katherine Crews, "Musical Activities in Knoxville, Tennessee, 1861–1891," ETHS *Publ.*, No. 34 (1962), 58–85; Crews, "The Golden Age of Music in Knoxville, Tennessee, 1891–1910," ETHS *Publ.*, No. 37 (1966), 49–76; John H. Ellis, "Memphis' Sanitary Revolution, 1880–1890," *THQ*, XXIII (March, 1964), 59–72; Folmsbee, *East Tennessee University*; Folmsbee, *Tennessee Establishes a State University* (Knoxville, 1961); Gilbert E. Govan and James W. Livingood, *The University of Chattanooga: Sixty Years* (Chattanooga, 1947); Marguerite Bartlett Hamer, "Thomas Hughes and His American Rugby," *NCHR*, V (Oct., 1928), 391–413; David Edwin Harrell, Jr., "The Disciples of Christ and Social Force in Tennessee, 1865–1900," ETHS *Publ.*, No. 38 (1966), 30–47; Harrell, *Quest for a Christian America* (Nashville, 1966); William B.

Hesseltine, "Methodism and Reconstruction in East Tennessee," ETHS *Publ.*, No. 3 (1931), 42–61; Isaac, *Prohibition and Politics*; Joseph C. Kiger, "Social Thought as Voiced in Rural Middle Tennessee Newspapers, 1878–1898," *THQ*, IX (June, 1950), 131–54; Kincaid, *Wilderness Road*, Ch. 24; Grace Leab, "Tennessee Temperance Activities, 1870–1899," ETHS *Publ.*, No. 21 (1949), 52–68; Lewis, "Tennessee Gubernatorial Campaign," *THQ*, XIII (June, 1954), 99–126; LeRoy Albert Martin, *A History of Tennessee Wesleyan College, 1857–1957* (Athens, 1957); Edwin Mims, *History of Vanderbilt University* (Nashville, 1946); Mims, *Chancellor Kirkland of Vanderbilt* (Nashville, 1940); Grace Sloan, "Tennessee: Social and Economic Laboratory," *Sewanee Review*, XLVI (Jan.–March, April–June, July–Sept., 1939), 36–44, 158–66, 312–36; Brian L. Stagg, "Tennessee's Rugby Colony," *THQ*, XVII (Fall, 1968), 209–24; A. A. Taylor, "Fisk University and the Nashville Community, 1866–1900," *JNH*, XXIX (April, 1954), 111–26; William R. Webb, Jr., "Sawney Webb: My Father and His Ideals of Education," *Sewanee Review*, L (April–June, 1942), 227–40.

24. ᛒᴥ Twentieth-Century Politics—
McMillin to Peay, 1899–1923

FEW PEOPLE found Tennessee politics boring during the first two decades of the twentieth century. Republicans, who a few years later were destined to endure lean years, struggled valiantly for control and, sometimes in league with insurgent Democrats, even fared sumptuously at the table of political success. Democratic factionalism, apparent during the 1880's but healed temporarily by the balm of Bob Taylor, made serious tears in the Democratic fabric during the first two decades of the twentieth century and was responsible to some degree for the success of the Republicans. New alignments and new issues—prohibition, particularly—combined to produce a Republican resurgence, claims of Democratic decadence, and enough excitement for years to come.

Democratic Control ᛒᴥ The twentieth century opened with a concerted effort by Republicans to carry the state for President McKinley. "Tennessee ought to be Republican," wrote editor William Rule of Knoxville in the summer of 1900. "There are one hundred thousand white men in the state of Tennessee who would rejoice to have the Republican party triumphant . . . ." Alf Taylor, John C. Houk, and Ben W. Hooper were among those who pointed to Republican industry and prosperity and who urged Tennesseans to reject the candidacy of William Jennings Bryan. Democrats were in control of the election machinery, however, and the Democratic organization carried the day for Bryan. Indeed, the Nebraskan received 144,751 (55.4 per cent) of the 265,945 votes. Republicans, temporarily disheartened but not disillusioned, soon found a way by which they could disenchant the majority party.

In the meantime the Democrat-controlled legislature turned its attention to state and local matters. Benton McMillin became governor in 1899 and was reelected by a comfortable majority in the following year. Governor McMillin had manifested a distinct interest in public schools, and, at his suggestion, several measures pertaining to education were enacted, including a law which empowered school boards in each county to establish a high school. To raise funds necessary for constructing school buildings, county courts were authorized to levy taxes not exceeding fifteen cents on each hundred dollars of taxable property. Other school laws provided for the election of school directors for each school district, uniformity in the use of textbooks throughout the state, increased appropriations for teachers' institutes, and the designation of one day each school year as "Arbor Day." A sinking fund for the retirement of bonded indebtedness was established, and the state capitol was refurbished.

McMillin was not a candidate for a third term, and Democrats therefore nominated James B. Frazier, who had practiced law in Chattanooga after his admission to the bar in 1881. Although without political experience, Frazier was elected in 1902[1] and again in 1904[2] by comfortable majorities. In 1904, Democrats for the first time adopted a platform which approved prohibition. In the campaign, Governor Frazier, apparently not wishing to alienate support of the liquor interests in the cities, supported the Four Mile Law as amended, but did not wish to apply it to the nine cities which it did not affect. Jesse M. Littleton, his Republican opponent, favored local option across the state.

One of the first matters commanding Governor Frazier's attention was the coal mines of East Tennessee where many mine owners, in their desire for profits, operated unsafe mines. Consequently, an act was passed providing for "the regulation and inspection of mines," and "for the safety, welfare, and protection of persons employed therein . . . ." Rigid standards and penalties were established. Two years later, Frazier pointed to the fact that since the enforcement of

---

[1] Frazier received 98,902 votes; Campbell, Republican, polled 59,007; and R. S. Cheves, Prohibitionist, 2,198.

[2] Frazier received 131,503 and Jesse M. Littleton, Republican, received 103,409.

the law no lives had been lost in the mines and no damaging explosions had occurred. Other matters to receive legislative attention were education and the reduction of the bonded indebtedness.

Shortly after his second inauguration, Governor Frazier resigned to take the seat of United States Senator W. B. Bate, who had died on March 9. John I. Cox, speaker of the state senate, filled out the unexpired gubernatorial term. No legislative innovations were suggested during his administration, except that the General Assembly did provide for a state flag, designed by LeRoy Reeves, and approved the purchase of 11,000 acres in Bledsoe, White, and Van Buren counties (the "Herbert Domain") as a place for convict labor. Cox was widely known as an anti-prohibitionist, and his election as speaker of the senate and his subsequent elevation to the governor's chair were partly responsible for the defeat of efforts to apply prohibition to the cities during the legislative term of 1905.

Malcolm Rice Patterson defeated Cox for the Democratic nomination in 1906 and then beat the Republican nominee, H. Clay Evans (who with Newell Sanders had gotten control of the party), in the general election.[3] Patterson was born in Alabama but was reared in Memphis and educated at Vanderbilt University; he was an experienced politician, having served as attorney general in Memphis and as congressman from the Tenth District for three terms until his resignation in November, 1906, after his election as governor. A bitter foe of the prohibitionists when elected, he later embraced their cause after his earlier stand had ended his political career.

Patterson's first term was a relatively progressive one and fairly free of strife except for the whiskey question which had been an issue off and on since the second quarter of the nineteenth century. Laws were passed prohibiting gambling at horse racing, creating a tax equalization board, prohibiting the manufacture or sale of adulterated or improperly branded food or drugs (the "State Pure Food and Drug Act"), and purchasing a mansion for the governor. The commission created for the latter purpose bought a house on Seventh Avenue, one-half block from the capitol. Succeeding governors lived there until 1922 when it was razed to make room for the erection of a war memorial building.

---

[3] Patterson received 111,856 votes and Evans, 92,804.

Prohibition and Democratic Division ⤳ Bob Taylor's conciliatory balm, applied so effectively to the divisive forces of Democratic factionalism in 1886 and again in 1896, had become ineffective by the time of the Democratic convention of 1908. In that year a new break appeared in the Democratic organization which was to result in the reelection of Patterson at the cost of good feeling, and ultimately to result in the slaying of Edward Ward Carmack, in statewide prohibition, and in the fusion of the Republicans and an independent wing of the Democrats. The bitterness was not to be healed for some years thereafter, despite the fact that Bob Taylor was brought forth again as a gubernatorial candidate in 1910. Even Bob himself had become irritated earlier at Governor Frazier because of the haste with which the governor's friends had pushed him into the Senate—a seat for which Bob had been anxious since his days as governor.

The Democrats in their convention in 1908 adopted the novel procedure of staging a statewide primary for the nomination of a gubernatorial candidate instead of selecting him in convention. Party leaders, well aware of the bitterness within the party over the fermenting liquor question, hoped that the primary would avoid an outright split. Everyone knew of course that Patterson wanted a second term. He had made enemies, however, and they coalesced around Edward Ward Carmack, who agreed to run (in spite of the advice of Kenneth McKellar and other friends) against Patterson.

Few Tennesseans have had so stormy a political career as Carmack. A native of Tennessee who was educated at Webb School, he began his colorful career as a lawyer and newspaper editor in Columbia; there he was also a member of the county court and was elected to the house of representatives. In 1888, Carmack founded a paper in Nashville called *The Democrat* and a few months later became editor-in-chief of the Nashville *American* when the *Democrat* and the *American* were merged. In 1892, he became editor of the Memphis *Commercial* (which soon was merged with the *Appeal*) where he wrote strong editorials on imperialism, free silver, and policies advocated by William Jennings Bryan. Carmack was elected to Congress in 1896 after resigning as editor of the *Commercial Appeal* in a quarrel over editorial policy, and remained until his election to the United States Senate in 1901. His stay there was limited to one term because he was defeated by Bob Taylor in 1906. As candidates in

1906, both Carmack and Taylor had sought to wear the mantle of the prohibitionists and both tried to associate the other with the saloons in this first senatorial primary in Tennessee.

In the gubernatorial contest, both Carmack and Patterson waged a warm and vigorous campaign from Memphis to Bristol. Carmack was a florid orator with a ready wit not unlike that of Bob Taylor; Patterson was slow and methodical, but equally competent. Their campaign managers—George Armistead of Franklin for Carmack and Austin Peay of Clarksville for Patterson—were known as able organizers across the state; Peay later became governor. The principal issue of the campaign became that of prohibition—a question which was not new to Tennesseans but which had become increasingly poignant in Tennessee with the advent of the twentieth century. The Four Mile Law as amended in 1887 had forbade retail liquor sales within four miles of any rural school whether public or private; twelve years later the law was amended to apply to newly incorporated towns of 2,000 or less. As a consequence, many towns chose to surrender their charters and apply for new ones under which the sale of whiskey within their borders would automatically be prohibited. Four years later, the law was applied to towns of not more than 5,000, which would include all but nine municipalities. Alarmed brewers urged Tennessee grog shops retailing their products to close on Sunday and otherwise try to improve public relations, but the Chattanooga Brewing Company boldly announced a $200,000 expansion program.

Shortly after the legislation of 1903 was enacted, leaders of the Anti-Saloon League announced plans to apply prohibition to every county in the state. They were successful in 1907 when the legislature passed the Pendleton Act, which extended the law to the cities, despite concerted opposition by the liquor interests and former Governor Cox who had returned to the senate. Knoxvillians immediately became embroiled in a referendum on the question and voted nearly 2 to 1 for a new charter with automatic prohibition. By the end of the year, only Memphis, Nashville, Chattanooga, and LaFollette were "wet." Governor Patterson, who, according to a later governor (Ben W. Hooper) had "personal habits in connection with intoxicants [which] were notoriously in conformity with his political tenets," had viewed the trends with alarm. Advocating local option instead of legislative prohibition, Patterson ran in 1908 with the full support of the liquor interests and of course the state machine; Carmack, admitting that earlier he had supported local option but now believed that statewide prohibition was necessary for the well being of all the people, had the support of the rural folk, the church groups, and the progressive Bryan Democrats. The immediate result—thanks to large majorities in Shelby, Hamilton, and Davidson counties—was a victory for Patterson by a majority of some 7,000 votes. Of more far-reaching concern, however, was the bitterness which engulfed the Democratic party and which became acute with the slaying of Carmack a short time later.

In the meantime, Republicans had become just as inharmonious —if not more so—than the Democrats. Among the Republicans who had quarreled bitterly for years over federal patronage, prohibition, and legislative apportionment were able leaders such as First District Congressman Walter P. Brownlow (a distant cousin of "Parson" Brownlow), former Second District Congressman John C. Houk, Second District Congressman Nathan W. Hale, former First District Congressman Alf Taylor, H. Clay Evans, and Newell Sanders (a Chattanooga businessman, a federal patronage dispenser under President Theodore Roosevelt, and chairman of the State Republican Committee). By 1908, the Republicans were divided into the Sanders Regulars and the "Home Rule Group" led by Houk. When they assembled in Nashville on March 25 for a convention, the result was, as the editor of the Knoxville *Journal* wrote, a "Free for All" which lasted "for an hour or more, in which heads were skinned, noses mashed, and clothing of delegates torn." Sanders was choked to the point of unconsciousness, locks and latches were hacked off the doors to the house chamber, and thousands of dollars of furniture was destroyed. Needless to say, little of a constructive nature was accomplished at the convention, but a few weeks later the Regulars under Sanders and Evans reassembled and nominated George N. Tillman for governor and endorsed William Howard Taft for President. In the general election, Patterson defeated Tillman by a vote of 133,166 to 113,233.

Carmack Slain ঙ৶ In the meantime, Carmack became editor of the Nashville *Tennessean*, a newspaper recently established by a young Nashville attorney and politician, Luke Lea. Carmack, extremely bitter over his defeat, had considered contesting the results of the primary but finally contained himself as best he could with a terse announcement that "the fight against liquor must go on." He had many things and many people to criticize, and among the first of his enemies to receive scathing denunciation were Governor Patterson and Duncan B. Cooper. Cooper was an intimate friend and adviser to Governor Patterson, and a former friend and employer of Carmack when the latter was editor of the Nashville *American*.

Enmity between Carmack and Cooper, which ultimately resulted in the death of the fiery editor, probably began in 1896 when Cooper championed the cause of Malcolm Patterson's father, Josiah, when the latter ran a close but unsuccessful race against Carmack for Congress. Later, in 1906, Cooper warmly supported Bob Taylor in his successful race against incumbent Carmack for the United States Senate and Patterson in his successful campaign for governor. The two victories made Cooper a powerful politician in Tennessee. Carmack in his race against Patterson in 1908 charged that "Bald-headed Dunc" (sometimes it was "a little bald-headed Angel named Dunc") was in unholy league with Governor Patterson against the people, and he urged the voters to support him in turning both out of power.

The references to himself rankled in Cooper's mind, and he dispatched a friend, E. B. Craig, to the *Tennessean* editor soon after Carmack's appointment with a threat that he would not tolerate continued criticism. Soon thereafter, however, Carmack wrote and published a flippant editorial dripping with ridicule in which he gave credit to Cooper for the reconciliation of Patterson and former Governor Cox, who had been political enemies since before Cox was governor. On the following day, Cooper and his son, Robin, a young Nashville lawyer, met Carmack by chance on the corner of Union Street and Seventh Avenue. The three were armed, Carmack having been persuaded by friends a few days earlier to carry a gun for his own safety and the Coopers apparently arming to avenge their honor. At any rate, several shots were fired and Carmack was killed instantly.

A long trial ensued in the Davidson County criminal court in which it was shown that Robin Cooper had fired three shots, all of which struck Carmack, and that Carmack had fired two shots, one of which struck Robin's right shoulder. A decision of second degree murder was rendered by the court, and the Coopers were sentenced to twenty years in prison. A few months later the supreme court affirmed the decision of the lower court with respect to Duncan Cooper (who had not fired a single shot), but remanded the case of Robin Cooper (who fired the shots which killed Carmack) for retrial. Within a few minutes after hearing the decision, Governor Patterson pardoned Duncan Cooper.[4] "It took the Supreme Court seventy-two days to decide this case and it decided it the wrong way," he asserted. "It took me seventy-two minutes and I decided it the right way." Few people were surprised at the pardon, but all were shocked at the unmitigated haste and flippant attitude Patterson took toward the deliberate judgment of the court.

Needless to say, Patterson signed his political death warrant when he pardoned Duncan Cooper. Equally important was the impetus which both the slaying and the pardon gave to the cause of prohibition; Carmack became a far more powerful political figure in death than he had been in life. When the legislators assembled on the first Monday in January, 1909, they were overwhelmed by hundreds of church and prohibition leaders on one hand, and the liquor lobbyists on the other. The result was the enactment of statewide prohibition to become effective July 1, 1909. Governor Patterson promptly vetoed the measure, as was expected, but the legislators passed it over his veto. Another measure prohibiting the manufacturing of intoxicating beverages went into effect six months later.

Of equal significance were the General Education Law of 1909 (to be discussed later) and a general election law which struck at the roots of the governor's political control. The election law gave the General Assembly the power to select the State Election Board which must consist of two members from the majority party and one from the minority party. The board, then, would select bipartisan commissions in the counties. Before, the board members had been appointed by the governor who always chose members of his own party. Patterson and the regular Democrats vigorously opposed the law, but it was passed by a coalition of Republicans and Independent Democrats. The coalition presaged the advent of fusion politics in the state.

---

[4] Charges ultimately were dropped against Robin Cooper. Later he died a violent and unexplained death. His body was found in his automobile in Richland Creek and a bloody brick, apparently the murder weapon, lay nearby.

In the meantime, as indicated, the Carmack Democrats had organized into what came to be called the "Independent Democrats," with Luke Lea and E. B. Stahlman as the chief spokesmen. The first test of strength came in the summer of 1910 when in the Democratic primary five candidates for the supreme court ran as independents against the nominees of the Regular Democrats handpicked by Patterson. Shortly before the decision in the Carmack case, Governor Patterson was said to have attempted to influence the decision of Chief Justice W. D. Beard, an old friend of his father, Josiah Patterson. The report was widely circulated among the Carmack group that Patterson, at the head of the Regular Democratic machine, was trying to control the courts. Beard, therefore, charging that he would stand only for a "free and untrammeled judiciary," repudiated Patterson and soon announced that he and other court members would not run as party nominees in a primary as directed by the State Democratic Executive Committee, but would run as independents. This stand by Beard united Independent Democrats as nothing else had; leaders immediately convened in Nashville and nominated three incumbent justices—Beard, John K. Shields, and M. M. Neil—and Grafton Green and David L. Lansdon. The Regulars nominated incumbents W. K. McAlister and Bennett D. Bell, and R. E. Maiden, R. M. Barton, and R. B. Cooke. An independent slate for the court of appeals also was selected.

Independents were desirous of winning at almost any cost, and apparently promised to support a Republican candidate for governor in the general election in return for Republican support in the judicial primary. At any rate, the Republican State Committee endorsed the Independent ticket and studiously took action to prevent the name of any Republican from being placed on the ballot. The Independent slate was victorious in the August primary by more than 40,000 votes, 25,000 being polled in East Tennessee where Republicans were strongest. There was little doubt but that Republicans en masse had crossed party lines to help elect the Independents.

Ben Hooper Elected Governor ₰ Both parties chose able gubernatorial candidates. The Regular Democrats had nominated Patterson in June, but Independents had abstained with the assertion that they might support a Republican if a strong prohibitionist were nominated. Republicans met in Nashville a few days after the Democratic primary in one of the largest and most significant conventions in the history of the party. Although more than a dozen names had been suggested before delegates assembled, the choice finally boiled down to Alf Taylor and Ben W. Hooper of Newport. Amid pledges to unite for the sake of the party, Hooper, an ardent prohibitionist, was nominated.

The nominee, a young (thirty-nine) lawyer, was not without political experience. He had served in the state legislature, had been an assistant United States attorney for the Eastern District of the state, was a captain in the Spanish American War, and had been a party leader for nearly two decades. His mild and genial manner made him generally acceptable and the fact that he was a prohibitionist made him acceptable to the Independent Democrats. Within a few weeks the Independents formally endorsed him.

In the meantime, Patterson faced the hopelessness of the contest. Championing local option when prohibition was gaining momentum, accused by some of having plotted Carmack's murder, charged with attempting to tamper with the judiciary, and faced with a division within his own party which could not be healed before the election, Patterson received a final blow when in early September the only newspaper supporting him (the Nashville *American*) was purchased by Luke Lea and merged with the anti-Patterson *Tennessean*. On September 10 the governor, pleading a desire "to harmonize the discordant elements in the Democratic party," withdrew. Three weeks later the Regular Democrats announced from a "Harmony Convention" that they had nominated the old conciliator and spellbinder of earlier times, Bob Taylor, then in the United States Senate.

The campaign between the two East Tennesseans waxed warm. Taylor, despite his sixty years and his desire to remain in the Senate (which he effectively concealed throughout the campaign), met Hooper in acrid debate across the state. Hooper attacked the pardoning record of both Taylor and Patterson, blamed the Democrats for "maladministration," and charged that Taylor if elected would be simply a tool of the Patterson machine. Taylor denied that he was in any way attached to Patterson, but in oratorical tones reminiscent of days of old he championed the cause of public education, good government, good roads, heaven, and separation of church and state, and in tones of righteous indignation effectively scored hell, sin, and Republicans. This time, however, even the magnetism and charm of Bob Taylor could not heal the Democratic breach, and Hooper was elected by a vote of 133,074 to 121,694. The orator of course had not resigned his Senate seat and thus returned to Washington where he served until his death on March 31, 1912. (Governor Hooper appointed Newell Sanders to the Senate seat to serve until an election could be held.)

Democrats achieved very little unity during Hooper's first administration. Conflict between the Fusionists (Independent Democrats and Republicans) who had a tenuous majority in the house and the Regular Democrats who controlled the senate developed soon after the legislative session opened. After the Regulars gave up hope of unseating Hooper, and Fusionists dropped plans to contest several disputed legislative seats, legislators turned their attention toward electing a successor to Senator Frazier, whose term expired March 4, 1911. The Regulars concentrated upon Benton McMillin, but the Fusionists, with the support of Mayor Ed Crump of Memphis, elected Luke Lea. Debate over the election law of 1909 and enforcement of prohibition soon caused the Fusionists to lose control of the legislature. When a bill was passed by the Regulars modifying the election law of 1909 to such an extent that Democrats would have complete control of the state's election machinery, thirty-four Fusionists (with money supplied by Newell Sanders) fled to Decatur, Alabama, to prevent the formation of a quorum. When Governor Hooper promptly vetoed the election measure, the breaking of the quorum meant that no action could be taken on a movement to override the veto.

Finally, after an absence of two months the legislators returned when an agreement was reached among Crump, Lea, Sanders, and Stahlman. Crump agreed to permit the Shelby delegation to vote with the Fusionists on the election law in return for an agreement that Fusionists would support measures beneficial to Memphis and which incidentally would enhance his own power. The session ended with the election law of 1909 and the prohibition laws intact.

Hooper was a candidate to succeed himself and McMillin was chosen by the Regular Democrats who were joined by a few Independents. Hooper, with the strong support of Newell Sanders (recently appointed to the Executive Committee of the Republican

National Committee), defended his record and charged that the election of McMillin would be a "return to lawlessness." McMillin decried the division within Democratic ranks and promised to end the "temporary reign of Republicans."

A new candidate, perhaps, unassociated with the Patterson machine might have united the Democrats, but not McMillin. Most Independents voted once again for Hooper; he won by a vote of 124,641 to 116,610.

The legislative session of 1913, like that of 1911, was one of considerable turbulence. Whether the Fusionists or Regulars controlled depended upon what Edward Crump of Memphis wished the Shelby delegation to do. The result was that Crump, who permitted open saloons in Memphis as an expedient to power, worked with the Fusionists during the first part of the session but switched to the Regulars after Hooper called for enforcement legislation designed to close the saloons in Memphis.

Before control laws could be enacted, serious controversy arose when Democrats passed a measure revising the election law of 1909 to regain complete control of the state election commission and the county election commissions. Again, as in 1911, Fusionists prevented the majority from passing the measure over the governor's veto by leaving the state (March 31), thus breaking the quorum. Three months later they returned and took their seats long enough to vote on a general appropriations measure. Before they could get away again—armed guards this time prevented their departure—the Regulars passed the election bill over the governor's veto, but the Supreme Court subsequently nullified it. The Fusionists departed from the state again and remained away until the rump session adjourned on August 23.

Governor Hooper's proposed measures to enforce the prohibition laws had not been acted upon, and he therefore called the legislature into special session early in September. Among other things, he asked for laws to close saloons, to remove local officials who refused to enforce prohibition, and to regulate the shipment of liquor into the state. Although the measures passed the senate, the special session ended on September 27 before they could be brought to a vote by the tumultuous members of the house.

Governor Hooper promptly called the legislature into a second extra session two weeks later. This time he was more successful, as

Democratic legislators realized that some type of enforcement was necessary. Despite opposition from Mayor Crump and other officials from the large cities, legislators—in an unusually brief session of only five days—passed several laws; the most important of these were the Nuisance Law and two anti-shipment laws. Under the Nuisance Act an attorney general, city or county attorney, or ten citizens might secure the closing of saloons, "bawdy houses," and gambling establishments by court order if it could be clearly shown that police officials had refused to act. The anti-shipment laws prohibited the shipment of liquor from county to county within the state and forbade the transportation of intoxicants into the state from "wet" states; an important exception provided that individuals could carry or have delivered to their places of residence quantities of one gallon or less at a time. The laws were designed of course to close the saloons but not necessarily prevent drinking at home.

Among other important action taken by the legislators in 1913 was the election of John K. Shields (who had succeeded as chief justice in 1910 upon the death of W. D. Beard) to a six-year United States senatorial term after having chosen W. R. ("Sawney") Webb to fill the remaining two months of the late Senator Bob Taylor's unexpired term.

State Democrats Unite Temporarily Behind Wilson ॐ

In the meantime, Democrats on the national level elected a President—the second one in more than fifty years. The advent of Woodrow Wilson upon the political stage pleased the Independent Democrats, and two years before his election they received rumors of his candidacy with enthusiasm. Wilson captured the attention of astute political observers across the country in November of 1910 when he was elected governor of New Jersey where Republicans normally dominated. Immediately the editor of the Chattanooga *Daily Times* hailed him as the hope of his party in 1912 and boldly predicted that he would win the presidential nomination. Luke Lea, owner of the newly merged *Tennessean and American*, joined the *Daily Times* in endorsing Wilson for the presidency. The Nashville *Banner*, on whose staff Wilson's brother, Joseph, worked as city editor, saw him as one who could return the country "to the statesmanship of the old days." During the next two years, news about Wilson (whose father, Dr. Joseph R. Wilson had taught at Southwestern Presbyterian Theological Seminary at Clarksville from 1885 to 1892) dominated the front pages of the Democratic press of Tennessee; his western tour in 1911—his first substantial bid for the nomination—was followed carefully, and his speeches were printed.

When in February, 1912, Wilson visited Nashville to dedicate the new Young Men's Christian Association building, he found Independents solidly behind him but the Regulars divided among three other major contenders for the nomination. Senator Bob Taylor led the forces of House Speaker Champ Clark; Hilary E. Howse, the defiant anti-prohibitionist mayor of Nashville, championed the cause of Senator Oscar Underwood of Alabama; and the *Commercial Appeal* of Memphis and Nathaniel Baxter of Nashville upheld the interests of Judson Harmon of Ohio. The division of Democratic ranks continued through the state convention in May and the Baltimore convention a few weeks later.

Those who hoped that Democratic division would cause Wilson to lose the state were to be disappointed. President Taft, of course, had been nominated by the Republicans, but Theodore Roosevelt's political ambitions had helped to create a breach in the party so that the Progressives nominated Roosevelt. The warm summer weather and the apparent hopelessness of the situation caused the rotund Taft to limit his speaking engagements considerably after early June, but Roosevelt, with the vigor which characterized his entire life, carried his campaign to Memphis, Jackson, Chattanooga, Knoxville, and points across the country. Because Tennesseans had elected a progressive Republican governor two years before, many observers believed the state would vote Republican or Progressive. Democrats were able to close ranks sufficiently, however, to gain for Wilson a little more than half the popular vote and thus, of course, all the electoral votes. Taft and Roosevelt shared the remaining popular votes about equally.

Thomas C. Rye Elected Governor ঙ৵ Democrats settled their quarrels sufficiently in 1914 to regain the governor's chair. They nominated a relatively unknown attorney general of the Thirteenth District, Thomas C. Rye of Henry County, a prohibitionist who was unassociated with the bitterness of party factionalism and who was generally acceptable to party leaders in all sections of the state. Democrats, in an obvious effort to heal the breach, wrote a platform favoring prohibition.

Both Republicans and Independents nominated Hooper for a third term, but Independents were so weakened by defectors—chief of whom was Luke Lea, who now turned the full strength of his powerful newspaper in favor of Rye—that they entertained little hope of success. Interestingly, former Governor Patterson, once the nemesis of the prohibitionists, but now a teetotaler and under the employ of the American Anti-Saloon League, also declared strongly for Rye.[5] The result was a victory for Rye by a vote of 137,656 to 116,667. Democrats also secured control of the General Assembly.

The most controversial legislation passed during Rye's administration was the Ouster Law, enacted in January, 1915. The general purpose of the measure was to remove public officials who failed to enforce the law, but more specifically it was aimed at Memphis Mayor E. H. Crump and other city officials who permitted saloons to operate in defiance of the law. Ouster suits could be filed by state, county, or city attorneys or upon petition by ten or more citizens who were freeholders.

Suit was filed against Crump by the state attorney general in October, 1915. The chancery court in which the suit was tried declared that Crump had not enforced prohibition laws and that he could no longer hold office. In the meantime the Memphis mayor had been reelected to another term which would begin January 1, 1916. The supreme court, however, to which the chancery decision was appealed, issued a stay order on January 1 preventing him from taking office; six weeks later the court sustained the decision of the chancery court and stated that Crump had been properly ousted. Suits against officials in Nashville, Knoxville, and other cities were not successful.

Shortly after Crump's removal, Governor Rye called the legisla-

[5] Patterson announced his conversion to teetotalism and strong law enforcement in the summer of 1913 after a series of unfortunate incidents. His son had become involved in difficulties in Washington and in 1911 was committed to a mental institution. Two years later, Patterson while in Nashville became intoxicated and was arrested "in a raid on a house of prostitution"—apparently by Mayor Hilary Howse in an effort to discredit him. Not long after this unfortunate episode, Patterson joined a Protestant church, and became a teetotaler and a strong defender of prohibition. He lectured under the auspices of the Anti-Saloon League and frequently was heard before civic and church groups in speeches supporting temperance and law enforcement.

ture into special session to inquire "into the official conduct and
fidelity of circuit and criminal court judges and district attorneys of
the state," particularly Judge Jesse Edgington and Attorney General
Z. Newton Estes of Memphis. The legislature convened on March
21 and brought impeachment proceedings against the two a few
weeks later. Both were convicted and removed from office. Considerable interest also was shown in an attempt to remove Sheriff J. A.
Reichman of Shelby County, but testimony before the chancery
court indicated that facts would not support the allegations.

Other legislation during Rye's two terms provided for the creation of a control board for charitable and penal institutions, a
state highway commission, the registration of automobiles and
trucks, a special highway tax to match federal funds, and a general
budget system. Of great significance was an act of 1917 requiring
that party nominations for major offices be made by primary elections instead of by conventions. A proposal for a woman's suffrage
amendment was defeated at the polls in 1917.

The election of 1916 created considerable interest. Wilson was
nominated again for President and defeated Charles E. Hughes, his
Republican opponent, by a comfortable majority in the state, although his national margin was indeed small. In the gubernatorial
election, Rye defeated John W. Overall, of Liberty, who for some
years had been a United States marshal for Middle Tennessee and
a prominent Republican.[6] Principal interest centered in the senatorial race in which Congressman Kenneth D. McKellar defeated
former Governor Ben W. Hooper.

McKellar was born in Alabama but moved to Memphis as a
young man. He earned three degrees at the University of Alabama
and became a successful lawyer in Memphis before his election in
1911 to Congress, where he served until his election to the Senate.
In the primary of 1916, McKellar defeated Luke Lea, the incumbent, in a bitter contest in which former Governor Patterson and
George L. Berry (later a member of the Senate) also were candidates. In a vigorous campaign before the general election, tempers
flared frequently; McKellar defeated Hooper by about the same
majority as Rye polled in the governor's race.

[6] The vote was 146,758 to 117,817.

Administration of Governor Albert H. Roberts ᘒ The entrance of the United States into World War I in April of 1917 did not dampen the interest of Tennesseans in state and national politics. Voters were not surprised when Governor Rye announced that he would seek election to the United States Senate instead of reelection to a third term as governor. The principal candidates for the Democratic gubernatorial nomination in 1918 were Chancellor Albert H. Roberts of Overton County and Austin Peay of Clarksville. The two men vigorously stumped the state before Democratic voters. Roberts won by about 12,000 votes and then defeated the Republican nominee, Judge H. B. Lindsay of Campbell County, by nearly 40,000 votes in the general election.

Senator Shields, the incumbent, defeated Rye in the senatorial primary by a small majority and won over H. Clay Evans in the general election by more than 30,000 votes. Shields had been elected to the Senate in 1913, the last time a General Assembly elected a United States senator. (The Seventeenth Amendment which gave the people the right to elect United States senators went into effect later in that year.) In the primary, he found Rye, who had the open support of former Governor Patterson and the tacit support of President Wilson, a formidable foe, and Shields was forced to cancel plans to remain in Washington and returned instead to campaign. His warm support from Ed Crump and Senator McKellar was sufficient to net him a victory, although he failed to win Middle Tennessee.

The first item of business under the Roberts administration was the ratification of the Eighteenth Amendment, which prohibited the manufacture, sale, and consumption of alcoholic beverages. Inasmuch as Tennessee had been legally "dry" since 1909, ratification was considered a perfunctory matter. By a vote of 28 to 2 in the senate and 82 to 2 in the house, Tennessee became the twenty-third state to vote favorably on the proposed amendment.

Of greater significance were laws which revised the tax structure of the state. For a decade the expenses of operating the government had exceeded the revenue to such an extent that the deficit amounted to several millions of dollars. Roberts made economy in government and tax reform his chief issues. Inadequate laws, poor collections, and incompetent and corrupt officials, he told legislators, were moving the state toward bankruptcy. He therefore discharged several unnecessary state employees and urged tax revision upon the legislature. The result was a "sliding scale" assessment law and legislation which gave the State Railroad Commission power to assess taxes on public utilities, including telephone and telegraph, electric power, gas, and water companies in addition to the railroads.

Other significant laws were passed. One million dollars was appropriated, to be matched jointly by Davidson County and the city of Nashville, for the erection of a war memorial building. Land was purchased and work was begun at once. Two measures were but a prelude to the bitter struggle for ratification of the Women's Suffrage Amendment. One granted women limited suffrage by giving them the right to vote in municipal and presidential elections, and the other, called the "Married Women's Emancipation Act," gave married women the same rights with respect to property as those held by unmarried women. Other laws repealed an act of 1915 which had abolished capital punishment, levied a special tax for school support, and established a state textbook commission.

Tennessee Ratifies the Nineteenth Amendment ई∾ The question of woman suffrage was not new to Tennesseans. As early as 1883 a bill had been introduced in the senate to permit women to vote in matters pertaining to schools, and a few years later a woman suffrage league was organized in Memphis. More than thirty-five years were to elapse, however, before suffrage leaders could claim even a partial victory.

In the meantime, faithful feminists sought to educate the people on the matter at hand. In 1906 they conducted a "Southern Woman Suffrage Conference" at Memphis and organized the Tennessee Equal Suffrage Association. Within the next decade numerous other organizations were formed on the local level in all of the major cities. Frequently, liberal college faculty members were at the head; the Vanderbilt Equal Suffrage League became a model for leaders at other colleges and universities throughout the state. Leaders from other states, including officers of the National American Woman Suffrage Association, addressed and encouraged Tennessee leaders from time to time. In the forefront of state and local activity was Sue Shelton White of Henderson. She frequented legislative and congressional halls alike, called upon President Wilson on many occasions, demonstrated with other women in front of the White House, and was arrested and sentenced—for lighting a fire on the White House lawn—to the Old Work House in Washington where she promptly went on a hunger strike until she was released.

Both Governor Hooper and Governor Rye favored enfranchisement during their administrations, but not until Governor Roberts was in office did women achieve their goal. In 1913 a proposed amendment which Hooper favored was defeated before the people. In 1917 feminists sponsored a bill with Rye's approval to give women the right to vote in presidential and municipal elections, but this bill also was defeated. When the measure passed two years later, leaders considered it a token only; they ignored it and concentrated the full measure of their force upon ratification of the proposed Nineteenth Amendment.

By the summer of 1920, thirty-five states had ratified the Nineteenth Amendment and eight had rejected it. (Thirty-six, or three-fourths of the states, of course was required for constitutional ratification.) Of the remaining five, Tennessee, Vermont, and Connecticut were the only ones suffrage leaders believed might ratify it. Inasmuch as legislators in Vermont and Connecticut refused to vote on the question until after the November elections, Governor Roberts was urged to call a special session so that Tennesseans might express their desire through their elected representatives. Even President Wilson, believing perhaps that membership in the League of Nations might be accomplished by the senators elected in 1920, telegraphed Roberts to urge the calling of a special session. Democratic presidential nominee James M. Cox of Ohio also urged Roberts to act, as did many prominent state leaders of both parties. One avid Democrat saw great significance in the matter for his party and wrote Roberts that if Tennessee did not ratify immediately, "some Republican state will," and "rob Tennessee of its chance for glory and the Democratic party of its . . . opportunity for success at the polls in November."

Roberts needed little persuasion. Once convinced of its legality, he called the special session to convene on August 9.[7] Former Gov-

---

[7] Roberts hesitated at first because the state constitution provided that an amend-

ernor Rye, as president of a "Men's Ratification Committee," and a variety of women's organizations began immediately to lobby for ratification. They were met by the Tennessee division of the "Southern Women's League for the Rejection of the Susan B. Anthony Amendment," and also by a variety of conservative politicians, preachers, and general citizens who argued that ratification would cause women to lose their femininity, violate the laws of God, elevate Negroes to high political offices, destroy democratic government, and even bring on a destructive war of the sexes. Those favoring ratification had the help of such prominent national figures as Carrie Chapman Catt, long associated with the movement for women's rights, and Senator McKellar. Those opposing ratification welcomed Congressman Finis J. Garrett and Major E. B. Stahlman to capitol hill.

Observers noted from the beginning that the real struggle would be in the house of representatives. Two days after convening, members of the senate voted 25 to 4 for ratification. After several days of debate, Seth Walker, the house speaker who earlier had favored ratification but who had changed his mind when the special session was called, moved the tabling of the resolution. This attempt to defeat woman suffrage failed by a vote of 48 to 48. Ratificationists then moved the adoption of the amendment. Harry T. Burn of McMinn County had voted to table, but now he voted with the forty-eight ratificationists; this vote accomplished the adoption of the amendment by 49 to 47, since the constitutional majority of 50 was not necessary for ratification. So that he might have the right to move reconsideration of the action and perhaps still defeat ratification after tempers had cooled and interest had abated, Speaker Walker then changed his vote also.

After several days, while Walker waited for interest to cool, suffrage leaders raised the question of reconsideration themselves so

---

ment to the Constitution of the United States cannot be acted upon by a legislature elected before the amendment is submitted. In an Ohio case (*Hawke* v. *Smith*, 253 U.S. 221) involving the Eighteenth Amendment, however, the Supreme Court held that states could not establish rules for the ratification of a federal amendment because the power to ratify derives solely from the United States Constitution. Section 32 of Article II of the state constitution was, in effect, voided, and a special session consisting of legislators who had been elected before the proposed amendment was submitted could be and was called.

that they might dispose of it by defeating it. Much to their surprise, however, they found that about thirty legislators opposed to ratification had entrained for Decatur, Alabama, to prevent the formation of a quorum. A few others who remained in Nashville secured a restraining order from a circuit court judge enjoining Governor Roberts from certifying a vote and reporting the results to the secretary of state in Washington. Despite the absence of a constitutional quorum, ratificationists disposed of the motion to reconsider anyway. They argued, as in *Hawke v. Smith*, that authority to adopt or reject a constitutional amendment comes from the federal and not the state constitution; a simple majority of those voting, they said, not a majority of the elected members as specified by the state constitution, was sufficient. The chief justice of the state supreme court granted a petition to dissolve the injunction issued earlier. Governor Roberts thereupon certified the vote of ratification to Secretary of State Bainbridge Colby in Washington, who accepted the results despite continued complaints and allegations of illegality from those opposing ratification. Further efforts to undo the work of the suffrage advocates were to no avail, and thus Tennessee became the pivotal state in the nation's acceptance of the Nineteenth Amendment.

A *Republican Victory* ≷ Scarcely had the smoke cleared from the ratification struggle when the November elections occurred. Democrats nominated Governor Roberts for a second term and confidently predicted a November victory by 50,000 votes. Several prominent Republicans sought the nomination, including T. F. Peck of Etowah and Jesse Littleton, but the aging Alfred Taylor was chosen instead. In the meantime, Senator Warren G. Harding of Ohio and Governor Cox of Ohio had been nominated for President by their respective parties. It was a Republican year in Tennessee as well as in the nation as a whole. The people, war-weary and apparently tired of the Democratic manna of idealism, turned to the fleshpots of Harding and the Republicans. Harding won the presidency by a landslide vote and carried Tennessee by a substantial majority. The success of the national Republicans, opposition to Roberts by the rising labor organizations, and the magnetism of the Taylor name swept Alf Taylor into the governor's mansion by more than 40,000 votes.[8]

During Taylor's administration, laws were passed creating the office of state tax commissioner, expanding the power of the Railroad and Public Utilities Commission, providing money for the establishment of Andrew Johnson's tailor shop in Greeneville as a shrine, and the creating of the Tennessee Historical Committee to collect and preserve antiquities of the state. Democrats controlled the legislature and inevitable friction between the governor and the General Assembly resulted. Governor Taylor was especially interested in the continuation and expansion of the Muscle Shoals project which was begun during the war as a nitrate manufacturing plant. He headed a delegation of Tennesseans to Washington in an effort to persuade Congress not to abandon the project. Sources close to the governor told of his effectiveness in helping to avoid serious labor difficulties between the expanding unions and Tennessee's growing industry.

Democrats Victorious in 1922 ⁊ Republicans nominated Governor Taylor to succeed himself in 1922. In a close contest in the Democratic primary, Austin Peay defeated former Governor Benton McMillin by about 4,000 votes. Taylor and Peay provided an interesting contrast before the voters. Alf Taylor, personally appealing, entertained the cheering crowds with jokes about his dog, "Old Limber," and with stories about his mountain friends and neighbors from Happy Valley. He sat on the platform and beamed as his three sons and a friend thrilled the crowds with their renditions of religious and mountain folk songs. Peay, however, told no stories but soberly promised an aggressive administration in which he would build highways, develop public education, and lower taxes. Most of the state press, including the Nashville *Tennessean* and the Memphis *Commercial-Appeal,* supported him. Although the crowds cheered Alf, they voted for Peay. The Clarksvillian was elected by a vote of 141,002 to 102,586.

At the same time, Senator McKellar defeated Newell Sanders by a substantial vote and continued a distinguished career which was

---

[8] The vote was Taylor 229,143 and Roberts 185,890.

not to end until his defeat by Albert Gore in 1952. The legislature also was Democratic, which assured party control of the state.

SUGGESTED READINGS

General Accounts

Folmsbee, Corlew, and Mitchell, *Tennessee*, II, Chs. 34, 44; Hamer, *Tennessee*, II, Chs. 45–46; Kenneth D. McKellar, *Tennessee Senators as Seen by One of Their Successors* (Kingsport, 1942), Chs. 34–41; Cartter Patten, *A Tennessee Chronicle* (Chattanooga, 1953), Ch. 29.

Specialized Accounts

Everett Robert Boyce (ed.), *The Unwanted Boy: The Autobiography of Governor Ben W. Hooper* (Knoxville, 1963); Isaac, *Prohibition and Politics*, Chs. 6–16; Eric Russell Lacy, "Tennessee Teetotalism: Social Forces and the Politics of Progressivism," *THQ*, XXIV (Fall, 1965), 219–40; Arthur S. Link, "Democratic Politics and the Presidential Campaign of 1912 in Tennessee," ETHS *Publ.*, No. 18 (1946), 107–30; James P. Louis, "Sue Shelton White and the Woman Suffrage Movement," *THQ*, XXII (June, 1963), 170–202; John Berry McFerrin, *Caldwell and Company: A Southern Financial Empire* (Chapel Hill, 1939); McRaven, *Nashville*; William D. Miller, *Mr. Crump of Memphis* (Baton Rouge, 1964); Miller, *Memphis During the Progressive Era* (Memphis, 1957); Miller, "The Progressive Movement in Memphis," *THQ*, XV (March, 1956), 3–16; J. Winfield Qualls, "Fusion Victory and the Tennessee Senatorship, 1910–1911," WTHS *Papers*, No. XV (1961), 79–92; Verton M. Queener, "The East Tennessee Republican Party, 1900–1914," ETHS *Publ.*, No. 22 (1950), 94–127; Leslie F. Roblyer, "The Fight for Local Prohibition in Knoxville, Tennessee, 1907," ETHS *Publ.*, No. 26 (1954), 27–37; Russell L. Stockard, "The Election and First Administration of Ben W. Hooper as Governor of Tennessee," ETHS *Publ.*, No. 26 (1954), 38–59; Stockard, "The Election and Second Administration of Governor Ben W. Hooper of Tennessee as Reflected in the State Press," ETHS *Publ.*, No. 32 (1960), 51–71; Taylor, *Woman Suffrage Movement*; Rufus Terral, *Newell Sanders: A Biography* (Kingsport, Tenn., 1935), Chs. 12–22.

25. ᠀᠊᠁ Education in Twentieth-Century Tennessee

Ｆ Tennessee has a creditable system of public education, it has been in large measure the product of the
men, events, and time that have moved across the horizons of the
twentieth century in the state. During the second half of the nineteenth century, the disrupting forces of civil war, the emancipation
of slaves, the bitterness of reconstruction, the economic distress of
the farmers, and the complacency of the people had kept educational
progress at a minimum. But with the dawn of the twentieth century, the state emerged from the Panic of 1893 with land values
and the price of farm products rising sharply. The state debt, a
problem to each General Assembly since the days of Reconstruction,
had been placed on a sound basis; state income had increased considerably; and a surplus of funds had accumulated in the treasury.

Increasing State Support, 1900–1930 ᠀᠊᠁ Prior to the beginning of the new century, education had not been involved deeply
in state politics. With the improvement of economic conditions and
the subsiding of the political battle between the small farmers and
the Bourbons, however, the less privileged people of the state began
to think in terms of improved educational opportunity for their
children. Benton McMillin, elected governor in 1898 on a platform
calling for better schools, secured the passage of acts establishing
high schools and requiring uniform textbooks, which stimulated
the people's interest in education.

The appointment of Seymour A. Mynders as state superintendent of public instruction by Governor James B. Frazier in 1903 marked the beginning of a new era in education in Tennessee. The first professionally trained and experienced educator to be elevated to that office, Mynders was determined to see his program of education enacted into law. After his training at The University of Tennessee, he had served as a teacher and administrator in the public schools and thus had a wide acquaintance with school people; Mynders was able to organize them into a well-directed political force.

When Superintendent Mynders took office, the status of the schools was low. Five months was the length of the school term prescribed by law, but the requirement was not enforced in many counties. There were 6,758 primary schools (grades one through five), 1,069 "secondary" schools (grades one through eight), but no high schools. The scholastic population, as defined by law, numbered 771,965, of which 484,663 were enrolled in schools, with 341,538 in regular attendance. Thus, less than 50 per cent of those eligible were attending school. The average monthly salary of teachers was $28.86, with a low in Van Buren County of $18.50 and a possible high in Shelby County of $40.72. The training of teachers appears to have been commensurate with the salaries. There were no state colleges for teacher training, except that the state in 1901 did provide George Peabody College for Teachers with $55,600 to be used for scholarships and to support teachers' institutes. It was not until 1903 that The University of Tennessee received its first appropriation from the state treasury, $10,000 for the acquisition of some additional farm land.

Confronted with this deplorable situation, Superintendent Mynders early in 1903 brought to Nashville a group of school administrators who drafted an eight-point platform for educational improvement and launched a campaign to achieve their objectives. In brief, the platform called for an increased state school fund, local taxation for education, school consolidation, better training for teachers, establishment of teachers' and school libraries, establishment of one or more high schools in each county, elimination of politics and nepotism from the schools, and intelligent and economical expenditure of school funds.

During the next several years, Mynders and his successors in the office of state superintendent, Robert L. Jones and John W. Brister, also trained educators, conducted periodic, statewide campaigns in the interest of education. They had the aid and leadership of Philander P. Claxton, the capable professor of education and director of the famous Summer School of the South at The University of Tennessee. Claxton previously had served with the Southern Education Board and later was to become United States commissioner of education. Also participating were many county superintendents, the State Teachers' Association (and also the sectional associations), the Public School Officers Association, and the Southern Education Board. As public apathy gradually decreased, business, professional, and civic leaders formed "The Cooperative Education Association," later called the School Improvement League. Public rallies were held repeatedly in practically every county in the state, and in election years efforts were made to induce every candidate for the legislature, in the enthusiasm of the moment, to pledge support of the specific items in the school improvement program.

Although much important legislation was passed, the outstanding achievement of this "campaign era" was the General Education Law of 1909, which brought together in one measure much of the program of reform which the education leaders had been advocating. The bill, in its broad scope, called for the annual appropriation of 25 per cent of the gross revenue of the state to the general education fund, to be distributed as follows: (1) 61 per cent to the counties in proportion to scholastic population; (2) 10 per cent to equalize the common schools in the several counties; (3) 8 per cent to assist the counties in maintaining high schools; (4) 1 per cent to establish and maintain public school libraries; (5) 13 per cent to establish and maintain four normal schools, one in each of the grand divisions and a fourth for Negroes, in Nashville; and (6) 7 per cent to maintain and improve The University of Tennessee.[1] It may be said that this law provided the core of the present educational system of Tennessee. While the amounts and percentages have varied in subsequent appropriations, the broad principles have remained constant, and the services and institutions established have been maintained and broadened.

The peculiar effectiveness of the "school lobby" is indicated by the passage of this legislation in 1909 in the midst of a bitter political

---

[1] Two years earlier the institution had received $100,000 as its first biennial appropriation for maintenance.

controversy between the wets and the drys, which resulted in the enactment of statewide prohibition over Governor Patterson's veto and a serious division in the Democratic party. This split led to the election of a Republican governor, Ben W. Hooper, in 1910 and 1912. Although Hooper had not made education a major plank in his platform, he and State Superintendent John Brister successfully sponsored legislation increasing the general school fund from 25 per cent to 33⅓ per cent of the gross revenue and providing for compulsory school attendance, uniform examination and certification of teachers, school consolidation, and the transportation of pupils.

The campaign era in Tennessee education was a period of rare accomplishment. County high schools were established. Normal schools for the three grand divisions were established at Johnson City, Murfreesboro, and Memphis; and the Agricultural and Industrial Normal School for Negroes was built in Nashville. School consolidation was started, transportation of pupils was originated, school libraries were created, the training of teachers was improved, and The University of Tennessee was given financial support by the state and made an integral part of the state school system.

During the two administrations of Governor Tom C. Rye (1915–19), there was a temporary reaction against educational progress. Although the charge was scarcely justified, Rye had campaigned on the promise to take the schools out of politics. In 1915, two laws passed despite the opposition of the school forces were an enlargement of the State Board of Education, which also was given the power to name the state superintendent, and the establishment of the Tennessee Polytechnic Institute (now the Tennessee Technological University) at Cookeville, to be financed by reducing the state appropriation for high schools by 25 per cent. Two years later a vigorous effort was made to reduce the support of higher education in order to increase the appropriation for elementary and secondary schools. This plan to "divide and conquer" failed, and the school forces reunited sufficiently to obtain the enactment of a progressive program of legislation, despite the imminence of American participation in a European war.

The legislation of 1917, more comprehensive than any since 1913, provided:

1. That all counties be required to levy a five-cent High School Tax, and that the maximum County High School tax be raised from fifteen cents to twenty-five cents.

2. That a $625,000 bond issue be authorized for a building and improvement program for the normal schools.

3. That a $1,000,000 bond issue be authorized for an expansion program for the State University.

4. That a five-cent General Property Tax be levied "to provide for the development and maintenance of the University and to retire the $1,000,000 bond issue."

5. That the 7 per cent of the General Education Fund formerly appropriated to the university be divided equally between the equalization fund for elementary schools and the state fund for high schools, 5 per cent to the former and 2 per cent to the latter.[2]

The comprehensive nature of the program aided its enactment. The newly established normal schools and high schools had developed widespread support, and interest in the University had become more statewide as a result of the establishment of agricultural experiment stations in West and Middle Tennessee and the moving of the institution's medical school from Nashville to Memphis.

Governor Albert H. Roberts in 1919 appointed to the state superintendency of public instruction the youthful but aggressive Albert Williams, who moved with alacrity in formulating a program and securing its legislative enactment. The law provided for a five-cent general property tax in addition to all other school revenues. The new funds were to be distributed one-third to the counties equally, one-third to the counties on the basis of scholastic population, and one-third as an equalizing fund to be given to those counties having less than a seven-months' school term. During the first year this law was in operation, the schools received $2,500,000 more than the previous year. A strengthening amendment to the compulsory school attendance law and legislation creating a five-member textbook commission were also enacted in 1919.

Under the leadership of Williams, education took on new life in Tennessee. The State Teachers' Association, which for three years had been dormant, was reorganized into a militant body. The Public School Officers Association gained renewed strength and became

[2] Holt, *Struggle for a State System of Public Schools*, 293. The bond issue for normal schools needed supplementary legislation in 1921.

again a powerful force for the advancement of education. United States Commissioner of Education P. P. Claxton, at the request of Governor Roberts and Superintendent Williams, returned to the state to launch a campaign for education. Claxton presided over a Tennessee Citizens' Conference at Monteagle in August, 1920, which adopted a program calling for a minimum school term of eight months, adequate support of high schools, teacher-training privileges for church and private colleges, adequate support of the state university and of the normal schools and provision for their expansion, uniformity of school legislation, and the supplying of funds sufficient to put Tennessee's schools in the front ranks of the nation. The campaign was in full swing with good promise of success when Governor Roberts was defeated for reelection by the Republican candidate, Alfred A. Taylor.

Fortunately, Governor Taylor had pledged his wholehearted support of the schools in the campaign, and he backed his state superintendent, J. B. Brown, in presenting a sound educational measure in the early days of the legislative session of 1921. Property taxes for school purposes were increased by three cents on the $100 assessed valuation; counties participating in the equalization fund were required to levy a thirty-cent property tax on the assessed valuation and to maintain a school session of 100 days; the long-promised $625,000 in bonds for the normal schools and the Tennessee Polytechnic Institute were made available; the state supplement to county superintendents' salaries was increased; most of the elementary school fund was to be apportioned among the counties on the basis of average daily attendance instead of scholastic population; and state aid was provided for teacher-training in certain first-class high schools. Thus, a Republican governor and a Democratic legislature cooperated to maintain the growth of education.

The inauguration of Governor Austin Peay in 1923 marked the dawn of a new era in educational administration in Tennessee. During his first term, however, he was mainly interested in a thorough reorganization of the state government. Within this plan, the state superintendent of public instruction was renamed commissioner of education and made a member of the governor's cabinet. Although this change resulted in improved school administration, it also gave the governor tremendous power in determining educational programs and appropriations. With few exceptions, this power has been used to the advantage of the schools of the state.

The first commissioner, Perry L. Harned, had a rich background of experience in both education and politics and succeeded in getting Peay's support for an educational reform program which, despite numerous amendments, became the General Education Law of 1925. It provided that the state would supply adequate funds for an eight-months' school term and for teachers' pay according to a state salary schedule to any county that would levy an elementary school tax of fifty cents on each $100 of property, a poll tax of one dollar, and such privilege taxes for school purposes as were allowed by law. In addition to setting up a state salary schedule, the act standardized the licensing of teachers, changed the normal schools to four-year teachers' colleges, increased the school fund by including most of the revenue from a newly enacted tobacco tax, and laid the groundwork for a general building program. While this measure was still pending in the legislature, the famous—or infamous—Anti-Evolution Act was passed. One reason why Governor Peay signed it was the fear that otherwise the education law would be jeopardized.

After defeating Hill McAlister in the Democratic primary of 1926, despite McAlister's charge that Commissioner Harned had put the schools in politics, Governor Peay pushed through the legislature another progressive education law. The allocation from the tobacco tax to the equalization fund was increased from $250,000 a year to $800,000; a million-dollar bond issue was authorized for the improvement of rural school buildings; a $600,000 appropriation was made for necessary improvements in the teachers' colleges; and $500,000 was to be appropriated annually for five years to The University of Tennessee as a building fund. The tobacco tax revenue was also to be used to pay off the bonds. By separate legislation not requested by the school lobby, the Austin Peay Normal School (now University) was established at Clarksville and a junior college branch of The University of Tennessee was located at Martin.

With the death of Austin Peay, on October 2, 1927, the cause of public education lost one of its best friends. His successor, Henry Horton, however, continued Harned in his office as commissioner and supported his efforts in 1929 to have the educational appropriation made a part of the state budget rather than being a percentage (33⅓) of the gross revenue of the state. Although later criticized, this change was essential. Because of departmental exceptions, the "gross revenue" had come to include only the receipts from the general property tax of twenty cents, which was reduced to eight cents in 1931 and later abolished entirely.

Education During Depression, Recovery, and Wars ♦
Education faced a serious crisis with the economic depression deepening in 1930, with state finances seriously affected by the loss of state funds through the failure of Caldwell and Company, and with Governor Horton being subjected to impeachment charges when the legislature convened in 1931. Under the circumstances it was indeed a triumph for Horton and Harned that school appropriations of 1931 were kept at the existing levels. The amounts appropriated were not actually paid when due, however, because of the increasing deficit in state funds. Local sources of revenue also became depleted. The salaries of teachers, including those at the institutions of higher learning, were radically reduced, and some school systems had to resort to the use of scrip. It was a period of hardship and suffering for school personnel.

It was during this critical period that Hill McAlister assumed the office of governor in January, 1933, after having been elected on a platform of economy and a balanced budget. During 1932, Dr. P. P. Claxton had returned to Tennessee to lead another educational campaign like those of 1906 and 1908, but because of the depression it was not very successful. McAlister, however, not unfriendly toward education, had promised during the campaign to do for the schools whatever the financial condition of the state would permit. He appointed as his commissioner of education the first commissioner in the state to hold a Ph.D. degree, Professor Walter D. Cocking of George Peabody College for Teachers.

When the legislature of 1933 convened, the cry for economy involved a serious attack on the state institutions of higher learning, including the demands that the teachers' colleges be closed for two years and appropriations for the state university be reduced by one-half. With the greatest of difficulty, the "school lobby" prevented the closing of the teachers' colleges. In the compromise finally enacted, appropriations for higher education were slashed approximately 66⅔ per cent, high schools 28 per cent, and elementary schools 19½ per cent. Since appropriations for highways were cut

50 per cent, education did not suffer much greater reductions, pro-
portionately, than other state functions. Within the educational
field, however, higher education received the most serious cuts. As
a "depression courtesy" all elementary and secondary teachers holding limited training certificates were allowed to teach during the
next biennium without complying with the state requirement of
attending summer school or renewing their certificates by examination. A redeeming feature of the legislation of the session was a bond
issue from which the teachers would receive $8,000,000 for the im-
mediate payment of long overdue salaries. Also, the general appropriation bill provided that school funds should be distributed
monthly instead of twice yearly. Finally, the legislature created a
special educational commission to direct a study of public education
in Tennessee and report its findings to the regular session of the
1935 legislature.

This commission, under the chairmanship of Dr. Cocking and
including eight appointed members, after an intensive study submitted a two-volume report in October and December, 1934. A
preview of the second volume, containing the recommendations,
was published in November in the newspapers in such a way as to
present a distorted impression concerning the commissioner's aims.
The leading recommendation was to shift the main responsibility
for maintaining a minimum school program from the local units of
government to the state. This was presented by the press merely as a
demand for a trebling of the state's appropriations for education.
The natural reaction was unfavorable. The chief means of financing
the program suggested by the commission and other school forces
was the enactment of a general sales tax. It was hoped that the
Shelby delegation, under the control of E. H. Crump, would support
such legislation, but it joined forces with the opposition. Thus the
sales tax was doomed and with it all immediate hopes of educational
reform. The commission's report, however, remained a mine of
information for the school forces and contributed greatly to later
educational progress.

Meanwhile, the State Teachers' Association had been reorganized
and revitalized under a new name, the Tennessee Education Association, and with the support of the sectional associations it rapidly
pushed to the fore as the leader of the educational forces in the

state. A new constitution in 1933 provided for the employment of a full-time executive secretary, for the creation of the representative assembly as the legislative body of the organization, and the administrative council as the agency to implement the policies thus determined. It also began the publication of *The Tennessee Teacher*.

Following the disappointing results of the 1935 session of the state legislature, Commissioner Cocking called a conference of superintendents to meet at Camp Clements on Caney Fork River in September of that year. A committee of nine drafted a seven-point program to be presented to the next legislature: 1. that the state should finance a minimum salary schedule for elementary teachers, provided there should be no restriction of local initiative; 2. that the minimum school term should be eight months for elementary schools and nine months for high schools; 3. that the minimum salary for teachers should be $60.00 a month, provided that as standards of qualifications were raised salaries should be raised in direct proportion to such increases in standards and improvements in training and experience; 4 that all beginning teachers must have completed at least two years of study in an approved institution of higher learning; 5. that adequate library facilities be made available for pupils in all the public schools; 6. that the state should encourage desirable consolidation of schools, efficient transportation, and skilled supervision; and 7. that adequate facilities for higher education be provided by the state. After the representative assembly of the Tennessee Education Association added an eighth point calling for the creation of "an adequate and actuarily sound retirement system," the "Eight-Point Program" was unanimously approved by that group.

Under the direction of Secretary W. A. Bass of the association, the program was well publicized, and each candidate for governor and each candidate for the legislature was asked to support it. Thus, when the legislature of 1937 convened, Governor Gordon Browning and a majority of the legislators were committed to it. Legislation to implement in part the program included the appropriation for the biennium of $7,000,000 for elementary schools, $750,000 for high schools, $750,000 for The University of Tennessee, and $110,000 for each four-year state college. Also, the legislature declared its intent to assume the entire cost of a minimum school program as soon as the finances of the state would permit it to do so.[3] Since the governor had promised a balanced budget, the legislature made provision for impounding portions of the appropriations if state revenues should not equal expenditures. The University, the state colleges, and school libraries suffered the most serious cuts under the impounding procedure.

The Tennessee Education Association directed its campaign of 1938 toward the complete realization of the Eight-Point Program. Although Prentice Cooper, the successful gubernatorial candidate in that year, had pledged support to the program, he had also promised a balanced budget and no new taxes. During his first administration he did little more than hold the line for schools, although he did inaugurate, with an appropriation of $325,000, a program of providing free textbooks for pupils in the lower grades. High schools received a $200,000 increase for the biennium, but libraries and the state colleges suffered slight decreases in appropriations. With the depression approaching an end, it was possible for the legislature of 1941 to add for the biennium $151,000 to the appropriation for the state university, $250,000 for the elementary schools, and another $200,000 for the high schools.

World War II brought havoc to the public schools of the state. Large numbers of young men and women left the teaching profession to enter the armed forces or to accept more remunerative employment in defense plants. Governor Cooper adhered to his program of economy, but gradually there appeared to be a little comprehension by those in authority of the tragic condition of the schools. The legislature of 1943 appropriated $850,000 per year as an emergency salary adjustment, and at a special session in 1944 made a special appropriation of $3,200,000 or as much as would be necessary to increase teachers' and principals' salaries by $20.00 per month. With the election of Jim Nance McCord as governor in 1944 a new day dawned for the schools of the state. On his strong recommendation the legislature of 1945 not only raised all basic educational appropriations by considerable amounts, but also made another special appropriation of $4,050,000 for the purpose of guaranteeing each full-time teacher or principal a salary increase of

---

[3] Also included were appropriations for transportation of pupils, school libraries, supervision and consolidation, supplementing the salaries of superintendents, and vocational education.

$25.00 per month. It also established a fund of $500,000 to go to the institutions of higher learning to be used for the benefit of returning war veterans.

The most important educational achievement of the McCord administrations was the enactment in 1947 of a general sales tax of 2 per cent, with the revenue going largely to the public schools. This followed his reelection in 1946 during a campaign that also involved a vigorous fight in the interest of better schools by the Tennessee Education Association and several civic groups. The same General Assembly appropriated $24,870,932 for the public elementary and secondary schools and stipulated that $19,500,000 must be contributed by local governments; The University of Tennessee was given an annual appropriation of $3,073,200, the largest in its history up to that time. The 1947 legislature also finally passed the eighth point in the Eight-Point Program of 1936 and instituted a retirement program for teachers. This law provided that each teacher would contribute 5 per cent of his annual salary, which would be matched by state funds. Provisions also were made for permissive and mandatory retirement at specified ages. Although neither adequate nor ideal, the system was a start in the right direction. Eventually, in 1957, this retirement program was combined with the federal social security system and became more adequate and actuarily sound. Governor McCord, in strongly recommending the sales tax, gambled his political future on the measure. Although he was defeated in the next election, McCord should be credited with saving the schools from chaos and lightening the burden of future governors.

His successor, however, Gordon Browning, who returned to the governor's office in January, 1949, had long been known as a friend of education. It was during his previous administration that much of the Eight-Point Program had been enacted. The legislatures of 1949 and 1951 greatly increased appropriations for education. Despite the complication of the Korean War, legislators in 1951 made $44,964,473 available to the elementary and secondary schools, and this was to be increased by one million during the second year of the biennium; the legislators also appropriated $4,386,163 annually for The University of Tennessee, with proportionate increases for the state colleges. Nevertheless, the rising cost of living was forcing many teachers to seek employment in private industry or to accept teaching positions in states paying higher salaries. Therefore, during the first administration of Governor Frank G. Clement a total of $52,610,433 was appropriated for the elementary and secondary schools for the first year of the biennium with a provision for an increase to $64,159,000 during the second year. The state university received $5,449,163 for each year, and the state colleges gained increased appropriations on the basis of enrollments at each institution.

Since the cost of living continued to mount, even these increases proved inadequate. Therefore, the Tennessee Education Association dedicated 1954 to a campaign for increased state revenues and increased salaries for teachers. Governor Clement gave the campaign hearty support, and after being reelected (this time to a four-year term), he called on the legislature to vote taxes sufficient to maintain the school program from the elementary level through the institutions of higher learning. The legislators responded by increasing the sales tax from 2 to 3 per cent, which made possible the appropriation of $69,531,000 annually for the elementary and secondary schools, $6,352,000 for the state university, and comparable increases for the state colleges. The honeymoon between the governor and the educators came to an end during the legislative session of 1957, when Clement insisted on cutting in half the Education Association's request for an appropriation which would make possible a $400 yearly increase in salary for every public school teacher. As a compromise the governor agreed on increases above the $200 limit if any excess in funds was accumulated over the anticipated collection figures. In subsequent years the teachers gained with some degree of regularity a bonus from such excess funds.

During the 1957 session the legislature received a two-volume report on public education in Tennessee, one volume dealing with grades one through twelve and the other with higher education, based on a study which had been authorized by the preceding General Assembly. The report, prepared by the Legislative Council (created in 1953) with the cooperation of the State Department of Education and the office of the director of the budget, emphasized among other things that the momentous change in the educational problem in Tennessee was due in part to the fact that the state, after having been largely rural in nature throughout most of its history, had become more industrial than agricultural in recent years. Each volume included detailed recommendations for educational reform.

The legislature of 1957 paid little attention to the report, and Buford Ellington, Clement's successor as governor, had promised a program of austerity. In spite of a vigorous campaign on the part of the Tennessee Education Association for a large increase in school funds, the teachers were given a salary raise of only $100 a year for the four years of the governor's term. Ellington, as had his predecessor in office, voiced the opinion that further raises would have to be on the local level. A number of county and city systems did raise salaries of their teachers from local funds. The appropriations for higher education were increased somewhat, but not as much as the several state institutions had requested.

Frank Clement returned to the governor's office for another four-year term in 1963 and induced the legislature to broaden the application of the 3 per cent sales tax, thus providing enough increased revenue to make possible a $400 increase in teachers' salaries during the first year of the next biennium and $100 during the second. The appropriation for the state university was also increased 24 per cent, enabling it to expand its facilities—especially in the graduate sphere —and the state colleges were also granted increased funds. Another measure enacted in 1963 authorized the consolidation of city and county schools. Although the extension of the sales tax was one factor in Clement's defeat in his race for the United States Senate in 1964, he obtained from the legislature further increases in educational appropriations in 1965. Teachers' salaries were raised $250 for each year of the biennium, and the state university's appropriation was increased to $44,487,000, which was $12,500,000 more than for the preceding two years. The University was also given a bond issue of $13,500,000 for physical plant expansion. During a special session of 1966, called to distribute a surplus of $39,000,000 in the state treasury, public school teachers were given another $250 a year increase in salaries, and additional appropriations were made for higher education.

Buford Ellington returned to the office of governor in January, 1967, with a program of increased support of public education to be financed by various increases in state taxes. Although the program had to be cut back because of the failure of the legislature to accept all of the tax proposals, Tennessee was still able to advance to the rank of 11th among the states in the amount of state funds appropriated for public education. The state still ranks 46th, however, in amount of support from federal, state, and local funds, due largely to the insufficiency of local appropriations.

Racial Integration, and a Survey of Higher and Private Education ੩ Before the Supreme Court on May 17, 1954, had delivered its historic decision outlawing the "separate but equal" doctrine regarding public education, The University of Tennessee had been required in 1952 by an earlier court decision to admit Negroes to its law and graduate schools. Also before the 1954 decision, a group of Negro parents in Clinton brought suit in a federal district court to obtain admission of their children to Clinton High School, because the children were then being required to travel all the way to Knoxville for a high school education. The case was not decided until after the 1954 decision, and in view of that case, the district court ordered the Clinton High School to admit the Negro children in August, 1956. Disorders largely incited by an outside agitator, John Kasper (who subsequently spent one year in a federal penitentiary), necessitated the sending of units of the National Guard to Clinton by Governor Clement to restore order. Thus, Clinton High School became the first school in the state, other than Oak Ridge, then under federal jurisdiction, to follow the dictum of the Supreme Court.

Meanwhile, the Nashville school board submitted to the district court a plan of gradual integration, beginning with the first grade and adding one grade each year. Following acceptance of the plan by the court, one elementary school in Nashville was opened to Negro first graders in September, 1957, despite disturbances that included the dynamiting of the school, also incited by Kasper, who was sentenced to a state prison term. A month later the Clinton High School was destroyed by dynamite, for which the guilty party was convicted of conspiracy. Subsequently, most of the other public school systems adopted the grade-a-year plan; this plan was later speeded up sufficiently to enable all of the public schools to avoid the withholding of federal funds under the application of the Civil Rights Act of 1964. Colleges and universities also were desegregated.

After a gradual plan of desegregation of the state colleges under its jurisdiction had been invalidated by the United States Supreme Court in May, 1957, the State Board of Education opened those schools to Negroes but permitted each institution to determine its own entrance requirements. Memphis State University was allowed to postpone integration until 1959. Under court order, the board of trustees of The University of Tennessee finally opened its undergraduate schools to Negroes in January, 1961. "Reverse" integration occurred in 1966, when Tennessee State University (formerly Tennessee Agricultural and Industrial State College for Negroes) at Nashville enrolled twenty-five white students.[4] Most of the private institutions of higher learning also adopted the integration policy, with Maryville College in the lead, immediately after the 1954 Supreme Court decision. Maryville had been open to Negroes following the Civil War until early in the twentieth century, when it was forced by a state law to exclude them.

In the field of higher education, during the first two-thirds of the twentieth century The University of Tennessee advanced from a position of being, in effect, despite its name, largely a localized East Tennessee institution to the status of a real state university, servicing and being supported by the whole area of Tennessee. Moreover, with a full-time student enrollment of 20,957 in 1967, it ranked 23rd among the colleges and universities in the nation.

The modernization of the University had begun during the administration of Charles W. Dabney, Jr., as president, 1887–1904, and was continued under his successors. The institution began to meet its statewide responsibilities through farmers' institutes and the programs of the agricultural experiment station, by working with the secondary schools for the improvement of educational facilities, and the organization of the alumni throughout the state. The obtaining of the first appropriation from the state treasury (even though only $10,000, in 1903) proved that state support was obtainable, and the immense popularity attained by the Summer School of the South, opened on the campus in 1902 through the influence of Professor Claxton and with the aid of the Southern Education Board, gave the institution a nationwide reputation.

The most essential reform, achieved in 1909, was the broadening

[4] Several years earlier Fisk University, a private college for Negroes, had admitted white students.

of the board of trustees to make the University representative of the whole state, thus removing the institution from the control of a Knoxville and East Tennessee clique. A few years later, the medical and dental units were moved from Nashville to Memphis, thereby giving the western part of the state an interest in the institution which it formerly had not had. The medical unit at Memphis was to become the largest in the nation. As time passed, the University, through its various extension activities and branches, made its slogan—the campus is the whole state—more meaningful. Moreover, the University's reputation as a school for graduate studies and scientific experimentation, including such new fields as atomic energy and outer space, has rapidly increased in recent years. In 1968, as a result of the proliferation of branches, the institution was reorganized as a university system, with an administration for each campus headed by a chancellor.

At the same time the other state institutions of higher learning have also made great progress, even though in 1968 the state of Tennessee was still near the bottom of the list of states in per capita expenditures for higher learning. The normal schools established under the act of 1909 advanced to the status of teachers' colleges and eventually to that of state universities, and have entered the field of postgraduate instruction. Recently, in order to make collegiate facilities more geographically available to high school graduates, the state has embarked on a program of establishing regional junior colleges.

Privately supported institutions of higher learning have also kept pace. Vanderbilt's graduate and medical schools (and George Peabody College for Teachers) early attained national reputations. The small sectarian or municipal colleges continue to make contributions in their individual spheres, but have difficulty competing with state-supported institutions. The once-famed law department at Cumberland University in Lebanon was moved in 1961 to Alabama to become a part of Samford University. Also, when the legislature and the newly created Higher Education Commission in 1968 authorized the establishment of a four-year branch of The University of Tennessee in Chattanooga, the trustees of the University of Chattanooga negotiated an agreement to merge with that branch in 1969, to become The University of Tennessee in Chattanooga.

Life at the institutions of higher learning has been greatly transformed since the beginning of the century. Not only has the state university ceased to be a military institute modeled after West Point, but life at all of the colleges has become much less rigidly controlled than it was in 1900. Extracurricular activities have expanded to the extent that the institutions have become to a considerable degree microcosms of life outside. Intercollegiate athletics, with their counterpart in the secondary institutions, have expanded until it seems that a school's reputation depends more on the size of its stadium, the appearance and skill of its band and majorettes, and the state and national ranking of its athletic teams than on scholastic achievement. Yet the educational process itself is undergoing transformation, with emphasis on the training of the whole person, the use of modern techniques, and the growing realization in this scientific era of public responsibility for providing educational opportunities beyond the secondary level.

SUGGESTED READINGS

General Accounts

Folmsbee, Corlew, and Mitchell, *Tennessee*, II, Ch. 36; Andrew D. Holt, *The Struggle for a State System of Public Schools in Tennessee, 1903–1936* (New York, 1938); John Trotwood Moore and A. P. Foster, *Tennessee: The Volunteer State* (4 vols., Nashville, 1923); White, *Tennessee Educational Organization.*

Specialized Accounts

Hugh D. Graham, *Crisis in Print: Desegregation and the Press in Tennessee* (Nashville, 1967); Graham, "Desegregation in Nashville: The Dynamics of Compliance," *THQ*, XXV (Summer, 1966), 135–54; Charles Lee Lewis, *Philander Priestly Claxton: Crusader for Public Education* (Knoxville, 1948); Mims, *Vanderbilt University*; Mims, *Chancellor Kirkland*; James R. Montgomery, *The Volunteer State Forges Its University . . . 1887–1919* (Knoxville, 1966); Montgomery, "The Summer School of the South," *THQ*, XXII (Dec., 1963), 361–81; Frank B. Williams, Jr., "The East Tennessee Education Association, 1913–1954," *ETHS Publ.*, No. 27 (1955), 49–76.

SEVEN STATE UNIVERSITIES

The forty-six public and private institutions of higher education in Tennessee include seven state universities, which are represented on this and the following pages.

Looking west at the Knoxville campus, The University of Tennessee, which has principal campuses also at Memphis, Martin, and Chattanooga

Engineering building at Tennessee Technological University, Cookeville

Portion of campus of Austin Peay State University, Clarksville

Aerial view of Middle Tennessee State University, Murfreesboro

Campus of Memphis State University, Memphis

A partial view of East Tennessee State University campus, Johnson City

The library building at Tennessee A & I State University, Nashville

Two Institutions for Medical Education

Students from many states receive their training at one of the two medical-education complexes in Tennessee.

Top: One of the research buildings at The University of Tennessee Medical Units, Memphis; *lower*: Aerial view of Vanderbilt University Medical School, Nashville.

26. &∾ The Volunteer State Goes to War

Long before the beginning of the twentieth century, the "volunteer spirit" of Tennesseans evidenced on numerous occasions had become a notable tradition. Recruitment for the King's Mountain campaign in 1780 by John Sevier and Isaac Shelby has received overwhelming response from the frontiersmen incensed over Patrick Ferguson's threat to ravage the Western country. Again in 1812, enthusiastic enlistment within the state evolved from the fervent desire to preserve the national honor in the face of gross disregard of the rights of Americans on the high seas by a monarchy that was also, Tennesseans believed, inciting Indians to attack frontier settlements. Consequently, as Robert H. White has shown, Tennessee was referred to in the press on the eve of the Mexican War as the "Volunteer State." When that war began and 2,800 Tennessee soldiers were requested by the national government, 30,000 volunteered, thus proving the appropriateness of the nickname.[1] Some of the men who went to Mexico later met on opposing sides in Civil War engagements, for by 1861 Tennesseans were steeped in the custom of fighting and were eager to wage war for the Confederacy or the Union.

Spanish-American War &∾ A new generation, outraged by gory details, as exaggerated by a yellow press, of the mistreatment

---

[1] White, "The Volunteer State," 53. The ardor for war declined, however (as had been the case in 1813–14), especially on the part of the Whigs, when the contest continued longer than anticipated. Billy H. Gilley, "Tennessee Opinion of the Mexican War as Reflected in the State Press," 7–26.

of the Cuban people by the Spanish overlords, chanted *"Cuba libre"* and "Remember the *Maine"* when they marched off to fight the Spaniards in Cuba, Puerto Rico, and the Philippines in 1898. These Tennesseans also were proud that the first shot in the war was fired from a gunboat named *Nashville.* The state contributed only 187 officers and 4,148 enlisted men for this "splendid little war," but most of them were volunteers. Some of the men who later attained noteworthy reputations were a future congressman, senator, and secretary of state (Cordell Hull), a future governor (Ben W. Hooper), and a future military figure of World War I and United States senator (General Lawrence D. Tyson).

World War I ᚥ When the opposing alliance systems in Europe became involved in a general war in 1914, Tennesseans for a time observed a fair degree of neutrality. Of the leading newspapers in the state, several assumed a strong pro-Ally (Great Britain and France) position from the beginning; others were more restrained; and a few were avowedly pro-German. When the submarine warfare waged by the Germans caused the loss of American lives in the sinking of the British liner *Lusitania* in 1915, however, public opinion shifted more strongly to the Allied side. Although two of the papers in the four major cities in the state continued to maintain a neutral position until the United States actually declared war, the state press as a whole became increasingly denunciatory of the policies of Germany and the other Central Powers. As a result, many Tennesseans marched in "Preparedness Parades" in 1916, and a few went to Canada to join the British forces.

On February 1, 1917, Germany resumed unrestricted submarine warfare, which had been halted temporarily by the *Sussex* pledge in 1916, and on March 16–17 three American ships, including the *City of Memphis,* were sunk. Responding to President Wilson's war message, Congress on April 6 declared that a state of war existed between the United States and Germany.[2] The Tennessee delegation voted unanimously in favor of the war.

[2] Later declarations of war were made against the other Central Powers. The beginning of hostilities silenced the few dissenting voices such as a group of "peace lovers" in Nashville who had caused a riot by calling for a referendum before any declaration of war.

The nation, now confronted with the herculean task of equipping, training, and transporting an army overseas, was almost totally mobilized. Thousands of young Tennesseans volunteered for duty in the armed forces while other thousands, including many women, went to work in industrial plants and munition factories. Women and children tended crops and "victory gardens," and the women collected thousands of pledge cards from citizens promising to co-operate with the conservation program of the Food Administration. Unfortunately, all did not go well. The new word "slacker" was frequently applied to patriotic citizens who had no intention of impeding the war effort. Persons with German names were automatically suspect, the teaching of German in the schools was suspended, and musical works by German composers could not be played. In general, the people of Tennessee responded to the war effort with enthusiasm, paid increased taxes without audible complaint, subscribed generously in Liberty Loan drives, worked for the Red Cross, and cheerfully accepted meatless, heatless, and wheatless days.[3] A serious distraction in the fall of 1918 was the flu epidemic which struck many thousands of Tennesseans and caused more than four hundred deaths.

Probably the most important war plant in Tennessee was a DuPont powder factory built at a cost of $80,000,000 on the Cumberland River near Nashville at a place now called Old Hickory. The plant brought about 20,000 newcomers to the region, thus over-taxing housing facilities. The federal government spent about $150,000,000 on war plants in the state. The most important training camp was Park Field, near Millington, for the training of pilots.

Civilians in the modern concept of war are heavily involved in duties designed to keep the armed forces properly supplied, to sustain civilian morale, and in general to implement the policies of the federal government. The coordinating agency was the National Council of Defense, which requested each state to form a similar council on the state level. Rutledge Smith of Cookeville was appointed chairman of the Tennessee Council of Defense, which was to coordinate all war-related activities and to prepare the people to

[3] There were, of course, a few dissidents who were dealt with by legal action as well as by public disapproval. One Williamson County resident paid a fine of $50.00 for questioning President Wilson's right to establish daylight saving time by executive action.

meet any emergency that might arise. In cooperation with Governor Rye, Chairman Smith soon perfected an excellent organization. W. E. Myer of Smith County became state chairman of the Fuel Administration; Harcourt A. Morgan, dean of the College of Agriculture of The University of Tennessee, headed the Food Administration in the state; Lee Brock of Nashville became chairman of the Fair Price Committee; and Percy Maddin of Nashville was appointed chairman of the Legal Advisory Board. These men, in cooperation with numerous other individuals, organized similar committees in virtually every county and municipality in the state.

A small but important part of the state's contribution to the armed forces had already been trained and equipped as the Tennessee National Guard. A few weeks before the United States became involved in the war, a portion of the Guard returned from service along the Mexican border where they had participated in General John Pershing's unsuccessful effort to catch the Mexican rebel, Francisco Villa, who had led a raid into New Mexico in 1916. With additional recruits the Guard was mustered into the federal service in April, 1917. The First Tennessee Ambulance Company left Memphis for Fort Oglethorpe on June 7 to become the first from the Volunteer State to go on active duty. Ultimately, the company became a part of the Forty-second Division. Most of the 7,065 Tennessee guardsmen called into service, however, became a part of the Thirtieth Division, called "Old Hickory" in honor of Andrew Jackson; this division also included Guard units from North and South Carolina, as well as draftees from several states.

The largest number of Tennesseans inducted into the armed forces entered through the selective service system enacted by Congress on May 18, 1917, and amended in 1918 to extend the age limits from 21 and 30 to 18 and 45. From the 472,716 Tennesseans registered under this system, 61,069 were inducted; 17,339 of these inductees were Negroes. The remainder of the nearly 80,000 who saw service in the war entered as volunteers. Of those in service 1,836 lost their lives; six received the Congressional Medal of Honor.

Although no regular training camps for infantry were located within the state, The University of Tennessee and other institutions of higher learning participated in the training of officers through the establishment of Reserve Officer Training Corps programs. At U.T. and the University of the South at Sewanee these activities were integrated with military programs already in existence. In the fall of 1918 the Reserve Army Training Corps was replaced for the remainder of the war by the Student Army Training Corps. Under this new program the army supervised the training of male students, who were to be allowed to continue in college until completion of their courses and then were to enter the armed services as commissioned officers. They were sworn into the army, paid $30.00 a month, and given academic as well as military training. The Memphis campus (medical and dental units) of The University of Tennessee had a program for the training of naval personnel.

After a period of intensive training in France, the Thirtieth Division relieved a British division on August 17, 1918. Its Fifty-ninth Brigade, commanded by General Lawrence D. Tyson of Knoxville, was involved in almost continuous action until the Armistice was signed on November 11. General Tyson was awarded the Distinguished Service Medal, and Colonel Cary F. Spence was cited for heroic service. The Fifty-fifth Brigade, which also included many Tennessee units, was equally distinguished. One of its officers, Colonel Luke Lea, acquired considerable publicity after the war ended by attempting to kidnap Kaiser Wilhelm II from his refuge in the Netherlands.

Admiral Albert Gleaves, the most notable of the many Tennesseans serving in the navy, was in charge of transporting United States troops to Europe. The fact that almost two million men were sent overseas offers adequate testimony to the efficiency of this officer. Admiral William B. Caperton of Spring Hill became Tennessee's first full admiral since David Farragut. The marine corps, the aviation corps, and many other units of the armed forces inducted large numbers of Tennesseans. Lieutenant Edward Buford of Nashville probably was Tennessee's most noted ace; among the Tennessee aviators who lost their lives were Lieutenants Claude O. Lowe and Charles M. McGhee Tyson, the son of General Tyson, who was honored by the naming of the McGhee Tyson Airport near Knoxville.

Alvin C. York, a farm boy from the Cumberland Mountain area, was destined to become not only Tennessee's but also the nation's outstanding hero of the war. During the Battle of Argonne Forest, York found his detachment decimated and, becoming separated from his remaining comrades, staged a one-man's offensive against the German army. He is reported to have killed twenty German soldiers, captured a German major, and prevailed upon his prisoner to persuade 131 other Germans to surrender. The young Tennessee corporal created a sensation when he proudly marched his prisoners to the American lines. York was promoted to sergeant and awarded the Distinguished Service Cross and the American Medal of Honor. Congress voted him a resolution of appreciation, and the people of Tennessee deeded a farm to him in his home county of Fentress and named an agricultural institute in his honor. In 1961, three years before his death, grateful friends in Tennessee and the nation raised enough money to compromise a tax obligation resulting from his mismanagement of the royalties from the motion picture which depicted his heroic exploits. In 1968, a bronze statue was erected in his honor at the state Capitol.

World War II and After ᶾᷛ Tennesseans were startled on Sunday afternoon, December 7, 1941, when the news came over the radio that the Japanese were attacking Pearl Harbor. This was a rude awakening for a people who had observed in complacent safety the turmoil of war in Europe for more than two years. Although Tennesseans were subjected to the conflicting propaganda activities of the American First Committee and the Committee to Defend America by Aiding the Allies, the majority had great confidence in the Roosevelt administration and particularly in the judgment and ability of Secretary of State Cordell Hull, a native of the Volunteer State. As elsewhere in the nation, the anti-war sentiment inculcated by the America Firsters was rapidly dispelled by the sneak attacks of the Japanese on American men and installations in Hawaii and the Philippines.

Previously, the United States had taken a few precautionary steps in the eventuality of American involvement: new defense plants had been put in operation and a Selective Service Act had been passed by Congress. As a result of the act, numerous young men, including the assigned quota from Tennessee, had been drafted into the armed forces and many others awaited induction. Following the Pearl Harbor attack, many of those waiting for the draft enlisted instead.

Tennessee, the first state to set up a state defense organization, created the Advisory Committee on Preparedness, on May 22, 1940; in July, 1941, the committee was renamed the State Defense Council. At that time Adjutant General T. A. Frazier, who was already serving as the state director of selective service, succeeded Major General Lytle Brown as chairman. William D. Price, who was executive director of the State Planning Commission, served as executive secretary both of the advisory committee and of the council. In September, 1940, the famous "Old Hickory" Division of the National Guard was called into service, and a new regiment, the first since the Civil War, was organized in Tennessee. To take care of the state's defense needs, the legislature in January, 1941, authorized the creation of a Tennessee State Guard, to be composed of volunteers; this Guard became the largest in the South and the first to receive federally supervised field training.

Following the attack on Pearl Harbor, December 7, 1941, and the declarations of a state of war against Japan, Germany, and Italy, all the defense agencies were galvanized into activity. Tennessee, then with the installations of the Tennessee Valley Authority and later with those at Oak Ridge, became a prime security area. Because of increasing demands on his time, Adjutant General Frazier resigned as head of the State Defense Council, and after an interim appointment of W. D. Price, Will R. Manier, Jr., a prominent lawyer of Nashville, was named "Coordinator" on February 3, 1942. Later, he also served as chairman of the War Services Advisory Council created in June, 1944.

As state director of selective service, Adjutant General Frazier established an efficient organization for the induction of young Tennesseans into the armed forces. Although Fort Oglethorpe in Georgia was again used as an induction center, it was later replaced by Camp Forrest,[4] near Tullahoma, as the chief induction center for Tennesseans. Many Tennessee women, however, went into the Women's Army Corps at the Georgia post.

In contrast to World War I, when very few soldiers were trained for combat service in the Volunteer State, World War II saw many thousands of servicemen trained at Camp Forrest (originally Camp Peay), Camp Tyson (near Paris, and named for General L. D. Ty-

[4] The camp was named in honor of the intrepid Civil War hero, Nathan Bedford Forrest—a fact which brought considerable criticism from Northern sectionalists.

son), or Camp Campbell (located along the Tennessee-Kentucky state line). Also, the Army Air Force had important training centers at Smyrna and Halls and a ferry command at Memphis from which planes were flown overseas. Nearby at Millington, the largest inland naval operation in the country included a naval air school as well as a naval base. The colleges again were pressed into service. In addition to its regular R.O.T.C. units, The University of Tennessee had a pre-flight school at Knoxville for the air force, and several other institutions also had similar academic training as well as military training for units of the air force, army, or navy. Thus the state was virtually an armed camp during the greater part of the war. Approximately 10 per cent of the population (315,501) went from Tennessee into the armed forces. To take care of some of the great numbers of the wounded, two service hospitals, Kennedy Army Hospital at Memphis and Thayer Hospital at Nashville, were established.

American reverses in the early days of the war soon made it evident that virtually every phase of life in the nation would have to be adjusted to the great task of winning the struggle against the totalitarian powers. Much civilian production had to be converted to war purposes, thus causing much inconvenience and considerable hardship. With the Japanese overrunning the sources of rubber in the Far East, rationing of automobile tires became a necessity, and General Lytle Brown was placed in charge of this allotment in Tennessee. Certificates were required for the purchase of new tires or to have old ones retreaded. German submarine warfare soon made the importation of coffee, sugar, and other necessities difficult, and the diverting of many goods to supply the expanding armed forces forced rationing of most food items. Tennesseans formed lines at the rationing office to secure the "strange" coupon books to be used in the purchase of foods. The people tightened their belts and ate less meat and used less sugar.

Gasoline rationing also became mandatory as a home front sacrifice. Car pools among workers in the cities became common, and city transit companies did a flourishing business as other people were compelled to use public service transportation. Moreover, individuals wanted to conserve their automobiles, for new ones were not being manufactured and offered for sale. The wartime scarcities necessitated a salvage program, and Leonard Sisk of Nashville was appointed state salvage officer to conduct drives to collect scrap

metal and scrap rubber. Many loyal Tennesseans not only participated in those drives, but also in drives for the sale of war bonds and
stamps. The people supported the activities of the new United
Service Organization (USO), as well as the Red Cross, for the sustaining of morale.

Although no American cities were bombed and the country was
not invaded, there was some apprehension that such events might
occur. Therefore, Coordinator Manier of the State Defense Council
also coordinated activities for civilian defense; approximately one
hundred leaders attended a school for civilian defense teachers held
in Nashville in May, 1942, and returned to their home communities
to hold similar schools to train the people to defend themselves
against bombing, fire, or gas attacks. Every city in the state had air
raid wardens, volunteer fire fighters, first aid workers, and other personnel to make them ready to repel any possible enemy attack.

A few defense plants had been built in Tennessee prior to Pearl
Harbor. In 1940, E. I. DuPont de Nemours and Company had
opened a large powder plant near Millington to produce powder for
the Allies, and Consolidated-Vultee Aircraft Corporation established a plant in Nashville which was making planes for the British
when the United States became involved in the war. With the entrance of the United States into the conflict, the industrial resources
of Tennessee were dedicated to the production of war materials.
Among the new plants put into production was a shell-loading plant
at Milan, operated by Procter and Gamble, soap manufacturers. It
employed more than 5,000 workers and was one of the largest war
industries of the state.

The greatest of all Tennessee war industries was the Oak Ridge
complex of plants that participated in the creation of the atomic
bomb. The site, eighteen miles west of Knoxville, headquarters of
TVA, was acquired in the autumn of 1942 by the national government, and by mid-1943 a group of large industrial plants had been
built and housing provided for a city of 75,000 inhabitants. This
development has been described as the best-kept secret of World
War II, the remarkable feature being that the inhabitants themselves, with the exception of a few key men, knew nothing of the
purpose of the new city. For more than three years Tennesseans
wondered about what was going on at Oak Ridge. Their curiosity
was satisfied when United States planes dropped atomic bombs on

the Japanese cities of Hiroshima and Nagasaki on August 6 and 9, 1945. Their use no doubt hastened the end of the war. Tennessee had made a vital contribution to the winning blow.

Oak Ridge was the residential center for the workers in the Clinton Engineer Works, one subdivision of the Manhattan District which had charge of the production of the bomb. It was also the administrative center, under the command of Major General Leslie Groves, of the entire Manhattan District, which had other subdivisions in various sections of the nation. The whole project was financed by a special, but largely secret, appropriation of a billion dollars. Senator Kenneth McKellar from Tennessee, chairman of the Appropriations Committee, had a large share in making possible such an enormous appropriation for an "unknown" purpose.

After the war the project came under the supervision of the Atomic Energy Commission, and the emphasis shifted to the exploitation of atomic energy for peaceful purposes. Oak Ridge eventually gained its independence of federal control. But this new city, with its Museum of Atomic Energy, its Institute of Nuclear Studies, and its many growing cultural activities, has become a great asset to the economic and social growth of Tennessee.

War contracts awarded to Tennessee firms approximated $1,250,-000,000. They were for ships, arms, munitions, clothing, food, and many other items which could be produced in the state for the use of the fighting forces. These industries employed more than 200,000 men and women. The work of the women in industry was especially outstanding, as well as the service of many Tennessee young women in the auxiliaries of the armed forces such as the WACS and the SPARS. Forty-five Tennessee industrial plants were awarded the Army-Navy "E" for excellence. More than $48,000,000 worth of ships were built in Memphis and Nashville. In the Navy, five destroyer escorts were named for Tennesseans killed in the war. The U.S. destroyers *Caperton* and *Gleaves* were named for Tennessee admirals of World War I fame; other destroyers named for Tennesseans were the *Farragut, Maury, Noe, Balch,* and *Lea.* The four major cities in the state, Memphis, Nashville, Knoxville, and Chattanooga, had cruisers named in their honor.

When the United States not only sponsored but actually joined the United Nations (of which Cordell Hull has been called the "Father"), in contrast to its policy concerning the League of Nations following the First World War, Tennesseans hoped that at last the day of world peace had arrived. Such was not to be the case, however, and with the development of the "Cold War" with the Communist powers, many Tennesseans were sent not only to the numerous American bases scattered all over the world, but also were included in the armed forces of the North Atlantic Treaty Organization (NATO) in Western Europe and in several UN police forces stationed in the Near East, Africa, and elsewhere.

The most important "police action" of the UN, under the leadership of the United States, occurred in Korea in 1950 and after. That country, freed from Japanese rule, had been divided at the 38th parallel into two zones, one occupied by the Soviet Union and the other by the United States, in which Communist and democratic regimes, respectively, had been set up. When peaceful efforts to unite the two zones proved fruitless, Russia sent its North Korean army across the boundary in an effort to unite the country by force under Communist rule. President Truman obtained from the UN Council, from which Russia was temporarily absent, a resolution declaring North Korea the aggressor. Thus the Korean War, or "police action," began. The forces opposing the Communists were largely from South Korea and the United States, although a few contingents from other democratic countries in the UN participated. When Red China intervened in the war and the contest dragged on interminably, considerable public sentiment against the war arose in the United States, but probably somewhat less in Tennessee than in most other states. Hostilities finally ceased with the signing of an armistice on July 27, 1953. In the exchange of prisoners, in which an overwhelming majority of the North Koreans and Chinese chose not to return to Communist rule, it was discovered that, on the other hand, some American prisoners, including a few Tennesseans, had been effectively "brain-washed" by the Asiatic Communists. These, however, were the exceptions to the general rule. The Tennessee economy during the Korean war benefited from war contracts. The Holston Ordnance Works at Kingsport and an arsenal at Milan were reactivated, and a guided missile plant was built near Bristol. The Avco Company of Nashville built parts for the B-47 bomber, and the Wheland Company built a gun-manufacturing plant near Chattanooga.

The United States became involved in another Asiatic "war" in the 1960's, because of her obligations as a member of the South East Asia Treaty Organization (SEATO), and also in support of the efforts of the non-Communist government of South Vietnam to avoid being overrun by the infiltration and the terroristic activities of the Communist regime which had been set up in the North. By 1967 approximately a half million American troops, including many from Tennessee, were fighting in Vietnam. Considerable public sentiment arose against United States involvement in another seemingly interminable war on the mainland of Asia, which it was feared might become the prelude to a third world war. Demonstrations against the war were not as prevalent in Tennessee, however, as elsewhere. The Tennessee legislature in 1967 adopted without a dissenting vote a resolution favoring the government's policy in Vietnam, and passed a law to provide stringent punishment for the desecration of the United States flag. Congressman James Quillen from the First District became a leading sponsor of similar federal legislation. Thus, the Volunteer State has continued to maintain the traditional patriotic fervor.

SUGGESTED READINGS

General Accounts
Folmsbee, Corlew, and Mitchell, *Tennessee*, II, Chs. 38, 42; Hamer, *Tennessee*, II, Ch. 54.

Specialized Accounts
George H. Butler, *The Military March of Time in Tennessee, 1939–1944: Report of the Adjutant General* (Nashville, 1945); Harry L. Coles, Jr., "The Federal Food Administration of Tennessee and Its Records in the National Archives, 1917–1919," *THQ*, IV (March, 1945), 23–57; Sam K. Cowan, *Sergeant York and His People* (New York, 1922); Gilley, "Tennessee Opinion of the Mexican War," ETHS *Publ.*, No. 26, pp. 7–26; Luke Lea, "The Attempt to Capture the Kaiser," ed. by William T. Alderson, *THQ*, XX (Sept., 1961), 222–61; Tom Skeyhall (ed.), *Sergeant York: His Own Story* (New York, 1928); State Planning Commission, *Civilian Defense in Tennessee, 1940–1945, Publication No. 157* (Nashville, 1945).

27. ❧ Twentieth-Century Politics— Peay to McCord, 1923–1945

THE DECADES of the twenties and thirties were years of reckless prosperity and excruciating depression; the first five years of the forties was a half decade of war. On the national scene, one of the weakest and also one of the ablest men ever to reside in the White House served as President. Scandals pervaded the administration of President Harding. The unfortunate Herbert Hoover cast about for a solution to problems no man could readily solve, and the confident and able Franklin D. Roosevelt led the American people into an experiment designed to relieve them of the ravages of panic and depression.

The election of Austin Peay by no means ended political strife in Tennessee, but it did bring several years of constructive government. Peay served until his death in 1927, at which time he was succeeded by the speaker of the senate, Henry H. Horton. Administrative reorganization, highway construction, and educational advancement marked his accomplishments.

Horton's administration began in prosperity and ended in depression. His efforts to continue the constructive policies of Peay met with little success. When the Bank of Tennessee and other financial institutions failed, some of which had millions of dollars of state funds on deposit, Horton was accused of poor judgment and fraud.

Hill McAlister served through the first New Deal, and was succeeded by Gordon Browning in 1937. The Huntingdon lawyer's attempts at a progressive administration were marred by his battles with Boss Ed Crump of Memphis, and Browning was defeated after one term by Crump-backed Prentice Cooper of Shelbyville. Cooper's administration, although overshadowed by World War II, was marked by solid achievements. He served the full constitutional limit of six years and was succeeded by Jim Nance McCord of Lewisburg.

Peay as Governor ❧ Shortly after the November elections (1922), Peay's friends urged him to make administrative reorganization a major goal. It was generally agreed that the matter was long overdue. During the half century after the revision of the state constitution in 1870, governmental agencies, boards, commissions, and bureaus had increased at such a rate that duplication of effort, confusion, and gross extravagance seemed the order of the day. Acting independently of the State Superintendent of Education, for example, were the Library Commission, State Librarian, Free Library Committee, and Text-Book Commission, to say nothing of the Historical Committee and various examining boards. More than one thousand employees worked in sixty-four departments, boards, commissions, and agencies at total salaries which exceeded one million dollars. Many observers believed the number of workers could be halved and greater efficiency obtained.

The new governor, therefore, in his first message to the legislature (January 16) urged the passage of a reorganization measure. Two weeks later the bill, entitled "An act to reorganize the administration of the state in order to secure better service and thorough coordination and consolidation, [and] to promote economy and efficiency in the work of the government . . . ," was enacted with the stipulation that it should go into effect February 1. Eight departments, including those of finance and taxation, agriculture, highways and public works, education, institutions, health, insurance and banking, and labor were established. Some of the existing agencies were abolished, but most were consolidated for more effective operation under these departments. The law became one of Peay's major accomplishments, and his supporters claimed that it saved the state millions of dollars.

In addition to proposing constructive legislation, Peay of course had to remain close to the people to retain the governor's chair. In 1924 he defeated John R. Neal of Rhea Springs in the primary and rode to an easy victory with other Democratic candidates in the general election. In that year much interest centered on the race for

United States senator in which General Lawrence D. Tyson successfully challenged John K. Shields. Tyson, a war hero, had commanded one of the two brigades which composed the Thirtieth ("Old Hickory") Division—in fact he had commanded all of the Tennessee National Guard when the troops first were mustered into service. He had received the Distinguished Service Medal and won other honors for his actions in the Meuse-Argonne sector. Shields had served competently, but had lost popularity after he voted against the peace treaty which would have placed the United States in the League of Nations. A highlight of the campaign was a letter written by President Wilson criticizing Shields for not supporting his policies while he was President. John W. Davis, although he lost to President Coolidge by a substantial vote, carried Tennessee comfortably.

Peay was opposed in his bid for a third term by Hill McAlister, of Nashville, the state treasurer. Peay ran on his record, but supporters of McAlister accused Peay of attempting to establish unwarrantable control over the state and were especially critical of a 10 per cent tax on tobacco, which the governor had pushed through the legislature the year before in order to finance an eight months' school term in every county. In a hard fought campaign Peay won by a vote of 96,545 to 88,448 and then defeated Walter White, of Dayton, in the general election by 40,000 votes. It was the first time since the days of Isham G. Harris that a governor had been elected to a third consecutive term.

In each election, Peay had the powerful support of Luke Lea, who returned from Europe in 1918 a war hero and became an even more powerful political figure than he had been before the war. Although Lea had been defeated by Kenneth D. McKellar in his bid to return to the Senate in 1916, the defeat had been forgotten in the exaggerated claims of his military exploits which included an almost successful attempt to capture the German Kaiser. Lea influenced many voters through the widely read Nashville *Tennessean*, and by 1927 he also had acquired control of the Knoxville *Journal* and the Memphis *Commercial Appeal*. Peay also had the support in 1922 and 1924 of Clarence Saunders of Memphis, who made and lost a fortune in Piggly-Wiggly Stores and then made a second fortune from the promotion of another grocery chain which he called "Clarence Saunders, Sole-Owner-of-My-Name, Stores." Saunders generally opposed Ed Crump but aligned himself with the Memphis dictator against Peay in 1926 on the grounds that two terms as governor were sufficient.

Peay was opposed each time by Crump, who became the most powerful political figure the state had ever known. In Nashville he was opposed by Hilary Howse, who for some years was mayor of Nashville, and E. B. Stahlman, publisher of the Nashville *Banner*. Peay charged during the campaign that the Memphis and Nashville bosses sought to dominate the state solely for the benefit of the urban centers and that if he were not reelected the rural counties would suffer. The *Tennessean*, a morning paper with a wide circulation among voters in rural counties, took the message into rural homes across Middle Tennessee and was responsible in no small measure for Peay's victories.

Accomplishments of Austin Peay ❧ Austin Peay generally is recognized as one of a half dozen outstanding men who have held the office of governor. Perhaps his greatest accomplishments lay in the reorganization measure referred to earlier, the general education measures, and the extension of the highway system. Under the General Education Law of 1925, facilities for higher education were expanded, and all counties were guaranteed elementary schools of eight months' duration. Two years later, Austin Peay Normal (later changed to Austin Peay State University) was established at Clarksville. An extensive highway construction program was paid for by a gasoline tax and bridge tolls and by the issuance of $15,000,000 of short-term notes; for his achievements, Peay has been called "the Roadbuilding Governor." Other measures enacted during Peay's tenure revised the tax structure, established a park in the Great Smoky Mountains and a game preserve at Reelfoot Lake, and expanded penal and charitable institutions.

Henry H. Horton as Governor ❧ Governor Peay died suddenly on October 2, 1927, and was replaced by Henry H. Horton, of Marshall County, the speaker of the senate. It became Horton's lot to serve as governor during one of the stormiest periods of the state's political history.

Luke Lea became much more intimately associated with Horton than he had ever been with Peay, and Lea also brought to the political stage Rogers Caldwell, a successful businessman with whom he had become associated in a variety of business deals. Caldwell, with his brothers Dandridge, Meredith, and C. W., had formed in 1917 Caldwell and Company, an investment bank interested mainly in municipal bonds of the Southern states. By the end of the next decade it had become a financial empire with holdings in several states ranging from banks to baseball. In 1926, Lea and Caldwell made the first of several joint ventures—the purchase of a controlling interest in the Holston National Bank of Knoxville—and by 1927 had entered into a half dozen or more additional transactions, including the purchase of the newspapers mentioned earlier. Horton's close association with Lea and Caldwell was to lead to a ground swell of opposition and a move toward impeachment.

A few months after Horton took the oath of office, he announced his candidacy for a full term in the August, 1928, primary. He was opposed by McAlister who, with the support of Stahlman, Howse, and Crump, made Horton's association with Lea and Caldwell the chief issue of the campaign. Then followed one of the bitterest campaigns in state political history.

Even before Peay's death, Lea had sought to force C. Neil Bass, the commissioner of highways, to specify without competitive bids the use of "Kyrock"—a product of the Caldwell-owned Kentucky Rock Asphalt Company—in building certain Tennessee highways. Continued pressure upon Bass led to his resignation in February, 1928, and to the allegation that Lea, not Horton, was the "real" governor of Tennessee. Stahlman's *Banner* led the assault, and described Lea as "Governor-in-Fact" and Horton as "Governor-in-Name." In a series of cartoons, Caldwell—the "Kyrock Kid"—was shown holding huge moneybags, Lea "the dictator" was dubbed "Musso-LEA-ni," and Horton—the "Governor-in-Name"—usually was mired in Kyrock. In Memphis, Crump worked more quietly behind the scenes than did Stahlman in Nashville, but he did hold rallies in support of McAlister, bought advertising space in which to criticize Saunders who supported Horton, and, through the Memphis *Press Scimitar* which supported McAlister, denounced the "three Rock-Asphalteers, Lea, Caldwell, and Horton," who were little more than "promoters and political hijackers."

Lea, of course, through his chain of newspapers extolled Horton. Through the Knoxville *Journal,* Lea advised Republicans to vote in the Democratic primary. In the *Tennessean,* he published statements by prominent Nashvillians in praise of Rogers Caldwell and even a terse statement by Caldwell himself in which the magnate said that it was "neither pleasant nor proper for a private citizen to be made an issue and to be used as a target for abuse and misrepresentation." McAlister was pictured as a weak politician who had been defeated once, would be defeated again, and who was only a tool in the hands of Ed Crump and the machine politicians of Memphis and Nashville.

Horton won the nomination by a majority of less than 6,000 votes in one of the closest races in the twentieth century. Crump delivered Shelby County to McAlister by a vote of 24,069 to 3,693; the Davidson vote was more than 2-to-1 against the governor, but the huge rural support for Horton brought him victory.

In November, Tennesseans again voted Republican in the presidential election, but elected Horton governor by a substantial majority. Prohibition continued to be an issue in the national contest, and Al Smith—never popular in the hinterlands anyway—was described as a Catholic who would repeal the Eighteenth Amendment. This vote for Hoover was the last time Tennesseans voted Republican until the Eisenhower era of the 1950's.

Earlier, Horton had promised to continue Governor Peay's policies of road construction and educational development. When efforts failed to secure the necessary funds through a revision of the tax structure, Horton turned to bonds. Accordingly, the legislature in 1929 provided for the floating of $28,796,000 of bonds, most of which would be used for roads and bridges. Several months later Governor Horton called the assembly into special session (December 2, 1929), to float additional bonds for highway construction.

By a state statute of 1913 as revised in 1929, money received from the sale of bonds could be deposited in approved state banks until it was needed to pay for the projects for which the bonds had been issued. This meant, of course, that favored banks sometimes had the use of state money for several months or even a year or longer if road construction or other projects moved slowly. The result was that considerable state funds found their way into the Bank of Tennessee and other Caldwell-controlled banks. The Bank of Tennessee, established in 1919 largely for the purpose of serving as a depository for Caldwell and Company instead of for the general public, showed in June of 1929 that the state's balance with it had increased from $40,000 in June of 1927 to $2,269,000. Other Caldwell-Lea banks showed state balances in excess of a total of $10,000,000. The collapse of the stock market in October, 1929, and the consequent onset of the Great Depression resulted in numerous bank failures across the country and a sizable loss for the state of Tennessee.

Before the financial storm broke, another election had been held and Horton was elected to another term. He was opposed in the primary by L. E. Gwinn, described by the editor of the *Tennessean* as "About an average lawyer from Covington," but supported by Stahlman and the Nashville *Banner*. To the amazement of political sages, Lea's *Commercial Appeal* warmly endorsed Crump for Congress, and Crump, announcing that he and Mayor Watkins Overton had appreciated Horton's efforts to build good roads into Memphis and to enlarge the mental hospital at Bolivar, supported Horton. Twenty-odd thousand Memphians changed their minds about Horton, at Crump's behest, and Gwinn was swamped by a majority of nearly 45,000 votes. So far as the junior Senate seat was concerned, Senator Tyson had died in August, 1929, and was replaced by William E. Brock of Chattanooga. In the August primary, two elections for the Senate seats were held: one, for the "short term" that would complete Tyson's term ending in 1931, and the other for the "long term," that is, for a full six-year term beginning in 1931. Brock won the short term easily over John R. Neal. For the long term, Congressman Cordell Hull defeated Andrew H. L. Todd of Murfreesboro, who had been speaker of the state house of representatives, by a 2-to-1 majority. Hull had served continuously in the House since 1907 except for one term from 1921–23, and had emerged as an authority on tax and tariff reform. In the general elections the Democratic candidates won handily, despite efforts of the Republican candidate (C. Arthur Bruce) to make a major issue out of the large amount of state funds in the Caldwell-Lea banks. The reaction against Hoover brought even the defeat of veteran Congressman B. Carroll Reese, of the First Congressional District.

Four days after the election, on November 8, the newspapers of the state carried accounts of the closing of the Caldwell-Lea owned Bank of Tennessee; the state of Tennessee had a balance of $3,418,-

ooo on deposit at the time. For several months prior to this time rumors circulated in financial circles that Caldwell and Company was in serious financial straits, but company officials warmly denied them. The failure of the Bank of Tennessee, however, brought panic to thousands of Tennesseans from Memphis to Bristol who had money on deposit. The Caldwell-controlled Holston-Union Bank of Knoxville suffered a run on November 10 when three-quarters of a million dollars were withdrawn, and it failed two days later. Other Caldwell-controlled banks either closed or merged with other solvent banks, and by November 14 Caldwell and Company had been placed in the hands of a receiver.

The state of Tennessee had had on deposit a total of $6,659,000 in the closed Lea-Caldwell banks at the time. When this fact became generally known, a storm of resentment arose against Horton, Lea, and Caldwell, and when the legislature convened in January, 1931, demands were made widely for Horton's impeachment. Ed Crump, who had supported Horton in the August primary, now sought to restore his position among "the people" by denouncing Horton and moving into the forefront of those who urged impeachment. Soon after the legislature convened it became readily perceivable that the fight for impeachment would be between the forces of Crump and those of Lea and Horton. Both Horton and Crump issued statements through the press highly condemnatory of each other.

A legislative committee to draft articles of impeachment was formed, and the members at once prepared articles of accusation. They charged Horton with conspiring with Lea and Caldwell to defraud the state, having extravagantly spent money on furnishings for the governor's mansion, issuing false statements with regard to the state's money in the Caldwell banks, improperly using his pardoning power, and in general not being "fit and capable longer to hold the office of Governor." At first, sentiment was strong in the house, but after several long delays the movement failed.

Several reasons may be given for the failure of the attempt at impeachment, although it was readily perceivable that the state had lost nearly $7,000,000 because of the lack of wisdom and judgment in financial matters of the governor and his associates. One reason was that many rural legislators believed that impeachment was merely a disguised plan to place the urban group in power. Too, inasmuch as Senate Speaker Scott Fitzhugh of Memphis was controlled by Crump, many believed that should Horton be convicted and Fitzhugh become governor little by way of improvement would accrue. A third reason was that those interested in impeachment moved so slowly that sentiment which earlier had favored impeachment had cooled when house members finally got around to voting on the matter.

Little else of significance was done during the legislative session. Perhaps the most constructive legislation tightened the rules having to do with the depositing of the state's funds in state banks. Horton had not been a candidate to succeed himself in 1932, and his departure from the governor's mansion early in the following year was not lamented.

McAlister as Governor ₴ By the August primary of 1932 the country was so deeply in the grips of the depression that bank and business failures were common across the country. In the governor's race, McAlister, twice defeated (in 1926 and 1928), ran with the endorsement of Ed Crump. Lewis Pope, Pikeville attorney and commissioner of institutions under Peay, ran on the slogan "Lewis S. Pope, the tax payer's hope" and promised a revision of the tax structure and aid to education. Malcolm R. Patterson, long in retirement in Memphis, ran as the administration candidate—with whatever support the wounded Horton group might give him. Crump delivered a majority of more than 25,000 votes in Shelby County to McAlister who won the nomination by less than 10,000.

The closeness of the race and Crump's methods of conducting elections in Memphis aroused a storm of protest and charges of fraud. Pope's campaign manager, Sam Carmack (a cousin of the slain Edward Ward Carmack), announced that the Pikeville attorney would contest the election because many of the Shelby precincts were "tainted with this revolting fraud." Crump had used "cossack methods," charged the editor of the *Commercial Appeal*, and had "rounded up voters by the truckload" and taken them "like so many dumb, driven cattle" to the polls to vote for McAlister. Crump, however, bought advertising space to deny that he had conducted anything but a fair election. He denounced "the Liars, Blackguards, and thieves" who criticized him, and described McAlister as a "clean,

honest, courageous and efficient" man who would "run the rascals
out of the state house in Nashville." Although Pope filed charges
of fraud, his claims were not sustained by the Democratic State
Committee. He then announced that he would run as an independent
in the November election.

Pope's race disappointed his supporters; he finished third behind
McAlister and John E. McCall, the Republican candidate. On
the national scene Franklin Delano Roosevelt swept the nation
with promises of a "new deal" that would restore the country to
prosperity. Tennesseans, who had voted quite strongly for Herbert
Hoover in 1928, now very overwhelmingly repudiated him in favor
of the winsome chief executive of New York. The Lea-controlled
Tennessean ignored McAlister's election but concentrated instead
upon the promised reforms of President-elect Roosevelt—whose
name, the editor cautioned his readers, was pronounced "Rose-evelt"
instead of "Ruse-evelt," as Theodore Roosevelt had pronounced it.

Like the rest of the country, Tennessee was in the depths of depression
when McAlister became governor and Franklin D. Roosevelt
became President. In 1928, President Hoover and millions of
other Americans in naive confidence had seen a vision of an America
where poverty would be eliminated. The euphoria had vanished
by the time McAlister took office, and many people were in need.
Indeed, by 1931, some people in Nashville, Memphis, Knoxville,
and Chattanooga were without adequate food, clothing, and shelter.
The Red Cross, Salvation Army, and other similar organizations
had spent the bulk of their resources, and many people looked to
the federal government for aid. In April, 1930, Tennessee was
granted more than one million dollars of federal funds, which was
soon spent in highway construction. Sometime later funds under
the Reconstruction Finance Corporation became available, and
late in 1932 work projects under the Emergency Relief and Construction
Act were begun in Knox and other counties. Even so,
destitution was widespread. The Fisher Body Company of Memphis
closed early in 1933, putting 1,200 men out of work; indeed, by the
end of the year more than one-third of the major industrial establishments
of the state had closed.

As mentioned earlier, financial institutions in Tennessee were in
dire straits by the time of McAlister's inauguration. The governor,
following the example of more than a dozen other governors, pro-

claimed a six-day banking holiday on March 1; indeed, by March 4 when President Roosevelt was inaugurated scarcely a bank in the country was engaged in normal operations. The President called Congress into extra session immediately and recommended legislation designed to restore popular confidence in the banks.

After a quick but thorough examination of all banks, treasury officials decided that sound banks would open during the week of March 12. On that evening (a Sunday) President Roosevelt assured the people in a "fireside chat" that their money was safer "in a reopened bank than under the mattress." Accordingly, banks adjudged sound located in the four major cities resumed operation on March 14, and other sound banks reopened later in the week. The Federal Depositors Insurance Corporation soon was established to insure deposits to the extent of $5,000 for each depositor. By summer, bank officials across the state told of the restoration of confidence in the banks and proudly reported that more money was being placed on checking account than was being withdrawn.

Several relief agencies were created within the first few weeks after President Roosevelt's inauguration. The Civilian Conservation Corps, designed to provide relief and vocational training for a vast number of unemployed young men and boys, was established by Congress two weeks after the banks reopened. Camps were constructed across the country where needy young men were put to work planting trees, building roads, and performing a variety of other chores. By the end of the year, thirty-three camps had been set up in all sections of the state. When McAlister's second term expired in 1937, more than 7,000 Tennesseans had been enrolled in the CCC. They had planted millions of pine seedlings, developed parks, erected fire observation towers, and accomplished many other worthwhile tasks.

Other agencies of relief established in 1933 included the Public Works Administration (PWA) and the Civil Works Administration (CWA). The former, created in May as a part of the National Industrial Recovery Act, provided work for thousands of unemployed. More than 500 projects were undertaken in Tennessee under the program, including the construction of bridges, public housing projects, and municipal water systems, and the paving of streets and roads. The CWA, although it received considerable criticism over the nation, employed hundreds of Tennesseans in cleaning county courthouses (of dirt), refurbishing jails and schools, landscaping roadsides, raking leaves, and other chores.

The most important problem which the Roosevelt administration faced—at least so far as Tennesseans were concerned—was that of restoring agriculture to a healthy and prosperous condition. Farm prices almost daily were declining, but the farmers' fixed costs—such as taxes and interest on borrowed money—remained constant. The situation in Tennessee, and indeed through the South, was critical when in May, 1933, the Agriculture Adjustment Act was passed. Under the act, payments were to be made to farmers who agreed under contract to curtail production of crops designed for market.

Cotton, the first crop to come under the provision of the act, was grown in thirty-six counties of southern Middle and West Tennessee and had declined in price from a high of thirty-five cents per pound in 1919 to six cents in 1932. A referendum indicated that nearly 90 per cent of the cotton growers of the state wished to come under the program. Within a few weeks 46,504 farmers signed contracts to remove 264,287 acres from production; for this they were paid $4,665,404.

Wheat, corn, tobacco, and other commodities also came within the program. Before the act was declared unconstitutional in 1936, Tennessee farmers had received payments in excess of $20,000,000 for limiting production. The Soil Conservation and Domestic Allotment Act and other legislation designed as replacement legislation soon were enacted.

Tennessee farmers also benefited from other New Deal legislation. The Emergency Farm Mortgage Act, the Farm Credit Administration, and the expansion of the Federal Land Banks enabled Tennesseans to borrow millions of dollars for agricultural purposes.

One of the soundest and most far-reaching of the New Deal agencies was the Works Progress Administration, established in 1935 with Harry Hopkins as director. Indeed, it was the chief work relief agency until World War II made it no longer necessary. Colonel Harry S. Berry, who had served briefly as commissioner of highways under Governor Horton, was named administrator for Tennessee. In September, Berry announced that plans had been completed for farm to market roads costing $22,000,000 and employing 5,000 men. The administrator stressed the fact that "every county" would benefit from the project. Among other projects were the construction of a variety of public buildings such as schools and courthouses, establishment of more than one hundred parks, and provisions for numerous playgrounds and playing fields. By 1939 employment had been provided for more than 25,000 persons in the state.

Under the WPA the employables were separated from those who were unable to work. Those in the latter category received surplus commodities in the form of food and clothing. In order to supplement provisions supplied by the federal government, Tennessee in 1935 established the State Welfare Commission, with operating funds provided from bonds, to administer assistance to the needy. Thousands of Tennessee's needy soon were placed on the roles.

The National Youth Administration was created as a part of the WPA and became effective in Tennessee in September (1935) in time for the school year. This program provided constructive training for unemployed youths not in school and also gave aid to those who required it to remain in school. Students performed clerical tasks for school administrators, swept buildings, prepared food in cafeterias, fired furnaces, and performed many other jobs for which the government paid them a few cents per hour to enable them to attend high school or college.

Tennesseans participated in practically all of the New Deal agencies. As a whole, the program was of course the economic salvation for the state, but it also established the hegemony of the federal government in state affairs.

Although poverty brought suffering and Washington dominated much of the attention of Tennesseans, much interest still continued in state and local politics. When the legislature assembled in 1935, there was no question but that Ed Crump was the undisputed political boss of Tennessee. Austin Peay was dead, the Caldwells experienced the collapse of their fortune and power, and Luke Lea and his son, Luke Lea, Jr., had been incarcerated, after exhausting all legal remedies, in the North Carolina State Prison in Raleigh.[1] No one was able to realize Crump's power more than Governor McAlister.

[1] After a series of legal maneuvers in several states, the Leas were convicted of conspiracy to defraud the Central Bank and Trust Company of North Carolina and in May, 1934, they were incarcerated. A few months later Luke Lea, Jr., was paroled, and about two years later Luke Lea, Sr., was also paroled. Both received full pardons in 1937. McAlister was reelected in 1934, again defeating Pope.

The governor received numerous letters from Crump advising him on a variety of state matters. When McAlister proposed a sales tax in order to reduce the state debt and also to provide assistance for the needy public schools, he incurred the lasting enmity of the Memphis boss. The powerful Shelby delegation, at Crump's behest, took up the cudgels against the sales tax and launched a successful fight that was destined to bring about new alignments. The legislature failed to enact a new revenue bill after a bitter fight. Thus, the governor was forced to call the lawmakers into an extra session, and at this session they agreed to reenact the appropriation measure of 1933 which did not include the governor's recommendations for increased expenditures.

Crump and McAlister also disagreed over the liquor question. The Eighteenth Amendment had been repealed, but with McAlister's support coming largely from the dry rural counties he refused to give in to Crump's demands that Memphis and other large cities be permitted to sell alcohol.

McAlister did not seek reelection; Crump had termed him "our sorriest governor"—one who had kept the sales tax "hidden in his stony heart" and "tried in a sneaking way to put" it over on the people. He retired to his home in Nashville, but later became a referee in bankruptcy.

The gubernatorial campaign of 1936 brought to the forefront two formidable foes—Burgin E. Dossett of Campbell County and Gordon Browning of Huntingdon. Dossett, a superintendent of county schools, former state commander of the American Legion, and manager of McAlister's campaign in 1934, announced early in the spring with the support of the governor and Senator McKellar. Browning announced a few weeks later. He had commanded a battery of artillery in a regiment commanded by Luke Lea, had served in Congress for twelve years, and had been an unsuccessful candidate for the United States Senate against Nathan Bachman in 1934. Boss Crump, who had denied Browning's appeal for help in 1934, refused to aid either candidate until he could make a careful assessment of the chances each had for election.

The candidates took the stump early in June, and it was apparent immediately that Browning was the stronger of the two. Crump, interested in supporting a winner, began a series of conferences with Senator McKellar and others on July 12, and one week later announced his support for Browning. Politicians were amazed that Crump would reverse his position of 1934 and support an old friend of Luke Lea. Crump, however, wanted a winner, and, as Joe Hatcher wrote in the Nashville *Tennessean* two days after Crump's announcement, Browning "was destined to go to Shelby with a substantial majority" even if Crump had supported Dossett. Browning won by more than a 2-to-1 majority and promptly telegraphed Crump that there were "60,000 reasons" why he loved Shelby County.

Browning as Governor   Browning had campaigned as a liberal candidate, and immediately after his inaugural he announced a progressive program. He favored larger appropriations for education, a merit system for state employees, a license for automobile operators, better roads, continued development of TVA, a reorganization of state government, a balanced budget, and the refunding of the state debt. In most of his proposals he was successful. Browning sought to restore the concept of a strong executive, abandoned since the administration of Austin Peay, by pushing through the legislature an administrative reorganization plan somewhat along the lines of the act of 1923. Among other things, the measure provided for a department of administration, an office of back tax collector, and several other new positions designed to streamline the administrative branch. Under the commissioner of administration would be a division of personnel whose director would attempt to establish a merit system for governmental employees. The director administered examinations to job applicants, certified persons eligible for employment, established a classification system, and recommended a plan for compensation on state jobs to the governor. The measure was enacted over the protests of the Shelby delegation. A revenue bill, by which the state would improve educational facilities, build roads, and make other changes, also was opposed by those from Memphis. Browning's bill provided for increased taxes on public utilities, a tax on chain stores, a corporation excise tax, an increase in the income tax on securities, an increase in the tax on beer, and an increase in the franchise tax. The Shelby County group vainly argued that a repeal of the prohibition laws would bring in sufficient revenue to replace all the taxes proposed by the administration. Despite Crump's opposition, the General Assembly closed with a record of solid achievement. A merit system had been created, a driver's license law had been enacted, the state debt had been refinanced in a manner that reestablished the credit of the state, the budget had been brought into balance, and increased appropriations had been made for schools and highways.

Of even greater interest to many Tennesseans than the legislative accomplishments, however, was Browning's bitter break with Crump and his defeat in his bid for a second term. The governor had hardly taken the oath of office when he incurred the wrath of the Memphis boss. His failure to take Crump's advice on a variety of matters, his appointment to high positions of several men who had been close to Governor Horton, and his friendship with Luke Lea disturbed the "Red Snapper" (as Crump not infrequently was called). The controversy over legislation was still another factor in the split, as was Crump's fear, whether justified or not, that Browning was influenced by private power interests against the development of TVA. When Browning on October 1, 1937, called a special session of the legislature to enact a county unit plan applicable to state elections whereby the power and strength of Shelby would be curtailed, the break became apparent and irrevocable. Crump denounced him as a man of "brass, gusto, and selfishness" whose "undercover plan to disfranchise voters in Shelby . . . is an abuse of power, a manifestation of secret ambition, and of crooked politics."

Browning explained to legislators the need for a revision of the primary voting law. Recounting the accomplishments of the regular legislative session, the governor alleged that the entire work of the assembly was threatened "because the Governor of the State could not pacify the resentment of an individual (Crump)." The Crump machine, which voted most Memphians as a bloc, already had registered 117,000 names as voters, Browning charged, when in the past seldom had more than one-half that number voted. "There is of course no one among you who believes that 117,000 voters have registered in any county in this state," he charged. His choice, he said, was whether he would "sit supinely" while Crump indulged in "such a sabotage" of his program, or whether he would attempt to curtail the "invidious" power of the Memphis dictator. He had called the legislators into special session, therefore, to recommend the passage of a unit plan where "a definite influence in determining the results of a primary would be assigned and guaranteed to each county, in proportion to the vote cast for party nominees in the preceding election," limited only "by the comparative population of that county to others." Crump was dumbfounded. Even "Huey Long in his desperation" had not conceived of a thing so diabolical.

The unit bill, obviously, was designed to weaken the influence of Shelby County and to give more strength to the small rural counties. On October 15 the senate enacted the governor's bill by a vote of 20 to 13, despite the fact that scores of Crump lieutenants roamed the legislative halls to defeat the measure. When the bill came before the house, United States Senator McKellar addressed legislators and denounced it as a violation of the principles of democracy. Despite the influence of Crump and McKellar, the unit bill squeaked by the house by a seven-vote majority. Crump's forces promptly announced plans to test the constitutionality of the measure, and early in the next year the state supreme court declared it unconstitutional.

The decision of the court was a stiff blow to Browning's political aspirations, but there were other means of counteracting the Crump power and the resourceful governor planned to use them. He had gained control of the State Board of Elections shortly after the unit bill was passed, and he later ordered the Shelby election commission to purge the registration lists of persons improperly registered. When he opened his campaign for a second term in June, he denounced Crump as a dictator and promised to free the people from what he termed political oppression.

Browning met formidable opposition in State Senator Prentice Cooper, of Shelbyville, after Walter Chandler, of Memphis, withdrew. Cooper was the son of W. P. Cooper, former speaker of the state house of representatives, and had served in both houses of the legislature in addition to a term as district attorney general. He had graduated from Princeton and had studied law at Harvard. Cooper could not match Browning on the platform, and he therefore made few speeches. He had the support, however, of the powerful Crump machine and the strong state organization of Senator McKellar; indeed, the senator employed the full force of his federal patronage to defeat the governor. Crump bought thousands of dollars of advertising space in newspapers across the state to portray Cooper as a man of dignity and refinement and Browning as a bigoted boor.

Browning, Crump wrote, was the type of person "who would milk his neighbor's cow through a hole in the fence." He was insincere; indeed, in his lifetime "his heart had beat over two billion times without a single sincere beat." He was traitorous; "in the art galleries of Paris," Crump wrote, "there are twenty-seven pictures of Judas Iscariot—none look alike but all resemble Gordon Browning."

The governor was unable to meet the invective of the Red Snapper and to maintain the dignity which his office required. His supporters in Shelby were being bullied and threatened with physical violence, he charged, and Crump's plan to conduct elections illegally seemed apparent. The campaign grew more bitter as election day approached. Finally, in desperation, Browning determined to station the National Guard in Shelby on election day to insure free elections. Senator McKellar protested to the War Department and Crump petitioned Federal Judge John D. Martin, an old friend, to enjoin the governor from sending troops. On the evening of August 1—three days before the election—Browning was scheduled to address a rally at the Mid-South Fair Grounds in Memphis. As he ascended the platform before an audience of 7,000 West Tennesseans (many of whom had come from other counties to hear him), he was accosted by a United States marshall who dramatically served him with a Martin-issued injunction.

The action of the courts—state and federal—caused the people of the state to lose faith in Browning and to assume that he sought in a dictatorial manner to run rough-shod over the courts and the people. The election was as one-sided as was the one of 1936, and Prentice Cooper became governor as Browning returned to Huntingdon in humiliation and defeat.

Cooper as Governor ❧ Cooper had only token opposition in 1940 and by defeating Judge Ridley Mitchell in 1942 with a substantial majority he became the first governor since Isham G. Harris to serve three consecutive terms. War and rumors of war dominated the Cooper years, but they were years of solid achievement. The state debt was reduced from $123,598,000 to $83,517,000 —the largest amount of debt reduction ever accomplished in the state's history. Aid to schools was increased by 66 per cent, appropriations for old age assistance were doubled, and free textbooks were provided for school children in the lower grades. A statewide system of tuberculosis hospitals was inaugurated, and the forest and park lands were increased to 341,000 acres. The governor remained in the good graces of Crump throughout his six years as chief executive and only rarely did he not enjoy complete harmony with the legislature, although in 1939 a county option liquor bill was passed over his veto. In 1944 he was nominated by Estes Kefauver in the Democratic convention for Vice President but received only favorite son support.

Jim Nance McCord of Lewisburg was elected to succeed Cooper. "Not since 1924 has the Tennessee Democracy staged a primary that was so unique," wrote veteran reporter Ralph Perry after the primary, unique "in that there was one candidate so far outstanding that the opposition was negligible." McCord had defeated Rex Manning of Nashville and John R. Neal of Knoxville by more than a 10-to-1 majority in the August primary. His victory in the general election in November over John Wesley Kilgo, a forty-three-year-old Greeneville Republican "country lawyer," was by almost as large a majority.

The Mississippi-born McCord, a "self-made man" from a poor family of eleven children, was billed as a "pure and wholesome" man and a "plain country Democrat." For a quarter of a century he had served as mayor of Lewisburg and as a member of the Marshall county court, and had worked as a traveling salesman, auctioneer, and newspaper publisher. He had served as president of the Tennessee Press Association, had been a delegate to the Democratic national convention in 1940, and had been elected to Congress without opposition in 1942 from the Fourth District. McCord made no sweeping promises of reform but promised only to give the people honest government and to preside with a firm and even hand.

SUGGESTED READINGS

General Accounts

Folmsbee, Corlew, and Mitchell, *Tennessee*, II, Ch. 44; Hamer, *Tennessee*, II, Ch. 45; V. O. Key, Jr., *Southern Politics in State and Nation* (New York, 1949).

Specialized Accounts

T. H. Alexander, *Austin Peay, Governor of Tennessee* (Kingsport, 1929); McFerrin, *Caldwell and Company*; William D. Miller, "The Browning-Crump Battle: The Crump Side," ETHS *Publ.*, No. 37 (1965), 77–88; Miller, *Mr. Crump*; Jennings Perry, *Democracy Begins at Home: The Tennessee Fight on the Poll Tax* (New York, 1944); Franklin O. Rouse, "The Historical Background of Tennessee's Administrative Reorganization Act of 1923," ETHS *Publ.*, No. 8 (1936), 104–20.

28. ?❧ Twentieth-Century Agriculture and Industry

PHENOMENAL CHANGES have evolved in the economy of the state during the twentieth century. Although much industrial progress was made in the three decades before 1900, Tennessee still remained predominantly an agricultural state at the dawn of the new century. During the two decades after World War II, however, the Volunteer State rapidly shifted to an industrial economy. By 1964, 31.4 per cent of the people earned their living from industrial jobs as compared to 29.3 per cent for the nation as a whole; only 5.7 per cent received their major income from farming.

Agriculture ?❧ Agriculture in the twentieth century has been marked by enormous advancements in technology and science. The greatest mechanical advance has been the invention of the internal combustion engine tractor, which soon after World War II almost entirely replaced the horse and mule as a source of power. At the turn of the century, electricity was unknown on the farms, but with the advent of the Tennessee Valley Authority during the 1930's that source of power was soon found on most farms. By the 1960's the dairy farmer, as well as the row crop farmer and the beef cattle farmer, was as dependent upon electricity as he was upon the soil.

Almost as important as the technological improvements was the revolution in the application of science to agriculture. County agents from Memphis to Bristol introduced farmers to a variety of new methods, farmers' cooperatives and other farm stores marketed commercial fertilizers to triple and quadruple production, and many new fungicides and weed killers were designed to decrease the amount of backbreaking toil once necessary. Corn and cotton farmers of the 1960's used "pre-emergence" and "post-emergence" sprays that required little or no cultivation of the crops between planting and harvesting.

Other major changes stand out in twentieth-century agriculture in Tennessee. There has been a steady decline in farms and farm acreage but a decided increase in production. The number of farms multiplied steadily until the 1920's. The number in 1860 (82,368) had tripled in 1910 (246,012) and had reached a high of 252,657 in 1920. By 1930, however, the number had declined to 243,657 and by 1960 to 157,688. There also has been a decline in the number of acres under cultivation and the size of farms. The number of acres in farms was at its height in 1900 when 20,342,058 was under cultivation with an average acreage per farm of 90.6. By 1930, however, 18,003,241 acres were under cultivation, with an average per farm of 73.3. In 1960, 16,081,285 acres were in farms, and by 1967 the number had decreased to 15,266,000 acres.

Although farms and farm acreage decreased steadily, production has increased phenomenally. The yield per acre of corn, cotton, wheat, tobacco, and all other crops has been swelled because of improved farm practices and modern fertilizers. Moreover, the source of income from farms has changed in the twentieth century—dairying, for example, although a negligible source of income in pre-Civil War days, brought returns to the farmers of over eight million dollars in 1900. Today, dairying is a chief source of income for farmers in all sections of the state.

Even with farm production increasing sharply during the twentieth century, farm income has not kept pace with industry, however, and this disparity has caused many people to leave the farms for the cities. Therefore, a multiplicity of government programs has been designed to aid the farmers. Although there was considerable talk in Congress and out, no aid of any consequence was forthcoming until the New Deal program of 1933 and after. Despite a continued depressed condition in comparison with the income of urban blue collar groups, the farmer of today in Tennessee has a standard of living undreamed of by the nineteenth-century farmer. Mainly responsible for this standard has been rural electrification, which has enabled farmers to enjoy running water, electric appliances, and practically all the other conveniences of urban life.

Agricultural development in Tennessee in the twentieth century may be divided for convenience into four broad periods. The first would include the first two decades of the century when farmers enjoyed relative prosperity in comparison to the difficult decades following the Civil War; these years between the conclusion of the Spanish-American War and World War I have been called the "golden era of American agriculture." A second period would include the one and one-half decades from the end of World War I to the New Deal; this period of course encompasses the depression of 1920, the subsequent efforts at relief by the federal government under the Republican administrations of Harding, Coolidge, and Hoover, and the first few years of the depression of 1929 and the 1930's. A third period would embrace the revolution occasioned by the New Deal and World War II. A fourth would be the two decades of mechanization, coming after World War II, that drove the horse and mule from the farm as a source of power in all but the very backward or very hilly agricultural areas.

As the nineteenth century closed, a farmers' revolt ceased, and farmers entered into an era of prosperity. Earlier, changes in agriculture were effected during the generations after the conclusion of the Civil War. The number of farms had doubled and the amount of cleared land had increased considerably. Corn continued to be the major crop and was grown in all sections of the state; in 1900 the crop was valued at $28 million. Cotton was second in value, followed by wheat, hay, and other crops. Cotton, however, continued to be the major crop of southern West Tennessee; the five counties of Shelby, Fayette, Haywood, Lauderdale, and Tipton produced more than one-half of the state's crop in that year.

Concentration upon the production of animals for slaughter was also a major change by 1900. Only a few years earlier most farmers had given little attention to selective breeding and had turned cattle and hogs loose during the year to roam in the forests and forage for themselves. Beef and dairying became important soon after the advent of the twentieth century, and by 1920 farmers throughout the state were producing good grades of cattle. Meat products in 1900 were valued at more than $9 million, which was greater than any other argricultural product except corn. Indeed, Tennessee in that year ranked third among Southern states in meat production, just behind Texas and Kentucky. Dairy products were valued at more than $8 million. Poultry and eggs brought farmers almost as much.

Tennessee farmers at the dawn of the new century raised a variety of crops in addition to those mentioned. Tobacco remained an important crop in the north central counties and was valued at $2.7 million in 1900. Fruits and vegetables, long important crops, continued to bring profits. Among fruits, the apple orchards were far more numerous than all others. In 1900 the apple crop was valued at more than $7 million; the total value of the peach, apricot, cherry, pear, and plum crop was a little less than $4 million. Other crops valued at one-half million or more included oats, Irish potatoes, sweet potatoes, peas, fruits, and sorghum.

"The farmers of our state are more prosperous," wrote Agriculture Commissioner John Thompson in 1908, "than at any time for 30 or 40 years past." The commissioner pointed to the increase in acreage under cultivation, the increase in production, and the growing farm income. The value of farm property and farm products doubled during the first decade of the new century. The enormous growth of urban areas had increased the domestic market enormously, and a profitable foreign market also was developing; thus the demand began to grow faster than the supply which brought the welcomed price increases.

Commissioner Thompson pointed to the state and county fairs and to the "Farmers' Institutes" as being extremely important in keeping farmers informed about new methods and markets. The first such institute, held in Jackson in 1899, proved to be very popular, and by 1908 the commission reported that 149 institutes had been conducted in ninety-four counties, in addition to regional institutes in each of the grand divisions of the state. The State Fair Association was organized in 1906 and offered prizes totaling $18,-000. In a few years the amount of prize money was tripled. Tennesseans had won two grand prizes—in tobacco and forest products—at the Louisiana Purchase Exposition in St. Louis in 1903.

The prosperity of the years before World War I was stimulated considerably by the European demands for farm products after the war began. Cotton, for which Tennessee farmers received less than 12 cents per pound in 1912, brought 19.6 cents in 1916, 27.6 cents

| Map 6. | West Tennessee | Middle Tennessee |

THE THREE GRAND DIVISIONS

at the close of the war, and reached an all-time high of 35.6 cents in 1919. Corn and tobacco likewise grew phenomenally in value. Corn, selling at 70 cents per bushel in 1914 had more than doubled in price four years later, and brought $1.51 per bushel in 1919. Tobacco jumped from 9.7 cents per pound in 1914 to 27.9 cents when the war closed, and then to a high of 31.2 in 1919. Along with the prices, the amount produced increased considerably too, especially of corn and tobacco. Animal products also advanced during the war, although Texas fever, which invaded the state's beef industry early in the twentieth century, was a major cause of beef cattle loss as late as 1914.

The period of 1920–30 opened and closed in agricultural depression, but between those years Tennessee farm prices held up reasonably well; prices, however, did not approach the highs of 1918 and 1919. The price of cotton dropped from 35.6 cents in 1919 to 13.9 cents in 1920; for the same years corn dropped from $1.51 to 62 cents per bushel, and tobacco from 31.2 cents to 17.3 cents per pound. In 1921, prices for cattle, sheep, and hogs had declined to about 50 per cent of their 1919 levels. The 1920's were a decade in which industry and most of the rest of the country prospered, but agriculture did not. The productive capacity of the American farmer obviously was out of balance with the foreign and domestic de-

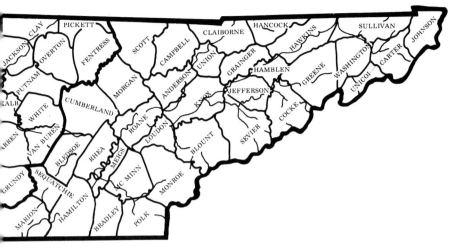

East Tennessee

AND COUNTIES IN TENNESSEE

mands. The war years had been years in which the European demands were heavy; in the postwar years the inflationary boom had spiralled prices upward. Production from foreign countries in the 1920's—particularly those of South America, Australia, and Canada, in addition to those of Europe—greatly curtailed foreign markets, and improvements in technology at home caused overproduction. Although Tennessee congressmen generally were sympathetic to efforts in Washington to aid farmers, little was accomplished there of a constructive and lasting nature.

In 1922, the State Agriculture Department issued a new edition of *Facts About Tennessee*, a pamphlet edited by Commissioner T. F. Peck and designed to encourage immigrants to come into the state. Peck pointed to land available at low prices, salubrious climate, and productive soil. "There is a certainty of profitable returns," Peck wrote, "from whatever is put into the soil." He emphasized the growth of the cities and the resulting good prices which were being realized for produce of the truck farmers. "Happiness, comfort, and health," he stressed, "await homeseekers in Tennessee, whose citizens gladly welcome newcomers to a region of schools, churches, social advantages, and good neighbors."

Although Tennessee farmers experienced relief from the depression by 1922, Peck's optimism was not warranted in the remainder of the decade. Prices of cotton, corn, and tobacco climbed to 23.8 cents, 74.5 cents, and 22.8 cents, respectively, in 1922 but made no appreciable gain for the remainder of the decade. In 1930 the prices of the three products had sagged to 9.5 cents, 59.6 cents, and 12.8 cents, respectively.

The 1920's marked high hopes among tobacco growers for increased profits. The introduction of burley tobacco, which, unlike the "dark fired" type, did not require "firing," was a cause for optimism. At the beginning of the decade, burley was grown only in two or three counties of East Tennessee, but in 1921, after a concerted drive by the East Tennessee Tobacco Association and the Agriculture Extension Service to encourage its growth, 4,550,000 pounds were produced. Two years later the crop was quadrupled. Greene County soon became the leading burley producer in the state, with Greeneville one of the largest markets in the country. Although burley was confined largely to East Tennessee, farmers in the counties of Sumner, Bedford, Maury, and Giles also produced millions of pounds during the decade. Even though burley at times brought as much as 40 cents per pound, it, like other products, experienced a decided decline in price at the end of the decade.

By 1933, drought and depressed prices had taken their toll among Tennessee farmers. Cotton had dropped to a new low—5.7 cents per pound—corn brought 31.9 cents per bushel, and tobacco fell to 10.5 cents per pound. A scorching drought in 1930 cut production to such an extent that experts in Nashville estimated the loss to farmers at one hundred million dollars. Along with prices, production had fallen considerably by 1933. The total value of farm products of the state declined from $313,661,000 in 1929 to $132,-015,000 in 1932; the value of products sold from Tennessee farmers for the same period dropped from $160,622,000 to $62,192,000. The registration of new passenger cars and trucks, always a necessity for rural people, indicated the gripping and developing poverty. Whereas 41,488 had been registered in 1928 and 55,211 in 1929, only 11,696 new vehicles were registered in the state in 1932.

Shortly after the presidential inauguration of 1933, President Roosevelt told Congress of the dire conditions in Southern agriculture. The South was the nation's number one economic problem, he said; therefore, "an unprecedented condition calls for the trial of new means to rescue agriculture." Representative Joseph W.

Byrns, of Nashville, a member of the House for twenty-two years and later its speaker, was among those who helped draft the Agricultural Adjustment Act (AAA), which President Roosevelt signed into law on May 12, 1933. This law, which was to have a profound effect upon agriculture in Tennessee, was mainly enacted to raise farm prices to parity. Parity was defined as reestablishing "prices to farmers at a level that will give agricultural commodities a purchasing power with respect to articles farmers buy, equivalent to the purchasing power of articles in the base period . . . August, 1909–July, 1914." The measure authorized production controls through voluntary contracts with farmers to restrict their production of certain basic commodities such as cotton, wheat, corn, tobacco, and hogs—all important farm products in Tennessee. Producers were to be paid for their reductions in output by rental payments derived from a tax to be collected from the processors. State Commissioner of Agriculture O. E. Van Cleve hailed the act, praised the Tennessee delegation in Washington for supporting it, and estimated that in the Volunteer State the income of farmers would be more than doubled on the three essential crops of corn, cotton, and wheat.

Most crops already had been planted when the law was passed, and therefore it was clearly necessary to explain to farmers what was being done. Meetings of farmers were held in every county during June to explain carefully that some crops would have to be plowed under in order that farmers might benefit from the program.

Cotton was the first crop to come under the AAA program. Governor McAlister, proclaiming July 12 as "Cotton Day," urged farmers to familiarize themselves with the program and to sign up to become eligible for payments. When the campaign ended, more than 46,500 farmers signed contracts to remove 264,287 acres from production. They were paid a total of $4,665,404 for an average of nearly $18 per acre during the first year. The law was changed in the following year, and nearly 90 per cent of the cotton farmers of the state signed contracts.

Tennessee farmers participated in all phases of the act until it was declared unconstitutional in January, 1936. Producers of corn, tobacco, wheat, and hogs benefited. Tennessee agriculture was being lifted "by its bootstraps," wrote the editor of the Clarksville *Leaf Chronicle* in July, 1935, "out of the morass of depression."

Replacement acts soon were passed. In 1938, Congress enacted the Agricultural Adjustment Act, which to this day remains the nation's basic agricultural legislation. On the provision that a referendum indicated that two-thirds of the farmers wished to participate, this law authorized payments to farmers who maintained a soil building program. While some claimed that the law would make farmers "tenants of a federal bureaucracy," Tennessee farmers voted to accept it by a large majority.

Tennessee farmers participated in all the New Deal farm programs applicable to the state, and received many benefits. Millions of dollars were borrowed under the Commodity Credit Corporation, which was originally established in October, 1933, as a subsidiary of the Reconstruction Finance Corporation. The Farm Credit Administration of 1933 and the Rural Electrification Administration of 1935 also were of tremendous benefit to Tennessee farmers. By 1936 the prices of cotton, corn, and tobacco were, respectively, 12.4 cents, $1.04, and 23.6 cents. Although prices declined during the brief recession of the following year, they regained their position by 1939 and continued to climb in the next decade.

During World War II there was of course considerable demand for agricultural products. Although the farm population decreased from 1,275,582 in 1940 to 981,501 in 1945, and the number of farms from 247,617 to 234,431 in the same period, production increased considerably; this gain was due largely to mechanization. The Tennessee Home Food Supply Program was begun in 1940 under which each participating farmer agreed to grow on his farm a minimum of 75 per cent of his family's food. Certificates of Recognition, signed by Governor Cooper, were given to those who participated. Governor Cooper was named chairman of the National Victory Gardens Committee, and more than 200,000 families in the state cultivated "victory gardens."

Many changes in agriculture have taken place since World War II. Mules and horses, once the chief source of power on the farms, rapidly disappeared after the war and were replaced by tractors. In 1940 the number of tractors on farms was only 11,814, but five years later the number had doubled. Ten years later (1955), there were 84,869 tractors on farms and by 1960 nearly 100,000. By the latter date, nearly 12,000 farm operators reported the use of two or more tractors, and 718 stated that they operated farms on which five or more were used. This would mean, then, that today most of the farms in Tennessee have at least one tractor. In 1945 there was an average of one tractor per nine farms in the state. The trend toward mechanization, improved methods of farming, superior seeds and selective breeding, and improved fertilizers and animal feeds have made greater production possible with less manpower and man-hours. Between 1910 and 1960, for example, the man-hours necessary to produce one hundred bushels of wheat declined from 106 to 11.

At mid-century 1,016,204 people lived on 231,631 farms; their land, buildings, livestock, and equipment were valued at two and one-third billion dollars. Many farmers were putting their land into permanent pasture for grazing dairy and beef cattle. Statistics indicated that livestock was the state's biggest single source of farm income. The gross value of dairy products was $105,148,000, and Tennessee ranked fifth in the nation in the production of cheese. Beef, pork, and mutton together were valued at $185,000,000 and poultry at $40,000,000. Cotton still was king, and the crop sold in 1951 for $117,624,000. Corn was second, at $105,630,000; tobacco came third at $66,898,000. Farmers were rapidly clearing their forest lands to take advantage of high lumber prices brought about by the postwar building boom. At mid-century, Tennessee was the world's largest producer of hardwood flooring and also supplied millions of board feet for furniture manufacture and other construction.

By 1968 cotton had abdicated as king and had been replaced by tobacco and soybeans. The cotton crop of 1967, curtailed by poor weather and decreasing acreage, was the smallest in more than 100 years, and the yield of 336 pounds per acre was the lowest since 1951. Tennessee's total crop value of $303,580,000 was down 4 per cent from 1966. Tobacco, the leader, was valued at $76,827,000; soybeans, $68,015,000; hay, $53,652,000; corn, $50,979,000; and cotton, $27,438,000. Tobacco, which had reached a low of 10.5 cents in 1932, brought 65 cents in 1966 and 72.8 on the New Tazewell market in 1967. Greeneville continued to be the leading burley market, with Johnson City and Mountain City close behind. In Middle Tennessee, where both burley and dark fired tobacco are grown, Franklin, Sparta, Columbia, Hartsville, and Clarksville were the largest markets. Livestock figures for 1967 indicated that the number of hogs had increased over 1966, but that the number of cattle produced declined slightly.

Perhaps of most concern in 1968 was the steady decline of farms which pointed poignantly to the fact that the small farmer is the modern "vanishing American," in Tennessee as well as in the nation as a whole.

Industry ஃ The industrial development of the last three decades of the nineteenth century, discussed in an earlier chapter, continued at even a greater rate of expansion after the beginning of the twentieth century. The capitalization of industry in 1899 had reached a new high of $71,182,966, and the value of manufactured products exceeded $92,500,000. Industrial workers numbered 45,963 and were paid a total of $14,727,506 in wages.

At the beginning of the century the leading industry was flour and gristmilling, which accounted for more than 20 per cent of the total products of the state's industries. Nashville was the chief center for flour milling, with Knoxville the leading center in the eastern part of the state and Memphis in the west. Most small towns, because of the abundance of corn and wheat and also an ample supply of water, had a flour or gristmill. The timber and lumber industry ranked second. Every county had an abundant supply of virgin timber and, consequently, many sawmills. Memphis was the largest inland hardwood lumber market in the world at the turn of the century; Nashville led in flooring and other hardwood products. Third place among the industries was iron and steel. Sixteen establishments employed nearly 2,000 wage earners, and their products were valued at $5,000,000. Ore was mined in both East and Middle Tennessee. Other important industries at the turn of the century included textiles (with an employment of 4251), cotton seed products, and tobacco processing; the latter industry experienced a gain of 252.7 per cent within the decade.

During the first three decades of the twentieth century, industrial growth especially was apparent. The number of manufacturing establishments increased approximately 45 per cent from 1904 to 1909, and then once again five years later, when the war began, factory growth showed considerable development and continued to do so throughout World War I. Many of the industries originating during the war, however, were of a temporary nature, and immediately after the war the plants closed. After the recession of 1920–21, industry again developed strongly in the state until the time of the depression in 1929. The average number of wage earners in manufacturing increased 179 per cent during the thirty-year period from 1899 to 1929. In the first decade alone of this period, the increase was 60 per cent. Again, from 1914 to 1919 the number of wage earners increased 28 per cent—largely because of the war prosperity and the demands of the Allies for war goods.

Considerable diversification took place in the first three decades of the century, and several new industries ranked foremost among manufactured goods of the state. Knit goods, as measured by the value of the annual output, ranked first in 1930, with an output value of $48,406,388. Lumber and timber products came second at $32,604,611. Flour and gristmill operations, which had ranked first in 1900, placed third in 1930 with products valued at $28,600,288. Rayon, shortenings and other vegetable cooking oils, animal and poultry feeds, and motor vehicles and parts were among the products scarcely heard of in 1900, but whose total products were valued in the millions in 1930.

Although some of the plants constructed during the war closed down by 1919, others were able to convert to products for civilian consumer use. Among these was the Du Pont Powder Plant at Old Hickory, which very shortly after arms were stacked was manufacturing rayon and cellophane goods. The plant, constructed in a record time of three months, was producing powder by July, 1918. By summer of the following year, the town of Old Hickory consisted of 30,000 people and nearly 4,000 buildings, including homes, schools, hotels, and city government buildings. A steel suspension bridge, 540 feet long with 1,260 feet of trestled approaches, spanned the Cumberland River which separated the town from Nashville. Thousands of Tennesseans soon were employed in the manufacture of rayon and cellophane. Although operations were curtailed during the depression of 1929 and after, the plant failed to close completely during that time.

The decade of the 1920's opened and closed in depression, but in the intervening seven-year period considerable industrial growth occurred. The number of commercial establishments increased 36 per cent in the two-year period from 1927 to 1929, but declined 45 per cent during the next four-year period. When the depression began, the number of wage earners in manufacturing had increased 179 per cent during the first thirty years of the twentieth century.

The trend away from agriculture and toward manufacturing is shown during the same thirty-year period by the increase of only 39.7 per cent in the population of the state. The increase in industrial development was largely responsible for the urban growth during the first three decades of the century. In 1929, Memphis, with a population of 162,351, produced manufactured products valued at nearly $200,000,000; Nashville, with a population of 118,342, produced goods valued at nearly $150 million; and Chattanooga ranked third with products well over $100 million. Memphis, the largest inland cotton market of the world, became the largest producer of cotton seed products in the world. By the early 1920's the E. L. Bruce Company of Memphis became the world's largest hardwood flooring manufacturer. Chattanooga, with a population of 57,895, was the leading knit goods center of the state and was second in the entire nation in the construction of steam boilers and in the manufacture of hosiery. Knoxville, with a population of 77,818, manufactured hundreds of different items—including textiles, iron and steel products, marble and other stone products, knit goods, and lumber. Moreover, many of the small urban areas were in the process of developing large industrial establishments. The Kingsport Press of Kingsport was reputed to be the largest plant in the country devoted exclusively to the manufacture of books. Johnson City, the fifth largest urban area, had large hosiery mills, textile mills, and other factories. Jackson, almost as large as Johnson City, was a railroad center and was outstanding for its production of cotton seed products.

The depression of the 1930's caused many manufacturing establishments to close, although when the brief recession of 1937 occurred considerable recovery was apparent. In that year 2,083 industrial plants in Tennessee were paying total wages of $109,247,514 and producing goods valued at $707,986,784. Two years later, when World War II began in Europe, the number of plants had expanded to 2,289, which paid wages in the amount of $109,661,769 and produced goods valued at $728,087,825. By that year rayon and allied products had become one of the most valuable industries in the state, producing goods valued at $59,724,728. Meat packing ranked second and chemical products third among the top industrial establishments of Tennessee. The need for materials of war brought new industries to Tennessee, and many of these, including the Oak Ridge

Atomic Energy Center and the Arnold Air Engineering Center at Tullahoma, remained operative after the war was over.

Immediately after World War II, state officials expanded their efforts to bring industry into the state. Before that time, the State Planning Commission had only conducted limited research studies to determine which industries would develop best and which would be interested in coming to Tennessee. A comprehensive industrial survey was undertaken in the early 1940's, and in 1943 the commission published the first directory of manufactures. In the following year, the commission began to maintain an inventory of available facilities for industries, and in 1945 published *Industrial Resources of Tennessee*. In 1953, the Tennessee Industrial and Agricultural Development Commission was established primarily to develop new industry and to encourage the expansion of industries already operating in the state. Therefore, the commission announced its plans to explain to all possible investors the advantages which the state held for industrial location. Advertising in the New York *Times* and other newspapers of wide circulation was begun before the year had passed, and in 1954, a traveling representative was employed to make frequent trips into northern cities to explain to potential investors the advantages of Tennessee. Not infrequently, state officials and prominent businessmen went as teams into the cities of New York, Chicago, Detroit, and other northern and eastern cities in search of investment capital. In 1945–46 the state had expended only $17,889 for industrial development; in the biennium of 1958–59 it spent $233,803. Further, the staff of the Industrial Commission expanded from four in 1948 to twenty in 1959.

By 1947—two years after the war ended—the manufacture of chemical and allied products clearly was the leading industry of the state. Food and kindred products and textile manufacturing ranked second and third, respectively. Industrial establishments had increased more than 50 per cent since World War II began in 1939, and the total value added by manufacturing had more than tripled. In 1947 six major urban counties accounted for 50 per cent of the total value added, 49 per cent of the employees, and 39 per cent of the establishments. Shelby (Memphis) rose to first place in value added, followed by Davidson (Nashville), Hamilton (Chattanooga), Sullivan (Kingsport and Bristol), and Knox (Knoxville).

Considerable growth continued in the 1950's. Among the states

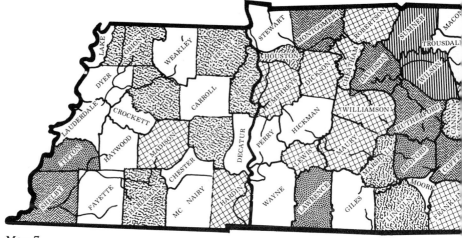

Map 7.

PER CENT CHANGE

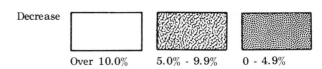

Decrease   Over 10.0%   5.0% - 9.9%   0 - 4.9%

which had 250,000 or more industrial jobs in 1955, Tennessee made greater industrial gains during the decade of 1955–65 than any other state. Tennessee had a gain of 28 per cent of manufacturing jobs, as compared with 25 per cent in Florida, North Carolina, and South Carolina, and 21 per cent in Texas.

In a publication released in 1961, the Division of Industrial Research hailed the year of 1960 as one which "will go down in the record books as one of the most dynamic in the history of the State" —"dynamic" inasmuch as during the "record-breaking period" of 1959–60 there were nearly 40,000 jobs created because of new plants moving in and the expansion of plants already established. In 1960 the number of new industries selecting locations in Tennessee was 162, as compared to 99 in 1954; the number of expansions during the same period was 224 as compared to 136 in 1954. Chattanooga led with 26 new plants and 29 expansions. East Tennessee had 152 new and expanded plants—only 28 less than the total in Middle and West Tennessee combined.

Middle Tennessee showed the greatest amount of growth since 1950, but it is interesting to note the increasing importance of East

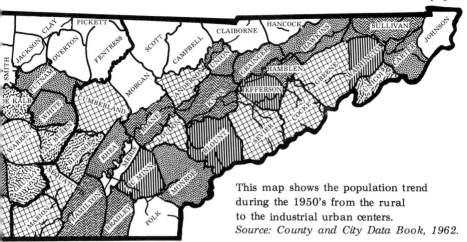

This map shows the population trend
during the 1950's from the rural
to the industrial urban centers.
Source: County and City Data Book, 1962.

IN POPULATION, 1950-60

Increase

0.1% - 4.9%   5.0% - 9.9%   Over 10.0%

Tennessee in manufacturing, especially when compared to West Tennessee. The manufacturing income in 1962 was $685,104,000 in East Tennessee, $405,524,000 in Middle Tennessee, and $344,372,000 in West Tennessee. The growth since 1952, however, was 154.6 per cent for Middle Tennessee as compared to 104.2 for East Tennessee. In the eastern section, manufacturing alone accounted for the income of 25 per cent or more in 21 of the 36 counties; this was true in only 2 of the 21 counties of West Tennessee.

The significance of industry and commerce in the lives of Tennesseans is apparent by the shift in population from the predominant rural counties to the urban counties. In the rural counties of all three divisions of the state, but especially those of the Cumberland Plateau and those west of the Tennessee River, the population decline is more apparent than elsewhere. In counties having large federal agencies (such as Coffee and Montgomery) and counties having large cities, the population increase is readily evident, as shown in Map 7 and in the following table.

In a study released by the Tennessee Valley Authority in January,

Population of Certain Rural and Urban Counties for 1950 and 1960 with Prognostications for Changes in 1970 and 1980

County	1950	1960	Per cent increase or decrease	1970	Per cent increase or decrease	1980	Per cent increase or decrease
Bradley	32,338	38,324	18.5	44,555	16.3	51,338	15.2
Chester	11,149	9,569	−14.2	7,973	−16.7	6,532	−18.1
Coffee	23,049	28,603	24.1	34,909	21.0	42,315	21.2
Davidson	321,758	399,743	24.2	485,853	21.5	594,431	22.3
Fayette	27,535	24,577	−10.8	20,892	−15.0	17,468	−16.4
Fentress	14,917	13,288	−11.0	11,571	−13.0	10,024	−13.4
Gibson	48,132	44,699	−7.1	39,529	−11.6	33,891	−14.3
Giles	26,961	22,410	−16.9	18,177	−18.9	14,369	−21.0
Hamilton	208,255	237,905	14.2	260,994	9.7	284,807	9.1
Henry	23,828	22,275	−6.5	19,813	−11.1	17,143	−13.5
Knox	223,007	250,523	12.3	273,149	9.0	293,196	7.3
Lauderdale	25,047	21,844	−12.8	18,349	−16.0	15,037	−18.1
McNairy	20,390	18,085	−11.3	15,646	−13.5	13,293	−15.0
Macon	13,599	12,197	−10.3	10,706	−12.2	9,190	−14.2
Madison	60,128	60,655	1.9	58,417	3.7	55,149	5.6

Maury	40,368	41,699	3.3	41,642	−.1	40,961	−1.6
Meigs	6,080	5,160	−15.1	4,296	−16.7	3,527	−17.0
Montgomery	44,186	55,645	25.9	72,027	29.4	94,835	31.7
Moore	3,948	3,454	−12.5	2,972	−3.1	2,479	−16.6
Morgan	15,727	14,304	−9.0	12,645	−11.6	11,013	−12.9
Overton	17,566	14,661	−16.5	12,149	−17.1	9,943	−18.2
Perry	6,462	5,273	−18.4	4,159	−21.1	3,229	−22.4
Putnam	29,869	29,236	−2.1	27,944	−4.4	26,100	−6.6
Roane	31,665	39,133	23.6	47,562	21.5	57,212	20.3
Robertson	27,024	27,335	1.1	26,706	−2.3	25,644	−3.10
Rutherford	40,696	52,368	28.7	67,933	29.7	90,779	33.6
Shelby	482,393	627,019	29.1	795,761	26.9	1,025,748	28.9
Smith	14,098	12,059	−14.5	9,979	−17.2	8,024	−19.6
Stewart	9,175	7,851	−14.4	6,562	−16.4	5,304	−19.2
Sullivan	95,063	114,139	20.1	132,722	16.3	151,707	14.3
Sumner	33,533	36,217	8.0	37,820	4.4	38,757	2.5
Trousdale	5,520	4,914	−11.0	4,234	−13.8	3,558	−4.0
Van Buren	3,985	3,671	−7.9	3,288	−10.4	2,942	−10.5
Weakley	27,962	24,227	−13.4	20,189	−16.7	16,328	−19.1
Williamson	24,307	25,267	3.9	25,792	2.1	26,163	1.4
Wilson	26,318	27,668	5.1	28,222	2.0	28,342	1.4

Source: Staff Division for Industrial Development, State of Tennessee

1968, industrial expansion in the TVA region achieved a record high in 1967. Among the principal new plants and expansions during the year cited by the TVA report were: Aluminum Company of America's $30 million expansion and modernization at Alcoa, Combustion Engineering's $20 million Chattanooga plant to build nuclear components for steam generators, Goodyear Tire & Rubber Company's $46 million plant at Union City, a $15 million General Electric plant at Hendersonville, and a $10 million structural steel plant to be built at Memphis by Chicago Bridge & Iron Company.

Ironically, the Center for Business and Economic Research of The University of Tennessee at the same time released a study which pointed to a trend toward a declining economy in Tennessee in the fall and early winter of 1967. Unemployment in every major city, the report stated, climbed above the national average. Even so, the per capita income of the state far exceeded that of any comparable period in the past. In 1950 the state's per capita income of $992 was only 66.8 per cent of the national figure. By 1960 it had increased to 69.2 per cent and to 72.4 per cent by 1964. Preliminary figures indicated that the 1968 figure will be well above 75 per cent. There seems to be little question but that the number of those employed in industrial pursuits will continue to increase and those employed in agriculture will continue to decrease. The state, therefore, appears to be on the threshold of continued industrial development.

SUGGESTED READINGS

General Accounts
Folmsbee, Corlew, and Mitchell, *Tennessee*, II, Chs. 33, 35, 41; Hamer, *Tennessee*, II, Chs. 51–53.

29. &➣ A New Era in Tennessee: TVA

THE BASIN of the Tennessee River originates in south-western Virginia and ends with the confluence of that river with the Ohio. On its way the Tennessee and its tributaries touch seven states, but it crosses the state of Tennessee twice and therefore affects the lives of its people more than those of the other six.

Before the coming of TVA, the valley was an underdeveloped area, with a relatively low level of agricultural and industrial development. There was beauty of landscape in the rugged mountains of Tennessee, but the soil was thin and the area was not realizing its potential in industrial development. The people of the valley were poor, many of them subsisting on a cash income of less than $100 a year. Although the allegation by Secretary of Labor Frances Perkins in 1933 that few valley residents wore shoes was a gross exaggeration, it is true that a large proportion of the population was on relief because of the depression.

The Origins of TVA &➣ A new era was to dawn for the people of the valley with the realization of a great plan envisioned by the new President of the United States, Franklin Delano Roosevelt. The difficulty in navigating the Tennessee River, the poverty of the area, the paucity of good soil, and soil erosion by uncontrolled rivers and streams were important factors in the creation of the Tennessee Valley Authority. With respect to TVA, the solution of these problems was to be combined with the opportunity to use the river for the production of electric power. The Authority would have the task of planning the complete development of the valley for the good of the nation.

The Tennessee River as a navigation channel was an age-old problem. With the end of the Civil War, the destruction of many railroads brought a revival of steamboat navigation on the Tennessee River. This led to a new interest in obviating the most serious obstruction to navigation, the Muscle Shoals, and thus in 1890 and 1911 new canals were built around them. In 1913, to aid navigation upstream, Hales Bar Dam, thirty-three miles below Chattanooga, was completed. Erected by the Tennessee Electric Power Company under supervision of army engineers, it was "the first combined navigation-and-power improvement on the Tennessee River system."[1]

These measures, and others which had been adopted, did not increase materially the amount of traffic on the Tennessee, and it was not long before the production of electric power became the most important consideration in the development of the river. This was especially true in regard to the beginning of construction at the Muscle Shoals under the National Defense Act of 1916 of Wilson Dam and nitrate plants for defense purposes,[2] but also peacetime production of cheap fertilizer for agriculture was anticipated. World War I ended before Wilson Dam was completed, and the government was left with the thorny problem of what to do with the "white elephant" at the Muscle Shoals. Then, Henry Ford, to the country's amazement, made the historic offer on July 8, 1921, to lease Wilson Dam and other power facilities (if the government would complete their construction), purchase the nitrate plants, and produce nitrogenous fertilizer. It was assumed that Ford would create a new "Detroit" at the Shoals.

Thus was inaugurated the notorious Muscle Shoals controversy, which continued for more than a decade before being resolved by the creation of the Tennessee Valley Authority in 1933. The con-

[1] Davidson, *The Tennessee*, II, 177. The first Muscle Shoals Canal, completed in 1836, had been of little use.
[2] Although navigation locks were included in the plans, power was the most vital consideration.

troversy involved the conflicting interests of farmers, land speculators, fertilizer producers, and advocates of public versus advocates
of private electric power. The controversy also raged around the
problem of navigation improvement, and later around the question
of multipurpose stream planning after the disastrous floods of 1927.
During the early stages of the controversy, Tennessee congressmen,
led by Senator Kenneth D. McKellar, who had introduced the
original Defense Act of 1916, enthusiastically and almost unanimously supported the Ford "dream," envisioning the great benefits
to Tennesseans expected to result from the waving of the manufac-
turer's magic wand over the Tennessee Valley. By the end of 1924,
however, McKellar had led most of his fellow Tennesseans in Congress into George W. Norris's public power camp. Norris, fearing
monopolies in the field of electric power, had favored government
operation of hydroelectric plants on the Tennessee River because
rates charged by the government would serve as a measuring rod for
the fairness of rates charged by privately operated power companies.
Although McKellar filibustered against one Norris measure in 1928
because it failed to give sufficient consideration to fertilizer production and more especially neglected to provide for compensation to
the states involved for tax losses which would result from the dam-
building program, he returned to the fold when the Nebraskan
amended his bill to take care of those objections. Thereafter, Mc-
Kellar was such a loyal supporter that he became a rival of Norris
for the title, "Father of TVA," and was disappointed in 1933 when
he was not given the honor of introducing the TVA bill. Nevertheless, in February of that year McKellar admitted on the floor of the
Senate that

> The entire Tennessee Valley, and indeed the entire South, owes to
> George W. Norris a deep debt of gratitude for the wonderful fight
> he has made for the last 10 years to keep Muscle Shoals in the hands
> of the Government to use it for the benefit of the people.[3]

[3] Quoted in Hubbard, *Origins of TVA*, 315. Although McKellar later parted company with the Authority over the patronage issue, he had been so influential in getting
increasing appropriations for the project that one writer (Edward Felsenthal, in
WTHS *Papers*, XX, 108–22) called him "The Rich Uncle of TVA." The brilliant,
but unconventional law professor, former state legislator, and perennial candidate
for public office, Dr. John R. Neal, also was an ardent proponent of public power; he
has been credited with drafting one section of the TVA law.

The Establishment of TVA ?? Although prior to 1933 Norris and the Progressive Republican-Southern Democratic coalition had twice managed to get his power "yardstick" and multipurpose stream planning bill for the Tennessee River through Congress, the measure had not become law because of the Coolidge and Hoover presidential vetoes. After Franklin D. Roosevelt entered the White House on March 4, 1933, a similar measure was passed on May 18 and quickly received the President's signature. In accordance with the President's message of April 10, following his visit to the Tennessee Valley and conferences with Norris and other proponents of Muscle Shoals legislation, the bill was somewhat broader in scope than some of those leaders had in mind. It envisioned not only power development (which would provide a "yardstick" to bring down the rates charged by monopolistic private companies), flood control, and navigation improvement, but also reforestation, a diversified industry, retirement of poor farm land, and the "development of the natural resources of the Tennessee River drainage basin and its adjoining territory for the general social and economic welfare of the Nation." To carry out this development, a government corporation, the Tennessee Valley Authority, was created and, in the President's words, was "clothed with the power of government but possessed with the flexibility and initiative of private enterprise." Significantly, the bill authorized TVA not only to "sell the surplus power not used in its operations," with preference to states, counties, municipalities, and cooperatives, but also to construct, purchase, or lease transmission lines by which to dispose of that power.

President Roosevelt appointed Arthur E. Morgan to the chairmanship of the three-man board of the Tennessee Valley Authority. Morgan, an engineer of outstanding ability then serving as president of Antioch College in Ohio, was a social thinker with utopian ideals. Fifty-five years of age, he had devoted the greater portion of his adult life to the improvement of society, an experience which had whetted his ideal for remaking the world. One of the other two members was Harcourt A. Morgan, for fourteen years president of The University of Tennessee and before that time dean of its College of Agriculture. Canadian-born and sixty-six years of age, he had been naturalized in 1920 and had lived long enough in Tennessee to become well acquainted with the basic problems of the region. The third member of the board was thirty-three-year-old David E. Lilienthal, a brilliant attorney, a graduate of Harvard Law School, and the protégé of Felix Frankfurter, Donald Richberg, and Philip La Follette. Lilienthal had led Wisconsin's fight to regulate private power companies, and subsequently his role in TVA was to supervise the Authority's power policy. H. A. Morgan was placed in charge of fertilizer production and agriculture, and A. E. Morgan was responsible for dam construction, education, rural living, and social and economic planning. No member had administrative authority over the other two.

Navigation and Flood Control Programs 📖 As a guideline for river improvement, TVA had the report of the Corps of Engineers submitted by its chief, Major General Lytle Brown of Tennessee, in 1930. The report described the alternatives for the Tennessee River as: (1) a series of low dams, which would be the most economical method of navigation improvement, or (2) a series of high dams, which in addition to improving the navigability of the river would be of much greater value for flood control and would produce much larger amounts of electric power, but which would be enormously expensive. The TVA board leaned toward the second alternative, but assumed that because of the great expense involved the work of construction would have to be spread out over a long period of time. Initially, in the opinion of Lilienthal, priority should be placed on electric power, since navigation was "not an immediate thing." As one writer expressed it, "Who in 1933 would have ventured the opinion that the federal government would spend $2,098,365,462 in the Tennessee Valley region over the next twenty-five years . . . ?"[4] Therefore, the Authority's dam-construction program of 1934 was of a rather limited nature. The TVA act had specified the building of the Cove Creek Dam (later named for Senator Norris) across the Clinch River, and President Roosevelt had ordered that the Wheeler Dam be built on the main stream. Chairman Morgan in May, 1934, reported that the board then had in mind only four more dams for the immediate future, two on the main stream between Wilson Dam and the mouth of the river and two on tributaries, the Little Tennessee and the Hiwassee. Navigation improvement from those projects would have been limited to

[4] Droze, *High Dams and Slack Water*, 21, 25.

the portion of the river below Guntersville, whereas the Corps of Engineers had estimated that more than half of the anticipated traffic on the river, if improved, would originate or terminate above that point, in the vicinity of Chattanooga and Knoxville. Under existing plans those cities would be left without water connections for more than a generation.

Chattanoogans, especially incensed because of the omission of the proposed Chickamauga Dam from the plans, began to exert political pressure through Congressman Sam D. McReynolds and Senator McKellar to have that dam included. The Chattanoogans were aided by two developments: first, the government planned to increase expenditures to alleviate the shortage of money circulation during the depression, and second, on February 26, 1935, District Judge William T. Grubb decided in the Ashwander case that the "surplus power" TVA was authorized to sell was only such excess power as was unavoidably produced in the pursuit of its legitimate aims. Grubb did not believe that these aims included the "yardstick" idea. Faced with this challenge, even though confident that Grubb would be overruled in the higher courts, TVA found it advisable to bolster the constitutionality of its power program. That constitutionality was based strongly on the thesis that the chief purposes of TVA were navigation improvement and flood control, to which the production and sale of power were incidental. It therefore became necessary to make navigation improvement a more "immediate thing" than originally designed, and Congress was induced to amend the TVA law so as to define its purposes more specifically. By the Amendment of 1935 it was stated that the Authority should seek "to regulate the stream flow primarily for the purposes of promoting navigation and controlling floods." Moreover, TVA was specifically instructed to "provide a nine-foot channel [in the Tennessee] and maintain a water supply for the same, from Knoxville to its mouth. . . ."

Ten years and many dams later the nine-foot channel to Knoxville had been attained, and the Tennessee had become the "world's most modern waterway" and an important extension of the nation's 5,100-mile system of inland waterways.[5] During the period from 1948 to 1957 the amount of tonnage carried on the Tennessee in-

[5] Ibid., 62–63. The completion of Melton Hill Dam in 1963 extended the nine-foot channel up the Clinch River to Clinton, near Oak Ridge. Also there has been

creased 430 per cent, from 2,399,250 to 12,742,767 tons. This increase was due in part to the efforts of TVA to promote river traffic by aiding in the establishment of terminals, by working for the removal of artificial handicaps such as the territorial rate system in use by the railroads, and by various other means. Also, the building of the TVA dams has not only reduced significantly the danger of disastrous floods, but the improved navigability of the river has also contributed greatly to the ingress of new industries and the acceleration of economic growth in the region. These developments were further aided by the construction by the Corps of Engineers of a series of dams on the Cumberland River, which also had a nine-foot channel from the Ohio River to Cordell Hull Dam, several miles above Carthage, by 1966.

The Power Policies of TVA ‌ Even more important in the economic growth of the area was the providing of increasing amounts of electric power at low rates. The threat to the power "yardstick" aim of TVA inherent in the Grubb decision in the Ashwander case was partly removed by the decision of the Supreme Court in February, 1936, upholding the Circuit Court ruling of 1935 that Congress might provide for disposition of any or all power generated at Wilson Dam "as freely as in the case of other Government property." Seizing upon the loophole that the decision applied to Wilson Dam only, eighteen power companies in the area brought suit in May, 1936, claiming that TVA was engaged in the electric power business in such a way that the companies' business interests would be irreparably injured. They claimed that TVA could improve navigation more cheaply (and provide flood control with a modest expenditure) with a series of low dams than by the high-dam method which had been adopted. Therefore, "the whole scheme was primarily a power project with no real relation to navigation or flood needs. . . ."

When TVA finally won a victory in this TEP (Tennessee Electric Power Company) case early in 1939, its stalled negotiations for the purchase of the Commonwealth and Southern system of utility interests in the region reached fruition on February 4 when Wendell

---

a recent revival of interest in a canal to connect the Tennessee and Tombigbee rivers (first proposed in 1807), which would join the TVA navigation system with the Gulf of Mexico at Mobile.

534

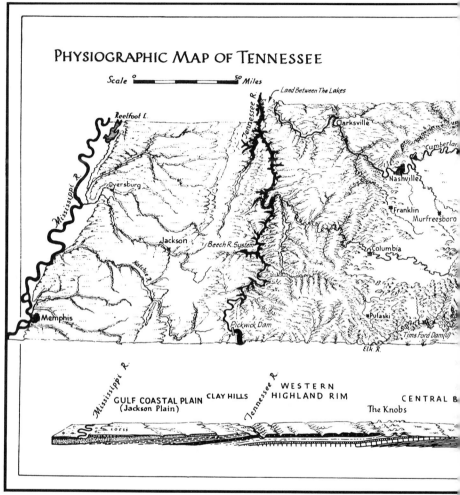

Physiographic map from *The Geography of Tennessee*, by H. C. Amick and L. H. Rollins, copyright 1937 by Ginn and Company.

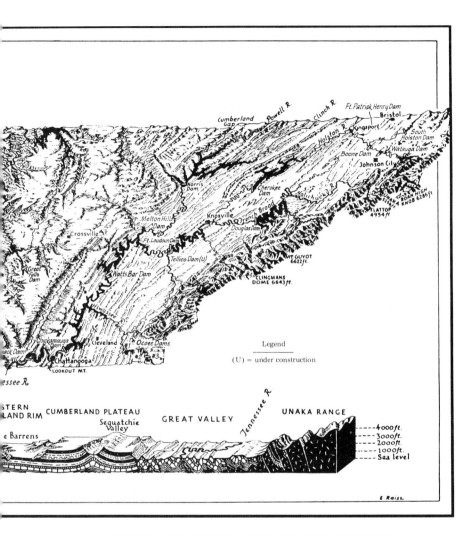

Map 8. PHYSIOGRAPHIC MAP OF TENNESSEE

Willkie, as the representative of that system, offered to sell its entire holdings to TVA or to its associated municipal or "Co-op" distributors. Thus, the Authority could acquire a practical monopoly on the distribution of electric power in its "natural service area" and avoid what otherwise would have been an uneconomical duplication of services. This situation, however, rendered obsolete the provision in the original TVA act of 1933 directing the Authority to pay 5 per cent of its gross revenue from power sales to the states in which the electric power was generated. Therefore, Congress in 1940 adopted an amendment providing that the much larger total payments in lieu of taxes should be apportioned among the states and also the counties affected by TVA operations.

One other result of the Supreme Court decisions and of the law of 1939 permitting TVA to purchase the private utilities in the area, which included steam plants as well as hydroelectric facilities, was the implication that TVA had the right to build as well as operate steam plants for the production of electric power. Because of the enormous increase in the demand for power caused by defense needs resulting from World War II, TVA found it necessary to build a great number of steam plants, and by the year 1955 it was producing more electricity by steam than by water power.[6]

Under the TVA law, the Authority was permitted to prescribe the rates at which its wholesale customers should sell electricity to the public. Thus, the rate-making policy of TVA was a matter of vital concern, involving the almost unsolvable problem of allocating costs among its various activities. Much more important, however, was the decision to set the rates low enough to cultivate an enormously increased demand for electric power and appliances. It is interesting to note that the Authority's competitors in the Southeast, even before they sold out to TVA, were forced to follow a similar policy and as a result learned, to their surprise, that the large volume, low price system brought in much larger profits than the previous small volume, high price policy. Utilities elsewhere then followed TVA's example. In contrast to a 2 per cent decline in electric power rates from 1926 to 1933, prices declined by one third from 1933 to 1951.

It was in the Tennessee Valley, however, that the "new era" was

[6] For the location of TVA's steam plants and numerous dams, see the accompanying map of Tennessee Valley region.

most evident. For generations the farm homes of the region had been lighted with kerosene lamps, food had been refrigerated in a spring house or ice box, and electric appliances had been virtually non-existent. In 1933 the area now served by TVA consumed only 1,500,000,000 kilowatt-hours of electricity, and the home use of electricity was 17 per cent below the national average. Within a two-year period home use had grown to 77 per cent above the national average. Total consumption in the area, aided of course by World War II and other influences besides low prices, reached 11,500,000,000 kilowatt-hours in 1945, and rose to 57,200,000,000 in 1959. As a result, the manner of living on the farms, and also in poorer sections of the cities of the region, was remarkably transformed.

Although some industries were brought into Tennessee as a result of the improved navigability of the Tennessee and Cumberland rivers, the most important magnet for industry was the availability of large amounts of cheap electric power. Industrial employment in the region served by TVA increased from 220,000 workers in 1929 to 440,000 in 1953, an increase of 99 per cent. Income in the region from manufacturing grew from $226,000,000 in 1929 to $1,363,000,000 in 1953, a growth of 502 per cent as compared to 321 per cent in the nation.

It is generally admitted that the selection in 1942 of Oak Ridge as the site of a plant which was to have a large share in the production of the atom bomb was due chiefly to the availability of TVA power. And, in turn, the peacetime uses of atomic energy, as well as its importance for defense purposes, have amazing potentialities for the future. Similarly, the selection in 1949 of Tullahoma in Middle Tennessee as the site of the Arnold Engineering Development Center, where The University of Tennessee has established a space institute, was not unrelated to the availability of electric power. That center has become a significant source of knowledge essential for the exploration of outer space.

Other Benefits of TVA ॐ In addition to industrialization and flood control, soil conservation and reforestation have been important contributions to the region. The TVA encouraged the adoption of better farming methods through research and farm demonstrations in an area which had suffered for years from poor farming methods and lack of fertilization. Through research, the proper types of fertilizer were developed for the various soils and were then made available to the farmer at a cheap price. Incidentally, also as a result of this improvement in fertilizers, the phosphate deposits in Tennessee have become more valuable with a greatly expanded and steady market. Therefore, through the programs of TVA, the Department of Agriculture, and other public agencies, farmers in the valley have increased greatly their use of fertilizers; have shifted a million acres from row crops to close growing crops; have terraced a million acres; and have established nearly a million acres of improved pastures. Research by TVA has also led to the invention of new equipment suited to better farming and has aided in the shift to soil-building agriculture. Further, the chief forester of TVA has worked with the forestry services of the states to develop plans for erosion control, reforestation, and forest improvement.

The great lakes formed by the dams have resulted in many ideal areas for fish and wildlife and for swimming and boating, thus making the region a sportsman's paradise. In combination with the Great Smoky Mountains National Park, opened in 1930, the TVA lakes and the Museum of Atomic Energy at Oak Ridge have made eastern Tennessee one of the most attractive regions for tourists in the nation. More people travel to the Great Smokies than to any other national park in the United States.[7] Another tourist haven is the "Between-the-Lakes" development between TVA's Kentucky Lake on the Tennessee River and Barkley Lake on the Cumberland River. Stimulated by TVA's recreation program, the state of Tennessee has greatly expanded the development of its state parks, the marking of historic sites, and the restoration of historic buildings. Thus, the tourist business has become an increasingly important source of revenue for the people of Tennessee.

Troubles of TVA ஜ The Tennessee Valley Authority has had—and still has—its troubles as well as its victories. In addition

---

[7] Also helpful in this regard, in addition to improved highways and the Appalachian Trail, have been the Cumberland Gap National Park, the Andrew Johnson National Monument at Greeneville, and the Chickamauga and Chattanooga National Military Park, and the privately developed and widely advertised "Rock City" on Lookout Mountain.

to the bitter fight over the constitutional question, TVA faced a serious feud within its first board of directors. The idealistic Arthur E. Morgan clashed with the other two, more practical directors. The incident that brought the conflict to the surface was the claim of Major George L. Berry, Tennessee labor leader and ex-senator, for remuneration for loss due to the flooding of lands under which he owned mineral rights. Chairman Morgan believed that Berry and his associates were guilty of bad faith and should be prosecuted on charges of conspiring to defraud the government, but the other two directors preferred a compromise settlement out of court. The latter were then openly charged with corruption and dishonesty by the chairman, while he, in turn, was accused of obstructing the implementation of determined policies. Unable to restore harmony, President Roosevelt finally replaced Arthur E. Morgan in March, 1938, with Senator James B. Pope of Idaho; Harcourt A. Morgan then became chairman. Congress, however, subjected TVA to a sweeping investigation by a joint congressional committee, which found no earth-shaking scandals. A veteran political observer commented that "it all boiled down to very little, except as a drama of personalities."[8]

Lilienthal, who succeeded Harcourt A. Morgan as chairman in 1941, also became involved in a feud with "The Rich Uncle" of TVA, Senator McKellar, who did not take very seriously the provision in the TVA act prohibiting politics from entering into the Authority's employment practices. McKellar complained bitterly when his recommendations for appointments were ignored, and several times tried unsuccessfully to make high-salaried TVA employees subject to confirmation by the Senate, and he made personal attacks on Chairman Lilienthal. He also opposed the construction of Douglas Dam on the French Broad River (as did many other Tennesseans because of the large amount of rich bottom land which would be inundated), and probably would have succeeded in preventing its construction had it not been for the Japanese attack on Pearl Harbor, December 7, 1941. In 1946 he opposed the appointment of Lilienthal to the chairmanship of the Atomic Energy Commission.

Although Dwight D. Eisenhower won Tennessee's electoral votes in 1952 by a small majority, partly because of his promise to main-

[8] Duffus, *The Valley and Its People*, 73.

tain TVA at maximum efficiency, as President he referred to the project as "creeping socialism." Subsequently, he started the Dixon-Yates controversy by instructing the Atomic Energy Commission to negotiate with the Dixon-Yates combine for the construction of a steam plant on the Arkansas side of the Mississippi near West Memphis as a means of preventing TVA from building a steam plant on the Tennessee side, north of Memphis. This precipitated a fight between advocates of public and private power and a congressional investigation. The Dixon-Yates contract was canceled in July, 1955, after Memphis announced its intention to build a steam plant; this plant then supplied the city with most of its power until Memphis resumed connections with TVA in 1963. During the Eisenhower administration, TVA also had some difficulty in getting a self-financing bill through Congress in a form acceptable to the President. This was finally achieved in August, 1959, when Eisenhower signed a bill authorizing TVA to issue $750,000,000 (an amount later increased) in revenue bonds for new steam plants, but limiting any further expansion of its service area.

The most recent TVA controversy of note involved its decision to build the Tellico Dam across the Little Tennessee River near its mouth, which would flood much bottom land along that stream and its Tellico branch. The proposals aroused the ire of fishing enthusiasts, who charged that the proposed lake would destroy a notable trout-fishing area, and also of many historians, who objected to the flooding of the sites of many Overhill Cherokee Indian towns and the placing of historic Fort Loudoun, built in 1756–57, on an isolated island even if a wing dam should be built as planned, to prevent it from being completely covered by water. Despite the protests and because of the expectation that the dam would serve to promote the industrial expansion of the area, which actually was being stymied during the controversy, the dam was authorized by Congress in 1965 and 1966 and is now under construction.

Thus, it is evident that TVA is here to stay. Although born in controversy and copied more enthusiastically elsewhere in the world than in the United States (a similar Missouri Valley Authority has been rejected by Congress), TVA has been and will continue to be a vital factor in the economy of Tennessee and the other states of the Tennessee Valley.

SUGGESTED READINGS

General Accounts

Davidson, *The Tennessee*, II, Chs. 11–19; Folmsbee, Corlew, and Mitchell, *Tennessee*, II, Ch. 40; David E. Lilienthal, *TVA: Democracy on the March* (New York, 1944, 1953; paperback, Chicago, 1966).

Specialized Accounts

Gordon R. Clapp, *The TVA: An Approach to the Development of a Region* (Chicago, 1955); Wilmon Henry Droze, *High Dams and Slack Water: TVA Rebuilds a River* (Baton Rouge, 1965); R. L. Duffus, *The Valley and Its People: A Portrait of TVA* (New York, 1944); Edward Felsenthal, "Kenneth Douglas McKellar: The 'Rich Uncle' of the TVA," WTHS *Papers*, No. XX (1966), 108–22; Preston J. Hubbard, *The Origins of TVA* (Nashville, 1961); David E. Lilienthal, *The Journals of David E. Lilienthal, I, The TVA Years* (New York, 1964); Roscoe C. Martin (ed.), *TVA, The First Twenty Years* (Knoxville and Tuscaloosa, 1956); John R. Moore (ed.), *The Economic Impact of TVA* (Knoxville, 1967); Charles Herman Pritchett, *Tennessee Valley Authority: A Study in Public Administration* (Chapel Hill, 1943); Joseph Sirera Ransmeier, *The Tennessee Valley Authority: A Case Study in the Economics of Multiple Purpose Stream Planning* (Nashville, 1942); Philip Selznick, *TVA and the Grass Roots: A Study in the Sociology of Formal Organization* (Berkeley, 1949).

30. ᥡᘘ Twentieth-Century Politics—
McCord to the Present

W HEN GOVERNOR McCORD was inaugurated in January, 1945, World War II was nearing its end, and
Tennessee was shortly to face the problems of reconversion from a
wartime to a peacetime economy. The horde of returning veterans
had to be assimilated, and the passage by Congress of the "G. I. Bill
of Rights" subjected the state's education system to considerable
strain. Also, many veterans were unwilling to condone the continuance of the traditional system of machine politics; in 1946 they
organized a "Good Government" group in McMinn County which
overthrew the county's political machine by force in the "Battle
of Athens."

The Administrations of Jim Nance McCord, 1945–49 ᥡᘘ
During McCord's first term, the state had the opportunity to look
backward as well as forward. In addition to celebrating V-E Day
and V-J Day, marking the ending of the European and Asiatic
phases of the war, Tennesseans observed the sesquicentennial of
the admission of the state to the Union, June 1, 1796. Also in 1945
Kenneth D. McKellar was chosen president pro tempore of the
Senate, and Cordell Hull was awarded the Nobel Peace Prize for
his part in the creation of the United Nations. McCord's leading
achievement during his first two years in office was in obtaining a
material increase in appropriations for public schools. His second
term was to be much more notable in that respect.

With the continuing support of Ed Crump, McCord had been

elected for a second term in 1946, after defeating former Governor Browning in the Democratic primary. At the time Browning was still in Europe serving as an official in the Military Government of Germany and was unable to campaign.[1] Impressed by the chaotic conditions prevailing in the public schools, McCord led a motor caravan all the way to Memphis, hoping to induce Crump to give up his opposition to the levying of a general sales tax for the support of education. The Memphis dictator agreed not to oppose the measure, and a 2 per cent sales tax was passed in 1947. By that law and the establishment of a state retirement law for teachers and other state employees McCord earned a place as one of the strongest friends of education in the history of the state.

As a result of unfavorable public reaction to the sales tax, however, and of labor's opposition to McCord because he signed an open shop or "right to work" bill, he was defeated in his try for a third term in 1948. His successful opponent was Gordon Browning, who was back in the state with an enhanced military reputation and able to campaign in earnest. It was in this election also that the Crump machine went down to defeat in its efforts to prevent the election of Estes Kefauver to the United States Senate. Although Kefauver did not join forces with Browning in the campaign, the latter was able to benefit from the decline of Crump's political power, and the extreme virulence of his old enemy's diatribes against him probably also won him votes.

The senatorial election of 1948 was one of the most noteworthy in Tennessee history, in view of Kefauver's successful challenge to the Crump machine's domination of Tennessee politics. While other city bosses throughout the nation had lost their grip, Crump had been able to hold on, largely because he had been able to provide Memphis with a firm and efficient government unblemished by scandal. Although the large election majorities in Memphis and Shelby County probably were obtained by the block purchase of poll tax receipts for use by the well-organized Negro and lower class voters and the inclusion on registration lists of many names allegedly copied from tombstones,[2] little objection was raised be-

[1] In this same year Kenneth D. McKellar was elected to a sixth term in the Senate, although President Roosevelt had called Ed Crump to Washington and asked him to oppose his reelection. Crump, however, refused. Miller, *Mr. Crump*, 306.

[2] Browning in the 1948 campaign described an imaginary scene in which Crump replied to his assistant, Willie Gerber, who protested that he could not make out the

TENNESSEE, A SHORT HISTORY

cause the business interests appreciated the many civil projects, the absence of local graft, and the low taxes and property assessments. The machine was so powerful, also, that only a limited amount of intimidation and harassment was necessary to keep the few dissenters or "wayward" in line. In 1948, however, the business and professional interests, in Memphis as well as elsewhere in the state, were able to organize effectively in their effort to topple Crump from power. This involved the weakening of the long-standing alliance between the Crump machine and the Republicans of East Tennessee, in which the latter voted for Crump-supported candidates in the Democratic primaries in exchange for Republican control of county races in East Tennessee.

The victor in this senatorial election of 1948, Estes Kefauver of Chattanooga, had made an outstanding record as a liberal in Congress after his election from the Third District in 1939. To oppose his candidacy in the Democratic primary, Crump selected Circuit Judge John A. Mitchell of Cookeville, even though this meant dropping the incumbent senator, Thomas Stewart, whose election in 1942 had been made possible only by the Crump-created majority in Shelby County—the only county in the state Stewart was able to carry. That was one reason why Crump dropped him in favor of a man with a good military record; another was Stewart's failure to give TVA adequate support. Stewart, however, refused to withdraw, and the three-cornered race gave Kefauver a distinct advantage.

Crump attempted to make Kefauver's alleged sympathy for Communism the chief issue, by comparing his votes in Congress with those of the pro-Communist Vito Marcantonio of New York, but he was unable to prove his charge. One of his statewide advertisements, calling Kefauver a "pet coon" who pretended to be a good American while really aiding the Communists, boomeranged against him. Kefauver replied that he was not Crump's "pet coon," and he adopted the coon as a symbol of his campaign. Wearing an old coonskin cap with a tail hanging down his back, he told the crowds it was from a genuine Tennessee coon, "whose rings were in its tail, not in its nose." Kefauver carried his cause to the people with his

name on a certain tombstone, "Willie, you've got to read it. We've got to have the right name. This has got to be an honest election." Memphis *Press Scimitar*, August 3, 1948, quoted in Miller, *Mr. Crump*, 329.

customary handshaking style; he attacked Stewart's anti-TVA bills and Mitchell's anti-labor stand and association with Crump; and he turned the Communism charge against Crump by pointing out that "Citizens of Communist states are threatened with reprisals if they dare to differ from the dictator."

In the final vote Mitchell and McCord carried Shelby County, but by less than normal majorities; in the statewide votes Kefauver won the senatorial and Browning the gubernatorial nominations by substantial margins.[3] Neither candidate had any significant Republican opposition in November. In the presidential election of the same year Truman and Barkley received eleven of the twelve Tennessee electoral votes, the other one going to the Crump-backed Dixiecrat ticket of Thurmond and Wright. In the time since the use of the general ticket system became universal, this was the only instance in American history in which the electoral votes of any state had been divided. It happened because two of the electors on the regular Democratic ticket elected by the Tennessee voters were also on the Dixiecrat ticket, and one of them actually cast his vote in the electoral college for Thurmond and Wright instead of Truman and Barkley. It was more than a coincidence that Estes Kefauver, elected to the Senate in the same year, was an ardent, though unsuccessful, champion of amending the Constitution in such a way as to end the general ticket procedure in presidential elections.

The Browning and Clement Administrations, 1949–59
&ᴥ Many political observers expected Browning to wage war on the Crump organization because of the bitter fights that had occurred in previous years. The new governor, however, gave no indication of renewing the fierce struggle. He concentrated on a rural roads program and on improvements of educational facilities. In 1951, after Browning was elected for another term, a law was passed which, in effect, removed the payment of a poll tax as a prerequisite for voting, but another bill which would have made Memphis State College a part of The University of Tennessee was rejected, due largely to the vigorous opposition of President James

---

[3] For senator the votes were: Kefauver, 152,489; Stewart, 111,787; Mitchell, 78,586; for governor: Browning, 214,465; McCord, 160,192.

D. Hoskins of the University and of the Knoxville Chamber of Commerce.

In 1952, following charges of fraud and mismanagement in connection with the state purchase of the Memorial Apartment Hotel in Nashville, Browning was defeated in the Democratic primary by an eloquent young lawyer from Dickson, Frank G. Clement. At the same time the aged Senator McKellar went down to defeat at the hands of young Congressman Albert Gore of Carthage, thus ending an uninterrupted senatorial career of thirty-six years. Those Democratic nominees had little difficulty in the general election in November, but for the first time since 1928 a Republican presidential candidate, General Dwight D. Eisenhower, carried Tennessee. He won, however, by a narrow margin of only 2,437 votes over Adlai Stevenson, who had defeated Estes Kefauver for the Democratic nomination even though the Tennessean had won most of the presidential primaries.[4]

A long campaign to revise the state's outdated fundamental law finally led to the meeting of a limited constitutional convention in 1953. Former Governor Prentice Cooper, who had returned to the state after serving as ambassador to Peru, was elected chairman and Ben W. Hooper, another ex-governor, vice chairman. All eight amendments proposed were then approved by the voters in November of the same year and were the first changes in Tennessee's constitution since 1870. These amendments made the constitution slightly easier to amend; raised the pay of legislators from $4.00 to $15.00 per day and authorized later changes by legislative action; increased the governor's term from two to four years, but made him ineligible for immediate reelection; gave the governor power to veto individual items of appropriation bills, but ended his use of the "pocket" veto; made unconstitutional the poll tax requirement for suffrage (however, this was already abolished, in effect, by legislative action); prohibited so-called "ripper" bills[5]; authorized home rule for cities; and authorized the consolidation of city and county functions.

Although these changes were significant reforms, they fell somewhat short of the recommendations made by a constitution revision

[4] In the first of those primaries, in New Hampshire, he defeated President Truman, which was one reason why the President decided not to run for another term.

[5] "Ripper" bills changed the structure of local governments without any consideration being given to the wishes of the inhabitants.

commission which had been created during McCord's first term. The commission had proposed, for example, a thoroughgoing revision of the taxation clause, which has been interpreted by the courts as prohibiting the use of a personal income tax and which has handicapped legislative action in other ways.

During Clement's first administration a bond issue was authorized to finance the supplying of free textbooks in all twelve grades in the public schools (supplementing previous legislation applying to the lower grades only), and a greatly improved mental health program was inaugurated. Legislative investigations were made of the preceding administration and also of textbooks in use in higher as well as lower education, but no texts with Communist leanings were uncovered. Also in 1953 an Industrial Development Division of the Department of Conservation was created, and the Clement administrations and those of his successor (on two occasions), Buford Ellington, have been active in bringing new industries into the state. After being reelected in 1954, again defeating Browning in the primary, Clement obtained the enactment of a law increasing the sales tax from 2 to 3 per cent, which made possible further improvements in the education program.

In the presidential election year of 1956 Clement was selected to deliver the keynote address at the Democratic National Convention, which again nominated Stevenson instead of Kefauver, but gave the latter the vice presidential nomination. Nevertheless, Eisenhower again carried the state, and by a slightly larger margin than in 1952. A States Rights ticket headed by T. Coleman Andrews, which was nominated by a convention held in Memphis, received less than 20,000 votes, of which more than one-third were in Shelby County and much more than half in West Tennessee.

In 1957, as a result of school integration difficulties, the legislature passed five school segregation statutes, which were not, however, specifically recommended by the governor. The most important one, a parents' preference law, was declared unconstitutional by a federal district court, thus opening the way for the gradual integration plan as pioneered by Nashville. Also, the teachers' retirement law was amended so as to authorize coverage under the federal social security program, and consolidated metropolitan governments were authorized, which later led to the creation of the metropolitan district of Nashville and Davidson County. Governor Clement's com-

missioner of agriculture, Buford Ellington, after narrowly defeating
Andrew ("Tip") Taylor and Mayor Ed Orgill of Memphis in the
Democratic primary, was elected governor in 1958 over ex-Governor
Jim Nance McCord, running as an Independent, and the Republi-
can candidate, Thomas Wall.

Politics and Reapportionment, 1959–68 ᭥ Governor
Ellington came into office pledged to avoid any increases in taxes.
Yet he was able to carry through considerable improvements in
education, highway building, and social welfare. He also sponsored
a thorough reorganization of the state government, consolidating
seventy agencies into eighteen. Another limited constitutional convention of 1959 considered but rejected a reduction of the voting
age to eighteen. It adopted one amendment, extending the term of
county trustees to four years, which was later approved by the voters.

A major development during the period since 1959 has been the
long-delayed reapportionment of legislative and congressional districts. This type of reform, initiated by Tennessee, spread throughout the nation, and reduced materially the rural domination of
legislative bodies. Although the Tennessee constitution provides for
a reapportionment of legislative districts every ten years, there had
been no reapportionment since 1901. Therefore, political leaders in
the major cities and the League of Women Voters inaugurated a
vigorous campaign which finally resulted in a Supreme Court decision, March 26, 1962, in *Baker* v. *Carr,* that the Tennesseans had
the right to seek redress in the federal courts for the failure of the
legislature to reapportion legislative seats. Following this decision,
the legislature in a special session enacted a new apportionment law
which, however, was so inadequate that a three-judge federal court
panel gave the legislature until June 3, 1963, to correct the deficien-
cies. It permitted the new law to be used, however, in the elections
of 1962.

In those elections former Governor Clement, again eligible, was
returned to the governorship. The Republicans, who in 1960 had
carried Tennessee in a third consecutive presidential election (Nixon
over Kennedy), won two additional seats in the state house of representatives. They also won the Third Congressional District from the

Democrats, electing William E. Brock, and they almost defeated Congressman Clifford Davis in the Ninth District.

To keep Tennessee progressive, Clement in 1963 pushed through a law extending the sales tax to utility bills and other items to gain revenue. Counties were also authorized to levy a 1 per cent sales tax (increased to 1½ in 1968), if approved by a referendum. Another legislative reapportionment failed to satisfy the federal court, which insisted on several modifications; the court, however, later permitted the law to be used in the 1964 elections and gave the legislature until June 1, 1965, either to accept the modifications or pass a new law which would be acceptable to the court.

Despite the return of the state to the Democratic column in the presidential election of 1964, largely because of fears concerning Barry Goldwater's Vietnam and TVA policies, the Republicans gained five seats in the legislature. One of the Democrats chosen was A. W. Willis, Jr., of Memphis, the first Negro elected and seated in the legislature since 1886–87. Liberals were also encouraged by the victory of Congressman Ross Bass over Governor Clement in the Democratic primary for the vacancy in the U. S. Senate caused by the death of Estes Kefauver,[6] even though Bass narrowly escaped defeat by the Republican candidate, Howard H. Baker, Jr., in the general election.

As a result of a Supreme Court decision in February, 1964, in the case of *Wesberry* v. *Sanders*, that congressional as well as legislative districts must be as nearly equal as possible in population, the legislature in 1965 reapportioned the state's nine congressional districts. There still remained such a disparity of population that a three-judge federal panel refused to approve the measure; and when the legislature in 1967 failed to meet the court's deadline for revision, the court imposed its own realignment, to be used for the first time in the elections of 1968.

The revision of legislative districts by the General Assembly of 1965 was accepted by the federal court, but one feature of it, the subdividing of counties for senatorial as well as house districts, was declared unconstitutional by the state supreme court in May, 1966. The constitutional barrier to that type of redistricting was removed,

[6] The seat had been temporarily filled by Herbert S. Walters by appointment in August, 1963.

however, by one of the amendments[7] proposed by the limited constitutional convention of 1965, and the division of urban counties
into senatorial districts became effective in 1968. As a result, two
Negroes—the first in Tennessee history—were elected to the state
senate in 1968. Also, six Negroes, the same number as in 1966, were
elected to the house.

In the election of 1966 considerable progress was made in the
direction of making Tennessee a two-party state, even though the
Republicans did not nominate a candidate to oppose Buford Ellington for the governorship. Howard H. Baker, Jr., however, became
the first popularly elected Republican senator from Tennessee, and
actually the first one elected since "Parson" Brownlow had been
chosen by the legislature in 1869. The only other Republican,
Newell Sanders, to serve in the Senate was appointed by a Republican governor, Ben W. Hooper, in 1912. Baker defeated ex-Governor
Frank Clement, who had defeated Ross Bass, the incumbent, in the
Democratic primary. Also, Dan H. Kuykendall defeated the incumbent Democratic representative from the Ninth District (Shelby
County), George W. Grider, thus giving the Republicans four of
the nine congressmen. Although the state senate remained divided
25 to 8 in favor of the Democrats, the Republicans increased their
membership in the house by sixteen, to a total of 41 of the 99. That
number was increased to 42 before the end of the second session of
that assembly, because one Democrat[8] changed his party affiliation
as a protest against the unfair tactics used by that party to restore
its majority control of all ninety-five county election commissions in
the state. An act of 1965 had given the Republicans control of the
commissions in the thirty-seven counties carried by Goldwater in
1964, in exchange for the Republicans' aid in breaking a deadlock
between two Democratic factions in the state senate.

[7] The amendments provided for election of members of both houses from separate
districts, even where a county is entitled to more than one, and required all members
to be qualified voters in the districts they represent; provided for the apportionment of
both houses according to population, but permitted one house to be apportioned on
some other basis if the U. S. Constitution should be amended to permit it; authorized
annual legislative sessions with the first session of the biennium to be split into two
periods; allowed county legislative bodies to fill vacancies in the legislature; and set the
pay for legislators at an annual salary of $1,800 plus an allowance for expenses. They
were approved in November, 1966.

[8] Charles Galbreath of Nashville was elected to the state court of criminal appeals
in August, 1968, running as a Republican in some counties and as an "Independent"
in others.

The first half of Governor Ellington's second term was characterized by considerable increases in appropriations for highways and education, although less than recommended because of the failure of the legislature to approve the entire tax-increase program proposed by the governor. The county-option system of 1939 for liquor regulation was amended so as to permit cities in dry counties to hold referendums on the legalization of "package stores." The four urban counties were also given the opportunity to legalize the sale of liquor by the drink, but an effort to repeal what was left of the state's "bone dry" law failed during the session of 1968. In 1967 the state's anti-evolution law of 1925, which had been the occasion for the historic "monkey trial" in Dayton, was finally repealed. The legislature also authorized a referendum in November, 1968, on the calling of another limited constitutional convention to be held in 1971. State commissions were established to coordinate higher education and to improve race relations. To supplement the latter a series of anti-riot laws was enacted in 1968 because of the increased danger of civil disturbances in urban communities.

Tennessee cities, which in previous years had seen many "sit-in" demonstrations in the interest of civil rights, were relatively quiet during the "long, hot summer" of 1967, possibly due in part to the work of the state and local interracial commissions, which had brought about the integration of most public facilities. The disturbances of that summer, however, were ushered in by less serious riots in Nashville at the time of a visit by the "black power" militant, Stokely Carmichael, in April. One year later the assassination of Dr. Martin Luther King, Jr., the apostle of non-violence, in Memphis, where he had gone to support a strike of garbage collectors—most of whom were Negroes—was the occasion for serious disorders not only in that city and in Nashville and Chattanooga, but also in Washington, D. C., and many other cities throughout the country. Although the "images" of Memphis and of Tennessee were seriously injured, the interracial cooperation in the observance of the "national day of mourning," especially in Memphis, and the many memorials in King's honor may pave the way toward improved relations in the future and toward more effective action regarding the problems of education, housing, and labor. A few days after the assassination, Congress completed action on a new civil rights bill which included an open housing section, but the only Tennessee representative to vote for it was Richard Fulton of Nashville. Previously, Howard Baker had helped break a Southern filibuster in the Senate by proposing a compromise housing clause, which was not included, however, in the bill as it passed the Senate, and later the House.

In the presidential election of 1968 Tennessee returned to the Republican column, giving its electoral votes to the successful candidate, Richard M. Nixon. The Independent party candidate, George Wallace, took second place over Vice President Hubert H. Humphrey. Five Democrats and four Republicans were reelected to Congress. The Republicans, however, for the first time in modern history, captured control of the lower house of the state legislature, with the election of 50 members (one elected an Independent) to 49 Democrats. The Republicans also increased their representation in the state senate from 8 seats to 13 of the total membership of 33. In 1970 the Democrats recovered control of the lower house (55D, 44R) but lost the governorship, Winfield Dunn (R) of Memphis defeating John J. Hooker (D). William E. Brock III (R) ousted Senator Albert Gore (D) and was succeeded in Congress by LaMar Baker (R).

SUGGESTED READINGS

General Accounts

Dewey W. Grantham, "The South and Reconstruction of American Politics," *JAH*, LIII (Sept., 1966), 144–66; Lee Seifert Greene and Robert Sterling Avery, *Government in Tennessee* (Knoxville, 1962; second edition, 1966); Perry, *Democracy Begins at Home*.

Specialized Accounts

Boyce, *Unwanted Boy*; Folmsbee, Corlew, and Mitchell, *Tennessee*, II, Ch. 44; Brett W. Hawkins, *Nashville Metro: The Politics of City-County Consolidation* (Nashville, 1966); Hawkins, "Public Opinion and Metropolitan Reorganization in Nashville," *JOP*, XXVIII (May, 1966), 408–18; Key, *Southern Politics*; Allen H. Kitchens, "Political Upheavals in Tennessee: Boss Crump and the Senatorial Election of 1948," WTHS *Papers*, No. XVI (1962), 104–26; Lawrence D. Longley, "The Effectiveness of Internal Groups in a State Legislature," *THQ*, XXVI (Fall, 1967), 279–94; Miller, *Mr. Crump*, Chs. 11–14; Norman L. Parks, "Tennessee Politics Since Kefauver and Reece: A 'Generalist' View," *JOP*, XXVIII (Feb., 1966), 144–66; Marie-Gregson Wingfield, "The Memphis Interracial Commission," WTHS *Papers*, No. XXI (1967), 93–107.

31. ❧ Social and Intellectual Developments in the Twentieth Century

THE TWENTIETH CENTURY opened in the liberalism of the Progressive Era; World War I and the conservatism of the 1920's followed. Then, the progressive New Deal came with Franklin D. Roosevelt, and the early 1940's brought World War II and the atom bomb. With the decades following 1945, threats of nuclear warfare and other crises have caused foreign and domestic problems never dreamed of before. Vast social change and intellectual achievement have evolved with these developments. Tennessee, where the atom bomb was made, has not escaped the social and intellectual trauma of the age. The population of the state has increased from scarcely two million in 1900 to nearly four million in 1968, and with the population explosion has come a shift from a rural to an urban society and culture.

Religious Development ❧ The Roman Catholic, Judaic, and major Protestant denominations had become well established in Tennessee by the twentieth century. The principal religious groups continued to be the Methodist, Baptist, and Presbyterian. By mid-twentieth century both union and division had taken place in some groups, and by 1968 leaders in the Methodist, Presbyterian, Episcopal, and other denominations had expressed interest in the work of the Consultation on Christian Union (COCU), which would unite many of the major Protestant bodies.

The last detailed religious census compiled by the federal government midway in the period here considered—1936—showed that

918,809 Tennesseans were affiliated with a religious body. The Southern Baptist Church was in the forefront with 226,896 members and the Methodist Episcopal Church, South, second with 160,951. Three Presbyterian bodies (Southern, Northern, and Cumberland) had a combined membership of more than 140,000, and Roman Catholics counted almost 32,000.

Southern Baptists and Methodists were well distributed across the state. Twenty-one thousand Baptists were concentrated in Knox County, 16,000 in Shelby, and about 14,000 each in Davidson and Hamilton counties. Of the Methodists, Davidson had nearly 20,000, Shelby 18,600, Hamilton almost 9,000, and Knox about 7,000. Eight thousand Presbyterians were in Shelby and Davidson each, and about 6,000 each were in Knox and Hamilton counties. The Church of Christ, which was formed late in the nineteenth century from the conservative wing of the Disciples of Christ, was listed for the first time in the census records of 1906 with nearly 10,000 members in Davidson County and with more than 2,000 each in Knox and Rutherford. All of the religious groups have experienced considerable growth, of course, since the federal census of 1936.

Union among the various denominations was discussed by leaders of all faiths. Among the successful unions was one among the Northern Methodists, the Southern Methodists, and the Methodist Protestants, in 1939. A somewhat unsuccessful union was attempted between the Northern Presbyterians and the Cumberland Presbyterians three decades earlier. The principal Methodist bodies (the Methodist Episcopal Church and the Methodist Episcopal Church, South) had divided and formed over the political sectional controversy more than a decade before the Civil War. The Methodist Protestant Church had been organized as a protest against the formality of the episcopacy. Most of the Tennessee churches were affiliated with the Southern branch, although the Holston Conference of the Northern branch was maintained in East Tennessee. Although the union in 1939 was opposed by some of the churches in the Deep South, Tennesseans as a whole supported the movement. The Southern church brought to the union more than fifty colleges and universities, three of which were located in Tennessee (Scarritt College for Christian Workers in Nashville, Lambuth College at Jackson, and Martin College at Pulaski). In 1968 the Methodists joined with the Evangelical United Brethren to form the United

Methodist Church, which probably made it the largest Protestant Christian body in the world.

A union among Presbyterian bodies had been considered for many years. Not long after the Cumberland group was formed in Tennessee in 1810, a few leaders discussed reunion with the mother church. After the Civil War brought division, a union between the Northern Presbyterians (Presbyterians in the United States of America) and the Cumberland Presbyterians seemed mutually advantageous. Negotiations began in earnest soon after the beginning of the twentieth century, and a revision of church doctrine was made in 1903 by the Northern church to meet some of the demands of the Cumberlands. Although union was effected by majority vote of the latter group, a vigorous minority has continued the Cumberland church to the present time. More successful was the union of the Northern and the United Presbyterians in 1958.

Another group strengthened by union in the twentieth century was the Pentecostal Church of the Nazarene. Several groups grew out of a Wesleyan revival of the late nineteenth century professing the necessity of a return to the spiritual simplicity of John Wesley. The Pentecostal Mission had been organized in Nashville at the turn of the century, and in 1915 a union was effected between that group and the Pentecostal Church of the Nazarene at Nashville. The former was concerned largely with foreign missions and the latter with home missions; thus the union greatly strengthened both bodies. Trevecca College is maintained in Nashville by the Nazarenes. According to the census of 1936, the membership of the church in Tennessee (5,416) was exceeded only by the membership in California, Oklahoma, and Kansas.

Fundamentalism versus modernism was a question of considerable concern to religious leaders of the state during the first three decades of the twentieth century. Within the small and basically fundamentalistic groups the question was rarely discussed, but within the bodies of the Presbyterians, Episcopalians, Methodists, and Disciples the matter came up with frequency, probably because of the antievolution statute and the Scopes trial. The School of Religion of Vanderbilt University became the center of modernism after the University gained complete independence in 1914 from the Methodist jurisdiction following litigation over a period of years. Chancellor J. H. Kirkland, who had been a leader in the movement to separate entirely from Methodist supervision, encouraged Dr. O. E. Brown, Dean of the School of Religion, and other faculty members of the school in their freedom of thought. The "Round Table," a literary club in Nashville whose membership included most of the faculty members, thoroughly discussed the matter, including of course the evolution law and Scopes trial. In 1926 the University published three lectures, by Dr. Brown, Dr. Kirkland, and Dr. Edwin Mims (professor of English), in which the three argued for freedom of thought. Mims championed the cause of higher criticism of the Bible and urged all men to consider the great truths of the Bible as a whole and not out of context, and insisted that they "rally . . . to this new standard of Jesus, emancipated from traditional interpretation" of the Scripture. Brown suggested that among the major issues between the fundamentalists and modernists were those concerned with the Virgin Birth, the alleged inerrancy of the Bible, and evolution. He and Kirkland denied further allegations of the fundamentalists, principally that those who believe in evolution are essentially materialists who have abandoned faith in God for modern science and that higher criticism of the Bible denied or ignored the sacredness of the Holy Scripture. Kirkland, seeking to accommodate science and religion, extolled the power of the mind of man. "In the beginning was force, and this force was mind," wrote the chancellor, "and this mind was God, and this God has been ever indwelling in the universe He has made, for without Him was not anything made that was made." The studies and assertions by Chancellor Kirkland, Dean Brown, and others seen resulted in fundamentalist groups dubbing Vanderbilt "a hotbed of Modernism," whose professors would undermine the faith of the fathers.

The talk of modernism did not deter but instead reemphasized the propensity of many for oldtime evangelistic revivals. T. DeWitt Talmadge, Billy Sunday, and N. B. Hardeman were among those who urged Tennesseans to depart from the paths of sin and to seek conversion. World War II and its aftermath brought Americans into confrontation with realities as never before and, according to the ministers, accentuated their need for superhuman strength in their hour of bewilderment. Thus, the way was paved for Billy Graham, who preached with tremendous success to thousands in

Nashville and Memphis in 1951 and again in 1954. Governor Frank G. Clement, having just been elected to a second term in 1954, developed a warm friendship for the evangelist, and was widely rumored as one who soon would join the Graham evangelistic team.

The churches experienced tremendous growth and expansion during the 1950's and 1960's, and the Salvation Army and the Gideon Bible Society also reported considerable gain in their activities and services. Church leaders, aware as never before of the social and economic demands of the unfortunate and underprivileged, redoubled their efforts to insure that the churches would serve greater Christian purposes in a confused world of turmoil and strife. The work of evangelists such as Billy Graham, the tireless labor of hundreds of lesser known but nevertheless toiling ministers of the gospel, and the realization among the laity of the need for God in an era when a solution for foreign and domestic problems alike seemed to require the strength and mind of One more powerful than mankind were at least partly responsible.

The Antievolution Law and the Scopes Trial 𝕰❧ Fundamentalists, steeped in a narrow interpretation of the faith, believed Christianity to be assailed on all sides, and they became self-appointed defenders of the faith. Especially objectionable were the higher criticism of the Bible and suggestions that there may have been other "creations" besides that described in Genesis. But most objectionable of all was Charles Darwin's theory of evolution which seemed to them not only to contravene the gospel, but to take stature and dignity from man, who was created a little lower than the angels and in the image of God.

Before the war, although some religious leaders were able to accommodate Darwinism to their faith, many others believed that the *Origin of the Species* was in direct conflict with the story of creation as told in the Book of Genesis. Articles, books, and lectures by William Graham Sumner, Lester Frank Ward, and others in and out of the large universities accentuated the matter. In 1909–12, fundamentalists reaffirmed their faith in the inerrancy of the Bible and the story of creation in twelve pamphlets, *The Fundamentals: A Testimony*, which received wide circulation in Tennessee, especially among Methodists and Baptists. A variety of organizations, such as the Anti-Evolution League and the Bible Crusaders of America, also enlisted a strong following in the Volunteer State, and speakers under the auspices of these groups were received warmly in all sections of the state. No living Democrat was more beloved in Tennessee than William Jennings Bryan—he had carried the state each time in three unsuccessful attempts to win the presidency—and people had read his addresses whether delivered on the hustings in behalf of political candidates or in churches in support of fundamentalism. Some had read with considerable interest of the debate conducted in the columns of the New York *Times* in 1922 between the Great Commoner and Harry Emerson Fosdick, the young "modernist" minister and writer in New York. After Bryan spoke in Nashville in 1924 on "Is the Bible True?" Protestant leaders in Middle Tennessee printed thousands of copies of the address and circulated them among legislators and other prominent people from Memphis to Bristol. Therefore, it was only natural that inasmuch as bills to outlaw the teaching of evolution were considered in Arkansas, Georgia, Minnesota, Mississippi, Missouri, New Hampshire, North Carolina, Oklahoma, West Virginia, and perhaps other states, legislators in Tennessee gave the matter consideration.

A few weeks after the General Assembly convened in January, 1925, a bill was introduced in the house and senate which made the teaching of evolution in the public schools a felony. The proposed bill was received by the public with mixed emotions, and newspaper editors, clergymen, educators, and public officials were found on both sides. After considerable debate, both houses passed the measure and transmitted it to Governor Austin Peay. The governor, after "due deliberation" and after examining "tens of thousands of letters" and hearing appeals and protests from countless delegations, and doubtless fearing that a veto would endanger the passage of his education bill, signed the measure nine days after its passage. He praised the law as one which would "protest against an irreligious tendency," but expressed doubt that it would ever be applied.

The law became a subject for much discussion in newspapers and journals outside the state. Conservative papers and religious journals praised the law, but eastern liberals deplored it. Joseph Wood Krutch, a Tennessee native then on the editorial staff of *Nation*, condemned the law and blamed it upon "ignorant fundamentalists."

Walter Lippmann, Henry L. Mencken, and other eastern journalists joined in the ridicule.

The governor's signature was hardly dry when the press heralded the news that John Thomas Scopes, a young teacher of biology at Dayton, had been indicted by the Rhea County grand jury for violation of the statute. On May 26, 1925—one day after the indictment was reported—Dayton was the dateline for almost every major newspaper in the country. Interest spread abroad when Bryan announced that he would assist Attorney General A. Tom Stewart in the prosecution, and Dudley Field Malone, Arthur Garfield Hays, and Clarence Darrow appeared to aid counsel for the defense.

The trial began on July 13, and for eight days Dayton indulged in a festive atmosphere. The details of the affair have been told in both truthful and exaggerated fashion by journalists, playwrights, novelists, and historians in both Europe and America. Scopes was found guilty and fined $100, and Tennessee, now termed the "Monkey State" by Eastern punsters, was subjected to much ridicule. In Tennessee, however, fundamentalist religious groups experienced considerable growth while more liberal ones declined in membership.

The law remained on the statute books until 1967. Various attempts at repeal during the four decades of the law's existence met with derision and opposition by conservatives. At late as 1959 some members of the Tennessee Academy of Science and others of various chapters of the American Association of University Professors who petitioned the legislature for repeal were summarily rebuffed. One high state official, for example, suggested to a college biology professor who had drafted a petition urging repeal that if he did not wish to teach according to the laws of the state he might seek employment elsewhere. At the same time the county court of Rutherford County, upon hearing that the Middle Tennessee State University chapter of the American Association of University Professors had petitioned the legislature for repeal, unanimously condemned the "free thinking" educators and asserted that members of the court—all "Godfearing men"—deplored such attempts to repeal the antievolution statute.

The repeal in 1967 came with relatively little effort and fanfare. Although last ditch stands in defense of the original measure were made by a few conservatives, the law was repealed forty-two years after its passage.

History and Literature ॐ Tennessee has produced scores of talented authors who have contributed richly to the American literary heritage. Its heroes, public figures, and picturesque environment frequently have been fascinating subjects to authors and readers alike.

Among the public figures of the state, Jackson has been studied to a greater extent than any other, with hundreds of books and articles published about him. James Parton, who knew Jackson personally and published before the Civil War a three-volume account of his life and times, despaired at the conflicting sources which his research uncovered and concluded that Jackson was indeed an enigma. He was "one of the greatest of generals," Parton wrote, but was "wholly ignorant of the art of war." He was "a most law-defying, law obeying citizen," a "democratic autocrat," an "urbane savage," and an "atrocious saint." John Eaton and Arthur S. Colyar were Tennesseans who also prepared biographies about the Hero during the nineteenth century.

Within the twentieth century, Jacksonian historiography has multiplied. The most successful work, despite certain shortcomings, has been Arthur M. Schlesinger, Jr.'s *Age of Jackson*, published in 1945. Earlier, John Spencer Bassett and Marquis James wrote two-volume biographies of Andrew Jackson. Historians have quarreled for decades over whether Jackson was a sincere democrat or an opportunist. Thomas P. Abernethy, in his *Frontier to Plantation in Tennessee* and other works, has argued the latter point of view, but Schlesinger and others have maintained that the Hero was a sincere democrat. Charles Grier Sellers, Jr., has discussed the controversy over Jackson in some detail in his article, "Andrew Jackson versus the Historians." Novelists also have supped at the table of Jackson lore. Two of the most successful have been Irving Stone's *The President's Lady* and Noel B. Gerson's *Old Hickory*.

James K. Polk, a Jackson supporter until the Chief's death and, hence, aptly called "Young Hickory," has been a subject for biographers and novelists. Polk for many years was neglected by historians, but the publication of his diary not long after the beginning of the twentieth century brought about a reevaluation; now, modern historians list him along with Washington, Jackson, Lincoln, and others among the ten most successful Presidents. The most competent of the Polk scholars, Charles Grier Sellers, Jr., has published recently nearly a dozen articles on Polk in addition to *James Knox Polk, Jacksonian,* and *James Knox Polk, Continentalist,* the definitive works on Polk. The Polk papers are being edited by Herbert Weaver and Paul Bergeron of Vanderbilt University. Of the novels based on the life of Polk, the most successful has been Noel B. Gerson's *The Slender Reed.*

The career of Tennessee's other President, Andrew Johnson, also has been examined thoroughly. Shortly after the turn of the century, James S. Jones prepared a *Life of Andrew Johnson,* and in 1916 Clifton Hall published *Andrew Johnson, Military Governor of Tennessee*—an account highly critical of the East Tennessean's stay in Nashville as an appointee of President Lincoln. During the 1920's, four scholars prepared works on Johnson as follows: Robert W. Winston, *Andrew Johnson, Plebian and Patriot*; Lloyd Paul Stryker, *Andrew Johnson, A Study in Courage*; George Fort Milton, *The Age of Hate, Andrew Johnson and the Radicals*; and W. M. Caskey, two articles on Johnson's gubernatorial administrations. LeRoy P. Graf and Ralph W. Haskins, editors of the Johnson papers, published the first volume in the series in December, 1967. Of the several historical novels based on the life of Johnson, the most successful was Gerson's *Yankee from Tennessee.*

John Sevier has become almost a legendary figure among writers of Tennessee biography. The Hero of the Battle of King's Mountain—who was also nicknamed "Nolichucky Jack" and "The Warrior of the Watauga"—was successful, according to the inscription on his monument, in all thirty-five of his battles with the Redskins and the Redcoats. Sevier plays an important role in Lyman C. Draper's *King's Mountain and Its Heroes* (1887), Theodore Roosevelt's *Winning of the West* (1895), Samuel Cole Williams's *History of the Lost State of Franklin* (1924), Donald Davidson's *The Tennessee,* I, (1946), Wilma Dykeman's *The French Broad* (1955), and North Callahan's *Smoky Mountain Country* (1952). Full length biographies of Sevier include F. M. Turner's *General John Sevier* (1910) and Carl Driver's *John Sevier, Pioneer of the Old Southwest* (1932). Among the novels centering around Sevier are Gerson's *The Cumberland Rifles* (1952), Florette Henri's *King's Mountain* (1950), and Helen T. Miller's *The Sound of Chariots* (1947). "Chucky Jack" has been the hero in a plethora of children's books and plays.

The careers of scores of other public figures have been scrutinized by historians and novelists. Among the historians, Joseph H. Parks, the most prolific biographer, penned a study of Felix Grundy (1940), and ten years later prepared a perceptive account of John Bell. Parks next wrote on General Edmund Kirby Smith (1954) and General Leonidas Polk (1962). William H. Masterson has prepared a well-written biography of William Blount (1954), and William N. Chambers has written *Old Bullion Benton* (1956), the definitive work on Thomas Hart Benton. Mabel G. Frantz (*Full Many a Name: The Story of Sam Davis*), Adelaide C. Rowell (*On Jordon's Stormy Banks*), and a dozen others have authored somewhat emotional accounts of Sam Davis. Dan Robison has written a careful study of Robert Love Taylor (1935), E. Merton Coulter a critical but accurate biography of William G. Brownlow (1937), Marquis James an account of Sam Houston (1929), Rufus Terral a biography of Newell Sanders (1935), Thomas Alexander a brief but perceptive account of Thomas A. R. Nelson, and William D. Miller the definitive work on Ed Crump of Memphis (1964). David Crockett, Daniel Boone, Nathan Bedford Forrest, and David Farragut are but a few of the other Tennesseans to whom biographers have turned their talents in recent years.

Numerous theses, dissertations, and articles have appeared on lesser figures. Frank B. Williams, Jr., in his inimitable style has written on a little known but important figure during Reconstruction, John B. Eaton, Jr., a Northern chaplain who was superintendent of education in Tennessee immediately following the Civil War. Aaron Boom has studied John Coffee; Sam Smith, Joseph B. Killebrew; Ray G. Osborne, James C. Jones; Clement Grant, Cave Johnson; Clyde Ball, Arthur S. Colyar; James W. Bellamy, Landon Carter Haynes; Norman Lexington Parks, John Bell; Frances Clifton, John Overton; G. R. Farnum, William B. Bate; Leota D. Maiden, Colonel John Williams; Enoch Mitchell, Robert Whyte; Chase C. Mooney, Adam Huntsman; Rufus Spain, R. B. C. Howell; Russell L. Stockard, Ben W. Hooper; and William R. Webb, Sawney Webb.

More than a dozen well-prepared accounts of geographic regions and counties have appeared in recent years. Superior to most have been Gilbert E. Govan and James W. Livingood's *The Chattanooga Country* (1954), William D. Miller's *Memphis During the*

Progressive Era (1957), and Garvin Davenport's *Cultural Life in Nashville on the Eve of the Civil War* (1941). Among the county histories have been Inez Burns's history of Blount County, Mary U. Rothrock and others on Knox County, Carl Sims's work on Rutherford County, Dixon Merritt and others on Wilson County, Helen and Joseph M. Krechniak on Cumberland County, Kate Johnston Peters about Lauderdale County, Walter Womack about McMinnville and Warren County, Emma Inman Williams on Madison County, William B. Turner about Maury County, and Robert E. Corlew on Dickson County.

The many general histories of Tennessee have included multi-volume works by Philip Hamer, John Trotwood Moore, Dixon Merritt, and by Folmsbee, Corlew, and Mitchell. A half-dozen authors have written one-volume works for use as texts in elementary schools. In 1899, Gentry R. McGee published a simple but comprehensive book called *A History of Tennessee*, which, as revised later by C. B. Ijams of Jackson, was used as a text for more than a quarter of a century. William R. Garrett and Albert V. Goodpasture issued their *History of Tennessee* in 1905. Then, in 1925 S. E. Scates's *A School History of Tennessee* and in 1936 Robert H. White's *Tennessee, Its Growth and Progress* were published. School histories currently in use include Joseph H. Parks and Stanley J. Folmsbee's *The Story of Tennessee* and Mary U. Rothrock's *This is Tennessee*, as well as her earlier *Discovering Tennessee*.

At the beginning of the twentieth century the novels and short stories of Mary Noailles Murfree, who wrote under the pseudonym of Charles Egbert Craddock, were the most widely read among works by Tennessee authors. She was born in Murfreesboro in 1850, and before she was thirty, she had placed short stories in the *Atlantic Monthly* and *Lippincott's Magazine*. A collection of short stories, *In the Tennessee Mountains* (1884), created a sensation and established her reputation as a writer. In the years that followed before her death in 1922, she wrote more than a dozen novels and scores of short stories, emphasizing particularly the Civil War and the colonial history of the Southwest. Her talent for graphic detail and her ability to captivate the reader with her charm as a master storyteller accounted for her popularity.

Among the writers of the 1920's and 1930's, perhaps none became better known nationally than two Nashville groups, the Fugitives

and the Agrarians; indeed, the former have been termed "the inau-
gurators of the Southern renaissance," and the latter the interpreters
of "a complex American region."[1] The Fugitives, a group of sixteen poets,[2] published nineteen issues (1922–25) of a journal called
The Fugitive and devoted it almost exclusively to poetry. The
Agrarians, a group of twelve writers,[3] most of whom were young
Vanderbilt instructors and students, published a variety of essays,
articles, and books, stressing a transcendentalist emphasis; the best
known of the books was an anthology entitled *I'll Take My Stand:
The South and the Agrarian Tradition*, (1930). The work of both
Fugitives and Agrarians was both praised and condemned but
scarcely ignored.

Creativity and individualism were the watchwords of the Fugitives. Indeed, as Davidson pointed out, they sought "to flee from
the extremes of conventionalism," and to accept and use the best
qualities of modern poetry "without . . . casting aside as unworthy
all that is established as good in the past"; thereby, they hoped to
capture and express the spirit of the "true Southern values." In the
early issues of their journal, the Fugitives were not particularly interested in exploiting their identity as Southerners. They rebelled,
they said, against "the high-caste Brahmins of the Old South." But
as the disillusionment following World War I became magnified
and the crass materialism of the mid-1920's became more apparent,
they were convinced that industrial and commercial preoccupa-
tions were stripping the American people—and Southerners in particular—of their traditional and cultural birthright. They saw in their
Southern heritage a society in which traditional and spiritual im-
pulses were predominant—a society which should be preserved. In
this way the Fugitives were the precursors of the Agrarians.

Four Fugitive poets—Davidson, Ransom, Tate, and Warren—
formed the nucleus of the Agrarians who undertook to publish a
criticism of American society and philosophy of the 1920's and

---

[1] See Thomas Lawrence Connelly, "The Vanderbilt Agrarians," for an able discussion of the Agrarians.

[2] John Crowe Ransom, Donald Davidson, Allen Tate, Robert Penn Warren,
Merrill Moore, Laura Riding, Jesse Wills, Alec B. Stevenson, Walter Clyde Curry,
Stanley Johnson, Sidney M. Hirsch, James Frank, William Yandell Elliott, William
Frierson, Ridley Wills, and Alfred Starr.

[3] John Crowe Ransom, Donald Davidson, Allen Tate, Robert Penn Warren,
Andrew Lytle, Stark Young, John G. Fletcher, Frank L. Owsley, Lyle Lanier, Herman
C. Nixon, John D. Wade, and Henry B. Kline.

1930's. In some respects they were in the tradition of novelist Sinclair Lewis and editor H. L. Mencken who saw in the emphasis upon materialism a departure from sound values. They were not debunkers and pessimists like Mencken, however; they were reformers who sought to turn society from the monotony of conformity and the loss of identity of the lonely crowd. The true South they described as conservative, rural, and spiritually motivated—qualities which had become traditional largely through an agrarian economy. These were qualities worth clinging to, but would necessitate the repudiation of machinery and its materialistic philosophy which threatened to strip man of his individuality. Learning from Sinclair Lewis and others of the standardization which industrialism had imposed upon other regions, the Agrarians rejoiced that it had been slow in developing in the South and questioned its worth in view of the problems in other regions where it had developed. Drawing upon the Bible, Thomas Jefferson, and John C. Calhoun, the Agrarians asserted that an economy of subsistence agriculture where men retained their self-respect and commanded the respect of their neighbors was superior to a surrender to "Progress"—which some even were calling "The American way of life," but which would reduce man to the monotony of the assembly line and strip him of his individuality. In returning to a conservative past, they shared the disillusionment of many people after World War I and believed that they could escape the problems concomitant to increasing population, urbanization, and racial turmoil.

Eastern critics dismissed the Agrarians as harmless literary diehards who could not forget the Confederacy. Such eminent historians as William B. Hesseltine, Henry Steele Commager, and Dixon Wecter dismissed them as provincial visionaries who would return to a "Golden Age" which never existed. Still others pictured them as scholars of considerable literary ability but who wished perpetually to shed tears over the Lost Cause, to blame the North for America's problems, and to perpetuate a feudalistic society. The Agrarians completely ignored, it was said, the many faults of the old system while extolling the virtues of courtesy, honor, and courage which they assigned to the Old South. Writers of the 1960's have been kinder to the Agrarians. Indeed, C. Vann Woodward, Thomas Lawrence Connelly, and Louis D. Rubin are among the scholars to view them as being within the reform tradition of America and who seriously sought quality instead of sheer quantity in American life. Woodward, in his perceptive *The Burden of Southern History*, has indicated a belief that critics have not fully understood the intent and purpose of the Agrarians. Connelly, in the article cited earlier, has described *I'll Take My Stand* as only an "experimental beginning of a thirty-year reappraisal of American society" and an "attempt to define a Southern tradition that was worth defending and to criticize American society in general."

Regardless of the initial comments about their anthology, the Agrarians continued to be heard. Perhaps Davidson's best-known contribution is a two-volume work entitled *The Tennessee River*, published in 1946 and 1948 as a part of the Rivers of America series. Davidson, a native of Campbellsville, was a member of the English department at Vanderbilt University for more than thirty years. Lytle, born in Murfreesboro, has authored more than a half-dozen novels and for many years has been editor of the *Sewanee Review*. Nixon taught for years at Vanderbilt and is remembered for his interpretation of the rural South in *Forty Acres and Steel Mules* and his plea for social planning in *Possum Trot*. Warren, a Rhodes scholar, has written with Cleanth Brooks, Jr., two widely used texts on poetry and fiction. Owsley, also a gifted teacher at Vanderbilt for many years, wrote *King Cotton Diplomacy*, *States Rights in the Confederacy*, and *Plain Folk of the Old South*, for which he relied heavily upon Tennessee materials to show the prevalence of a strong middle class in the Old South. Ransom, born in Pulaski, is best remembered for his work on the *Kenyon Review*, which he founded and edited until 1959.

T. S. Stribling was born in 1881 and became a Tennessee novelist who in many ways contrasted the more refined and gentle approach of the Fugitives. This son of a country merchant at Clifton saw little of value in the old South which the Fugitives and Agrarians depicted as so worthy of emulation. After several novels of adventure with South American settings, Stribling returned to Tennessee locale in *Teeftallow* (1926), a story of poor whites surrounded by bigotry, and *Bright Metal* (1928), a tale of a cultured "foreigner" who married into a difficult Tennessee environment; the latter book was somewhat reminiscent of *Main Street* by Sinclair Lewis, his mentor. Both works by Stribling struck hard at the myth that the Southern hill folk were gentle and hospitable. Other novels included *Back-

water (1930), *The Forge* (1931), *The Store* (1932), and *Unfinished Cathedral* (1934). He saw nothing but bitterness and hardship in the Southern environment; his whites are vulgar villains who operate only in terms of force, violence, and brutality. No Agrarian, he probably sought for the South the very industry and commerce which the Agrarians and Fugitives despised.

The people and the picturesque countryside of the state frequently have been a subject for writers of considerable prominence who have lived outside the state, particularly, William Faulkner, of Oxford, Mississippi. Memphis was the "big city" nearest Faulkner, and he knew it as a boy better than any other. East Tennessee also was a frequent point of reference, but less known to Faulkner than Memphis. Few who have read his last novel, *The Reivers, A Reminiscence* (1962), will forget the fictionalized account of the muddy roads leading into Memphis from Mississippi, the experiences of Boon Hogganbeck and Lucius Priest, the carefree Mississippians, and Everbe Corinthia, the prostitute with a heart.

James Agee was a Tennessee native who did not forget his homeland. His *Letters of James Agee to Father Flye* (1962) made occasional reference to Tennessee and demonstrated the literary talents of the youth in addition to the richness of his heart and soul. His Pulitzer prize-winning novel, *A Death in the Family*, which was later cast into a broadway drama and a motion picture, opened with a scene of young Agee as a child in Knoxville happily enjoying the companionship of his father. After his father died, he moved for a short time with his mother to Sewanee, where he attended St. Andrews school for boys; it was there that Agee met an instructor who became his close friend and confidante, Father James Harold Flye.

David J. Harkness, an authority on literature by and about Tennesseans and about the South, has discovered certain characteristics which set Tennessee fiction apart in American literature. In contending that writers about Tennessee show "a preoccupation with kinship" and have a sense of the family as a shaper of society, he has cited Wilma Dykeman's *The Far Family* and Agee's *A Death in the Family* as examples. The preoccupation with historic image also appeals to writers about Tennessee, according to Harkness, and Andrew Lytle's *The Long Night* and *The Velvet Horn* and Alfred L. Crabb's *Dinner at Belmont, Home to Tennessee,* and *Journey to Nashville* are examples. Too, Tennessee writers are concerned with regional development, perhaps because of the distinct political and physical regions of the state. Here, Harkness points to Dykeman's *The Tall Woman,* Ed Bell's *Fish on the Steeple,* and Mildred Haun's *The Hawk's Done Gone* as typical. The variety of cultures in the state—those of the rich and poor, the landed gentry and the subsistence mountain folk—are depicted by Wilma Dykeman, Andrew Lytle, Edd Winfield Parks, Anne Goodwin Winslow, T. S. Stribling, Robert Penn Warren, and others. Especially notable is Roark Bradford's depiction of Negro life.

Music, Drama, and Other Cultural Aspects 〰 As in the field of literature, Tennesseans have been active in other aspects of culture. The Federal Theater Project of the 1930's, attempting to salvage a profession made bankrupt by the depression, provided drama at government expense for the people in the major urban areas of the state—as indeed throughout the country. By mid-century many cities had their own "Little Theaters" and "Barn Theaters." The Tennessee Theater Association, with Paul Crabtree as president, was formed at Crossville in 1968, with three vice presidents for each section of the state. The Cumberland Playhouse at Crossville has been among the most successful of the summer stock theaters.

Many motion pictures have been made in Tennessee and with Tennessee performers. "All the Way Home," originally a play based on Agee's novel *A Death in the Family,* was filmed in Knoxville. Both the novel and the drama had won Pulitzer prizes—the first time the award had been won by both the original novel and its dramatization. Claude Jarman, Pat Boone, and Dinah Shore of Nashville, Elvis Presley of Memphis, Elizabeth Patterson of Savannah, Patricia Neal, Polly Bergen, and Jerome Courtland of Knoxville, and Peggy Dow of Athens have been featured in major motion pictures. Jarman at mid-century was widely acclaimed for his role in "The Yearling" and Miss Patterson for hers in "Intruder in the Dust," "Welcome Stranger," and "Miss Tatlock's Millions." Patricia Neal in 1964 won an Oscar for her performance in "Hud."

Tennesseans have excelled in the field of music. Grace Moore, James Melton, and Frances Geer have had outstanding careers in opera. Many choral groups have performed before local audiences from Memphis to Bristol; perhaps the best known has been the Fisk Jubilee Singers, who have captivated audiences in both Europe and America. Roland Hayes, the internationally known tenor and former member of the Boston University Music Faculty, was a member of the famed Fisk Jubilee Singers while an undergraduate at Fisk University. Charles Bryan, a native of Warren County and for many years a professor of music at George Peabody College for Teachers, wrote "The Bell Witch," a folk cantata, and was the first Tennessean to receive a Guggenheim Award for music. Francis Craig, for many years a well-known orchestra leader in Nashville, penned such hit songs as "Near You" and "Tennessee Tango," and Beth Slater Whitson composed "Meet Me Tonight in Dreamland" and "Let Me Call You Sweetheart." William C. Handy, Memphis Negro, became known as "the Father of the Blues" after he wrote "The Memphis Blues" in 1910 and "The St. Louis Blues" a few years later. Beasley Smith's orchestra was heard throughout the country during the 1920's and early 1930's. He composed "Night Train to Memphis" and "Sunday Down in Tennessee," and in 1952 won a Freedom's Foundation Award for "God's Country." Tennessee has four state songs by native composers: "My Homeland, Tennessee" by Nell Grayson Taylor and Roy L. Smith, "My Tennessee" by Frances Hannah Trainum, "When It's Iris Time in Tennessee" by Willa Mai Waid, and "Tennessee" (sung to the tune of "Beulah Land") by A. J. Holt. The state has been the inspiration for many lyrics, including "Tennessee Moon," "Tennessee Waltz," "Memphis in June," and "Chattanooga Choo-Choo."

With its variety of country music, the Grand Ole Opry, broadcast weekly from Nashville, has become famous in American radio and television. The Opry began in November, 1925, as a country music show sponsored by WSM Radio station and has operated continuously since that time. Among the well-known artists appearing here have been Roy ("Wabash Cannon Ball") Acuff, Hank Williams, Lester Flatt, Earl Scruggs, Ernest Tubb, Uncle Dave Macon and his son Dorris, and Minnie Pearl (well known for her friendly salutation, "I'm so proud to be here"). Commedienne Minnie Pearl (Mrs. Henry Cannon), a Ward Belmont graduate, from 1944 to 1947 published the Grinder's Switch *Gazette*, a newspaper "filled with all the news of Grinder's Switch [her hometown near Centerville] and all our friends on the Grand Ole Opry." Some have questioned the cultural aspects of the Opry, but none can deny its impact upon the music world and its influence in making Nashville the country music center of the world. The "Athens of the South" is consequently also known as "Music City, U.S.A.," for its country music business of over $100,000,000 per year. More than a dozen commercial recording studios and four record pressing plants are located there, together with the "Country Music Hall of Fame and Museum," established in 1967 by the Country Music Association Foundation.

Tennesseans have done comparatively little in the fields of sculpture and painting, although the sculpture of Puryear Mims in character studies of Tennessee Negroes, farmers, and mountain folk has been an exception. In painting, Aaron K. Douglass, a Negro artist, has painted symbolic scenes (now on display in Fisk University Library), George De Forest Brush scenes of Indian life, and Fred Rubens of Murfreesboro painted portraits. There are excellent art galleries and museums in all the major cities of Tennessee.

Hundreds of other Tennessee novelists, poets (for instance, Arna Bontemps, the librarian at Fisk University for many years), historians, and artists—all perhaps as significant as those discussed here but too numerous to mention—have contributed much to the cultural life of the nation.

Tennessee Becomes Conscious of Its Past ३० During the second quarter of the twentieth century, Tennesseans became increasingly conscious of their past. Previously, both the *American Historical Magazine* and the *Tennessee Historical Magazine* had been discontinued. The Tennessee Historical Society, which actually traced its beginnings to the Tennessee Society for the Diffusion of Knowledge formed in 1835 and the Tennessee Antiquarian Society formed in 1820, was revitalized and began once again to meet periodically and to collect source materials.

The Tennessee Historical Committee was created in 1919 with its principal purpose being to collect and preserve materials about Tennesseans in World War I. In 1941 the name was changed to the Tennessee Historical Commission, and its areas of interest were expanded to incorporate general historical materials, the marking of historic sites, publication of historical works, and the broad function of diffusing historical knowledge about the state. The commission is composed of twenty-seven members, including the governor and commissioner of education who serve ex-officio.

The commission has accomplished much in all of these areas of interest. One of its first significant acts was to encourage the writing of county histories, then to subsidize one-half of the printing costs. Among its publications have been the monumental *Messages of the Governors*, edited by State Historian Robert H. White, who to date has prepared seven volumes covering the messages to the end of the nineteenth century. The commission also is cooperating with the National Historical Publications Commission in the editing and publishing of the papers of James K. Polk and Andrew Johnson. The commission donates copies of each of its publications to every university, college, high school, and public library of the state and has erected more than 1,000 historic markers across the state. Further, the commission assumed a major role in the preservation of historic sites such as the Carter House in Franklin, Oaklands in Murfreesboro, Belle Meade Mansion in Nashville, and the Blount Mansion in Knoxville.

Largely through the commission's efforts, a new State Library and Archives Building supplanted the crowded one-room facilities maintained for many years in the State Capitol. Established in 1854 with an appropriation of $5,000 at the insistence of Governor Andrew Johnson, the State Library developed quite slowly over the years. The State Archives Department, created about fifty years later, had preserved their important documents in the basement of the War Memorial Building until the construction of the new building.

Today, the library and archives are under the direction of the state librarian and archivist, who supervises four divisions—the State Library Division, Public Libraries Division, Division of Administrative Services, and Archives Division. Until 1969 the state librarian served as chairman of the Historical Commission.

There are three major historical societies in the state, plus societies in many counties. These, appropriately enough, are called the East Tennessee Historical Society, the West Tennessee Historical Society, and the Tennessee Historical Society. Each publishes a journal—the Tennessee Historical Society quarterly and the other two annually—subsidized by funds from the commission. Under the terms of a recent agreement, the Tennessee Historical Society also houses an extensive collection of historical materials in the State Library. The societies, through their journals and many activities, play an important role in stimulating interest in Tennessee history.

The celebration of the state sesquicentennial in 1946 did much to create and quicken interest in the state's history. The official ceremonies were held in Nashville from May 30 to June 3 under the direction of the sesquicentennial committee of the Historical Commission, of which Stanley F. Horn was chairman. Busts of Admiral David G. Farragut and Commander Matthew Fontaine Maury were unveiled in the house of representatives, a pageant entitled "Tennessee Through the Years" was staged at Dudley Stadium, and Dr. Walter R. Courtenay, pastor of the First Presbyterian Church of Nashville, preached a sesquicentennial sermon.

Ceremonies also were held in other Tennessee cities and in Washington, D. C., in the Library of Congress under the auspices of members of the Tennessee State Society of Washington. Within the state, in addition to the ceremonies held in Nashville, the occasion was marked in Knoxville, Memphis, Chattanooga, Johnson City, Murfreesboro, Franklin, Monteagle, and elsewhere. In Knoxville, a monument to the memory of Sarah Hawkins Sevier, first wife of John Sevier, was unveiled on the courthouse lawn. In Johnson City, celebrants unveiled a monument and also paid tribute to Judge Samuel Cole Williams, chairman of the Historical Commission, author, and guiding spirit in promoting interest in the history of the state. In Memphis, the annual cotton carnival highlighted "One Hundred and Fifty Years of Tennessee History," and celebrants heard Mayor Walter Chandler, also a member of the commission, deliver an address in commemoration of the occasion. At Murfreesboro, a monument to the memory of General Griffith Rutherford, Revolutionary soldier and one of Middle Tennessee's early settlers, was unveiled, and an address was delivered by Edward Ward Carmack, Jr.

Tennessee's Population Trends > A noticeable urban trend had taken place by mid-century. The population in 1960 was

3,567,089, an increase of more than 70 per cent over that of 1900, and a majority of the people lived principally in cities of 25,000 or more. The first six censuses of the twentieth century, especially those of the second three decades, indicate a marked urban trend. Although the population increased approximately 12.6 per cent during the 1940's, 43 of the 95 counties actually decreased in population. During the 1950's, the population increased nearly 8 per cent, but 54 counties had a smaller count in 1960 than in 1950. Counties showing the largest gains during the twenty-year period were Anderson (which, containing Oak Ridge, showed a gain of 123.6 per cent in 1950 over the population of ten years earlier), Coffee, Davidson, Hamblen, Hamilton, Knox, Roane, Rutherford, Sullivan, and Shelby.

Three belts of population gain during the period of 1940–60 are readily discernible. The first begins with Sullivan County on the Virginia line and extends in a southwestward direction through Washington, Hamblen, Greene, Anderson, Knox, Roane, Loudon, and Bradley counties. A second belt begins at Bradley and Hamilton and runs in a northwestward direction through Sequatchie, Warren, Coffee, Rutherford, Davidson, and Montgomery counties; thus, the two belts together compose a "V" with the two branches moving in a northwestern and northeastern direction from the beginning point on the Georgia line. A third belt is Shelby County which gained almost 30 per cent during the 1950's; state statisticians estimate that this county will experience a population increase of 112 per cent in 1980 over the population of 1950.

Significant is the proportional decline of the Negro population in the state. The Negro population of 480,243 in 1900 was 23.8 per cent of the total, but in 1960 it was only 16.5 per cent. High wages and good working conditions in Northern factories during and after World War II were particularly responsible for the exodus. Although World War I and the industrial prosperity of the 1920's lured many Tennessee Negroes to Northern cities, the depression of the 1930's caused many to return to the cotton fields of West Tennessee. Once again war brought mobility, and this time many of those who left did not return. Those who did return, however, enjoyed better wages and living conditions than ever before, but the white attitude toward them changed very little. In fact, a racial disturbance just at the war's end in Columbia's Negro district ("Mink Slide") lasted for a week and necessitated Governor McCord's sending the home guard to restore law and order.

Indeed, at mid-century most Tennessee whites clung to the attitude toward blacks that dated back some fifty years earlier. Respect for Negro rights had not characterized the American people in 1900, and the people of Tennessee were no exception. The "separate but equal" decree of the Supreme Court (1896) had become the accepted dogma in Tennessee and throughout the country. Most newspaper editors called the blacks "coons" and "nigger," and politicians and civic leaders generally referred to them, if at all, with equal condescension; whites who associated with the blacks were considered as lowering the dignity of the Caucasian race. Politicians and editors alike roundly excoriated President Theodore Roosevelt when in 1901 he invited Booker T. Washington to lunch in the White House. The orator and Democratic leader Edward Ward Carmack, for example, denounced the President for attempting to turn the White House into a "nigger restaurant," and the editor of the Memphis *Commercial Appeal* was mortified weeks later when he discovered that Roosevelt had issued no information that the executive mansion had "been disinfected or even the chair, knife, fork, plate, and napkin deodorized." As late as 1917, after nearly two decades of "progressivism," aroused Shelby countians could lynch a Negro accused of rape and murder and in the same week listen to a prominent Memphis lawyer and civic leader urge them to support the war effort to prevent Germany from turning back "the hands of Civilization . . . a hundred years."

The Supreme Court decision of 1954 (*Brown v. the Board of Education of Topeka*) that ordered integration with all deliberate speed found most of the people entirely unready for such enormous social change. The decision was received with mixed emotions by Tennessee's political and civic leaders and newspaper editors. Except for Senators Gore and Kefauver and Representative J. Percy Priest, the Tennessee delegation in Washington expressed their disapproval by signing the Southern Manifesto in which 97 Southern congressmen pledged to continue to fight for segregation. Although the majority of the major newspapers neither endorsed nor denounced the decision, most of the few which did take a stand approved it. The small weekly Lexington *Progress* expressed the sentiments of many people when the editor wrote that the decision came as no surprise to Tennesseans because "by any and all standards we live by—those of our Constitution, . . . Christianity, and even those leading to the settlement of our country—Segregation was doomed."

Commendation and implementation proved to be two entirely different matters. While state lawmakers talked of enacting laws to defy the will of the Court, Negroes, under the leadership of the National Association for the Advancement of Colored People, filed suits to implement the decision. These suits brought about a gradual desegregation of the schools and colleges, but not without considerable disorder.

In the meantime, the Tennessee Federation for Constitutional Government, headed by Donald Davidson, a respected author and professor of English literature at Vanderbilt University, sought by legal means to prevent or at least to postpone desegregation by emphasizing a strict interpretation of the Constitution. The Federation led the legal battle at Clinton in August, 1956, when fifteen Negroes registered at the high school. Disorder was encouraged at Clinton (and a few months later in Nashville) by a rabble-rousing native of New Jersey, John Kasper, who inspired extreme segregationists wherever he appeared.

Integration spread slowly across the state in the late 1950's. As a result, by the fall of 1959 only four of the state's school districts had been integrated, and only 169 of the state's 146,700 Negro children of school age attended integrated schools. The decade of the 1960's, however, was to bring about considerably more progress.

For many Negroes, especially those of high school and college age, the wheels of justice ground far too slowly to meet their demands. Restive over discrimination in buses, restaurants, downtown stores and theaters, Negroes began in 1960 a new tactic—the "sit-in." Beginning in Nashville in February where several hundred students from Fisk and Tennessee A & I converged on lunch counters in downtown Nashville and spreading on to Chattanooga, Knoxville, and Memphis, the sit-ins brought poignantly to the public mind and conscience the second-class citizenship to which Negroes were subjected. Arrests, fines, and verbal and physical abuses did not deter them, and in May several Nashville merchants agreed voluntarily to desegregate lunch counters. When in 1961 "freedom riders" began excursions into Southern cities to test segregation on buses and interstate carriers, Nashville Negroes and others joined in.

The four-year period of 1964–68 was one of marked progress for the Negro in attaining equality in the White Establishment. A. W. Willis, Jr., a NAACP lawyer in Memphis, was elected to the legislature in 1964—the first Negro to be elected to the General Assembly in the twentieth century—and in 1966 six others were elected, including Dr. Dorothy Brown, the first Negro woman in the history of the state to serve in the legislature. In 1967, Stokely Carmichael addressed Vanderbilt students without incident in the highly publicized *Impact* series, despite widespread criticism from conservative Vanderbilt alumni scattered throughout the country. The untimely assassination of Martin Luther King, Jr., in Memphis on April 4, 1968, not only removed an able leader and proponent of non-violence but became a signal for violent reaction and racial disturbances throughout the country. Preliminary estimates of damage in New York amounted to $15 million, and in the nation's capital it was almost as much. Buildings in Nashville (particularly at Tennessee A & I University), Chattanooga, Memphis, and elsewhere were looted and burned, and damage resulting from the riots and looting was estimated at $700,000 in Tennessee. Night curfews were ordered in a dozen towns and cities across the state.

Society in Tennessee in 1968 was far from static and exhibited none of the placidity which the rural scene posed in 1900. Few signs appeared which pointed to anything other than a continuation of an effervescent society attempting to right itself in a turbulent world. The urbanization of the state and the many foreign and domestic problems, for which few if any of the people were prepared, were at least partly responsible for the social and intellectual ferment of the times.

SUGGESTED READINGS

General Accounts

Folmsbee, Corlew, and Mitchell, *Tennessee*, II, Chs. 33, 37, 47; Robert M. Miller, *American Protestantism and Social Issues, 1919–1939* (Chapel

Hill, 1958); Rufus B. Spain, *At Ease in Zion: Social History of Southern Baptists* (Nashville, 1967).

Specialized Accounts

Kenneth K. Bailey, "The Enactment of Tennessee Anti-evolution Law," *JSH*, XVI (Nov., 1950), 472–90; Oswald E. Brown, James H. Kirkland, and Edwin Mims, *God and the New Knowledge* (Nashville, 1926); Louise Cowan, *The Fugitive Group: A Literary History* (Baton Rouge, 1959); Thomas Lawrence Connelly, "The Vanderbilt Agrarians: Time and Place in Southern Tradition," *THQ*, XXII (March, 1963), 22–37; Ray Ginger, *Six Days or Forever: Tennessee v. John Thomas Scopes* (New York, 1958); Graham, *Crisis in Print*; David Harkness, *Tennessee in Recent Books, Music and Drama* (Knoxville, 1950); Harkness, *Literary Profiles of the Southern States* (Knoxville, 1953); Harkness, *Tennessee in Literature* (Knoxville, 1949); Harrell, "Disciples of Christ and Social Force," ETHS *Publ.*, No. 38, pp. 30–47; Elmo Howell, "William Faulkner and Tennessee," *THQ*, XXI (Sept., 1963), 251–62; Rayburn W. Johnson, "Population Trends in Tennessee from 1940 to 1950," *THQ*, XI (Sept., 1952), 254–62; Thomas A. Krueger, *And Promises to Keep: The Southern Conference for Human Welfare, 1938–1948* (Nashville, 1967); John W. Porter, *Evolution—A Menace* (Nashville, 1922); Henry Lee Swint, "The Historical Activities of the State of Tennessee," *THQ*, XVII (Dec., 1958), 291–300.

Bibliography

BOOKS

ABERNETHY, THOMAS P., *The Burr Conspiracy*, New York, 1954
————, *From Frontier to Plantation in Tennessee*, Chapel Hill, 1932; reprinted, Memphis, 1955; University, Ala., 1967
ABSHIRE, DAVID, *The South Rejects a Prophet: The Life of Senator D. M. Key, 1824–1900*, New York, 1967
ADAIR, JAMES, *History of the American Indians*, ed. by S. C. Williams, Johnson City, Tenn., 1930
ALDEN, JOHN RICHARD, *John Stuart and the Southern Colonial Frontier: A Study of Indian Relations, War, Trade, and Land Problems in the Southern Wilderness, 1754–1775*, Ann Arbor, 1944
————, *The South in the Revolution*, Baton Rouge, 1957
ALDERSON, WILLIAM T., AND ROBERT M. MCBRIDE (eds.), *Landmarks of Tennessee History*, Nashville, 1965
ALEXANDER, T. H., *Austin Peay, Governor of Tennessee*, Kingsport, Tenn., 1929
ALEXANDER, THOMAS B., *Political Reconstruction in Tennessee*, Nashville, 1950
————, *Thomas A. R. Nelson of East Tennessee*, Nashville, 1956
ALVORD, CHARLES W., *The Mississippi Valley in British Politics*, 2 vols., Cleveland, 1916–17
ALVORD, CHARLES W., AND LEE BIDGOOD, *The First Explorations of the Trans-Allegheny Region by the Virginians, 1650–1674*, Cleveland, 1912
ARMSTRONG, ZELLA, *Who Discovered America? The Amazing Story of Madoc*, Chattanooga, 1950
ARNOW, HARRIETTE, *Flowering of the Cumberland*, New York, 1963

————, *Seedtime on the Cumberland*, New York, 1960

BAKELESS, JOHN, *Master of the Wilderness: Daniel Boone*, New York, 1939

BANCROFT, FREDERIC, *Slave Trading in the Old South*, Baltimore, 1931

BARCLAY, R. E., *Ducktown: Back in Raht's Time*, Chapel Hill, 1946

BARNES, WILLIAM W., *The Southern Baptist Convention, 1845–1953*, Nashville, 1954

BARNHART, JOHN H., *Valley of Democracy*, Bloomington, Ind., 1953

BARTRAM, WILLIAM, *Observations on the Creek and Cherokee Indians*, American Ethnological Society, *Transactions*, III, New York, 1853

BASS, ALTHEA, *Cherokee Messenger*, Norman, 1936

BASSETT, JOHN SPENCER (ed.), *Correspondence of Andrew Jackson*, 7 vols., Washington, D. C., 1926–35

————, *Life of Andrew Jackson*, 2 vols., New York, 1911

BEALE, HOWARD K., *The Critical Year: A Study of Andrew Johnson and Reconstruction*, New York, 1930

BENTLEY, GEORGE R., *A History of the Freedmen's Bureau*, Philadelphia, 1955

BINKLEY, WILLIAM C., *The Texas Revolution*, Baton Rouge, 1952

BONE, WINSTEAD PAINE, *A History of Cumberland University, 1842–1935*, Lebanon, Tenn., 1935

BOURNE, EDWARD G. (ed.), *Narratives of the Career of Hernando De Soto*, 2 vols., New York, 1922

BOWERS, CLAUDE G., *Making Democracy a Reality: Jefferson, Jackson and Polk*, Memphis, 1954

————, *The Party Battles of the Jackson Period*, Boston, 1922

————, *The Tragic Era*, Cambridge, 1929

BOYCE, EVERETT ROBERT (ed.), *The Unwanted Boy: The Autobiography of Governor Ben W. Hooper*, Knoxville, 1963

BROOME, ISAAC, *The Last Days of the Ruskin Cooperative Association*, Chicago, 1903

BROWN, AARON V., *Speeches, Congressional and Political, and Other Writings*, Nashville, 1854

BROWN, JOHN P., *Old Frontiers: The Story of the Cherokee Indians from Earliest Times to the Date of Their Removal to the West, 1838*, Kingsport, Tenn., 1938

BROWN, OSWALD E., JAMES H. KIRKLAND, AND EDWIN MIMS, *God and the New Knowledge*, Nashville, 1926

BROWNLOW, WILLIAM GANNAWAY, *The Great Iron Wheel Examined, or Its False Spokes Extracted, and an Exhibition of Elder Graves, Its Builder*, Nashville, 1856

————, *Ought American Slavery to be Perpetuated? A Debate Between*

Reverend William G. Brownlow and Reverend A. Pryne, Philadelphia, 1858

——, *Sketches of the Rise, Progress and Decline of Secession: with a Narrative of Personal Adventures among the Rebels*, Philadelphia, 1862

BUCK, SOLON J., *The Agrarian Crusade*, New Haven, 1921

BURNETT, J. J., *Sketches of Tennessee's Pioneer Preachers*, Nashville, 1919

BURNS, INEZ, *History of Blount County, Tennessee*, Maryville, Tenn., 1957

BURT, JESSE C., JR., *Nashville: Its Life and Times*, Nashville, 1959

BUTLER, GEORGE H., *The Military March of Time in Tennessee, 1939–1944: Report of the Adjutant General*, Nashville, 1945

CALDWELL, JOSHUA W., *Studies in the Constitutional History of Tennessee*, Cincinnati, 1895

CALLAHAN, NORTH, *Henry Knox: General Washington's General*, New York, 1958

CAMPBELL, CLAUDE A., *The Development of Banking in Tennessee*, Nashville, 1932

CAMPBELL, MARY R., *The Attitude of Tennesseans Toward the Union, 1847–1861*, New York, 1961

CAMPBELL, T. J., *The Upper Tennessee*, Chattanooga, 1932

CAMPBELL, THOMAS H., *Studies in Cumberland Presbyterian History*, Nashville, 1944

CAPERS, GERALD M., JR., *The Biography of a River Town—Memphis: Its Heroic Age*, Chapel Hill, 1939; reprinted New Orleans, 1966

CARR, HOWARD E., *Washington College*, Knoxville, 1935

CARR, I. N., *History of Carson-Newman College*, Jefferson City, Tenn., 1959

CARROLL, E. MALCOLM, *Origins of the Whig Party*, Durham, 1925

CARTER, CLARENCE EDWIN (ed.), *The Territorial Papers of the United States, IV, The Territory South of the River Ohio: 1790–1796*, Washington, D. C., 1936

CARTER, CULLEN T., *History of the Tennessee Conference and a Brief Summary of the General Conference of the Methodist Church from the Frontier in Middle Tennessee to the Present Time*, Nashville, 1948

CARTWRIGHT, PETER, *Autobiography of Peter Cartwright, the Backwoods Preacher*, Nashville, 1946

CARUSO, JOHN A., *The Appalachian Frontier*, Indianapolis, 1959

CAUGHEY, J. W., *McGillivray of the Creeks*, Norman, 1938

CHAMBERS, WILLIAM NISBET, *Old Bullion Benton: Senator from the New West*, New York, 1956

CHITTY, ARTHUR BENJAMIN, JR., *Reconstruction at Sewanee*, Sewanee, Tenn., 1954

CLAPP, GORDON R., *The TVA: An Approach to the Development of a Region*, Chicago, 1955

CLARK, BLANCHE HENRY, *The Tennessee Yeoman, 1840–1860*, Nashville, 1942

CLARK, THOMAS D., *The Beginnings of the L & N*, Louisville, 1933

———, *A Pioneer Southern Railroad, from New Orleans to Cairo*, Chapel Hill, 1936

———, *The Rampaging Frontier*, Indianapolis, 1939

CLAYTON, W. W., *History of Davidson County, Tennessee*, Philadelphia, 1880

CLEAVES, FREEMAN, *Rock of Chickamauga: The Life of General George H. Thomas*, Norman, 1948

CLEVELAND, CATHARINE C., *The Great Revival in the West, 1797–1805*, Chicago, 1916

COLE, ARTHUR C., *The Whig Party in the South*, Washington, D. C., 1913

CONNELLY, THOMAS LAWRENCE, *Army of the Heartland: The Army of Tennessee, 1861–1862*, Baton Rouge, 1967

COOPER, WALTER RAYMOND, *Southwestern at Memphis, 1848–1948*, Richmond, 1949

CORKRAN, DAVID H., *The Cherokee Frontier, 1740–1762*, Norman, 1962

CORLEW, ROBERT E., *A History of Dickson County*, Dickson, Tenn., 1956

COTTERILL, ROBERT S., *The Southern Indians*, Norman, 1954

COULTER, E. MERTON, *The South During Reconstruction, 1865–1877*, Baton Rouge, 1947

———, *William G. Brownlow: Fighting Parson of the Southern Highlands*, Chapel Hill, 1937; rpt. Knoxville, 1971

COWAN, LOUISE, *The Fugitive Group: A Literary History*, Baton Rouge, 1959

COWAN, SAM K., *Sergeant York and His People*, New York, 1922

COX, JACOB D., *The Battle of Franklin, Tennessee*, New York, 1897

CRANE, VERNON W., *The Southern Frontier*, Durham, 1928

CRAVEN, AVERY O., *The Coming of the Civil War*, Chicago, 1957

CREEKMORE, BETSEY BEELER, *Knoxville*, Knoxville, 1958; second edition, 1967

CROCKETT, DAVID, *Autobiography of David Crockett*, New York, 1923

CUMMING, WILLIAM P., *The Southeast in Early Maps*, Princeton, 1958

DAHIR, JAMES, *Region Building, Community Development Lessons from the Tennessee Valley*, New York, 1955

DANA, CHARLES A., *Recollections of the Civil War*, New York, 1899

DANIELS, JONATHAN, *Devil's Backbone: The Story of the Natchez Trace*, New York, 1961

DAVENPORT, F. GARVIN, *Cultural Life in Nashville on the Eve of the Civil War*, Chapel Hill, 1941

DAVIDSON, DONALD, *The Tennessee, I: The Old River, Frontier to Secession*, New York, 1946; *II: The New River: Civil War to TVA*, New York, 1948

DEVORSEY, LOUIS, JR., *The Indian Boundary in the Southern Colonies, 1763–1775*, Chapel Hill, 1966

DORRIS, JONATHAN T., *Pardon and Amnesty under Lincoln and Johnson*, Chapel Hill, 1953

DOUGLAS, BRYD, *Steamboatin' on the Cumberland*, Nashville, 1961

DOWNEY, FAIRFAX, *Storming the Gateway: Chattanooga, 1863*, New York, 1960

DRAKE, JAMES VAULX, *Life of General Robert Hatton, Including His Most Important Public Speeches: Together with Much of His Washington and Army Correspondence*, Nashville, 1867

DRAPER, LYMAN C., *King's Mountain and Its Heroes*, Cincinnati, 1881; reprinted, New York, 1929, Spartanburg, S. C., 1967

DRIVER, CARL, *John Sevier: Pioneer of the Old Southwest*, Chapel Hill, 1932

DROZE, WILMON HENRY, *High Dams and Slack Water: TVA Rebuilds a River*, Baton Rouge, 1965

DUFFUS, R. L., *The Valley and Its People: A Portrait of TVA*, New York, 1944

DUMOND, DWIGHT, *The Secession Movement, 1860–61*, New York, 1931

DUVALL, SYLVANUS M., *The Methodist Episcopal Church and Education, up to 1869*, New York, 1928

DYER, JOHN P., *The Gallant Hood*, Indianapolis, 1950

DYKEMAN, WILMA, *The French Broad*, New York, 1955; reprinted, Knoxville, 1965

EATON, CLEMENT, *Henry Clay and the Art of American Politics*, Boston, 1957

FAIRBANKS, GEORGE R., *History of the University of the South*, Jacksonville, 1905

FARRAR, ROWENA RUTHERFORD, *A Wondrous Moment Then*, New York, 1967

FAULKNER, CHARLES H., *The Old Stone Fort: Exploring an Archaeological Mystery*, Knoxville, 1968

FERTIG, JAMES W., *The Secession and Reconstruction of Tennessee*, Chicago, 1898

FITZGERALD, O. P., *John B. McFerrin: A Biography*, Nashville, 1890

FOLK, R. E., *Battle of New Orleans: Its Real Meaning*, Nashville, 1935

FOLMSBEE, STANLEY J., *Blount College and East Tennessee College, 1794–1840*, Knoxville, 1946

————, *East Tennessee University, 1840–1879, Predecessor of the University of Tennessee*, Knoxville, 1959

————, *Sectionalism and Internal Improvements in Tennessee, 1796–1845*, Knoxville, 1939

————, *Tennessee Establishes a State University: First Years of The University of Tennessee, 1879–1887*, Knoxville, 1961

FOLMSBEE, STANLEY J., AND LUCILE DEADERICK, *The Founding of Knoxville*, Knoxville, 1941

FOLMSBEE, STANLEY J., ROBERT E. CORLEW, AND ENOCH L. MITCHELL, *History of Tennessee*, 2 vols., New York, 1960

FOREMAN, CAROLYN T., *Indians Abroad, 1493–1838*, Norman, 1943

FOREMAN, GRANT, *Indian Removal*, Norman, 1932

————, *Sequoyah*, Norman, 1938

FOSTER, A. P., *Counties of Tennessee*, Nashville, 1923

FRIEND, LLERENA, *Sam Houston: The Great Designer*, Austin, 1954

FULLER, THOMAS O., *History of the Negro Baptists of Tennessee*, Memphis, 1936

————, *The Story of the Church Life Among Negroes in Memphis, Tennessee*, Memphis, 1938

GABRIEL, RALPH H., *Elias Boudinot, Cherokee, and His America*, Norman, 1941

GAINES, GEORGE TOWNES, *Fighting Tennesseans*, Kingsport, Tenn., 1931

GARRETT, WILLIAM R., AND ALBERT V. GOODPASTURE, *History of Tennessee*, Nashville, 1905

GARRISON, WINIFRED E., AND ALFRED T. DEGROOT, *The Disciples of Christ: A History*, St. Louis, 1948

GILBERT, WILLIAM H., JR., *The Eastern Cherokees*, Washington D. C., 1943

GINGER, RAY, *Six Days or Forever: Tennessee v. John Thomas Scopes*, New York, 1958

GIPSON, LAWRENCE H., *The British Empire Before the American Revolution*, 12 vols. to date, New York, 1936——

GOHMANN, SISTER MARY DE LOURDES, *Political Nativism in Tennessee to 1860*, Washington, D. C., 1938

GOODSPEED, WESTON A., *et al.* (eds.), *History of Tennessee*, Nashville, 1887

GOVAN, GILBERT E., AND JAMES W. LIVINGOOD, *The Chattanooga Country*, New York, 1952; reprinted, Chapel Hill, 1963

————, *The University of Chattanooga: Sixty Years*, Chattanooga, 1947

GRAF, LEROY P., AND RALPH W. HASKINS (eds.), *The Papers of Andrew Johnson*, 3 vols. to date, Knoxville, 1967–

GRAHAM, HUGH D., *Crisis in Print*, Nashville, 1967

GRAY, LEWIS C., *History of Agriculture in the Southern United States to 1860*, 2 vols., Washington, D. C., 1933

GREENE, LEE SEIFERT, AND ROBERT STERLING AVERY, *Government in Tennessee*, Knoxville, 1962; second edition, 1966

GREENE, LEE S., *et al.*, *Rescued Earth*, Knoxville, 1948

HALE, WILL T., *History of DeKalb County, Tennessee*, Nashville, 1915

HALE, WILL T., AND DIXON MERRITT, *A History of Tennessee and Tennesseans*, 8 vols., Chicago, 1913

HALL, CLIFTON R., *Andrew Johnson: Military Governor of Tennessee*, Princeton, 1916

HALLUM, JOHN, *Diary of an Old Lawyer*, Nashville, 1895

HALSEY, LEROY (ed.), *The Works of Philip Lindsley, D.D.*, 3 vols., Philadelphia, 1866

HAMER, PHILIP M., *Fort Loudoun on the Little Tennessee*, Raleigh, N. C., n.d.

————, *Tennessee: A History, 1763–1932*, 4 vols., New York, 1933

HAMILTON, JAMES J., *The Battle of Fort Donelson*, New York, 1968

HARKNESS, DAVID, *Literary Profiles of the Southern States*, Knoxville, 1953

————, *Tennessee in Literature*, Knoxville, 1949

————, *Tennessee in Recent Books, Music and Drama*, Knoxville, 1950

HARPER, FRANCES (ed.), *The Travels of William Bartram*, New Haven, 1958

HARRELL, DAVID E., JR., *Quest for a Christian America*, Nashville, 1966

HAWKINS, BRETT W., *Nashville Metro: The Politics of City-County Consolidation*, Nashville, 1966

HAY, THOMAS R., *Hood's Tennessee Campaign*, New York, 1929

HAYWOOD, JOHN, *Civil and Political History of the State of Tennessee*, Knoxville, 1823; reprinted, Nashville, 1915, Knoxville, 1969

————, *Natural and Aboriginal History of Tennessee*, ed. by Mary U. Rothrock, Jackson, Tenn., 1959

HENDERSON, ARCHIBALD, *The Conquest of the Old Southwest*, New York, 1920

HENRY, ROBERT SELPH, *"First with the Most" Forrest*, New York, 1944

————, *The Story of the Confederacy*, Indianapolis, 1931

HERR, KINCAID A., *The Louisville and Nashville Railroad*, Louisville, 1943

HESSELTINE, WILLIAM B. (ed.), *Dr. J. G. M. Ramsey: Autobiography and Letters*, Nashville, 1954

———— (ed.), *Pioneer's Mission: The Story of Lyman Copeland Draper*, Madison, Wis., 1954

HICKS, JOHN D., *The Populist Revolt*, Minneapolis, 1931

HOLT, ALBERT C., *The Economic and Social Beginning of Tennessee*, Nashville, 1923

HOLT, ANDREW D., *The Struggle for a State System of Public Schools in Tennessee, 1903–1936*, New York, 1938

HORN, STANLEY F., *The Army of Tennessee*, Indianapolis, 1941

————, *The Decisive Battle of Nashville*, Baton Rouge, 1956; reprinted, Knoxville, 1968

————, *The Invisible Empire*, Boston, 1939

HORSMAN, REGINALD, *The Causes of the War of 1812*, Philadelphia, 1962

————, *Expansion and American Indian Policy, 1789–1812*, East Lansing, Mich., 1967

HUBBARD, PRESTON J., *The Origins of the TVA*, Nashville, 1966

HUGHES, THOMAS, *Rugby, Tennessee: Being an Account of the Settlement Founded on the Cumberland Plateau*, London, 1881

ISAAC, PAUL E., *Prohibition and Politics: Turbulent Decades in Tennessee, 1885–1920*, Knoxville, 1965

JACOBS, WILLIAM S. (comp.), *Presbyterianism in Nashville*, Nashville, 1904

JAMES, MARQUIS, *The Life of Andrew Jackson*, 2 vols., New York, 1933–37

————, *The Life of Andrew Jackson*, New York, 1940

————, *The Raven: A Biography of Sam Houston*, New York, 1929

JOHNSTON, WILLIAM P., *Life of General Albert Sidney Johnson*, New York, 1879

JONES, JAMES S., *Life of Andrew Johnson*, Greeneville, Tenn., 1901

JORDAN, GENERAL THOMAS, AND J. P. PRYOR, *The Campaigns of Lieutenant-General N. B. Forrest*, New Orleans, 1868

JORDAN, LEWIS G., *Negro Baptist History, 1750–1930*, Nashville, 1930

KEATING, J. M., *History of Memphis and Shelby County, Tennessee*, Syracuse, 1888

KELLEY, PAUL, *Historic Fort Loudoun*, Vonore, Tenn., 1958

KEY, V. O., JR., *Southern Politics in State and Nation*, New York, 1949

KILLEBREW, JOSEPH B., *Introduction to the Resources of Tennessee*, Nashville, 1874

KINCAID, ROBERT L., *The Wilderness Road*, Indianapolis, 1947

KNOX, JOHN BALLENGER, *The People of Tennessee*, Knoxville, 1949

KRUEGER, THOMAS A., *And Promises to Keep: The Southern Conference for Human Welfare, 1938–1948*, Nashville, 1967

LACY, ERIC R., *Vanquished Volunteers: East Tennessee Sectionalism from Statehood to Secession*, Johnson City, Tenn., 1965

LAW, HARRY L., *Tennessee Geography*, Oklahoma City, 1954; reprinted, 1963

LESTER, J. C., AND D. L. WILSON, *Ku Klux Klan, Its Origin, Growth, and Disbandment*, New York, 1905

LESTER, WILLIAM S., *The Transylvania Colony*, Spencer, Ind., 1935

LEWIS, CHARLES LEE, *Philander Priestly Claxton: Crusader for Public Education*, Knoxville, 1948

LEWIS, THOMAS M. N., AND MADELINE KNEBERG, *Hiwassee Island: An Archaeological Account of Four Tennessee Indian Peoples*, Knoxville, 1946

————, *Prehistory of the Chickamauga Basin in Tennessee*, Knoxville, 1941

————, *Tribes that Slumber: Indians of the Tennessee Region*, Knoxville, 1958; reprinted, 1960, 1966

LILIENTHAL, DAVID E., *The Journals of David E. Lilienthal, I, The TVA Years*, New York, 1964

————, *TVA: Democracy on the March*, New York, 1944, 1953

LIVERMORE, THOMAS L., *Numbers and Losses in the Civil War in America: 1861–65*, Bloomington, Ind., 1901

LORD, WALTER, *A Time to Stand: The Epic of the Alamo*, New York, 1961

McCALLUM, JAMES, *A Brief Sketch of the Settlement and Early History of Giles County, Tennessee*, Pulaski, Tenn., 1928

McCLURE, WALLACE, *State Constitution-Making, with Especial Reference to Tennessee*, Nashville, 1916

McCORMAC, EUGENE I., *James K. Polk: A Political Biography*, Berkeley, 1922

McDONNOLD, B. W., *History of the Cumberland Presbyterian Church*, Nashville, 1899

McFERRIN, JOHN B., *History of Methodism in Tennessee*, 3 vols., Nashville, 1869

McFERRIN, JOHN BERRY, *Caldwell and Company: A Southern Financial Empire*, Chapel Hill, 1939

McGEE, GENTRY R., *A History of Tennessee from 1663–1924*, New York, 1924

McGUFFEY, CHARLES D., *Standard History of Chattanooga*, Knoxville, 1911

McILWAINE, SHIELDS, *Memphis Down in Dixie*, New York, 1948

McKELLAR, KENNETH D., *Tennessee Senators, as Seen by One of Their Successors*, Kingsport, Tenn., 1942

McKelvey, Blake, *American Prisons: A Study in American Social History Prior to 1915*, Chicago, 1936

McMurray, W. J., *History of the Twentieth Tennessee Regiment Volunteer Infantry, C.S.A.*, Nashville, 1904

McNeilly, James H., *Religion and Slavery*, Nashville, 1911

McRaven, Henry, *Nashville: Athens of the South*, Chapel Hill, 1949

McRaven, William H., *Life and Times of Edward Swanson*, Nashville, 1937

Malone, Henry T., *Cherokees of the Old South: A People in Transition*, Athens, Ga., 1956

Marshall, Park, *A Life of William B. Bate, Citizen, Soldier, and Statesman*, Nashville, 1908

Martin, Isaac P., *Methodism in Holston*, Knoxville, 1945

Martin, LeRoy Albert, *A History of Tennessee Wesleyan College, 1857–1957*, Athens, Tenn., 1957

Martin, Roscoe C. (ed.), *TVA: The First Twenty Years*, Knoxville and Tuscaloosa, 1956

Masterson, William H., *William Blount*, Baton Rouge, 1954

Matthews, Thomas E., *General James Robertson*, Nashville, 1934

Merritt, Frank, *Early History of Carter County, 1760–1861*, Knoxville, 1950

Michaux, F. A., *Travels to the Westward of the Alleghenys*, London, 1805

Miller, Ernest J., *The English Settlement at Rugby, Tennessee*, Knoxville, 1941

Miller, William D., *Mr. Crump of Memphis*, Baton Rouge, 1964

———, *Memphis During the Progressive Era*, Memphis, 1957

Milling, Chapman J., *Red Carolinians*, Chapel Hill, 1940

Milton, George F., *The Age of Hate: Andrew Johnson and the Radicals*, New York, 1930

Mims, Edwin, *Chancellor Kirkland of Vanderbilt*, Nashville, 1940

———, *History of Vanderbilt University*, Nashville, 1946

Montgomery, James R., *The University of Tennessee Builds for the Twentieth Century*, Knoxville, 1957

———, *The Volunteer State Forges Its University . . . 1887–1919*, Knoxville, 1966

Mooney, Chase, *Slavery in Tennessee*, Bloomington, Ind., 1957

Moore, John R. (ed.), *The Economic Impact of TVA*, Knoxville, 1967

Moore, John T., and A. P. Foster, *Tennessee: The Volunteer State*, 4 vols., Nashville, 1923

Morris, Eastin, *The Tennessee Gazetteer*, Nashville, 1834

Murphy, B. H., *The Emancipator*, Nashville, 1932

NEELY, THOMAS B., *American Methodism: Its Divisions and Unification*, New York, 1915

NEVINS, ALLAN (ed.), *Polk: The Dairy of a War President, 1845–1849*, New York, 1929

OWSLEY, FRANK L., *Plain Folk of the Old South*, Baton Rouge, 1949

PARKS, EDD WINFIELD, *Long Hunter: The Story of Big-foot Spencer*, New York, 1942

PARKS, JOSEPH H., *Felix Grundy: Champion of Democracy*, Baton Rouge, 1949

————, *General Edmund Kirby Smith, C. S. A.*, Baton Rouge, 1954

————, *General Leonidas Polk, C. S. A.*, Baton Rouge, 1962

————, *John Bell of Tennessee*, Baton Rouge, 1950

PARTON, JAMES, *Life of Andrew Jackson*, 3 vols., New York, 1860

PATTEN, CARTTER, *A Tennessee Chronicle*, Chattanooga, 1953

PATTERSON, CALEB P., *The Negro in Tennessee, 1790–1865*, Austin, 1922

PATTON, JAMES W., *Unionism and Reconstruction in Tennessee, 1860–1869*, Chapel Hill, 1934

PEAKE, O. B., *A History of the United States Indian Factory System, 1795–1822*, Denver, 1954

PERRY, JENNINGS, *Democracy Begins at Home: The Tennessee Fight on the Poll Tax*, New York, 1944

PETERS, KATE JOHNSON, *Lauderdale County: From Earliest Times*, Ripley, Tenn., 1957

PHELAN, JAMES, *History of Tennessee: The Making of a State*, Boston, 1889

PHILLIPS, ULRICH B., *American Negro Slavery*, New York, 1918

————, *A History of Transportation in the Eastern Cotton Belt to 1860*, New York, 1908

POAGE, GEORGE R., *Henry Clay of the Whig Party*, New York, 1936

PORTER, JOHN W., *Evolution—A Menace*, Nashville, 1922

POSEY, WALTER B., *The Baptist Church in the Lower Mississippi Valley, 1776–1845*, Lexington, 1957

————, *The Development of Methodism in the Old Southwest, 1783–1824*, Tuscaloosa, 1933

————, *Frontier Mission: A History of Religion West of the Southern Appalachians to 1861*, Lexington, Ky., 1966

————, *The Presbyterian Church in the Old Southwest, 1788–1838*, Richmond, 1952

POUND, MERRITT B., *Benjamin Hawkins—Indian Agent*, Athens, 1951

PRITCHETT, CHARLES HERMAN, *Tennessee Valley Authority: A Study in Public Administration*, Chapel Hill, 1943

PRUCHA, FRANCIS P., *American Indian Policy in the Formative Years*, Cambridge, 1962

PUTNAM, A. W., *History of Middle Tennessee; or, Life and Times of Gen. James Robertson*, Nashville, 1859; rpt. Knoxville, 1971

QUAIFE, MILO M. (ed.), *The Diary of James K. Polk During His Presidency, 1845–1849*, 4 vols., Chicago, 1910

QUARLES, ROBERT T., AND R. H. WHITE (eds.), *Three Pioneer Tennessee Documents: Donelson's Journal, Cumberland Compact, Minutes of the Cumberland Court*, Nashville, 1964

RAGAN, ALLEN E., *History of Tusculum College, 1794–1944*, Greeneville, Tenn., 1945

RAMSEY, J. G. M., *Annals of Tennessee to the End of the Eighteenth Century*, Charleston, 1953; reprinted, with biographical sketch by W. H. Masterson and "Annotations Relating Ramsey's *Annals* to Present-Day Knowledge" by Stanley J. Folmsbee, Knoxville, 1967

RANSMEIR, JOSEPH SIRERA, *The Tennessee Valley Authority: A Case Study in the Economics of Multiple Purpose Stream Planning*, Nashville, 1942

REMINI, ROBERT V., *Andrew Jackson*, New York, 1966

RIVES, GEORGE L., *The United States and Mexico*, New York, 1913

ROBISON, DANIEL M., *Bob Taylor and the Agrarian Revolt in Tennessee*, Chapel Hill, 1935

ROCHESTER, ANNA, *The Populist Movement in the United States*, New York, 1943

ROOSEVELT, THEODORE, *The Winning of the West*, 4 vols., New York, 1904; one-vol. abridgement, New York, 1963

ROTHROCK, MARY U. (ed.), *The French Broad-Holston Country: A History of Knox County, Tennessee*, Knoxville, 1946

RULE, WILLIAM, *Standard History of Knoxville, Tennessee*, Chicago, 1900

SCHLESINGER, ARTHUR M., JR., *The Age of Jackson*, Boston, 1945

SCROGGS, WILLIAM O., *Filibusters and Financiers: The Story of William Walker and His Associates*, New York, 1916

SELLERS, CHARLES G., JR., *James K. Polk, Continentalist, 1843–1849*, Princeton, 1966

———, *James K. Polk, Jacksonian, 1795–1843*, Princeton, 1957

SELZNICK, PHILIP, *TVA and the Grass Roots: A Study in the Sociology of Formal Organization*, Berkeley, 1949

SEYMOUR, DIGBY G., *Divided Loyalties: Fort Sanders and the Civil War in East Tennessee*, Knoxville, 1963

SHACKFORD, JAMES A., *David Crockett: The Man and the Legend*, ed. by John B. Shackford, Chapel Hill, 1956

SHAW, HELEN L., *British Administration of the Southern Indians, 1756–1783*, Lancaster, Pa., 1931

SIMS, CARL C. (ed.), *A History of Rutherford County*, Murfreesboro, Tenn., 1947

SKEYHALL, TOM (ed.), *Sergeant York: His Own Story*, New York, 1928

SKINNER, CONSTANCE L., *Pioneers of the Old Southwest*, New Haven, 1919

SMITH, JUSTIN H., *The Annexation of Texas*, New York, 1941

SOSIN, J. M., *Whitehall and the Wilderness*, Lincoln, Neb., 1961

SPAIN, RUFUS B., *At Ease in Zion: Social History of Southern Baptists*, Nashville, 1967

SPENCE, W. J. D. AND DAVID L., *A History of Hickman County, Tennessee*, Nashville, 1900

STARKEY, MARION L., *The Cherokee Nation*, New York, 1946

STATE PLANNING COMMISSION, *Civilian Defense in Tennessee, 1940–1945*, *Publication No. 157*, Nashville, 1945

STEPHENSON, NATHANIEL W., *Texas and the Mexican War*, New Haven, 1921

STRYKER, LLOYD P., *Andrew Johnson, A Study in Courage*, New York, 1929

SWANTON, JOHN R., *Early History of the Creek Indians and Their Neighbors*, Washington, D. C., 1922

———— (ed.), *Final Report of the U. S. De Soto Expedition Commission, House Ex. Doc., No. 71*, Washington, D. C., 1939

SWINT, HENRY L., *The Northern Teacher in the South, 1862–1870*, Nashville, 1941

TAYLOR, A. ELIZABETH, *The Woman Suffrage Movement in Tennessee*, New York, 1957

TAYLOR, ALF A., HUGH L., AND JAMES P., *Life and Career of Senator Robert Love Taylor*, Nashville, 1913

TAYLOR, ALRUTHEUS A., *The Negro in Tennessee, 1865–1880*, Washington, D. C., 1941

TAYLOR, O. W., *Early Tennessee Baptists, 1769–1832*, Nashville, 1957

TAYLOR, OLIVER, *Historic Sullivan*, Bristol, Tenn., 1909

TEMPLE, OLIVER P., *East Tennessee and the Civil War*, Cincinnati, 1899

————, *Notable Men of Tennessee from 1833 to 1875*, New York, 1912

TERRAL, RUFUS, *Newell Sanders: A Biography*, Kingsport, Tenn., 1935

THOMPSON, ERNEST T., *Presbyterians in the South, 1607–1861*, Richmond, 1963

THORNBOROUGH, LAURA, *The Great Smoky Mountains*, Knoxville, 1956; revised edition, 1962

THOROGOOD, JAMES E., *A Financial History of Tennessee Since 1870*, Sewanee, Tenn., 1949

TIGERT, JOHN J., *Bishop Holland Nimmons McTyeire, Ecclesiastical and Educational Architect*, Nashville, 1955

TRACY, JOSEPH, *History of the American Board of Commissioners for Foreign Missions*, Worcester, Mass., 1940

TURNER, WILLIAM BRUCE, *History of Maury County, Tennessee*, Nashville, 1955

VAN DEUSEN, GLYNDON G., *The Jacksonian Era, 1828–1848*, New York, 1959

————, *The Life of Henry Clay*, Boston, 1937

WALKER, ROBERT S., *Torchlights to the Cherokees: The Brainerd Mission*, New York, 1931

WARD, JOHN W., *Andrew Jackson, Symbol of an Age*, Oxford, 1955

WARE, CHARLES C., *Barton Warren Stone: Pathfinder of Christian Union*, St. Louis, 1932

WATKINS, SAMUEL R., *Co. Aytch: Side Show of the Big Show*, Jackson, Tenn., 1942

WEST, WILLIAM G., *Barton Warren Stone: Early American Advocate of Christian Unity*, Nashville, 1954

WESTON, FLORENCE, *The Presidential Election of 1828*, Washington, D. C., 1938

WHITAKER, ARTHUR P., *The Mississippi Question, 1795–1803*, New York, 1934

————, *The Spanish-American Frontier, 1783–1795*, Boston, 1927

WHITE, MOSES, *Early History of the University of Tennessee*, Knoxville, 1879

WHITE, ROBERT H., *Development of the Tennessee State Education Organization, 1796–1929*, Nashville, 1929

———— (ed.), *Messages of the Governors of Tennessee*, 7 vols. to date, Nashville, 1952—

————, *Tennessee: Its Growth and Progress*, Nashville, 1936

WHITE, ROBERT H., *et al.* (eds.), *Tennessee: Old and New*, 2 vols., Nashville, 1946

WILEY, BELL I., *The Life of Billy Yank: The Common Soldier of the Union*, Indianapolis, 1952

————, *The Life of Johnny Reb: The Common Soldier of the Confederacy*, Indianapolis, 1943

————, *The Plain People of the Confederacy*, Baton Rouge, 1944

WILLIAMS, SAMUEL C., *Beginnings of West Tennessee in the Land of the Chickasaws, 1541–1841*, Johnson City, Tenn., 1930

————, *The Dawn of the Tennessee Valley and Tennessee History*, Johnson City, Tenn., 1937

———— (ed.), *Early Travels in the Tennessee Country*, Johnson City, Tenn., 1928

————, *History of the Lost State of Franklin*, Johnson City, Tenn., 1924

———— (ed.), *Lieutenant Henry Timberlake's Memoirs, 1756–1765*, Johnson City, Tenn., 1927; reprinted, Marietta, Ga., 1948

————, *Phases of Southwest Territory History*, Johnson City, Tenn., 1940

————, *William Tatham: Wataugan*, Johnson City, Tenn., 1947

————, *Tennessee During the Revolutionary War*, Nashville, 1944

WINDROW, JOHN E., *John Berrien Lindsley: Educator, Physician, Social Philosopher*, Chapel Hill, 1938

WINSTON, ROBERT W., *Andrew Johnson, Plebeian and Patriot*, New York, 1938

WOODWARD, GRACE D., *The Cherokees*, Norman, 1963

WOOLDRIDGE, JOHN (ed.), *History of Nashville, Tennessee*, Nashville, 1890

PERIODICALS

ABEL, ANNIE H., "The History of Events Resulting in Indian Consolidation West of the Mississippi," American Historical Association, *Annual Report*, 1906, 2 vols., Washington, D. C., 1908

ABERNETHY, THOMAS P., "Andrew Jackson and the Rise of Southwestern Democracy," *AHR*, XXXIII, October, 1927

————, "The Early Development of Commerce and Banking in Tennessee," *MVHR*, XIV, December, 1927

————, "The Origin of the Whig Party in Tennessee," *MVHR*, XII, March, 1926

AHERN, L. H., AND R. F. HUNT, JR., "The Boatyard Store, 1814–1825," *THQ*, XIV, September, 1955

ALDEN, G. H., "The State of Franklin," *AHR*, VIII, January, 1903

ALEXANDER, THERON, JR., "The Covenanters Come to Tennessee," *ETHS Publ.*, No. 13, 1941

ALEXANDER, THOMAS B., "Kukluxism in Tennessee, 1865-1869," *THQ*, VIII, September, 1949

————, "The Presidential Campaign of 1840 in Tennessee," *THQ*, I, March, 1942

————, "Thomas A. R. Nelson as an Example of Whig Conservatism in Tennessee," *THQ*, XV, March, 1956

————, "Whiggery and Reconstruction in Tennessee," *JSH*, XVI, February, 1950

ALLEN, WARD, "Cragfont: Grandeur on the Tennessee Frontier," *THQ*, XXIII, June, 1964

ALLISON, JOHN, "The Mero District," *AHM*, I, April, 1896

ANDERSON, DOUGLAS, "The Centennial Idea and the Centennial 'Dream,'" *THM*, Ser. 2, III, January, 1935

ARMYTAGE, W. H. G., "New Light on the English Background of Thomas Hughes' Rugby Colony in Tennessee," ETHS *Publ.*, No. 21, 1949

BAILEY, KENNETH K., "The Enactment of Tennessee's Antievolution Law," *JSH*, XVI, November, 1950

BAKER, THOMAS H., "Refugee Newspaper: The Memphis *Daily Appeal*, 1862–65," *JSH*, XXIX, August, 1963

BALL, CLYDE, "The Public Career of Colonel A. S. Colyar, 1870–1877," *THQ*, XII, March, June, September, 1953

BARBEE, DAVID RANKIN, "The Line of Blood: Lincoln and the Coming of the Civil War," *THQ*, XVI, March, 1957

BARKER, EUGENE C., "Notes on the Colonization of Texas," *MVHR*, X, September, 1923

————, "President Jackson and the Texas Revolution," *AHR*, XII, July, 1907

————, "The United States and Mexico, 1835–1837," *MVHR*, I, June, 1914

BARNHART, JOHN D., "The Tennessee Constitution of 1796: A Product of the Old West," *JSH*, IX, November, 1943

BAUGHN, MILTON L., "An Early Experiment in Adult Education: The Nashville Lyceum, 1830–32," *THQ*, XI, September, 1952

BEARD, WILLIAM E., "Joseph McMinn, Tennessee's Fourth Governor," *THQ*, IV, June, 1945

————, "A Saga of the Western Waters," *THQ*, II, December, 1943

BEARSS, EDWIN C., "Cavalry Operations in the Battle of Stones River," *THQ*, XIX, March, June, 1960

————, "Unconditional Surrender: The Fall of Fort Donelson," *THQ*, XXI, March, June, 1962

BEJACH, LOIS D., "The Seven Cities Absorbed by Memphis," WTHS *Papers*, No. VIII, 1954

BELISSARY, CONSTANTINE G., "Industry and Industrial Philosophy in Tennessee, 1850–1860," ETHS *Publ.*, No. 23, 1951

————, "The Rise of Industry and the Industrial Spirit in Tennessee, 1865–1885," *JSH*, XIX, May, 1953

————, "Tennessee and Immigration, 1865–1880," *THQ*, VII, September, 1948

BELLAMY, JAMES W., "The Political Career of Landon Carter Haynes," ETHS *Publ.*, No. 28, 1956

BERTHOFF, ROWLAND T., "Southern Attitudes Toward Immigration, 1865–1914," *JSH*, XVII, August, 1951

BEST, EDWIN J., "New Providence Presbyterian Church," ETHS *Publ.*, No. 30, 1958

BIGGS, R. O., "The Cincinnati Southern Railway: A Municipal Enterprise," ETHS *Publ.*, No. 7, 1935

BOOM, AARON, "John Coffee, Citizen Soldier," *THQ*, XXII, September, 1963

BOUTWELL, LANE L., "The Oratory of Robert Love Taylor," *THQ*, IX, March, 1950

BOWMAN, ELIZABETH S., AND STANLEY J. FOLMSBEE, "The Ramsey House: Home of Francis Alexander Ramsey," *THQ*, XXIV, Fall, 1965

BRADEN, GUY B., "The Colberts and the Chickasaw Nation," *THQ*, XVII, September–December, 1958

BRATTON, MADISON, "The Unionist Junket of the Tennessee and Kentucky Legislatures in January, 1860," ETHS *Publ.*, No. 7, 1935

BROOKS, ADDIE L., "The Building of Trunk Line Railroads in West Tennessee, 1852–1861," *THQ*, I, June, 1942

————, "Early Plans for Railroads in West Tennessee, 1830–1845," *THM*, Ser. 2, III, October, 1932

BROWN, JOHN P., "Cherokee Removal, an Unnecessary Tragedy," ETHS *Publ.*, No. 11, 1939

BRUESCH, S. R., "Early Medical History of Memphis (1819–1861)," WTHS *Papers*, No. II (1948)

BURKE, JOHN E., "Andrew Jackson as Seen by Foreigners," *THQ*, X, March, 1951

BURT, JESSE C., JR., "East Tennessee, Lincoln, and Sherman," ETHS *Publ.*, Nos. 34, 35, 1962, 1963

————, "The Nashville and Chattanooga Railroad: The Era of Transition, 1854–1872," ETHS *Publ.*, No. 23, 1951

————, "Sherman's Logistics and Andrew Johnson," *THQ*, XV, September, 1956

BUTLER, FRANCELIA, "The Ruskin Commonwealth: A Unique Experiment," *THQ*, XXIII, December, 1964

CAMPBELL, CLAUDE A., "Banking and Finance in Tennessee during the Depression of 1837," ETHS *Publ.*, No. 9, 1937

CAMPBELL, JAMES B., "East Tennessee During the Federal Occupation, 1863–1865," ETHS *Publ.*, No. 19, 1947

————, "East Tennessee During the Radical Regime, 1865–1869," ETHS *Publ.*, No. 20, 1948

CAMPBELL, MARY R., "The Significance of the Unionist Victory in the Election of February 9, 1861, in Tennessee," ETHS *Publ.*, No. 14, 1942

————, "Tennessee and the Union, 1847–1861," ETHS *Publ.*, No. 10, 1938

————, "Tennessee's Congressional Delegation in the Sectional Crisis of 1859–1860," *THQ*, XIX, December, 1960

CANNON, WALTER F., "Four Interpretations of the History of the State of Franklin," ETHS *Publ.*, No. 22, 1950

CAPERS, GERALD M., "Yellow Fever in Memphis in the 1870's," *MVHR*, XXIV, March, 1938

CASKEY, W. M., "First Administration of Governor Andrew Johnson," ETHS *Publ.*, No. 1, 1929

————, "The Second Administration of Governor Andrew Johnson," ETHS *Publ.*, No. 2, 1930

CASSELL, ROBERT, "Newton Cannon and the Constitutional Convention of 1834," *THQ*, XV, September, 1956

————, "Newton Cannon and State Politics, 1835–1839," *THQ*, XV, December, 1956

CATE, WIRT A., "Timothy Demonbreun," *THQ*, XVI, September, 1957

CHAMBERS, WILLIAM N., "Thwarted Warrior: The Last Years of Thomas Hart Benton in Tennessee, 1812–1815," ETHS *Publ.*, No. 22, 1950

CLARK, THOMAS D., "The Building of the Memphis and Charleston Railroad," ETHS *Publ.*, No. 8, 1936

————, "The Development of the Nashville and Chattanooga Railroad," *THM*, Ser. 2, III, April, 1935

CLIFTON, FRANCES, "John Overton as Andrew Jackson's Friend," *THQ*, XI, March, 1952

COLES, HARRY L., JR., "The Federal Food Administration of Tennessee and Its Records in the National Archives, 1917–1919," *THQ*, IV, March, 1945

COLLINS, HERBERT, "The Southern Industrial Gospel before 1860," *JSH*, XII, August, 1946

CONNELLY, THOMAS L., "The Vanderbilt Agrarians: Time and Place in Southern Tradition," *THQ*, XXII, March, 1963

CORBITT, D. C. AND ROBERTA (trs. and eds.), "Papers from the Spanish Archives Relating to Tennessee and the Old Southwest, 1783–1800," ETHS *Publ.*, Nos. 9–40, 1937–68

CORLEW, ROBERT E., "Some Aspects of Slavery in Dickson County, Tennessee," *THQ*, X, September, December, 1951

COULTER, E. MERTON, "The Georgia-Tennessee Boundary Line," *GHQ*, XXXV, December, 1951

———, "Parson Brownlow's Tour of the North During the Civil War," ETHS *Publ.*, No. 7, 1935

———, "The Granville District," *James Sprunt Historical Papers*, III, Chapel Hill, 1913

CRABB, ALFRED L., "The Twilight of the Nashville Gods," *THQ*, XV, December, 1956

CRANE, VERNON W., "The Tennessee River as the Road to Carolina," *MVHR*, III, March, 1916

CREWS, E. KATHERINE, "Early Musical Activities in Knoxville, Tennessee, 1791–1861," ETHS *Publ.*, No. 32, 1960

———, "The Golden Age of Music in Knoxville, Tennessee, 1891–1910," ETHS *Publ.*, No. 37, 1966

———, "Musical Activities in Knoxville, Tennessee, 1861–1891," ETHS *Publ.*, No. 34, 1962

CROWE, JESSE C., "The Origin and Development of Tennessee's Prison Problem, 1831–1871," *THQ*, XV, June, 1956

CROWNOVER, SIMS, "The Battle of Franklin," *THQ*, XIV, December, 1955

DAVENPORT, F. GARVIN, "Cultural Life in Nashville on the Eve of the Civil War," *JSH*, III, August, 1937

———, "Culture Versus Frontier in Tennessee, 1825–1850," *JSH*, V, February, 1939

DEFRIECE, PAULINE M., AND FRANK B. WILLIAMS, JR., "Rocky Mount: The Cobb-Massengill Home: First Capitol of the Territory of the United States South of the River Ohio," *THQ*, XXV, Summer, 1966

DESCHAMPS, MARGARET B., "Early Days in the Cumberland Country," *THQ*, VI, September, 1947

DEVORSEY, LOUIS, JR., "The Virginia-Cherokee Boundary of 1771," ETHS *Publ.*, No. 33, 1961

DOAK, H. M., "The Development of Education in Tennessee," *AHM*, VIII, January, 1903

DOSTER, JAMES F., "The Chattanooga Rolling Mill: An Industrial By-product of the Civil War," ETHS *Publ.*, No. 36, 1964

DOWNES, RANDOLPH C., "Cherokee-American Relations in the Upper Tennessee Valley," 1776–1781," ETHS *Publ.*, No. 8, 1936

———, "Indian Affairs in the Southwest Territory," *THM*, Ser. 2, III, January, 1937

EATON, CLEMENT, "Southern Senators and the Right of Instruction, 1789–1860," *JSH*, XVIII, August, 1952

EDWALL, HARRY R., "The Golden Era of Minstrelsy in Memphis: A Reconstruction," WTHS *Papers*, No. IX, 1955

———, "Some Famous Musicians on the Memphis Concert Stage Prior to 1860," WTHS *Papers*, No. V, 1951

ELLIS, JOHN H., "Memphis' Sanitary Revolution, 1880–1890," *THQ*, XXIII, March, 1964

EMERSON, O. B., "Frances Wright and Her Nashoba Experiment," *THQ*, VI, December, 1947

ENGLAND, J. MERTON, "The Free Negro in Ante-Bellum Tennessee," *JSH*, IX, February, 1943

EUBANKS, DAVID L., "J. G. M. Ramsey as a Bond Agent: Selections From the Ramsey Papers," ETHS *Publ.*, No. 36, 1964

EWING, CORTEZ A. M., "Early Tennessee Impeachments," *THQ*, XVI, December, 1957

EWING, FRANCES H., "The Senatorial Career of the Honorable Felix Grundy," *THM*, Ser. 2, II, July, 1932

FAKES, TURNER J., JR., "Memphis and the Mexican War," WTHS *Papers*, No. II, 1948

FEISTMAN, EUGENE G., "Radical Disfranchisement and the Restoration of Tennessee, 1854–1866," *THQ*, XII, June, 1953

FELSENTHAL, EDWARD, "Kenneth Douglas McKellar: The 'Rich Uncle' of the TVA," WTHS *Papers*, No. XX, 1966

FINK, HAROLD S., "The East Tennessee Campaign and the Battle of Knoxville," ETHS *Publ.*, No. 29, 1957

FINK, PAUL M., "The Bumpass Cove Mines and Embreeville," ETHS *Publ.*, No. 16, 1944

———, "Jacob Brown of Nolichucky," *THQ*, XXI, September, 1962

———, "Methodism in Jonesboro, Tennessee," ETHS *Publ.*, No. 21, 1949

———, "Russell Bean, Tennessee's First Native Son," ETHS *Publ.*, No. 37, 1965

———, "Smoky Mountains History as Told in Place Names," ETHS *Publ.*, No. 6, 1934

———, "Some Phases of the History of the State of Franklin," *THQ*, XVI, September, 1957

FOLMSBEE, STANLEY J., "The Beginnings of the Railroad Movement in East Tennessee," ETHS *Publ.*, No. 5, 1933

———, "Blount College and East Tennessee College, 1794–1840: The First Predecessors of the University of Tennessee," ETHS *Publ.*, No. 17, 1945; reprinted in the University of Tennessee *Record*, Vol. 49, No. 1, Knoxville, 1946

————, "East Tennessee University: Pre-War Years, 1840–1861," ETHS *Publ.*, No. 22, 1950

————, "The Journal of John Cotten, the 'Reluctant Pioneer'—Evidences of its Unreliability," *THQ*, XXVIII, Spring, 1969

————, "The Origin of the First 'Jim Crow' Law," *JSH*, XV, May, 1949

————, "The Origins of the Nashville and Chattanooga Railroad," ETHS *Publ.*, No. 6, 1934

————, "The Turnpike Phase of Tennessee's Internal Improvement System of 1836–1838," *JSH*, III, November, 1937

FOLMSBEE, STANLEY J., AND ANNA GRACE CATRON, "David Crockett: Congressman," ETHS *Publ.*, No. 29, 1957

————, "David Crockett in Texas," ETHS *Publ.*, No. 30, 1958

————, "The Early Career of David Crockett," ETHS *Publ.*, No. 28, 1956

FOLMSBEE, STANLEY J., AND SUSAN HILL DILLON, "The Blount Mansion: Tennessee's Territorial Capitol," *THQ*, XXII, June, 1963

FOLMSBEE, STANLEY J., AND MADELINE L. KNEBERG (eds.) AND GERALD W. WADE (trans.), "Journals of the Juan Pardo Expeditions, 1566–1567," ETHS *Publ.*, No. 37, 1965

FRANK, JOHN G., "Adolphus Heiman: Architect and Soldier," *THQ*, V, March, 1946

FRANKLIN, JOHN H., "The Southern Expansionists of 1846," *JSH*, XXV, August, 1959

FRANKLIN, W. NEIL, "Virginia and the Cherokee Indian Trade," ETHS *Publ.*, No. 4, 1932; No. 5, 1933

GALPIN, W. FREEMAN (ed.), "Letters of an East Tennessee Abolitionist," ETHS *Publ.*, No. 3, 1931

GANYARD, ROBERT L., "Threat from the West: North Carolina and the Cherokee," *NCHR*, XLV, January, 1968

GARRETT, W. R., "The Genesis of the Peabody College for Teachers," *AHM*, VIII, January, 1903

————, "The Northern Boundary of Tennessee," *AHM*, VI, January, 1901

GASS, EDMUND C., "The Constitutional Opinions of Justice John Catron," ETHS *Publ.*, No. 8, 1936

GILLEY, BILLY H., "Tennessee Opinion of the Mexican War as Reflected in the State Press," ETHS *Publ.*, No. 26, 1954

GOODPASTURE, ALBERT V., "Dr. James White: Pioneer, Politician, Lawyer," *THM*, I, December, 1915

————, "Genesis of the Jackson-Sevier Feud," *AHM*, V, April, 1900

————, "John Bell's Political Revolt, and his Vauxhall Garden Speech," *THM*, II, December, 1916

———, "The Watauga Association," *AHM*, III, April, 1898

GOVAN, GILBERT E., "Some Sidelights on the History of Chattanooga," *THQ*, VI, June, 1947

GOVAN, GILBERT E., AND JAMES W. LIVINGOOD, "Chattanooga Under Military Occupation, 1863–1865," *JSH*, XVII, February, 1951

GRAEBNER, NORMAN A., "James K. Polk's Wartime Expansionist Policy," ETHS *Publ.*, No. 23, 1951

GRAF, LEROY P., "Andrew Johnson and the Coming of the War," *THQ*, XIX, September, 1960

——— (ed.), " 'Parson' Brownlow's Fears: A Letter About the Dangerous, Desperate Democrats," ETHS *Publ.*, No. 25, 1953

GRAHAM, HUGH D., "Desegregation in Nashville: The Dynamics of Compliance," *THQ*, XXV, Summer, 1966

GRANT, CLEMENT L., "Cave Johnson and the Presidential Campaign of 1844," ETHS *Publ.*, No. 25, 1953

———, "The Politics Behind a Presidential Nomination as Shown in Letters from Cave Johnson to James K. Polk," *THQ*, XII, June, 1953

———, "The Public Career of Cave Johnson," *THQ*, X, September, 1951

GRANTHAM, DEWEY W., "The South and Reconstruction of American Politics," *JAH*, LIII, September, 1966

GRESHAM, LUNIA PAUL, "Hugh Lawson White as a Tennessee Politician and Banker, 1807–1827," ETHS *Publ.*, No. 18, 1946

———, "Hugh Lawson White: Frontiersman, Lawyer, and Judge," ETHS *Publ.*, No. 19, 1947

———, "The Public Career of Hugh Lawson White," *THQ*, III, December, 1944

HALL, HOWARD, "Franklin County in the Secession Crisis," *THQ*, XVII, March, 1958

HAMER, MARGUERITE B., "The Correspondence of Thomas Hughes Concerning His Rugby," *NCHR*, XXI, July, 1944

———, "The Presidential Campaign of 1860 in Tennessee," ETHS *Publ.*, No. 3, 1931

———, "Thomas Hughes and His American Rugby," *NCHR*, V, October, 1928

HAMER, PHILIP M., "Anglo-French Rivalry in the Cherokee Country, 1754–1757," *NCHR*, July, 1925

———, "The British in Canada and the Southern Indians," ETHS *Publ.*, No. 2, 1930

———, "Correspondence of Henry Stuart and Alexander Cameron with the Wataugans," *MVHR*, XVII, December, 1930

————, "Fort Loudoun in the Cherokee War, 1758–1761," *NCHR*, October, 1925

————, "John Stuart's Indian Policy During the Early Months of the American Revolution," *MVHR*, XVII, December, 1930

————, "The Wataugans and the Cherokee Indians in 1776," ETHS *Publ.*, No. 3, 1931

HARLAN, LOUIS R., "Public Career of William Berkeley Lewis," *THQ*, VII, March, June, 1948

HARRELL, DAVID E., "The Disciples of Christ and Social Force in Tennessee, 1865–1900," ETHS *Publ.*, No. 38, 1966

————, "Disciples of Christ Pacifism in Nineteenth-Century Tennessee," *THQ*, XXI, September, 1962

————, "James Winchester: Patriot," *THQ*, XVII, December, 1958

HASKINS, RALPH W., "Andrew Johnson and the Preservation of the Union," ETHS *Publ.*, No. 33, 1961

————, "Internecine Strife in Tennessee: Andrew Johnson Versus Parson Brownlow," *THQ*, XXIV, Winter, 1965

HATFIELD, JOSEPH T., "William C. C. Claiborne, Congress and Republicanism," *THQ*, XXIV, Summer, 1965

HAUNTON, RICHARD H., "Education and Democracy: The Views of Philip Lindsley," *THQ*, XXI, June, 1962

HAWKINS, BRETT W., "Public Opinion and Metropolitan Reorganization in Nashville," *JOP*, XXVIII, May, 1966

HAYS, WILLARD, "Andrew Johnson's Reputation," ETHS *Publ.*, No. 31, 1959; No. 32, 1960

HENDERSON, ARCHIBALD, "Richard Henderson: The Authorship of the Cumberland Compact and the Founding of Nashville," *THM*, II, September, 1916

————, "The Spanish Conspiracy in Tennessee," *THM*, III, December, 1917

————, "The Treaty of the Long Island of the Holston, 1777," *NCHR*, VIII, January, 1931

HENRY, H. M., "The Slave Laws of Tennessee," *THM*, II, September, 1916

HENRY, J. MILTON, "The Revolution in Tennessee, February, 1861 to June, 1861," *THQ*, XVIII, June, 1959

HENRY, ROBERT SELPH, "Tennesseans and Territory," *THQ*, XII, September, 1953

HERRON, W. W., "A History of Lambuth College," WTHS *Papers*, No. X, 1956

HESSELTINE, WILLIAM B., "Methodism and Reconstruction in East Tennessee," ETHS *Publ.*, No. 3, 1931

————, "Some New Aspects of the Pro-Slavery Argument," *JNH*, XXI, January, 1936

————, "Tennessee's Invitation to Carpet-Baggers," ETHS *Publ.*, No. 4, 1932

HIGHSAW, MARY W., "A History of Zion Community in Maury County, 1806–1860," *THQ*, V, 1946

HOFFMAN, W. S., "Andrew Jackson, State Rightist: The Case of the Georgia Indians," *THQ*, XI, December, 1952

HOLLAND, JAMES W., "The Building of the East Tennessee and Virginia Railroad," ETHS *Publ.*, No. 4, 1932

————, "The East Tennessee and Georgia Railroad, 1836–1860," ETHS *Publ.*, No. 3, 1931

HOLMES, JACK D. L., "The Ebb-Tide of Spanish Military Power on the Mississippi: Fort San Fernando de las Barrancas, 1795–1798," ETHS *Publ.*, No. 36, 1964

————, "Fort Ferdinand on the Bluffs: Life on the Spanish-American Frontier, 1795–1797," WTHS *Papers*, No. XIII, 1959

————, "Spanish-American Rivalry Over the Chickasaw Bluffs, 1780–1795," ETHS *Publ.*, No. 34, 1962

————, "The Underlying Causes of the Memphis Race Riot of 1866," *THQ*, XVII, September, 1958

HOLT, ALBERT C., "The Economic and Social Beginnings of Tennessee," *THM*, VII–VIII, 1921–24

HORN, STANLEY F., "Isham G. Harris in the Pre-War Years," *THQ*, XIX, September, 1960

————, "Nashville During the Civil War," *THQ*, IV, March, 1945

HOUSE, ALBERT V., JR., "President Hayes' Selection of David M. Key for Postmaster General," *JSH*, IV, February, 1938

HOUSTON, REV. SAMUEL, "The Provisional Constitution of the State of Franklin," *AHM*, I, January, 1896

HOWELL, ELMO, "William Faulkner and Tennessee," *THQ*, XXI, September, 1962

HOWELL, ISABEL, "John Armfield, Slave-trader," *THQ*, II, March, 1943

HOWELL, SARAH M., "The Editorials of Arthur S. Colyar, Nashville Prophet of the New South," *THQ*, XXVII, Fall, 1968

HUMPHREYS, CECIL C., "The Formation of Reelfoot Lake and Consequent Land and Social Problems," WTHS *Papers*, No. XIV, 1960

HUNT, RAYMOND F., JR., "The Pactolus Ironworks," *THQ*, XXV, Summer, 1966

HUTSON, A. C., JR., "The Coal Miners' Insurrections of 1891 in Anderson County, Tennessee," ETHS *Publ.*, No. 7, 1935

————, "The Overthrow of the Convict Lease System in Tennessee," ETHS *Publ.*, No. 8, 1936

IMES, WILLIAM L., "Legal Status of Free Negroes and Slaves in Tennessee," *JNH,* IV, July, 1919

JOHNSON, RAYBURN W., "Population Trends in Tennessee from 1940 to 1950," *THQ,* XI, September, 1952

JONES, THOMAS B., "The Public Lands of Tennessee," *THQ,* XXVII, Spring, 1968

JORDAN, WEYMOUTH T., "The Freedmen's Bureau in Tennessee," ETHS *Publ.*, No. 11, 1939

KARSCH, ROBERT F., "Tennessee's Interest in the Texas Revolution," *THM,* Ser. 2, III, January, 1937

KEGEL, CHARLES H. (ed.), "Earl Miller's Recollections of the Ruskin Cooperative Association," *THQ,* XVII, March, 1958

KELLEY, PAUL, "Fort Loudoun: The After Years, 1760–1960," *THQ,* XX, December, 1961

KELSAY, ISABEL T., "The Presidential Campaign of 1828," ETHS *Publ.*, No. 5, 1933

KIGER, JOSEPH C., "Social Thought as Voiced in Rural Middle Tennessee Newspapers, 1878–1898," *THQ,* IX, June, 1950

KINCAID, ROBERT L., "The Wilderness Road in Tennessee," ETHS *Publ.*, No. 20, 1948

KITCHENS, ALLEN H., "Political Upheavals in Tennessee: Boss Crump and the Senatorial Election of 1948," WTHS *Papers,* No. XVI, 1962

KLUTTS, WILLIAM A., "Fort Prud'homme, Its Location," WTHS *Papers,* No. IV, 1950

KOLLMORGEN, WALTER M., "Observations on Cultural Islands in Terms of Tennessee Agriculture," ETHS *Publ.*, No. 16, 1944

LACY, ERIC R., "The Persistent State of Franklin," *THQ,* XXIII, December, 1964

————, "Tennessee Teetotalism: Social Forces and the Politics of Progressivism," *THQ,* XXIV, Fall, 1965

LAMBERT, ROBERT S., "The Democratic National Convention of 1844," *THQ,* XIV, March, 1955

LANDIS, EDWARD B., "The Influence of Tennesseans in the Formation of Illinois," Illinois Historical Society's *Transactions,* 1933, Springfield, 1933

LAUGHLIN, S. H., "Diaries of S. H. Laughlin, of Tennessee, 1840, 1843," *THM,* II, March, 1916

LEA, LUKE, "The Attempt to Capture the Kaiser," ed. by William T. Alderson, *THQ,* XX, September, 1961

LEAB, GRACE, "Tennessee Temperance Activities, 1870–1899," ETHS *Publ.*, No. 21, 1949

LEWIS, J. EUGENE, "The Tennessee Gubernatorial Campaign and Election of 1894," *THQ*, XII, June, September, December, 1954

LINK, ARTHUR S., "Democratic Politics and the Presidential Campaign of 1912 in Tennessee," ETHS *Publ.*, No. 18, 1946

LIVINGOOD, JAMES W., "Chattanooga: A Rail Junction of the Old South," *THQ*, VI, September, 1947

———, "The Chattanooga *Rebel*," ETHS *Publ.*, No. 39, 1967

———, "Chattanooga, Tennessee: Its Economic History in the Years Immediately Following Appomattox," ETHS *Publ.*, No. 15, 1943

LONGLEY, LAWRENCE D., "The Effectiveness of Internal Groups in a State Legislature," *THQ*, XXVI, Fall, 1967

LOUIS, JAMES P., "Sue Shelton White and the Woman Suffrage Movement," *THQ*, XXII, June, 1963

LOWE, GABRIEL C., JR., "John H. Eaton, Jackson's Campaign Manager," *THQ*, XI, June, 1952

LUTTRELL, LAURA E., "One Hundred Years of a Female Academy: The Knoxville Female Academy, 1811–1846 [and] The East Tennessee Female Institute, 1846–1911," ETHS *Publ.*, No. 17, 1945

McCLARY, BEN H., "Nancy Ward," *THQ*, XXI, December, 1962

McCORD, FRANKLYN, "J. E. Bailey: A Gentleman of Clarksville," *THQ*, XXIII, September, 1964

McCORMICK, RICHARD P., "New Perspectives on Jacksonian Politics," *AHR*, LXV, January, 1960

McCOWN, MARY H. (ed.), "The 'J. Hartsell Memora': The Journal of a Tennessee Captain in the War of 1812," ETHS *Publ.*, No. 11, 1939; No. 12, 1940

——— (ed.), "A King's Mountain Diary," ETHS *Publ.*, No. 14, 1942

McGAW, ROBERT A., AND RICHARD W. WEESNER, "Tennessee Antiquities Re-Exhumed: The New Exhibit of the Thruston Collection at Vanderbilt," *THQ*, XXIV, Summer, 1965

McGILL, J. T., "Franklin and Frankland: Names and Boundaries," *THM*, VIII, January, 1925

McNEILL, SARAH BROWN, "Andrew Jackson and Texas Affairs, 1819–1836," ETHS *Publ.*, No. 28, 1956

McWHINEY, GRADY, "Braxton Bragg at Shiloh," *THQ*, XXI, March, 1962

MAIDEN, LEOTA D., "Colonel John Williams," ETHS *Publ.*, No. 30, 1958

MALONE, HENRY T., "Return Jonathan Meigs: Indian Agent, Extraordinary," ETHS *Publ.*, No. 28, 1956

MARTIN, ASA E., "The Anti-Slavery Societies of Tennessee," *THM*, I, December, 1915

———, "Pioneer Anti-Slavery Press," *MVHR*, II, March 1916

MASTERSON, WILLIAM H., "William Blount and the Establishment of the Southwest Territory," ETHS *Publ.*, No. 23, 1951

MATLOCK, J. W. L. (ed.), "The Battle of the Bluffs, From the Journal of John Cotten," *THQ*, XVIII, September, 1959

MEHRLING, JOHN C., "The Memphis and Charleston Railroad," WTHS *Papers*, No. XIX, 1965

———, "The Memphis and Ohio Railroad," WTHS *Papers*, No. XXII, 1968

MILES, GUY, "The Tennessee Antiquarian Society and the West," ETHS *Publ.*, No. 18, 1946

MILLER, WILLIAM D., "The Browning-Crump Battle: The Crump Side," ETHS *Publ.*, No. 37, 1965

———, "J. J. Williams and the Memphis Movement," WTHS *Papers*, V, 1951

———, "The Progressive Movement in Memphis," *THQ*, XV, March, 1956

MITCHELL, ENOCH L. (ed.), "Letters of a Confederate Surgeon of the Army of Tennessee to His Wife," *THQ*, V, March, 1946

———, "Robert Whyte, Agrarian, Lawyer, Jurist," *THQ*, X, March, 1951

MOFFITT, JAMES W., "Early Baptist Missionary Work among the Cherokees," ETHS *Publ.*, No. 12, 1940

MONTGOMERY, JAMES R., "The Nomenclature of the Upper Tennessee River," ETHS *Publ.*, No. 28, 1956

———, "The Summer School of the South," *THQ*, XXII, December, 1963

MOONEY, CHASE C., "The Political Career of Adam Huntsman," *THQ*, X, June, 1951

———, "The Question of Slavery and the Free Negro in the Tennessee Constitutional Convention of 1834," *JSH*, XII, November, 1946

———, "Some Institutional and Statistical Aspects of Slavery in Tennessee," *THQ*, I, September, 1942

MOONEY, JAMES, "Myths of the Cherokee," U. S. Bureau of American Ethnology, *19th Annual Report*, Pt. I, Washington, D. C., 1900

MOORE, MRS. JOHN TROTWOOD, "The First Century of Library History in Tennessee, 1813–1913," ETHS *Publ.*, No. 16, 1944

MOORE, POWELL, "James K. Polk and the 'Immortal Thirteen,'" ETHS *Publ.*, No. 11, 1939

————, "James K. Polk and Tennessee Politics, 1839–1841," ETHS *Publ.*, No. 9, 1937

————, "James K. Polk: Tennessee Politician," *JSH*, XVII, November, 1951

————, "The Political Background of the Revolt against Jackson in Tennessee," ETHS *Publ.*, No. 4, 1932

————, "The Revolt against Jackson in Tennessee," *JSH*, II, August, 1936

NASH, CHARLES H., "The Human Continuum of Shelby County, Tennessee," WTHS *Papers*, No. XIV, 1960

NASH, CHARLES H., AND RODNEY GATES, JR., "Chucalissa Indian Town," *THQ*, No. XXI, June, 1962

NEWBERRY, FARRAR, "The Nashville Convention and Southern Sentiment of 1850," *The South Atlantic Quarterly*, XI, July, 1912

O'DONNELL, JAMES H., III, "Taylor Thistle: A Student at the Nashville Institute, 1871–1880," *THQ*, Winter, 1967

————, "The Virginia Expedition Against the Overhill Cherokee, 1776," ETHS *Publ.*, No. 39, 1967

OSBORNE, RAY G., "Political Career of James Chamberlain Jones, 1840–1857," *THQ*, VII, September, 1948

OWSLEY, FRANK L., "The Pattern of Migration and Settlement on the Southern Frontier," *JSH*, XI, May, 1945

OWSLEY, FRANK L. AND HARRIET C., "The Economic Basis of Society in the Late Ante-Bellum South," *JSH*, VI, February, 1940

————, "The Economic Structure of Rural Tennessee, 1850–1860," *JSH*, VIII, May, 1942

OWSLEY, HARRIET C., "Peace and the Presidential Election of 1864," *THQ*, XVIII, March, 1959

PARKS, EDD W., "Dreamer's Vision: Frances Wright at Nashoba, 1825–1830," *THM*, Ser. 2, II, January, 1932

————, "Sawney Webb: Tennessee School Master," *NCHR*, XII, July, 1935

————, "Zollicoffer: Southern Whig," *THQ*, XI, December, 1952

PARKS, JOSEPH H., "A Confederate Trade Center Under Federal Occupation: Memphis 1862–1865," *JSH*, VII, 1941

————, "John Bell and the Compromise of 1850," *JSH*, IX, August, 1943

————, "John Bell and Secession," ETHS *Publ.*, No. 16, 1944

———— (ed.), "Letter Describes Andrew Jackson's Last Hours," *THQ*, VI, June, 1947

————, "Memphis Under Military Rule, 1862 to 1865," ETHS *Publ.*, No. 14, 1942

———, "The Tennessee Whigs and the Kansas-Nebraska Bill," *JSH*, X, August, 1944

——— (ed.), "Some Tennessee Letters, 1849–1864," *THQ*, IV, September, 1945

PARKS, NORMAN L., "The Career of John Bell as a Congressman from Tennessee," *THQ*, I, September, 1942

———, "Tennessee Politics Since Kefauver and Reece: A 'Generalist' View," *JOP*, XXVIII, February, 1966

PATTON, J. W., "Progress of Emancipation in Tennessee," *JNH*, XVII, January, 1932

———, "Tennessee's Attitude Toward the Impeachment and Trial of Andrew Johnson," ETHS *Publ.*, No. 9, 1931

PEASE, WILLIAM H. AND JANE H., "A New View of Nashoba," *THQ*, XIX, June, 1960

PENNINGTON, EDGAR L., "The Battle at Sewanee," *THQ*, IX, September, 1959

PHELPS, DAWSON A., "The Chickasaw, the English, and the French, 1699–1744," *THQ*, XVI, June, 1957

———, "Genesis of the Natchez Trace Parkway," WTHS *Papers*, No. XIX, 1965

———, "The Natchez Trace in Tennessee History," *THQ*, XIII, September, 1954

PHILLIPS, PAUL DAVID, "White Reaction to the Freedmen's Bureau in Tennessee," *THQ*, XXV, Spring, 1966

POSEY, WALTER B. (ed.), "Bishop Asbury Visits Tennessee, 1788–1815: Extracts from His Journal," *THQ*, XV, September, 1956

PRICE, PRENTISS (ed.), "The Provisional Constitution of Frankland," *AHM*, I, January, 1896

PUTNAM, A. W. (ed.), "The Correspondence of Gen. James Robertson," *AHM*, I–IV, 1896–1900

QUALLS, J. WINFIELD, "The Beginnings and Early History of the Lemoyne School at Memphis," WTHS *Papers*, No. VII, 1953

———, "Fusion Victory and the Tennessee Senatorship, 1910–1911," WTHS *Papers*, No. XV, 1961

QUEENER, VERTON M., "Brownlow as an Editor," ETHS *Publ.*, No. 4, 1932

———, "A Decade of East Tennessee Republicanism, 1867–1876," ETHS *Publ.*, No. 14, 1942

———, "The East Tennessee Republican Party, 1900–1914," ETHS *Publ.*, No. 22, 1950

———, "The East Tennessee Republicans as a Minority Party, 1870–1896," ETHS *Publ.*, No. 15, 1943

————, "The East Tennessee Republicans in State and Nation, 1870–1900," *THQ*, II, June, 1943

————, "East Tennessee Sentiment and the Secession Movement, November, 1860–June, 1861," ETHS *Publ.*, No. 20, 1948

————, "Gideon Blackburn," ETHS *Publ.*, No. 6, 1934

————, "Origin of the Republican Party in East Tennessee," ETHS *Publ.*, No. 13, 1941

RANCK, JAMES S., "Andrew Jackson and the Burr Conspiracy," *THM*, Ser. 2, I, October, 1930

RANKIN, ROBERT S., "The Oldest College West of the Alleghenies," ETHS *Publ.*, No. 1, 1929

RISJORD, NORMAN K., "1812: Conservatives, War Hawks and the National Honor," *William and Mary Quarterly*, Ser. 3, XVII, 1961

RITTER, CHARLES C., " 'The Drama in our Midst,' The Early History of the Theater in Memphis," WTHS *Papers*, No. XI, 1957

ROBERTSON, JAMES I., JR., "Frolics, Fights, and Firewater in Frontier Tennessee," *THQ*, XVII, June, 1958

ROBISON, DANIEL M., "The Political Background of Tennessee's War of the Roses," ETHS *Publ.*, No. 5, 1933

————, "Tennessee Politics and the Agrarian Revolt in Tennessee, 1886–1896," *MVHR*, XX, December, 1933

ROBLYER, LESLIE F., "The Fight for Local Prohibition in Knoxville, Tennessee, 1907," ETHS *Publ.*, No. 26, 1954

ROGERS, WILLIAM F., "Life in East Tennessee Near the End of the Eighteenth Century," ETHS *Publ.*, No. 1, 1929

ROPER, JAMES E., "Isaac Rawlings, Frontier Merchant," *THQ*, XX, September, 1961

————, "Marcus Winchester and the Earliest Years of Memphis," *THQ*, XXI, December, 1962

ROSE, KENNETH, "Jenny Lind, Diva," *THQ*, VIII, March, 1949

————, "A Nashville Musical Decade, 1830–1840," *THQ*, II, September, 1943

ROTHROCK, MARY U., "Carolina Traders among the Overhill Cherokees, 1690–1760," ETHS *Publ.*, No. 1, 1929

ROUSE, FRANKLIN O., "The Historical Background of Tennessee Administration Reorganization Act of 1923," ETHS *Publ.*, No. 8, 1936

ROYCE, CHARLES C., "The Cherokee Nation," U. S. Bureau of American Ethnology, *5th Annual Report*, Washington, D. C., 1887

————, "Indian Land Cessions in the United States," U. S. Bureau of American Ethnology, *18th Annual Report*, Washington, D. C., 1899

RUTLEDGE, ROSA DYER, "Union University through the Century, 1834–1950," WTHS *Papers*, No. IV, 1950

SCROGGS, WILLIAM O. (ed.), "With Walker in Nicaragua: The Reminiscences of Elleanore (Callaghan) Raterman," THM, I, December, 1915

SELLERS, CHARLES G., JR., "Andrew Jackson Versus the Historians," MVHR, XLIV, March, 1958

———, "Banking and Politics in Jackson's Tennessee, 1817–1827," MVHR, XLI, June, 1954

———, "Jackson Men with Feet of Clay," AHR, LXII, April, 1957

———, "James K. Polk's Political Apprenticeship," ETHS *Publ.*, No. 25, 1953

———, "Jim Polk Goes to Chapel Hill," NCHR, XXIX, April, 1952

———, "Who Were the Southern Whigs?" AHR, LIX, January, 1954

SHARP, J. A., "The Downfall of the Radicals in Tennessee," ETHS *Publ.*, No. 5, 1933

———, "The Entrance of the Farmers' Alliance into Tennessee Politics," ETHS *Publ.*, No. 9, 1937

———, "The Farmers' Alliance and the People's Party in Tennessee," ETHS *Publ.*, No. 10, 1938

SHEELER, J. REUBEN, "The Development of Unionism in East Tennessee, 1860–1866," JNH, XXIX, 1944

SILVER, JAMES W., "Edmund Pendleton Gaines: Railroad Propagandist," ETHS *Publ.*, No. 9, 1937

SIOUSSAT, ST. GEORGE L., "Andrew Johnson and the Early Phases of the Homestead Bill," MVHR, II, December, 1918

——— (ed.), "The Journal of Daniel Smith," THM, I, March, 1915

——— (ed.), "Letters of James K. Polk to Cave Johnson, 1838–1848," THM, I, September, 1915

——— (ed.), "Letters of John Bell to William B. Campbell, 1839–1857," THM, III, September, 1917

———, "Memphis as a Gateway to the West," THM, Ser. 1, III, March, June, 1917

——— (ed.), "Mexican War Letters of Col. William Bowen Campbell, of Tennessee, Written to Governor David Campbell, of Virginia, 1846–1847," THM, I, September, 1915

———, "Tennessee and the Removal of the Cherokee," *Sewanee Review*, XVI, July, 1908

———, "Tennessee, The Compromise of 1850, and the Nashville Convention," MVHR, II, December, 1915; reprinted in THM, IV, December, 1918

SLOAN, GRACE, "Tennessee: Social and Economic Laboratory," *Sewanee Review*, XLVI, January–March, April–June, July–September, 1938

SMITH, CULVER H., "Propaganda Technique in the Jackson Campaign of 1828," ETHS *Publ.*, No. 6, 1934

SMITH, SAMUEL B., "Joseph Buckner Killebrew and the New South Movement in Tennessee," ETHS *Publ.*, No. 37, 1965

SOMIT, ALBERT, "Andrew Jackson: Legend and Reality," THQ, VII, December, 1948

SPAIN, RUFUS B., "R. B. C. Howell: Nashville Baptist Leader in the Civil War Period," THQ, XIV, December, 1955

———, "R. B. C. Howell: Progressive Baptist Minister of the Old Southwest," THQ, XIV, September, 1955

———, "R. B. C. Howell: Virginia Baptist Tradition Comes to the Old Southwest," THQ, XIV, June, 1955

STAGG, BRIAN, "Tennessee's Rugby Colony," THQ, XVII, Fall, 1968

STANTON, WILLIAM M., "The Irish of Memphis," WTHS *Papers*, VI, 1952

STENBERG, R. R., "Jackson's Rhea 'Letter' Hoax," JSH, II, November, 1936

STOCKARD, RUSSELL L., "The Election and First Administration of Ben W. Hooper as Governor of Tennessee," ETHS *Publ.*, No. 26, 1954

———, "The Election and Second Administration of Governor Ben W. Hooper of Tennessee as Reflected in the State Press," ETHS *Publ.*, No. 32, 1960

SWINT, HENRY L., "Ezekial Birdseye and the Free State of Frankland," THQ, III, September, 1944

———, "Higher Education in the Tennessee-Kentucky Region a Century Ago," THQ, II, June, 1943

———, "The Historical Activities of the State of Tennessee," THQ, December, 1958

——— (ed.), "Reports from Educational Agents of the Freedmen's Bureau in Tennessee, 1865–1870," THQ, I, March, June, 1942

TAYLOR, A. A., "Fisk University and the Nashville Community, 1866–1900," JNH, XXIX, April, 1954

TAYLOR, HILLSMAN, "The Night Riders of West Tennessee," WTHS *Papers*, No. VI, 1952

TAYLOR, JOE G., "Andrew Jackson and the Aaron Burr Conspiracy," WTHS *Papers*, No. I, 1947

THOMPSON, E. BRUCE, "An Early Temperance Society at Nashville," THM, V, October, 1919

———, "Reforms in the Care of the Insane in Tennessee, 1830–1850," THQ, III, December, 1944

————, "Reforms in the Penal System of Tennessee, 1820–1850," *THQ*, I, December, 1942

THOMPSON, ISABEL, "The Blount Conspiracy," ETHS *Publ.*, No. 2, 1930

THRUSTON, G. P., "The Development of History at the Tennessee Centennial," *AHM*, III, January, 1898

TRACY, STERLING, "The Immigrant Population of Memphis," WTHS *Papers*, No. IV, 1950

TRIMBLE, SARAH RIDLEY (ed.), "Behind the Lines in Middle Tennessee, 1863–1865: The Journal of Bettie Ridley Blackmore," *THQ*, XII, March, 1953

TURNER, FREDERICK J., "Western State Making in the Revolutionary Era," *AHR*, I, October, 1895

UTLEY, BUFORD C., "The Early Academies of West Tennessee," WTHS *Papers*, No. VIII, 1954

VANCE, RUPERT B., "Tennessee's War of the Roses," *Virginia Quarterly Review*, XVI, Summer, 1940

VAN DEUSEN, GLYNDON G., "Some Aspects of Whig Thought and Theory in the Jacksonian Period," *AHR*, LXIII, January, 1958

WAGNER, HARRY C., "The Beginnings of the Christian Church in East Tennessee," ETHS *Publ.*, No. 20, 1948

WALKER, ARDA S., "Andrew Jackson: Frontier Democrat," ETHS *Publ.*, No. 18, 1946

————, "John Henry Eaton, Apostate," ETHS *Publ.*, No. 24, 1952

WALKER, PETER F., "Building a Tennessee Army: Autumn, 1861," *THQ*, XVI, June, 1957

————, "Command Failure: The Fall of Forts Henry and Donelson," *THQ*, XVI, December, 1957

————, "Holding the Tennessee Line," *THQ*, XVI, September, 1957

WALKER, W. A., JR., "Martial Sons: Tennessee Enthusiasm for the War of 1812," *THQ*, XX, March, 1961

WASHBURN, CLARA B., "Some Aspects of the Campaign of 1844 in Tennessee," *THQ*, IV, March, 1945

WAX, RABBI JAMES A., "The Jews of Memphis, 1860–1865," WTHS *Papers*, No. III, 1949

WEBB, WILLIAM R., JR., "Sawney Webb: My Father and His Ideals of Education," *Sewanee Review*, L, April–June, 1942

WEEKS, STEPHEN B., "Tennessee: A Discussion on the Sources of Its Population and Lines of Immigration," *THM*, II, December, 1916

WHITAKER, ARTHUR P., "The Muscle Shoals Speculation, 1783–1789," *MVHR*, XIII, December, 1926

————, "The Public School System of Tennessee, 1834–1860," *AHM*, July, 1899

————, "Spanish Intrigue in the Old Southwest: An Episode, 1788–1789," *MVHR*, XII, September, 1925

WHITE, CHARLES P., "Early Experiments with Prison Labor in Tennessee," ETHS *Publ.*, No. 12, 1940

WHITE, ROBERT H., "Tennessee's Four Capitals," ETHS *Publ.*, No. 6, 1934

————, "The Volunteer State," *THQ*, XV, March, 1956

WILLIAMS, CHARLOTTE, "Congressional Action on the Admission of Tennessee into the Union," *THQ*, II, December, 1943

WILLIAMS, EDWARD F., "Memphis' Early Triumph over Its River Rivals," *WTHS Papers*, No. XXII, 1968

WILLIAMS, FRANK B., JR., "The East Tennessee Education Association, 1913–1954," ETHS *Publ.*, No. 27, 1955

————, "John Eaton, Jr., Editor, Politician, and School Administrator, 1865–1870," *THQ*, X, December, 1951

————, "The Poll Tax as a Suffrage Requirement in the South, 1870–1901," *JSH*, XVIII, November, 1952

————, "Samuel Hervey Laughlin, 'Polk's Handyman,' " *THQ*, XXIV, Winter, 1965

WILLIAMS, SAMUEL C., "The Admission of Tennessee into the Union," *THQ*, IV, December, 1945

————, "Ann Robertson: An Unsung Tennessee Heroine," *THQ*, III, June, 1944

————, "Brigadier-General Nathaniel Taylor," ETHS *Publ.*, No. 12, 1940

————, "Early Iron Works in the Tennessee Country," *THQ*, VI, March, 1947

———— (ed.), "Executive Journal of Gov. John Sevier," ETHS *Publ.*, Nos. 1–7, 1929–35

————, "The First Territorial Division Named for Washington," *THM*, Ser. 2, II, April, 1932

————, "The First Volunteers from the 'Volunteer State,' " *THM*, VII, July, 1924

————, "A Forgotten Campaign," *THM*, VIII, January, 1925

————, "The Founder of Tennessee's First Town: Major Jesse Walton," ETHS *Publ.*, No. 2, 1930

————, "French and Other Intrigues in the Southwest Territory," ETHS *Publ.*, No. 13, 1941

————, "Henderson and Company's Purchase Within the Limits of Tennessee," *THM*, V, April, 1919

————, "Moses Fisk," ETHS *Publ.*, No. 20, 1948

————, "Nathaniel Gist: Father of Sequoyah," ETHS *Publ.*, No. 5, 1933

————, "Shelby's Fort," ETHS *Publ.*, No. 7, 1935

————, "The South's First Cotton Factory," *THQ*, V, September, 1946

————, "Stephen Holston and Holston River," ETHS *Publ.*, No. 8, 1936

————, "Tennessee's First Military Expedition (1903)," *THM*, VIII, October, 1924

————, "Tidence Lane—Tennessee's First Pastor," *THM*, Ser. 2, I, October, 1930

————, "Western Representation in North Carolina Assemblies," ETHS *Publ.*, No. 14, 1942

WILLIAMS, T. HARRY, "Andrew Johnson as a Member of the Committee on the Conduct of the War," ETHS *Publ.*, No. 12, 1940

WILLIAMS, VIRGINIA, "Tennessee's Public School Lands," *THQ*, III, December, 1944

WINDROW, J. E., "Collins D. Elliott and the Nashville Female Academy," *THM*, Ser. 2, III, January, 1935

WINGFIELD, MARIE-GREGSON, "The Memphis Interracial Commission," WTHS *Papers*, No. X, 1967

WINGFIELD, MARSHALL, "Tennessee's Mormon Massacre," *THQ*, XVII, March, 1958

WISH, HARVEY, "The Slave Insurrection Panic of 1856," *JSH*, V, May, 1939

WOOLVERTON, JOHN F., "Philip Lindsley and the Cause of Education in the Old Southwest," *THQ*, XIX, March, 1960

WORK, MONROE N. (comp.), "Some Negro Members of Reconstruction Conventions and Legislatures and of Congress," *JNH*, V, January, 1920

YOUNG, CAROL FURLONG, "A Study of Some Developing Interpretations of the History of Revolutionary Tennessee," ETHS *Publ.*, No. 25, 1953

Index